Contents

KT-229-282

Published by Lonely Planet Publications Pty Ltd
ABN 36 005 607 983

Australia Head Office, Locked Bag 1, Footscray,
Victoria 3011, ☎ 03 8379 8000, fax 03 8379 8111,
talk2us@lonelyplanet.com.au

USA 150 Linden St, Oakland, CA 94607,
☎ 510 893 8555, toll free 800 275 8555,
fax 510 893 8572, info@lonelyplanet.com

UK 72–82 Rosebery Ave, Clerkenwell, London,
EC1R 4RW, ☎ 020 7841 9000, fax 020 7841 9001,
go@lonelyplanet.co.uk

France 1 rue du Dahomey, 75011 Paris,
☎ 01 55 25 33 00, fax 01 55 25 33 01,
bip@lonelyplanet.fr, www.lonelyplanet.fr

© Lonely Planet 2004
Photographs © Richard Nebesky, Guy Moberly and as
listed (p245)

Printed through Colorcraft Ltd, Hong Kong
Printed in China

The Authors

DAMIEN SIMONIS

The medieval bastion of Toledo was home to Damien when he was not on the road in Spain, North Africa or the Middle East in the early 1990s. Small town life was OK but the pull of the big city was hard to resist and Damien shifted his Spain base north to the capital. What a place! Traffic jams at 5am! Whole districts seemingly dedicated to the business of fun – drinking, music, dancing, late night food.

This author's undying admiration goes to those many *gatos* who manage the extraordinary trick of combining early morning appearances in the office with seemingly unending late nights. It's not something Damien ever had to master.

Times changed and Damien moved on, back to London but with a twist, making Madrid's eternal northern rival, Barcelona, his on-again-off-again Spanish base. But he gets down to the capital whenever he can, part of Madrid is still home to this wandering soul.

Damien was the coordinating author of this book. He wrote the Introducing Madrid, City Life, History, Arts & Architecture, Madrid's Barrios, Walking Madrid, Eating and Directory chapters.

SARAH ANDREWS

As a wide-eyed college student on her first trip to Madrid Sarah carried Lonely Planet's Spain guide and dutifully toured the sights of the city, falling in love with the Prado, the cave restaurants around Plaza Mayor and the bars of Cava Baja (not necessarily in that order). Little did she suspect that she'd eventually move to Spain to not only read about but write about this city that never sleeps.

But life is funny that way, and Sarah, who's from Raleigh, North Carolina, has been living in Barcelona since 2000. When not on wild goose chases for Madrid's loudest techno club or most authentic bullfighters' shop she works from her apartment by the Mediterranean, writing articles and the occasional guidebook about her adopted country.

Convincing her to spend a couple of months getting the inside scoop on Madrid's nightlife, entertainment and shopping scenes was no easy task, but hey, someone has to do all the hard work!

Sarah wrote the Drinking & Nightlife, Entertainment, Shopping, Sleeping and Excursions chapters.

PHOTOGRAPHER

Richard Nebesky was born one snowy night in the grungy Prague suburb of Zizkov, but surprisingly he didn't have a camera in his hand. It was, however, not long after he got out of his cot that his father, an avid photo enthusiast, gave him his first point and shoot unit. Ever since, the camera has been by his side on wander treks, ski adventures, cycling trips and while researching Lonely Planet books around the globe. Richard has also worked for various magazines, travel guide book publishers and many social photography projects.

The magic of Madrid's architecture and the uniqueness of art works by Dali and Picaso always draw him back. This time Richard's stay had a wonderful twist to it – the Royal wedding.

Lonely Planet Publications
Melbourne | Oakland | London | Paris

Damien Simonis &
Sarah Andrews

Madrid

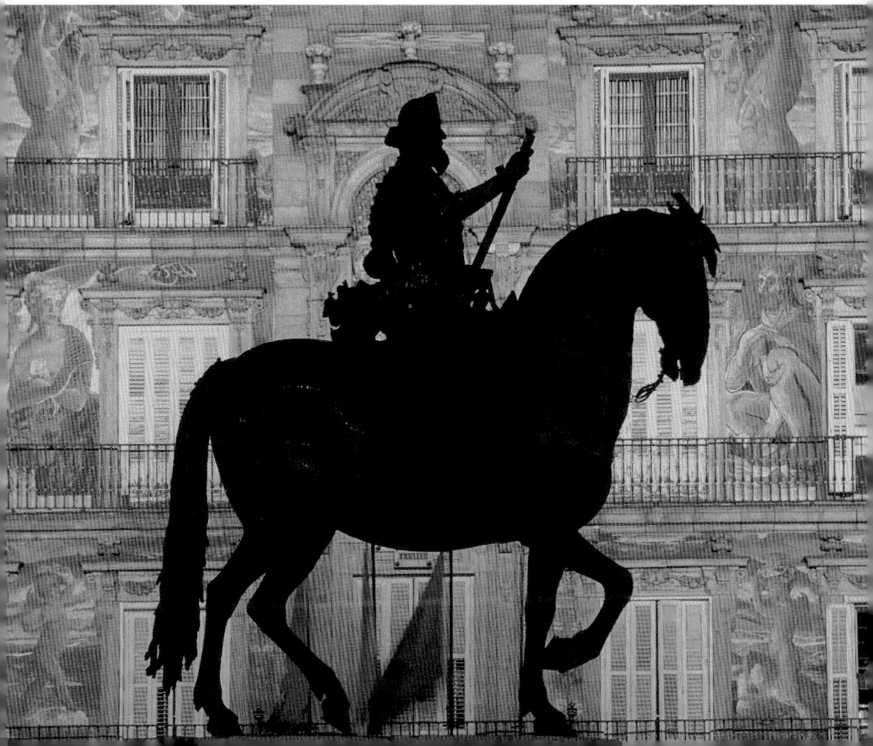

The Top Five

1 El Prado
Marvel at the Spanish Old Masters, from Velázquez to Goya (p26)
2 Parque del Buen Retiro
Take a colourful Sunday stroll in the green heart of Madrid (p22)
3 Plaza Mayor
Stop for a coffee and paper on the capital's emblematic square (p112)
4 Palacio Real
Wander the sumptuous halls of the centuries old Royal Palace (p112)
5 Salamanca
Let your credit card loose around chichi Calle de Serrano (p177)

Introducing Madrid

'*¡Dame una de boquerones!*' blurts out a chap crammed up against the bar in one of Madrid's jammed tapas joints ('Give me a plate of white anchovies!'). A buzz is in the air. Beer-filled *cañas* clink, everyone talks in a whirl of chatter. Outside, Plaza de Santa Ana is bathed in glorious sunshine. Madrileños work hard at enjoyment, eating and drinking. They work hard, full stop. The Spanish capital has never felt so purposeful.

Shaken by the terror blasts of 11 March 2004, the Spanish capital has shown a resilience and indomitable spirit that has surprised many. The city and its people dealt with the crisis without hysteria and mourned in dignity and without seeking reprisals. There has been no wave of xenophobia, no cries for revenge. Madrileños have chosen to continue living their lives as before, undeterred by the fear of further attack.

Madrid has long basked in the deep sunny heat of its long summer days and endless partying nights, but nowadays it exudes an unfettered self-confidence. A live-for-the-moment insouciance mingles with a hitherto unknown dynamism. And this in spite of the terrorists' cruel assault.

International business and tourists flock to a city that is exploding with energy. New metro stations seem to open up every other day, ambitious urban-expansion plans are spreading the city limits further into the surrounding country and the city's airport capacity is being doubled.

Jacques Rogge, President of the International Olympic Committee, could not hide his admiration on a visit in late 2003. Commenting on its candidacy for the 2012 summer games, he enthused: 'This is a well-prepared bid. Madrid is a strong contender.'

Lowdown

Population 3.03 million

Time Zone (GMT + one hour)

Average 3-star double room Around €120 to €180

Bocadillo (filled bread roll) €3 to €5

Litter bugs In many old-time tapas bars it's perfectly all right to throw your paper serviettes, prawn shells and the rest on the floor by the bar – at the end of the day it's all swept away

Coffee At the bar around €1

Metro ticket €1.15 (single ride)

Metrobús 10-ride ticket €5.35

No-no Blocking the left side on escalators – Madrileños are sticklers for keeping to the right to let the hurried pass by

To listen to Madrid town hall, not in the least daunted by rival claims from Paris, London, New York and Rio, the bid is so convincing that it's all but in the bag.

A latecomer to the concert of modern European nations, held up by decades of dictatorship and comparative poverty, there is a sensation that Madrid is coming into its own. No more cringing introspection here. Madrileños have been celebrating their town with gusto since the late 1970s, but only in recent years have they seemed to shake off what was left of a deeply felt inferiority complex in the face of Europe's other capitals.

The city is young by European standards, heaved from its medieval, village somnolence into the limelight by Felipe II's decision to make it his permanent capital in 1561. For a long time the city did not breach boundaries laid out between El Prado and the Palacio Nacional. Its heart was and remains the broad, gracious Plaza Mayor. The grand multi-lane boulevards of the Paseo de la Castellana and Gran Vía were later additions that conferred on it the pomp of the capital in the 19th and 20th centuries.

For all its youth, Madrid bears more than its share of high culture and history. For art buffs, it is the Big Three that put Madrid on the map – El Prado, with its grand collection of Spanish Old Masters; the Centro de Arte Reina Sofía, a homage to modern Spanish art; and the Museo Thyssen-Bornemisza, a prestigious and eclectic collection. Museums abound and Renaissance, baroque, neo-Classical and Art Deco touches lend it depth and gravitas.

Did we say *gravitas*? Step out into the Madrid night and nowhere could seem less serious. This is Europe's party town. Swarms of locals and an increasing dose of outsiders throng the restaurants and bars of the city. Good-natured hedonism is Madrid's nocturnal calling card. Far from the sobriety of national government at the Moncloa, town hall rituals in Plaza de la Villa or serious boardroom business on Paseo de la Castellana, it is the chaotic laneways of La Latina, Malasaña (with its bright and visible gay contingent around Chueca) and Huertas that hold the city's attention. Revellers there are joined in spirit by still more in the swank restaurants of Salamanca or the posh watering holes that litter Chamberí.

Madrid has always been a magnet for immigrants. For a long time most of them came from elsewhere in Spain. Hardly surprising, since all the main highways and railways converge on this central point in the Iberian peninsula. They brought with them all the cuisines and quirks of the rest of Spain. On a given evening you can eat Galician seafood, sip Catalan *cava* and experience the blood-rush of flamenco. Now the wider world is coming too. Kebab stands, Japanese cuisine and New York–style cocktail bars are enriching the local scene.

Need a break from Madrid madness? It happens to be an ideal base for more peaceful day trips. Toledo, Segovia, El Escorial, Ávila, Aranjuez, the Sierra de Guadarrama and even Córdoba are all within easy striking distance.

DAMIEN'S TOP MADRID DAY

The nature of a great day depends on the night before! When I'm being sensible and not hitting the sack later than 3am, I love to make for the Café Comercial on Glorieta de Bilbao for a morning café con leche and a read of *El País*. Batteries charged, it's a metro ride across town for the Parque del Buen Retiro, a late morning dose of green peace and a wander towards El Prado, where I refresh my acquaintance with the Old Masters. By now I'm working up a hunger and march across town for a meaty lunch at Casa Parrondo. An afternoon of strolling along Calle Mayor, Plaza Mayor and the Palacio Real leaves me with a thirst. Time for a few cañas (beers) with pals at the bars with views of Las Vistillas before retiring for a siesta. That night, I have agreed to meet friends at Bodega de la Ardosa at 11pm for a vermouth start to a long evening. Bar-hopping through the night, we decide to switch location late, grab a taxi and wind up dancing in Kapital. Emerging at 6am, I crawl to the metro station and head for a shower and bed. Thank God I don't have to work today!

Essential Madrid

- El Prado (p25)
- Plaza Mayor (p112)
- Carousing in the bars of Malasaña (p145)
- Sunday in the Parque del Buen Retiro (p22)
- Palacio Real (p112)

City Life

City Life

MADRID TODAY

Never has Madrid looked and felt more like a capital. They used to say that *'sólo Madrid es corte'* (only Madrid can be home to the royal court), but for a long time after its nomination as permanent royal capital by Felipe II in 1561, it had anything but the air of a capital. And while by Franco's day there was no denying the stature of the place, the little dictator seemed to have a knack for making even the brightest light sink into a depressed, colourless melancholy.

How things have changed in the three decades since Franco went to Jesus. The place is a hive of activity, sprucing itself up, pouring money into infrastructure and doing a mighty job of showing itself a worthy bidder for the 2012 Olympics.

It is also a scarred city. Long the occasional target of Basque terror group ETA for assassinations and bomb blasts, Madrid was shaken to the core by a series of blasts on three commuter trains on 11 March 2004 that killed 190 people and injured 1400. This time, however, the assault came from Muslim fundamentalists. Madrileños picked up the pieces with remarkable speed, undeterred and unbowed. And three days later the country voted the right-wing government out and the Socialists in (much to the chagrin of US president George W Bush).

The biggest overnight change after Franco was a hedonistic explosion later dubbed *la movida*. While that may be a thing of the past and linked to characters like the then up-and-coming film director Pedro Almodóvar, the city's gift for partying remains largely undiminished. To wander Malasaña, La Latina and Huertas is to enter an all-night jungle of bars and clubs. But not everyone is happy about it. Local residents continue to complain bitterly of all-night noise, the acrid smell left behind by people urinating in public and the piles of rubbish, especially bottles, plastic cups and the like left behind by outdoor revellers.

For several years the town hall, run by the right-wing Partido Popular (PP), has slowly clamped down on the excesses. Where a few years ago it was still common for people to light up joints in bars, the practice has all but disappeared. Since 2002 the city has also clamped down (up to a point) on the phenomenon of the *botellón,* basically hundreds of thousands

Fresco-covered Real Casa de la Panadería houses at Plaza Mayor (p70)

Hot Conversation Topics

- Months after the bomb blasts that gutted three commuter trains heading into Madrid at morning rush hour, Madrileños are out there working and partying like before.
- Beckham's a good lad and works hard on the field, but he's not shooting too many of his famous penalty goals is he?
- Why, oh why, do they have to build an 8km rail tunnel in the middle of the city? As though we don't have enough road works to scramble around!
- Did Goya really do those scary Black Paintings, or were they just his son Javier's doodlings?
- The 2012 Olympics? Nice idea but we'll believe it when we see it.
- So now we have brand spanking new radial toll roads to ease the traffic. There's only one problem – no-one uses them!
- And now we'll see what right-wing Esperanza Aguirre, the first woman president of a Spanish region, will get up to – hopefully more than just shooting her mouth off against her predecessor and now mayor of Madrid, Alberto Ruiz-Gallardón!

of youngsters who pour into Madrid on the weekend with their own tipples (including awful concoctions like *calimocho*, cheap red wine with Coca Cola) and get noisily wasted in the streets outside the bars they can't afford to frequent.

But life in Madrid is not all eating, drinking, dancing and keeping the neighbours awake. Some people are kept awake just by the cost of living. Since the mid-1990s the city has experienced an unprecedented boom in house prices. Year after year, Madrileños would reassure each other: this surely can't go on. But so far there is no sign of this loopy market slowing down. Spaniards are among the lowest wage-earners in the 'old' (pre-May 2004) European Union, so it is hardly surprising that the spiralling price of accommodation has left locals aghast. In the five years to 2004, house prices as much as doubled.

This has been accompanied by a construction boom on the increasingly distant frontiers of the city. What many families want is a *chalet* – generally a semi-detached house with garden in one of the many modern developments *(urbanizaciones)* that ring the city. But they too have become too pricey for many Madrid families, some of whom have opted for villages in regions as far off as Extremadura! Anecdotal evidence of Madrileños cheerfully proclaiming their readiness to rise at 3am to commute along the country's highways to get to work in Madrid, all for the sake of a quiet suburban life at an affordable price, leave one gasping in disbelief!

All of this has helped fuel the PP's ambitious building programmes – whole suburbs are being raised around the periphery of Madrid in projects that will stretch to at least 2020. The development runs hand in hand with the recent massive expansion of the metro system, new ring roads, top-shelf projects like the planned skyscrapers at the northern end of Paseo de la Castellana and a new stadium if the city wins the Olympics.

Just as much fun as the crazy finances and extraordinary construction frenzy are city and regional politics. In May 2003 both the city and the surrounding region (the Comunidad de Madrid) went to the polls. The Madrileños, predictably, elected the popular former president of the Comunidad, Alberto Ruiz-Gallardón, as their mayor, replacing the maladroit José María Álvarez Manzano. In the Comunidad de Madrid's regional elections the country's first-ever woman regional president, the right-wing Esperanza Aguirre, emerged victorious (just). Her undisguised dislike of party fellow Ruiz-Gallardón promises to add spice to the monochrome political landscape. The PP's glee was darkened by the bomb attacks and subsequent Socialist victory in the country's general elections.

After the housing obsession and terrorism, what most worries Madrileños nowadays is crime. Although statistics show recorded crime falling in the city, Spanish police and Europol admit a growing number of organised crime bands are operating in Madrid and beyond. Many are home-grown, and Europol claims that most European mafias across the continent have dealings with Spanish bands. In Madrid, the Colombian mafia deals in heroin, the Moroccans dominate the dope department and various Eastern European groups deal in anything from prostitution to arms. Still as with the mafia world elsewhere, it rarely touches the lives of ordinary citizens and Madrileños pursue the twin activities of work and pleasure with the same gusto they always have.

CITY CALENDAR

Given the way Madrid seems to boom with unrestrained youthful energy on any old weekend of the year, you'd hardly think the city needed any more partying incentive. But Madrileños receive plenty. From Carnaval in cool February to the local fiestas in central Madrid *barrios* (neighbourhoods) in the stifling heat of August, the locals are ready for a good party under any circumstances and regardless of the temperature.

Given that there is almost always something going on, it can be an idea to choose the moment for travelling to Madrid with an eye on the weather. Winter, for instance, can sometimes have a nasty bite to it when cold winds blow in off the Sierra del Guadarrama. February can, however, be quite sunny and pleasant. July and August are the hottest months of the year and make you understand why air conditioning was invented. August is an odd time to be in Madrid, as the city virtually shuts down. Locals head for the sea, the hills, anywhere they can cool down a little. As a result, many restaurants close and offices run in neutral. Accommodation, at least, is generally pretty easy to find.

For a full list of official public holidays in Madrid, turn to the Directory (p230).

JANUARY

NEW YEAR'S DAY (AÑO NUEVO)

Like New Year's Eve *(noche vieja)* anywhere, this occasion can create but not always fulfil expectations. Many Madrileños gather in Puerta del Sol to wait for the 12 *campanadas* (bell chimes) that mark midnight. All try to stuff 12 grapes (one for each chime) into their mouths and make a wish for the new year.

REYES

The Epiphany (Epifanía) on 6 January is also known as the Día de los Reyes Magos (Three Kings' Day), or simply Reyes, perhaps the most important day on a Madrileño kid's calendar. Santa Claus may race around distributing gifts in December, but, traditionally, young Spaniards wait until the Epiphany. Of course if they've been bad they get lumps of coal *(carbón)*. Nowadays even the coal is sweet, and you can see piles of the stuff in pastry stores in the run-up to the feast day. Three local politicians from different parties dress up as the three kings (three wise men) and head a parade of horse-drawn carriages and floats from the Parque del Buen Retiro to Plaza Mayor at 6pm on 5 January.

FIESTA DE SAN ANTÓN

St Anthony is known as the patron saint of animals, and local faithful take their beasties to be blessed at the Iglesia de San Antón in Calle de Hortaleza on 17 January, the saint's feast day.

FEBRUARY

CARNAVAL

Carnaval spells several days of fancy-dress parades and merrymaking in many places across the Comunidad de Madrid, usually ending on the Tuesday 47 days before Easter Sunday. It is not as big in Madrid as in other Spanish cities, with celebrations tending to be a fairly localised affair in several districts. Depending on the dates, it can spill over into March.

FESTIVAL FLAMENCO

This is a yearly event that has been gaining in prestige since it was first staged in the early 1990s. A combination of big names and rising talent gets together for five days of fine flamenco music in one of the city's theatres (often the Teatro Albéniz but check). The festival covers all facets of the art, from singing to dance, with both men and women performers. The dates are moveable so watch out.

ARCO

www.arco.ifema.es

Staged in the Parque Ferial Juan Carlos I exhibition centre near Barajas airports, this is one of Europe's biggest homages to contemporary art and has gained enormously in prestige since it was first held in 1982. Known also as the Feria Internacional de Arte Contemporánea, it brings together galleries and exhibitors from all over the world. It's a wonderful occasion to get clued up on what is happening in art across the globe, as well as being a major forum for the art-business bods themselves. It lasts for five days, usually around the middle of the month.

MARCH & APRIL

JUEVES SANTO (GOOD THURSDAY)

This day kicks off the official holiday period known in Spain as Semana Santa (Holy Week). For many Madrileños it means a chance to get away from the city for a few days' rest and recreation. Nevertheless, local *cofradías* (lay fraternities) organise religious processions on this day and throughout he Easter period. They can be a colourful affair with an Andalucian flavour, with hooded men (looking scarily like KKK adepts) and barefoot women dragging chains around their ankles and bearing crosses among the parading figures.

VIERNES SANTO (GOOD FRIDAY)

Good Friday and Easter in general are celebrated with greater enthusiasm in some of the surrounding towns. Chinchón, in particular, is known for its lavish Easter processions.

ARTEMANÍA

www.pcm.tourspain.es

The Feria de Arte y Antigüedades is the nation's top date for the antique lover. Dealers from all over Spain converge on the Palacio de Congresos y Exposiciones on Paseo de la Castellana. You can admire anything from Picasso lithographs to ebony furniture items or even ancient pottery. The fair usually lasts for a week towards the end of the month.

JAZZ ES PRIMAVERA

Three weeks of jazz across the city.

MAY

FIESTA DEL TRABAJO (LABOUR DAY)

You'll probably hardly notice 1 May is a holiday except for all the closed offices, banks and shops.

FIESTA DE LA COMUNIDAD DE MADRID

On 2 May (El Dos de Mayo) in 1808, Napoleon's troops put down an uprising in Madrid, and commemoration of the day has since become an opportunity for much festivity. Celebrations begin with a speech, by a local personality, from the balcony of the Casa de Correos in the Puerta del Sol. The day is celebrated with particular vim and vigour in the bars of Malasaña. There follows a fistful of cultural events, lasting as long as two weeks.

FIESTAS DE SAN ISIDRO LABRADOR

The merry month of May is nowhere merrier than in Madrid. In the wake of the Dos de Mayo festivities come the city's big holiday, 15 May, when it celebrates the feast day of its patron saint, San Isidro (the 'peasant'). Proceedings kick off with the *pregón*, a speech delivered by a VIP that is the starting signal for a week of cultural events around the city. On 15 May the townfolk gather in central Madrid to watch the colourful procession. Lots of the town citizenry also traipse across the Puente de San Isidro to the chapel across the Manzanares dedicated to the saint and spend the day there picnicking. There, many in traditional dress, they sip holy water and munch on *barquillos* (sweet pastries). Goya depicted this feast day by the river at the tail end of the 18th century. In those days you looked across green fields back to Madrid – that view is now largely obstructed by high-rises!

Cool Cats

Especially around the Fiestas de San Isidro, *chulapos* and *manolas* come out of the woodwork. The gents dress in traditional short jackets and berets and the women in *mantones de Manila*, and both put their best feet forward in a lively *chotis*.

Huh? The *mantón de Manila* is an embroidered silk shawl, which few people now wear except during fiestas. The *chotis* is a traditional working-class dance not unlike a polka. One of the most common versions involves a quick three-step to the left, the same to the right, and is topped off with a brisk twirl. Only a small portion of the really *castizo* (true-blue) Madrileños bother with this any more, but those who do so do it with a certain pride.

The *chulapo* – or dyed-in-the-wool, born-and-bred Madrileño – is today more commonly known as a *chulo*. Now this is a word to beware of. It generally implies a degree of bravado and even arrogance of character, although in the eyes of Madrileños this is no bad thing. As an adjective it can simply mean 'cool' (usually in reference to an object). But to many people (especially beyond Madrid) the word bears quite negative qualities – brash, showy. The word can also mean 'pimp', so you'd want to be sure of your company and context before bandying it around too much. The fast-talking, hard-living Madrid version of James Dean is also typecast as a *macarra*, which at its worst also means a spiv.

These breezy types, especially the kind you'd come across in the inner working-class neighbourhoods, such as Lavapiés, were also once generally referred to as *manolos* (Manolo is a common first name). So it stands to reason that their girls should be known as *manolas*!

To complete the picture, full-blooded Madrileños are also known as *gatos* – cats – a nice image to reflect their city savvy. The term quite appeals to the locals, as it has come to reflect their tendency to crawl around the city like cats until all hours. They say the term was coined as one of Alfonso VI's soldiers artfully scaled Muslim Magerit's formidable walls in 1085. 'Look,' cried his comrades, 'he moves like a cat!'

Capgros *or 'big head' during the annual Fiestas de San Isidro Labrador (p11)*

The country's most prestigious *feria* (bullfighting season) also commences now and continues for a month, at the bullring Plaza de Toros Monumental de Las Ventas (Map p260).

FESTIMAD

This is Madrid's big contribution to Spain's year-round circuit of major music festivals. In this case, bands from all over the country and beyond converge on Móstoles (on the Metro-Sur train network), just outside Madrid, for two days of indie music indulgence.

JUNE

DÍA DE SAN JUAN

Celebrated in other parts of Spain with fireworks and considerable gusto, the eve of this holiday (24 June) is a minor affair in Madrid. The action in Madrid, such as it is, takes place in the Parque del Buen Retiro.

DÍA DEL ORGULLO DE GAYS, LESBIANAS Y TRANSEXUALES

The city's gay and lesbian pride festival and parade take place on the last Saturday of the month. It is an international gig, with similar parades taking places in cities across Europe, from Berlin to Paris, on the same day.

JULY

VERANOS DE LA VILLA

As if the traditional local fiestas were not enough to amuse those Madrileños who stay behind in the broiling city heat in summer, the town authorities stage a series of cultural events, shows and exhibitions, known as 'Summers in the City'. Concerts, opera, dance and theatre are performed in the Centro Cultural de la Villa, in the Palacio del Conde Duque and other venues around town. The programme starts in July and runs to the end of August.

AUGUST

FIESTAS DE SAN LORENZO, SAN CAYETANO & LA VIRGEN DE LA PALOMA

Not all of Madrid leaves town in the heat of midsummer, and not all those who stay behind remain in a sunstroke-induced torpor. These three local patron saints' festivities (which revolve around La Latina, Plaza de Lavapiés and Calle de Calatrava in La Latina respectively) keep the central districts of Madrid busy during the first fortnight of August. Food and drink stands are set up in the streets and almighty din fills the hot night air as locals eat, drink, dance and generally let their hair down. Why not? It's too hot for sleep anyway.

LA ASUNCIÓN (FEAST OF THE ASSUMPTION)

Also known as the Fiesta de la Virgen de la Paloma, 15 August is a solemn date in the city's religious calendar, celebrating the Assumption of the Virgin Mary.

SEPTEMBER

LOCAL FIESTAS

Several local councils organise fiestas in the first and second weeks of September. They include Fuencarral–El Pardo, Vallecas, Arganzuela, Barajas, Moncloa–Aravaca and Usera. In the last week of the month you can check out the Fiesta de Otoño (Autumn Festival) in Chamartín. These are very local affairs and provide a rare insight into *barrio* life of the average Madrileño.

FIESTA DEL PCE
www.pce.es (in Spanish)

In mid-September the Partido Comunista de España (PCE; Spanish Communist Party) holds its annual fundraiser in the Casa de Campo.

Baaaaa!

A couple of times a year (in spring and autumn), shepherds drive their flocks through central Madrid as they move from winter to summer pastures or vice versa. Heedless of modernity, nine of the centuries-old Cañadas Reales (Royal Ways) and numerous smaller routes along which cattle and sheep were traditionally driven remain on the books and the right of passage guaranteed by law. Since 1993 shepherds have re-activated their rights and drive up to 2000 head of sheep through the city en route between the north of the country and Extremadura. So if you find yourself in a woolly road block in downtown Madrid on a chilly November day, don't be surprised!

This mixed bag of regional-food pavilions, rock concerts and political soap-boxing lasts all weekend.

FIESTA DE OTOÑO (AUTUMN FESTIVAL)

Since the early 1980s the city has thrown off the torpor of summer with a busy calendar of musical and theatrical activity right up to the approach to Christmas. The nature and scope of the programme depends in no small measure on budget constraints..

NOVEMBER
DÍA DE LA VIRGEN DE LA ALMUDENA

Castizos (true-blue Madrileños) gather in Plaza Mayor to hear Mass on the feast day (9 November) of the city's female patron saint.

EMOCIONA JAZZ

Groups from far and wide converge on the capital for a series of concerts in venues across town.

DECEMBER
FESTIVAL DE GOSPEL AND NEGRO SPIRITUALS

In the week running up to Christmas Madrid is treated to a feast of jazz, blues and gospel, usually in the Centro Cultural de la Villa.

NAVIDAD (CHRISTMAS)

This is a fairly quiet family time. Many celebrate with a big midday meal, although some prefer to eat on Christmas Eve (Nochebuena). Nativity scenes (cribs) are set up in churches around the city and an exhibition of them is held in Plaza Mayor.

Top Five Unusual Events

- **Reyes (Epifanía)** When the Three Wise Men parade around Madrid.
- **Fiesta de San Antón** Blessing of the beasts at the Iglesia de San Antón.
- **Jueves Santo (Good Thursday)** When local religious brotherhoods take to the streets in colourful and emotion-charged processions.
- **Fiestas de San Isidro Labrador** Madrid's biggest party, with processions and the country's premier bullfighting season.
- **Fiestas de San Lorenzo, San Cayetano & La Virgen de la Paloma** Summer fun with eating, drinking and dancing in the streets.

CULTURE
IDENTITY

The city of Madrid is Spain's biggest, with a population of 3.09 million. The surrounding region, the Comunidad de Madrid, counts a further 2.65 million, making it the most densely populated part of the country (whose total population is 42.7 million), with about 13.5% of the country's inhabitants in an area that covers less than 2% of the territory. In absolute terms the Comunidad de Madrid ranks third behind Andalucía and Catalonia, both much larger territories.

With people continuing to flock to the capital from around the country and urban expansion in top gear, some predict the metropolitan area will count six million inhabitants by 2012, although at present rates of growth that claim seems a little far-fetched. Some 600,000 foreign migrants live in the Comunidad de Madrid (more than two-thirds of them in the city) and now make up 10% of the population. Half are registered with work or residency permits, but they get along illegally as *clandestinos*. The biggest groups are Ecuadorians, Colombians and Moroccans. In the working-class neighbourhoods of Lavapiés and around, you will encounter North Africans rubbing shoulders with Pakistanis, Black Africans and Latin Americans. Others live in the poorer outer dormitory suburbs. The growth in the phenomenon has been spectacular. In the early 1990s the number of foreigners living in Spain was negligible. Since 2000 the migrant population has more than doubled.

Madrid, like the rest of Spain, is mostly Catholic, at least in name. It has known the presence of the three great monotheistic faiths, the Jewish, Muslim and Christian religions. The completion of the Reconquista in 1492 and subsequent expulsions of Muslims and Jews radicalised religion in Spain and set the stage for the Inquisition and the military-style Jesuit order. Under Franco, Catholicism was again made a state religion and the Church played a major role in society.

The wealth of the Church fuelled the violent anticlericalism of the 19th century that saw countless churches and convents expropriated and destroyed. The ill-feeling continued into the 20th century, and it was hardly surprising that the Church should align itself with Franco. In doing so it won itself many bitter enemies and its clergy paid a heavy price.

Nowadays, younger Spaniards especially pay, at most, lip service to their Catholicism and many Spanish theologians criticise the Church for its conservatism on issues such as sex, abortion and divorce, warning that it will lose even more ground with Spaniards if it does not 'modernise'.

And yet, as in the rest of Spain, the visible religiosity of Madrileños remains strong. Great Easter processions, in which penitents of religious fraternities dress up in strange habits, put on conical masks *(capilotes)* and march solemnly around the city bearing crosses and beating drums, still attract enormous crowds of people who otherwise might rarely set foot in a church.

Wishful Kissing

As many as 100,000 people flock to the Iglesia de Jesús de Medinaceli, in Plaza de Jesús (Map pp270–2) on the first Friday of Lent to kiss the right foot of a wooden sculpture of Christ. The church stays open until 2.30am on Saturday as the faithful file in for the *besapié* (kissing of the foot). Queues stretch good-naturedly for blocks and one morning in early March 2004 the pilgrims got a surprise when heir to the throne Prince Felipe and his bride to be Letizia Ortiz turned up plant a kiss on Jesus' toes. An Our Father and a Mass (held hourly) complete the devotion, at the end of which pilgrims make three requests to Jesus Christ. He is said to grant one of them.

LIFESTYLE

Madrileños manage that rare city combination – they lead generally frenetic lives but give the impression of being quite relaxed about it all. People dash about all over the city, but rigorously stop for a couple of hours around 2pm, either for lunch, a sleep or both. They then somehow manage to climb back into gear for the evening session of madness, until around 8pm.

People who live in central Madrid generally do so cheek-by-jowl. Just about everyone lives in an apartment, although what this means can vary greatly. Because of the way Madrid apartment blocks (especially the older ones dating to the 1950s and beyond) tend to be a mix of *exterior* and *interior* elements, you can find people living in all sorts of places. Exterior means something that looks onto the street, while interior can mean anything from a grand internal courtyard to a *patio de luz*, little more than a shaft in the middle of a building that allows a little light in and lots of pipes out. Some people live in tiny *áticos* (attics) from which they might have wonderful views across town but (without air con) swelter in summer.

Groups of students from the provinces crowd into large, often run-down flats in the most incredible ways. Unluckier ones may wind up with a *habitación ciega* (a 'blind room', ie without a window). Your average middle-class inhabitant of central Madrid, especially if they managed to purchase before the housing market went nuts in the mid-1990s, may well have a splendidly spacious apartment rambling over 150 sq metres, with balconies and wooden shutters, hardwood floors, high ceilings and interior bedrooms giving onto quiet courtyards. Luxury apartments of several hundred square metres with all the latest designer fittings and occasionally even rooftop pools also exist. To look at buildings from the street you simply have no idea what might lurk inside.

Many Madrileños prefer the new to the old. New *chalets* (detached or semi-detached houses) in *urbanizaciones* outside Madrid, luxury villas to the north of the city in places like La Moraleja or just plain new apartment blocks have a big market in Madrid, where many people equate old with crummy. It's all a matter of taste. And in no other culture are people so prepared to buy sight unseen or *sobre plano* (on the plan). This involves looking at architect's drawings for a planned development, picking the floor and the flat's characteristics, setting up the mortgage and waiting for the thing to be built. It is no doubt a cheaper way of buying, but risky too. In the past, building cooperatives have collapsed leaving behind some very out-of-pocket customers.

In the heart of Madrid live all sorts of people, filling it with human soul: the elderly who have never moved; families with children, cats and dogs; young, hip couples; executives who prefer the city centre to the traffic commute; student groups; migrants in search of work. Every possible social class and type is present.

And just as for their extraordinary religious parades, Madrileños like to get out into the streets. You can see high-class dames preening themselves along Calle de Serrano as they shop in Madrid's endless multiplying boutiques. Or grungy types hanging about the bars of Malasaña and Chueca. Even in winter, when the sun pops out, well-rugged-up Madrileños may be espied stopping for a coffee or drink at an outside table.

On summer evenings, they remain outside, eating and drinking at terraces amid a joyful chattering din until deep into the night. While the too-cool-for-school crowd may be seen at terraces along the Paseo de la Castellana, a more mixed crowd hangs about areas like La Latina, where in Plaza de San Andrés and Plaza de la Paja you are as likely to stumble over football-playing ankle biters at 11pm as run into drinking buddies. It is one of the endearing qualities of Madrid that children are so easily melded in to their parents' nocturnal diversions.

Madrileños are true urban animals and not necessarily waiting about to meet you just because you have blown in from abroad. On the other hand, as big cities go it can be surprisingly friendly. Meeting locals in bars – especially if you have some mastery of Spanish – is a lot easier than in towns like London. Don't expect lifelong friendship, however. People here live fully for the moment. Today's encounter can be tomorrow's distant memory.

An invitation to someone's home is a rare mark of friendship, but then the locals are not so in to entertaining at home. They are much more likely to head out in gregarious bands to *tapear* (eat tapas – bar snacks – in one bar after another), or just pick a restaurant. You can't then just head home and so it's off to the one of the seemingly endless bars splashed across the city. Relatively few Madrileños allow themselves to get blind drunk. They love a tipple – and blimey the tipples are generous – but keep it under control. After all many have to last until the next dawn and the object is enjoyment, not making themselves ill in as short a time a possible. They have little comprehension for northern Europeans tanking up fast and stumbling in a stupor through the remainder of the evening.

How Do They Do It?

As foreigners crawl red-eyed back to their hotel after a long night on the tiles, they can frequently be heard muttering to themselves in a semi-coherent mix of admiration and irritation: 'How do they do it?' How on earth do the locals stay out all night and then turn up for work the next day? The answers are varied. For the majority of Madrileños with day jobs, the nocturnal frolics don't generally start until Thursday – one day of suffering is perfectly tolerable. But there are other tricks. Many people work on *horario intensivo* (intensive timetable) in summer because of the heat. This can see them starting work as early as 7am and finishing up by 2pm at the latest. Those with energy stop in at home for a shower and coffee on the way to work directly from the club, scream through the day on adrenalin (or fake it) and then head home for a long sleep. Since many folk don't go out until around midnight, that makes for a full 'night's' sleep, only in the afternoon! For others, the *siesta* does exist – a couple of hours snooze time between 2pm and as late as 5pm can be enough to keep grey matter in operation. Another snooze after work isn't a bad idea before hitting the town. Of course, on the weekend many night owls are just that, sleeping by day and vamping around by night!

One should not be fooled into thinking Madrid is El Dorado. For Madrileños it can be a tough place to survive. Especially with the high cost of lodgings (a decent flat of 100 sq metres in an average part of central Madrid is not likely to sell for under €300,000 or rent for less than €800 to €1000), locals often struggle to make ends meet. After decades of austerity under Franco and the subsequent emergence into the mainstream Western world, Madrileños have acquired a taste for the nice things in life – new cars, foreign holidays and all the other standard fripperies. But many have to make do on low wages. The minimum wage, at €460 a month, is among the lowest in Europe. Many people in modest jobs (secretarial, teaching and so on) don't gross much more than €1000 a month. Better paid middle-ranking professionals might as much as double that. Spain may be hurtling towards parity with the rest of Western Europe in terms of the cost of living, but it continues to lag behind in pay packets (whatever the statistics might say – see Economy & Costs, p19).

Beers and snacks at Stop Madrid (p148)

Perhaps that's why the city, like the rest of Spain, has one of the lowest birth rates (1.2%) in the world. Although many Madrileños condemn the influx of legal and illegal immigrants, without them, Spain's population would be in decline.

Madrileños can seem gruff and be economical with etiquette and thank yous but this does not signify unfriendliness. One way in which you may notice people expressing their fellow feeling is the general *'buenos días'* they often utter to all and sundry when they enter a shop or bar, and the *'adiós'* when they leave.

FASHION

Madrileños did not exactly stride out of the Franco era the best-dressed folk in Europe – understandable after centuries of troubles and decades of fascist austerity. It makes the rapid rise of Madrid (and Spain) as a new force in world fashion all the more surprising.

The Spaniards, in a sense, are naturally inclined towards fashion. Even when in straitened financial circumstances, they like to dress well and with style. Since the beginning of the 1990s there has been a shopping explosion in Madrid, with options to suit all budgets. The money, as ever, still hangs around the boutiques of Calle de Serrano and adjacent streets in chichi Salamanca.

Elsewhere in town, a racier scene is also blossoming. Calle del Almirante and nearby streets close to Chueca are alive with fun, imaginative shops. Slightly more grunge, or simply young and playful, are the 60 fashion stores in the Mercado. Since the so-called market opened in 1998 it has become a magnet for a hip, urban brigade. Names like Energie, Puma, Gas and the like light up the eyes of youthful Madrileños searching for the latest look without having to mortgage themselves in the process.

The shops reflect different tendencies in the street. Spanish fashion of the upper middle and upper classes has a classic, somewhat uniform look about it. Browns and beiges dominate, furs are common in winter and all in all there is a vaguely conservative Mediterranean feel about it. At the same time, a more international, rootless and uncomplicated air predominates among much of the city's younger folk.

Although Madrid is still a way from rivalling the big fashion meccas like Milan and Paris, the Pasarela Cibeles (www.cibeles.ifema.es in Spanish) runway fashion shows staged in the Parque Ferial Juan Carlos I have established themselves since the late 1990s as an important event on the threads circuit. Mostly Spanish but some foreign designers sign up in increasing numbers to display their spring and autumn collections. The show gets some pretty fierce competition from eternal rival, Barcelona, in the form of the almost simultaneous Pasarela Gaudí, but not many countries can boast *two* major fashion centres at international level.

Some big names in *prêt-a-porter* fashion arrived in the course of the 1990s. None of them are locals and a surprising concentration have their origins in the distant northwest region of Galicia, traditionally seen as one of the poorest parts of Spain, dedicated to subsistence farming and fishing and constantly bathed in Atlantic drizzle. The biggest of these success stories is Zara, with more than 800 stores throughout the world.

There is plenty of haute couture activity. One of the grand names in this business is Agatha Ruiz de la Prada, appreciated by Warhol, and designer of everything from children's clothes through flouncy accessories to top of the line men's and women's threads.

A long list of designers from all over Spain has emerged in the 30 years since Franco took his awful military uniforms and pot belly from public view by expiring in 1975. Names to look for include Pedro del Hierro, Kina Fernández, Nacho Ruiz and Montesinos Alama, but there are many, many more.

For the Pasarela Cibeles these designers have no need to look for the Naomi Campbells of this world. They have plenty of home-grown talent to choose from, such as Nieves Álvarez, Verónica Blume, Martina Klein and Madrid-born Eugenia Silva.

A Ladies' Man

Born in Madrid in 1969, Javier Larraínzar has, since 1992, become one of the city's top haute couture icons. Having lived part of his youth abroad, Larraínzar studied his trade in all the obvious places, doing long stints in Milan, New York and elsewhere before finally deciding to return home. He has concentrated on women's fashion and found demand for his inspired creations so high that he opened a **boutique** (☎ 91 577 88 35; Calle de Castello 16) in the Salamanca *barrio* in 1996. At the same time, he struck a deal with El Corte Inglés, Spain's top department store chain, to install his boutiques in their stores. His style is relaxed but classically Spanish, with warm natural colours and quality fabrics the principal ingredients.

SPORT
Football

Although many TVs in Madrid bars will have the day's bullfight on, a Real Madrid (www .realmadrid.com) football (soccer) match usually has locals switching channels. Not all Madrileños are Madridistas (Real Madrid followers) – the town has two other sides and a tiny minority of the population dares to barrack for other sides too. But, on the whole, football-mad Madrileños are justifiably proud of the team nominated by FIFA in 1998 as the greatest side of all time. The team has taken more cups and trophies than any other in Spain and is studded by a cast of local and international heroes, ranging from France's Zinedine Zidane and Brazil's goal king Ronaldo (who in March 2004 signed up for another four years) to newly hired Manchester golden boy David Beckham. Beckham is doing well for himself with tourism-promotion contracts and the like, but is proving anything but a star on the field. Renowned for his penalty goal kicking, he has barely managed to score at all so far and in February 2004 blamed Spanish referees for not enforcing the minimum 10-yard distance between penalty kicker and the wall of defenders. Any excuse will do...

Their grand Estadio Santiago Bernabéu, named after the club's greatest chairman, takes pride of place just off the Paseo de la Castellana in the northern half of central Madrid and getting tickets to big matches can be all but impossible. So long as you can steer clear of the radical *hinchas* (fans), the Ultras del Sur, the local equivalent of the nastiest of UK soccer bovver boys, a Real Madrid match can be an exciting high point of a stay in the city.

Madrid is home to two other teams, Atlético de Madrid (which at the time of writing was doing well in the top six of the league table) and Rayo Vallecano, languishing in the second division.

For details of how to see a match, turn to p164.

Right Royal Footballers

There was a strange symmetry about David Beckham's arrival in the Real Madrid side in the 2003–04 season. Never mind the £25 million price tag for the three-year contract that Real Madrid paid Manchester United. The sport itself came to Spain late in the 19th century from perfidious Albion. The jury is out so far on how big a contribution the pony-tailed genius will make to a team already loaded with stars...

The first Spanish clubs sprang up at the beginning of the 20th century. Among them was Madrid Foot-Ball, which came into being on 8 March 1902. It would later become Real Madrid. In 1902 Athletic de Bilbao won the first-ever Spanish championship cup, the Campeonato de Copa de España (later known as the Copa del Rey, Spain's equivalent of the English FA Cup), staged to celebrate the arrival on the throne of Alfonso XIII. Madrid took its first national cup against Athletic three years later.

In those early days, Madrid Foot-Ball team members wore white shirts, long trousers and blue berets. Later on, the blue berets went and a splash of purple was added to the team strip. Nowadays, depending on the day, they don anything from all white to light-blue jerseys with navy-blue trousers.

In 1920, King Alfonso XIII conceded the title of 'royal' to the Madrid club, which henceforth would be known as the Real Madrid Football Club.

The national league (Liga) got into full swing in 1928, but it was not until 1931 that *los blancos* (whites) or *merengues* (meringues), as Real Madrid were known, came out on top for the first time. It was hardly the last. Indeed, with 29 victories, Real Madrid has dominated the Spanish Primera División (First Division) with almost alarming consistency. Fans of arch-rival FC Barcelona will tell you that in the years of Primo de Rivera's dictatorship, and later under Franco, their team was frequently the victim of dodgy decisions.

Meanwhile, as the rest of Europe tore itself apart in WWII, Spain kept playing football. In September 1943 Santiago Bernabéu took the helm as club president, a post he retained for 32 years. A year later work started on the stadium along the Paseo de la Castellana that would bear his name and which remains to this day a mecca of Spanish football.

Bernabéu's time was the club's golden age. With hefty backing from Franco during the 1950s and 1960s, the side swept from one victory to the next at national and international level.

Real Madrid has dominated just about every other available competition too. The Copa del Rey has fallen into the whites' hands on 17 occasions. The introduction of the Champions League in 1956 only gave the side more space to display its bravura. Real Madrid managed to take the cup five times in a row, a record unequalled by any other European club. In all, the side has taken this cup nine times (the last in 2002). The club has been equally keen to lay its hands on the Spanish Supercopa (seven times), the UEFA Cup (twice) and Cup Winners' Cup (for the first time in 2002).

Bullfighting

Hemingway called it *Death in the Afternoon*. Some refer to it as an art and fewer as a sport. The quintessentially Spanish activity of bravado, the bullfight, is indeed hard to qualify. To the animal rights groups that oppose *la lidia*, it is simply a cruel and bloody spectacle.

Whatever your take, an afternoon of bullfighting (*la corrida*) is an essential part of Madrid life, particularly during the month-long season at Las Ventas bullfighting ring that begins with the Fiesta de San Isidro on 15 May (p11). This is the world's premier bullfighting season. Spanish and foreign bullfighters (*toreros*) aspire to (but rarely achieve) an appearance here.

On an afternoon ticket there are generally six bulls and perhaps three star matadors (those bullfighters who do most of the fighting and then kill the bull at the end). The matador leads a team (*cuadrilla*) of fighters who make up the rest of the colourful band who appear in the ring. It is a complex business but in essence the matadors aim to impress the crowd and jury with daring and graceful moves up close to as aggressive a fighting bull as possible. Although the death of the bull is generally inevitable (its meat is later sold), this in no way implies the bullfighter always gets off free. It is a genuinely dangerous business and being gored and tossed by several hundred kilos of bull is no fun.

While few modern fighters match the courage and skill of former greats like Luis Miguel Dominguín (1926–96) or Rafael Ortega (1921–97), there are some stars to look out for. They include: Jesulín de Ulbrique, Julián 'El Juli' López, 'Joselito' (José Miguel Arroyo) and El Cordobés (Manuel Díaz).

For more details on when and where to see a bullfight in Madrid, see p165.

Basketball

Although they don't get the same publicity, Real Madrid's basketball players are as much national champions as their footballing counterparts. The team has won 28 premier league competitions since it entered the league in 1956. It has also taken a host of other trophies, including the Copa del Rey (22 times) and eight European titles. Also popular is the less successful Adecco Estudiantes side (for match information see p165).

LANGUAGE

Español (Spanish), referred to by the more politically sensitive as Castellano (Castilian) to distinguish it from other languages spoken in the Spanish state (principally Catalan and its dialects, Basque and Gallego), is the language of the city. The Real Academia Española, located near the Prado, watches over Cervantes' tongue with deadly solemnity (and perhaps less humour than is good for its members when it comes to foreign lexical intruders) and issues the country's version of the Oxford English Dictionary, the weighty *Diccionario de la Lengua Española*. Ceding reluctantly to reality, the academy finally admitted the strange word *internet* to the dictionary in 2004.

Madrileños tend to talk at high velocity, a lively Spitfire of a language that, if you are interlocuting with a born-and-bred, colourful local, can be so laced with local slang *(cheli)* that you might wonder how much Spanish you ever learned!

While you will find plenty of Madrileños, especially younger people and hotel and restaurant employees, who understand some English, you cannot bank on it. Learning a little Spanish is worthwhile and will be rewarded, as some Spaniards tend to think a little like Anglo-Saxons: it is assumed people should speak Spanish (it is the world's third language after English and Chinese after all). See the Language chapter for the basics (p239).

ECONOMY & COSTS

Madrid is the uncontested financial capital of Spain. As the political capital this might seem to go without saying, but until recent decades the economic motors of the country were Barcelona and the Basque country. Indeed, eternal rival Barcelona has watched with

Plaza de Toros bullfighting ring (p165)

dismay as Madrid soars away as the country's prime economic mover, shedding its long-held image as the nation's bureaucratic deadweight. An interesting indicator of the capital's dynamism is the fact that 30% of national research and development takes place in Madrid. Mind you, R&D funding remains appallingly low in Spain, and a traditional brain drain to other European countries and the USA continues unabated.

The Banco de España (central bank) a nd the Ibex stock exchange are based here and, increasingly, international corporations with interests in Spain are establishing their main headquarters in Madrid. Madrid's Barajas airport is the main hub for international and domestic air transport and most railways and highways spread out of central Madrid like spokes of a wheel. The big edge that competing cities like Barcelona and Bilbao have over Madrid is something the landlocked capital will never be able to do anything about – their busy commercial ports. But this has not stopped Madrid from becoming the country's biggest economic hot spot.

The area around Madrid is home to a range of farming and industry. Principal crops include wheat, barley, corn, potatoes, alfalfa, melons, lettuce, garlic and grapes, but the region's share of national agricultural output is small. Livestock and dairy holdings are also scattered about the region. Principal industries include metallurgy, chemicals, textiles, tobacco, paper and some foodstuffs.

Average pay (up to €2500 gross per month for professionals) in this services and finance oriented city is 17% higher than the national average and slightly above the European average, but costs such as rent are also considerably higher. The national minimum wage, at €460 a month, is the second lowest (only the Portuguese are worse off) among the 15 'older' members of the European Union (before the May 2004 expansion). In 2003 unemployment began to rise again (7% in Madrid and 11.2% nationally according to one set of official figures). Worse, Spanish employers are masters of short-term contracts. Only 14% of job contracts signed in 2003 in Madrid were for full-time indefinite positions.

For the European visitor, Madrid remains affordable. Although the cost of accommodation has grown by leaps and bounds, it is still possible to eat well for reasonable prices. Lunchtime especially offers the possibility of the *menú del día*, a fixed-price, all-in set lunch that can cost under €10. Public transport and taxis are cheap compared with most other European cities and it is sometimes possible to visit some museums for free (see the 'It's Free Top Five' boxed text, p63, for more information).

How Much?

El País newspaper €1

Souvenir T-shirt €10 to €24

Entrance to the Prado €3

One litre of mineral water in supermarket €0.35

One litre of petrol €0.82

A caña (small glass of beer) of Mahou €1

A tapa €1 to €3

Admission to dance clubs €10 to €20

Normal letter (up to 20g) within Europe €0.52

Cocktail €6 to €8

GOVERNMENT & POLITICS

Three governments rule from Madrid. The national government (in the hands of the Partido Socialista Obrero Español, or Socialist Party, since March 2004 and headed by José Luis Rodríguez Zapatero) has its home in the Cortes (parliament), which is divided into two houses, the Congreso de los Diputados (lower house) on Carrera de San Jerónimo, and the Senado (senate), off the Plaza de España.

The city government is led by the mayor *(alcalde)*, who at the moment is the right-wing Partido Popular's Alberto Ruiz-Gallardón. He and his councillors (including Ana Botella, wife of José María Aznar, the former PP Spanish president) operate out of the Ayuntamiento (town hall) on Plaza de la Villa in the heart of the old city. Ruiz-Gallardón, who had been a popular president of the Comunidad de Madrid region until the May 2003 elections (regional and city), romped home with 30 seats (out of 55).

His colleague (with whom he does not exactly see eye to eye), Esperanza Aguirre, replaced him at the helm of the Comunidad de Madrid but did not have such an easy time of it. Defeated by a potential left-wing coalition in May, Aguirre got a second chance when two Socialist deputies defected, forcing an election replay in October 2003. Aguirre is the first-ever woman president of a Spanish region.

Madrileños are more than a trifle curious to see how their two high-profile women politicians will pan out, especially since their party no longer runs the nation. In a society that retains a strongly *macho* culture, Esperanza Aguirre and Ana Botella (who has taken on the tough assignment in a city like Madrid of social affairs) have, however unfair it may seem, a lot to prove.

Permanent seat of Spain's ruling royal house since the latter half of the 16th century, Madrid got a promotion in 1833 when it was decided to create a province around it. The Castilian provinces surrounding Madrid (in particular Segovia, Toledo and Guadalajara) all lost territory to make way for the newcomer. The decision was taken to bring the royal estates *(reales sitios)* of El Pardo, Aranjuez and San Lorenzo de El Escorial under the direct administration of the capital. In addition, it was hoped the move would lend the capital greater dignity.

Until the fall of Franco, the province of Madrid remained a part of Castilla La Nueva (New Castile), the predecessor of the modern region of Castilla-La Mancha. With devolution in 1983, the province of Madrid became a separate autonomous region *(comunidad autónoma)*. The new regions of Castilla y León and Castilla–La Mancha refused to take in the province, fearing Madrid would siphon off funds and attention from far-flung and needy corners of their respective regions.

Elections to the city and regional governments take place every four years (the last were in 2003). They are free and by direct universal suffrage. The members of each house thus elected then vote for the president of the province and the mayor (although their candidates for these jobs are generally established before the elections). The city of Madrid is divided into 21 districts, each with its own local council *(junta municipal)*.

ENVIRONMENT

THE LAND

Madrid lies at the heart of a single-province autonomous region (the Comunidad de Madrid) in the rough shape of a triangle. It covers 8028 sq km (less than 2% of Spanish territory) on a high continental plateau some 650m above sea level. The northwest boundary is closed off by a series of mountain ranges known collectively as the Sierra. They take in ranges of the Somosierra, the Sierra de Guadarrama and the Sierra de Gredos (all of which Madrid shares with the autonomous region of Castilla y León). They run from the northeast to the southwest for 140km and are part of the longer chain known as the Cordillera Central, which runs across much of central Spain. In winter some mighty cold winds blow off the mountains and into the city below.

Little opposes the continuing spread of suburban construction in any direction – and that is clearly observed when flying in. Indeed, Madrid continues to spread into the surrounding country and absorb what were once separate villages.

Historically, the narrow trickle that is the Río Manzanares, which runs roughly north to south, formed the natural western boundary of the city but phalanxes of high-rise apartment blocks have long swamped the river.

The steepest bit of terrain in the whole city is the ridge along which the original Islamic fortress town (the *alcázar*) was raised. From the Palacio Real, the Catedral de Nuestra Señora de la Almudena and Vistillas, the land falls away into parks towards the Manzanares. A tributary once raced down what is now Calle de Segovia.

Walking up Calle de Segovia, the Cuesta de San Vicente or any of the nearby parallel streets is about the only time you might work up a sweat from climbing while in Madrid.

To the east, the heart of old Madrid rises almost imperceptibly before dropping down again to the great north–south boulevard, the Paseo de la Castellana (which changes name several times in its long journey), itself laid in a former river bed. To the east of the Castellana is one of the city's principal green areas, the Parque del Buen Retiro. The other, the much more extensive and unkempt Casa de Campo, stretches west of the Manzanares.

GREEN MADRID

Although Madrid does not immediately strike one as the greenest of cities (it isn't!), its citizens do have access to several wide open spaces. The most central and attractive is the Parque del Buen Retiro, which once constituted the eastern boundary of the city and was the preserve of royalty and nobles. The carefully crafted green park, with sculpted gardens, artificial lakes and roaming paths, is a wonderful escape from the din of central Madrid. Just across the road from the Retiro is the charming little Real Jardín Botánico, a botanical garden packed with all sorts of exotic species.

Equally green and enticing for the romantic stroller is the Campo del Moro, which slopes away west of the Palacio Real. Shady paths wind around these artfully planned gardens.

Altogether wilder is the Casa de Campo, a much drier and grander expanse that stretches west of the Manzanares.

ENVIRONMENTAL ISSUES

Problems of air pollution in Madrid are typical of a comparatively crowded and busy city. Although restrictions apply to parking and driving throughout the centre of town, Madrid is generally full to bursting. Cars jostle about the place and the air is none too clean.

Rubbish disposal remains a fairly haphazard affair. Large, brightly coloured containers have been scattered about the city for the separated collection of paper, glass and cans – but use of them depends entirely on the citizenry. Discouragingly, it is not unusual to see mounds of rubbish piling up around these and other general-refuse containers – the stuff is eventually hauled off, but it is hard to escape the feeling that it is not a big priority.

The city seems locked in a continual struggle with its inhabitants. Every night the city streets are hosed down in what must represent a monumental consumption of water! And every day the good people of Madrid (some of them at least) diligently bestrew the place with paper, cigarette butts, food, plastic and so on. And not only do their dogs make an

There's a Bear in There

'Fui sobre agua edificada, mis muros de fuego son.' ('I was built on water and my walls are of fire.'). Thus went what was long Madrid's slogan and call sign. The town was rich in freshwater streams (now mostly covered up) and the flinty stone used to build its walls was excellent for sparking fires. It's a nice line, but sooner or later the town needed a worthy symbol.

It got a rather complicated one. The present city emblem is a she-bear nuzzling a *madroño*, or strawberry tree (so named because its fruit looks a little like strawberries), bordered by a frame bearing seven five-point stars and topped by a crown.

When Alfonso VI took Madrid from the Muslims in 1085, the town was symbolically seen by some as the first of a long line of conquests that would take the Christians south. Thus Madrid became an example of things to come, or a north point. As it happens, a group of seven stars that lies close to the North Star in the northern hemisphere form a shape known as the Ursa Minor, or small she-bear. Thus the bear (once also a common sight in the El Pardo area north of the city) and seven stars came to symbolise Madrid.

Above the frame is a crown. They say Carlos I allowed Madrid to use the symbol of the imperial crown in its coat of arms after he cured a fever using *madroño* leaves (a popular medicinal herb).

The five points of the stars represent the five provinces that surround Madrid (Segovia, Ávila, Toledo, Cuenca and Guadalajara).

This coat of arms appears on a deep-violet background to form the city's flag. When the Comunidad de Madrid was created as a region under the Autonomies Statute in the early 1980s, the town fathers had to come up with another flag. They chose to put the seven stars on to a red background, which symbolises the territories of Castile from which the new province was carved.

unpleasant contribution to the walkways, countless local chaps on late-night bar-hopping expeditions find it necessary to let open their flies in the streets of Madrid, generally *after* the official hosing down has taken place! The result is not always an olfactory pleasure.

Madrid is justly acclaimed for its nightlife. But this brings with it dubious pleasures for anyone trying to get some shuteye. Combined with the international bongo brigade, which hangs around the squares and streets of Malasaña in particular, the pleasure of some is most definitely the torture of others.

Noise pollution is a big problem throughout the city. Rowdy traffic, late-night rubbish collection, lusty use of sirens by the emergency services and trigger-happiness with car horns all help to keep nerves well jangled. To live in many streets in central Madrid is to invite insomnia. The general hubbub of bar-goers, cars and scooters starting up and passing by can go on until 4am or even later. If you're unlucky enough to live above a general store, you will often have delivery trucks, engines turning over, parked outside your place by 7am. And two hours later the intense traffic that is a call sign of downtown Madrid will have swept away any last chance you might have had to snooze. Long live double glazing.

URBAN PLANNING & DEVELOPMENT

The city is pushing its way out in all directions. Its peripheral ring road was long the M-30 until it was swallowed up by development; the much wider M-40 was completed in the 1990s, followed by the M-45, a more distant branch road running around the southeast edge of the city. Seeing that even this was not enough, another ring road, the M-50, has been started, with a first tranche to the southwest of the city opened in early 2004, along with the first of several new access tollways to the city. Environmentalists and other opponents of these projects claim they are an excuse to foment still greater urban expansion and that the M-50 in turn will prove inadequate if long-distance public transport does not get more attention.

The city continues to consume neighbouring towns and municipalities. Places such as Leganés and Getafe, to the south, are now barely distinguishable from the municipality of Madrid itself. The city seems to be surrounded by phalanxes of new apartment blocks, malls and armies of cranes creating still more. Whole new suburbs are being planned or already

Boats on the lake in Parque del Buen Retiro (p81)

under construction – a total of 300,000 apartments in massive building programmes that will swallow up pretty much all that remains of the available land in the Madrid municipal area by around 2020. Such an approach (with its inevitably speculative side) is fairly typical of the PP, and opposition parties have slammed the programme. They say the creation of soulless suburbs will do nothing for the city. They add that more work should be done to accelerate renovating the centre of the city, where in some areas like Lavapiés generally elderly people still live in Third World conditions without heating or private toilets.

Arts & Architecture

Arts & Architecture

One of Spain's youngest cities, Madrid presents the strange conundrum of being at once comparatively poor in historic architecture and at the same time the home of the country's greatest art treasures. In the Museo del Prado especially there is a veritable army of Spanish Old Masters of the calibre of Velázquez and El Greco, through to the precocious genius of Goya. But it doesn't stop there. Madrid is a metropolis in rapid development, looking forward to new horizons. It is fitting that it should also be a storehouse of modern and contemporary Spanish art, the biggest concentration of which hangs in the Centro de Arte Reina Sofía. Writers from across the country and beyond call Madrid home. The national cinema industry also gravitates to Madrid, although the city does not boast the kind of world-class studios of other European capitals (such as London and Rome).

VISUAL ARTS

From medieval obscurity Madrid has become the main repository of Spain's art treasures. The bulk of the grand works of past centuries was done for the royal court rather than the city, but today the city's galleries and their visitors reap the benefit of royal collections and modern bequests. After the frenetic if largely fading activity of the years of *la movida*, the city's many private foundations and little galleries keep Madrid bubbling along with artistic activity.

COURTING FELIPE II

Madrid doesn't really figure on the artistic radar prior to it being made capital in 1561. Even then, Felipe II remained refractory in the face of home-grown talent, preferring the work of Italians such as Titian and a series of lesser Mannerists. About the only Spaniard to attract the king's attention was Logroño-born El Mudo (the Mute), Juan Navarrete (1526–79), who became one of Spain's first practitioners of Tenebrism, a fashion that largely aped Caravaggio's chiaroscuro style.

Perhaps the most extraordinary, and temperamental, of the 'Spanish' artists of the 16th century was the Cretan-born Domenikos Theotokopoulos (1541–1614), known as El Greco (the Greek). On arriving from Italy, where he had trained, he decided that Toledo, 70km south of Madrid and Spain's ecclesiastic capital, would be the most lucrative place to ply his trade. He tried but largely failed to interest the king's court in his ethereal figures, and as Toledo's fortunes waned after 1561, so did his.

VELÁZQUEZ & THE GOLDEN AGE

As Spain declined politically, the royal court promoted fine arts to such a point that the 17th century is seen as Spain's Golden Age. The brightest and longest lasting star was Seville-born Diego Rodríguez de Silva Velázquez (1599–1660), who moved to Madrid as court painter and stayed. Velázquez stands in a class of his own. He composed scenes that owe their vitality not only to his photographic eye for light and contrast but also to a compulsive interest in the humanity of his subjects. His masterpieces include *Las Meninas* and *La Rendición de Breda* (The Surrender of Breda), both on view in the Prado (p77).

A less exalted contemporary and friend of Velázquez, Francisco de Zurbarán (1598–1664), moved to Seville as an official painter but wound up at the end of his life in poverty in Madrid. He is best remembered for the startling clarity and light in his portraits of monks, a series of which hangs in the Real Academia de Bellas Artes de San Fernando (p74).

Other masters of the era whose works hang in the Prado, although they had little to do with the capital, include José (Jusepe) de Ribera (1591–1652), who was influenced by Caravaggio and produced fine chiaroscuro works, and Bartolomé Esteban Murillo (1618–82).

Museo Sorolla (p97)

THE MADRID SCHOOL

While the stars were at work, a second tier of busy baroque artists beavered away in the capital and came to be known collectively as the Madrid School.

The monk Fray Juan Rizi (1600–81) did most of his work for Benedictine monasteries across Castile, including Madrid's Convento de San Martín. Some hang in the Real Academia de Bellas Artes de San Fernando (p74). Although his brother, Francisco Rizi (1614–85), also did his fair share of church work, he had more fun as a set painter for theatre pieces given in the Palacio del Buen Retiro for the capital's elite.

Claudio Coello (1642–93), the last important artist of the Madrid School, specialised in the big picture. Some of his enormous canvases adorn the complex at San Lorenzo de El Escorial (p213), among them his magnum opus, *La Sagrada Forma* (The Holy Form).

GOYA, SOROLLA & SOLANA

A provincial hick from the village of Fuendetodos in Aragón, Francisco José de Goya y Lucientes (1746–1828) could have had little idea of the impact he would make in Madrid and beyond. He is one of the towering figures of European art, in a class of his own.

Goya started his career as a cartoonist in the Real Fábrica de Tapices (Royal Tapestry Workshop) in Madrid. In the early stages of his rise, his portrayals of everyday scenes recall something of the candour of Hogarth and in some cases betray the influence of Tiepolo, whom Carlos III attracted to Spain to work on the Palacio Real.

In 1776 Goya began designing for the tapestry factory and by 1799 was appointed Carlos IV's court painter. Illness in 1792 left him deaf and many critics attribute this to a wild, often merciless style increasingly unshackled by convention.

Several distinct series and individual paintings mark his progress. In the last years of the 18th century he painted such enigmatic masterpieces as *La Maja Vestida* (The Young Lady Dressed) and *La Maja Desnuda* (The Young Lady Undressed), identical portraits but for the lack of clothes in the latter. The rumour mill suggests the subject was none other than the Duchess of Alba, with whom

Top Five Museums & Galleries

- Museo del Prado (p77)
- Museo Thyssen-Bornemisza (p79)
- Centro de Arte Reina Sofía (p73)
- Museo Arqueológico Nacional (p92)
- Real Academia de Bellas Artes de San Fernando (p74)

he allegedly fooled around, although no-one has ever been able to prove such scandalous claims. Whatever the truth of Goya's sex life, the Inquisition was not amused by the artworks, which it ordered to be covered up. Nowadays all is bared in the Prado (p77).

At about the same time as his mysterious *Majas*, Goya executed the playful frescoes in Madrid's Ermita de San Antonio de la Florida (p96) and *Los Caprichos* (The Caprices), a biting series of 80 etchings lambasting the follies of court life and ignorant clergy.

The arrival of the French and war in 1808 had a profound impact on Goya. Unforgiving portrayals of the brutality of war are *El Dos de Mayo* (The Second of May) and, more dramatically, *El Tres de Mayo* (The Third of May). The latter depicts the execution of Madrid rebels by French troops.

After he retired to the Quinta del Sordo (Deaf Man's House), as he called his modest country lodgings west of the Manzanares in Madrid, age and perhaps bitterness prompted the creation of his nightmarish *Pinturas Negras* (Black Paintings). Executed on the walls of the house, they were later removed and now hang in the Prado. A scandal erupted recently when it was claimed that these chilling works were actually doodled by the artist's son, Javier, and sold as genuine Goyas by his grandson. The Prado strenuously denies the claims. Goya spent the last years of his life in voluntary exile in France, where he continued to paint until his death. Carlos Saura's 1999 film, *Goya en Burdeos*, is not a bad treatment of the artist's final years in Bordeaux.

Although no-one of the stature of Goya can be cited in his wake, new trends were noticeable in the latter decades of the 19th century. Joaquín Sorolla (1863–1923) flew in the face of the French Impressionist style, preferring the blinding sunlight of the Valencian coast to the muted tones favoured in Paris. His work can be studied in Madrid's Museo Sorolla (p97).

Leading the way into the 20th century was Madrid-born José Gutiérrez Solana (1886–1945). Typical of his disturbing and avant-garde approach to painting are low lighting, sombre colours, and the deathly pale figures who people his works, emblematic of what historians now refer to as *España negra* (black Spain). See a selection of his canvases in the Centro de Arte Reina Sofía (p73).

Top Five Art Books

- *The Arts in Spain,* John Moffit – this is a handy and highly accessible single-volume introduction to the history of art in Spain
- *Goya,* Robert Hughes – the colourful art critic takes you on a rich discovery tour of one of Spain's greatest painters
- *Guernica – The Making of a Painting,* Joaquín de la Puente – a slim volume that reveals the story behind the creation of one of the 20th century's best known paintings
- *Picasso,* Carsten-Peter Warnke & Ingo I Walther – a generously illustrated study (in English) of the towering figure of modern Spanish art
- *Breve Historia de la Pintura Española,* Enrique Lafuente Ferrari – readers of Spanish with a serious wish to come to grips with the whole gamut of Spanish painting could do worse than this two-volume set

PICASSO, DALÍ & JUAN GRIS

Málaga-born Pablo Ruiz Picasso (1881–1973) arrived in Madrid from Barcelona in 1897 at the behest of his father for a year's study at the Escuela de Bellas Artes de San Fernando. But the precocious Picasso was already bored with school and instead took himself to the Prado to learn from the masters, and to the streets to depict life as he saw it. Picasso went on to become the master of Cubism and sundry other faces of 20th-century art. One of the best known of his works is *Guernica,* a complex painting portraying the horror of war and inspired by the German aerial bombing of the Basque town Gernika in 1937. It hangs in the Centro de Arte Reina Sofía (p73).

In 1922, Salvador Dalí (1904–89) arrived in Madrid from Catalonia. He didn't like studying at the Escuela de Bellas Artes de San Fernando any more than Picasso, but his time in the capital was important for other reasons. For four years he lived in the 'Resi', the renowned students' residence (which still functions today) where he met poet Federico García Lorca and future film director Luis Buñuel. The three self-styled anarchists and bohemians romped through the cafés and music halls of Twenties Madrid. Brothels, pranks, jazz and *tertulias* (endless literary chats) were their daily bread. Dalí, a wacky artist and later a consummate self-promoting showman, was finally expelled from art school and left Madrid, never to return. The only remaining link of the artist with Madrid is a handful of his hallucinatory works in the Centro de Arte Reina Sofía (p73).

In the same gallery is a fine selection of the Cubist creations of Madrid's Juan Gris (1887–1927), who was turning out his best work in Paris while Dalí and Co. were up to no good in Madrid. Along with Picasso and Georges Braque, he was the principal exponent of the Cubist style.

ART IN CONTEMPORARY MADRID

The death of Franco in 1975 unleashed a frenzy of activity, much of it frivolous and destined not to last, in the Madrid art scene. Indeed, artistic creativity was caught up in the drink, drugs and sex explosion that was *la movida*. The Moriarty Gallery in trendy Calle del Almirante became a central point of artistic exuberance. A parade of artists marched through the gallery, among them such leading *movida* lights as Ceesepe (born 1958), whose real name is Carlos Sánchez Pérez. Aside from his busy paintings, at first full of people and activity and recently veering to a more surrealist side, he captured the spirit of 1980s Madrid in eight short films. Another Moriarty protégé was Ouka Lele (born 1957), a self-taught photographer whose sometimes weird works stand out for her tangy treatment of colour. Some of her photos are held in the collections of various museums around Madrid, including the Centro de Arte Reina Sofía and Museo Municipal. Another *movida* photographer who still exhibits *chez* Moriarty is Alberto García-Alix (born 1956).

The explosion of rebellious, effervescent activity in the 1980s tends to cloud the fact that the visual arts in the Franco years were far from dead. Many artists spent years in exile. One of Spain's greatest 20th-century sculptors, Toledo-born Alberto Sánchez (1895–1962) lived his last years in Moscow. He and Benjamín Palencia (1894–1980), an artist whose paintings occasionally show striking similarities with some of Sánchez's sculptures, were part of the so-called *Escuela de Vallecas* (Vallecas was once a village and is now a roughish outer suburb of Madrid). Pablo Palazuelo (born 1916) produced a steady flow of paintings and iron sculptural works. His latest works are characterised by hard abstract lines and he frequently bases sculptures on his own paintings. The art of Eduardo Arroyo (born 1937) is steeped in the radical spirit that kept him in exile from Spain for 15 years from 1962. His paintings tend in part to pop art, brimming with ironic socio-political comment.

José María Sicilia (born 1955), a radical Expressionist who has spent much time in Paris and New York, was another big name of the 1980s. He divides his time between Mallorca and Paris and claims rather archly that his paintings existed before he did them, in the sense that frequently the surfaces he chooses contain all sorts of potential images and reliefs. Carlos Franco (born 1951) did the frescoes on the Casa de la Panadería on Playa Mayor. Antonio López García (born 1936) takes a photographer's eye to his hyperrealistic paintings. Settings as simple as *Lavabo y Espejo* (Wash Basin and Mirror, 1967) convert the most banal of everyday objects into scenes of extraordinary depth. His Madrid street scenes are equally loaded with detail, light play and subtle colour. His contemporary Alfredo Alcain (born 1936), whose textured paintings could at times be mistaken, in the distance, for aerial shots of patchwork fields. He won the coveted Premio Príncipe de Asturias for art in 2004.

The Moriarty gallery is still going strong and has been joined by phalanxes of other galleries. The big event in Madrid is the annual mid-winter Arco contemporary art fair, which goes from strength to strength as a showcase for both emerging and established Spanish talent, mixed with an international flavour.

ARCHITECTURE

Madrid's delayed emergence as a European capital has perhaps influenced its attitude to its own urban heritage as much as the physical development of the city itself. Madrid doesn't waste too much time reflecting self-indulgently on its not always glorious past and instead looks forward. Much of the modern metropolis we see today was in any case built from the late 19th century on. Its grand boulevards, especially the north–south axis of the Paseo de la

Top 10 Notable Buildings

Castellana (under all its various names) are lined with the city's recent urban history.

Ambitious Art Deco structures lend a sometimes pompous, sometimes genuine, grand-eur to the lower end of this avenue and Gran Vía. For all the neo-Gothic silliness of a building like the grandiloquently named Palacio de Comunicaciones (ie the post office!), the whole effect resplendent with swirling roundabouts and fountains, is the unmistakable feel of the capital that other Spanish cities, however replete with history, could never exude.

Uninhibited by needing to respect historic heritage architecture, the Paseo de la Castellana, as it sweeps north away from the Prado, is a smorgasbord of modern metropolitan building. The occasional tower (such as the Torres de Colón) mushrooms out of nowhere but much of the building is rather more medium-rise. Some of it is downright ugly but parts have a not displeasing, bustling air.

Not all has been neglected or destroyed (although many fine old 19th-century and still older buildings have, down the years, been sacrificed to the virtues of modernisation). The elite *barrio* of Salamanca retains all the huffy high-class splendour accorded it by the fine apartment buildings raised in the late 19th and early 20th centuries. Much the same can be said of *barrios* west of the Castellana, such as Chamberí.

Since the 1980s the city has rediscovered its historic core. Slowly but surely, the small concentration of monuments that makes up historic Madrid, and the often splendid housing around them, have been given a makeover and restored to their former glory. Some areas, the notably colourful but down-at-heel Lavapiés and parts of Malasaña, still have a way to go.

MADRID TO THE 16TH CENTURY

Madrid came to life as a Muslim fortification (see History, p85) and evolved as a small Castilian town until Felipe II took the surprising decision in 1561 to establish the court of Imperial Spain permanently in what was little more than a squalid ensemble of timber housing interspersed with the odd grand church or palace and laced with fetid lanes. Even then it took the city a long time to develop significantly.

The only reminder of the Muslim presence in Madrid is a modest stretch of the town wall below the Catedral de Nuestra Señora de la Almudena (p66). Visitors to Madrid with a yen for Muslim architecture should get the high-speed AVE train down to Córdoba (p212) to see the magnificent Mezquita (mosque). Day trippers ican get a taste of some of Spain's past architectural glories by visiting surrounding cities: Segovia (p203) for the incredible Roman aqueduct and fine Romanesque churches; Toledo (p202) for remnants of Visigothic art and the heritage in rich *mudéjar* building. Both cities also boast grand Gothic cathedrals.

All that remains of the *mudéjar* style in Madrid are the bell towers of the Iglesia de San Pedro El Viejo (p84) and Iglesia de San Nicolás de los Servitas. The *mudéjares* (Muslims who remained behind in re-conquered Christian territory) displayed priceless architectural skills and their influence is evident across much of Spain. One unmistakable *mudéjar* feature is the preponderance of brick, as is clear in the two Madrid churches. Around the country, castles, churches and mansions were built of this material. Extravagantly decorated timber ceilings, often ornately carved, are another hallmark of the *mudéjar* hand and can be seen in various buildings in Toledo and Segovia. The term *armadura* refers to any of these wooden ceilings, especially when they have the appearance of an inverted boat.

As noted, Toledo and Segovia, along with Ávila, boast fine examples of Gothic architecture, a style that sprang from the humbler Romanesque in France and saw the erection of great soaring churches across medieval Europe. The style largely passed Madrid by. All that remains from the era is the much-interfered-with, late-Gothic Casa de los Lujanes (p112), and the beautiful, hidden away Capilla del Obispo (p84).

RENAISSANCE & BAROQUE

The few signs of style that Madrid began to develop in the course of the 16th century came in spite of its otherwise preoccupied ruler, good King Felipe II. He found it impossible not to become involved in the minutiae of the running of his empire and its wars. Not only that, but he had to build his mausoleum/palace/summer getaway at El Escorial. In short, he had precious little time to give thought to improving the grubby town he had chosen for his capital. Indeed, even before Felipe's momentous decision, the town fathers had been making a bit of an effort as the Renaissance blossomed in Spain.

What had begun in Italy as an extraordinary flowering of the arts and architecture in the previous century could roughly be divided into three distinct styles in Spain. First was the Italian-influenced special flavour of Plateresque, best appreciated in Salamanca, west of Madrid (see Lonely Planet's *Spain*). One of its main exponents, Alonso de Covarrubias (1488–1570), was busy in his home city of Toledo (he designed the Alcázar, p206). Another more purist form of Renaissance building under the likes of Diego Siloé (1495–1563) developed in Andalucía.

Finally, Juan de Herrera (1530–97) was the last and perhaps greatest figure of the Spanish Renaissance. Herrera developed a style unlike anything else of the period. His austere masterpiece was the palace-monastery complex of San Lorenzo de El Escorial (p213).

Even after his death, Herrera's style lived on in Madrid. The sternness of his Renaissance style fused with a timid approach to its successor, the more voluptuous, ornamental baroque. Together they formed a characteristic style known as *barroco madrileño*. The façades of the Real Casa de la Panadería, the Palacio del Duque de Uceda (now the Capitanía General; p69), the Ayuntamiento and the Convento de la Encarnación (p67) loosely fall into this category. The last two were designed by Juan Gómez de Mora (1586–1648), whereas his uncle Francisco de Mora (1560–1610) had a hand in the Palacio del Duque de Uceda. Gómez de Mora was also behind the royal prisons facing Plaza de la Santa Cruz, now the Ministerio de Asuntos Exteriores (Ministry of Foreign Affairs).

The Basílica de San Isidro, completed in the 1660s, is another example of restrained baroque, although it clearly moves a little closer to the gaudier style of Franco–Italian influence with which most people are more familiar. In Madrid one of the few other clear tastes of the style is the main entrance of what is now the Museo Municipal (p88).

Ventura Rodríguez (1717–85) dominated the architectural scene in 18th-century Madrid much as Goya lorded it over the world of art. He redesigned the interior of the Convento de la Encarnación and did the Palacio de Liria. His style was controlled and clearly heading towards neo-classicism. His main competition came from the Italian Francesco Sabatini (1722–97), who finished the Palacio Real (p68) and raised the triumphal Puerta de Alcalá.

Juan de Villanueva (1739–1811) designed the neo-Classical pile that would bear his name and eventually house the Museo del Prado (p77), as well as numerous outbuildings of the royal residences such as San Lorenzo de El Escorial.

Museo del Prado (p77)

Moneo's Modern Miracles

It took a brave individual to shoulder the burden of modernising the Museo del Prado, Spain's premier art collection housed in the venerable late 18th-century Palacio Villanueva. Rafael Moneo, born in the northern town of Tudela in 1937, was that fellow. The Madrid-based architect was no stranger to urban challenges. One of his first major tasks was the construction of the Bankinter building (Map p263) in Madrid in 1976. After the mania of the 1960s for destroying 19th-century mansions and replacing them with bland blocks, Moneo demonstrated there was another way. He created a seemingly monolithic façade for the bank on one side and a series of linking buildings to incorporate a still-standing 19th-century mansion into the property. Just for once, the needs of the modern business concern were successfully wedded to aesthetic considerations. Moneo, who was behind projects as diverse as Barcelona's Auditori (1999) and the bizarre, bulging cathedral of Los Angeles (2000), met another major Madrid challenge with his remodelling of the Antigua Estación de Atocha in 1992. Again, he combined the needs of the modern era (a station capable of handling the new high-speed AVE train to Seville and a host of other links) with pleasure. The 19th-century iron and glass station building was preserved and converted into a tropical garden, a huge glasshouse (p72). The Prado is one of his biggest undertakings to date. Modernising the main gallery and linking it with the Casón del Buen Retiro and what little remains of the cloisters of the Iglesia de San Jerónimo el Real has been an enormously delicate task, not made any easier by the need to keep the Prado open throughout.

BELLE ÉPOQUE

As Madrid emerged from the chaos of the first half of the 19th century, a building boom got under way. The use of iron and glass, a revolution in building aesthetics that symbolised the embracing of modernity, became all the fashion. The Palacio de Cristal in the Parque del Buen Retiro was built at this time, along with train stations, markets and other public edifices.

By the dawn of the 20th century, known to many as the *belle époque* (that brief period of supreme European optimism before the continent collapsed into the frenzied killing of WWI), Madrid was abuzz with construction. A gaggle of architects from all over the country was at work. Headed by the prolific Antonio Palacios (1874–1945), they transformed Madrid and gave it its airy feeling of the capital rediscovered.

Many looked to the past for their inspiration. Neo-*mudéjar* was especially favoured, in Madrid and beyond, for bullrings. The ring at Las Ventas, finished in 1934, is a classic example. The most obvious of the neo-Gothic creations is the Catedral de Nuestra Señora de la Almudena (p66), only completed in 1992. A more bombastic interpretation of the style is Palacios' Palacio de Comunicaciones (p81) on the Cibeles roundabout. You can't miss this glorified general post office, finished in 1917, with its plethora of pinnacles and prancing ornament. Still, at the time it was reckoned a masterpiece reflecting the glory of Spain. For that reason its style is sometimes referred to as *españolista*.

Across the way is the more sober but nonetheless grandiose temple to Mamon, the Banco de España, finished in 1891 in what some call the 'eclectic' style, a polite way of saying mishmash. But mishmash can be pleasing. Architects felt free enough to look to past styles, mix and match and create new, difficult-to-categorise hybrids. Many of them are today thrown together as being Art Deco, although that is not always strictly accurate. Among these joyous and eye-catching buildings (Gran Vía is jammed with them) are examples such as the 1916 Edificio Grassy and the Edificio Metrópolis (1905).

The brief but florid blooming of modernismo (the local version of Art Nouveau construction) in Barcelona towards the end of the 19th century was a largely regional affair that left most of Spain as untouched as it was unmoved. Gaudí and Co had few counterparts outside Catalonia, and just one seriously sinewy mansion in the style was raised in Madrid, the Sociedad General de Autores y Editores building in Malasaña (p90).

CONTEMPORARY MADRID

Emblematic of Madrid's entry into the 20th century is the Telefónica building (p108) on Gran Vía. Built in the 1930s, it is a squat but impressive citadel, used by Franco's troops in the Casa de Campo to aim artillery fire into the heart of the city from 1936 to 1939.

Franco's victory ushered in a period of austerity. By the 1950s the construction business was again active and the 1960s brought a positive boom, albeit often of questionable taste.

The Edificio de España in the square of the same name is an extraordinary piece of what we might call dictatorial architecture. It would not look out of place in Soviet Moscow.

Much of what is new and skyscrapery in Madrid has gone up along the city's main axis, Paseo de la Castellana, especially in the Nuevos Ministerios area. Capping the boulevard to the north are the strange leaning Torres Puerta Europa on Plaza de Castilla.

Madrid is undergoing a period of unprecedented urban expansion (see p23). Some big names are at work on calling-card projects. Henry Cobb is planning a tower of glass, the Torre Espacio, for the northern end of the Paseo de la Castellana, where at least three other 45-storey skyscrapers will join it in part of a plan to cover the railway lines of Chamartín and create apartment blocks, offices and shopping centres. Ricardo Bofill is working on converting dumps in the south of the city into landscaped parks, while Richard Rogers' new terminal for Barajas airport is the biggest public works project under way in Europe. Rogers (who is working with Spanish architect Carlos Lamela on the project) can barely hide his pleasure at working in Madrid 'at this time of rebirth'.

Rogers may be chuffed but not everyone is happy with what's happening. One truly Madrileño architectural team is the couple Ignacio García Pedrosa and Ángela García de Paredes, who completed the modern re-design of the Teatro Olímpico in Lavapiés in 2004. They see the city's growth as raging out of control. 'The city expands in spasms and most of the urban projects lack character,' claims Pedrosa. 'Other cities have grown with a greater and more professional overall vision,' adds his wife.

LITERATURE

FROM THE SIGLO DE ORO TO PÉREZ GALDÓS

Spanish letters blasted off in the late 16th century and many writers inevitably gravitated to the capital. The Siglo de Oro or 'Golden Century' of Spanish writing begins with perhaps the greatest of all Spanish poets, Seville-born Luis de Góngora (1561–1627). Unconcerned by theories, morals or high-minded sentiments, Góngora manipulated words with a majesty that has largely defied attempts at critical 'explanation'; his verses are above all intended as a source of sensuous pleasure.

The Siglo de Oro was very much Madrid's century. The greatest scribblers of the epoch were either born or spent much of their time in the young capital (for playwrights, see Theatre p39). Francisco de Quevedo (1580–1645) spent much of his time in Madrid taverns scribbling some of the most biting, nasty and entertaining prose to come out of 17th-century Spain. His *La Historia de la Vida del Buscón Llamado Don Pablos*, tracing the none-too-elevating life of an antihero, El Buscón, is laced with venom and is his most lasting work.

The man thought of as the father of the novel was born in Alcalá de Henares and ended his turbulent days in Madrid. Miguel de Cervantes Saavedra (1547–1616) started writing *El Ingenioso Hidalgo Don Quijote de la Mancha* (Don Quixote) as a short story to earn a quick peseta. It turned instead into an epic tale in 1605. The ruined *ancien régime* knight and his equally impoverished companion, Sancho Panza, embark on a trail through the foibles of his era – a journey whose timelessness and universality marked the work out for greatness.

Benito Pérez Galdós (1843–1920), Spain's Balzac, spent virtually all his adult life in Madrid. His more mature works, such as *Fortunata y Jacinta*, display a bent towards naturalism and, in the early 20th century, even symbolism. The novel recounts much more than a tormented love triangle, throwing light on the mores of late 19th-century Madrid. It has been brought to the screen several times, notably in a 10-part TV series in 1980 starring Ana Belén and Maribel Martín.

Top Five Madrid Novels

- *Fortunata y Jacinta*, Benito Pérez Galdós (1887)
- *La Colmena*, Camilo José Cela (1957)
- *Capital de la Gloria*, Juan Eduardo Zúñiga (2003)
- *El Capitán Alatriste*, Arturo Pérez-Reverte (1996)
- *Historias del Kronen*, José Ángel Mañas (1994)

MODERN MADRID WRITING

The censors of Francoist Spain kept a lid, albeit far from watertight, on literary development in Spain, and Madrid was no exception. Much of what was good in Spanish writing was penned by writers in exile. Since then, there has been a flowering of Spanish letters and Madrid is at the heart of it. Not only does the city produce bucketloads, but various foreign writers, such as Peruvian Mario Vargas Llosa, have settled there.

Although not a Madrileño by birth, Camilo José Cela (1916–2002) wrote one of the most talked about novels on the city in the 1950s, *La Colmena* (The Beehive). This classic takes the reader into the heart of Madrid, the beehive of the title, in what is like a photo album filled with portraits of every kind of Madrid punter in those grey days. Cela took the Nobel for literature in 1989 and the most important Spanish literature prize, the Premio Cervantes, six years later.

Francisco Umbral (born 1935), a prestigious journalist and winner in 2000 of the Premio Cervantes, is yet another chronicler of the city. *Trilogía de Madrid*, which explores a whole range of different circles of Madrid life in the Franco years, is just one of several Madrid centric novels to his credit. Some have praised Umbral as the greatest prose writer in Spanish of the 20th century (Cela would no doubt snort in disagreement).

In *Capital de la Gloria*, Juan Eduardo Zúñiga (born 1929) presents a moving portrayal of Madrid and its people in 10 stories set during the last months of Republican resistance against Franco's forces in the Civil War.

Murcia´s Arturo Pérez-Reverte (born 1951), long-time war correspondent and general man's man, has become one of the most internationally read Spanish novelists. In *El Capitán Alatriste* we are taken into the decadent hurly-burly of 18th-century Madrid. The captain in question has become the protagonist of several novels.

Almudena Grandes (born 1960), in her most recent novel, *Los Aires Difíciles,* traces the growth of a relationship between two Madrileños who have moved to the south coast near Cádiz, both of them with an uncomfortable past in the big city. She has published four others and several series of short stories.

Although born in Extremadura, Madrid likes to think of Dulce Chacón (1954–2003) as one of its own. Poet, playwright and novelist, she truly came into her own in the mid-1990s. Her last novel is perhaps her most moving. In *La Voz Dormida,* Chacón traces the at times harrowing stories of women across Spain mistreated by the victors of the Civil War.

The author of *the* cult urban tribal novel in Madrid is with little doubt José Ángel Maña (born 1971). In *Historias del Kronen* a band of young disaffected Madrileños hangs out in the Kronen bar and throws itself into a whirlwind of sex, drugs, violence and rock 'n roll.

Another emerging talent is José Machado (born 1974), whose *Grillo* is a heavily autobiographical look at a young Madrileño lad of good family determined to be a writer. It's a little like looking into a mirror that looks into a mirror...

A curious work is Roger Osbourne's *The Dreamer of the Calle de San Salvador*. Set in the Madrid of Felipe II, it is difficult to categorise. The account of a young Madrid girl, Lucrecia de León, given to having portentous dreams that a series of clerics took to transcribing and interpreting, is disconcerting and chilling. Based on the 16th-century transcripts of the clerics who interviewed Lucrecia, one is left with the questions largely unanswered at the time. Was Lucrecia just a dreamer? Was she part of the conspiracy to damage the king? Osbourne takes us back to Madrid's early days as capital.

Tower of Telefónica building (p96)

MUSIC

CLASSICAL & OPERA

If Spain has been noticeable mostly by its absence from the world of great classical music and opera, Madrid has been even less blessed. The few Spanish composers of note (such as Isaac Albéniz, Enrique Granados, Joaquín Rodrigo and Manuel de Falla) all came from other parts of the country.

The single obvious exception to the rule is Plácido Domingo (born 1934), the country's leading opera tenor and born *gato*. Early childhood was where the charming singer's relationship with Madrid more or less ended, as his parents, *zarzuela* performers, moved to Mexico, where he made his singing debut years later.

Critics lament the lack of much home-grown talent in Madrid or beyond the capital. Although it is true that Madrileños now have more opportunities to appreciate world class performances of classical music and opera, audiences are comparatively limited and little seems to be being done to increase the general level of education in, or awareness of, 'serious music'.

Techno Takes Off

Luis Rozalen goes by many names. One of the pioneers of the electronic music scene in Madrid, he did the rounds of the few clubs indulging in techno in the early 1990s. As a solo operator his mixes first saw the light of day in a compilation album with other DJs, *Electronic Generators*, in 1994. Two years later his first CD, *Eleven*, hit the dance floors of Spain and beyond. Since then he and his group, known as HD Substance, have hit the European circuit, playing anywhere from London to Berlin and back to Madrid again, and establishing their names as leaders in Spanish techno. When flying solo he works under the pseudonym of Milinko. Under that name he brought out his first CD, *A New Life*, in 2001. The following year Rozalen appeared at topline electronic festivals such as Barcelona's Sonar fest and the Arezzo Wave in 2002. He continues to appear both as Milinko and as the group HD Substance in such mythical locations as Florida 135, reputedly one of the biggest discos in all Spain in the town of Fraga (Aragón).

CONTEMPORARY MUSIC

Madrileños may be reticent about the highbrow stuff but they are no slouches when it comes to contemporary music. The crazy days and the hell-for-leather lifestyle of the city's youth even today seems to have marked the place out as a bastion of rock.

Since the days of *la movida* in the 1980s, Madrid's home-grown rock scene has been vibrant. Seguridad Social is a good old-fashioned hard-rock group that has remained a surprisingly constant force since they first started playing in 1982. Their latest CD, *Otro Mares*, is as powerful as any of their other 14 albums. Another legend in Madrid is rock poet Rosendo Mercado, who started off with the group Leño in the late 1970s, later went solo and hasn't stopped since.

After the delirious 1980s, in which such iconic groups as Radio Futura, El Último de la Fila, Nacha Pop and Mecano (and punkier ensembles such as Alaska and Kaka de Luxe) came and went, the Madrid pop scene went a little quiet. One curious exception that has kept the rock flag flying with Seguridad Social is Dover, a Madrid quartet that belts out energetic indie rock in English and was enjoying the height of popularity during their national tour in 2004. Their latest CD, *The Flame*, was recorded in Madrid after a period in which they did most of the studio work in the USA.

Recently emerged from the rock bar scene in Malasaña with their first CD, *Just Married*, is the pop quartet Balboa. Led by guitarist Carlos del Amo and his singer girlfriend Lua Ríos, they have combined the energy of rock with a strong guitar lead and a soft poppie touch in Lua's voice and lyrics. Another Madrid rock group that has bounced back into the limelight are Alcorcón boys Sôber. These four lads with chunky goatees first played in the 1980s, when heavy metal ruled. Nowadays they play a softer rock and count Madrid's young among their biggest fans.

Not everyone in Madrid is a head-banger. Three years after his band Nacha Pop split Madrid-born Antonio Vega (born 1957) put out his first solo disc in 1991. Vega was one of the sensations of the mid-1990s with his soft pop-rock, and in 2001 he was nominated for the Grammy Latinos.

Out of the working class periphery of Madrid has emerged another little music sensation, La Excepión, a hip-hop trio that goes beyond the sometimes senseless, egotistical lyrics frequently associated with the genre. Their songs are full of social critique and humour, and at times allow a whisper of other influences, including flamenco, to colour their melodies.

A hip-hop star who likes to mix in a little reggae and lounge into his electronic wizardry is Roty 340.

Most of these acts are likely to be seen in larger venues like La Riviera (p163).

(p163)

Top Five CDs

- *De Un Lugar Perdido*, Antonio Vega – an icon of Madrid pop, his 2001 record is one of his best
- *Otros Mares*, Seguridad Social – good clean rock n' roll from Madrid's never say die band
- *The Flame*, Dover – for those who like their Spanish indie rock in English
- *Nacha Pop 1980–1988*, Nacha Pop – the classic *movida* band's only live album, recorded at their last concerts and containing a selection of their best songs
- *A New Life*, Milinko – the best in Madrid techno from one of its veterans (at the tender age of 30)

FLAMENCO

The musical and dance form most readily identified with Spain is rooted in the *cante hondo* (deep song) of the *gitanos* (Roma people) of Andalucía, and probably influenced by North African rhythms.

The melancholy *cante hondo* is performed by a singer, who may be male *(cantaor)* or female *(cantaora)*, to the accompaniment of a blood-rush of guitar from the *tocaor* (guitar player). The accompanying dance is performed by one or more *bailaores* (flamenco dancers).

It is impossible here to delve into the different kinds of song and music (ranging from the anguished *siguiriyas* and *soleás* to the more toe-tapping *bulerías, boleros, fandangos, alegrías* and *farrucas*). A good website (in Spanish) is at www.deflamenco.com.

Although flamenco emerged in southern Spain, it is not the exclusive preserve of Andalucía. Since the mid-19th century, the best performers of flamenco have turned up at one time or another in Madrid – and many were born there. At first, the *gitanos* and Andalucians were concentrated in the area around Calle de Toledo. The novelist Benito Pérez Galdós found no fewer than 88 Andalucian taverns along that street towards the end of the 19th century. The scene shifted in the early 20th century to Plaza de Santa Ana, where the singer Antonio Chacón (1869–1929) performed in Los Gabrieles and the Villa Rosa (both of which still exist).

The genre flourished in the 1920s but with the Civil War things went downhill. Not until the 1950s did flamenco come to life again. In those dark years of austere dictatorship, even fun was considered suspect and so the hidden world of smoky cabarets and *tablaos* (flamenco shows) was born. These shows, now often geared to tourists, usually lack the genuine emotion of real flamenco, although a few are worth seeing if you have no alternative. Many of the original places have disappeared, but some, such as the Corral de la Morería and Café de Chinitas, are still in business today (see p157).

Want to learn? There are a dozen dance schools that teach flamenco in Madrid. The best known (and probably hardest to get into) is the **Academia Amor de Dios** (☎ 91 530 16 61; Calle de Fray Luís de León 13).

FLAMENCO STARS

Since the 1980s flamenco has enjoyed an extraordinary flowering both in Spain and abroad.

Paco de Lucía (born 1947) is the best-known flamenco guitarist internationally. He has a virtuosity few can match and is the personification of *duende*, that indefinable capacity to transmit the power of flamenco. After many years abroad he decided to return to Spain in 2004, promising not to do any more concerts outside his native country.

The list of fine flamenco guitarists is long, among them the Montoya family (some of whom are better known by the sobriquet of Los Habichuela), especially Juan (born 1933) and Pepe (born 1944).

Paco de Lucía's friend El Camarón de la Isla (1950–92) was, until his death, the leading light of contemporary *cante hondo*; plenty of flamenco singers today try to emulate him. Another artist who has reached the level of cult figure is Enrique Morente (born 1942), referred to by a Madrid paper as 'the last bohemian'. A venerable *cantaora* is Carmen Linares (born 1951).

Of Spain's countless flamenco dancers and choreographers, one of the greatest names is with little doubt Antonio Ruiz Soler (1921–96). One of the great all-time *bailaoras* was the fiery Barcelona-born Carmen Amaya (1913–63). Leading contemporary figures include the flighty, adventurous Joaquín Cortés (born 1969) and Antonio Canales (born 1962), more of a flamenco purist.

> ## Top Five Flamenco CDs
>
> - *Canciones Hondas*, Ketama – this CD is one of the best ever by the rocky flamenco fusion group Ketama – miles better than the Gypsy Kings!
> - *Lágrimas de Cera*, El Lebrijano – a mix of classic flamenco, Easter songs and Arabic music
> - *Territorio Flamenco* – a great introduction to flamenco, including such names as Carmen Linares, Estrella Morente and Miguel Poveda
> - *Piano Jondo*, Diego Amador – modern flamenco with piano, a delicious experiment
> - *Caja Integral de Paco de Lucía. Fuente y Caudal del Flamenco*, Paco de Lucía – for the *apasionado*, you can get hold of this collection of 26 CDs and book of the man many consider the most important living performer of flamenco guitar (search for it online at www.deflamenco.com)

NUEVO FLAMENCO & FUSION

Possibly the most exciting developments in flamenco have occurred during its visits to other musical shores. The purists loathe these changes. In the proud *gitano* world, innovation has often met with abrasive scorn.

Two of the best-known groups that have experimented with flamenco-rock fusion since the 1980s are Ketama and Pata Negra, whose music is labelled by some as *Gypsy rock*. In the early 1990s, Radio Tarifa emerged with a mesmerising mix of flamenco, North African and medieval sounds. A more traditional flamenco performer, Juan Peña Lebrijano, better known simply as El Lebrijano, has created some equally appealing combinations with classical Moroccan music.

Young performers are taking it a step further. Rakel Winchester, a group led by singer Raquel Riquelme, is almost impossible to categorise, a kind of flamenco mixed up with rock and punk. Raquel herself is a *paya* (in the view of the *gitanos* anyone who is not a *gitano* is a *payo*), and some have described the band's music as *paya punk* – definitely one to watch.

More to the liking of flamenco purists willing to countenance a little modernising is Diego Amador (born 1973), a self-taught pianist. The piano is not a classic instrument of flamenco but Amador makes it work.

DANCE

Nacho Duato, head and principal dancer of the Madrid-based Compañía Nacional de Baile since 1990, has transformed it from a low-profile classical company into one of the world's most technically dazzling and accomplished contemporary dance groups. Founded in 1978, the Ballet Nacional de España mixes classical ballet with Spanish dance. Both perform regularly in Madrid and around the country.

CINEMA & TELEVISION

Spanish cinema, with several exceptions, was fairly limited by censorship in the Franco years. In the last three decades the industry has shown great vitality but suffered perpetual financial constrictions. Mercedes Sampietro, president of the Academia de Cine, lamented the overall state of the industry at the beginning of 2004. 'There are years when one or two Spanish films save the whole industry at the box office, and that just cannot be.'

As elsewhere in Europe, the overwhelming preoccupation in Spain is the crushing predominance of Hollywood blockbusters. Spanish movie-making is generally done on modest budgets and manages some great hits, but public funding has fallen in real terms under the conservative Partido Popular government since 1996. Sampietro is hoping the government will make good on promises to increase the budget for the country's cinema protection fund in 2004. In 2003, in spite of an overall drop in audience numbers, 16% of box office takings were for Spanish films. Perhaps the downside is that the lion's share went to a home-grown slapstick comedy, *Mortadelo y Filemón*.

Although Madrid is the uncontested capital of the nation's film industry, comparatively few Madrileños actually make the flicks.

Madrid's senior cinematic bard is Juan Antonio Bardem (born 1922). He wrote the script for Luis García Berlanga's 1952 classic, *Bienvenido Mr Marshall* (Welcome Mr Marshall), and followed in 1955 with *Muerte de un Ciclista* (Death of a Cyclist). His son, Javier, has become one of the best-known faces in Spanish cinema, starring in many local and several foreign flicks. The Bardems have their fingers in several pies and run a trendy *tapas* bar in downtown Madrid.

Fernando Trueba (born 1955) has signed some fine Spanish films, the best of which was his 1992 *Belle Epoque*. A good dose of gentle romps and bed-hopping on a country estate in Spain in 1931 as four sisters pursue a slightly ingenuous young chap against a background of growing political turbulence. Behind the scenes on this and many Spanish movies is the publicity-shy, Madrid-based Rafael Azcona, surely one of the cinema's most prolific screenplay writers. *Belle Epoque* took an Oscar.

Pedro Almodóvar (born 1951) repeated the trick in 2000 with his 1999 hit, *Todo Sobre Mi Madre* (All About My Mother). The capital likes to think of Almodóvar as one of its own. He lived the years of *la movida* in the capital, but was born and raised in the south of Castilla–La Mancha. He won many early fans with such quirkily comic looks at modern Spain, generally set in the capital, as *Mujeres al Borde de un Ataque de Nervios* (Women on the Verge of a Nervous Breakdown; 1988) and *Átame* (Tie Me Up, Tie Me Down; 1990). In his latest, *La Mala Educación* (Bad Education; 2004), he returns to Madrid, although much of the twisted story of a drag queen, his brother and a school friend turned film maker, takes place elsewhere.

An astounding line-up of some of Spain's best actresses comes from Madrid. They include: Victoria Abril (born 1959), Ana Belén (born 1950), Penélope Cruz (born 1974), Carmen Maura (born 1945) and Maribel Verdú (born 1970). In the late 1990s Penélope took a leap of faith and headed for Hollywood where she has had success in such films as *Captain Corelli's Mandolin* (2001) and *Vanilla Sky* (2001).

Top Five Films Set in Madrid

- *La Colmena* (The Beehive; 1982) Based on the classic novel by Camilo José Cela, the film is an extraordinarily faithful rendition of this portrait of a Madrid in the grey years of the 1950s, sparkling with all sorts of characters, including a cameo appearance by the author himself.
- *Amantes* (Lovers; 1991) Vicente Aranda's film is set in 1950s Madrid and is based on the real story of a doomed love triangle.
- *Historias del Kronen* (1994) In Montxo Armendariz's film, a slightly depressing story of alienated urban youth emerges from the heart of Madrid. Based on the novel of the same name.
- *Carne Trémula* (Live Flesh; 1997) Loosely based on a Ruth Rendell novel and set in Madrid in 1992, many hailed this as Pedro Almodóvar's best movie to date when it appeared. The tortured themes of sex, violence and love are all there in a twisted love thriller starring Javier Bardem.
- *La Comunidad* (The Community; 2000) Directed by the generally wacky Alex de la Iglesia, this is a cheerfully off-the-wall tale of greed in a Madrid apartment block starring Carmen Maura as the newcomer in the block, where all the neighbours are trying to get their hands on the lottery stash of the elderly chap upstairs who dies shortly after Julia (Maura) moves in.

Watching and waiting outside the Teatro Español (p148) on Plaza de Santa Ana

International TV gloop landed in Madrid some years ago and for a while the entire city seemed to be glued to the *caja tonta* (silly box) absorbed by the antics of *Gran Hermano* (Big Brother) and *Operación Triunfo* (which propels singing unknowns to intergalactic fame). The good news in 2004 is that finally people seem to be tiring of reality TV and going back to sitcoms and soaps, a far superior form of pop culture when you look at it. The musical comedy *Paco y Veva* is top of the charts and in early 2004 *Manolito Gafotas*, extracted from a popular local cartoon character, was also pipping *Gran Hermano*, which has lost half its audience since it first aired in 2000. Manolito, with his outsize glasses, is the most popular kids' cartoon character in Spain. He has twice been converted into a movie subject and now a TV series that follows this feisty boy's antics in the Madrid suburb of Carabanchel.

THEATRE

The literary Golden Age that characterised 17th-century Madrid also filled the sails of theatrical creation with the winds of genius. Some of the country's all-time greatest playwrights were at work in much the same period. Lope de Vega (1562–1635), also an outstanding lyric poet, was perhaps the most prolific: more than 300 of the 800 plays and poems attributed to him remain. He explored the falseness of court life and roamed political subjects with his imaginary historical plays. You can visit his house even today (p72). Perhaps of greater substance is the work of Tirso de Molina (1581–1648), in whose *El Burlador de Sevilla* (The Seducer of Seville) we encounter the immortal Don Juan, a likeable seducer who meets an unhappy end.

The works of Pedro Calderón de la Barca (1600–81) were laced with agile language and inventive dramatic techniques. His storylines were, however, comparatively run-of-the-mill. His most powerful are *La Vida es Sueño* (Life's a Dream) and *El Alcalde de Zalamea* (The Mayor of Zalamea). In both Calderón upholds the idea of righteousness and justice irrespective of class and caste.

Food & Drink

Food & Drink

Spain is a little rougher and readier at the table than its closest Mediterranean neighbours. But while it does not always reach the heights of self-conscious sophistication of some French cooking or the pleasing comfort of the best in Italian cuisine, food in Madrid is always fun and often very good. Whether you stand at a bar nonchalantly chomping on seafood tapas or sit down for a meal at one of the city's zillions of restaurants and taverns, the experience is generally pleasant (for the palate and wallet) and frequently delightful.

It is impossible to talk of a single 'Spanish cuisine', as it is made up of many regional varieties. It is even more difficult to talk of a Madrid cuisine, which aside from a handful of traditional dishes takes pride in being a culinary crossroads of Spain's myriad gastronomic traditions. Combined with a growing range of foreign cuisines, this means Madrid offers the best of Spain and the wider world in its countless eateries. So dig in!

HISTORY & CULTURE

Madrid has attracted as many cuisines from the provinces as hopefuls to royal, liberal, republican and dictatorial courts. Good thing too, because the city's history is hardly one of culinary richness. Medieval Madrid was a simple place and the bulk of its inhabitants scraped by on a limited diet, the staple of which was cereals (often barley). All the wonderful bread so common today was a rarity, as was meat. Seafood was utterly unheard of. Fruit and vegetables, typically grown along the Manzanares, were by no means available to all. Olive oil, a standard element of much Mediterranean cooking and an integral part of the Muslim diet, was an expensive luxury to Madrileños. In such a calorie-poor diet, wine (bad wine) played an important nutritional role, but even that was in chronic short supply. That was then!

In spite of the harsh history of inland Spain, the nation's cuisine as a whole is typically Mediterranean, liberal in its use of olive oil, garlic, onions, tomatoes and peppers. A particular spin comes from the country's long history of Muslim occupation, reflected in the use of such spices as saffron and cumin and, in desserts, the predominance of honeyed sweets. The high place accorded to almonds and fruit also betrays a lasting Muslim influence. The other big source of culinary richness was South America, whence came such elements taken for granted today as potatoes and tomatoes (not to mention coffee and chocolate).

The regions of Spain all have their own specialities. The Catalans and Basques are the most serious and inventive about their food. Their tables are replete with seafood and meat and in both cases various sauces play an important role. Fish and seafood rule further west along the coast, especially in Galicia, where tuna, squid, octopus, shellfish and all sorts of other bizarre sea critters play a star role. The rainy north is also the epicentre of dairy production. Fish dominates in Andalucía too, although with lesser variety. Valencia brought us probably the country's single most famous dish, paella. At its best it is a huge wok-like pan of saffron-coloured rice dripping with morsels of seafood.

Inland, meat (especially roasts) and game dominate – simple and heavy fare which when it's good is very good. From the south comes the obsession with ham (*jamón*), as well as the *tapa*, to accompany your drink at the bar. The *tapa* has become a phenomenon of its own and can range from a few free olives with your tipple through to the elaborate concoctions the Basques come up with (better known as *pintxos*).

Landlocked Madrid is one of the biggest fish- and seafood-consuming cities in the world. Tonnes of the stuff are daily trucked and trained into town from the distant coast. Spain's fishing fleet is the EU's biggest and they cast their nets far and wide (even to the point of causing diplomatic incidents with Canada) to keep Madrileños (among others) happily munching on the catch of the day (or yesterday).

This is no recent phenomenon. Laurie Lee mentions it in *As I Walked Out One Midsummer Morning*, a delightful tale of his pre-Civil War rambles across Spain, and the tradition goes back a couple of centuries. Just how fresh the fish transported from the coast by horse-drawn cart could have been is a moot point. The Maragatos of northwest Castile, who dominated the northern Spanish carrying trade, had a spark of inspiration when they began buying up and salting cod in the ports, then sending it on to Madrid. This *bacalao* was prepared in various ways, and one local version that has remained is bite-sized fried portions with a thin strip of red capsicum on top, known as *soldaditos de Pavía*. What bits of cod have to do with little soldiers from Pavia (Italy) is anyone's guess. Other favoured fish in Madrid are *merluza* (hake) and *besugo* (sea bream).

Madrid is undergoing something of a tastebud revolution. In the mid-1990s local food lovers would drool over a handful of restaurants offering exotic (read non-Spanish) cuisine. What started as a trickle has taken on critical mass and foreign (especially Asian) eateries are springing up all over the place. The designer restaurant with hard-to-define 'international' and mixed Med cuisine has also emerged as a genre, as have stylish chains. And those all-time favourite snack options in London, Paris, New York and Sydney, kebabs and falafels, have now landed in force. This writer observed an elderly couple peering inside one such joint with evidently diffident curiosity. Ah, what is coming over this city! they must have thought.

It is a virtual food fest for appreciative Madrileños looking for the occasional distraction from their old favourites. For the visitor, it simply means greater choice, which can only be good news. You can find purveyors of good Middle Eastern, Italian, Chinese, Indian, Japanese, Cuban, Korean, Thai and Indonesian food around town. Fast-food options, from McDonald's to home-grown versions offering *bocadillos* (rolls) with various fillings, also abound (although Madrileños are less attached to the idea of eating fast than their counterparts in Barcelona in the north of the country).

Vegetarians, and especially vegans, can have a hard time in Spain, but in Madrid a growing battery of vegetarian restaurants offers welcome relief to meat-loathers.

Ham it up with *a* bocadillo de jamon *(ham roll)*

ETIQUETTE

Grabbing the attention of waiters can be a time-consuming business in some restaurants, al
though in smarter places they are usually pretty quick to attend. Generally diners order a bottl
of wine and water and you will be provided separate glasses for each (in Spain the larger glass i
for the water). In mid-summer (mostly at lunch time) you might also ask for some Casera (like
Sprite) to mix with and dilute your heavy red wine and make *tinto de verano* (summer red).

A full meal generally comprises an *entrante* (starter), *plato principal* (main course) an
postre (dessert). You can skip the starter without causing offence. If you opt for the *men*
del día (set lunch) you pay a set price for the three courses plus house wine and water
Coffee is extra.

In many simpler restaurants you will keep the same knife and fork throughout the meal
As each course is finished you set the cutlery aside and they whisk away the plates. Once you
order is taken and the first course (a starter that could range from a simple *ensalada rusa* – a
cold vegetable salad thick with potatoes and mayonnaise – to an elaborate seafood item) is ir
place, you may find service accelerates disconcertingly. This especially becomes the case as you
reach the end of any given course. Hovering waiters (where were they when you wanted to see
the menu?) swoop like lean eagles to swipe your unfinished dish or lift your glass of wine, stil
tinged with that last sip you wanted to savour. *'Todavía no he terminado'* ('I haven't finished
yet') you may point out – you'll be flashed a cheerful smile and your waiter will be off.

Don't get too excited by dessert. Clearly in more sophisticated restaurants you will have
all sorts of temptations but in your average Madrid eatery, especially at lunch, it might be
nothing more than a simple choice of fruit, *flan* (crème caramel) or *helado* (ice cream). I
you opt for the ice cream, don't be surprised to be shown a list of manufactured goodies
of the sort you'd grab at the beach.

Non-smokers be warned. Spain is a smokers' paradise and restaurants seem to be a favourite place for this activity. Not only do Spaniards smoke with satisfaction at the conclu-
sion of a filling meal, many smoke between courses, regardless of whether their co-diners
have finished or not. Some classier restaurants have non-smoking sections, but this is the
exception rather than the rule.

Don't jump out of your seats if people coming and going past your table address you
with a hearty *'buen provecho!* They're just saying 'Enjoy your meal!'

HOW MADRILEÑOS EAT

You might not arrive in Madrid with jet lag but, due to the different Spanish eating habits,
your tummy will think it has abandoned all known time zones.

Breakfast *(desayuno)* is generally a no-nonsense affair taken at a bar on the way to work.
A *café con leche* with a pastry *(bollo)* is the typical breakfast. You may get a croissant or
some cream-filled number. Some people prefer a savoury start – you could go for a *sandwich*
mixto, a toasted ham and cheese. A Spanish *tostada* is simply buttered toast (you might
order something to go with it). Others, especially party animals heading home at dawn after
a night out, go for an all-Spanish favourite, *churros y chocolate*, a lightly deep-fried stick of
plain pastry immersed in thick, gooey hot chocolate.

Lunchtime *(comida/almuerzo)* is basically from 2pm to 4pm and is generally the main
meal of the day, although modern work and living habits are changing this for some
Madrileños. The traveller's friend is the *menú del día*, a set-price meal comprising three
courses, with a drink thrown in and generally only available at lunchtime. You can often
find them for around €9 to €12. So you can eat solidly and economically at lunch and then
splash out at dinner! A simpler version still is the *plato combinado*, basically a meat-and-
three-veg dish that will hardly excite taste buds but will have little fiscal impact.

On the subject of dinner *(cena)*, no local would even start thinking about it before 9.30pm
and most people don't head out to eat until after 10pm. Most (but not all) kitchens close
by midnight or 1am.

Instead of heading for a sit-down restaurant meal, many locals prefer to *tapear* or *ir de*
tapeo (go on a tapas crawl). This is the delightful business of standing around bars and
choosing from a range of tasty little goodies. You can stay in one place or move around from
one to another. You basically keep munching and drinking until you've had enough.

The origin of the *tapa* appears to lie in the old habit of serving drinks with a lid *(tapa)* on the glass, perhaps to keep out pesky bugs. The *tapa* might have been a piece of bread and at some point a couple of morsels on the *tapa* became par for the course – usually salty items bound to work up a greater thirst. In some bars in Madrid you will still get a few olives or other snack with your beer, free. For more sophisticated tapas, you pay, and this is more the norm than the exception nowadays.

A *tapa* is a tiny serving and if you particularly like something you can have a *media ración* or even a full *ración*. Two or three of the latter, depending on what they are, can easily constitute a full meal. Clearly they cost more too!

Don't panic! If your gastric juices can't hold out for the 'late' starting times, there are intermediate options. Many bars and restaurants serving tapas and *raciones* have them out before and after the appointed main meal times, which means you can always pick up something. Some restaurants open early enough to cater for northern European eating habits – although you sometimes pay for this with mediocre food and the almost exclusive company of other tourists.

As mentioned, many bars and other establishments offer some form of solid sustenance. This can range from *bocadillos* (filled rolls), tapas and *raciones* to full meals in *comedores* (sit-down restaurants) out the back. *Cervecerías* (beer bars), *tabernas* and *tascas* (taverns), *bodegas* and *cuevas* (wine cellars) are some of the establishments in this category.

For a full meal you will most frequently end up in a *restaurante*, but other names will pop out at you. A *marisquería* specialises in seafood, while a *mesón* (big table) might indicate (but not necessarily) a more modest eatery.

STAPLES & SPECIALITIES

The basics are simple enough: bread and olive oil. And lots of garlic. No Spaniard would eat a meal without bread, and olive oil seems to make its way into just about everything. Spices, on the other hand, are generally noticeable by their absence. If you're told something is *picante* (spicy, hot) you can generally be sure it is little more than mild.

The typical *carta* (menu) begins with starters such as *ensaladas* (salads), *sopas* (soups) and *entremeses* (hors d'oeuvres). The latter can range from a mound of potato salad with olives, asparagus, anchovies and a selection of cold meats – almost a meal in itself – to simpler cold meats, slices of cheese and olives.

The basic ingredients of later courses can be summarised under the general headings of *pollo* (chicken), *carne* (meat), *mariscos* (seafood), *pescado* (fish) and *arroz* (rice). Meat may be subdivided into *cerdo* (pork), *ternera* (beef) and *cordero* (lamb). If you want a side order *(guarnición)*, you may have to order separately. This may be the only way to get a decent serve of vegetables *(verduras)*, which for many locals seem to be detested.

If you opt for tapas, it is handy to identify some of the common items: *boquerones* (white anchovies in vinegar…delicious and tangy); *albóndigas* (good old meat balls); *pimientos de Padrón* (little green peppers from Galicia – some are hot and some are not); *patatas bravas* (potato chunks bathed in a slightly hot red sauce, sometimes mixed with mayonnaise); *gambas* (prawns, either done *al ajillo*, with garlic, or *a la plancha*, grilled); *chipirones* (baby squid, served in various ways); *calamares a la Romana* (deep-fried calamari rings)…the list goes on.

Of the truly local dishes, *cocido a la Madrileña* is the best known. It is a kind of hotpot or stew. Into the broth are tossed various vegetables, chickpeas, chicken, beef, lard and possibly other sausage meats too. In the old poor man's version you were lucky to find any meat at all. A real favourite with Madrileños but something of an acquired taste is *callos* – tripe. A typical Castilian opener is *sopa de ajo* (garlic soup) or *sopa castellana*, basically broth with an egg floating about in it. All this stuff, as you may have guessed, is pretty basic. A good deal of Castilian cooking reflects the poverty in which many of its people lived for centuries, indeed until the last 40 years or so.

As already hinted, however, the range of cuisine available in Madrid covers the entire nation's richness and a host of modern, inventive, mixed Med and international options. Refined cooking in splendid surroundings is as much an option as a noisy Cuban meal or a typical serving of steaming hot *callos*.

DRINKS
NONALCOHOLIC

Clear, cold water from a public fountain or tap is a Spanish favourite – but check that it' *potable* (fit to drink). For tap water in restaurants, ask for *agua de grifo*. *Agua mineral* (bot tled water) comes in innumerable brands, either *con gas* (fizzy) or *sin gas* (still).

Coffee, Tea & Hot Chocolate

The coffee in Spain is strong and slightly bitter. A *café con leche* (generally drunk at breakfas only) is about half coffee, half hot milk. Ask for *grande* or *doble* if you want a large cup, *e vaso* if you want a smaller shot in a glass, or a *sombra* if you want lots of milk. A *café sol* (usually just *un solo*) is a short black; *un (café) cortado* is a short black with a little mill (*macchiato* in Italy). For iced coffee, ask for *café con hielo*; you'll get a glass of ice and a ho cup of coffee, to be poured over the ice – surprisingly it doesn't all melt straight away!

Madrileños prefer coffee, but you can get hold of many different styles of *té* and *infusione* (herbal teas such as camomile). Locals tend to drink tea black. If you want milk, ask for i to come separately *(a parte)* to avoid ending up with a cup of tea-flavoured watery milk.

A cup of *chocolate caliente* (hot chocolate) is an invitation to sticky fingers – it is a thick dark sweet tooth's dream and could just as easily be classed as a food product as a drink.

Fruit & Soft Drinks

Orange juice *(zumo de naranja)* is the main freshly squeezed juice available, often serve with sugar. To make sure you are getting the real thing, ask for the juice to be *natura* otherwise you run the risk of getting a puny little bottle of runny concentrate.

Refrescos (cool drinks) include the usual international brands of soft drinks, local brand such as Kas, and, in summer, *granizado* (iced fruit crush).

A *batido* is a flavoured milk drink or milk shake. *Horchata* is a Valencian drink of Islami origin. Made from the juice of *chufa* (tiger nuts), sugar and water, it is sweet and tastes lik soya milk with a hint of cinnamon. You'll come across it both fresh and bottled (but thi is a drink that should be consumed freshly made). A naughtier version is a *cubanito* an involves adding a fat dollop of chocolate ice cream.

Hot chocolate time at the Chocolatería de San Ginés (p125)

ALCOHOLIC

One rule of drinking etiquette to observe closely in bars: never ask for or suggest having just one last drink. Madrileños always order the *penúltima* (next but last), even if it really is the last of the evening. To mention the *última* (last) is bad luck, it sounds like one's last drink on Earth. Of course, the problem with ordering a *penúltima* is that it frequently leads to ordering another subsequently…

Wine

Spain is a wine-drinking country and *vino* (wine) accompanies almost every meal (even most Spaniards draw the line at breakfast). Spanish wine, whether *blanco* (white), *tinto* (red), or *rosado* (rosé) tends to have some kick, in part because of the climate and in part because of grape types and production methods. That said, the long adhered to policy of quantity over quality has in many wine-making regions for some time given way to a far subtler approach. It is still possible to find cheap, rough, kick-ass stuff that makes your mouth pucker and which a disparaging Spaniard would write off simply as *garrafón* (plonk). But the palette of wine styles coming out of Spain has become much more sophisticated in recent decades.

At the bottom end of the market (apart from true *garrafón* in the form of almost giveaway Tetrabrik wine casks), an entirely drinkable bottle of table wine can easily enough be had for around €3 to €4 in supermarkets and wine merchants (especially the old kind, a slowly dying breed, where they will fill your bottle for you). The same money in a restaurant won't get you far, however. Apart from house wine *(vino de la casa)*, which it is common to order at lunchtime by the litre or half litre, you will be looking at an average of €10 for a reasonable bottle and considerably more for something classy.

You can also order wine by the glass *(copa)* in bars and restaurants, although the choice of wines will be more limited.

A complicated system of wine classification is in place. As in the other major wine-producing countries of the EU, there are two broad categories: table wine and quality wine. The former ranges from the straightforward *vino de mesa* (table wine) to *vino de la tierra*, which is a wine from an officially recognised wine-making area. If they meet certain strict standards for a given period, they receive DO status. An outstanding wine region gets the DOC *(denominación de origen calificada)*. The number of DO regions is growing, although some may cover little more than a few vineyards. The only DOC wines come from the Rioja region in northern Spain, which was demarcated in 1926, and the small Priorat area in Catalonia.

Classifications are not always a guarantee of quality, unfortunately, and many drinkers of Spanish wine put more faith in the name and reputation of certain producers or areas than in the denomination labels. This has been more recently reflected in some *vinos de la tierra*, produced by adventurous vintners little bothered by the old rules. They are with increasing frequency superior to DO or DOC wines.

Most of the best wine is produced in the north of the country, the Penedès area in Catalonia (whites and sparkling wine), Rioja, Navarra, Ribera del Duero (reds) and Galicia (whites). Sherry rules in Andalucía, while the Valdepeñas area of southern Castilla–La Mancha produces some interesting drops.

Locals may try to sell you on some of the young, light *vinos de Madrid* from the surrounding region. These wines have DO standing and some aren't bad at all, but it is fair to say that the Comunidad de Madrid is not renowned for its quality wine production. Traditionally, the Valdepeñas area was long the capital's principal supplier. The thing about Madrid today, however, is that you can get your hands on wines from across the country, giving you a chance to sample the best Spain has to offer.

The occasional foreign wine is sneaking its way into specialist wine merchants' stores and certain restaurants but overall Spanish wines rule. As one Madrid importer of Australian wines often laments, Spaniards tend not to be adventurous, preferring to stick to their tried and true favourites rather than taking leaps into the unknown. Many remain doggedly faithful to the tipples of a region they know well, avoiding even the risk of trying wines from other parts of the country!

Food & Drink – Drinks

Beer

If Madrid could be said to have a flagship drink, apart from the strange animal that is *licor de madroño* (see Other Drinks below), it would be lager style beer. The most widespread local draught and bottled brand is Mahou, first produced in Madrid by a French entrepreneur in 1890. Lighter is Cruzcampo, which was first produced in Seville in 1904.

Otherwise, two Catalan companies, Damm and San Miguel, each produce about 15% of all Spain's beer. San Miguel is common; Damm's main brand, Estrella, is a little harder to come by. If you can get hold of beers by Galicia's Estrella, you'll be pleased. Plenty of foreign beers are also widely available.

Frothing & Bubbles

To slake your thirst at the bar you can just ask for a *cerveza* (beer) but it's better to know exactly what you are after.

The most common order is a *caña*, a small glass (*vaso*) of draught beer (*cerveza de barril*). In the heat of the summer, this is the best way to make sure they keep coming cold. A larger beer (about 300ml), more common in the hipper bars and clubs, usually comes in a *tubo* (a long, straight glass).

The equivalent of a pint is a *jarra*, unless of course you're in a pseudo-Irish pub, in which case you can also ask for a *pinta*.

If you do just ask for a *cerveza* you may get bottled beer, which is more expensive. A small bottle of beer is called a *botellín* or *quinto* because it contains a fifth of a litre. A larger one (330ml) is often referred to as a *tercio* (as in a third of a litre).

A *clara* is a shandy, a beer cut with *gaseosa*, which is virtually the same as Sprite (pronounced in Spain *e-sprite*) or 7-Up.

And who said the Spaniards don't have a sense of humour? Many bars also provide extremely large plastic beakers of beer (usually for the youngsters). The beer is not always great (and often cut with water), but is cheap and abundant. These huge containers are called...*minis*.

Other Drinks

Sangria is a red wine-and-fruit punch (usually with lemon, orange and cinnamon), sometimes laced with brandy. It's refreshing going down but can leave you with a sore head. Indeed, the origins of the drink go back to the days when wine quality was not always what one might have hoped for and the vinegary taste needed a sweetener to make it all palatable. Another version you might come across is *sangría de cava*, the same drink made with sparkling white. *Tinto de verano* is a mix of wine and Casera, a brand of *gaseosa* (like Sprite).

There is no shortage of imported and Spanish-produced top-shelf stuff – *coñac* (brandy) is popular. Larios is a common brand of gin but it doesn't get too many rave reviews from resident Brits!

You will on occasion be asked if you'd like a *chupito* to round off a meal. This is a little shot of liqueur or liquor but the idea is to help digestion. Popular and refreshing Spanish ones are *licor de manzana verde* (green apple liqueur) and *licor de melocotón* (peach), both transparent, chilled and not relatively light in alcohol terms (around 20%).

Madrid's emblematic drink, but one few locals actually bother with, is *licor de madroño* (strawberry-tree liqueur), a light-brown, high-octane drop extracted from the fruit of Madrid's symbolic strawberry tree. A couple of *madroño* bars exist in Madrid. El Madroño (Plaza de Puerta Cerrada 7) is one of the few bars specialising in *licor de madroño*. Outside, one of the ceramic illustrations on the walls reproduces Veláquez's *Los Borrachos* (The Drunkards).

Anisado de Chinchón is a very popular *anis* (aniseed-based drink) produced in the town of the same name south of Madrid. A nationally popular drink that swings between sweet liqueur and something a little harder is Ponche Caballero. If you wander into a Galician restaurant you might come across their version of grappa, a clear firewater made with crushed grapes and called *orujo*.

History

History

Ah Madrid. It's always been a city which defies comparison. It's true that Madrid has none of the noble legacy of cities, such as London and Paris, founded by mighty Rome. Selected from rural obscurity to become capital in the second half of the 16th century, it has shaken off its humble origins – indeed to many, Madrid is now regarded as one of the most exciting cities in Europe.

THE RECENT PAST

On 11 March 2004, Madrid was touched by a whiff of the horror visited on New York in September 2001. At rush hour that morning, just three days before the country was due to go to the polls, 10 separate bombs went off on three commuter trains heading into the capital's Atocha station, killing 190 people and wounding 1400. It was the biggest such terror attack in the nation's history and left the city reeling.

At first it was assumed the Basque terror group ETA was responsible and so the ruling right-wing Partido Popular government insisted in the following days. That insistence began to ring hollow as suspicion grew that the attack might have come from a radical Islamic group in reprisal for the government's unswerving support of US President George W Bush's invasion of Iraq. That policy had never enjoyed popular support (quite the contrary) and the PP was clearly worried that the assassins' bombs could leave shrapnel in its election campaign too.

Whether that was the case or not, the PP was defeated in an extraordinary upset by the PSOE (Partido Socialista Obrero Español), whose candidate José Luis Rodríguez Zapatero thus led the Socialists back to power after eight years in the wilderness on 14 March 2004.

Thank heavens! PSOE supporters in the capital must have thought. For the previous year had been an electoral disaster for the left. The PP's Alberto Ruiz-Gallardón won the mayoral elections with an absolute majority in May and his colleague, Esperanza Aguirre, became the country's first ever woman regional president in close-run regional elections for the Comunidad de Madrid in October 2003.

Since 1996 the three levels of government in Madrid (local, regional and national) had been in the same party's hands and observers from other regions claim they overtly favoured development of the capital. Whatever the truth of such accusations, the city has moved ahead in leaps and bounds.

As the national economy took off in the late 1990s, Madrid felt the effects. Extraordinary expansion programmes for the metro, highways, airport, outer suburbs and for inner city renewal are unmistakable signs of confidence. According to one set of statistics, up to 75% of inward foreign investment into Spain is directed at the capital.

The extraordinary pace of development in the capital is no doubt aimed in part at the International Olympic Committee, which will decide in 2005 on whether to award the 2012 games to Madrid.

Madrid's PP period, which began at town hall level in 1991, was preceded by a long and liberating time under the PSOE. The first free municipal elections after Franco's death were held in Madrid in 1979, and the Marxist Enrique Tierno Galván became mayor of a left-wing council. A charismatic leader, he was in charge of the city until his death in 1986. His successor, Juan Barranco, kept power in socialist hands until 1991.

TIMELINE	c4000 BC	854	932
	Neolithic tribes present around the Río Manzanares	Muhammad I, Emir of Córdoba, establishes fortress of Magerit (Mayrit)	Christian king Ramiro II of Castile tries in vain to take the fortress of Magerit

Esperanza in Charge

On Saturday 22 November 2003 Spain's first ever regional woman president took power. Esperanza Aguirre (born 1952), mother of two, let a few tears drop as she thanked her parents, children and key party members for their support. But Aguirre is anything but a liberal softie. A tough right-wing PP member and former national education minister, she has a long political history. After years as a public servant she became an opposition member of the Madrid town hall in 1983. With 1.6 million votes at the 1996 general elections, she was the most voted for woman senator in Spanish history and became minister of education and culture in José María Aznar's first PP government. By 1999 she was the speaker of the Senate, a post she abandoned to dedicate herself to the elections in the Comunidad de Madrid in 2003. She makes little attempt to hide her dislike for her predecessor, the present mayor of Madrid Alberto Ruiz-Gallardón. She dismissed all but one of his staffers in the regional government on taking over and, asked subsequently what she thought of Gallardón's chances of being nominated by the PP as national presidential candidate, La Presidenta replied shortly 'his time hasn't come'.

Galván's time at the helm coincided with an explosion of zesty nightlife that came to be known as *la movida*. Indeed some say he kicked it off by telling Madrileños to 'get stoned and watch out'. Drinking, drugs and sex suddenly were OK. After decades of grey repression, young Madrileños discovered the 60s, 70s and early 80s all at once. Much of the most outlandish behaviour revolved around small cliques such as that attached to the as yet relatively unknown film director Pedro Almodóvar. He enjoyed himself doing drag acts in smoky bars that people in the know would frequent. The dope- and cocaine-fuelled *movida* charged along through most of the 1980s. All night partying was the norm, cannabis was virtually legalised and the city howled. Up and down the Paseo de la Castellana, summer terraces roared to the chattering, drinking, carousing in-crowds. Some of the terraces, although quieter, are still there.

There was a downside to all this. Freely available high-quality drugs were one thing, but the apparent collapse of control led to a spiralling junkie problem in Madrid. When AIDS struck, it struck with a vengeance. Whereas the beautiful people sipped *cubatas* at 5am, bag snatchers prowled the city squares and streets looking for money to finance their habit.

Most people identify the end of the fun with the arrival of the PP's José María Álvarez del Manzano in power in the Ayuntamiento in 1991 with an absolute majority. In the following years rolling spliffs in public became increasingly dangerous and creeping clamps were imposed on the almost lawless bars.

Of course, it's all relative. Things may have quietened down a little since those heady days but Madrid and its people still maintain a healthy appetite for hedonism.

Ayuntamiento (town hall) at Plaza de la Villa (p68)

1085	1309	1348	1474
Alfonso VI of Castile occupies Magerit and Toledo	The Cortes (royal court and parliament) sit for the first time in Madrid	The plague hits Madrid; the town's first *regidor* (governor) is appointed by the king	Isabel is crowned Queen of Castile

FROM THE BEGINNING

To imagine the kind of settlement that might have preceded what is now Madrid, wander down to the Río Manzanares. Archaeologists have found abundant material around the river that demonstrates a human presence, probably nomadic, as far back as Palaeolithic times. Neolithic tribesmen brought their flocks to drink at the river and graze, but it is uncertain whether any settled.

Many voices have affirmed that the Romans established a town called Mantua Carpetana here but proof is nonexistent (although isolated villas dating from Roman times were scattered about the countryside). Such claims grew out of a desire on the part of imperial hagiographers to assign the city a more 'fitting' origin than that accepted by historians today – that of Islamic garrison.

MUSLIM FRONTIER TOWN

Whatever the occasional nomadic group of farmers may have been up to around the Manzanares, events of great moment dot the history of the Iberian Peninsula. Ancient Phoenicians, Greeks and Carthaginians established coastal trading enclaves, while in the interior roamed Celtiberian tribes. The Romans made a concerted effort to bring the peninsula under their control and founded cities such as Toletum (Toledo) and Complutum (near present Alcalá de Henares), but nothing on the site of Madrid. The empire was followed by waves of barbarian invasion culminating in the dominance of the Visigoths, who in turn were ousted by Muslim invaders in the 8th century.

In 756 the emirate of Córdoba was established in the south of what the Muslims called Al-Andalus, which covered most of the peninsula until the beginning of the 9th century.

The 15th-century Arab historian Ibn Khaldun traced the foundation of Madrid to the 9th century. Convention has it that Muhammad I, emir (prince) of Córdoba, established a fortress here in 854. Magerit (Mayrit), as it came to be known, was one of a string of such forts across the so-called Middle March, a frontier land between the core of Al-Andalus in the south and the small Christian kingdoms north of the Río Ebro and Río Duero. The Middle March's capital was Toledo.

The forts were built as part of a defensive line against Christian incursion, but medieval Spain was a complex animal. Most of the people living in the Middle March were *muladíes* (*muwallads*), locals converted to Islam, who generally got on better with their Christian neighbours to the north than their Arab and Berber overlords in the south.

Until well into the 10th century, Magerit remained a fortified garrison. With the exception of a stretch of the city wall below the modern Catedral de Nuestra Señora de la Almudena, nothing of it survives. In place of the Palacio Real stood the fort (*al-qasr* – hence the Spanish *alcázar*). Immediately south was a tiny tangle of lanes huddled behind citadel walls and known as the *al-mudayna* (hence Almudena) in which the soldiery and, with time, their families lived. The fort's high position made it virtually impregnable from the north, west and south. The eastern side (where Plaza de Oriente is now) had to be more heavily fortified.

Magerit grew under the rule of Abderrahman III. South of what is now Calle de Segovia (then a stream), in the Vistillas area, emerged the busiest of the *arrabales* (suburbs beyond the city walls). A bridge was thrown over the stream to connect the two hills. To this day the warren of streets around Vistillas is known as the *morería* – Moorish quarter. The main mosque was built on what is now the corner of Calle Mayor and Calle de Bailén (nothing remains of it).

When in 1008 the emirate of Córdoba broke up into a series of smaller kingdoms called *taifas*, Magerit ended up attached to Toledo. In 1085, King Alfonso VI of Castile was virtually handed the *taifa*. It appears the latter's ruler preferred Valencia and in return for Alfonso's help in taking it, abandoned Toledo and its territory.

1479	1516	1519	1520
Isabel marries Fernando, king of Aragón; the two become the Catholic monarchs of Spain	Carlos I, grandson of Catholic monarchs, becomes king of Spain	King Carlos I of Spain crowned Habsburg emperor	Madrid and Toledo rebel against Carlos I

MEDIEVAL CHRISTIAN MADRID

Tiny Madrid, constantly under threat of encroachment by the more established nearby cities such as Segovia and with only uneven protection from the Castilian Crown, long remained a second-rate town. Whereas other Castilian cities received generous *fueros* (self-rule ordinances), Madrid had to content itself with fairly offhand royal rulings laid down in 1118 and 1202. By that time a small number of local families had concentrated municipal power in their hands and were furnishing the members of the town council, the Consejo de Madrid.

In 1348, the horrors of the Black Death struck Madrid with as much fury as the rest of urban Europe, and in that same year the king began to name *regidores* (governors) of Madrid and other cities in an attempt to tighten central control over them.

The same families (the Luzón, Vargas and others) ended up monopolising power as *regidores* and ruled as petty oligarchs. Less favoured families and the lower classes continually protested to the Crown over abuses of power, but although a *corregidor* (royally appointed co-governor) was occasionally sent in to bring the *regidores* to heel, in practice the latter continued to do as they pleased. In Madrid as in other Castilian towns there emerged a basically feudal system of government, the Comunidad de Villa y Tierra, in which the town *(villa)* lorded it over the peasants who worked the surrounding land *(tierra)*.

In 1309, the Cortes (royal court and parliament) sat in Madrid for the first time. Between then and 1561, when Felipe II made the town the permanent seat of the court, Madrid hosted this event 10 times. Madrid (or rather the *alcázar*) was a popular residence with the Castilian monarchs, particularly Enrique IV. They found it a relaxing base from which to set off on hunting expeditions, especially for bears in the El Pardo district.

Although trade was brisk in medieval Madrid, it was on a small scale and the town remained comparatively poor throughout the Middle Ages. The few reports from travellers to the town that survive to this day indicate it had little to offer. Observed one 15th-century writer, 'in Madrid there is nothing except what you bring with you'. It simply bore no comparison with other major Spanish, let alone European, cities.

Beyond the small world of Madrid, great things were happening. Christian Spain was united by the marriage of Isabel and Fernando (aka Isabella and Ferdinand), who as the Catholic Monarchs expelled the last of the Muslim rulers from Granada, financed Christopher Columbus' voyages of American discovery and ordered the expulsion of Jews who would not convert to Christianity from Spain – all this in 1492.

Isabel died in 1504 and Fernando seemed to complicate local and European politics, by marrying off his offspring to regal houses across Europe. It gets a little complex but the outcome left their grandson, Carlos, as king of Spain in 1516.

Top Five Books on the History of Madrid

- *Madrid,* Elizabeth Nash (2001) – an informative, entertaining and joyfully written account of various aspects of the city's past and present
- *Philip of Spain,* Henry Kamen (1998) – an intriguing look at the king who made Madrid his royal capital, oversaw the running of an empire stretching from America to Amsterdam and failed spectacularly to invade England with his Grand Armada
- *Franco,* Paul Preston (1995) – the definitive biography, in English at least, of the man who dominated 20th century Spain and for a while contemplated moving the capital out of Madrid
- *Madrid: Historia de una Capital,* Santos Juliá, David Ringrose & Cristina Segura (1997) – a comprehensive survey of the city's history in Spanish and one of the best in any language
- *Historia Breve de Madrid,* Fidel Revilla, Ramón Hidalgo & Rosalía Ramos (1994; re-edited in 2003) – a straightforward overview, in Spanish, of the key events in the city's history until the present day

1561	1616–19	1630	1702
Felipe II establishes his permanent court at Madrid, a town of 12,000 people	Construction of Plaza Mayor	The Palacio del Buen Retiro is completed	Felipe V, of the Bourbon family, is throned unleashing the War of the Spanish Succession

Carlos I succeeded to the Habsburg throne three years later and so became Carlos V, Holy Roman Emperor. His territories stretched from Austria to the Netherlands, and from Spain to the American colonies. He spent only 16 years of his 40-year reign in Spain and managed to alienate the Spanish nobility to such an extent that it revolted, carrying many cities with it in what came to be known as the rising of the *Comuneros*. In March 1520 Toledo rose and Madrid closely followed. The fight lasted a year but Carlos won.

The nobles lost more than a battle. From then on power was increasingly concentrated in the hands of the monarch. Carlos used much of that power and the wealth pouring in from the Americas on endless wars throughout Europe and against the Turks. All of Spain would eventually pay for such short-sighted 'investments'.

FILTHY RICH & JUST PLAIN FILTHY

Carlos' son and successor, Felipe II, ascended the Spanish throne (which included the American possessions and the Low Countries) in 1556. Five years later he abandoned the tradition of the moving royal court and made his capital in Madrid, a squalid town of 12,000 that was ideal for someone who wished to run into no interference from well established nobles in the big cities or the Church, 70km south in Toledo. In Madrid there was no-one to oppose the king's whims and wishes.

Between a handful of grander churches, the *alcázar* and noble residences, the bulk of the town was made up of precarious houses that were little more than mud huts. They lined chaotic, ill-defined and, for the most part, unpaved lanes and alleys. More concerned with the business of empire and building his monastic retreat at San Lorenzo de el Escorial, Felipe II had done little to improve the state of his capital by the time he died in 1598. When Pedro Texeiro drew the first map of the city in 1656 (the year in which Felipe IV created the fifth and last ring of city walls), the place was still largely a cesspit of narrow foetid lanes for most of its inhabitants.

Felipe II's successors, Felipe III and Felipe IV, lost control of events. They tended to hand management over to a trusted noble, like Count-Duke Olivares, who tried but failed to arrest the rapid decline of Spanish power.

Paradoxically, royal Madrid reached the height of sumptuousness as the court retreated increasingly from the nasty reality that surrounded it. The Palacio del Buen Retiro was completed in 1630 and replaced the *alcázar* as the prime royal residence (the Museo del Ejército building and Casón del Buen Retiro are all that now remain). Countless grand churches, convents and mansions were built.

But Madrid was fantasy land for some. Amid the squalor in which the bulk of its people toiled, royalty and the aristocracy gave themselves over to sickening displays of wealth and cavorted happily in their make-believe world of royal splendour. The national economy, especially in Castile, was collapsing, and plebs poured into Madrid in

Equestrian statue of Felipe III and house at Plaza Mayor

1734	1767	1808	1808
The Alcázar destroyed by fire; plans laid to replace with a new Palacio Real	Carlos III expels the Jesuits from Spain	Napoleonic troops under General Murat march into Madrid	Joseph Bonaparte, Napolean's brother, is crowned King of Spain

the hope of eking out a living. If you took away the court, the city amounted to nothing. In 1601 Felipe III, tired of Madrid, moved the court to Valladolid. The move lasted only five years but in that time the population of Madrid halved. *'Sólo Madrid es corte'* (roughly, 'Only Madrid can be home to the court'), it was said, however, and the good king moved back.

In 1598 Madrid was home to 60,000 souls, more than five times the number when Felipe II decided to make it capital. It was largely a city of immigrants and by 1656 the numbers had swollen to 150,000. The need of the court and its followers to exude an image of power and wealth created employment for all sorts of specialists and trades people, who streamed in from all corners of the country.

Nobles of every possible rank, and many a son of well-educated families with no title (*hidalgos* – sons of something), flocked to Madrid in the hope of gaining patronage or a post in the burgeoning machinery of government. The gentry and Church, who were exempt from taxation and entitled to a levy on production of their rural holdings, led a nice, if generally futile, life. One of Madrid's (and Spain's) problems was that the gentry looked down their noses on any form of work. If you had to earn a living you weren't worth knowing – hardly a recipe for a dynamic economy.

Madrid suffered several handicaps compared with more illustrious capitals elsewhere in Europe. It was bereft of a navigable river, port, decent road links or the slightest hint of entrepreneurial spirit. Agricultural land around the town was poor. The immense wealth from the Americas was squandered on wars and the court. Madrid was, in fact, little more than a large grubby leech, bleeding the surrounding provinces and colonies.

Count-Duke Olivares could see the relatively short-lived Spanish empire was in tatters but many could not. This was the golden age of art in Spain (while the people starved, the aristocracy patronised artists). Velázquez, El Greco, José de Ribera, Zurbarán, Murillo and Coello were all active in the 17th century.

THE BURGEONING BOURBONS

Carlos II's big underachievement was to leave Spain without an heir on his death in 1700. Felipe V, grandson of Louis XIV of France and Maria Teresa, a daughter of Felipe IV, took over but by 1702 all Europe was warring over the Spanish Succession. After 12 years of debilitating conflict, Felipe V kept Spain (his family, the Bourbons, remain at the head of the Spanish state today) but lost many of its territories. The country was in worse shape than ever.

Felipe set about with some diligence to put things right. He centralised state control and attempted (with little success) land reform. He preferred to live outside the noisy and filthy capital but when in 1734 the *alcázar* was destroyed in a fire, the king laid down plans for a magnificent new Palacio Real (Royal Palace) to take its place.

His immediate successors, especially Carlos III (r 1759–88), gave Madrid and Spain a period of comparatively common-sense government. Carlos (with the big nose – his equestrian statue dominates the Puerta del Sol) came to be known as the best mayor Madrid had ever had. He not only cleaned up the city (which still had a reputation for being among the filthiest in Europe), but also completed the Palacio Real, inaugurated the Jardín Botánico (Botanical Gardens) and carried out numerous other public works. He fostered local and foreign artists (including Goya and Tiepolo).

The *rey-alcalde* (king-mayor) did occasionally run into trouble with the restive populace of Madrid. His unpopular Italian minister, Squillace, at one point declared long capes illegal in an attempt to reduce crime. He argued that since the street cleaning had been improved, the capes were no longer necessary for keeping muck off other garments. He further claimed that the average *majo* (spiv) used the capes to hide weapons. The Madrileños would have none of it and after long and violent riots the measure was repealed. It was later reintroduced peacefully by the Conde de Aranda.

1815	1824–26	1834	1851
Inquisition summons Goya over the 'obscene' paintings, *La Maja Vestida* and *La Maja Desnuda*	French troops occupy Madrid	Cholera epidemic sweeps across Madrid and causes mob riots	Madrid gets its first railway line, to Aranjuez

In all, by the time Carlos III died in 1788, Spain and its capital were in better shape than they had been for a while. He had expelled the backward-looking Jesuits in 1767 and embarked on a major road-building programme. His attempts at land reform were less successful and Spain remained, for all the improvements, an essentially poor country with a big-spending royal court.

NAPOLEON & EL DOS DE MAYO

A year later the French Revolution sent all of Europe into a state of fevered panic. Carlos III's successor, Carlos IV, proved in no way equal to the challenge. He and his self-seeking minister, Manuel Godoy, contrived to bring upon Spain the wrath not only of revolutionary France but also, as the Spanish cravenly switched sides, of Britain. Godoy's machinations could not have done more damage. Allied with France, Spain was crushed by Nelson in the epic Battle of Trafalgar in 1805.

Next, Napoleon convinced Godoy to allow in his troops so that France and Spain could devour Portugal. It soon became evident that the diminutive Corsican had other things on his mind. By 1808 the French presence had become an occupation and Napoleon's brother, Joseph Bonaparte, had been crowned king of Spain.

Early that year, a French detachment under the command of Murat took control of Madrid. General Tomás de Morla's bands of hearty but unruly armed citizenry were no match for Napoleon's war machine and were quickly overwhelmed.

An uneasy calm descended on the city, but tension built in April and on the morning of 2 May townspeople attacked French troops around the Palacio Real and what is now Plaza del Dos de Mayo. Murat moved quickly and by the end of the day the rebels were quashed. The uprising marked the beginning of the Guerra de la Independencia (War of Independence, or Peninsular War), a long and nasty guerrilla campaign to oust the French. British and to a lesser extent Portuguese forces played a key role in the campaign, finally evicting the French in the Battle of Vitoria (in the Basque Country) in 1813. The war left Madrid exhausted. In 1812, 30,000 Madrileños perished from hunger alone.

FERNANDO, FEUDS & HALTING PROGRESS

King Fernando VII returned to Spain in 1814 and, a true reactionary, called a halt to just about every civic initiative launched by Joseph Bonaparte. Bonaparte had ordered the destruction of various churches and convents to create public squares, had widened streets, improved sanitation and moved cemeteries to the outskirts of the city – all necessary measures.

An absolutist, Fernando had occasional moments of enlightenment, such as when he opened part of the renewed Parque del Buen Retiro (it had been largely destroyed during the war) to the public and founded an art gallery in the Prado. But Spain under Fernando lost many of its colonies after defeat in Peru in 1824, and French troops marched into Spain at one point to prop him up. When he died in 1833, Fernando left Spain a three-year-old daughter, a recipe for civil war and an economy in tatters.

Isabel II, a toddler, was obviously not quite up to running the country, and so began the long years of the regency of her mother, María Cristina. Fernando's brother Don Carlos and his conservative supporters disputed Isabel's right to the throne and this sparked the Carlist wars. María Cristina turned to the liberals for help and so absolutist rule was over.

Political upheaval remained part of the city's daily diet, characterised above all by alternating coups between conservative and liberal wings of the army. One came in 1840, another in 1843, the year in which Isabel began to rule in her own right. In 1848, as revolution swept across Europe, a liberal rebellion shook Madrid. In the following 20 years until the revolt that sent Isabel into exile in France, you could just about have set your clock by the coups and riots.

1858	1870	1888	1891
Canal de Isabel II, still the main source of the city's running water, is opened	Café Comercial opens for business – it's still going today	Café Gijón opens for business	The Banco de España is completed and throws open its doors

Madrid was incredibly backward. A discernible middle class only began to make a timid appearance from the 1830s. It was aided when the government ordered the disentailment *(desamortización)* of Church property in 1837. The Church would lose 1600 properties in Madrid alone in the following four decades. A speculative building boom ensued and its beneficiaries constituted the emerging entrepreneurial class (although entrepreneurship went little beyond real-estate speculation).

Miraculous development was not the order of the day, however. As late as 1860 a quarter of Madrid's working populace was employed as servants in aristocratic households – a staggering indication of economic inactivity.

Not all was bad news. In 1851, the city's first railway line, between Madrid and Aranjuez, opened. It was followed in 1858 by the Canal de Isabel II that still supplies the city with water from the Sierra de Guadarrama. National roads radiating from the capital were improved. Public works, ranging from the reorganisation of the Puerta del Sol to the building of the Teatro Real, Biblioteca Nacional and Congreso de los Diputados (lower house of parliament), were carried out. Street paving, the sewage system and rubbish collection were improved, and gas lighting was introduced. More importantly, foreign (mostly French) capital was beginning to fill the investment vacuum.

In the 1860s, the first timid moves to create an Ensanche, or extension of the city, were undertaken. The initial spurt of building took place around Calle de Serrano, where the enterprising Marqués de Salamanca bought up land and built high-class housing aimed at both old and new money. Poor old Salamanca was a little ahead of his time and managed to lose everything in his gamble. By the time the area came good (as he had foreseen), he had already gone to Jesus. Try buying an apartment there now!

FROM RESTORATION TO REPUBLIC

A turbulent six years followed Isabel's flight to France in 1868. Government was handed to an Italian prince, Amedeo di Savoia. He found the task beyond him and in 1873 a republic was called. Matters didn't improve and the army decided to restore the Bourbon monarchy, putting Alfonso XII, Isabel's son, on the throne. A period of relative tranquillity ensued.

Building of the Ensanche gathered momentum. The city's big train stations were constructed and the foundation stones of a cathedral (Madrid's first) were laid – it would take more than a century to finish! Another kind of 'cathedral', the Banco de España, was completed with greater alacrity and opened its doors in 1891.

In 1898 the first city tramlines were electrified. In 1910 work began on the Gran Vía and nine years later the first metro line started operation. Inward migration would double the city's population from half a million at the turn of the century to almost one million in 1931, when the second republic was called. A study in 1930 showed that less than 40% of the capital's population was from Madrid. The 1920s were a period of frenzied activity, not just in urban construction but in intellectual life. As many as 20 newspapers circulated on the streets of Madrid, writers and artists (including Lorca, Dalí and Buñuel) converged on the capital, which hopped to the sounds of American jazz. The Twenties roared as much in Madrid as elsewhere in Europe.

Not all was fun and games, whatever big-spending students like Buñuel might have thought. By 1931, Madrid's politics had been radicalised. The rise of the socialists in Madrid and anarchists (especially popular among Barcelona's industrial workers and farmers in the country's south) had sharpened social tensions throughout the country. Recession late in WWI and the disastrous Spanish campaign in Morocco in the 1920s had worsened things to such an extent that in 1923 the captain-general of Catalonia, General Miguel Primo de Rivera, launched a coup that would lead to an uneasy six-year dictatorship. Alfonso XIII had him removed in 1930.

1898	1907	1917	1919
Spain loses its remaining colonies of Cuba, Puerto Rico and the Philippines to the USA	First car number plates issued in Madrid	Luis Buñuel studies at La Residencia de Estudiantes, as do Salvador Dalí and Federico García Lorca	Madrid's first metro line starts running

Madrid greeted the decision with joyful demonstrations. Municipal elections were called and on 12 April 1931 a coalition of republicans and socialists carried the day. Three days later a second republic was proclaimed and Alfonso XIII fled. The republican government opened up the Casa de Campo – until then a private royal playground – to the people and passed numerous reformist laws. But divisions soon crippled the left and helped a right-wing coalition into power in 1933. The following year General Francisco Franco violently put down a miners' revolt in Asturias with merciless Spanish Foreign Legion troops.

Again the pendulum swung and in February 1936 the left-wing Frente Popular (Popular Front) just beat the right's Frente Nacional (National Front) into power. One of its first actions was to remove suspect generals – Franco was sent to the Canary Islands. One way or another, a violent face-off appeared inevitable. Either the army would stage a coup or the extreme left would have the revolution for which it was clamouring.

Pablo Iglesias & the Birth of Spanish Socialism

Madrid, for hundreds of years the political nerve centre of Spain, has produced surprisingly few of the country's leading political figures (José María Aznar, the former PP Prime Minister is an exception): kings and queens were almost always from elsewhere. In more recent times, Franco came from Galicia, while the long-running charismatic socialist prime minister until 1996, Felipe González, is from Andalucía.

The founder of González' party, however, was a local boy. Well, almost. Born in Franco's home town of O Ferrol in 1850, Pablo Iglesias was brought to Madrid in his infancy and remained there. A printer by trade, he began trade-union activities at the age of 20. One year later he got La Emancipación, a workers' paper, off the ground. With the rise of Marxist ideas across Europe, in 1879 Iglesias was elected president of a new association that constituted Spain's first clandestine workers' party.

Two years later, the Partido Socialista Obrero Español (PSOE; Spanish Socialist Workers' Party) went public. Its advances were rapid. Within seven years it had branches across the country and Iglesias was running its mouthpiece, El Socialista. The Unión General de Trabajadores (UGT; General Workers' Union) was organised thereafter, with strong PSOE influence. By the turn of the century socialist candidates were winning seats in local government.

Iglesias himself was elected several times to the Cortes (national parliament) from 1910 to 1916. By then ailing and increasingly shy of the limelight, Iglesias had become a working-class myth. Even in the wake of the general strike called in 1917 by the UGT, which was suppressed without any ceremony, Iglesias was left in peace. He remained president of the PSOE and UGT, albeit in a largely honorary fashion, until his death in 1925.

THE CIVIL WAR

In the end the army moved first. In July 1936, garrisons in North Africa revolted, quickly followed by others on the mainland. There followed three years of nasty warfare, characterised by horrendous atrocities carried out by the republican and nationalist sides.

Having stopped nationalist troops advancing from the north, Madrid came under threat from Franco's forces moving up from the south. By early November 1936 they were in the Casa de Campo. The government fled to Valencia, but the resolve of the city's defenders, a mix of hastily assembled recruits, sympathisers from the ranks of the army and air force, the International Brigades (which started arriving on 9 November) and Soviet advisers held firm. Fighting was heaviest in the northwest of the city, around Argüelles, but Franco's frontal assault failed – until 28 March 1939, that is, by which time Franco had most of the country in his hands, and Madrid finally surrendered.

In the two and a half years of siege, Madrileños lived a bizarre reality. People went about their daily business, caught the metro to work and got on with things as best they could while skirmishes continued around Argüelles and nationalist artillery intermittently shelled the city, particularly Gran Vía ('Howitzer Alley'), from the Casa de Campo.

1929	1931	1931	1936
Gran Vía is completed	After nationwide municipal elections a republic is called and King Alfonso XIII flees	New government opens up Casa de Campo as a public park	The Spanish Civil War breaks out; Nationalist forces bombard Madrid from the Casa de Campo

THE FRANCO YEARS

A deathly silence fell over the city as the new dictator made himself at home. He at first considered shifting the capital south to the more amenable Seville, but decided instead to convert Madrid into a capital worthy of its new masters.

In those dark years, as Western Europe was again tearing itself apart in a world war and Franco and his right-wing Falangist Party maintained a heavy-handed repression, Madrid's problems remained acute. Observers described the Madrid of the early 1940s as a 'city of a million cadavers', impoverished and long unable to do much to repair the damage of more than two years of artillery bombardment. The Nationalists were not beyond a little megalomaniac dreaming. In one urban reconstruction plan attributed by some to Antonio Palacios (who died in 1945), the entire Puerta del Sol area was to be razed to the ground to make way for a 'heroic symphony' of monuments to Spanish imperial grandeur. Luckily, pauperism made even getting started on such projects impossible.

The 1940s and 1950s proved the most trying. These were the years of *autarquía* (economic self-reliance, largely induced by Spain's international isolation after the end of WWII) or, more simply, for most Spaniards, the *años de hambre* – the years of hunger. Only in 1955 did the average wage again reach the level of 1934!

Repression was at its harshest throughout the 1940s. Many thousands of suspects, ranging from supporters of the Frente Popular through to union members, were harassed, imprisoned, employed in forced labour (such as housing projects from which private enterprise made enormous profits, or the construction of the nationalist Valle de los Caídos monument northwest of Madrid), tortured and shot. Prior to 1945, thousands of political prisoners were shipped off to Nazi concentration camps – few returned.

The government of Madrid, as in all municipalities, was put in the hands of a mayor directly named by a *gobernador civil* (civil governor), who represented the state. In Madrid more than anywhere this effectively meant that local government was in central state hands.

Hundreds of thousands of starving *campesinos* (peasants) flocked to the capital, increasing the already enormous pressure for housing. In the 10 years from 1950 alone, more than 600,000 arrived. Most contented themselves with erecting *chabolas* (shanty towns) on the outskirts of the city. Ugly satellite suburbs began to grow and the private sector seemed to specialise in building cheap, unplanned housing. As early as the 1950s, discontent began to express itself openly in Madrid. It began in the universities and, perhaps surprisingly for some, in new Catholic youth and workers' organisations set up to fight the official line followed by government-sponsored trade unions.

Franco might not have liked communists, but he and Spain could thank their lucky stars for the existence of the Soviet Union. In 1953, the USA decided to grant economic aid to Franco's Spain in exchange

Over the top ... the baroque doorway of the Museo Municipal (p88)

1939	1953	1960	1973
Franco's troops finally enter Madrid in March, putting an end to the Civil War	USA grants financial aid to Spain in return for use of military bases	Real Madrid wins the European Cup for the fifth year running, setting a still-unmatched record	Basque liberation movement ETA assassinates Admiral Carrero Blanco in Madrid

for the use of Spanish air and naval bases during the Cold War. By the early 1960s industry was taking off in and around Madrid. Foreign investment poured in (factories of the American Chrysler motor company were Madrid's single biggest employers in the 1960s) and the services and banking sector blossomed. It was now that Paseo de la Castellana took on much of its present aspect. Fine old palaces were routinely demolished and replaced by such buildings as the Torres de Colón. These were the boom years of Spain's 'economic miracle', in part guided by the government's 1959 economic Stabilisation Plan.

The boom years brought greater prosperity to Madrileños. In 1960 fewer than 70,000 cars were on the road in Madrid. Ten years later more than half a million clogged the capital's streets. Bread alone doesn't do the trick though and, from 1965 on, opposition to Franco's regime became steadily more vocal. Again, the universities were repeatedly the scene of confrontation, but clandestine trade unions, such as Comisiones Obreras (CCOO; Workers Commissions) and the outlawed UGT, began to make themselves heard again too.

The waves of protest were not restricted to Madrid. In the Basque Country the terrorist group Euskadi Ta Askatasuna (ETA; Basques and Freedom) began to fight for Basque independence. Their first important action was the assassination in Madrid in 1973 of Admiral Carrero Blanco, Franco's prime minister and designated successor.

In 1974 Franco fell ill and later died on 20 November 1975. In the meantime, Spanish politics went on the boil.

RETURN TO DEMOCRACY

The PSOE, Partido Comunista de España (PCE; Spanish Communist Party), trade unions and a wide range of opposition groups and figures emerged from hiding and exile in the months before and after Franco's death. No-one was entirely sure what turn events would take, but King Juan Carlos I, of the Bourbon family that had left the Spanish political stage with the flight of Alfonso XIII in 1931, and long groomed by Franco, surprised everyone.

The king entrusted Adolfo Suárez, a former Francoist with whom he had long been in secret contact, with government in July 1976 and Suárez, with the king's explicit approval, quickly rammed a raft of changes through parliament. By 1977, when elections were called, opposition parties and trade unions had been legalised. Suárez and his centre-right coalition won the elections and set about writing a new constitution in collaboration with the opposition. It provided for a parliamentary monarchy with no state religion and guaranteed a large degree of devolution to the 17 regions into which the country was now divided.

Spaniards got a fright in February 1981 when a pistol-brandishing, low-ranking Guardia Civil (Civil Guard) officer, Antonio Tejero Molina, marched into the Cortes in Madrid with an armed detachment and held parliament captive for 24 hours. The king made it clear he did not back Tejero and the coup fizzled. A year later Felipe González's PSOE won the national elections. González remained in power until 1996, when the right-wing PP under José María Aznar picked up the baton.

1979	1981	1991	2003
Socialist Enrique Tierno Galván becomes mayor of Madrid	Guardia Civil officer Antonio Tejero holds parliament captive in February	Right-wing Partido Popular takes control of town hall under José María Álvarez de Manzano	Alberto Ruiz-Gallardón (PP) is elected mayor of Madrid

Madrid's Barrios

Madrid's Barrios

The heart of Madrid, where the village of Magerit came to life in medieval times and more than five centuries later became the capital of one of Europe's then most powerful nations, is squeezed into an area about 2km by 1.5km between the green spaces of the Parque del Buen Retiro and the Casa de Campo. Since the 19th century, and especially since the 1950s, the city has spread inexorably in all directions. Dormitory suburbs have been thrown up and villages have been engulfed in a process of urban expansion that continues apace today.

Madrid is divided up into *distritos* (districts) and these are subdivided into *barrios* (neighbourhoods), the official names of which are largely ignored by Madrileños. Indeed the word *barrio* has a very strong feel of local identity about it. '*¡Soy del barrio!*' locals proclaim in notes displayed on the dash of their cars, signalling at once to thieves that they should move on but seemingly making a more general and proud declaration to anyone who cares to read. Madrileños have their own city map in their heads and, since they know best, we follow them. Most of what is of in terest is in a more contained area.

We start in Los Austrias and Centro, which encompasses much of the compact historical heart of the city, with its palaces and churches and focusing on the grand central square, the Plaza Mayor. Next we spread out a little to the east to take in Sol, Huertas and Atocha. Sol is the central point of the city and of Spain, and in the labyrinth of lanes stretching south and east huddle masses of bars and eateries, a veritable feast for the hedonist. Just beyond lies the Paseo del Prado and El Retiro, a haven of culture in some of the city's finest museums, including the Prado itself, and a refuge of green parkland and gardens. From there we explore La Latina and Lavapiés, two separate but neighbouring *barrios*, the former a now hip part of the old town since Madrid's

Top Five for Children

- Warner Brothers Movie World (p109)
- Parque del Buen Retiro (p81)
- Parque de Atracciones (p109)
- Teleférico (p98)
- Faunia (p109)

Picasso's Guernica, *Centro de Arte Reina Sofía (p73)*

early days, the latter a fascinating working class quarter. Next up we head north, first to the gritty but slowly gentrifying nightlife zone of Malasaña and Chueca, with its bars, endless restaurants and bubbling gay scene. The chic 19th-century residential quarters of Salamanca & Ventas follow, along with Chamberí & Argüelles. Finally we follow the city's grand axis, the Paseo de la Castellana up into Northern Madrid and a range of spots Beyond the Centre, including some parks and children's attractions such as Warner Brothers Movie World.

It's Free Top Five

Admission to many galleries, museums and other sights is free at least one day per week. In a few cases this is restricted to EU citizens. In the following list anyone can visit free on the given days.

- **Museo del Prado** (Sat afternoons & Sun)
- **Centro de Arte Reina Sofía** (Sat afternoons & Sun)
- **Museo del Libro**
- **Museo Municipal de Arte Contemporáneo** (Tue-Sun)
- **Museo Arqueológico Nacional** (Sat afternoons & Sun)

ITINERARIES

ONE DAY

Wherever you are in the city, take the metro to Sol and start doing some footwork. The historic centre of Madrid is a compact, chattering, seething adventure. The streets, lanes and squares are alive with colour and vocal, gesticulating people. On a good-mood sunny day, which is most days in Madrid, the simplest activity is infused with a surprising intensity. Soak up the grandeur of **Plaza Mayor** (p70), wander in and out of cafés and pastry shops, browse boutiques. Head for the **Palacio Real** (p68) and stop for coffee on the **Plaza de Oriente** (p69). Double back along Calle Mayor to Sol and get lost amid the bars and restaurants of the Huertas area around Plaza de Santa Ana, have a long lunch and then make downhill for an afternoon of high culture at **Museo del Prado** (p77), the home of a grand collection of predominantly Spanish Old Masters. Afterwards, take a stroll in the **Parque del Buen Retiro** (p81) before heading up along Gran Vía into Chueca for a little window shopping, an evening tipple or two and dinner.

THREE DAYS

With three days you can truly begin to come to grips with the city. How you use the time will depend on your priorities. For art buffs the answer is clear. After the first day getting to know the layout of the town and attacking the Museo del Prado, spend the remaining days at the other two main art galleries in what has been dubbed locally the Art Triangle, the eclectic collection of the **Museo Thyssen-Bornemisza** (p79) and the mostly Spanish modern and contemporary art in the **Centro de Arte Reina Sofía** (p73). Between these two and the Prado, you have the cream of Madrid's art collections, although by no means exhaust them. Probably the best approach is to see one each morning. You could do both in one day, but they are difficult morsels to easily digest in one hit. After a morning in the Thyssen, it might be time for a coffee in the historic **Gran Café de Gijón** (p132). Getting hungry? What about a metro across town to the Príncipe Pío stop and a quick stroll to **Casa Mingo** (p138) for a simple but filling lunch of chicken and cider? There's more to this side trip, as the Goya paintings in the **Ermita de San Antonio de la Florida** (p96) are just nearby. From there walk south to the enchanting gardens of the **Campo del Moro** (p66). A walk uphill along Calle de Segovia brings you smack into La Latina, perfectly timed for a tipple at a wine bar along **Calle de la Cava Baja** and a meal in the same area – there's plenty to choose from. On day three, after a morning in the Reina Sofía and lunch around Plaza de Santa Ana, you might want to dedicate the afternoon to shopping. Head for **Calle de Serrano** in Salamanca and follow your nose. The street is lined with stores, as are the streets running immediately to the east. The atmosphere is quite different in this chichi part of town.

ONE WEEK

OK, with a week you've got room to move. You've covered the A-list art and already done a little exploring in your first three days. You've probably got a favourite café for your morning cuppa over a paper already sorted out. With four days to go you can spread your wings. Madrid is surrounded by fascinating cities that beg to be visited on day trips from the capital. Even if you threw all four days at excursions (and there is still plenty to do in the city), you couldn't do them all. Of the towns, the best three are **Toledo** (p200), **Segovia** (p203) and **Córdoba** (p210). Córdoba, you ask? Isn't that a bit of a trek? Not if you take the high-speed AVE train from Atocha station it ain't. A taste of Andalucía and Spain's Moorish past is less than two hours away. Then there are the royal residences, of which the most impressive (and most visited) is **San Lorenzo de El Escorial** (p213). Well worth considering, and much quieter, are the **Palacio Real del Pardo** (p214) and the palace complex at **Aranjuez** (p215), south of Madrid. Make the day trip on your last day one of the less exacting ones (say, the Palacio Real del Pardo), because on your last night you've got to party! You can't leave Madrid without having spent at least one night on the tiles…all night. You can take your pick of the zones (Huertas, La Latina, Malasaña, Chueca, Chamberí or up around Calle de Orense in northern Madrid). Have a snooze before you head out because nothing much is happening before 10pm anyway!

Discounts & Closing Times

The Paseo del Arte ticket covers the big three galleries (Museo del Prado, Museo Thyssen-Bornemisza and Centro de Arte Reina Sofía) for €7.66 and is valid for a year (one visit each). For unlimited visits to either the Prado or the Reina Sofía, a year's ticket costs €24.04. A yearly ticket to both these galleries and eight other museums throughout the country costs €36.06.

Most, but not all, museums and monuments close on Monday. Just about everything is also shut on Sunday afternoon. In July and August, some close parts of their displays for want of staff, most of whom take annual leave around this time. A few minor museums close entirely throughout August.

ORGANISED TOURS

Arte Alcance (☎ 91 448 84 36) organises tours to museums and art galleries. They have a year-round programme of visits, aimed largely at families and groups. The association works a lot with schools and principally in Spanish.

The Patronato Municipal de Turismo has more than 120 walking itineraries around the capital. The **Descubre Madrid** tours are mostly conducted in Spanish and cost around €2 to €3 per person. You can pick up calendars detailing when and where the walks are held at any branch of the Caja de Madrid bank, and at the Patronato tourist office (Plaza Mayor 3).

Londoner Mike Chandler offers a guided two-wheel tour of Madrid. He also offers a one-hour cycling fitness session in the Parque del Buen Retiro with a personal trainer (€30) and several tours beyond Madrid. Contact **Madrid Bike Tours** (☎ 680-581782; www .madridbiketours.com; tours & picnic lunch €55 per person; ⌚ 4hr).

Backed by the Ayuntamiento, orange tour buses run along three routes around the city, with frequent stops (many connecting with the other routes). Tickets entitle holders to hop on and off the buses as often as desired (the average time on each circular route is 75 minutes). More information, including route maps, is available at tourist offices or in most travel agencies. Purchase tickets directly on the bus, Madrid Visión info points around town (such as in the Prado) and in some hotels. The ticket also entitles you to a series of discounts to some museums, restaurants and shops. contact **Madrid Vision Buses** (☎ 91 779 18 88; www.madridvision. es; adult 1-/2-day ticket €10.60/13.60, child 7-16 & senior over 65 1-/2-day ticket €5.60/6.80, child under 7 free, weekend & holiday surcharge adult/child & senior €1.20/0.60; ⌚ 9.30am-midnight late Jun–late Sep, 10am-7pm late Dec-late Mar, 10am-9pm rest of the year).

The Patronato Municipal de Turismo organises Saturday-morning walks (€3.10) around the centre of old Madrid. Known as **Paseos por el Madrid de los Austrias** they start at 10am (English) and noon (Spanish). Meet outside the **Patronato tourist office** (Map pp270-2; Plaza Mayor 3) half an hour before. This is part of the Descubre Madrid programme (p64).

Pullmantur (Map pp268-9; ☎ 91 541 18 07; Plaza de Oriente 8) is one of several private companies offering bus tours of Madrid and excursions beyond. These range from jaunts around Madrid (€19 per person) through to a day tour including the Museo del Prado, the Palacio Real, and lunch (€62). Most central Madrid travel agencies can fill you in on the details of these and similar trips.

LOS AUSTRIAS & CENTRO

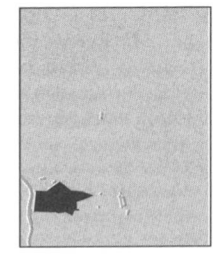

Under Carlos I and Felipe II, the first two kings in the Habsburg dynasty (1517–1700), Spain reached the heights of imperial greatness, its possessions spreading from Vienna to the Low Countries, from Seville to the Americas. Felipe's immediate Habsburg successors were prepared to invest in their unassuming new capital of Madrid. The area has come to be known as Madrid de los Austrias, in reference to the Habsburgs. Just beyond it, in the bustling area cradled between Calle de Arenal and Gran Vía, is an area we have dubbed Centro, indeed part of the official Centro district. At the very core of it all is the grand Plaza Mayor, while the royal jewel in the crown is the Palacio Real. Along with Spain's temporal rulers, the Catholic church had a finger in the central Madrid real estate pie, building churches and convents seemingly on every street corner. Many have since disappeared but some impressive structures remain.

Orientation

As a central starting point the grand, arcaded Plaza Mayor is hard to miss. A couple of hundred metres west of the official centre point of Spain, Puerta del Sol, Plaza Mayor is ringed by handy metro stops (Sol, Ópera, Tirso de Molina). It makes a good spot to start a tour of historic Madrid and you will probably pass through it again and again. Arcades lead off the square to the surrounding streets. To the north runs the east–west Calle Mayor (Main St), lined by apartments, shops and eateries. On its slightly downhill, lazily traced route towards Calle de Bailén and the grand Palacio Real it passes Plaza de la Villa, with its 17th-century Ayuntamiento and Gothic remains. Most of the narrow lanes around here are pedestrianised but not exactly deathly quiet. At night they fill with the laughter and gay banter of revellers wandering to and from the bars and eateries of La Latina, on the other side the Calle de Segovia.

The other main axis through this part of central Madrid is Calle del Arenal, which with Calle Mayor appears like the legs of a pair of compasses. It spills into Plaza de Isabel II and the spectacle of the Teatro Real, home of opera in Madrid. Renovation of the theatre and the broad Plaza de Oriente on its western flank in the late 1990s have had the effect of a spring storm, returning to it a sense of space and majesty that had long been lost. Plaza de Oriente looks across to the Palacio Real and is a perfect spot to sit down for a drink. West of the palace and some way below it (it is easy to see why the Muslims chose the site to build their *alcázar* – see p50), stretches what might be called the palatial backyard, the beautifully maintained and carefully studied Campo del Moro.

North of Calle del Arenal a web of streets stretches towards Gran Vía, a noisy avenue punched through the heart of Madrid early in the 20th century. It is one of the few parts of the city that is vaguely hilly, with lanes rising gradually to Plaza de Callao and Plaza de Santo Domingo. The pedestrian streets around Calle de Preciados bristle with department stores and are thronged with shoppers but the area's vocation was once a great deal more spiritual. Of the several convents once scattered around here, two remain. The most important is the Convento de las Descalzas Reales, which stands squat and mute like a fort one block north of Calle del Arenal. This part of the centre is a strange mix. By day and night Calle de la Montera is alive with hookers and pimps (in spite of anguished demands for a clampdown from exasperated residents and shopkeepers). Some of the streets dropping down to Plaza de España from Plaza de Santo Domingo have a slightly louche feel too. Bars of doubtful repute mix it with shops that look like they haven't been renovated since before the Civil War. The Senate buildings occupy its eastern extremity and by day the entire area is chirpy and largely respectable.

Top Sights

- Palacio Real (p68)
- Plaza Mayor (p70)
- Convento de las Descalzas Reales (p67)
- Campo del Moro (p66)
- Plaza de la Villa (p68)

CAMPO DEL MORO Map pp262-4

☎ 91 454 88 00; Paseo de la Virgen del Puerto;
🕓 10am-8pm Mon-Sat, 9am-8pm Sun & holidays
Apr-Sep, 10am-6pm Mon-Sat, 9am-6pm Sun & holidays
Oct-Mar; Metro Príncipe Pío

In 1110 an Almoravid army drew up in this field, later known as Campo del Moro (Moor's Field), below the walls of the former Muslim outpost. They occupied all but the fortress, whose Christian garrison held on until the Almoravid fury abated and their forces retired south. All that remains to remind us of the siege is the garden's name. The only entrance is from Paseo de la Virgen del Puerto.

Acquired by Felipe II, the partly English-style 20 hectares of gardens were not laid out as they are now until 1844, with alterations in 1890. The fountain known as Fuente de las Conchas, between the visitors' entrance and the palace, was designed by Ventura Rodríguez.

CATEDRAL DE NUESTRA SEÑORA DE LA ALMUDENA Map pp262-4

☎ 91 542 22 00; www.patrimonionacional.es; Calle de Bailén; 🕓 9am-9pm; Metro Ópera

South of the Palacio Real, Madrid's stark and cavernous cathedral was completed in mid-1992 after more than 110 years of construction. Indeed Carlos I had proposed building a cathedral back in 1518 but no-one could find the money.

Still, a place of worship has existed here or nearby since the city's earliest settlement. When the Christians arrived in the 11th century, they converted the grand mosque into a church in the name of Santa María. It came to be known as Santa María de la Almudena, an allusion to the Muslim name for this part of the town of Magerit. Situated on the corner of what are now Calle Mayor (a plaque marks No 88) and Calle de Bailén, the ex-mosque was soon torn down and replaced by a new church that lasted until the 18th century, when town planners demolished it to widen Calle Mayor.

Since Madrid had, until 1851, been considered part of the archdiocese of Toledo, it had never had its own cathedral. The church of Santa María de la Almudena had more or less fulfilled the roll unofficially, after which the baton was passed on to the Basílica de Nuestra Señora del Buen Consejo, on Calle de Toledo (p84). Inside, the modern cathedral is a pristine, bright white neo-Gothic job.

Between the cathedral and the Palacio Real you can normally get expansive views of the Casa de Campo to the west, but access has been blocked while excavation work is carried out on what appear to be remains of the Palacio's predecessor, the *alcázar*.

CONVENTO DEL CORPUS CRISTI (LAS CARBONERAS) Map pp270-2

☎ 91 548 37 01; Plaza del Conde de Miranda; admission free; 🕓 9.30am-1pm & 4-6.30pm; Metro Ópera

The church that hides behind sober walls on the western end of the quiet square is a fairly ordinary affair. What's curious is that a closed

Catedral de Nuestra Señora de la Almudena (above)

order of nuns occupies the convent building around it. When Mass is held, the nuns gather in a separate area at the rear of the church. More intriguing still, they maintain a centuries-old tradition of making sweet biscuits that can be purchased from the entrance just off the square on Calle del Codo. You make your request through a grill and the products are delivered through a little revolving door that allows the nuns to remain unseen by you.

CONVENTO DE LA ENCARNACIÓN

Map pp268-9

☎ 91 547 05 10; Plaza de la Encarnación; adult/student & EU senior €3.60/2, EU citizens free Wed, combined ticket with Convento de las Descalzas Reales €6; ☻ 10.30am-12.45pm & 4-5.30pm Tue-Thu & Sat, 10.30am-12.45pm Fri, 11am-1.45pm Sun & holidays; Metro Ópera

Founded by Empress Margarita de Austria, this 17th-century mansion built in the Madrid style of baroque is still inhabited by nuns of the Augustine order (Agustinas Recoletas). Inside you'll find a large art collection, mostly from the 17th century, and a host of gold and silver reliquaries. The most famous of these contains the blood of San Pantaleón, which purportedly liquefies every year on 28 June.

CONVENTO DE LAS DESCALZAS REALES Map pp268-9

☎ 91 547 53 50; Plaza de las Descalzas 3; adult/student & EU senior €5/2.50, EU citizens free Wed, combined ticket with Convento de la Encarnación €6; ☻ 10.30am-12.45pm & 4-5.30pm Tue-Thu & Sat, 10.30am-12.45pm Fri, 11am-1.45pm Sun & holidays; Metro Callao

Halfway between Calle del Arenal and Plaza del Callao, the grim walls of this one-time palace serve as a mighty buttress to protect the interior from the modern-day chaos outside. Behind the sober plateresque façade lies a sumptuous stronghold of the faith.

Doña Juana, daughter of Carlos I and mother of Portugal's ill-fated Dom Sebastian (whose disastrous military adventures saw Portugal absorbed into the Spanish empire), commandeered the palace for conversion into a convent in the 16th century. She was followed by the Descalzas Reales (Barefooted Royals), a group of illustrious women who became Franciscan nuns. A maximum of 33 nuns can live here, perhaps because Christ is said to have been 33 when he died. Those in residence still live according to the rules of the closed order.

The compulsory guided tour (in Spanish) of the convent takes you up a gaudily frescoed Renaissance stairway to the upper level of the cloister. The vault was painted by Claudio Coello and at the top of the stairs is a portrait of Felipe II and family members on the royal balcony.

You then pass several of the convent's 33 chapels. The first contains a remarkable carved figure of a dead Christ recumbent, which is paraded in a moving Good Friday procession each year. At the end of the passage you're led into the antechoir, then the choir stalls themselves, where Doña Juana is buried and a *Virgen la Dolorosa* by Pedro de la Mena is seated in one of the 33 oak stalls.

The former sleeping quarters of the nuns house a museum with some of the most extraordinary tapestries you are likely to see. Woven in the 17th century in Brussels, they include four based on drawings by Rubens. Four or five artisans could take as long as a year to weave a square metre of premium-quality tapestry, so imagine how many years must have gone into these! While on the subject of impressive numbers, Spain and the Vatican were the biggest patrons of the tapestry business: Spain alone is said to have collected four million of them.

IGLESIA DE SAN GINÉS Map pp270-2

☎ 91 366 48 75; Calle del Arenal 13; admission free; ☻ for services only; Metro Sol or Ópera

Between Calle Mayor and Calle del Arenal, directly north of Plaza Mayor, San Ginés is one of Madrid's oldest churches: it has been here in one form or another since at least the 14th century. In fact, it is speculated that, prior to the arrival of the Christians in 1085, a Mozarabic community (Christians in Muslim territory) lived around the stream that later became Calle del Arenal and that their parish church stood on this site. What you see today was built in 1645 but largely reconstructed after a fire in 1824. The church houses some fine paintings, including an El Greco.

IGLESIA DE SAN NICOLÁS DE LOS SERVITAS Map pp270-2

☎ 91 548 83 14; Plaza de San Nicolás 6; admission free; ☻ 8am-1.30pm & 5.30-8.30pm Mon, 8-9.30am & 6.30-8.30pm Tue-Sat, 9.30am-2pm & 6.30-9pm Sun; Metro Ópera

Considered to be the oldest surviving church in Madrid, it may have been built on the site of Muslim Magerit's second mosque – if such a mosque existed. Apart from the restored 12th-century *mudéjar* bell tower, the present church dates in part from the 15th century, vaulting is late-Gothic and the fine timber ceiling, which survived a fire in 1936, is from about the same period. Other elements inside this small house of worship include plateresque and baroque touches. The architect Juan de Herrera (see p31) was buried in the crypt in 1597.

MURALLA ÁRABE Map pp262-4
Cuesta de la Vega; Metro Ópera
Behind the cathedral apse and down Cuesta de la Vega is a short stretch of the so-called Arab Wall, the city wall built by Madrid's early-medieval Muslim rulers. Some of it dates as far back as the 9th century, when the initial Muslim fort was raised. Other bits date from the 12th and 13th centuries, by which time the city was in Christian hands. The Muslims had been quite crafty: money was scarce so, while the outside of the walls was made to look dauntingly sturdy, the inside was put together with cheap materials. It seems to have worked, as the town was rarely taken by force. In summer, the city council organises open-air theatre and music performances here.

PALACIO DE SANTA CRUZ Map pp270-2
☎ 91 379 95 50; Plaza de la Provincia; Metro Sol
Just off the southeast corner of Plaza Mayor and dominating Plaza de Santa Cruz is this baroque edifice which houses the Ministerio de Asuntos Exteriores (Ministry of Foreign Affairs). A landmark with its grey slate spires, it was built in 1643 and initially served as the court prison.

PALACIO REAL Map pp270-2
☎ 91 454 88 00; Calle de Bailén; adult/student & EU senior €9/3.50, EU citizens free Wed; ☽ 9am-6pm Mon-Sat, 9am-3pm Sun & holidays Apr-Sep, 9.30am-5pm Mon-Sat, 9am-2pm Sun & holidays Oct-Mar; Metro Ópera
When the *alcázar*, the oft-altered forerunner of the Palacio Real (Royal Palace), burned down in 1734, few mourned its demise. Felipe V, the first of the Bourbon kings, took the opportunity to indulge in a little architectural magnificence, planning to build a palace that would dwarf all its European counterparts. He drafted in the Italian architect Filippo Juvara (1678–1736), who had made a name for himself with his works in Turin, such as the Basilica di Superga and the Palazzo di Stupinigi. On his death, another Italian, Giovan Battista Sacchetti, took over, finishing the job in 1764.

The result, which Felipe did not live to see completed, was the Palacio Real, an Italianate baroque colossus with some 2800 rooms – of which you are allowed to visit around 50. It is occasionally closed for state ceremonies of pomp and circumstance and for official receptions, but the present king is rarely in residence, preferring to live elsewhere.

The **Farmacia Real** (Royal Pharmacy) is the first set of rooms to the right at the southern end of the **Plaza de Armas** (Plaza de la Armería) courtyard. The pharmacy is a seemingly endless parade of medicine jars and stills for mixing royal concoctions. West across the plaza is the **Armería Real** (Royal Armoury), a hoard of weapons and armour, mostly dating from the 16th and 17th centuries. The full suits of armour, such as those of Felipe III, are among the most striking items.

Access to the apartments is from the northern end of the Plaza de Armas. The main stairway, a grand statement of imperial power, leads first to the Halberdiers' rooms and eventually to the **Salón del Trono** (Throne Room). The latter is nauseatingly sumptuous with its crimson-velvet wall coverings complemented by a ceiling painted by the dramatic Venetian baroque master, Tiepolo. Shortly after, you'll encounter the **Salón de Gasparini**, with its exquisite stucco ceiling and walls resplendent with embroidered silks. The **Sala de Porcelana** is a heady setting, with myriad pieces from the one-time Retiro porcelain factory screwed into the walls. As you progress from one room to another through the palace, the decorative themes change. In the midst of it all comes the spacious **Comedor de Gala** (Gala Dining Room). Only students with passes may enter the **Biblioteca Real** (Royal Library).

If you're lucky, you might just catch the colourful changing of the guard in full parade dress. This takes place at noon on the first Wednesday of every month (except in July and August) between the palace and the Catedral de Nuestra Señora de la Almudena.

Several separate free entrances give access to the somewhat neglected, French-inspired **Jardines de Sabatini** (☽ 9am-9pm May-Sep, 9am-8pm Oct-Apr) on the northern flank of the Palacio Real. They were laid out in the 1930s to replace the royal stables that once stood on the site.

PLAZA DE LA VILLA Map pp270-2
☎ 010; ☽ free guided tour of Ayuntamiento 5pm & 6pm Mon; Metro Ópera
It is thought the town fathers chose this square for the permanent seat of city government in the late Middle Ages but it took them several centuries to scrape together the necessary cash to build an appropriate seat of government.

The 17th-century **Ayuntamiento** (town hall), on the western side of the square, is a typical Habsburg edifice with Herrerian slate-tile spires. When originally planned in 1644 by Juan Gómez de Mora, it was to be used as a prison, but in the end it took on both functions. The style is the so-called Madrid baroque *(barroco madrileño)*, a fairly sober local version of the more flowery baroque. Another reason for the relative sobriety of this granite and brick affair was the scarcity of funds for municipal buildings. In fact, the town council *(consejo)* had for three centuries since 1346 met in the Iglesia de San Salvador, facing the square on Calle Mayor. The church no longer exists. The final touches to the Casa de la Villa (as the town hall was also known) were only made to the building in 1693, and Juan de Villanueva made some alterations a century later.

You can join a free tour (in Spanish) of the Ayuntamiento. You are led through various reception halls and into the **Salón del Pleno** (council chambers). The latter were restored in the 1890s and again in 1986. The Ayuntamiento is decorated in a sumptuous neo-Classical style with late 17th-century ceiling frescoes. Just outside the chambers you can see a ceramic copy of Pedro Teixera's landmark 1656 map of Madrid.

Leaning more to the Gothic style with a clear *mudéjar* influence, on the opposite side of the square is the 15th-century **Casa de los Lujanes**, the brickwork tower which is said to have been 'home' to the imprisoned French monarch François I and his sons after their capture in the Battle of Pavia (1525). They say that as the star prisoner was escorted down Calle Mayor by his captor, Carlos I, the locals were struck by the splendour of his attire, which apparently left the Spanish Habsburg emperor looking a little drab.

The **Casa de Cisneros**, built in 1537 by the nephew of Cardinal Cisneros, who was a key adviser to Queen Isabel, is platersque in inspiration, although it was much restored and altered at the beginning of the 20th century. The main door and window above are what remains of the Renaissance-era building. It was acquired by the town council in 1917 and now houses the office of the *alcalde* (mayor). It is also home to the **Salón de Tapices** (Tapestries Hall), hung with fine 15th-century Flemish tapestries bought in 1945 from the cathedral of the western Castilian city of Zamora. It is visited as part of the Ayuntamiento tour.

About 100m east along Calle del Codo and across Plaza del Conde de Miranda is the bustling 19th-century **mercado** (central produce market) in Plaza de San Miguel.

One block southeast of Plaza de la Villa looms the 18th-century baroque remake of the **Iglesia del Sacramento,** the central church of the Spanish army.

Along Calle Mayor, as you approach Calle de Bailén, stands the **Palacio del Duque de Uceda**, identifiable by the soldiers milling around outside as it is now used as a military headquarters (the Capitanía General). Designed by Juan Gómez de Mora in 1608 in the Madrid baroque style, the building was originally a private residence, later acquired by the Crown and converted into government offices. The Palacio replaced an earlier building, outside which five assassins killed Juan de Escobedo, envoy of Don John of Austria envoy, on 31 May 1578. Don John, then in charge of the rebellious Dutch provinces, had sent Escobedo to report to King Felipe II. It appears Antonio Pérez, the king's secretary, organised the killing with the king's approval, having convinced him Escobedo was up to treasonous no good. Pérez seems to have been worried that his secret dealings with Dutch rebels were about to be revealed. Eventually prosecuted, Pérez fled to Aragón and thence to France and England.

If you duck down behind this massive mansion, you will end up in Calle de la Villa. At No 2 is the site of what was once the Estudio Público de Humanidades. This was one of Madrid's more important schools in the 16th century. Cervantes studied here for a while.

PLAZA DE ORIENTE Map pp268-9
Metro Ópera

East across Calle de Bailén from the Palacio Real is the majestic Plaza de Oriente, once partly occupied by dependencies of the *alcázar* and given its present form under French occupation in the early 1800s. The square is dominated by an equestrian statue of Felipe IV and littered with 20 statues of mostly ancient monarchs, many of which had been destined to adorn the Palacio Real until it was found that they were too heavy. They say that at night the statues get down off their pedestals and stretch their legs a bit.

Velázquez designed the horse for the statue of Felipe IV and Martínez Montañés its rider. Italian sculptor Pietro Tacca actually did the hard work with the bronze. And if you were wondering how a heavy bronze statue of a rider and his horse rearing up can actually maintain that stance, the answer is simple – the hind legs are solid while the front ones are hollow. That idea was Galileo Galilei's, showing what a team effort the sculpture was!

PLAZA DE RAMALES Map pp270-2
Metro Ópera

A quick hop south of Plaza de Oriente, this little square owes its existence to Joseph Bonaparte. He ordered the destruction of the Iglesia de San Juanto make way for this public space and a little fresh air! It is believed Velázquez was buried in the church, but his remains have been lost. Excavations in 2000 revealed the crypt of the former church and the remains of various people buried in it centuries ago, but no Velázquez.

PLAZA DE SANTO DOMINGO
Map pp268-9
Metro Santo Domingo

There is nothing to indicate it now, but this square is named after a huge Dominican convent that once stood here. That nothing remains but the name is a telling indication of the power of anticlericalism in 19th-century Spain.

PLAZA MAYOR Map pp270-2
Metro Sol or Ópera

The heart of imperial Madrid beats in the 17th-century Plaza Mayor, west of Puerta del Sol. Designed in 1619 by Juan Gómez de Mora and built in typical Herrerian style, of which the slate spires are the most obvious expression, it was long a popular stage for royal festivities, *autos-de-fe* (the ritual condemnation of heretics, frequently ending with them burning at the stake) and bloody bullfights. In 1790 a fire largely destroyed the square, which was subsequently reproduced under the supervision of Juan de Villanueva.

In the Middle Ages, the site was known as Plaza del Arrabal, since it lay beyond the then city walls (*arrabal* signified extramural suburbs). It was a favourite haunt of traders, who could carry on their business without fear of the taxation enforced within the city walls.

The *alhóndiga del pan,* where wheat and flour needed to make bread was sold, was located here (to be replaced in the 17th century by the **Real Casa de la Panadería**, or royal bakery), along with butchers' stalls, fishmongers, wine stores and other shops. These activities continued in one form or another for much of the life of the square, which today is still lined with shops.

In 1673, King Carlos II issued an edict allowing food vendors to raise tarpaulins above their stalls to protect their wares and themselves from the refuse that people habitually tossed out of the windows above! For some reason such tarpaulins had been banned since the days of the Catholic Monarchs.

In the middle of the present-day square stands an equestrian statue of the man who ordered its construction, Felipe III. The statue was created by the Italian sculptors Giambologna and Pietro Tacca and originally placed in the Casa de Campo. It was moved to the Plaza Mayor in 1848. Many years later, when a car park was built under the square the statue had to be temporarily removed. It was found to be filled by a colony of dead sparrows that had managed to fly in through the horse's mouth. And so it was decided to shut the horse's mouth for good.

The colourful frescoes on the Real Casa de la Panadería were painted in 1992, replacing earlier ones. On a sunny day the plaza's cafés do a roaring *alfresco* trade, in spite of the occasionally exorbitant prices.

TEATRO REAL Map pp270-2

☎ 91 516 06 96; www.teatro-real.com in Spanish; Plaza de Oriente; admission by guided tour (generally in Spanish) adult/student up to 26 years & senior €4/2; ⊙ every half hour 10.30am-1pm Mon & Wed-Fri, 11am-1.30pm Sat, Sun & holidays; Metro Ópera

Backing onto the eastern side of Plaza de Oriente is the city's premier, and in some respects unhappiest, opera house, the Teatro Real. Started in 1818, it was several decades in the making and has since been burned down, blown up in the Civil War and shut several times for restoration. Right now it seems to be doing fine after a long refurbishment programme that concluded in the 1990s. Its origins couldn't have been more humble. Back in 1708 the Italian Bartoli company was granted permission to build a theatre more or less on this site in what had been public wash houses. It was replaced with a sturdier building in 1735, in turn demolished in 1816. The building begun in 1818 was not finished until 1850. Numerous problems halted construction along the way and the partially built theatre was used as a powders store, Guardia Civil barracks and dance hall. Enough was enough and a royal decree ordered the opera house be completed immediately – five months later it opened. Fire struck in 1867 but the theatre continued. By 1925 it was in a bad state and work to restore it was interrupted by the Civil War, during which time it again housed gunpowder (which led to an explosion). Turned into an orchestral concert hall in 1965, it was closed in 1988 for complete restoration, combining the latest in theatre technology with a remake of the most splendid of its 19th century decor. Its doors reopened in 1997…and so far, so good! The guided tours take about 50 minutes.

Teatro Real (p70) from Plaza de Isabel II

SOL, HUERTAS & ATOCHA

They call it the Puerta del Sol (the Sun Gate) although the gate is long gone. It is the navel of Madrid and Spain, but few locals have time to gaze too long at it. A favoured meeting spot (under the clock of the Casa de Correos), it is above all a crossroads. People here are forever heading somewhere else, on foot, by metro (three lines cross) or bus (many lines terminate and start here). Speaking of transport, the whole area has been thrown into confusion by work to create an underground rail interchange between Sol and Gran Vía. Madrileños are not amused. Hidden away in the streets to the southeast of Sol are the culinary and liquid delights of the endless restaurants and bars of Huertas, one of the liveliest corners of the city. It all ends as suddenly as it began at Atocha and its train station.

Orientation

Puerta del Sol is the central point not only of Madrid but of all Spain. A plaque marks the spot in front of the Casa de Correos. The vague hemisphere that makes up this 'square' (the result of some town-remodelling under Carlos III) clearly delimits various *barrios* in the minds of locals and strangers alike. If Madrid de los Austrias, the regal and historical centre, lines off to the west, to the east the avenues of Calle de Alcalá and Carrera de San Jerónimo (slipping by the Cortes, or lower house of the national parliament on the way) strike off to the east and lead to the city's north–south artery, here called Paseo del Prado.

South of Carrera de San Jerónimo lies a world unto its own. Centred on the leafy, pretty and utterly unpredictable Plaza de Santa Ana, locals refer to the whole area vaguely as Huertas, after the street of the same name.

Simply mention Huertas and chances are people think Cervecería Alemana, a classic beer bar on Santa Ana, of the tiles of Los Gabrieles, the sherry at La Venencia or the jazz at Café Populart. For at night all is good-natured boisterousness on and around this square. During the Feria de San Isidro, the ultimate bullfighting season in the capital of bullfighting, many of the toreros and their retinues stay at the Gran Hotel Reina Victoria and drink around here. The square itself can be a hangout for the occasional stray junkie but there is nothing at all threatening in the air. At any rate, from Thursday night to Sunday morning it all heaves, sweats, knocks back *cañas*, laughs, gobbles down *gambas al ajillo*, shuffles around to the next bar… It is busier here at 3am on Sunday than New York Stock Exchange at 10am on Monday. Sure, it was long ago discovered by resident and visiting *guiris* (foreigners). True, some *gatos* haughtily avoid it for that very reason. But many a true-blue *gato* winds up here for a long, long evening.

By the time the long narrow streets leading east and southeast off Plaza de Santa Ana reach Paseo del Prado, the bars and restaurants have thinned to almost nothing. From that avenue off the thundering roundabout of Plaza del Emperador Carlos V, you'd never guess what lies hidden away from view. Just out of bounds, across clanking, honking Calle de Atocha from Huertas and facing the same roundabout is a former hospital turned modern art lover's mecca, the Centro de Arte Reina Sofía. And on the other side of the roundabout is the 19th-century gateway into the capital, Atocha train station, itself a sight since its partial conversion into a tropical garden hothouse in 1992.

ANTIGUA ESTACIÓN DE ATOCHA

Map pp262-4

Plaza del Emperador Carlos V; Metro Atocha Renfe

It would have been easy to just demolish the old train station at Atocha and start over. Instead, the grand iron and glass relic from the 19th century was preserved and artfully converted in 1992 into a surprising tropical garden with more 500 plant species. Around the greenery, various shops and Renfe information offices have been installed, along with a pretty mezzanine restaurant. From its tracks, instead of the ponderous steam trains of the past, now depart the high-speed AVE trains to Seville. The project was the work of architect Rafael Moneo, who is now behind the still more ambitious Gran Prado project. The tropical garden station certainly makes a pleasant, although slightly humid, departure or arrival point.

ATENEO CIENTÍFICO, LITERARIO Y ARTÍSTICO DE MADRID Map pp270-2

☎ 91 429 17 50; Calle del Prado 21; Metro Sevilla

This venerable club of learned types was founded in the 19th century and in atmosphere it seems hardly to have changed since. It is also home to a library. You can usually manage to wander into the foyer, which is lined with portraits of terribly serious-looking fellows, and you may be able to wander upstairs to the library, a jewel of another age, with dark timber stacks, weighty tomes and creakily quiet reading rooms dimly lit with desk lamps.

CASA DE LOPE DE VEGA Map pp270-2

☎ 91 429 92 16; Calle de Cervantes 11; adult/student & senior €2/1; 🕑 9.30am-2pm Tue-Fri, 10am-noon Sat; Metro Antón Martín

One of the greatest playwrights in Spanish, Lope de Vega, lived and wrote in Madrid. He spent 25 years, until his death in 1635, in this house on a street subsequently named after one of the country's greatest novelists. Lope shared the house with Marta de Nevares, a much younger woman, and four children from three different mothers. Lope de Vega's private life was busy and often far from private (the gossip mills in Madrid's literary world were every bit as effective as the magazine *¡Hola!* is today). All Madrid seemed to know about his affair with Marta except her husband. When he finally found out the scandal was enormous but in the end he accepted separation and Marta, who already had a little daughter by the writer, moved in to Lope's colourful household. Today the house, restored in the 1950s, is filled with memorabilia related to his life and times. Lope de Vega was sufficiently successful to be a home-owner, a rare thing in those days. His house was a typical *casa de malicia* (roughly, sneaky house). A city ordinance made it possible for the authorities to lodge strangers in houses of more than two floors, so many people deliberately refused to build any higher and Madrid's houses acquired the sobriquet. Out the back is a tranquil garden, a rare haven of birdsong in this cramped city centre. The street's name is no coincidence either as it is believed the author of Don Quixote died in No 2.

CENTRO DE ARTE REINA SOFÍA

Map p273

☎ 91 467 50 62; http://museoreinasofia.mcu.es; Calle de Santa Isabel 52; adult/student €3/1.50, free Sat 2.30-9pm & Sun, under 12 & senior over 65 free daily, handset guide to collection €3 (handset has recorded information that you take around the collection to hear explanations of works); ⏰ 10am-9pm Mon & Wed-Sat, 10am-2.30pm Sun

Adapted from the remains of an 18th-century hospital, Centro de Arte Reina Sofía houses the best Madrid has to offer in modern Spanish art, principally spanning the 20th century up to the 1980s. The occasional non-Spaniard makes an appearance, but most of the collection is strictly peninsular.

The gallery refers to the ground floor as the 1st floor; we'll use its floor-numbering system here. The permanent display ranges over the 2nd (Rooms 1 to 17) and 4th floors (Rooms 18 to 45). The 1st floor houses a café, an excellent art bookshop and a temporary exhibition space. There is more temporary exhibition space on the 3rd floor. Relax in the peaceful courtyard after the art ingestion, and enjoy the views over the city from the external lift, especially on the top floor.

The big attraction for most visitors is Picasso's *Guernica* (see boxed text below). Don't just rush straight for it, though, as there is plenty of other good material.

The first room on the 2nd floor serves as an ice-breaker, taking you through late-19th-century movements in painting that were to some extent dominated by what was happening in Barcelona. *Modernistas* such as Ramón Casas (1866–1932) and Santiago Rusiñol (1861–1931) are mixed together with their stylistic successors – *Noucentistas* (a Catalan movement that preached a return to more classic themes and styles) such as Isidro Nonell (1873–1911) – and a string of other painters from around the country. Among the latter is the important Basque painter Ignazio Zuloaga (1870–1945).

The following room concentrates on the Madrileño José Gutiérrez Solana (1886–1945). He depicts himself in gloomy fashion in *La Tertulia del Café de Pombo* (The Circle of the Café Pombo; 1920). Room 3 presents a mix of Spanish and foreign painters whose work came before, during and after the notable period of Cubism. The latter trend is perhaps best represented by the works of Juan Gris, a series of which you can admire in Room 4. Among the bronzes of Pablo Gargallo (1881–1934) in Room 5 is a head of Picasso. Speaking of whom, the genius takes up all of the long hall that is Room 6.

Joan Miró takes up a parallel corridor (Room 7) to the Picasso collection. Amid his often delightfully bright primary-colour efforts are some of his equally odd sculptures. In Room 9 you can see a couple of small canvasses by Vassily Kandinsky (1866–1944), one of the few foreigners on show here. Some 20 canvases by Salvador Dalí (1904–1989) hang in Room 10, including the surrealist extravaganza *El Gran Masturbador* (1929). Amid this collection is a strange bust of a certain *Joelle* done by Dalí and his pal Man Ray (1890–1976). Other surrealists, including Max Ernst (1891–1976), appear in Room 11.

Room 12 has a display dedicated to Buñuel, including a portrait of the film-maker by Dalí and sketches by the poet Frederic García Lorca. Room 13 hosts a long list of artists active in the turbulent decades of the 1920s and 1930s, including Benjamín Palencia. Luis Fernández (1900–73) dominates Room 14. Rooms 15 to 17 are set aside for temporary exhibits.

The collection on the 4th floor takes up the baton and continues from the 1940s until the 1980s. A new approach to landscapes evolved in the wake of the Civil War, perhaps best exemplified by the work of Juan Manuel Díaz Caneja (1905–88) in Room 18. In the following room you can study works by two important groups to emerge after WWII, Pórtico and Dau al Set. Among artists of the latter was Barcelona's Antoni Tàpies (born 1923), some of whose later pieces also appear in Rooms 34 and 35.

Rooms 20 to 23 offer a representative look at abstract painting in Spain. Among the more

Guernica

Guernica fully dominates Room 6 and is surrounded by a plethora of the artist's preparatory sketches. Already associated with the Republicans when the Civil War broke out in 1936, Picasso was commissioned by the Republican government of Madrid to do the painting for the Paris Exposition Universelle in 1937. He incorporated features from some of his other works into this, an eloquent condemnation of the horrors of war – more precisely, of the German bombing of Gernika (Guernica), in the Basque Country, in April of the same year. It has been surrounded by controversy from the beginning and was at the time viewed by many as a work more of propaganda than of art. The 3.5m by 7.8m painting subsequently migrated to the USA and only returned to Spain in 1981, to languish in the Casón del Buen Retiro until its transfer to the Reina Sofía. Calls to have it moved to the Basque Country continue unabated.

significant contributors are Eusebio Sempere (1923–85) and members of the Equipo 57 group (founded in 1957 by a group of Spanish artists in exile in Paris), such as Pablo Palazuelo.

Rooms 24 to 35 lead us through Spanish art of the 1960s and 1970s. Some external reference points – such as works by Francis Bacon (1909–92) and Henry Moore (1831–95), both in Room 24 – are thrown in to broaden the context.

Coming down to the present day, Room 38 is given over to work by Eduardo Arroyo, while works of the Basque sculptor Eduardo Chillida (1924–2002) fill Rooms 42 and 43.

CÍRCULO DE BELLAS ARTES Map pp268-9

☎ 91 360 54 00; www.circulobellasartes.com in Spanish; Calle de Alcalá 42; admission to café €1; ⏰ 9.30am-1am Mon-Sun Sep-Jul (café), 5-9pm Tue-Fri, 11am-2pm & 5-9pm Sat, 11am-2pm Sun (expositions)

Antonio Palacios, who seems to have built half of the monumental Madrid of the late 19th and early 20th centuries, was also behind this neo-baroque flurry, built in 1919. The Fine Arts Circle is a multifunctional cultural centre, which puts on theatre, cinema and other events. Visit the grand old-style café replete with chandeliers and the charm of a bygone era (p125).

CONGRESO DE LOS DIPUTADOS

Map pp270-2

☎ 91 390 60 00; Plaza de las Cortes; admission free; ⏰ for guided visits 10am-12.30pm Sat; Metro Sevilla

Where Carrera de San Jerónimo runs into Plaza de las Cortes is the Lower House of Parliament. Originally a Renaissance building, it was completely revamped in 1843 and given a façade with a neo-Classical portal. The modern extension tacked onto it seems a rather odd afterthought. Bring your passport to visit.

PLAZA DE LA PUERTA DEL SOL

Map pp270-2
Metro Sol

It is hard to imagine that in the late-medieval period the Puerta del Sol (Sun Gate) was the easternmost extent of the city. From here a road passed through the peasant hovels of the outer 'suburbs' en route to Guadalajara, to the northeast.

The name of the gate appears to date from the 1520s, when Madrid joined the revolt of the Comuneros (see History p53) against Carlos I and erected a fortress in the east-facing arch in which the sun was depicted. The fort,

which stood about where the metro station is today, was demolished around 1570.

Just outside the gate, where Calle de Alcalá and Carrera de San Jerónimo meet, stood the Iglesia del Buen Suceso, in front of which, in 1616, was raised a fountain topped by a statue of Diana (or, according to some, Venus). Locals (the area at the time was a pestilent mire made worse by the presence of a rambling produce market) dubbed her **Mariblanca** (White Maria), and the statue became something of a symbol of the city. The church was demolished in 1854 and the statue moved to Plaza de las Descalzas and then to Paseo de los Recoletos. It finally ended up inside the Ayuntamiento and a copy, which you can see today, was erected in the Puerta del Sol.

The main building on the square houses the regional government of the Comunidad de Madrid (the Asamblea de Madrid, or regional parliament, meets in a new building in the suburb of Vallecas). The **Casa de Correos**, as it is called, was built as the city's main post office in 1768. The clock, which marks a classic meeting place for Madrileños, was added in 1856. On New Year's Eve, people thronging the square wait impatiently for the clock to strike midnight, and at each gong swallow a grape – not as easy as it sounds! The semicircular junction owes its present appearance in part to the Bourbon king Carlos III (r 1759–88), whose equestrian statue (the nose is unmistakable) stands in the middle. In the 1860s the square was further broadened and the housing around it built.

Just to the north of Carlos, the statue of a bear nuzzling a *madroño* (strawberry tree) is not only the city's symbol but also another favourite meeting place.

REAL ACADEMIA DE BELLAS ARTES DE SAN FERNANDO Map pp270-2

☎ 91 524 08 64; http://rabasf.insde.es in Spanish; Calle de Alcalá 13; adult/student/senior & under 18 €2.40/1.20/free, free to all on Wed; ⏰ 9am-7pm Tue-Fri, 9am-2.30pm Sat-Mon Sep-Jun, varied hours in summer; Metro Sevilla

For a fascinating excursion into another age of art, step inside this fusty but engaging institution, long the academic centre of learning for up and coming artists. Fernando VI founded it in the 18th century as a centre of excellence and little seems to have changed since then. Picasso and Dalí were both sent here to study in their younger days, but neither flourished in its stiff-necked academic atmosphere.

The academy's gallery is not without interest. The 1st floor, mainly devoted to a mix of 16th- to 19th-century paintings, is the most noteworthy. Among relative scattered unknowns you will come across a hall of works by Zurbarán (especially arresting is the series of full-length portraits of white-cloaked friars) and a *San Jerónimo* by El Greco.

At a 'fork' in the exhibition a sign points right to Rooms 11–16, the main one of which is presided over by Alonso Cano (1601–67) and José de Ribera. In the other rooms, a couple of minor portraits by Velázquez and the odd isolated Rubens, Tintoretto and Bellini have managed to smuggle themselves in. Rooms 17–22 offer a roomful of Bravo Murillo and last, but most captivating, more than a dozen pieces by Goya, including self-portraits, portraits of King Fernando VII and the infamous minister Manuel Godoy, along with a take on bullfighting.

The 19th and 20th centuries are the theme upstairs but with the exception of a room given over to drawings by Picasso (one assumes they were done well after his young school days), the pickings are slim. Among artists represented are Joaquín Sorolla, Juan Gris, Eduardo Chillida and Ignacio Zuloaga – in most cases with only one or two items each.

PASEO DEL PRADO & EL RETIRO

What a contrast to the seething centre next door. Apart from the constant rumble of traffic up and down Paseo del Prado, something an urban renovation project should diminish, this is an island of greenery, fresh air and high culture. The big guns, the Museo del Prado and the Museo Thyssen-Bornemisza, are a heavily laden larder of art. Several other museums lurk in the quietly elegant streets just behind the Prado (wouldn't you want to live in a swish apartment in this central paradise?). Just beyond lie the gardens of the Parque del Buen Retiro.

Orientation

The *prado* (field) long marked the eastern extremity of Madrid. Indeed, until late into the 19th-century, building to the east or north of it was virtually non-existent. The southern end of the city began here and that is why Atocha station was built where it is – these were the Madrid city limits. Much as the Palacio Real formed the royal west wing of the city, so the gardens and palace than once stood here were the eastern equivalent. It was basically a fantasy playground for Madrid's swollen nobility. If you were going to spend most of the day doing nothing in particular, what nicer place to do so?

The Parque del Buen Retiro is rightly now a public domain, barely 1km by 1.5km. To its north and east lie the grid plan streets typical of the Ensanche (see Salamanca & Las Ventas p91) urban growth plan of the late 19th and early 20th centuries. The posher part, the *barrio* of Salamanca, begins across Calle de Alcalá to the north. Four blocks east of the park is one of the city's main hospitals, the Hospital General Gregorio Marañón (p231). In all, it is quiet, distinguished and residential. Apart from a handful of discreet restaurants and the museum patch around the Museo del Prado, not a lot goes on. Well, except in the park itself, which on weekends fills with everyone from extended families to clowns and roller-skaters. At night part of the southern end becomes a gay cruising patch.

Top Sights

- Museo del Prado (p77)
- Museo Thyssen-Bornemisza (p79)
- Parque del Buen Retiro (p81)
- Real Jardín Botánico (p82)
- Real Fábrica de Tapices (p82)

ERMITA DE SAN ISIDORO Map pp262-4
Cnr Calle O'Donnell & Avenida de Menéndez Pelayo;
Metro Príncipe de Vergara

The remnants of this small country chapel are about the only modest example of Romanesque architecture to be found in Madrid, just inside the Parque del Buen Retiro. Parts of the wall, a lateral entrance and part of the apse stand here since the restoration in 1999. At the time it was built, probably around the 13th century, Madrid was a little village more than two km away.

IGLESIA DE SAN JERÓNIMO EL REAL

Map p273

☎ 91 420 35 78; Calle de Ruiz de Alarcón; Metro Atocha

The Spanish royals might call this one of their chapels. Here, amid the Isabelline splendour of the grand church King Juan Carlos I was crowned in 1975 upon the death of Franco.

The church itself was once the nucleus of one of the most powerful monastic groups in Madrid. And when we say 'apparently Isabelline' style, we mean that what you see inside, disappointingly, is actually a 19th-century reconstruction that took its cues from San Juan de los Reyes in Toledo. The original had been largely destroyed during the Peninsular War, and suffered more with the subsequent expropriations. What remained of the cloisters next door was demolished (despite vociferous local protests) to make way for the Gran Prado extension.

A block east of the roundabout on Calle de Felipe IV is the custodian of the Spanish language – a learned academy where worthies pontificate on matters related to the language, and the place that produces the most authoritative Spanish dictionary – the **Real Academia Española de la Lengua**. The erudite persons who sit here decided in 2004 that Internet was officially a Spanish word. Precipitate they ain't.

MUSEO DE ARTES DECORATIVAS

Map p273

☎ 91 532 64 99; Calle de Montalbán 12; adult/student/senior €2.40/1.20/free, free to all on Sun; ⏱ 9.30am-3pm Tue-Fri, 10am-3pm Sat-Sun & holidays; Metro Retiro

This museum is full of sumptuous period furniture, ceramics, carpets, tapestries and the like, spanning the 15th to the late 19th centuries. Spread over five floors, it presents the visitor with an enormous variety of objects.

Ceramics from around the country and dating from different periods are on display throughout the building. The re-creations of kitchens from several regions are curious – it is surprising how much the kind of utensils used and the layout of a well-stocked kitchen varied! Reconstructions of regal bedrooms, women's drawing rooms and 19th-century salons all help shed light on how the privileged classes of Spain have lived down through the centuries.

MUSEO DEL EJÉRCITO Map p273

☎ 91 522 89 77; Calle de Méndez Núñez 1; adult/student/senior €1/0.50/free, free to all on Sat; ⏱ 10am-2pm Tue-Sun; Metro Retiro

In 1803 the chief minister, Manuel Godoy, ordered the establishment of an army museum in one of the few remaining parts of the one-time Palacio del Buen Retiro. It's now filled with weapons, flags, uniforms and other

Doorway detail of the Iglesia de San Jerónimo el Real (above)

emnants of Spanish military glory, and housed n what was the Salón de Reinos del Buen Retiro.

An interesting room containing portraits of Franco is devoted to the glorious nationalist campaign in the Civil War, while the Sala Árabe (decorated Alhambra-style) holds various curios, including the sword of Boabdil, the last Muslim ruler of Granada. He signed the instrument of surrender to the Catholic Monarchs that marked the end of the Reconquista in 1492.

It is planned to shift the museum to the *alcázar* in Toledo some time in 2005.

MUSEO DEL PRADO Map p273

☎ 91 330 28 00; http://museoprado.mcu.es; Paseo del Prado; adult/student €3.01/1.50, free Sat 2.30-7pm, Sun & some national holidays, also free for under 18 & senior over 65; ☽ 9am-7pm Tue-Sun; Metro Banco de España

Completed in 1785 in the Prado de los Jerónimos, the neo-Classical Palacio de Villanueva was originally conceived as a house of science, incorporating a natural history museum and laboratories. Events overtook the noble enterprise and during the Napoleonic occupation (1808–13) the building was converted ignominiously into cavalry barracks.

King Fernando VII resolved in 1814 to create a museum in the Palacio de Villanueva to put on public display a representative chunk of the country's artistic wealth. This idea was not prompted by civic ideals of sharing this heritage with the people. Rather, hundreds of works had been removed from the walls of royal palaces and needed to be stored somewhere! Five years later the Museo del Prado opened with 311 Spanish paintings on display. As the years passed, more works from the royal and other collections were added.

There are more than 7000 works in the collection today, but fewer than half are ever on view. This will change with architect Rafael Moneo's €50 million Gran Prado extension project, which hopefully will be completed in March 2005.

Moneo is building a new section of the museum on the site of what were the cloisters of the Iglesia de San Jerónimo El Real, and connecting it to the main building via a subterranean passage. Administration will move to the new building and a new library, drawings gallery and temporary exhibition space and seminar centre will also be set up there. Basement space is also being prepared in the nearby Casón del Buen Retiro, the ballroom of the now nonexistent Palacio del Buen Retiro

and until the mid-1990s home to a selection of lesser-known 19th-century Spanish works. Finally, more space will be acquired when the nearby Museo del Ejército (Army Museum) is transferred to Toledo.

You can enter the main part of the museum by the northern Puerta de Goya or the southern Puerta de Murillo. The latter leads you into the ground floor and you can access the ground and 1st floors from the former. There is little free printed information. The hand-out map guides you to the main schools and major artists. Otherwise, attractive little booklets (€1) in several languages can be extracted from machines located in a couple of the rooms. You'll find one on Goya in the rooms devoted to him on the 2nd floor. Others include Bosch, Titian, Velázquez and El Greco, all located in the appropriate areas.

One of the collection's beauties is the generous coverage of certain masters. Strings of rooms are devoted to the works of three of Spain's greatest – El Greco, Velázquez and Goya. This is the cream of the Prado's collection, but there is plenty of good stuff by other major Spanish artists (such as José de Ribera, Murillo and Zurbarán), as well as a fair serving of Flemish and Italian masters. A sprinkling of artists of other nationalities completes the picture.

At present the bulk of the collection is held on the ground and 1st floors. The ground floor is dominated by Italian and Flemish painters (including the likes of Titian, Tintoretto and Bosch). Three rooms are dedicated to El Greco. A handful of Spanish artists is also represented here.

Head for the 1st floor to see the main body of Spanish art. With the exception of five small rooms given over to Italian and French artists, and a section mostly devoted to Flemish art, this is an all-Spanish show, with big sections on Velázquez and Goya. The latter extends up into the south wing of the 2nd floor.

El Greco is represented on the ground floor, in Rooms 60A, 61A and 62A. The long, slender figures characteristic of this singular Cretan artist, who lived and worked in Toledo, are hard to mistake. Particularly striking are *La Crucifixión* and *San Andrés y San Francisco*, finished towards the end of the 16th century.

Diego Rodriguez de Silva y Velázquez became an official artist at the royal court at the age of 24. Of this 17th-century master's works, *Las Meninas* is what most people come to see, and rightly so. Executed in 1656, it is more properly known as *La Família de Felipe IV*

(The Family of Felipe IV). It depicts Velázquez himself on the left and, in the centre, the Infanta Margarita. There is more to it than that: the artist in fact portrays himself painting the king and queen, whose images appear, according to some experts, in mirrors behind Velázquez. His mastery of light and colour is never more apparent than here. An interesting detail of the painting, aside from the extraordinary cheek of painting himself in royal company, is the presence of the cross of the Order of Santiago on his vest. The artist was apparently obsessed with being given a noble title. He got it shortly before his death, but in this oil painting, he has awarded himself the order years before it would in fact be his! The painting takes pride of place in Room 27, halfway along the main hall on the 1st floor.

The bulk of Velázquez' works are in Rooms 26–28 (in the main hall) and 14–16. Among some of his outstanding portraits are *La Infanta Doña Margarita de Austria* (who stars in *Las Meninas*) and *Baltasar Carlos a Caballo*. *Cristo Crucificado* manages to convey the agony of the Crucifixion with great dignity. *La Rendición de Breda* (The Surrender of Breda) is another classic.

Francisco José de Goya y Lucientes is the most extensively represented of the Spanish masters in the Prado. Late to reach the heights of his grandeur, Goya, more than anyone, captured the extremes of hope and misery his country experienced before, during and after the Napoleonic invasion. In Room 21, on the 1st floor, hang what are probably his best-known and most intriguing oils, *La Maja Vestida* and *La Maja Desnuda*. These portraits of an unknown woman commonly believed to be the Duquesa de Alba (who may have been Goya's lover) are identical save for the lack of clothing in the latter.

The horrors of war had a profound effect on Goya's view of the world. *El Dos de Mayo* and, still more dramatically, *El Tres de Mayo* bring to life the 1808 anti-French revolt and subsequent execution of insurgents in Madrid. They're in Room 39. In Room x16B hang his *Pinturas Negras* (Black Paintings), so-called because of the dark browns and black that dominate, and the distorted animalesque appearance of their characters. Among the most disturbing of these works is *Saturno Devorando a Su Hijo* (Saturn Devouring His Son).

The 2nd floor's south wing contains many of Goya's preparatory paintings for tapestries, and religious paintings and drawings.

In the shadow of these greats come a small group of important Spanish artists and a gaggle of minor ones. Of the former, there are substantial collections of work by Bartolomé Esteban Murillo (Rooms 29 and 28) and José de Ribera (Rooms 25), Francisco de Zurbarán (Rooms 17A and 18A) and Claudio Coello (along with others of the Spanish baroque period; Room 16A. All these are on the 1st floor.

In Room 51C on the ground floor are the re-creation of a Romanesque church apse and some intriguing murals taken from the 12th century Mozarabic Ermita de San Baudelio, an enchanting little chapel in Soria province northeast of Madrid.

The wealth of Flemish art in the Prado should not be missed. The pick of the work of Hieronymus Bosch (c1450–1516) lives in Room 56A, on the ground floor. Among these paintings is *The Garden of Earthly Delights*, for which no-one has yet been able to provide a definitive explanation, although many have tried. While it is, without doubt, the star attraction of this fantastical painter's collection, all his work rewards inspection. The closer you look, the harder it is to escape the feeling that he must have been doing some extraordinary drugs. Around this room, five others are filled with Flemish works from the 15th and 16th centuries.

Up on the 1st floor, Peter Paul Rubens (1577–1640) gets a big run. His works dominate Rooms 8B, 9, 9A, 9B, 10, 10B and 11. The most sought after is his *Las Tres Gracias* (The Three Graces) in Room 9. He is joined by Anton Van Dyck (Rooms 9B, 10A and 10B) and others of the same epoch in the surrounding rooms (Rooms 7A through to 11).

The Italians of the Renaissance haven't been left out either – they fully occupy many rooms on the ground floor. Among the plethora of Madonnas with babes and Christ in many poses, are some sensational works worth checking out, like Botticelli's *The Story of Nastagio degli Onesti* in three parts. There's classic chiaroscuro from Caravaggio, while Tintoretto and Titian play with perspectives. Felipe II was partial to Titian and Venetian artists in general, which in part explains why they dominate the Italian scene in the Prado. But don't linger too long here – this is Spain, after all, and the best of the Spanish masters await.

In one small room on the ground floor containing German works (Room 55B), you can see a couple of small pieces by Albrecht Dürer (1471–1528) and Lucas Cranach the Elder (1472–1553). On the 1st floor, Rembrandt

1606–1669) scrapes in for Holland in Room 7, while Carlos III's court painter, Anton Rafael Mengs (1728–79) shares Room 86 with Tiepolo on the 2nd floor.

A small collection of paintings from Spain's eternal enemy, France, huddles together in Rooms 2 to 4 on the 1st floor. Artists include Nicolas Poussin (1594–1665), Louis Michel Van Loo (1707–71) and Jean-Antoine Watteau (1684–1721).

Down in the basement, the Tesoro del Delfín constitutes a remarkable collection of objets d'art from the 16th and 17th centuries. They belonged to the Grand Dauphin, the eldest son of Louis XIV of France. In the south wing of the 1st floor is an extensive display of ancient Greek and Roman statuary.

MUSEO NAVAL Map p273

☎ 91 379 52 99; Paseo del Prado 5; admission free; ☻ 10am-2pm Tue-Sun; Metro Banco de España

A block south of the big Plaza de la Cibeles roundabout, seafaring folk may well find this museum curious. It is jammed with quite extraordinary models of ships from the earliest days of Spain's maritime history to the 20th century. Accompanying them is a plethora of maps, arms, uniforms, flags (including a Nazi flag from the German warship *Deutschland*, which was bombed by Republican planes off Ibiza in 1937) and other naval paraphernalia.

Of greatest historical interest is Juan de la Cosa's parchment map of the known world, put together in 1500. The accuracy of Europe is quite astounding, and it is supposedly the first map to show the Americas (albeit with considerably greater fantasy than fact).

MUSEO THYSSEN-BORNEMISZA

Map pp270-2

☎ 91 369 01 51; www.museothyssen.org; Paseo del Prado 8; adult/student & senior €4.80/3, temporary exhibitions adult/student & senior/child under 12 €3.60/2.40/free, combined admission to museum & temporary exhibition adult/student & senior/child under 12 €6.60/3.60/free, headset guide €3; ☻ 10am-7pm Tue-Sun; Metro Banco de España

This is one of the most wide-ranging private collections of predominantly European art in the world. It has been accumulated over two generations by the Thyssen-Bornemiszas, a family of German–Hungarian magnates. Spain managed to acquire the prestigious collection when it offered to overhaul the neo-Classical Palacio de Villahermosa specifically to house most of it. Almost 800 works have hung here

since October 1992, with a further 80 at the Monestir de Pedralbes in Barcelona (destined to be moved to the Museu Nacional d'Art de Catalunya).

In early 2000 the museum acquired two adjoining buildings, which are being prepared to house approximately half of the collection of Carmen Thyssen-Bornemisza. This collection, which ranges from the 14th to the 20th centuries in much the same eclectic style as the permanent exhibition, numbers about 300 works. The emphasis is on 19th-century works and Spanish American, Impressionist and Expressionist art. The new exhibition opened in mid-2004. The 1st and 2nd floors of the extension are connected to the same floors in the original building and, eventually, the two collections will be fused into chronological order across the entire complex.

The original collection is spread out over three floors, so you could do worse than follow the museum pamphlet's advice to start on the 2nd floor (there is a lift) and work your way down chronologically from 13th- and 14th-century religious paintings to the avant-garde and pop art on the ground floor. The eclectic nature of the collection is such that many artists of a great number of epochs and schools are represented – if only by one or two samples.

The first three rooms on the 2nd floor are dedicated to medieval art, with a series of remarkable triptychs and paintings (predominantly Italian, German and Flemish) to get the ball rolling. They include some by Duccio di Buoninsegna (c1255–1318), who led the Sienese school into a gentle break from Byzantine forms in the late 13th and early 14th centuries.

In Room 4, the move away from Gothic painting in Italy is illustrated with works by Paolo Uccello (1397–1475), Benozzo Gozzoli (1420–97) and others from Milan, Venice, Perugia and Ferrara.

Room 5 contains, among others, one work by Italy's Piero della Francesca (1410–92) and a *Henry VIII* by Holbein the Younger (1497–1543). Room 6 (the long Galería Villahermosa) hosts a series of portraits, including a few by Venetian masters Lorenzo Lotto and Il Veronese. Here and in Room 4 you can also see a couple of examples of the glazed terracotta sculptures for which Florence's Della Robbia family became famous.

In Room 7 are some exemplary works by the brothers Gentile (1429–1507) and Giovanni Bellini (1430–1516) who, together with their father, Jacopo (1400–70), launched the Venetian Renaissance in painting. Titian and Bronzino (1503–72) are also represented.

Rooms 8 and 9 are given over to German 15th- and 16th-century masters. Among them are a few works by Lucas Cranach the Elder and the Younger, Hans Holbein the Elder and Dürer. Room 10 contains Dutch masters from the same period.

Room 11 is dedicated to El Greco (with three pieces) and his Venetian contemporaries Tintoretto, Titian and Jacopo Bassano.

Caravaggio and José de Ribera, who was much influenced by the former, dominate the next room, while Rooms 13 to 15 mainly contain works by Italians of the 17th century, among them Luca Giordana (1634–1705). Murillo and Zurbarán each have one painting here, along with some by various French artists.

Look out for the fine views of Venice by Canaletto (1697–1768), accompanied by some of the best works of Francesco Guardi (1712–93), in Rooms 16 and 17. The following room has a mixture of 18th-century predominantly Venetian painters.

Rubens leads the way in rooms 19 to 21 on this floor, which are devoted to 17th-century Dutch and Flemish masters. Anton van Dyck, Jan Brueghel the Elder (1568–1625) and Rembrandt (one painting) also get a showing. The Dutch theme continues on the 1st floor, with interiors and landscapes, followed (in Room 27) by a still-life series.

In Room 28 you'll find a Gainsborough (1727–88) – one of the few British works in the collection – along with a few paintings by Jean Antoine Watteau (1684–1721) and Jean-Honoré Fragonard (1732–1806).

Next (Rooms 29 and 30) comes a representative look at North American art of the 19th century, including three pieces by John Singer Sargent (1856–1925). In Room 31 Gustave Courbet (1819–77) and Goya (with a bust of Fernando VII and a couple of other works) get a run.

A series of great Impressionist and postimpressionist names get a showing in Rooms 32 and 33, with works by Camille Pissarro (1830–1903), Pierre-Auguste Renoir (1841–1919), Edgar Degas (1834–1917), Claude Monet (1840–1926), Edouard Manet (1832–83), Henri de Toulouse-Lautrec (1864–1901), Paul Cézanne (1839–1906), Paul Gauguin (1848–1903) and Vincent Van Gogh (1853–90).

Expressionism rules the remainder of the floor. In Room 35 you'll find canvases by Egon Schiele (1890–1918), and Edvard Munch (1863–1944).

Ernst Ludwig Kirchner (1880–1938) and Max Pechstein (1881–1955) lead the way in Rooms 36 and 37. Room 38 includes works by August Macke (1887–1914) and one by Vassily Kandinsky (1866–1944), while Max Beckmann (1854–1950) lords it over Room 39. The final room on the floor features a couple of works by George Grosz (1893–1959). His *Metropolis* is a nightmare vision of a city if ever there was one.

On the ground floor you move firmly into the 20th century, from Cubism through to pop art. Chronological order seems to be largely abandoned here. In Room 41 you'll see a nice mix of the big three of Cubism, Picasso, Georges Braque (1882–1963) and Madrid's own Juan Gris, along with several other contemporaries.

Picasso pops up again in Room 45, which also hosts works by Marc Chagall (1887–1985), Kandinsky, Paul Klee and Joan Miró (1893–1983). He turns up again in Room 46, along with Jackson Pollock (1912–56), Willem de Kooning (1904–97), Mark Rothko (1903–70) and Georgia O'Keefe (1887–1980). Lucian Freud (born 1922), Sigmund's Berlin-born grandson, Yves Tanguy (1900–55), Dalí and Francis Bacon (1909–92) are joined by David Hockney (born 1937) and Roy Lichtenstein (1923–97) in Rooms 47 and 48.

PALACIO DE LINARES & CASA DE AMÉRICA Map pp268–9

☎ 91 595 48 00; www.casamerica.es in Spanish; Paseo de los Recoletos 2; admission free; ☽ 11am-2pm & 5-8pm Tue-Sat, 11am-2pm Sun & holidays; Metro Banco de España

This 19th-century pleasure dome that stands watch over the northeast end of Plaza de la Cibeles was built in 1873 and is a worthy member of the line-up of grand façades on the plaza. To locals and tourists alike, its innards are notable particularly for the copious decoration in Carrara marble. The problem is that you don't get to see very much of it. Perhaps they keep it closed to the public because of an old story that tells us the place has a curse on it. The first duke of Linares is said to have had a bastard daughter, with whom his son later fell in love. They only found out she was his half-sister after they were wed – the cause of much subsequent gnashing of teeth. Anyway, what you can visit is the **Casa de América**, a modern exposition centre in the palace's grounds. All sorts of events and concerts are organised here.

PANTEÓN DE HOMBRES ILUSTRES

Map pp262-4

Calle de Julián Gayarre 3, admission free; ☿ 9am-7pm Mon-Sat, 9am-4pm Sun & holidays Apr-Sep, 9.30am-6pm Mon-Sat, 9am-3pm Sun & holidays; Metro Atocha Renfe

This is a rather sombre and mannish sort of place, a neo-Byzantine pantheon to some of the great and good of Madrid and Spain in the cloister of what would have been a grand basilica that was never built. Next door is the early-20th-century Basílica de Nuestra Señora de Atocha (which contains a Romanesque carving of the Virgin Mary left over from the 16th-century Dominican monastery that once stood here). Few of the names of the 19th- and 20th-century statesmen in the pantheon and writers will mean anything to those not fairly well acquainted with modern Spanish history, but it's a tranquil spot and worth dropping by if you happen to be here (say for the Real Fábrica de Tapices).

PARQUE DEL BUEN RETIRO Map pp262-4

Admission free; ☿ 6am-midnight May-Sep, 6am-10pm Oct-Apr; Metro Retiro

After a heavy round of the nearby art galleries the perfect antidote might be a wander in Madrid's reduced version of Central Park, the city's central green area and popular gathering place for Sunday strolling families, clowns, bongo players, arm-in-arm lovers and lone crepuscular cruisers. The gardens are at their busiest on weekends, when street performers appear.

Once the preserve of kings, queens and their intimates, the park is now open to all. You can hire boats (€4 for 45 minutes) to paddle about on the artificial lake (estanque), watched over by the massive structure of **Alfonso XII's mausoleum**. On the western side of the lake, you may notice an odd structure decorated with sphinxes. It is the **Fuente Egipcia** (Egyptian Fountain) and legend has it that an enormous fortune buried in the park by Felipe IV in the mid-18th century rests here. Park authorities assure us the legend is rot.

Weekend buskers and tarot readers ply their trade around the same lake, while art and photo exhibitions are held at a couple of places, in particular the Palacio de Exposiciones. Puppet shows for the kids are a summertime feature (look for Tiritilandia, or Puppet Land).

The **Palacio de Cristal** (☎ 91 574 66 14; ☿ 11am-8pm Mon-Sat, 11am-6pm Sun & holidays May-Sep, 10am-6pm Mon-Sat, 10am-4pm Sun & holidays Oct-Apr), a charming metal and glass structure to the south of the lake, was built in 1887 as a winter garden for exotic flowers. It is also the scene of occasional exhibitions. Not far off, the **Palacio de Velázquez** (☎ 91 573 62 45; same hours as Palacio de Cristal) was built in 1883 for a mining exposition and is now used for temporary expositions. Another building occasionally used for temporary expositions is the **Casa de Vacas** (☎ 91 409 58 19; ☿ 11am-10pm).

At the southern end of the park, near **La Rosaleda** (the rose gardens), a statue of **El Ángel Caído** (the Fallen Angel, aka Lucifer) brings a slightly sinister note to the place. The southwest end of the park is a popular cruising ground for young gay men.

PLAZA DE LA CIBELES Map pp268-9

Metro Banco de España

The spectacular fountain of the Cybele is one of Madrid's most beautiful. Ever since it was erected in 1780 by Ventura Rodríguez, this assessment has remained much the same. Carlos III liked it so much that he wanted to have it moved to the gardens of the Granja de San Ildefonso, on the road to Segovia, but the Madrileños kicked up such a fuss that he let it be.

The goddess Cybele had Atalanta and Hippomenes (recently paired off thanks to the intervention of Aphrodite) converted into lions and shackled to her chariot for having profaned her temple. They had been put up to this by Aphrodite, who was irritated by the apparent ingratitude of the newlyweds for her good work.

One might expect a degree of respect for ancient mythology and centuries-old public art. Unfortunately football, however, seems more sacred to its many supporters. Ever since the Spanish national competition got under way at the beginning of the last century, the Cibeles fountain has been the object of a kind of ritual rape by the players and supporters of Real Madrid when the side has won anything of note. Down through the years, these people have celebrated by clambering all over the fountain in a frenzy and chipping bits off as souvenirs. Oddly, the club itself has never done anything to stop this. The city council now occasionally boards up the statue on the eve of important matches.

The building you are least likely to miss on the square is the sickly-sweet **Palacio de Comunicaciones**, built in 1904–17 by Antonio Palacios and combining elements of a North American monumental style of the period with Gothic and Renaissance touches. Newcomers find it hard to accept that this is merely the central post office. Across the Paseo del Prado is the fittingly overbearing home to the national **Banco de España**, which was completed in 1891.

PLAZA DE NEPTUNO Map pp262-4

Metro Banco de España or bus No 10, 14, 27, 34, 37 & 45

Officially known as Plaza de Cánovas del Castillo, the next roundabout south of Cibeles is commanded by an 18th-century sculpture of the sea god by Juan Pascual de Mena. It is a haughty focal point, flanked not only by the Museo Thyssen-Bornemisza and the Prado, but also by the city's famous competitors in the hotel business, the Ritz and the Palace. Both opened for business in the heady years prior to WWI and attracted a mixed clientele. The saucy Dutch exotic dancer and alleged spy Mata Hari is said to have stayed at either one or the other during the war.

The Neptune fountain is to the fans of Atlético Madrid what the Cibeles is to Real Madrid's mob. The results are equally painful.

REAL FÁBRICA DE TAPICES Map pp262-4

☎ 91 434 05 50; www.realfabricadetapices.com; Calle de Fuenterrabía 2; admission €2.50; ⏱ 10am-2pm Mon-Fri Sep-Jul; Metro Menéndez Pelayo

Founded in the 18th century to provide the royal family and other bigwigs with tapestries befitting their grandeur, this workshop is still producing and restoring tapestries and carpets today. Its heyday lasted until the Napoleonic invasion of Spain, from which it only began to recover towards the end of the 19th century. If you like tapestries and carpets of a high quality and price, a visit is well worth your while. With luck you will get to see how they are made, and have been made over the centuries.

REAL JARDÍN BOTÁNICO Map pp262-4

☎ 91 420 30 17; Plaza de Bravo Murillo 2; adult/student/senior & child under 11 €1.50/0.75/free; ⏱ 10am-9pm May-Aug, 10am-8pm Apr & Sep, 10am-7pm Oct & Mar, 10am-6pm Nov-Feb; Metro Atocha

Ask most Madrileños about the city's botanical gardens and they won't know what you are talking about. All the worse for them, as the Real Jardín Botánico is a refuge more beautiful than El Retiro, although not as extensive. Created in 1755 under Fernando VI at El Huerto de Migas Calientes, on the banks of the Río

Plaza de Neptuno's fountain dates from the 1700s (left)

Manzanares, the original gardens consisted of some 2000 plants. Today more than 30,000 species are kept here.

Carlos III ordered the transfer of the gardens to their present location, which was completed in 1781. His proud statue presides over the centre of the gardens. The rather bombastic Ministerio de Agricultura building, which was built in 1882, robbed the gardens of two precious hectares, leaving a total of eight. Over the more than two centuries of their existence the gardens have gone through highs and lows, and were closed for regeneration from 1974 to 1981.

In the Pabellón Villanueva, on the northern flank of the gardens, art exhibitions are frequently staged – the opening hours are the same as for the park and usually the exhibitions are free.

LA LATINA & LAVAPIÉS

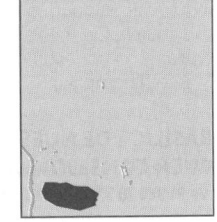

Named after a remarkable 15th-century noblewoman (see Plaza de la Cebada, p86), la Latina includes the one-time Moorish quarter of medieval Christian Madrid and some of the earliest 'suburban' expansion of the original town nucleus. A lively and in places rather gritty (but rapidly gentrifying) part of town, La Latina is a crossroads between the desirable Madrid de los Austrias and working-class *barrios* such as Lavapiés.

The deep long streets that slither downhill from Huertas into Lavapiés give you the feeling that you are descending into another, slightly dodgier world. On Sundays Madrid's best known weekly flea market is held in what is called El Rastro. Antique furniture shops throw open their doors and stands sell anything from old coins to utter rubbish. Although steps have been taken to breathe some life into the *barrio* since the early 1990s, hundreds, if not thousands, of residents still live in precarious circumstances, in some cases without even the most basic services.

Inevitably, as a somewhat rundown part of town, it has attracted a variegated community of migrants, legal and otherwise, that have lent the place a new dimension. Black Africans, Moroccans, South Americans and Chinese live cheek by jowl with locals in what has come to be a fascinating mix. Not without its difficulties but engaging all the same.

Orientation

The area of La Latina forms a rough triangle bordered by Calle de Segovia, Ronda de Segovia and Calle de Toledo, which separates it from Lavapiés. Bordering on Madrid de los Austrias, La Latina is in part older. The web of lanes around Calle de Segovia and Calle de Bailén once constituted the Morería, the Moorish quarter of the small town shortly after it fell into Christian hands. A set of medieval city walls once loosely followed Calles de la Cava Baja and de la Cava Alta. The sloping gardens of Vistillas at the western end of the *barrio* offer nice views west to the Sierra de Guadarrama. Just south of the gardens stands the outsize baroque Basílica de San Francisco el Grande.

From Plaza de Tirso de Molina and Calle de la Magdalena a series of long narrow lanes drops downhill from the centre of the city into Lavapiés. The barrio's most obvious nerve centre is the small triangular Plaza de Lavapiés (where the metro stop is), partly edged by the Teatro Olímpia (being renovated). A hotchpotch of interesting bars and eateries is scattered about in the vicinity. Further west, the streets of El Rastro, between Calle de los Embajadores and Ribera de los Curtidores, have their own distinct character.

The area is cordoned off to the south by Ronda de Toledo and Ronda de Atocha, noisy and ugly avenues that head east to Atocha station.

Top Sights

- Basílica de San Francisco El Grande (p83)
- El Rastro (p84)
- Iglesia de San Andrés (p84)

BASÍLICA DE SAN FRANCISCO EL GRANDE Map pp262-4

☎ 91 365 38 00; Plaza de San Francisco; admission €3; ⌚ 11am-1pm & 5-7pm Tue-Sat; Metro La Latina or bus 3, 60 & 148

Completed under the guidance of Francesco Sabatini, the recently restored baroque basilica has some outstanding features. Of particular note are the frescoed cupolas (restored in 2000–01) and the appealing chapel ceilings by Francisco Bayeu.

Raised on the site where legend claims St Francis of Assisi built a chapel in 1217, it is one of the city's biggest churches and has a curious ground plan. When you enter, the building arcs off to the left and right in a flurry of columns. Off this circular nave lie several chapels. You'll probably be directed to a series of corridors (lined with works of art) behind the high altar. A guide will take you to the sacristy, which features fine Renaissance *sillería* – the sculpted walnut seats where the church's superiors would meet.

A 19th-century plan to create a grand linking square supported by a viaduct between this church and the Palacio Real never left the drawing board – you can see a model in the Museo Municipal (p88).

BASÍLICA DE NUESTRA SEÑORA DEL BUEN CONSEJO Map pp270-2

☎ 91 369 20 37; Calle de Toledo 37; 🕒 8am-noon & 6-8.30pm; Metro Tirso de Molina

Calle de Toledo, which runs south from Plaza Major, was the main road to Madrid's one-time competitor for the title of national capital. The boulevard may no longer be the highway out of Madrid but it bustles all the same. Towering above its northern end is the imposing church that long served as the city's de facto cathedral (and is largely still known to locals as the Catedral de San Isidro), until Nuestra Señora de la Almudena was completed in 1992 (see p66). In fact, Madrid was only granted status as an archdiocese independent of Toledo in 1851, which explains why the city went for so long without a cathedral at all.

The austere baroque basilica was founded in the 17th century as the headquarters for the Jesuits and today is home to the remains of the city's main patron saint, San Isidro '(in the third chapel on your left after you walk in). Next door, the **Instituto de San Isidro** once went by the name of Colegio Imperial and, from the 16th century on, was where many of the country's leading figures were schooled by the Jesuits. You can wander in and look at the elegant courtyard.

Just beyond the church, the road forks. Calle de Toledo continues off to the right and ends about 800m further downhill at the triumphal arch at the **Puerta de Toledo**, completed in 1817 to celebrate the defeat of Napoleon. The irony is that its construction was actually begun by Joseph Bonaparte to celebrate French victory! Beyond, the 18th-century **Puente de Toledo**, completed in 1732 by Pedro de Ribera, spans the Río Manzanares. Until the highways of the 20th century were built, this was the way to Toledo. The left fork, Calle de los Estudios, leads into El Rastro (see below).

BASÍLICA DE SAN MIGUEL Map pp270-2

☎ 91 548 40 11; Calle de San Justo 4; 🕒 10.30am-12.45pm & 6-8.30pm Mon-Sat; Metro Latina or Sol

This basilica stands on the site of an earlier Romanesque church. This version, with a convex, late-baroque façade and rococo interior, was completed in 1745 by Italian architects and originally dedicated to the saints Justo an Pastor, who appear in a relief on the façade. Also on the façade are statues representing the four virtues.

EL RASTRO Map pp270-2

Ribera de los Curtidores; 🕒 8am-2pm Sun & holidays; Metro La Latina

The crowded Sunday flea market (see also p174) was, back in the 17th and 18th centuries, largely dedicated to a meat market (the word *rastro* referred to the trail of blood left behind by animals dragged down the hill). The road at the heart of the area, Ribera de los Curtidores (Tanners' Alley) provides further evidence of the one-time animal activity around here. Although increasingly bereft of objects of real interest, and busy with tourists, El Rastro flea market is worth wandering around just for the atmosphere.

IGLESIA DE SAN ANDRÉS Map pp270-2

☎ 91 365 48 71; Plaza de San Andrés; 🕒 8am-1pm & 5.30-8pm; Metro La Latina

This proud church was largely gutted during the Civil War and like many of Madrid's churches, it looks its best when lit up at night as a backdrop for the local café life.

It is nevertheless worth a peek inside. Enter from Plaza de San Andrés and as you turn left inside the church to face the altar you are confronted by an extraordinary work of baroque decoration. Stern, dark columns with gold-leaf capitals against the rear wall lead your eyes up into the dome, all rose, yellow and green, and rich with sculpted floral fantasies and cherubs poking out of every nook and cranny.

Around the back, on Plaza de la Paja (Straw Square), is the **Capilla del Obispo**, a fine and (for Madrid) rare example of the transitional style between Gothic and Renaissance – look at the (largely Gothic) vaulting in the ceilings and the fine Renaissance reredos (screens). The Vargas family had the chapel built to house San Isidro's remains, which it did for a short while (see the boxed text, opppsite). The chapel is often closed – you may only be able to get in if there is a temporary exhibition on.

IGLESIA DE SAN PEDRO EL VIEJO

Map pp270-2

☎ 91 365 12 84; Costanilla de San Pedro; Metro La Latina

The outstanding feature of this church is it clearly *mudéjar* bell tower. Along with the fine brick bell tower of the Iglesia de San Nicolás de los Servitas, a little way to the north, it is one

A Humble Saint

Towards the end of the 11th century a farm labourer called Isidro travelled from northern Spain to the newly reconquered Madrid to seek his fortune. He was one of many Christian Spaniards encouraged to repopulate territories wrested from Muslim control.

Isidro entered the service of the Vargas family. The story goes that one day, out in the fields just beyond the town walls, Isidro's boss, Iván de Vargas, was feeling so thirsty that Isidro called forth spring water for him where before there had been none. Iván was no doubt impressed, but not as much as the rest of town as word got around. 'It's a miracle!' they cried. And others followed. One such miracle involved Iván's son falling into a well. Isidro prayed and prayed until the water rose and lifted his son to safety. Successive generations maintained the memory of this and other miraculous deeds and by the 13th century Isidro had become a cult figure.

It was perhaps only natural, then, that such fervour should be repaid with further spectacles. Isidro had been buried in the cemetery of the Iglesia de San Andrés. In the late 13th century, his body was 'discovered' there and, more incredibly, the rot had not yet begun to set in. King Alfonso XI ordered the construction in San Andrés of an ark to hold his remains and a chapel in which to venerate his memory.

Later, the chapel was replaced by a baroque version at the back of the church, erected by the Vargas family in an effort to bask in the reflected saintly glory of their one-time family servant. His remains were moved in 1535, but only lasted 25 years here. After an argument between the parish priest of San Andrés and the chaplain of the new chapel (the Capilla del Obispo), his body was moved back to the church. In 1669 (47 years after the saint was canonised) yet another chapel was built for him there (it can be seen, in its restored form, today). A dividing wall went up between the church and the Capilla del Obispo, just in case anyone had any doubts about the severity of the tiff.

San Isidro Labrador (St Isidro the Farm Labourer) made his last move, to the Basílica Nuestra Señora del Buen Consejo, about 100 years later. His body, apparently remarkably well preserved, still rests there today (except on those occasions when, as in 1896 and 1947, he is paraded about town in the hope he will bring rain). San Isidro's whole family was canonised. His wife was Santa María de la Cabeza and his son San Millán. Another holy family.

f the few surviving testaments to the industriousness of *mudéjar* builders. Both towers have een carefully restored, but all other traces of nudéjar Madrid have disappeared. For a much etter idea of what these builders were capble of, head 70km south to Toledo (p200). The hurch interior (it is generally closed) is 15th-entury Gothic, although largely disguised by 7th-century renovation.

A CASA ENCENDIDA Map pp262-4

☎ 91 506 38 75; www.lacasaencendida.com in panish; Ronda de Valencia 2; ☾ 10am-10pm; Metro Embajadores

his cultural centre is utterly unpredictable, if only because of the quantity and scope of its ctivities. It puts on expositions, cinema sesions, workshops and more.

AVAPIÉS Map pp262-4

Metro Lavapiés

With the exception of **La Corrala** (Calle de Mesón le Paredes 65), an intriguing traditional (if nuch tidied up) tenement block, built around central courtyard, which functions now as a nakeshift stage for (mainly summertime) theare, there are no specific sights in this lively quarter. La Corrala is opposite the ruins of a

church. Another less prettied up one can be seen on Calle de Miguel Servet.

The real attraction of Lavapiés (they say the name comes from *aba-puest*, 'place of the Jews') is the earthy feel of what is one of the city's last true *barrios*, where people live crowded in on top of one another and everyone seems to know one another. People hang out the windows and talk (or shout) to one another across the washing hung out to dry over the narrow streets. Madrileños have long referred to Lavapiés and the area south as the *barrios bajos* (the low *barrios*), for the simple reason that they drop down from the high ground of the Austrias and Puerta del Sol to the narrow Manzanares river.

The bulk of the city's Jewish population once lived in the eastern half of Lavapiés (the existence centuries ago of at least one synagogue in the area is documented) in what was then known as the *judería* (Jewish quarter). The bulk of them left after the Catholic Monarchs ordered the expulsion of Jews and Muslims from all Spain in 1492. Those who remained behind became *conversos* (converts to Christianity) but were largely suspected of giving only lip service to the new faith. They too eventually left. You can also see a *casa de malicia* at Calle de Tribulete 11.

Later on, the life of this working class barrio was dominated by the Real Fábrica de Tabacos on Calle de Embajadores, where a mostly female staff worked until well into the 20th century, animating the surrounding streets with their comings and goings. Today the former factory is a largely abandoned hulk but one day it will house the Museo Nacional de Artes Decorativas and a new Museo de Reproducciones Artísticas.

Lavapiés is now the residence of an interesting mix of working-class *gatos*, *gitanos* (Roma people) and migrants from far and wide (including North Africans, Black Africans, Chinese and South Americans). In fact, according to one count more than 50 countries are represented in an area made up of a couple of dozen streets. It remains a largely poor part of town, in spite of efforts to renovate it and the bohemian attraction it has for many young people.

MUSEO DE SAN ISIDRO Map pp270-2

☎ 91 366 74 15; Plaza de San Andrés 2; admission free; ☼ 9.30am-8pm Tue-Fri, 10am-2pm Sat & Sun; Metro La Latina

Next door to the Iglesia de San Andrés (p84) is a modest building on the spot where they say San Isidro ended his days in around 1172. Here is also the 'miraculous well', in which popular tradition says the saint saved his master's son from drowning. The building now houses a small museum containing assorted archaeological finds from old Madrid. The largely new building has a 16th-century courtyard and a 17th-century chapel. The most interesting item in the archaeological section is a mosaic found on the site of a Roman villa in Carabanchel, now a southern suburb of the city. Various Iron Age, Bronze Age and Roman artefacts dug up around the Manzanares, along with a few Visigothic and Muslim-era odds and ends, make up the collection. Most of the building is taken up with temporary exhibition space.

PLAZA DE LA CEBADA Map pp270-2

Metro La Latina

The ill-defined 'Barley Square' is where city-dwellers came to purchase barley – an important staple – from local farmers in medieval days. In the wake of the Christian conquest the square was, for a time, the site of the Muslim cemetery. The nearby Plaza de la Puerta de Moros (Moors' Gate) underscores that this area was long home to the city's Muslim *(mudéjar)* population. The square eventually became a popular spot for public executions. Until well into the 19th century, the condemned would be paraded along Calle de Toledo, before turning into the square and there mounting the gallows. In an era when decent entertainment was hard to come by, it appears Madrileño rather enjoyed a good execution.

The **Teatro de la Latina**, at the Calle de Toledo end of the elongated square, stands where one of Queen Isabel's closest advisers, Beatriz Galindo, built a hospital in the 15th century. Her aims were twofold – to provide the city with a charitable institution for the sick and poor (as her deceased husband had ordered in his will), and to provide herself with decent digs for her coming years as a widow. A noted humanist, Galindo was known as 'La Latina' for her prodigious knowledge of Latin (which she taught Queen Isabel) and general erudition. In its heyday, the hospital occupied a large chunk of land between Calle de Toledo and Carrera de San Francisco (the former Islamic cemetery had been taken over after the order of 1492 imposing the conversion or expulsion from Spain of Muslims and Jews). All that remains of the late-Gothic building is a fine stone doorway, which was moved to the gardens of the Escuela de Arquitectura, in the Ciudad Universitaria in the north of the city. Only Galindo's nickname reminds us of what once stood here.

Museo de San Isidro (left)

Not far from the theatre, the narrow streets of Calle de la Cava Alta and Calle de la Cava Baja delineate where the second line of medieval Christian city walls ran. They continued up along what is now Calle de los Cuchilleros (Knifemakers St) and along the Cava de San Miguel, and were superseded by the third circuit of walls, which was raised in the 15th century. The *cavas* were initially ditches dug in front of the walls, later used as refuse dumps and finally given over to housing when the walls clearly no longer served any defensive purpose.

VIADUCT & CALLE DE SEGOVIA

Map pp270-2

Metro Ópera

The leafy area around and beneath the southern end of the viaduct that crosses Calle de Segovia (Jardines de las Vistillas) is an ideal spot to take a break.

Both the original 19th-century viaduct and its 1942 replacement were popular launch pads for suicides until plastic barriers were erected in the late 1990s. They obscure the views but one assumes the local death rate has dropped too. Before the viaduct was built, anyone wanting to cross over was obliged to make their way down to Calle de Segovia and back up the other side. In the town's earliest days, a punt ferried people across what was then a trickling tributary of the Manzanares.

While you're here, head down to Calle de Segovia and cross to the southern side. Just east of the viaduct, on a characterless apartment block (No 21) wall, is one of the city's oldest coats of arms. The site once belonged to Madrid's Ayuntamiento.

Calle de Segovia itself runs west to a nine-arched bridge, the **Puente de Segovia**, which Juan de Herrera built in 1584. The writer Lope de Vega thought the bridge a little too grand for the 'apprentice river'. He suggested the city buy a bigger river or sell the bridge!

Climb up the southern side from Calle de Segovia and you reach Calle de la Morería. The area from here south to the Basílica de San Francisco el Grande (p83) and southeast to the Iglesia de San Andrés (p84) was the heart of the *morería* (Moorish quarter). Strain the imagination a little and the maze of winding and hilly lanes even now retains a whiff of the North African medina. This is where the Muslim population of Magerit was concentrated following the 11th-century Christian takeover.

Across Calle de Bailén, the *terrazas* (cafés with outside tables) of **Las Vistillas** offer one of the best vantage points in Madrid for a drink, with views to the Sierra de Guadarrama. During the Civil War, Las Vistillas was heavily bombarded by Nationalist troops from the Casa de Campo, and they in turn were shelled from a republican bunker here.

MALASAÑA & CHUECA

Just north of Gran Vía spreads a warren of long, narrow streets intersected by even narrower lanes. Known officially as the Barrio de Universidad, but more generally as Malasaña (after Manuela Malasaña, a heroine of the city's brief 1808 anti-French uprising), it is a lively *barrio* that has still not shaken off a slightly louche feel.

Long one of Madrid's dingier slums, the heart of Malasaña retains an atmosphere of decay, but mostly in a charming sort of way. Away from the small, seedy red-light zone around Calle de la Luna, it is, for the most part, a lively haven of bars, restaurants

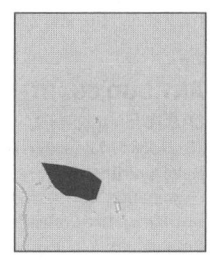

and other drinking dens. All up, after the craziness of the years of *la movida*, there is a sense that new blood and life is being injected into the area. The edginess is just enough to lend it a little extra colour and flavour.

Orientation

For the purposes of this guide, the definition of Malasaña extends some blocks west across Calle de San Bernardo into the area bounded by Gran Vía, Calle de la Princesa and Calle de Alberto Aguilera. Chueca is a small zone around the square and metro station of the same name.

The area is laced with extraordinary contrasts. The northeast corner is dominated by the Palacio de Justicia, the country's supreme law courts. Calle de Génova, which forms part of its northern boundary, is home to the headquarters of Spain's ruling Partido Popular. T the southeast, Malasaña butts against the walls of the national army headquarters (which includes in its grounds the Palacio de Buenavista, once home to the Alba family, grande of Spain).

Just four parallel streets lie between the courts and the army HQ. Mention Calle d Almirante and Calle de Piamonte to locals and they will think of bright, challenging fashio boutiques, shops full of bibelots and the occasional designer restaurant. They were hip in th 1980s and still are today. Cross Calle del Barquillo heading west and a slight incline take you into Plaza de Chueca. You have reached the epicentre of gay Madrid. All around her is concentrated an infinity of watering holes of all types, ranging from ageless vermout bars to outrageous gay clubs with very dark rooms and oodles of leather.

Calle de Hortaleza, which runs north from Gran Vía to airy Plaza de Santa Bárbara an ultimately the avenues that separate this *barrio* from the more conservative Chamberí, als marks a dividing line here. Cross it and Chueca is behind you, the atmosphere changes. A you head west things get a little seedier. Blue movie shops abound and hookers still wor the area around Calle de la Luna. Further north beats the heart of Malasaña around Plaz del Dos de Mayo. Rowdy bars are the theme around here – seek them out on streets lik Calle de San Vicente Ferrer, Calle de la Palma and Calle del Divino Pastor. And pity th neighbours!

In the grey Franco years, the centre of gravity of the *barrio* was a little north, around th Glorieta de Bilbao roundabout. Of all the literary cafés that once did a roaring trade her only the Café Comercial remains. Around it were the Europeo, the central stage of Camil José Cela's *La Colmena* (p33) and El Marly, where a black sax player lifted the oppresse spirits of the 1950s with a little swing.

Cross busy Calle de San Bernardo and things begin to quieten down. The bars and restau ants thin out, although Plaza de las Comendadoras is lively in summer. A few junkies han out in the square sometimes but rarely give grief to anyone much but themselves.

Finally Malasaña is closed off on its western edge by the Antiguo Cuartel del Conde Duque and the Palacio de Liria. The spacious internal courtyard of the former, once used to call troops to muster, is nowadays frequently the stage for concerts.

Top Sights

- **Museo Municipal** (p88)
- **Museo Romántico** (p89)
- **Sociedad General de Autores y Editores** (p90)

ANTIGUO CUARTEL DEL CONDE DUQUE Map pp268-9

☎ 91 588 57 71; Calle del Conde Duque 9-11; Metro Noviciado

Dominating the western edge of the Malasaña district is this grand former barracks. Nowadays it has a day job housing government archives, libraries, the Hemeroteca Municipal (the biggest collection of newspapers and magazines in all Spain) and the Museo Municipal de Arte Contemporáneo (p89). Now and then the one-time barracks does a night gig as a music venue.

MUSEO DE CERA Map pp268-9

☎ 91 319 26 49; www.museoceramadrid.com; Paseo de los Recoletos 41; adult/child under 10 €12/8 all attractions, €10/6 museum only; ⏰ 10am-2.30pm & 4.30-8.30pm Mon-Fri, 10am-8.30pm Sat-Sun & holidays; Metro Colón

If wax museums are your thing, this is a fair standard version of the genre. Some 450 cha acters have been captured in the sticky stu although some are less convincing than ot ers. In addition, you can board the **Tren del Terr** (€3) or the **Simulador** (€3) – the latter shakes yo up a bit, as though you were inside a washin machine. Another side show is the **Multivisi** animated 'experience' (€2). All a bit dire real although it might amuse the kids.

MUSEO MUNICIPAL Map pp268-9

☎ 91 588 86 72; Calle de Fuencarral 78; admission free; ⏰ 9.30am-8pm Tue-Fri, 10am-2pm Sat & Sun Sep-Jun, 9.30am-2.30pm Tue-Fri, 10am-2pm Sat & Su Jul & Aug, closed holidays; Metro Tribunal

The main attraction here is the restored ba oque entrance, raised in 1721 by Pedro c Ribera. Until its conversion into a museu in 1929, the building served as a hospice. C

St Valentine's Bones

Nobody much thinks about poor old St Valentine on what in Spain is called 'Lovers' Day' (El Día de los Enamorados) – 14 February. This 3rd-century bishop and academic was born in Terni, Italy, and according to legend had quite a thing about young people. Apparently, he was so enchanted by the blossoming of young love that he'd help to write love letters, hand out flowers to young newlyweds and even send a little money to struggling lovers.

That's the soap version. The more believable account tells us that the Roman Emperor, Claudius II, was recruiting a large army and forbade his soldiers to marry, believing that such links would weaken their resolve in the field. Valentine secretly performed marriages, flying in the face of this edict. Whatever the reason, Bishop Valentine was not popular with the Roman administration – and Christianity had yet to become Rome's official faith. So the authorities had Valentine arrested and executed on 14 February 269.

Valentine then disappeared from sight and mind until the 18th century, when his bones, along with those said to belong to hundreds of other saints, were dug up during excavations in Rome. Since the Eternal City had insufficient churches to each host one of these venerable skeletons, the Church decided to send some of them on a trip to other good Catholic countries.

And so St Valentine's bits landed in the crypt of the Iglesia de San Antón (more properly known as San Antonio Abad), in Malasaña. (Several other churches around Europe also claim to have been the lucky recipients.) In 1986 it was decided to put the skull-and-crossbones arrangement on public view (Calle de Hortaleza 65; 5-6.30pm).

e original building, founded in 1673, only e chapel remains. It lies dead ahead when ou walk in and is dominated by a grand can- as, *San Fernando Ante La Virgen* (St Ferdinand efore the Virgin Mary), by the Neapolitan aroque artist Luca Giordano (1634–1705). efore you step into the chapel proper, you ill see two sculpted sepulchres. The one on e right is of Beatriz Galindo (see Plaza de la abada p86) and the other of her husband, ancisco Ramírez.

Inside the museum, you are taken on an teresting but hardly masterful tour through e history of Madrid. On the ground floor, adrid de los Austrias (Habsburg Madrid) is rought to life, up to a point, through paintings d models. The theme continues on the floor bove, where the various rooms take you from urbon Madrid through to the final years of e 19th century. Of interest are a couple of oyas and, possibly more than anything else, huge model of Madrid made in 1830 by a ilitary engineer called León Gil de Palacios 778–1849). It took him the best part of two ears to complete. The top floor is set aside for mporary exhibits and a room devoted to the tirist and artist Enrique Herreros (1903–77). he selected drawings take an ironic look at e Madrid of the 1950s and 1960s.

USEO MUNICIPAL DE ARTE ONTEMPORÁNEO Map pp268-9
ⓣ 91 588 59 28; www.munimadrid.es/museoarte ntemporaneo; Calle del Conde Duque 9-11; admission ee; 10am-2pm & 5.30-9pm Tue-Sat, 10.30am-30pm Sun & holidays; Metro Noviciado

Spread over two floors, this is a surprisingly rich collection of modern Spanish art, mostly paint- ings, along with some photography (including a typically fantastical representation of the Cibeles fountain by Ouka Lele). The 1st floor is a mix of works acquired over the years 1999–2001, while the 2nd floor contains a chronological display (starting with the postwar period). One strand theme, particularly evident on the 2nd floor, is the city of Madrid. It is curious to see, side by side, avant-garde splodges and almost old- fashioned looking visions of modern Madrid. Examples of the latter include Juan Moreno Aquado's (born 1954) *Chamartín* (2000) and Luis Mayo's *Cibeles* (1997). The many talented artists represented include Eduardo Arroyo and Basque sculptor Jorde Oteiza.

MUSEO ROMÁNTICO Map pp268-9
☎ 91 448 10 45; Calle de San Mateo; closed for refurbishment at the time of writing; Metro Tribunal

The late-18th-century building housing this curi- ous little museum is housed was rented back in 1920 by the Marqués de la Vega-Inclán to house the tourism body he himself had founded, the Comisaría Regia de Turismo. Vega-Inclán was at the forefront of initiatives to promote Spain as a tourist destination, although perhaps a little ahead of his time. He was involved in the cre- ation of the chain of luxury hotels known as the *paradores*, and was also behind the creation of the Casa y Museo de El Greco in Toledo.

In 1924 Vega-Inclán turned the building into the Museo Romántico, a minor treasure trove of mostly 19th-century paintings, furniture, porcel- ain and other bits and bobs from a bygone age. The downstairs rooms contain books, photos and documents relating to the life of Vega-Inclán, while his collection is upstairs. It offers an insight into what upper-class houses were like in the 19th century.

PALACIO BUENAVISTA & CASA DE LAS SIETE CHIMENEAS Map pp268-9
Plaza de la Cibeles; Metro Banco de España
Set back amid gardens on the northwest edge of Plaza de la Cibeles stands the Palacio Buenavista, now occupied by the army. It once belonged to the Alba family, and the young Duchess of Alba, Cayetana, later said to have had an affair with the artist Goya, lived here for a time. A block behind it to the west, on the tiny Plaza del Rey, is the Casa de las Siete Chimeneas, a 16th-century mansion that takes its name from the seven chimneys it still boasts. Nowadays, it is home to the Ministry of Culture. They say that the ghost of one of Felipe II's lovers still runs about here in distress on certain evenings. It's unlikely, as it was purpse built for government. Carlos III's unpopular minister Squillace resided here. When he prohibited the wearing of long capes in Madrid (see p55), the mob came looking for him here (he was not in at the time). Today, the building houses offices of the Ministry of Education, Culture and Sport. From the Plaza del Rey you can see the rear of the Iglesia de San José, whose façade is actually on Calle de Alcalá but is easily missed.

PALACIO DE LIRIA Map pp268-9
☎ 91 547 53 02; Calle de la Princesa 20; admission o guided visit by prior arrangement only; ☺ 11am & noon Fri; Metro Ventura Rodríguez
This 18th-century mansion, rebuilt after fire 1936 and surrounded by an enviably gree oasis, holds an impressive collection of a period furniture and *objets d'art*. To join guided visit you need to send a formal re quest with your personal details to the palac which is home to the Dukes of Alba, one the grandest names in Spanish nobility. Th waiting list is long and most mortals conten themselves with staring through the gates in the grounds.

SOCIEDAD GENERAL DE AUTORES Y EDITORES Map pp268-9
☎ 91 349 95 50; www.sgae.es; Calle de Fernando VI ☺ 8am-2.30pm; Metro Alonso Martínez
A couple of blocks east of the Museo Romá tico, this joyously self-indulgent ode t Modernismo looks akin to a huge ice-crea cake half-melted by the hot summer sun. is virtually one of a kind in Madrid and w directly inspired by the work of Antoni Gau in Barcelona. You could try sneaking in du ing office hours for a peek but as a gener rule you may only visit the interior on th first Monday of October, which is Internation Architecture Day.

Exterior of Sociedad General de Autores y Editores building (above)

SALAMANCA & LAS VENTAS

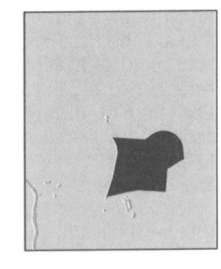

Madrid's most chichi quarter, the *barrio* of Salamanca northeast of the city centre is lined with elegant apartments and smart department stores. Named after the Marqués de Salamanca, a 19th-century aristocrat and general with enormous political clout and a penchant for property development (he went broke in the effort), it was always meant to end up as it did. As Madrid slowly came to grips with the need to extend the city in the course of the 19th century (the whole expansion project was labelled, in rather lapidary fashion, El Ensanche, simply, the Extension), one of the few areas to be developed initially was this *barrio*.

The Marqués de Salamanca threw everything he had into the promotion of his barrio. In 1871 he had the city's first horse-drawn tramways created, with a special service linking Puerta del Sol and Salamanca. Having bought up the land cheaply, he took out enormous loans to build houses and apartment blocks to attract people from the centre and so recover his initial investment. They contained the latest innovations. Water closets, the latest in domestic plumbing, water heating for bathrooms and kitchens. In the year of his death, 1883, the streets got electric lighting but for the marquis it was not enough. The *barrio* didn't begin to take off until after his death, and he could barely manage to sell the houses he built for a half of cost. He wrote towards the end of his life: 'I have managed to create the most comfortable barrio in Madrid and find myself the owner of 50 houses, 13 hotels and 18 million feet of land. And I owe more than 36 million reales on all of this. The task is completed but I am ruined.'

The snappy dressers wandering the grid-pattern boulevards around here seem to be on an utterly different planet from the people of inner-city districts such as Lavapiés. Apart from shopping, you can take in a little culture here.

Orientation

Looking at a map, Salamanca is easily enough recognised. It's the neat grid of streets tacked on to the northern and eastern sides of the Parque del Buen Retiro, cordoned off on the west side by the Paseo de la Castellana. Calle de María de Molina, Calle de Francisco Silvela and Calle del Doctor Esquerdo rule it off neatly to the north and east.

Serious shoppers need to know about this part of town for Calle de Serrano, the Oxford St (and then some) of Madrid. Still more retail therapy can be had in the nearest parallel and cross streets. Calle de Serrano was the first boulevard to be laid out in the Ensanche, and the Marqués de Salamanca could observe from the beginning the progress of his project, as he and his family and retinue lived in a grand mansion on the corner of Calle de Villanueva. Calle de Serrano was originally called Bulevar Narváez and later received its present name from one of the country's many 19th-century coup leaders.

The area is also home to a good number of embassies and, at the northern end, a couple of significant art galleries. All in all, it is a place to stroll and breathe in the atmosphere of the posh side of Spain. Not too many people around here vote PSOE. And in winter count the furs – the animal rights crowd haven't made any inroads here either!

Work on the Ensanche obliged the city to pull down its bullring on Calle de Alcalá and eventually the present one was built at a point then deemed beyond the city limits, at Las Ventas, about half a kilometre from the eastern boundary of Salamanca. Of course nowadays it is well within the city, which has exploded way past the M-30 ring road that runs just east of the bullring and once marked the outer city limits.

Top Sights

- Museo del Libron (p92)
- Museo Arqueológico Nacional (p92)
- Museo de la Escultura Abstracta (p93)
- Plaza de Toros & Museo Taurino (p93)

CASA DE LA MONEDA Map pp262-4

☎ 91 566 65 44; www.fnmt.es; Calle del Doctor Esquerdo 36; admission free; ⏰ 10am-7.30pm Tue-Fri, 10am-2pm Sat & Sun & holidays; Metro O'Donnell

If you like coins, this is the place for you: the national mint (or more literally the 'house of coin'). The collection begins with coins from

Ancient Greece and Roman Spain and proceeds through the Byzantine, Visigothic (including gold coins) and Islamic periods in Spain. The latter period is particularly well represented. Coins from the days of the Catholic Monarchs abound, and the collection continues through to the establishment of the peseta as the Spanish currency – only recently consigned to history by the euro. Paper money ranges from a 14th-century Chinese note to revolutionary Russian dosh. Also on display is an extensive collection of prints and *grabados* (etchings), lottery tickets since 1942 and stamps. You can also follow the processes involved in coining money and even strike your own medal.

BIBLIOTECA NACIONAL & MUSEO DEL LIBRO Map pp268-9

☎ 91 580 78 00; www.bne.es; Paseo de los Recoletos 20; admission free; 🕑 10am-9pm Tue-Sat, 10am-2pm Sun; Metro Colón

One of the most outstanding of the many grand edifices erected in the 19th century on the avenues of Madrid, the Biblioteca Nacional (National Library) was commissioned by Isabel II in 1865 and completed in 1892. Some of the library's collections have been imaginatively arranged in displays recounting the history of writing and the storage of knowledge. They constitute the fascinating Museo del Libro, a worthwhile stop for any bibliophile yearning to see a variety of Arabic texts, illuminated manuscripts, centuries-old books of the Torah and still more. If your Spanish is up to it, the displays come to life with interactive video commentaries.

FUNDACIÓN JUAN MARCH Map pp262-4

☎ 91 435 42 40; www.march.es in Spanish; Calle de Castelló 77; admission depends on exposition; 🕑 11am-8pm Mon-Sat, 11am-3pm Sun & holidays; Metro Núñez de Balboa

The foundation has its own collection and is responsible for organising some of the better temporary exhibitions each year. The foundation also stages concerts and other events throughout the year.

FUNDACIÓN LA CAIXA Map pp262-4

☎ 902 223040; www.fundacio.lacaixa.es; Calle de Serrano 60; 🕑 11am-8pm Mon & Wed-Sat, Sun & holidays 11am-2.30pm; Metro Serrano

The Catalan building society, the Caixa, has extensive art archives and treasures, some of which it likes to put on show every now and then at this gallery (it has others in Catalonia

and Mallorca). The emphasis is on contemporary art, whether local or international. As with the Fundación Juan March, it is worth keeping your eyes on the listings pages of local papers to see what exhibitions are on.

MUSEO ARQUEOLÓGICO NACIONAL Map pp268-9

☎ 91 577 79 12; www.man.es in Spanish; Calle de Serrano 13; adult/senior €3/free, free from 2.30pm Sat & all day Sun; 🕑 9.30am-8.30pm Tue-Sat, 9.30am-2.30pm Sun & holidays; Metro Colón

Out the back of the building that house the Biblioteca Nacional you'll find the rather forbidding looking entrance to the National Archaeology Museum. Don't be put off, as inside lies a delightfully varied collection spanning everything from prehistory to the Iberian tribes, Imperial Rome, Visigothic Spain, the Muslim conquest and specimens of Romanesque, Gothic and *mudéjar* handiwork.

The basement contains displays on prehistoric man and spans the Neolithic period to the Iron Age. Modest collections from ancient Egypt, Etruscan civilisation in Italy, classical Greece and southern Italy under Imperial Rome can be seen. Some Spanish specialities – ancient civilisation in the Balearic and Canary Islands – complete the picture.

ETA's Big Hit

By late 1973, Madrid and all Spain had a reached a high point of tension. An unwell Franco had appointed admiral Luis Carrero Blanco president of the Spanish government. Anti-regime protests multiplied as opposition groups more openly organised themselves. Most determined of all were the armed activists of the Basque Country independence movement, ETA. Three decades after the death of Franco, most Spaniards consider a still active ETA to be little more than a band of murderous delinquents, but in the dying years of the regime many sympathised with the movement. At around 9.30am on 20 December 1973, President Carrero Blanco's official car, an unarmoured black Dodge, proceeded slowly north along Calle de Claudio Coello in the heart of the Salamanca barrio. A small double-parked Morris 1300 obliged the official car to manoeuvre around it. And just as it did so a deafening blast shattered the morning peace and the presidential car was blown clean out of the street. Within minutes police arrived on the scene and confirmed their worst fears – the president was dead. ETA had made its most daring assault yet on the fascist regime.

The ground floor is the most interesting. Sculpted figures such as the *Dama de Ibiza* and *Dama de Elche* reveal a flourishing artistic tradition among the Iberian tribes – no doubt influenced by contact with Greek, Phoenician and Carthaginian civilisation. The latter bust continues, a century after it was found near the Valencian town, to attract controversy over its authenticity.

The arrival of Imperial Rome brought predictable changes. Some of the mosaics here are splendid, particularly the incomplete *Triumph of Bacchus* in Room 22. The display on Visigothic Spain, and especially material from Toledo, marks a clear break, but only previous experience with Muslim Spain (for example, the great cities of Andalucía) or other Muslim countries can prepare you for the wonders of Islamic art. The arches taken from Zaragoza's Aljafería are a centrepiece.

The influences of pure Islamic precepts persist in the later *mudéjar* style of the once again Christianised Spain, which stands in remarkable contrast with Romanesque and later Gothic developments – all of which can be appreciated by soaking up the best of this eclectic collection.

Finally, another room presents all sorts of items pertaining to Spanish royalty and court life from the 16th through to the 19th centuries.

Outside, stairs lead down to a partial copy of the prehistoric cave paintings of Altamira (Cantabria), which will be as close to the paintings as many people get.

MUSEO DE LA ESCULTURA ABSTRACTA Map pp262-4
Paseo de la Castellana; Metro Rubén Darío
This interesting open-air collection of 17 abstracts includes works by Eduardo Chillida, Joan Miró, Eusebio Sempere and Alberto Sánchez. The sculptures are beneath the overpass where Paseo de Eduardo Dato crosses Paseo de la Castellana. All but one are on the eastern side of Paseo de la Castellana.

MUSEO LÁZARO GALDIANO Map pp262-4
☎ 91 561 60 84; www.flg.es in Spanish; Calle de Serrano 122; adult/student €4/3; ⏰ 10am-4.30pm Wed-Mon; Metro Gregorio Marañón
A surprisingly rich, formerly private collection awaits you in this museum. Don José Lázaro Galdiano (1862–1947), a successful and cultivated businessman, had this Italianate mansion built in 1903. It became his home and at the same time a museum for his growing art

collection. He left the lot to the state on his death. Some 13,000 works of art and *objets d'art* constitute the collection, although only a quarter of these items are on show at any time. The ground floor is largely given over to a display setting the social context in which Galdiano lived, with hundreds of curios on show. The 1st floor is dominated by Spanish artworks up until Goya, the 2nd floor continues with Goya and paintings from the rest of Europe. The top floor is jammed with all sorts of ephemera (such as Mrs Galdiano's fan collection). Lawyer and journalist, Galdiano also collected a library of some 20,000 volumes.

The ceilings were all painted according to their room's function. The exception is Room 14, where the artist created a collage from some of Goya's more famous works, including *La Maja* and the frescoes of the Ermita de San Antonio de la Florida, in honour of the genius. Artists represented include Van Eyck, Bosch, Zurbarán, Ribera, Goya, Claudio Coello, El Greco *(San Francisco en Éxtasis)*, Gainsborough and Constable.

PLAZA DE COLÓN Map pp268-9
Metro Colón
The modern Plaza de Colón (Columbus Square), with the almost surreal **Torres de Colón** towers on its western side, is at first glance a rather uninspired affair. Its physical aspect, although softened by the fountains of the **Centro Cultural de la Villa**, is certainly nothing to write home about. The **Monumento a Colón** (statue of Columbus) seems neglected and the **Monumento al Descubrimiento** (Monument to the Discovery – of America, that is), for all its cleverness, does not leave a lasting impression. It was cobbled together in the 1970s. Still, the area is an artistic nerve centre. The Centro Cultural de la Villa (p158) plays host to a broad spectrum of theatrical and musical events, and just south of the square loom the national library and two museums. These can be looked upon as the beginning of museum row – the walk south from Colón to the Prado is laced with them.

PLAZA DE TOROS & MUSEO TAURINO Map p260
☎ 91 725 18 57; www.las-ventas.com in Spanish; Calle de Alcalá 237; ⏰ 9.30am-2.30pm Mon-Fri Oct-May, 9.30am-2.30pm Tue-Fri & 10am-1pm Sun Jun-Sep; Metro Las Ventas
The Plaza de Toros Monumental de Las Ventas, the most important bullring in the world, is, typically for this kind of structure, a classic

Sculpture at Museo de la Escultura Abstracta (p93)

example of the neo-*mudéjar* style. It was opened in 1931 although the first official fights did not take place until 1934. Up to 25,000 people can crowd into the ring's seats, which cascade down four storeys to ground level. The grand Puerta de Madrid, with its Moorish look, is thought of by aficionados as the gate of glory. This is where *toreros* the world over want to exit the ring, for they are only allowed to do so after an exceptional performance. Aficionados might like to wander into the **Museo Taurino**, a collection of paraphernalia, costumes, photos and other bullfighting memorabilia up on the top floor above one of the two courtyards by the ring. During the bullfighting season it also opens at the weekend.

The area is known as Las Ventas because, in times gone by, several wayside taverns (*ventas*), along with houses of ill repute, were to be found here. In those days, a fairly pungent stream flowed by, which was a deterrent to more clean-living folk moving into the area.

PUERTA DE ALCALÁ Map pp268-9
Plaza de la Independéncia; Metro Retiro

When Carlos III arrived in Madrid from Italy in 1759 to begin his reign, he paraded through a triumphal gate raised in 1599 and known as the Puerta de Alcalá (since the road that

passed under it led to Alcalá de Henares), Carlos, used to the grandeur of Palermo and Naples, where he had ruled previously, was not overly impressed by either Madrid or its gate. Perhaps it was this disappointment that unleashed his fervour for urban improvement (p55).

In any event, he so disliked the arch that he had it demolished in 1764 to be replaced by another, the one you see today. It was designed by Francesco Sabatini and completed in 1778. It was moved in the late 19th century to its present spot on Plaza de la Independencia as the city grew. Twice a year cars abandon the roundabout and are replaced by flocks of sheep being transferred in an age-old ritual from their summer to winter pastures (and vice versa).

It's hard to believe that the city's first permanent *plaza de toros* (bullring) was built just off Plaza de la Independencia, on the block now outlined by Calle de Serrano, Calle de Alcalá, Calle de Claudio Coello and Calle del Conde de Aranda, in 1749. Up to 16,000 Madrileños could cram in, and among them was often Goya, who came to make his copious sketches (in a series named *La Tauromaquia*) of this bloody activity. It was closed in 1874 as work on the Ensanche (urban extension), began to gather pace.

CHAMBERÍ & ARGÜELLES

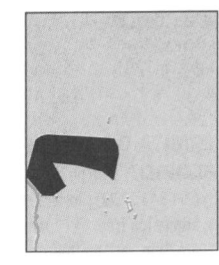

Not as chic as Salamanca perhaps, the district of Chamberí is certainly no slum. In the early 19th century it was an insignificant village beyond the then city boundaries. Napoleon himself is supposed to have spent the night here in December 1808, in the early months of his occupation of Spain. It had received its name a century earlier from María Luisa Gabriela, wife of Felipe V, who in the turbulent years of the War of the Spanish Succession liked to make little country jaunts in this area, as it reminded her of childhood stays at Chambéry in France. The comparison stuck and the Madrileño drawl converted it into Chamberí.

In the 1840s it began to attract poor migrants to Madrid who could not afford rents in the city itself. Indeed the housing shortage in Madrid itself was already acute and led to several laws aimed at building housing for the poor on the city limits. Chamberí was one of the areas chosen for urban development in the 1850s but, as in Salamanca on the other side of Paseo de la Castellana, progress was slow. A couple of streets were laid out from Paseo de la Castellana across the farmland into the dishevelled and growing township and by the turn of the century the area was more or less integrated into the city. By that time too, the *barrio* of Argüelles was in the making further southwest, when Crown land was acquired for the purpose.

While Chamberí is fairly well off today, it lacks the snootiness of Salamanca. Argüelles is quite different again, a relatively quiet corner near the main campus (also known as the Ciudad Universitaria) of the Universidad Complutense and the pretty Parque del Oeste. A series of parallel streets stretch down from the park to Plaza de España, a large but somehow unconvincing, some may say even misplaced square bordering on the historic centre of town.

Orientation

For ease of use we have delimited this area in the following way: from Paseo de la Castellana in the east, Chamberí stretches westward and runs into Argüelles. This in turn doglegs south to Plaza de España. Sloping parkland (which at its southern end hosts the rather awkward looking ancient Egyptian Templo de Debod) along Paseo del Pintor Rosales closes off the area to the west, with only the railway lines out of the Estación del Príncipe Pío separating it from the trickle of the Manzanares river below. From the same park the Teleférico cable car (p98) sets off for its little jaunt across to the Casa de Campo (p66). The Parque del Oeste also drops away from Argüelles. A pleasant place for a stroll and perhaps a drink at a terrace bar, it becomes a haunt for prostitutes at night (although less so recently, as the police have moved to clean the area up). Across the Avenida del Arco de la Victoria are Museo de América and the Faro, an observation tower open to the public.

Aside from a couple of curious museums, the area offers little else in the way of specific sights. It's not a bad area to search out some good restaurants and bars however, especially in the small area around the Quevedo and Iglesia metro stops. Being a mostly residential area, it has the distinct advantage of not attracting too many *guiris*, giving the nightlife a subtly local feel, although the folk are clearly not into grunge.

Top Sights

- Ermita De San Antonio De La Florida (p96)
- Museo de América (p97)
- Museo Sorolla (p97)
- Templo de Debod (p98)
- Faro de Madrid (p96)

CEMENTERIO DE LA FLORIDA

Map pp262-4
Calle de Francisco; Metro Príncipe Pío

Across the train tracks from the Ermita de San Antonio de la Florida is the cemetery where 43 rebels executed by Napoleon's troops lie buried. They were killed on the nearby Montaña del Príncipe Pío in the pre-dawn of 3 May 1808, after the Dos de Mayo rising. The event was immortalised by Goya and a plaque placed here in 1981. The forlorn cemetery, established in 1796, is usually closed.

ERMITA DE SAN ANTONIO DE LA FLORIDA Map pp262-4

☎ 91 542 07 22; Glorieta de San Antonio de la Florida 5; admission free; ☷ 10am-2pm & 4-8pm Tue-Fri, 10am-2pm Sat-Sun (hours in Jul-Aug vary); Metro Príncipe Pío

Some of the finest works produced by Goya are in this small hermitage, also known as the Panteón de Goya, about 10 minutes' walk north from the Campo del Moro. You'll see two small chapels. In the southern one, the ceiling and dome are covered in paintings done by the master in 1798 (and restored in 1993) on the request of Carlos IV.

Those on the dome depict the miracle of St Anthony. The saint who lived in Padua, Italy, heard word from his native Lisbon that his father had been unjustly accused of murder. The saint was whisked miraculously to his hometown from northern Italy, where he tried in vain to convince the judges of his father's innocence. He then demanded that the corpse of the murder victim be placed before the judges. Goya's painting depicts the moment in which St Anthony calls on the corpse (a young man) to rise up and absolve his father. Around them swarms a typical Madrid crowd. Usually in this kind of scene the angels and cherubs appear in the cupola, above all the terrestrial activity. But Goya places the human above the divine.

The painter is buried in front of the altar. His remains were transferred in 1919 from Bordeaux (France), where he had died in self-imposed exile in 1828. The odd thing is that apparently the skeleton that was exhumed in Bordeaux was missing one important item – the head.

FARO DE MADRID Map p261

☎ 91 544 81 04; Avenida de los Reyes Católicos; admission (lift) €1.20; ☷ 10am-2pm & 5-7pm Tue-Sun; Metro Moncloa

The odd tower ('lighthouse') just in front of the Museo de América is designed not to control air traffic but to transport visitors up for panoramic views of Madrid. It was built in 1992 to commemorate the 500th anniversary of the discovery of America and to celebrate Madrid's role that year as European Cultural Capital. There is no café up here, so be warned.

Forgetting Franco

Barely 200m southeast of the Faro de Madrid, enveloped by legions of traffic pouring into Madrid from the west, stands a proud-looking triumphal gate, topped by a *quadriga* (a chariot drawn by four horses) and known to most locals as the Puerta de Moncloa (Moncloa Gate). Actually, its proper name is the Arco de la Victoria and it was built in 1956 to commemorate the entry of Franco's victorious troops into the capital in March 1939 at the end of the Civil War. Since the death of Franco in 1975, monuments to him around the country have slowly disappeared and streets named after him have been discreetly changed. But the process has been slow and many reminders of the great dictator remain. It would seem that Madrileños have found it more practical to come up with their own name for the arch rather than demolish it.

GRAN VÍA Map pp268-9
Metro Gran Vía or Callao

Gran Vía arches uphill and southeast from Plaza de España, tops the rise dominated by the Telefónica building and dips down east to meet Calle de Alcalá just before the latter spills into the grand Cibeles roundabout. Gran Vía, a chokingly busy boulevard with more energy than elegance (although it gains some of the latter in the approach to Calle de Alcalá), was one of the rare bold and largely successful examples of urban planning in central Madrid since the late 19th century.

From luxury hotels to cheap *hostales*, pinball parlours and dark old cinemas to jewellery stores and high fashion, from fast food and sex shops to banks, Gran Vía has it all. Behind the grand façades are some of the tackier scenes of Madrileño life, especially in some of the side streets winding north off the boulevard.

The street was pushed through in the first decades of the 20th century. Whole neighbourhoods were swept away and replaced by grand *belle époque* piles. Among the more interesting ones is the French-designed **Edificio Metrópolis** (1905), which marks the southern end of Gran Vía. The winged victory statue atop its dome was added in 1975. A little way up the boulevard is the **Edificio Grassy** (with the Piaget sign), built in 1916. With its circular 'temple' as crown, and decorated with a profusion of arcs and slender columns, it is one of the most elegant buildings on the Gran Vía.

On a rise about one-third of the way along Gran Vía stands the **Telefónica** building. The national phone company was formed in the

920s, when this colossus was constructed.
was for years the highest building in the
ity (and a constant target for nationalist artil-
ery during the Civil War) and even today can
e seen from points all over central Madrid.
urther along you see another eye-catching
uilding, the **Carrión** (cnr Gran Vía & Calle de
acometrezo). This was the city's first tower-
lock apartment hotel and caused quite a stir
vhen it was put up in the pre-WWI years. Dur-
1g the Civil War the boulevard became known
s 'Howitzer Alley', so frequently would artillery
hells arrive from the front lines around the
iudad Universitaria to the north.

MUSEO DE AMÉRICA Map pp262-4

☎ 91 549 26 41; Avenida de los Reyes Católicos 6;
dult/student/senior & child under 18 €3.01/1.50/free,
ree to all on Sun; ☽ 10am-3pm Tue-Sat, 10am-
.30pm Sun & holidays; Metro Moncloa

or centuries, Spanish vessels plied the Atlan-
c between the mother country and the newly
von colonies in Latin America. Most carried
dventurers one way and gold the other, but
he odd curio from the indigenous cultures
ound its way back. The idea of creating a
ingle museum to hold these items went as
ar back as Cardenal Cisneros, but it was only
nder Franco that the decision was taken in
941 to establish the museum. A new building
vas required for it and it would be another 24
ears before it opened.

The two levels of the museum show off a
epresentative display of ceramics, statuary,
ewellery and instruments of hunting, fishing
nd war, along with some of the paraphernalia
f the colonisers. The display is divided into
ve thematic zones: **El Conocimiento de América**
vhich traces the discovery and exploration of
he Americas), **La Realidad de America** (a big screen
ummary of how South America wound up as
: has today) and others on society, religion and
anguage, which each explore tribal issues, the
lash with Spanish newcomers and its results.

The Colombian gold collection, dating as far
ack as the 2nd century AD, and a couple of
hrunken heads are particularly eye-catching.

Temporary exhibitions with various Latin
merican themes are regularly held here.

MUSEO DE CERRALBO Map pp262-4

☎ 91 547 36 46; http://museocerralbo.mcu.es in
panish; Calle de Ventura Rodríguez 17; adult/student
2.40/1.20, free Wed & Sun; ☽ 9.30am-3pm Tue-Sat,
0am-3pm Sun & holidays Oct-May, 10am-1pm Mon,
.30am-2pm Tue-Sat, 10am-2pm Sun & holidays Jul-Sep

You could walk past this noble mansion and
barely notice it amid the bustle in the tight, narrow streets just northwest of Plaza de España.
Inside is a haven of 19th-century opulence.
The 17th Marqués de Cerralbo (1845–1922) –
politician, poet and archaeologist – was also
an inveterate collector. You can see the results
of his efforts in what were once his Madrid
lodgings.

The upper floor of the museum boasts a
gala dining hall and a grand ballroom. The
mansion is jammed with the fruits of the collector's eclectic meanderings – from Oriental
pieces to religious paintings and clocks.

On the main floor are spread suits of armour from around the world and dating as far
back as the 15th century, along with a range
of arms. The Oriental room is full of carpets,
Moroccan kilims, tapestries, musical instruments, 18th century Japanese suits of armour
and items from Turkey, much of it obtained at
auction in Paris in the 1870s. The music room
is dominated by a gondola of Murano glass
and pieces of Bohemian crystal. The house is
also replete with porcelain, including Sèvres,
Wedgwood, Meissen and local ceramics.

Among the works of art are pieces by classic
masters, including Zurbarán, Ribera and van
Dyck. Occasionally there's a real gem, such as
El Greco's *Éxtasis de San Francisco*.

MUSEO SOROLLA Map pp262-4

☎ 91 310 15 84; http://museosorolla.mcu.es in
Spanish; Paseo del General Martínez Campos 37;
adult/student/under 18s & seniors €2.40/1.20/free;
☽ 9.30am-3pm Tue-Sat, 10am-3pm Sun & holidays;
Metro Iglesia

The Valencian artist Joaquín Sorolla (1863–
1923), after an academic education in fine arts,
developed a yen for painting natural outdoor
scenes and, after long stints in Paris and Rome,
he found himself back in Spain. Of his work,
the best known paintings are those depicting
the sea and beaches of his native Valencia,
full of brilliant Mediterranean light. Sorolla also
spent a great deal of time in his Madrid house,
a quiet mansion surrounded by lush gardens
that he designed himself, inspired by what he
had seen in Andalucía.

Over three floors, the house now contains
the fullest collection of the artist's works,
along with many he collected and received
from other artists throughout his life. Inside
on the ground floor you enter a cool *patio
cordobés*, an Andalucian courtyard off which
is a room containing collections of drawings.
The 1st floor is the main one, with the main

salon and dining areas, mostly decorated by the artist himself.

On the other side of the floor are three separate rooms that Sorolla used as studios. In the second one is a collection of his Valencian beach scenes. The third was where he usually worked. Upstairs his works, from early days until his latest output, are organised across four adjoining rooms.

PARQUE DEL OESTE Map pp262-4

⏱ 10am-8pm; Avenida del Arco de la Victoria; Metro Moncloa

Spread out between the university and Moncloa metro station, this is a tranquil and, in parts, quite beautiful park for a wander or shady laze in the heat of the day. Indeed, after its creation in 1906 it was long a favourite objective of strolling Madrileños including one of the country's greatest ever writers, Benito Pérez Galdós. He took his last ride out in Madrid here in August 1919. He soon fell ill and died in his house in the Salamanca district in January 1920.

Until quite recently the park would undergo a nocturnal transformation, when the city's transsexual prostitute population and their clients came out to play. The problem seems to have been largely resolved by shutting the park to wheeled traffic from 11pm on Friday until 6am on Monday.

PLAZA DE ESPAÑA Map pp268-9

Metro Plaza de España

A curiously unprepossessing square given its grand title, Plaza de España is flanked to the east by the 1953 **Edificio de España** (Spain Building), reminiscent of some of the larger efforts of Soviet monumentalism but somehow not unpleasing to the eye, and to the north by the rather ugly and considerably taller 35-storey **Torre de Madrid** (Madrid Tower). Taking centre stage in the square is a statue of Cervantes. At the writer's feet is a bronze of his immortal characters, Don Quixote and Sancho Panza. The monument was erected in 1927.

TELEFÉRICO Map pp262-4

☎ 91 541 74 50; www.teleferico.com in Spanish; adult €2.85/4.10 one-way/return, child 3-7 years €2.50 return; ⏱ hours vary; Metro Argüelles

One of the world's most horizontal cable cars (it never hangs more than 40m above the ground) putters out from the slopes of La Rosaleda 2.5km across into the depths of the Casa de Campo (p66), Madrid's enormous green (in summer more a dry olive hue) open space to the west of the city centre. Although not the most exciting ride around, it's relaxing and a very local thing to do. It certainly makes a change from the intense summer cooker feel of central Madrid on a broiling July day. Try to time it so you can settle in for a cool lunch or evening tipple on one of the *terrazas* along Paseo del Pintor Rosales.

TEMPLO DE DEBOD Map pp262-4

☎ 91 366 74 15; Paseo del Pintor Rosales; admission free; ⏱ 10am-2pm & 6-8pm Tue-Fri, 10am-2pm Sat & Sun Apr-Sep, 9.45am-1.45pm & 4.15-6.15pm Tue-Fri, 10am-2pm Sat & Sun Oct-Mar; Metro Ventura Rodríguez

Looking out of place at the heart of the Parque de la Montaña, in the Jardines del Paseo de Pintor Rosales, this 4th-century-BC Egyptian temple was saved from the rising waters of Lake Nasser, formed by the Aswan High Dam. It was sent block by block to Spain in 1970 thanks for the participation of Spanish archaeologists in the Unesco team that worked to save the extraordinary monuments that would otherwise have disappeared forever.

The temple was built in honour of the god Amon of Thebes, about 20km south of Phila in the Nubian desert of southern Egypt. According to some authors of myth and legend the god Isis gave birth to Horus in this very temple. The temple was first dismantled and moved to the island of Elephantina in 1960. Egypt's President Nasser then offered it to Spain, where it was sent two years later.

Plaza de Espana façade (left)

1 Plaza de Toros (p93) *2* Busking at Plaza Mayor (p70) *3* Hammam Medina Mayrit Baths (p168) *4* Traditionally dressed Madrileño kids

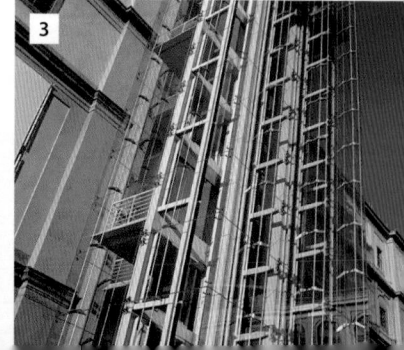

1 *Symbol of Madrid – the bear and strawberry tree monument stands in Plaza de la Puerta del Sol (p74)* 2 *Rooftop of the Basílica de San Francisco El Grande (p83)* 3 *Centro de Arte Reina Sofía (p73)* 4 *Museo Thyssen-Bornemisza (p79)*

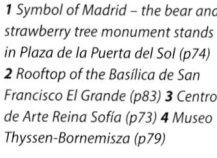

1 Fountain at Plaza de la Cibeles (p81) 2 Façade of the Ayuntamiento at Plaza de la Villa (p69) 3 Statues at Plaza de Oriente and Palacio Real (p69) 4 Detail of Las Meninas painting by Velázques, Museo del Prado (p77)

1 *Plaza de la Puerta del Sol (p74)*
2 *Zara (p17)* 3 *Shopping in Salamanca (p177)* 4 *Gran Via in sunlight (p170)*

1 Campo del Moro (p66) 2 Real Jardín Botánico (p82) 3 Parque del Buen Retiro (p81) 4 Overview from the chairlift ride at Casa de Campo (p108)

1 El Rastro market (p84)
2 Cervezas at Taberna de la Daniela (p135) **3** Madrileños eating at outdoor terrace (p120) **4** Painted fans, El Rastro market (p84)

1

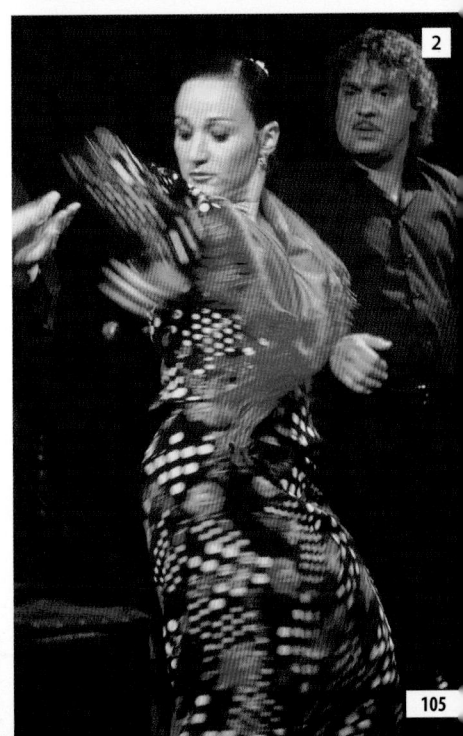

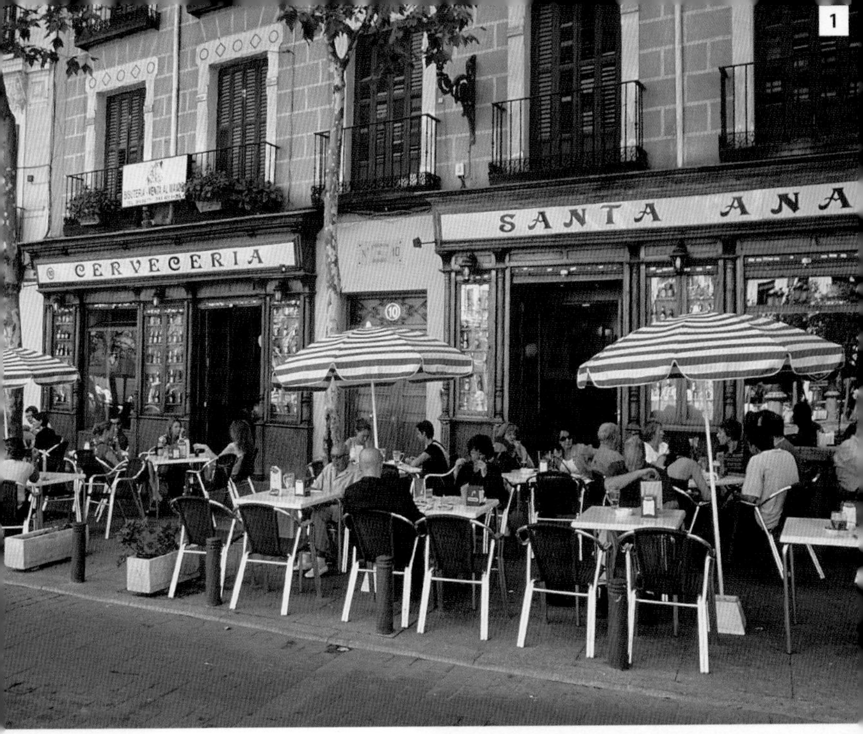

4

__1__ Early evening drinks on Plaza Santa Ana (p142) __2__ Flamenco show, Casa Patas (p157) __3__ Bar at Calle 54 jazz club (p161) __4__ Pouring beer at Café La Palma (p152)

2

3

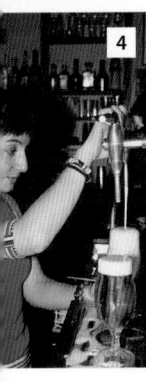

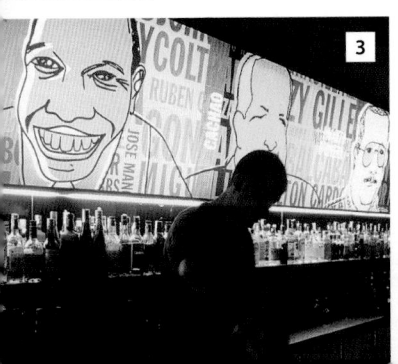

1 Souvenir flags of the football club Atlético de Madrid at Estadio Vicente Calderón (p164)
2 Spectators at bullfight, Plaza de Toros bullring (p165) **3** Real Madrid football club's stadium, Estadio Santiago Bernabéu (p164)
4 Bullfighting poster at Plaza de Toros (p165)

NORTHERN MADRID

Pretty much everything that you see in northern Madrid today has appeared since the 1940s. At the end of the Civil War in 1939, the Paseo de la Castellana ended around what is today Plaza de San Juan de la Cruz. The Ciudad Universitaria, a grand university project just beyond Argüelles, was finished by 1936, just in time for Franco's artillery to arrive to the west and spend the next three years destroying most of it (much of it was then rebuilt in the 1940s). The area around the modern Glorieta de Cuatro Caminos was lightly populated, as indeed was a stretch on either side of Calle de Bravo Murillo (which used to be the highway leading to France!). Mostly it was just fields.

Orientation

In 1932 the republic began building a modern ministry complex, Nuevos Ministerios, at the top end of Paseo de la Castellana. War interrupted its construction and it was only completed in 1953. This was the beginning of the project to extend the Paseo de la Castellana north which was begun under the Republic and finished in 1953 under Franco. From here the dead straight prolongation of the Paseo de la Castellana was to begin. It was completed in 1954, along with Plaza de Castilla at its northern end. Landmarks include the Estadio Santiago Bernabéu, home of Real Madrid and the leaning Torres Puerta de Europa on Plaza de Castilla.

A mix of modern office blocks, malls and residential housing has grown up on either side of Paseo de la Castellana. The east side is palpably wealthier and addresses such as Paseo de la Habana much sought after. It almost has a suburban feel to it. To the west of the Castellana it's a different story. The streets around Calle de Orense are largely commercial, although at night Calle de Orense in particular metamorphoses into a seething mass of partying Madrileños wafting in and out of megabars. The streets around Calle de Bravo Murillo, in the district known as Tetuán are another story again: tight and sometimes ragged lanes attest to the longer presence here of peripheral housing dating back to the 1930s and even earlier. It is a largely working class area with a notable seasoning of Latin American immigration.

The Paseo de la Castellana has since been extended further, beyond the city's second major train station (east of the avenue) and north beyond the city boundaries.

ESTADIO SANTIAGO BERNABÉU

Map p261

☎ 91 398 43 00 or 902 291709; www.realmadrid.com; tour admission adult/child under 14 €9/7, guided tour €14/10, admission Exposición de Trofeos only €7/5; ⏰ 10.30am-6.30pm daily, Exposición de Trofeos only on match days, up to 5hr before kick-off & day after matches; Metro Santiago Bernabéu

Football fans and budding Madridistas (Real Madrid supporters) will want to stop by the Estadio Santiago Bernabéu (which is undergoing a major programme of renovation) to inspect the champion team's home ground. You can wander around the grandstand, inspect the dressing rooms, stroll along the tunnel through which the players emerge onto the field and sit on the team benches. Afterwards you head for the **Exposición de Trofeos**. The display is held over two floors, an extraordinary array of competition cups and shields. Upstairs are the league trophies, while downstairs you can inspect the victory takings beyond Spain, the European Cups and the intercontinental trophies. In the Rincón de Raúl, have a look at the stars' personal collection of awards.

MUSEO DE LA CIUDAD Map p261

☎ 91 588 65 99; Calle del Príncipe de Vergara 140; admission free; ⏰ 10am-2pm & 4-7pm Tue-Fri, 10am-2pm Sat & Sun; Metro Cruz del Rayo

Described perfectly by one traveller as 'a must for the infrastructure buff', this city museum has a rather dry side. The permanent display is spread over three floors. On the first level is the driest stuff, which goes into everything from the airport to how the gas, electricity and telephone systems work. On the following two floors it gets more interesting. The first part covers Madrid from its beginnings until the Enlightenment and the top floor from the 19th century to the present. The outstanding items are the scale models of single buildings or items (such as the Plaza de Toros or equestrian statues of Felipe IV and Carlos III), as well as whole urban areas, like Plaza de la Villa and Paseo de la Castellana.

PASEO DE LA CASTELLANA Map p261
Metro Plaza de Castilla

This boulevard follows the course of a one-time stream and carves its way up to the north of the city, where it runs into Plaza de Castilla. This busy roundabout is remarkable for the leaning Torres Puerta de Europa, designed by John Burgee and carried out by Spanish architects in 1996. At 115m high and with a 15° tilt, they have become a symbol of modern Madrid. To the right (east) of the plaza, the huge square tower is a water tank used as part of the Canal de Isabel II. For more on Madrid's central artery, see the Walking Madrid chapter (p111).

BEYOND THE CENTRE

Beyond the centre the poles of attraction are limited mainly to a series of parks and green spaces. By far the most extensive is Casa de Campo, west of the Manzanares and home to the city zoo and amusement park. Other parks are scattered about the periphery of the city, although they are rapidly being bypassed and included within Madrid's every broadening boundaries.

Orientation

Aside from the Casa de Campo, worthwhile parks include the Dehesa de la Villa, north of the Ciudad Universitaria in the city's northwest, the Parque del Capricho and Parque Juan Carlos I east of the city near the airport and the Parque Biológico, to the southeast. Locomotive buffs should steam along to the Museo del Ferrocarril, about 1km south of Atocha station in the former Las Delicias train station. South of Madrid near the town of San Martín de la Vega is Madrid's answer to Disney World, Warner Brothers Movie World.

CASA DE CAMPO Map pp262-4
Metro Batán

This huge, unkempt semi-wilderness stretching west of the Río Manzanares undergoes similar night-time metamorphoses to the Parque del Oeste. It was in royal hands until 1931, when the new republic threw open its 1700 hectares to the people. It's about 2km from Plaza de la Puerta del Sol. How long it takes to get there depends on where you pick up the metro – about 10 to 15 minutes from the centre.

By day, cyclists and walkers eager for something resembling nature, but with no time or desire to leave Madrid, clog the byways and low roads that crisscross the park. There are also tennis courts and a swimming pool, as well as a zoo and the Parque de Atracciones (amusement park). Many people just come to sip a drink by the small artificial lake (Metro Lago). There are several lakeside *terrazas* and eateries, frequented by an odd combination of punters, working girls and clients. It's estimated that as many as 400,000 people visit the park on weekends!

For decades, the nocturnal scene has been quite a phenomenon. The occasional drug

Top Sights

- Casa de Campo (opposite)
- Warner Brothers Movie World (p109)
- Museo del Ferrocarril (p109)
- Parque del Capricho (p109)
- Parque de Atracciones (p109)

abuser, prostitute or pimp that one might have espied near the lake during the day would turn into an avalanche. As prostitutes jockeyed for position, punters kept their places around the lakeside *chiringuitos* (open-air bars or kiosks) as though nothing out of the ordinary were happening. The traffic in the middle of the night here was akin to rush hour in the city centre! We describe all this in the past tense because in late 2003 the police received orders to shut this scene down. No more louche nocturnal traffic jams. How long the ban will last?

On a different note, the Andalucian-style ranch known as Batán (Metro Batán) is used to house the bulls destined to do bloody battle in the Fiestas de San Isidro (p10).

DEHESA DE LA VILLA

🕐 9am-dusk; Metro Francos Rodríguez

If you want to meander around a relaxing green space, strewn with *terrazas* and the occasional family out for a Sunday stroll far from the city's hustle and bustle, this is one of the last relatively untouched stretches of parkland in the city.

FAUNIA

☎ 91 301 62 10; www.faunia.es in Spanish; Avenida de las Comunidades 28; adult/child under 12 & senior €17.50/12; 🕐 10am-5pm Wed-Sun, open later in summer; Metro Valdebernardo or bus 8, 71 & 130

Faunia is a modern animal theme park, where you can promenade from one thematic area to the next. They include an aviary, an insectarium, a penguin parade (with more than 70 penguins), an Amazon jungle scene (complete with simulated tropical storm) and the predictable performing dolphins and sea lions. You'll be happy to know that three skunks were born in captivity here in late 2003. It is located east of the M-40, well out of the centre.

MUSEO DEL FERROCARRIL

☎ 90 222 88 22; www.ffe.es; Paseo de las Delicias 61; adult/student & senior €3.50/2, free Sat; 🕐 10am-8pm Tue-Sun Sep-Jul; Metro Delicias

Train buffs should chug south of Lavapiés for this railway museum, housed in the otherwise now disused 1880s Estación de Delicias. Along the platforms are lined up about 30 pieces of rolling stock, from the earliest steam locomotives to a sleeping car from the late 1920s and the Talgo II, which ran on the country's long-distance routes until 1971. Several rooms off the platforms are set aside for dioramas of train stations, memorabilia, station clocks and the like. This is one for the kids, who will probably beg you to buy them model trains and track at the shop on the way out.

PARQUE DE ATRACCIONES

☎ 91 463 29 00; www.parquedeatracciones.es; Casa de Campo; admission €4.50, unlimited all-rides stamp adult/child under 8 €19.50/11.50, single-ride tickets €1.50, most rides cost adults such tickets; 🕐 hours vary; Metro Batán

Travellers can let kids off the leash at this amusement park, full of rides, shows and all the usual diversions you would expect of an amusement park. In the **Zona de Máquinas** (the rather ominous sounding Machines Zone) you'll find most of the bigger rides, such as the

Siete Picos (Seven Peaks, a classic roller coaster), the **Lanzadera** (which takes you up 63 metres and then drops you in a simulated bungee jump), **La Máquina** (a giant wheel that spins on its axis) and the favourite of all, the **Tornado**, a kind of upside down roller coaster that zips along at up to 80kmh for those with exceptionally cast-iron stomachs.

After all that gut-churning stuff, you may want to slope off to the **Zona de Tranquilidad**, where you can climb aboard a gentle Ferris wheel, take a theme ride through the jungle or just sit back for a snack. Of course, tranquillity is relative – you could try your heart out for shock and horror in **El Viejo Caserón** (a haunted house). **La Zona de la Naturaleza** (Nature Zone) offers, among other things, dodge 'em cars and various water rides.

Finally, in the **Zona Infantil**, the little ones can get their own thrills on less hair-raising rides, such as a Ford-T, the Barón Rojo (Red Baron) and Caballos del Oeste (Horses of the Wild West).

The park, in the Casa de Campo, has all sorts of timetable variations so it is always a good idea to check before committing yourself.

PARQUE DEL CAPRICHO

Avenida de Logroño; 🕐 9am-9pm Sat-Sun & holidays Apr-Sep, 9am-5pm Sat-Sun & holidays Oct-Mar; Metro Canillejas

This extraordinary park was inspired by Versailles but fell rather short of the model. After an age of abandon the motley spread of buildings and labyrinth have been cleaned up – there's even a neo-medieval hermitage. It's a fairly short walk north of the metro station.

PARQUE JUAN CARLOS I

☎ 91 721 00 79; 🕐 9am-dusk; Metro Campo de las Naciones

Just west of the Parque del Capricho is this modern caprice, a massive green area laid out near the city's main trade fair. Well-kept gardens are sprinkled between open fields. People come to lounge around, fly kites and visit the Estufa Fría, a modern greenhouse. For €3 you can ride in a catamaran, on a little train and check out the Estufa Fría.

WARNER BROTHERS MOVIE WORLD

☎ 91 821 12 34; www.warnerbrospark.com; San Martín de la Vega; adult/child & senior €32/24 or €48/36 for 2 consecutive days; 🕐 from 10am, the closing hours vary; *cercanías* train (line C3 for Pinto) from Atocha to stop in park near San Martín de la Vega (around 20 min)

Transport

The most efficient way to get to the sights in this chapter, with the exception of Warner Brothers Movie World, is by metro. In some cases you have a short walk afterwards but overall it is quicker than the bus or even driving. The appropriate metro stations are indicated in each entry.

Hang out with Tom and Jerry, experience the Wild West or remakes of the studio sets for such Beverly Hills greats as *Police Academy* at this film buff's dream theme park, about 25km south of central Madrid. Like many theme parks across Europe, Warner is losing money hand over fist and opinions are well divided on whether it is worth spending the considerable sums required to visit it. Should you decide to do so, you enter by Hollywood Boulevard, not unlike LA's Sunset Boulevard, and can then explore four different worlds: Cartoon World, the Old West, Hollywood Boulevard, Super Heroes (featuring Superman, Batman and the finks of Gotham City) and finally Warner Brothers Movie World Studios.

Roller coasters of the most excruciating kind, such as Superman and Batman, twist and throw you around through loops and corkscrews at high speed (up to 90kmh!). For the light headed, restaurants and shops provide more stable, terrestrial entertainment.

To get here by car, take the N-IV (the Carretera de Andalucía) south out of Madrid and turn off at Km22 for San Martín de la Vega about 15km east of the exit. Follow the signs to the car park, where parking is available for €5.

Opening times are complex and change – always check before heading out here.

ZOO AQUARIUM DE MADRID

☎ 91 512 37 70; www.zoomadrid.com; adult/child 3-7 years & senior/infant €13.10/10.55/free; ☉ 10.30am-dusk; Metro Batán

There has been a zoo of one sort or another in Madrid since 1770. The present one was opened in the Casa de Campo, about 300 metres from the **Parque de Atracciones** (see above) in 1972. It is home to about 3000 animals (everything from koalas to wolves) and a respectable aquarium (which was opened in 1995). Animals range from Emperor scorpions to green mambas. All the old favourites are there – zebras, giraffes, rhinoceros, leopards, flamingos, big grey kangaroo and rattlesnakes. You can watch dolphins and sea lions get up to their tricks in the **Delfinario**. Shows are held at least a couple of times a day. The 3000-sq-metre **Aviario** (aviary) was opened in 1998 and houses some 60 species of eagles, condors and vultures. In the adjacent modern **Acquarium** you can admire several hundred species of mostly tropical fish along with big boys like sharks.

Walking Madrid

Walking Madrid

Getting out and using a little shoe leather is the best way to get to know Madrid, although judicious use of the city's excellent Metro system can save on sweat. The following walks offer quite different visions of the city. The time you spend on them will depend greatly on whether you stop to visit sights or have a coffee along the way. Times given are for an estimated non-stop stroll.

OLD MADRID WALK

Unless you want to head for the big art galleries first, the most fitting place to begin exploring the city is the **Plaza de la Puerta del Sol 1** (Sol; p74), the official centre of Madrid. Walk up Calle de Preciados and take the second street on the left, which will bring you onto Plaza de las Descalzas. Take a look at the baroque doorway in the **Caja de Madrid building 2** – it was built for King Felipe V in 1733 and faces the **Convento de las Descalzas Reales 3** (p67). Moving south, you come to the **Iglesia de San Ginés 4** (p67) in Calle de los Bordadores, built on the site of one of Madrid's oldest places of Christian worship, dating back to at least the 14th century. Behind it is the wonderful **Chocolatería de San Ginés 5** (p125), place of worship for lovers of *churros y chocolate*.

Continue down to and across Calle Mayor until you reach the grand **Plaza Mayor 6** (p70). After a coffee on the square, head back to Calle Mayor and walk west to the historic **Plaza de la Villa**, home of Madrid's 17th-century **Ayuntamiento 7** (town hall; p69). On the same square stand the 16th-century **Casa de Cisneros 8** (p69) and the Gothic **Casa de los Lujanes 9** (p69), one of the city's oldest surviving buildings.

Take the street down the left side of the Casa de Cisneros, cross Calle del Sacramento at the end, go down the stairs and follow the cobbled Calle del Cordón out onto the Calle de Segovia. Almost directly in front of you is the *mudéjar* tower of the 15th-century **Iglesia de San Pedro El Viejo 10** (p84). Proceeding down Costanilla de San Pedro, you reach the **Museo de San Isidro 11** (p86). Next door is the **Iglesia de San Andrés 12** (p84), where the city's patron saint San Isidro Labrador, was interred.

From here you cross Plaza de la Puerta de Moros and head southwest to the **Basílica de San Francisco el Grande 13** (p83), or you can walk east past the market along Plaza de la Cebada which was once a popular spot for public executions to get into the Sunday flea market **El Rastro 14** (p84).

From San Francisco el Grande, plunge into the small tangle of lanes that forms what was once the *morería* (Moorish quarter), and emerge back onto Calle de Bailén and the wonderful *terrazas* (outdoor cafés). Bar Ventorrillo (Map , Corral de la Morería), probably the best located *terraza*, is on the edge of the **Jardines de las Vistillas 15**. This is a wonderful spot to relax and drink in the views of the Sierra de Guadarrama.

After a soothing *cerveza* (beer) follow the viaduct north to the **Catedral de Nuestra Señora de la Almudena 16** (p66), the **Palacio Real 17** (p68) and **Plaza de Oriente 18** (p69), with its statues.

Along the Way

Before you get started, we suggest you wander into **La Mallorquina** (p125) for a scrummy pastry over a cup of coffee. It's the perfect way to start any day. Should thirst or a little hunger strike while you're in La Latina, duck into **Taberna Matritum** (p130) for some good bar nosh. Depending on the time of day, an excellent spot for beer and views are the *terrazas* (outdoor cafés). Otherwise, wait until you get about half a kilometre up Calle de Bailén and park yourself at **Café de Oriente** (p122) for drinks or lunch. Along Gran Vía you'll find no shortage of snack and fast food places. Of course, once in the Huertas area you are spoiled for choice. A good spot that never fails if all you want is a beer and a bite in good company is the **Cervecería Alemana** (p144).

untains and hedge mazes. The east side f the plaza is closed off by the **Teatro Real 19** p70). The square is a wonderful place to top for a drink, contemplate the Palacio .eal and do a little people watching.

At its northern end, Calle de Bailén runs ast the **Senado 20** (Senate; ☎ 91 538 10 00; rww.senado.es; Plaza de la Marina Española ; visits by prior arrangement only). The enate building, in which the 17 regions and panish North African enclaves of Ceuta nd Melilla are represented, was originally arved out of a 16th century monastery in he 19th century. It was substantially modified in the 1840s and again in the 1950s. The nodern extension of the Senate facing Calle de Bailén was built between 1987 and 1991.

By continuing from **Plaza de España 21** up Calle de Ferraz, you could visit the curious col-ection of the **Museo de Cerralbo 22** (p97) and drop by the oddly displaced ancient Egyptian emplo de Debod 23 (p98).

Head back to Plaza de España. The eastern flank of the plaza marks the start of **Gran Vía**. This Jaussmannesque boulevard was slammed through the tumbledown slums to the north of Sol n the 1910s and 1920s. Today it is a busy thoroughfare, chocked with traffic and humming vith passers-by darting in and out of side streets, shops and eateries. About halfway along is he mighty Telefónica building (p96), still easily visible from its hilltop position. At the east nd of Gran Vía, note the superb dome of the **Edificio Metrópolis building 24** (p96). Continue east long Calle de Alcalá until you reach **Plaza de la Cibeles 25** (p81), Madrid's favourite roundabout. s you approach the roundabout, the country's late-19th-century **Banco de España 26** (p81) tands proudly on the right. On your left are the gardens and mansion of **Palacio de Buenavista** 7 (p90), now home to the army and Ministry of Defence.

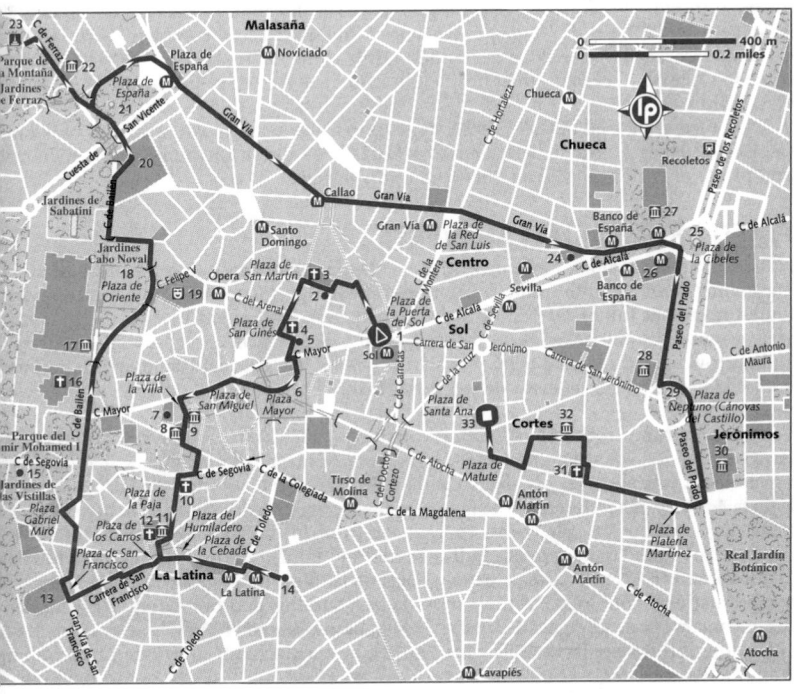

Walk Facts

Start Point Puerta del Sol

Finish Point Plaza de Santa Ana

Distance 7km

Duration 3½hr

Transport to Metro Sol

Transport from Metro Sol

Walking Madrid – Old Madrid Walk

Plaza de la Puerta del Sol (p74)

Wander down the west side of Paseo del Prado past the **Museo Thyssen-Bornemisza 28** (p79) and the Neptune fountain on **Plaza de Neptuno (Cánovas del Castillo) 29** (p82). Cross Paseo de Prado to reach the **Museo del Prado 30** (p77) or continue until you reach Calle de las Huertas (through the tiny Plaza de Platería Martínez). The 17th-century **Convento de las Trinitarias 3** is where writer Miguel de Cervantes lies buried (it's closed to the public). Turn right up Costanilla de las Trinitarias and continue north along Calle de San Agustín until you come to Calle de Cervantes, then turn left. At No 11 is the **Casa de Lope de Vega 32** (p72), the playwright's house.

A left turn at the end of Calle de Cervantes into Calle de León will bring you back onto Calle de las Huertas. Along here, on **Plaza de Santa Ana 33** and in surrounding lanes you will find plenty of options for taking the weight off your feet!

PASEO DE LA CASTELLANA WALK

By traversing north along the boulevard that cuts Madrid in two, you can travel past buildings dating from the 18th to the late 20th centuries in just 6km. This tour is no standard tourist route but full of interesting sights nonetheless. You might be tempted by one of several museums and galleries on the way, or just like to wander slightly off the straight and narrow for a drink or a meal. We start this walk in Paseo del Prado, which becomes Paseo de los Recoletos at Plaza de la Cibeles before changing name definitively to Paseo de la Castellana.

Emerging from Atocha Metro station you find yourself at the southern end of the leafy Paseo del Prado. Not a city known for its greenery, Madrid certainly makes an effort here. The boulevard itself is heavily shaded and on the right stretches the little visited **Real Jardín Botánico 1** (p82). Where it ends, the gracious, low-slung Palacio Villanueva, better known to art-lovers as the **Museo del Prado 2** (p77), takes over. At the Plaza de Neptuno (Cánovas del Castillo) roundabout two of Madrid's finest old hotels face one another, the **Hotel Ritz 3** (p190) and the **Westin Palace 4** (p191). The hotels, built in the early 20th century, are symptomatic of a pre-WWI optimism in Madrid, and this part of town underwent grandiose construction. The grand Palacio de Villahermosa, which now houses the eclectic collection of the **Museo Thyssen-Bornemisza 5** (p79), lies just across Carrera de San Jerónimo from the Palace.

At **Plaza de Cibeles 6** (p81), which is the one nearest to the heart of Madrileños (and supporters of Real Madrid football team), Madrid's pre-WWI construction boom is even more evident. Both the **Banco de España 7** (p81) and the **Palacio de Comunicaciones 8** (p81) are products of this period. Older but fitting in nicely with the monumental feel of the plaza is the **Palacio de Linares 9** (p80), north of the Palacio de Comunicaciones. On the other side of the plaza is the army headquarters, **Palacio de Buenavista 10** (p90).

The boulevard now becomes Paseo de los Recoletos (derived from a convent that once stood here) and maintains all the dignity of Paseo del Prado on its way to Plaza de Colón. You will twice be tempted to stop for a drink or meal at either the **Gran Café de Gijón 11** (p132) or the **Café-Restaurante El Espejo 12** (p131) further along. Both are steeped in history and atmosphere.

In the early 19th century we would already have been in the countryside by now. The Salamanca *barrio* to the east and the Chueca area to the west only began to take shape in the latter half of the century. So it comes as little surprise that, after passing the impressive façade of the **Biblioteca Nacional 13** (p92), we arrive in a thoroughly modern **Plaza de Colón 14** (p93). It is dominated by two equally modern monuments to Christopher Columbus and the discovery of America, together known as the Jardines del Descubrimiento (Discovery Gardens), although there's not much garden-like about any of it. On the west side of the traffic junction rise the **Torres de Colón 15** (p93), shiny glass office towers that announce with a flourish that we have arrived in the 20th century.

From here on the boulevard takes on the mantle of Paseo de la Castellana. It snakes gently to Plaza de San Juan de la Cruz, mostly flanked by low, modern buildings. On the

Walk Facts

Start Point Paseo del Prado

Finish Point Plaza de Castilla

Distance 6km

Duration 2hr

Transport to Metro Atocha

Transport from Metro Plaza de Castilla

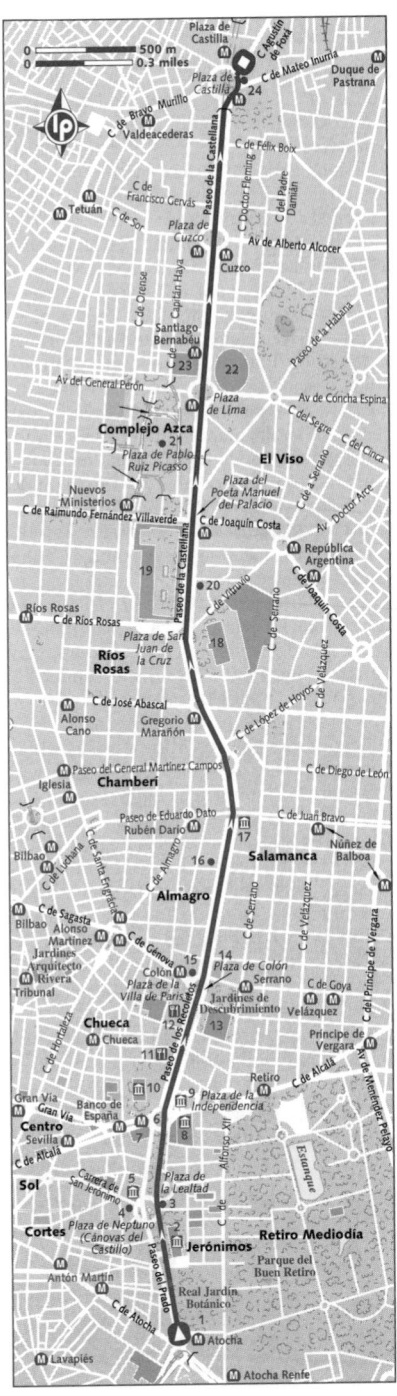

Salamanca side (your right) they tend to be fronted by gardens and behind them lurk embassies and big business. The Chamberí side is more densely packed and less opulent. Although during the Franco years any reminders of the past, mostly 19th-century mansions and villas, were sacrificed to the bulldozer, occasionally a slightly more enlightened attitude prevailed. Architect Rafael Moneo showed what could be done with his **Edificio Bankinter 16** (see the boxed text Moneo's Modern Miracles p32) at Paseo de la Castellana 29, combining the old with the new. Another clever idea comes under the bridge at Paseo de Eduardo Dato – the open air modern sculpture collection that makes up the **Museo de la Escultura Abstracta 17** (p93), most of it on the Salamanca side of the avenue. Some grander buildings of an earlier epoch can be seen further north, closer to Plaza de San Juan de la Cruz. The sprawling, domed **Escuela Técnica Superior de Ingenieros Industriales 18**, is fronted by a sloping garden and an 1883 statue of Queen Isabel I.

Biblioteca Nacional (p92) is one of the grandest 19th century buildings

The 20th-century extension of Paseo de la Castellana starts at Plaza de San Juan de la Cruz, from where it shoots ramrod straight to the north. On its west flank is the rambling grey site of the **Nuevos Ministerios 19**, a project started in the 1930s and finished under Franco to rehouse several government ministries. Inexplicably, a **crumbling private country residence 20** survives stubbornly on the corner of Castellana and Calle de Jorge Manrique.

Beyond the Nuevos Ministerios is where high-rise Madrid begins, with apartment and office blocks and towers mostly owned by banks. The first chunk of them together form the **Azca Centre 21**, intended as high-class residential property but somehow soulless nowadays, especially if you wander around its concrete labyrinth at night. Part of the same urban plan was the **Estadio Santiago Bernabéu 22** (p107), the home of Real Madrid.

Across from the stadium is the **Palacio de Congresos y Exposiciones 23**, a signal that we are now in largely high-end business territory. Various ministries, the World Tourism Organisation and other official bodies and private business have set up home in an area often referred to simply as Cuzco, after the square of the same name.

East of the stadium is some of the most desired real estate in Madrid. Apartment blocks with doormen, swimming pools, tree covered terraces and spacious apartments are dotted about an essentially residential area. West of Castellana it's a somewhat different story. Offices take up more space and Calle de Orense is at the core of a heaving nightlife zone.

At the end of the trail is Plaza de Castillo marked by the leaning glass **Torres Puerta de Europa 24** (p108), once home to a scandal-ridden Middle Eastern bank. This huge plaza is a bus and Metro interchange but it far from marks the end of the Castellana. Traffic roars through the tunnel under the roundabout and re-emerges on the boulevard's northern continuation, flanked mostly by colourless apartment blocks. Here the Madrid of the 21st century will emerge, with skyscrapers and sparkling apartments, entertainment and shopping complexes along the avenue and above the railway lines of Chamartín train station.

Along the Way

Apart from the already mentioned **Gran Café de Gijón** (p132) and **Café-Restaurante El Espejo** (p131), the pickings for restorative drinks and food right on Paseo de la Castellana are sometimes a little slim. Restaurants and bars abound in and around the streets leading off the boulevard, so you will never be far from sustenance. A good restaurant to consider for a lunch stop is **De Vinis** (p139).

IN VELÁZQUEZ'S FOOTSTEPS WALK

Diego Velázquez turned up in Madrid in 1623, having left his native Seville in search of fame and fortune. He found them here. This walk takes you around the Madrid of his time. You need to bring along a little imagination, as many of the locations the artist knew have since disappeared.

In his day, the stage coaches to Madrid all pulled up in **Plaza Mayor 1** (p70), so although we don't have documentary evidence of it, we can be pretty sure that this was where he and his family set foot on Madrid soil. Connections in Seville had secured him a job to paint the portrait of the young Felipe IV. From the square he and his family set off down Calle de Toledo to an apartment on **Calle de la Concepción Jerónima 2**.

He would walk to work, passing along Plaza del Conde de Barajas, Plaza del Conde de Miranda and Plaza de la Villa before

Walk Facts

Start Point Plaza Mayor

Finish Point Museo del Prado

Distance 4km

Duration 1½hr

Transport to Metro Sol

Transport from Metro Banco de España

crossing Calle Mayor and heading north along Calle de los Señores de Luzón and past what is now **Plaza de Ramales 3** (p70). This is where the Iglesia de San Juan Bautista used to stand and where Velázquez was laid to rest, but his remains have never been found since the church was destroyed in Napoleon's day. Velázquez's office was the **Palacio Real 4** (p69), which looked a good deal different in his day. After his appointment as Court Usher in 1627, he was granted rooms in the palace complex at Casa del Tesoro, located at the northern end of what is now **Plaza de Oriente 5** (p70).

Velázquez painted mostly for the court, but one of his canvases – a Crucifixion – wound up in the baroque **Convento de San Plácido 6**, north of Gran Vía on Calle del Pez. To

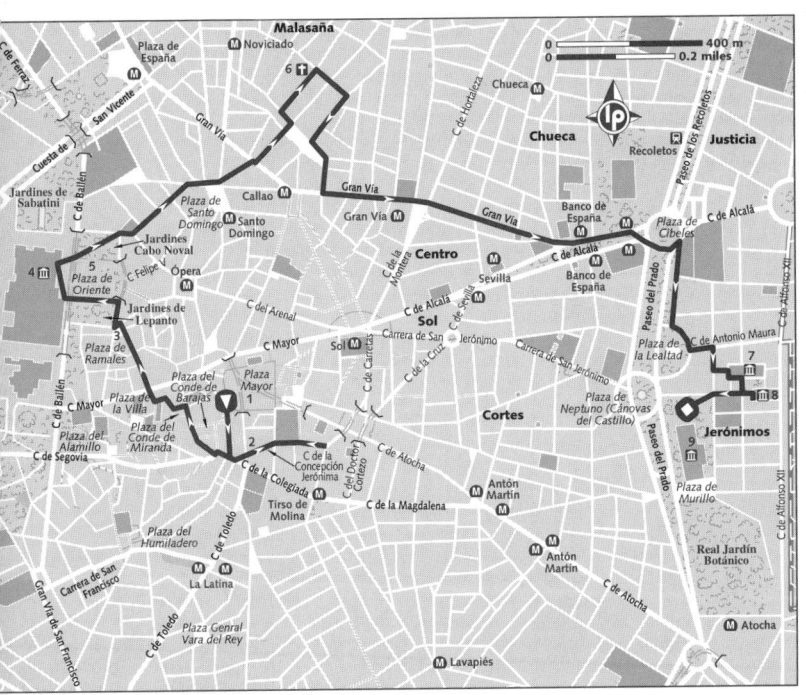

Along the Way

You might start the walk by sitting down in Plaza Mayor for a cup of coffee. If you wander by around lunchtime, you could do worse than pop into **Casa Paco** (p123) for a drink and a bite. Or take up an outdoor seat at the splendid **Café de Oriente** (p122). While climbing up Calle de la Bola – immediately after Plaza de la Encarnacion – a classic old Madrid lunch spot to consider is the **Taberna la Bola** (p124). Anyone for a hot steaming plate of tripe?

get there from Plaza de Oriente, head up the hill to Plaza de Santo Domingo, down Call de Silva across Gran Vía, left into Calle de la Luna and right up Calle de la Madera. Th church is still there today and worth a quick look inside, although the painting is now i the Prado museum.

To get to the Prado, you can catch the Metro (line 2) at Noviciado for Banco de España or take the scenic route walking down Gran Vía. One of Velázquez's masterpieces is th celebrated *La Rendición de Breda* (The Surrender at Breda). This was his contribution to series of paintings done between 1634 and 1635 to glorify Felipe IV in the Palacio del Bue Retiro. All that remains of the palace today are part of the north wing, now home to th **Museo del Ejército 7** (p76), and the former ballroom, or **Casón del Buen Retiro 8** (p75). Now migh be the time to enter the **Museo del Prado 9** (p75) for a look at his masterpieces.

Eating

Eating

Madrid is as much about eating and drinking as it is about wandering around gawping at fine art. Indeed, the real magic and rhythm of the place flow not through its Goyas and El Grecos (with all due respect) but through its bustling taverns, *marisquerías* (seafood eateries) and restaurants.

For those who like to just wander and pick a place at random, some parts of town are better than others. In the streets around Plaza de Santa Ana in the Huertas area there is no shortage of options. The huddle of streets around Calle de la Cruz is loaded with tapas bars and a series of cheap and cheerful Galician restaurants where seafood is the main choice – many of these, it has to be said, have let quality drop over the years in the face of unending waves of tourists. Those yearning for a more relaxed sit-down meal in the same area can head for the streets around Calle de Echegaray, which hosts any number of Spanish and foreign (especially Japanese) eateries. The long narrow lanes slipping east down to the Paseo del Prado also offer plenty of choice, from vegetarian to simple *menús del día* (menus of the day), from bar snacks to refined repasts.

Cava de San Miguel offers a string of cellar-like restaurants that can be fun but which, ultimately, are designed mostly with the foreign visitor in mind. A short walk away in La Latina, however, there are plenty of options. Start your search along Calle de la Cava Baja.

North of Gran Vía, the area around Chueca fairly hums along with masticating mandibles. The zone bounded roughly by Gran Vía, Calle de Hortaleza, Calle de Fernando VI and Calle del Barquillo is especially full of all sorts of eateries – from no-nonsense tapas bars open late into the night, to outrageously camp, weirdly lit, modern Med cuisine dives where presentation is at least as important as flavour, and where seeing and being seen is all part of the dining experience.

Many of the more expensive and name restaurants are cast like so many dice across the *barrio* of Salamanca and around the Paseo de la Castellana in northern Madrid. In these cases it is better to know what you are after, because, although there are many to choose from, they tend not to be too closely concentrated in any given street or area.

Bocaito (p133)

Cafés and bars are frequently hard to distinguish from one another in Madrid. After all, in most you can grab a beer or a coffee whatever the time of day. But some have that decidedly café feel, a place to huddle over a coffee, *bollo* (pastry) and the paper. Of course even some of these metamorphose in the night into crowded drinking establishments too. The cafés listed in this chapter have been chosen because they invite you, above all, to sit down over a coffee or tea, inside or out. The dividing line is fairly arbitrary, as the kind of distinctions between café and pub/bar present in Anglo-Saxon countries are pleasantly absent in these sunnier climes.

Opening Hours

Most restaurants and other types of eatery open their kitchens from 1pm to 4pm and again between 8pm to midnight. Few locals would sit down to lunch before 2pm, or dinner before 10pm. Bars and cafés that offer tapas generally adhere to similar hours as far as food goes, although you will often find at least something still at the bar outside the normal meal times. Cafés tend to open from 8am or 9am through to at least 9pm, and often to midnight or beyond if they double as bars. Many restaurants take a day off during the week. Where this is the case it is indicated in the reviews in this chapter. Most restaurants are shut on Christmas Eve and many on New Year's Eve (or Christmas Day and New Year's Day). Some close over Easter and a good many shut for at least part of August too.

Meal Times

Meal times are an important event in the daily round of your average Madrileño. Here people take the time to enjoy their food and where possible still have a full sit down show at lunchtime. Lunch can easily last a couple of hours. Dinner frequently is a lighter affair. For more details on how Madrileños eat, see the Food & Drink chapter (p41).

How Much?

In the following pages a 'meal' is understood to mean a starter, main course and dessert, including a little modestly priced wine. Prices have risen pretty steadily in Madrid over the past few years and the biggest offenders are the modern designer restaurants that frequently offer pricey design and indifferent food.

One traveller's budget restaurant may be another's splurge, so these categories are a little arbitrary. Those hoping to have a full meal as defined above for less than €20 could try the spots listed under Cheap Eats.

Opening your purse wider will improve your options greatly. If you are prepared to spend up to €45 you can eat at a wide range of places. Of course, still greater flexibility opens up the top dining options in the city, which compared with eating out in places like London, Paris or Milan can still work refreshingly easy on your personal fortune. You will rarely spend more than €100 on a top-quality meal.

There is one great way to cap prices at lunchtime – the *menú del día*, a full set meal (usually with several options), water and wine. They start from around €8. Many restaurants listed in this chapter, where you might otherwise pay much more *a la carta*, offer this cost-saving midday option. So just because they are not listed in the Cheap Eats section does not rule out sampling some of the pricier spots by day.

At fancier restaurants you will occasionally have the chance to opt for a *menú de degustación*, a set tasting meal of several different dishes. This can be a great way to get a broader view of what the restaurant does and has the advantage of coming with a fixed price.

Booking Tables

At many of the mid-range restaurants and simpler taverns with *comedores* (dining rooms) you can generally turn up and find a spot without booking ahead. At better restaurants and for dinner especially it is safer to make a booking.

Tipping

Many eating establishments have a cover charge, usually ranging up to a few euros per head. A service charge is generally already calculated into the bill (but take a look at it if you are unsure), so any further tipping becomes strictly personal. Spaniards themselves are no overwhelming tippers. If you are particularly happy, 5% on top would be fine. Remember this if you are presented a credit card receipt with space to add in the tip. In any case, it is always preferable to leave a tip in cash for the person who has waited your table.

Self-catering

Making your own snacks is the cheapest way to keep body and soul together. Shop in big produce markets such as: **Mercado de San Miguel** (Map pp270-2; 9am-2.30pm & 5.15-8.15pm Mon-Fri, 9am-2.30pm Sat) on the square of the same name, just off Plaza Mayor; **Mercado de la Cebada** (Map pp270-2; 9am-2pm & 5-8pm Mon-Fri, 9am-2.30pm Sat), on the square of the same name; and **Mercado de la Paz** (Map pp268-9; 9am-8pm Mon-Sat). For freshly baked bread head for a *panadería* (bakery). For a gourmet touch, the food departments of **El Corte Inglés** department store have some tempting local and imported goodies. Branches with food departments include those in Argüelles and Calle de Preciados.

Top Five Tapas

- **Bocaito** (p133)
- **La Trucha** (p126)
- **El Doble** (p137)
- **La Casa del Abuelo** (p126)
- **Casa Labra** (opposite)

LOS AUSTRIAS & CENTRO

The heart of old Madrid lends itself to a search for eateries with a little history and character. Many of the places listed have been doing business for a good while with tried and true Madrileño or broader Spanish cooking. But it's not all tripe and roast lamb, for instance, there are Japanese eateries to be found. Some atmospheric cafés, especially near the Teatro Real, make perfect breakfast spots.

CAFÉ DEL REAL Map pp270-2 *Café*
91 547 21 24; Plaza de Isabel II;
daily; Metro Ópera

Head for a window seat in the low-ceilinged upstairs section of this cosy café. Or, squeeze in around one of the ground-floor tables out the back for a quiet chat over a coffee or, later in the day, a glass of wine. It gets busy at night but also makes a pleasant spot for breakfast.

CAFÉ DE LOS AUSTRIAS Map pp270-2 *Café*
91 559 84 36; Plaza de Ramales 1;
9am-midnight; Metro Ópera

A vaguely stiff, even imperial, attitude reigns in this fine café looking onto the square that hides one of the city's little secrets – the undiscovered tomb of Velázquez. Take up a window seat at a marble-top table for a coffee and pastry.

CAFÉ DE ORIENTE
Map pp270-2 *Café & Spanish*
91 541 39 74; Plaza de Oriente 2;
9am-midnight; Metro Ópera

Located strategically on one of Madrid's most sublime squares in what was once part of a long-disappeared, 17th-century convent, the place feels like a set out of Mitteleuropa. It's the perfect spot for a coffee and paper, inside in winter or taking in the sun on the *terraza* in the warmer months. Some partake of the creative menu but generally the food does not match the prices.

CASA CIRÍACO Map p272 *Madrileño*
91 548 06 20; Calle Mayor 84; meal €25-30;
Thu-Tue; Metro Ópera or bus No 3

Casa Ciríaco was founded in 1917 in a building previously popular with would-be assassins: one threw a bomb from a balcony at Alfonso XIII as he passed by with his queen, Victoria Eugenia, on their wedding day in 1906. The attack failed, but 24 people died. The sounds of loud, intersecting conversation, the bustle of waiters and the simple home cooking still stand this place in good stead. The food is classic Madrileño cuisine, including old faves such as *callos* (tripe).

CASA LABRA Map pp270-2 *Tapas & Spanish*

☎ 91 531 00 81; Calle de Tetuán 11; meal €25-30;
☯ noon-3.30pm & 5.30-11pm Mon-Sat (restaurant),
daily (bar); Metro Sol

Push open the door to this wonderful old tapas bar. It has been going in much the same style since 1860. Locals pile in after a day's work and, on the subject of work, more than 100 years ago Pablo Iglesias and pals founded the Spanish socialist party while sipping on wine here. Later on, poet Lorca and his coterie used to frequent the place too. You can sit down to a full meal (or the €16.50 *menú del día*) at the back.

CASA PACO Map pp270-2 *Madrileño*

☎ 91 366 31 66; Plaza de la Puerta Cerrada 11; meal €25-30; ☯ Mon-Sat Sep-Jul; Metro La Latina

The gaily painted exterior of this old Madrid tavern is hard to miss and harder to resist. You could just wander in and sidle up to the bar for a couple of tapas and a shot of wine. Or head out back for a full meal of straightforward Madrileño cooking, which in this case could mean a big juicy steak.

CASA PARRONDO Map pp266-7 *Asturian*

☎ 91 522 62 34; Calle de Trujillos 9; meal €25-30;
☯ Mon-Sat Sep-Jul; Metro Ópera

Take a trip to the northern Spanish climes of Asturias in this grand old cider tavern and restaurant. In the dark-timber-filled dining area beyond the tight bar space sit down to a selection of tapas (lots of chorizo and cheese) and well-prepared food (mostly meat). You could be in an Asturian house in the mountains and, if the photos of the owner killing pigs and turning them into sausages don't put you off, you will eat well. They offer a lunch *menú del día* for €9.

DELFOS Map pp266-7 *Greek*

☎ 91 548 37 64; Cuesta de Santo Domingo 14; meal €25;
☯ Tue-Sat & Sun lunch, Sep-Jul; Metro Santo Domingo

Why not make a quick sidestep to the other side of the Med? The predictably cheery white

and blue decor here sets the scene for a round of *gyros* or a generous *souvlaki*. Aimed more at locals looking for variety than tourists, they make an effort to maintain reasonable quality.

LA CRUZADA Map pp270-2 *Spanish*

☎ 91 548 01 31; Calle de la Amnistía 8; meal €20-25;
☯ Mon-Sat & Sun lunch, Sep-Jul; Metro Ópera

The original La Cruzada was founded a couple of blocks away in 1827 and shifted (complete with the remarkable sculpted wooden bar) to its present address in 1972, from which point the rot gradually set in. Tarted up now as a bar and restaurant, it offers original *raciones* such as *conejo relleno* (stuffed rabbit) or *empanada de bacalao y pasas* (a kind of cod and raisin pie).

LA VIUDA BLANCA Map pp266-7 *Creative*

☎ 91 548 75 29; Calle de Campomanes 6; meal €25;
☯ Tue-Sun; Metro Ópera

Walk down the unpromising hall, pull back the black curtain and you are taken aback by the bright dining room ahead. By day, sunshine floods in through the conservatory ceiling onto diners chomping on whatever takes the chef's fancy. The rice dishes are well rounded. If white dominates the dining area, orange is the colour of the lounge off to the right. Sidle over for the place's conversion into La Viuda Negra bar (p150).

RESTAURANTE SOBRINO DE BOTÍN

Map pp270-2 *Spanish*

☎ 91 366 42 17; Calle de los Cuchilleros 17;
meal €35-45; ☯ daily; Metro Tirso de Molina

One of Madrid's oldest restaurants is featured in Benito Pérez Galdós' Fortunata y Jacinta and Hemingway's more recent The Sun Also Rises. They say that Goya once worked here as a dishwasher, but that story is a little hard to swallow. A string of dining rooms, all timber and oozing history, fills with locals and tourists for hearty meals of *cochinillo* (suckling pig) and *cordero asado* (roast lamb) done in the wood-fired ovens.

SEGÚN EMMA Map pp270-2 *Mediterranean*

☎ 91 559 08 97; Plaza del Conde Miranda 4; meal €20-25; ☯ Wed-Mon; Metro Ópera or bus 3

The only thing wrong with this lively little tapas tavern, apart possibly from the lime-green decor, is the airless smokiness of the place. Come in when it's not too crowded and please the palate with an array of tempting *raciones*, including several with *ventresca*, the tastiest

Top Five in Los Austrias & Centro

- La Gloria de Montera (p124)
- Café de Oriente (opposite)
- Restaurante Sobrino de Botín (opposite)
- Casa Paco (above)
- Casa Parrondo (above)

Eating – Los Austrias & Centro

Casa Labra (p123), popular for more than 100 years

part of any ocean-going tuna. Other options could include *queso Manchego* or guacamole.

TABERNA DEL ALABARDERO
Map pp266-7   *Tapas & Spanish*
☎ 91 547 25 77; Calle de Felipe V 6; meal €40-45;
☻ daily; Metro Ópera
You enter by the busy bar, where you could stop in your tracks and settle in for a few drinks and tapas. Otherwise, proceed inside. The place oozes a carefully maintained pre-war atmosphere in its series of dining rooms that spread out the back. In all, with period photos and elegant but cosy table settings, you could almost be at grandmother's. Fare is largely classic, although even a venerable family institution like this can't seem to resist the fashion for creative touches and mile-long names like *rabo de toro estofado con miel y canela, puré de patata al cardomomo y zanahorias tempranas* (bull's tail stew with honey and cinnamon, cardamom-spiced mashed potatoes and young carrots).

TABERNA LA BOLA Map p265   *Madrileño*
☎ 91 547 69 30; Calle de la Bola 5; meal €35;
☻ Mon-Sat & Sun lunch; Metro Santo Domingo
This rollicking old Madrid tavern has been stirring up a storm with its traditional *cocido a la madrileña* (stew; €16) since 1880. On the menu are plenty of hearty meat dishes too. The atmosphere reflects the years, making this a worthwhile once-off in spite of the prices.

TABERNEROS Map pp270-2   *Mediterranean*
☎ 91 542 21 60; Calle de Santiago 9; meal €25;
☻ Tue-Sun; Metro Ópera
No one's fooling anyone. This tavern may have been in business since 1897 but its successful gastro-pub-style overhaul has all the hallmarks of yesterday. The bare brick walls are lined with bottles of fine wine from around the country, and diners huddle on small timber stools at the equally diminutive tables. So long as you don't get backache, the carefully prepared *raciones* (*bonito tataki* for a Japanese black pepper tuna touch, *zampone napolitano* for a southern Italian approach to stuffed pig's trotters) are worth the trouble.

CHEAP EATS
LA GLORIA DE MONTERA
Map pp266-7   *Mediterranean*
☎ 91 523 44 07; Calle del Caballero de Gracia 10; meal €15-20; ☻ daily; Metro Gran Vía
A youthful, snappy atmosphere reigns in this white-walled minimalist restaurant with old-fashioned library-style table lamps and shelves of artsy fake books. The forty-odd tables are always packed and there's a reason: value for money. The menu ranges across fish (*lenguado a las almendras* – sole in an almond sauce) and meat (a chicken fillet prepared in *finas hierbas*). All sorts of delightful *amuses-gueules* precede the main courses.

Sticky Fingers

Tapas are fine, but sweet teeth also need sustenance. Madrid pastry shops are just the ticket, especially at breakfast time.

Antigua Pastelería del Pozo (Map pp270-2; ☎ 91 522 38 94; Calle del Pozo 8; ⏰ 9.30am-2pm & 5-8pm Mon-Sat, 9.30am-3pm Sun; Metro Sol) has lost none of its old charm or touch for turning out all sorts of great pastries. Tucked away from the madding crowds in one of the rare relatively quiet lanes near Puerta del Sol, it has been in operation since 1830 (and for 20 years before that as a simple bread bakery), making it the city's oldest dealer in tooth-decaying items.

La Mallorquina (Map pp270-2; ☎ 91 521 12 01; Puerta del Sol 8; ⏰ 9am-9.15pm; Metro Sol) is another classic pastry shop. Treat yourself to a takeaway *ensaimada* (a light pastry dusted with icing sugar) from Mallorca, or lean at the bar to munch on sugary items over a coffee. This is truly an old-world, pastry paradise.

Muñiz (Map pp270-2; ☎ 91 365 66 47; Calle de Calatrava 3; ⏰ 6.30am-midnight; Metro La Latina) purveys the Spanish sweet tooth's favourite: *churros y chocolate*. What is it about these deep-fried doughnut strips dipped in thick syrupy chocolate? Dunk and you'll find out. Want a deeper-fried, fatter version? Try the *porras*.

Chocolatería de San Ginés (Map pp270-2; ☎ 91 365 65 46; Pasadizo de San Ginés 5; ⏰ 6pm-7am; Metro Sol) is perhaps the best known of Madrid's *churros y chocolate* vendors. You can stop by in the evening for one of these calorific bombs, but its main market is clubbers with the munchies, pouring out of the nearby dance palaces.

SOL, HUERTAS & ATOCHA

Huertas is known to everyone for its watering holes, but there is no shortage of places to take in solids as well. A collection of tapas bars, some of them specialising in only one or two items but done so well, are to be found in the lanes between Puerta del Sol and Plaza de Santa Ana. The same area is loaded with straightforward, mostly Galician seafood, restaurants. Further east, Calle del Prado is the backbone of a concentration of restaurants (interspersed between the bars), that range from cheerful Cuban to rather more elegant dining options. Several good vegetarian diners are scattered about, and those looking for economical options will have little trouble.

AKI Map pp270-2 *Japanese*
☎ 91 429 58 06; Calle de Echegaray 9; meal €25-30; ⏰ Thu-Tue; Metro Sevilla

The sight of a Japanese punter is a good sign for those interested in a sushi or sashimi break from *jamón, jamón* and *tortilla*. Try the sushi special for €22, or put together your own choice either at the bar or the tables out back. They have some cheaper *menús del día* too.

CÍRCULO DE BELLAS ARTES
Map pp266-7 *Café*
☎ 91 521 69 42; Calle de Alcalá 42; ⏰ 9am-1am; Metro Sevilla

This daring and convoluted structure, designed by Antonio Palacios Ramilo in 1919, boasts a wonderful *belle époque* café replete with chandeliers and the charm of a bygone era. You have to buy a token temporary club membership (€1) to drink here, but it's worth every cent.

CLUNY Map pp270-2 *Creative*
☎ 91 429 28 38; Calle del Prado 15; meal €20-25; ⏰ daily; Metro Sevilla

You never know what you might find in this smart spot, with its spacious dining area. Turkish dishes mix with *ensalada con cangrejos de río y mollejas de cordero* (river crab salad with lamb's sweetbread). A nice touch is the complimentary pâté with mustard and crackers to start.

EAST 47 Map pp270-2 *Mediterranean*
☎ 91 429 07 47; Calle de José Abascal 56; meal €30-45; ⏰ daily; Metro Sevilla

Tucked into a ground-floor corner of the classy Hotel Villa Real is this New York-style bar and eatery where you can enjoy blinis with 30g of Beluga caviar for a mere €75. All right, caviar is overrated anyway, so try instead an airy, light *carpaccio de solomillo con balsámico* (a thinly sliced raw sirloin bathed in balsamic vinegar) and finish with a cheese platter.

EL CENADOR DEL PRADO
Map pp270-2 *Spanish Creative*
☎ 91 429 15 61; Calle del Prado 4; meal €35-40; ⏰ Mon-Sat & Sun lunch; Metro Antón Martín

Here is a discreet location for a quietly elegant and romantic meal. What comes out of the kitchen is a mix of fairly traditional Spanish cooking with a few international twists and turns, like the *escalope de berenjenas con setas gratinadas* (aubergine escalope with gratin mushrooms). You can choose from several set-lunch menus (which include a vegetarian option at €19) and keep the cost below €30. The same staff also run a charming café next door.

EL TOCORORO Map pp270-2 *Cuban*
☎ 91 369 40 00; Calle del Prado 3; meal €25; ☽ Tue-Sun (closed two weeks each in Feb & Sep); Metro Antón Martín

Squeeze into one of the few tables or just sit at the little bar for a taste of Cuba. It's bright, cheerful and fairly authentic. The speciality is *langosta con enchilada* (lobster and enchilada), but you can choose from plenty of old Havana favourites such as *ropa vieja* (a kind of stringy meat number) and *arroz congri* (rice and black beans). Filling, single-dish meals cost €15. Don't omit to savour a post-prandial *mojito*.

Top Five in Sol, Huertas & Atocha
- La Finca de Susana (opposite)
- Cluny (p125)
- La Vaca Verónica (p127)
- Gula Gula (opposite)
- El Cenador del Prado (p125)

LA CASA DEL ABUELO Map pp270-2 *Tapas*
☎ 91 521 23 19; Calle de la Victoria 12; meal €20-25; ☽ 11.30am-3.30pm & 6.30-11.30pm; Metro Sol

Squeeze your way past the chattering punters to the bar at this ageless place and ask for a *chato* (small glass) of the heavy, sweet El Abuelo red wine, made in Toledo province. Then request the only possible accompaniment in the house: heavenly *gambas* (prawns) *a la plancha* (grilled) or *al ajillo* (sizzling in garlic in little ceramic plates). They go for €6 a *ración* (portion).

LA TRUCHA Map pp270-2 *Tapas*
☎ 91 532 08 82; Calle de Núñez de Arce 6; meal €20-25; ☽ Tue-Sat; Metro Sol

'The trout' is one of Madrid's great tapas bars and something of an icon in this part of town. Limber up to the bar and choose from the long list of delicious snacks, or allow yourself to be advised by the lively staff. There are numerous tables if you feel like taking a load off and having a full sit-down meal. Most people crowd into the bar, indulge in a few items and push on elsewhere. If this branch is too crowded, try the other **branch** (☎ 91 429 58 33; Calle de Manuel Fernández y González 3; ☽daily) nearby.

LHARDY Map pp270-2 *Gourmet Spanish*
☎ 91 522 22 07; Carrera de San Jerónimo 8; meal €35-45; ☽ Mon-Sat & Sun lunch; Metro Sevilla

A wonderland of delicatessen items, Lhardy has been serving up gourmet tapas since 1839. Prosper Merimée convinced a pal, one Mr Lhardy, to come to Madrid, assuring him he would have no competition! You can also sit down to full meals (the house specialities are Madrid dishes such as *callos* and *cocido* as well as *perdiz estofado* – partridge stew), or shop around for take-home items.

CHEAP EATS

EL BRILLANTE Map p273 *Bocadillos*
☎ 91 528 69 66; Calle del Doctor Drumén 7; bocadillos around €3-5; ☽ 6.30am-12.30am; Metro Atocha

Just by the Centro de Arte Reina Sofía, El Brillante is a stalwart for *bocadillos* and other snacks (*raciones* cost around €6 to €10) in the wee hours after a hard night on the tiles, or simply to fuel up during the day.

GULA GULA Map pp270-2 *Creative*
☎ 91 420 29 19; Calle del Infante 5; meal €15-20; ☽ 9am-3am Tue-Sun; Metro Antón Martín

Gula Gula was one of the first designer restaurants to hit Madrid in the mid-1990s and continues to offer fun food. The bare brick walls, parquet floor, stage lighting and sexily dressed waiters and waitresses turn dining into quite a night out. The atmosphere is camp and snappy, the food a mixed bag but leaning to vegetarian. The salad buffet remains a strong point, but you could opt for a beef Stroganoff. On some evenings dinner is followed by a show, anything from drag to go-go boys and/or girls. Lunchtime is more restrained.

LA BIOTIKA Map pp270-2 *Vegetarian*
☎ 91 429 07 80; Calle del Amor de Dios 3; meal €10-15; ☽ daily; Metro Antón Martín

You walk through a small shop selling all sorts of healthy things to get to the restaurant. This is a long-standing vegetarians' paradise, where you can opt for such faves as seitan ('wheat meat'), tofu-based dishes and generous salads.

LA FINCA DE SUSANA
Map pp270-2 *Mediterranean*
☎ 91 369 35 57; Calle de Arlabán 4; meal €15-20; ☽ daily; Metro Sevilla

'Susana's farm' remains a hip draw. Soft lighting and a veritable jungle of greenery create a soothing atmosphere. Try the salads, grilled vegetables and variations on the *carpaccio* (thinly sliced raw meat) theme. An intriguing starter is the *mousse de atún con gengibre y tabasco suave* (tuna mousse with ginger and a light tabasco sauce), followed by a rich chicken breast in roquefort sauce.

LA NEGRA TOMASA Map pp270-2   *Cuban*

☎ 91 523 58 30; Calle de Cádiz 9; meal €15; ☉ noon-3.30am Sun-Mon, noon-5.30am; Metro Sol

Treat it as restaurant or as a bar – it's basically both. In this boisterous Cuban locale, the waitresses dress in traditional Cuban gear (definitely pre-Castro), the shelves are loaded with dolls reminiscent of the tourist markets of Havana and the food is quite decent. How about a dish of *cojimar* (shrimps in a tomato sauce with rice and slices of banana fritter)... or just have yourself a *mojito* (Hemingway's favourite tipple)!

LA VACA VERÓNICA

Map pp270-2   *Mediterranean*

☎ 91 429 78 27; Calle de Moratín 38; meal €15-20; ☉ Sun-Fri & Sat evening; Metro Antón Martín

Step inside – it's all yellow, but no submarine. You could be forgiven for thinking it's all just a little too playful, and the decor a trifle garish, but the limited menu is good. It ranges from Argentinian (try the steak fillet) to international. Follow with a *tarta de chocolate blanco con frambuesas* (white chocolate cake with strawberries).

LAS BRAVAS Map pp270-2   *Tapas*

☎ 91 532 26 20; Callejón de Álvarez Gato 3; meal €15; ☉ 10am-11.30pm; Metro Sol

Las Bravas has long been the place for a *caña* and the best *patatas bravas* (fried potatoes with a spicy tomato and mayonnaise sauce) in town. The antics of the bar staff are enough to merit a pit stop, and the distorting mirrors are a minor Madrid landmark. Elbow your way to the bar, be snappy about your orders, which will be shouted down the line, and you'll have your bravas n' beer in no time. They do other tapas and *raciones* too.

MACEIRA Map pp270-2   *Galician*

☎ 91 429 15 84; Calle de Jesús 7; meal €15-20; ☉ Tue-Sun & Mon evening; Metro Antón Martín

Get in here early as the simple wooden benches and tables creak under the pressure of the crowds. Get stuck into classic *raciones* of Galician seafood, such as *pulpo a la gallega* (bite-size chunks of slightly spicy boiled octopus; €8.25) downed with a crisp white Ribeiro.

RESTAURANTE INTEGRAL ARTEMISA

Map pp270-2   *Vegetarian*

☎ 91 429 50 92; Calle de Ventura de la Vega 4; meal €15-20; ☉ daily; Metro Sevilla

With a couple of options for meat-eaters (such as chicken in an Armagnac-based sauce), this mostly vegetarian restaurant does a brisk trade with its salads (€8.50 to €11) and more substantial mains such as the *calabacines a la Siciliana* (stuffed courgettes in a Parmesan gratin).

RESTAURANTE LA SANABRESA

Map pp270-2   *Spanish*

☎ 91 429 03 38; Calle del Amor de Dios 12; meal €12-15, set menu €7.60; ☉ Mon-Sat; Metro Antón Martín

Starving at lunchtime and in no mood to spend a fortune? For a filling, comforting meal with all the basic nutritional groups covered, this is the place. A no-nonsense atmosphere attracts all sorts of locals, from the well-dressed but financially challenged gentleman in the corner to a table-load of students. They tuck in to a long list of dishes, anything from *callos* (€3.60) to sizzling *churrasco* (barbecued) beef (€7).

VINITIS Map pp270-2   *Mediterranean*

☎ 91 420 40 90; Calle de Ventura de la Vega 15; meal €15-20; ☉ daily; Metro Sevilla

Spread over two floors, with dark exposed brick and stained-timber pillars, Vinitis offers a nice variety of national and foreign wines to try by the glass (choose from the blackboard or allow yourself to be advised) to go with a broad range of *raciones* (two of which could make a light meal). The *arroz cremoso de setas* (creamy rice with mushrooms) goes nicely with the *berenjenas al parmesano* (aubergine baked with Parmesan cheese).

PASEO DEL PRADO & EL RETIRO

The discreet residential enclave, cradled by the Parque del Buen Retiro and the Museo del Prado, is not exactly bristling with restaurants but, unsurprisingly, is home to a handful of fairly exclusive spots. For more down-to-earth options you need to get further away from the park.

CLUB 31 Map pp268-9 *Spanish*

☎ 91 532 05 11; Calle de Alcalá 58; meal €50-60; ☺ daily; Metro Retiro

A classic that steadily declined since its opening in 1959, Club 31 has changed management and been reborn. Philippe Stark decor (long black seats, leaning wall mirrors and bright white designer lamps hanging from the ceiling) have added a contemporary note but the cuisine is classic. The accent is on fish and venison, with the occasional modern touch (like the lobster *soufflé*). You could set your watch by the old-style, professional (if slightly haughty) service.

MICONO Map p273 *Middle Eastern*

☎ 91 429 90 70; Calle de Alberto Bosch 14; meal €30-35; ☺ Mon-Sat; Metro Atocha

The timber seats look like letters from the Chinese alphabet, but the rugs hanging from the red-painted walls are decidedly Middle Eastern. Where are we? The foundation, in culinary terms, is Lebanese, with options such as *mezze* (a mix of starters) and skewered chicken. But then come the curve balls, like green salad with Dijon mustard. And there's not much Middle Eastern about their apple pie!

VIRIDIANA Map p273 *Creative Spanish*

☎ 91 531 10 39; Calle de Juan de Mena 4; meal €60; ☺ Mon-Sat; Metro Retiro

Viridiana is a classic establishment for cuisine using the freshest market produce and the occasional international touch. Old favourites include *solomillo de ternera con salsa de foie y trufas negras* (beef prepared in a foie gras sauce with black truffles) and the *rabo de buey estofado* (stewed bull's tail) are tempting. Dress up and bring your credit card.

CHEAP EATS

RESTAURANTE LA MAZORCA

Map pp262-4 *Vegetarian*

☎ 91 501 70 13; Paseo de la Infanta Isabel 21; meal €10-15; ☺ Tue-Sat, Mon & Sun lunch only; Metro Atocha Renfe

The simply decorated, little dining area fills with locals looking for a good-value, healthy meal. The *crepe de espinacas en salsa de queso* (spinach crepe in a cheese sauce) is good, as are the vegetable-based paella starter and chunky *canelones* (a pasta dish similar to Italian cannelloni). It offers a couple of different *menús del día*.

LA LATINA & LAVAPIÉS

Many of the animated bars and taverns in and around Calle de la Cava Baja also serve food. The restaurants of La Latina, among them some classics (such as Casa Lucio) tend to stick to Spanish fare, sometimes with a regional twist. As you bowl down the streets into Lavapiés, you find a greater mix. The presence of a burgeoning multicultural community has inevitably had an impact. Middle Eastern restaurants, perhaps with a little belly dancing, have since the late 1990s been joined by a phenomenon already common in other major European cities – Turkish-kebab outlets.

CASA LUCIO Map pp270-2 *Madrileño*

☎ 91 365 32 52; Calle de la Cava Baja 35; meal €35-45; ☺ Sun-Fri & Sat evening Sep-Jul; Metro La Latina

Lucio has been wowing Madrileños with his light touch, quality ingredients and down-home local cooking for ages. The place, softly lit and with a warm atmosphere, is often full, so you may find yourself taking liquid comfort at the bar before proceeding to your table, even if you book ahead. You'll just have to wait for your cloud-light *revuelto* (basically scrambled eggs with all sorts of goodies mixed in – Lucio is famous for his eggs!), which you'll wash down with a gutsy Rioja.

EL ESTRAGÓN Map pp270-2 *Vegetarian*

☎ 91 365 89 82; Plaza de la Paja 10; meal €20-25; ☺ daily; Metro La Latina or bus 31, 50 & 65

A delightful spot for crepes and other vegetarian specialities, El Estragón does make a few slips for the attentive vegan (the butter for instance), but is good for the less-strict observers of the lifestyle.

LA BURBUJA QUE RÍE

Map pp270-2 *Asturian*

☎ 91 366 51 67; Calle del Ángel 16; meal €20; ☺ daily; Metro La Latina

'The Laughing Bubble' is an excellent Asturian tavern that serves up wonderful nourishing and hearty dishes (try the *setas con almejas* – mushrooms and clams) with cider. All right, you can have beer or wine too if you insist but it takes the fun out of the proceedings! Either way the atmosphere is good naturedly rollicking.

LA CAMARILLA Map pp270-2 *Spanish*

☎ 91 354 02 07; Calle de la Cava Baja 21; meal €40-0; ☺ daily; Metro La Latina

A grand lamp hangs precariously from the roof at the entrance to what is most easily described as a gastro-pub, Madrid style. The cooks have an attractive approach to food, combining elements of the old (such as their Saturday menu of *cocido*, which is a little like turning bubble 'n' squeak into a major culinary event) with more inventive interpretations of national cooking.

NUEVO CAFÉ BARBIERI Map pp270-2 *Café*

☎ 91 527 36 58; Calle Ave María 45; ☺ 3pm-2am Sun-Thu, 3pm-3am Fri & Sat; Metro Lavapiés

Once the haunt of the artistic and hopefully artistic, this cavernous old café attracts a mostly young urban crowd. It provides newspapers to riffle through as you sip on a long *café con leche*. With its high ceilings, rough timber tables and dark heavy curtains, it is especially enticing on a chilly winter afternoon. It also makes a relaxing place for a few glasses of wine and can get pretty busy on the weekend.

POSADA DE LA VILLA

Map pp270-2 *Spanish*

☎ 91 366 18 60; Calle de la Cava Baja 9; meal €35-40; ☺ Mon-Sat & Sun lunch Sep-Jul; Metro La Latina

The Posada is a wonderfully restored 17th-century inn *(posada)* where, down through the centuries, all sorts of people, from travelling salesmen to fellows of ill repute, found lodging. The food coming out of the open-plan kitchen is solid, meaty fare but people come especially for the setting. All is heavy timber and brickwork, and Partido Popular bigwigs love the place.

RESTAURANTE JULIÁN DE TOLOSA

Map pp270-2 *Navarran*

☎ 91 365 82 10; Calle de la Cava Baja 8; meal €35; ☺ Mon-Sat & Sun lunch; Metro La Latina

Carnivores in particular will appreciate this Navarran institution. Settle down in the warm, exposed-brick-and-timber surrounds and order a *chuletón* (basically a huge chop of top-quality, juicy meat) for two. You might want to precede with some vegetables, like the *espárragos blancos* (white asparagus). Fill up your glass with Chivite red and enjoy.

Eating – La Latina & Lavapiés

Bar and bartender at Posada de la Villa (p129)

TABERNA MATRITUM

Map pp270-2   *Mediterranean*

☎ 91 365 82 37; Calle de la Cava Alta 17; meal €20-25; ☺ Wed-Sun & Tue lunch; Metro La Latina

Barely a dozen tables welcome punters for gastro-pub style food. Beneath the high ceilings in this one-time smoky tavern, palates are delighted with such creations as *carpaccio de ciervo con boletus edulis y vinagreta de frambuesa* (thinly sliced raw venison with mushrooms and a raspberry vinaigrette). It doesn't accept phone reservations.

CHEAP EATS

BABILONYA Map pp270-2   *Middle Eastern*

☎ 91 539 62 04; Calle del Ave María 50; meal €15-20; ☺ daily; Metro Lavapiés

Just north off Plaza de Lavapiés, this welcoming spot is a perfect example of the several fun Middle Eastern/North African eateries in this part of town. Crowd in around the low tables and enjoy reasonable Middle Eastern fare (followed by the inevitable gooey honeyed sweets). With a little luck you'll be treated to a performance of belly dancing – somebody shaking their falafel while you scoff yours!

OLIVEROS Map pp270-2   *Spanish*

☎ 91 354 62 52; Calle de San Millán 4; meal €15-20; ☺ 1-5pm & 8pm-midnight Tue-Sat, noon-6pm Sun mid-Sep–mid-Aug; Metro La Latina

The typical Madrid frontage is itself an attraction. Let yourself be tempted by the chef or the tile decoration and pop inside this tiny warm, bottle-lined den, which has changed little since the Oliveros family took over in 1921. It has been serving up food since 1857 and the cuisine remains faithfully local. You could dine easily on tapas, ranging from *panceta ahumada* (smoked streaky bacon) through *chorizo al infierno* (sausage from hell). Or sit down for some, say, *callos de la Abuela* (grandma's tripe).

MALASAÑA & CHUECA

The culinary heart of this area beats loud and clear in and around Chueca. Pretty much anything goes around here, and that means the food too. Foreign restaurants, whether Brazilian, French or Japanese, rub along happily with designer diners that on occasion revel in a picaresque campness. If none of that is your style, no problem. Smoky, rowdy tapas bars alternate with lively, down-home restaurants serving up bundles of hearty, regional cooking.

A BRASILEIRA Map pp266-7   *Brazilian*

☎ 91 308 36 25; Calle de Pelayo 49; meal €20-25; ☺ daily; Metro Chueca

The main problem with this place is that its diminutive dimensions are in no way capable of dealing with the numbers trying to get a look in. Once you have managed to carve out a hole for yourself, sit back for some rich dishes like *vatapá* (mixed seafood) and, for some punters better still, the long list of cocktails (among them some alcohol-free ones). It's a happy-go-lucky place and will put you in the mood to explore the surrounding phalanxes of bars when you're finished.

ARABIA

Map pp266-7   *Middle Eastern & North African*

☎ 91 532 53 21; Calle de Piamonte 12; meal €20-25; ☺ Tue-Fri dinner only, Sat & Sun lunch & dinner; Metro Chueca

Like a long tunnel in the heart of hip shopping territory just off Chueca, Arabia is where local fashionistas seek their exotic Middle Eastern fix. The food is not strictly identifiable with any one Arabic region, and mixes and matches between Lebanon and Morocco. While chilling to the Oriental airs you could try *cuscus libio de verduras y carne* (Libyan couscous with vegetables and meat) or such unlikely options as *manzana asada rellena de ollo, pasas y piñones* (baked apple stuffed with chicken, raisins and pine nuts).

ARCE Map pp266-7   *Seafood & Venison*

☎ 91 522 59 13; Calle de Augusto Figueroa 32; meal €50; ☺ Mon-Fri & Sat evening; Metro Chueca

Trip downstairs to this quiet basement hideaway for exquisitely prepared dishes ranging from hunter's venison to ocean catch. How about a subtle *vol au vent de pescado y marisco* (with fish and seafood)?

AZUL PROFUNDO Map pp266-7   *Tapas*

☎ 91 532 25 64; Calle de Plaza de Chueca 4; meal €35-40; ☺ Tue-Sat & Sun lunch; Metro Chueca

This 'deep blue' newcomer has an unusual approach to the serious business of eating. The main option is a set menu of varied and creative tapas by one of the town's hottest young chefs, Andrés Madrigal (better known for his up-market diner, Balzac). The composition of this set meal changes every couple of weeks so it's impossible to know exactly what will be on offer at any given time. Just have faith.

BAZAAR

Map pp266-7 *Mediterranean Creative*
☎ 91 523 39 05; Calle de la Libertad 21; meal €20-25;
☯ daily; Metro Chueca

Occupying a privileged corner location, with hardwood floors, grand windows and theatre lighting, Bazaar is part of a chain of bright new restaurants (all with different names and styles) that has sprung up recently in Madrid and Barcelona. The place packs out with a mostly casual young crowd who come for the broad, mixed menu. *Rosbif de atún con chutney de mango* (slices of tuna with mango chutney) is just one example of the dishes issuing from the kitchen.

BOGA BAR

Map pp268-9 *Seafood & Rice Dishes*
☎ 91 532 18 50; Calle del Almirante 11; meal €35-40;
☯ Mon-Sat & Sun lunch; Metro Chueca

The round arches, fire-red walls and deep-green fronds have a strange, basement Med air about them. To get your buns onto a bench for a feast of seafood you will have to book ahead. After your succulent *rodaballo al horno* (oven-cooked turbot) you could try a *browny* (sic) *con helado* (with ice cream).

CAFÉ COMERCIAL Map pp266-7 *Café*
☎ 91 521 56 55; Glorieta de Bilbao 7; ☯ 8am-1am Sun-Thu, 8am-2am Fri-Sat; Metro Bilbao

This glorious old Madrid café seems to be fighting a rearguard action against modern times (well, except for the computers)! The sprawling corner café and bar, with seats outside on the roundabout, has been left all alone. The cafés of the Glorieta de Bilbao were in the 1950s and 1960s a centre of coffee house intellectualism, with writers, artists, charlatans and probably the occasional informer all gathered for endless chats. The Comercial has changed little since those days, although the clientele has broadened to include just about anyone and everyone.

CAFÉ-RESTAURANTE EL ESPEJO

Map pp268-9 *French-Basque*
☎ 91 308 23 47; Paseo de los Recoletos 31; meal €40;
☯ café 8am-midnight, restaurant 1-4pm & 9pm-midnight; Metro Colón

With all its mirrors, chandeliers and discreet charm of another era, this café restaurant offers a little of everything. In the dining area you will be treated to reasonable French Basque cuisine. Or you could simply take your place in the café and reminisce over how this was once a haunt of writers and intellectuals. Outside, the turn-of-the-20th-century-style Pabellón del Espejo (it was actually opened in 1990), is marvellous for dining on summer evenings or late night drinks – this becomes one of Madrid's popular drinking *terrazas* in high summer.

CASA PERICO Map pp266-7 *Spanish*
☎ 91 532 81 76; Calle de la Ballesta 18; meal €25;
☯ Mon-Fri & Sat lunch; Metro Callao

In this dingy street lurks a minor Madrid legend. Since the 1940s, punters have been gathering at the dark little tables for such house specialities as *arroz a lo cutre* ('grotty rice', actually a delicious creamy rice dish). When you push open the door it isn't entirely clear you're in a restaurant – the handful of check-cloth-covered tables are huddled behind a mess of wine bottles, crates and God knows what else. A great, quirky place to eat!

EL MENTIDERO DE LA VILLA

Map pp266-7 *Modern Spanish*
☎ 91 308 12 85; Calle de Santo Tomé 6; meal €50;
☯ Mon-Fri & Sat evening; Metro Chueca

Tucked away off Plaza de las Salesas, this is one of Madrid's open quality secrets. The name (roughly the 'city gossip shop') was actually applied in the 16th century to the Puerta del Sol part of town, where people from all walks of life gathered and exchanged news and views. The news here is that the Spanish nouvelle cuisine can be delicious. How about duck-liver toast with caramelised apple?

EL PEPINILLO DEL BARQUILLO

Map pp266-7 *Spanish*
☎ 91 310 25 46; Calle del Barquillo 42; meal €20-25;
☯ daily; Metro Alonso Martínez

You can opt for a limited selection of tapas at the bar or sit down. The green-grey walls are bedecked with giant mirrors, designer lamps emitting a muted glimmer and sketches of little black bulls. The limited menu runs the gamut of juicy sirloin steak *(solomillo)* through *almejas* (clams), en passant by a series of Mediterranean salads. You might espy the occasional show-business personality tucking in.

GRAN CAFÉ DE GIJÓN

Map pp268-9   *Café & Spanish*
☎ 91 521 54 25; Paseo de los Recoletos 21; meal €30;
🕑 7am-2am; Metro Chueca or Banco de España
Just down the road from El Espejo, this 'grand café' is equally graceful. It has been serving coffee and meals since 1888 and was long another favourite with Madrid's literati, before, during and after Franco's time. Pop in for a drink or a meal. The latter is a bit of a national smorgasbord, ranging from *cabrito asado a la segoviana* (roast kid) to *bacalao al pil pil* (the typically steamed Basque cod in a garlic sauce).

LA CARRETA Map pp266-7   *Argentine*
☎ 91 532 70 42; Calle de Barbieri 10; meal €20-25;
🕑 1-5pm & 9pm-4am Wed-Mon; Metro Chueca
Meat-eaters in search of a truly late night meal have come to the right place. At 'the Cart' you find an extensive array of meats ready to be grilled to perfection, and way after most sensible diners' bedtime. Crowd in around the long tables and enjoy the general chaos around you as punters file in and out of this Argentine joint. With luck you'll be around for a late live tango show.

LA DAME NOIRE Map pp266-7   *French*
☎ 91 531 04 76; Calle de Pérez Galdós 3; meal €20-25,
menú del día €18; 🕑 evenings only; Metro Gran Vía
Steak tartare and other French temptations by candlelight in this intimate location, all reds, blues and golds, make this a popular option. You might start with a velvet soft *crema de calabaza* (pumpkin soup) and follow with *lengua de buey al vino de Madeira* (bull's tongue). The *tarte Tatin* is hard to resist. Throughout the evening the music of Piaf, Serge Gainsbourg and other Gallic greats wafts through the place.

LA FONDUE DE TELL Map pp266-7   *Swiss*
☎ 91 594 42 77; Calle del Divino Pastor 12; fondue & wine per person €20-25; 🕑 daily; Metro Bilbao

Get past the heavy wooden door and a small, welcoming space, complete with cowbells hanging from the rafters, greets you. You could almost be in an Alpine chalet. Apart from the fondue (of which there are several cheese varieties), you could opt for that other intrinsically Swiss cheese dish, *raclette* (which involves scraping bits of melted cheese on to your plate and scoffing with potatoes and pickles). Wash down with a choice of Swiss and Spanish wines.

OSTERIA DEL REGNO DI NAPOLI

Map pp266-7   *Italian*
☎ 91 445 63 00; Calle de San Andrés 21; meal €20-25;
🕑 Sun-Fri & Sat evening; Metro Bilbao
For a cheerful taste of southern Italy, this could be the spot for a change. Even on a rainy day you'd feel happy inside with all the bright, pastel colours. The pasta is not bad and the *pollo al marsala* (chicken prepared in Marsala, a sweet Sicilian wine) captures the vaguely honeyed nuance that characterises much south Italian cooking.

PIÙ DI PRIMA Map pp266-7   *Italian*
☎ 91 308 33 72; Calle de Hortaleza 100; meal €45;
🕑 Mon-Fri & Sat dinner; Metro Chueca
A hushed atmosphere dominates this slightly pricey but rather popular spot. Chueca fashionistas pop in for good-quality, mixed Italian dishes (there is no attempt at a single regional identity here). Opt for the *vitello tonnato* (thin veal slices smothered in a cream of tuna sauce) or risotto. The pasta is homemade and the tiramisu melts away in the mouth.

RESTAURANTE ROBATA

Map pp266-7   *Japanese*
☎ 91 521 85 28; Calle de la Reina 31; meal €35-40;
🕑 Wed-Mon; Metro Gran Vía
Japanese restaurants have been popping up since the late 1990s, but locals agree that Robata, one of the first, remains one of the best. The sight of tour groups from the home country piling in is all the confirmation we need. The decor is light and bright and the atmosphere subdued – good for a business lunch.

RESTAURANTE EXTREMADURA

Map pp266-7   *Extremaduran*
☎ 91 531 88 82; Calle de la Libertad 13; meal €30;
🕑 daily; Metro Chueca
Inland cooking from the region of Extremadura, with special emphasis on *caza* (venison) and other meat is the benchmark of this

restaurant. *Jamón* is a key fixture and straight-forward roast lamb *(cordero asado)* is worth trying. The atmosphere is convivial and often a little rowdy – it's ideal for groups sat around the long tables.

RESTAURANTE MOMO

Map pp266-7   *Creative*
☎ 91 532 71 62; Calle de Augusto Figueroa 41; meal €25; ☽ daily; Metro Chueca

Even after all these years, Momo continues to be a beacon of relatively low-cost inventive cuisine in Chueca, which nowadays is jammed with competition. Popular with the local gay community and straights alike, it attracts an art and dance crowd too. Long, convivial tables make it great fun for groups to try things like *pavo con salsa de pistachos* (turkey with pistachio sauce).

SALVADOR Map pp266-7   *Madrileño*

☎ 91 521 45 24; Calle de Barbieri 12; meal €25; ☽ Mon-Sat Sep-Jul; Metro Chueca

It looks like a dive from the outside but it is a legend. Since the dark days of 1941 locals have been coming to the 'Saviour' for lashings of hearty Madrid cooking. One of them was Hemingway, who along with bullfighting pals used to wander over from the nearby Chicote bar. He appears in some of the numberless photos and paintings of the bullfighting world that decorate the walls on both floors of this stood-still-in-time diner. Aficionados and toreros still come here to dine, especially during the Fiesta de San Isidro (p10). So tuck into a plate of *rabo de toro* (bull's tail), a meaty delicacy. The cooking is simple, no-nonsense fare.

TETERÍA DE LA ABUELA

Map pp266-7   *Tea Room*
Calle del Espíritu Santo 19; crepes around €5-7; ☽ 5pm-2am Tue-Sun; Metro Tribunal or Noviciado

This enchanting tea room with tiny marble-top tables, rickety wooden seats and an old fashioned till has a touch of the 19th century and a hint of the 1960s. Along with the great range of teas, you can indulge in scrummy crepes.

WOKCAFE Map pp266-7   *Creative Asian*

☎ 91 522 90 69; Calle de las Infantas 44; meal €25; ☽ Mon-Sat; Metro Chueca

With its hip NYC feel and vaguely pan-Asian cuisine (the wok in question is the key kitchen tool), Wokcafé (a bit of a misnomer now as the café part no longer operates) attracts a

chirpy, inner-urban crowd. Blood-red decor rules, with conical dangling lampshades, bordello mirrors and grand windows right onto the busy street.

CHEAP EATS

BOCAITO Map pp266-7   *Tapas*

☎ 91 532 12 19; Calle de la Libertad 4-6; meal €15-20; ☽ Mon-Fri & Sat evenings; Metro Chueca or Banco de España

Film-maker Pedro Almodóvar finds this bar and restaurant in the traditional Madrid style 'the best anti-depressant'. Forget about the sit-down restaurant and just jam into the bar, order a few *raciones* off the menu, slosh them down with some gritty red or a *caña* and enjoy the theatre that these busy barmen perform.

CHIACCHERE Map pp266-7   *Italian*

☎ 91 521 26 90; Calle de la Libertad 9; meal €10-15; ☽ noon-8pm Mon-Thu, noon-midnight Fri & Sat; Metro Chueca

A bright, bustling breath of Italy on a gastronomically crowded street. Italian residents in Madrid wander in for a taste of home, and the emphasis is on self-service (the lunch set meal of bruschetta, pasta, coffee and a soft drink costs €10.50), but you can also sit down for a simple meal of pasta.

Wokcafe shines bright (p133)

PATATUS Map pp266-7 *International*
Calle de Fuencarral 98; big platters up to €16.50;
☾ daily; Metro Bilbao

Spread out like a modern Soho theme pub (it could almost pass for a Walkabout or something of the ilk), there is no shortage of beer to go with a singular pub grub–style menu. Fill up on carbs with potato (and meat) platters accompanied by a variety of sauces. It's big, brassy and crowded. You'll have to fight your way to the bar.

TAQUERÍA DE BIRRÄ Map pp266-7 *Mexican*
☎ 91 522 80 49; Plaza de las Comendadoras 2; meal
€15; ☾ 1-4pm & 8pm-1am; Metro Noviciado

Mexican food and margaritas that pack a punch are the business here. It's a light-hearted affair. Choose your poisons from the big plastic menus and out come your tacos, fajitas and guacamole in (generally) quick time. It's not high-class cuisine but a lot of fun, especially in summer when you can sit out in the square.

SALAMANCA & LAS VENTAS

As you would expect in Madrid's snootiest 'hood, there is no shortage of black tie restaurants, a few of which we list. But it is not too difficult to run into earthier establishments that are often a great deal more fun and still offer good food. They tend to be scattered all about although the closer you get to Calle de Serrano the more likely you are to hit highs on the financial Richter scale. Out around the bullring at Las Ventas are some knock-about places for eating before or after an afternoon's combat.

BIOTZA Map pp268-9 *Basque Tapas*
☎ 91 781 03 13; Calle de Claudio Coello 27; meal €25;
☾ 9am-midnight Sun-Thu, 9am-1am Fri & Sat;
Metro Serrano

Pale-green tile decoration and no-nonsense angular benches and stools are the bones of this tiny Basque snackery. This is a piece of San Sebastián in Madrid, with the elaborate *montaditos* (canapés) and *pintxos* (tapas) typical of that northern town. They cost around €3 apiece, or you could opt for a full meal with the occasional fusion touch – such as the *tempura de berenjenas* (aubergine tempura).

CAFÉ SAIGÓN Map pp262-4 *Vietnamese*
☎ 91 563 15 66; Calle de María de Molina 66; meal
€20-25; ☾ daily; Metro Gregorio Marañón

Settle down inside this bold glass-fronted uptown eatery for a mix of Vietnamese and a handful of Chinese dishes. Inside, the restaurant spreads over two floors. The lemongrass chicken is light and subtle (it's easy to go heavy on the lemon) and the prawns in green curry have a bit of a kick.

CASA JULIÁN Map pp268-9 *Spanish*
☎ 91 431 35 35; Calle de Don Ramón de la Cruz 10;
meal €25; ☾ Mon-Sat & Sun lunch; Metro Serrano

A busy, no-nonsense restaurant in the heart of Salamanca, Casa Julián is utterly unpretentious and the slogan is *'solo carne'* (just meat). Well, you can order a few vegetables to accompany if you must!

Top Five in Salamanca & Las Ventas

- El Amparo (below)
- La Trainera (opposite)
- Restaurante El Pescador (opposite)
- Thai Gardens (p136)
- Lago de Sanabria (below)

EL AMPARO
Map pp268-9 *Basque & Creative*
☎ 91 431 64 56; Calle de Puigcerdà 8; meal €80-100;
☾ Mon-Fri & Sat evening; Metro Serrano

Hidden away down this charming side alley in the heart of Salamanca, El Amparo is one of the more exclusive restaurants in town. The cuisine has been variously described as Basque and *nueva cocina madrileña* ('nouvelle Madrid cuisine'), indicating that you can expect a bit of a mix. The service and wine list are admirable, and the food is generally excellent. Try the *risotto de cigalas*, a crayfish rice delight. Some of the homemade desserts are divine.

LAGO DE SANABRIA Map pp268-9 *Spanish*
☎ 91 576 74 21; Calle de Ayala; meal €25-30;
☾ Tue-Thu & Sat lunch only, Fri lunch & evening;
Metro Velázquez or Serrano

Named after a lake west of Zamora, on the road to northern Portugal, it seems like any old local bar and eatery when you first walk inside. Looks can be deceiving. The slightly rough and tumble appearance belies a menu of good traditional cooking, done with care. It does a great *ventresca* (tuna) for €15.

LA PALOMA Map pp262-4 *Spanish*
☎ 91 576 86 92; Calle de Jorge Juan 39; meal €45-60; Mon-Sat Sep-Jul; Metro Velázquez

BMWs and Jags park outside this low grey house as lunchtime at the Dove is essentially a suits' affair. Customers come for a mix of traditional national cooking and the occasional creative culinary adventure. They especially like to play around with seafood flavours, such as with their *rape relleno de centollo sobre verduras y salsa de marisco* (monkfish stuffed with spider crab on a bed of vegetables and seafood sauce).

LA TRAINERA Map pp262-4 *Seafood*
☎ 91 576 80 35; Calle de Lagasca 60; meal €50; Mon-Sat Sep-Jul; Metro Velázquez

Seafaring decor gives the game away as you enter this labyrinth, with dining areas succeeding one another along hallways and passages. Run, predictably enough, by Galicians, the 'Trawler' assures you plenty of fresh fish and abundant white wine to wash it down. The only exception to the rule is ham, for those who would like to nibble on some high-quality *jamón ibérico* before their main course.

LOS TIMBALES Map pp262-4 *Spanish*
☎ 91 362 30 42; Calle del Cardenal Belluga 3; meal €25-30; daily; Metro Ventas

Outside, the ceramic decoration of bullfighting scenes might put you in the mood for trying the house version of *rabo de toro estofado* (bull's tail stew). After all, you're just a block from the Ventas bullring. Take tapas at the bar or head for one of several dining areas, where the bullfight theme continues in picture and portraits in among the exposed brick and tiles. Dishes range from Galician fish options to the bean bonanza of *fabada Asturiana*.

MUMBAI MASSALA Map pp268-9 *Indian*
☎ 91 435 71 94; Calle de los Recoletos 14; meal €30-35; daily; Metro Retiro

One thing you are not going to find in Madrid is a cheap curry house around every corner. Still, occasionally one is struck with a desire for Britain's (ahem) national cuisine and this busy *hindú* is a good spot to satisfy the urge with fresh naan, decent curries (not all that spicy though, as the Spaniards don't care too much for hot food) and a selection of set menus that can bring the cost down (the cheapest is a lunch *menú del día* for €12).

PARADIS ERRE EFE Map pp268-9 *Creative*
☎ 91 575 45 40; Paseo de los Recoletos 2; meal €50-60; Mon-Fri & Sat evening; Metro Retiro

Housed in the Casa de América in Palacio Linares, the minimalist decor exudes modishness. Barcelonan chef Ramón Freixa offers 'interactive' cooking. You want a veal fillet? Fine, now you choose what goes with it, which could be anything from a soya-based sauce with pears dripping in wine or a Bearnaise. The elegant main dining room, dominated by whites and blacks, is surrounded by smaller annexes.

RESTAURANTE EL PESCADOR
Map pp262-4 *Seafood*
☎ 91 402 12 90; Calle de José Ortega y Gasset 75; meal €30-40; Mon-Sat Sep-Jul; Metro Lista

Galician seafood is the order of the day here. No point in coming if you want a steak. Madrileños remain faithful to 'The Fisherman', with its seafaring decor, because they know the raw materials are good and treated with respect. There are no needless frills here – expect robust servings of whatever fish (much of it sold by weight) or sea critter you choose.

RESTAURANTE OTER EPICURE
Map pp268-9 *Navarran*
☎ 91 431 67 71; Calle de Claudio Coello 73; meal €40-45; Mon-Sat; Metro Serrano

Head downstairs to a long, elegant, halogen-lit dining hall, an up-market temple of Navarran high cuisine. An imaginative mix of seafood and meat dishes is prepared with style. From the sea try the *bacalao confitado con berzas y su pil pil* (caramelised cod with cabbage and a garlic sauce).

TABERNA DE LA DANIELA
Map pp262-4 *Tapas*
☎ 91 575 23 29; Calle del General Pardiñas 21; meal €20-25; daily; Metro Goya

The colourful tile decor is a sign of other times and the Taberna de la Daniela indeed is a relic of other days. People pile in here for lunch and dinner, and finding even standing room can be an effort. Because the place is generally overwhelmed, table service can be tardy at best. It's more fun to munch tapas at (or at least near!) the bar.

TEATRIZ Map pp268-9 *Fusion*
☎ 91 577 53 79; Calle de la Hermosilla 15; meal €30-40; daily; Metro Serrano

Teatriz takes the theatrical recherché biscuit. Designed by Philippe Stark, the former Teatro Beatriz has an eerily lit bar right on the stage. Tables are spread out over several levels and it's the kind of place you'd want to look like George Clooney to fit in. The food follows the fashion, falling into distinct categories, ranging from Made in Spain to Fusion. You can mix and match, taking a traditional starter and following with a vaguely Vietnamese main. While you're there, check out the loos, where you leave luminous footprints!

THAI GARDENS Map pp268-9 *Thai*
☎ 91 577 88 84; Calle de Jorge Juan 5; meal €30-35;
daily; Metro Serrano
Madrid's top Thai is lavish – they're not joking about the gardens. They say the ingredients are flown in weekly from the home country and at lunchtime they offer a good set menu for €22.

Fashionable dining at Teatriz (p135)

Late Bites & Dawn Dining
Way past midnight and your stomach's growling? To get a meal as late as 2am (maybe later if you're in luck) you could try **La Carreta** (Map pp262-4), **El Brillante** (Map p273), **La Negra Tomasa** (Map pp270-2) and **Gula Gula** (Map pp270-2). For snacks and *bocadillos* after the disco, you could try out **Restaurante Iberia** (Map pp262-4) and **El Brillante**.

CHEAP EATS
ALFREDO'S BARBACOA Map pp268-9 *BBQ*
☎ 91 576 62 71; Calle de Lagasca 5; meal €10-15;
Tue-Sat & Sun lunch; Metro Retiro
Alfredo's is a great American-style lunch stop just north of El Retiro. On the menu are lightly spiced spare ribs for €6.75 and good steaks and burgers. Pining after a serving of coleslaw? This is the place. You can eat in or takeaway.

CHAMBERÍ & ARGÜELLES
Unlike, say, the area around Plaza de Chueca, these *barrios* are not so densely populated with restaurants. Scattered about, however, are some gems that repay a bit of treasure hunting. Since most of this area is relatively little transited by tourists, an added bonus is the chance to sit down to your meal among mostly local diners. Options range from cheap snack food through some of the best tables in Madrid.

ANNAPURNA Map pp268-9 *Indian*
☎ 91 319 87 16; Calle de Zurbano 5; meal €20-30;
Mon-Fri & Sat dinner; Metro Alonso Martínez
Long considered the best of a handful of Indian restaurants in town, it remains good. The place is relaxed (some would say a little too relaxed given the time it can take for dishes to arrive) and animated, attracting the occasional Brit from the language school across the road. Tandoori is the house speciality, although the menu goes well beyond that. As usual though, don't expect anything too hot, as Spaniards like things to be nice without too much spice.

CAFÉ VIENA Map pp262-4 *Spanish*
☎ 91 559 38 28; Calle de Luisa Fernanda 23; meal €30; Mon-Sat; Metro Ventura Rodríguez
Whether you pop in for a relaxing coffee or sip of wine or for a meal in the restaurant out back, this is a trip back in time. A once-grand old bastion of Castilian cuisine (the restaurant specialises in venison and items such as *perdiz de monte a la toledana* – Toledo mountain partridge), the Viena still oozes the rough charm of another epoch with its gritty mirrors, polished timber and straight-back dining chairs.

CHANTARELLA

Map pp262-4   *Mediterranean*

☎ 91 541 80 03; Calle de Luisa Fernanda 27; meal €20-25; Thu-Sun & Mon-Wed lunch; Metro Ventura Rodríguez

It's a trifle perplexing categorising this little food den. Step inside to a vaguely funky atmosphere and let your taste buds do the walking. If you're after trad you could try its *cocido a la madrileña*, which it does specially on a Thursday. Otherwise you could range from a serving of *lomo de buey en salsa de queso azul* (ox meat bathed in a blue cheese sauce) to the occasional surprising fusion number.

CUENLLAS Map pp262-4   *Gourmet Spanish*

☎ 91 547 31 33; Calle de Ferraz 5; meal €45-50; Mon-Sat; Metro Ventura Rodríguez

This place is for gourmets and wine lovers but it can become almost insufferably crowded at lunchtime – you'd never know from the outside how rowdy it can get around 2pm. The *ensalada de pato* (duck salad) is intriguing, while the *centro de solomillo* is a succulent cut of beef.

DANTXARI Map pp266-7   *Basque*

☎ 91 542 35 24; Calle de Ventura Rodríguez 8; meal €35-45; Mon-Sat Sep-Jul; Metro Ventura Rodríguez

Although a tad cramped, this is an excellent spot to sample some of the rich and tender dishes of the Basque Country at reasonable prices. The cheery red-check tablecloths and timber wall panelling create a warm atmosphere, although all the clocks on one dining room wall are overwhelming! Cooking is strictly traditional and never fails to please with such dishes as *bacalao al pil-pil* (salted cod in a sauce of garlic and olive oil based sauce) or *solomillo de buey al vapor* (steamed sirloin of ox).

EL DOBLE Map p261   *Tapas*

☎ 91 441 47 18; Calle de Ponzano 58; meal €20-25; Tue-Sat & Sun lunch; Metro Alonso Cano

El Doble is a busy tapas bar run, judging by the photos, by intense bullfighting aficionados.

The *raciones*, such as the *gambas* (prawns) and *ventresca* (tuna) are good at around €7 to €8. The two bars with the same name on this street serve good food. They close early – expect to be out by midnight.

JOCKEY Map pp268-9   *Spanish*

☎ 91 319 24 35; Calle de Amador de los Ríos 6; meal €70; daily Sep-Jul; Metro Colón

Fine Spanish cooking, with the occasional wink to nearby imports (how about a dozen Bourgogne snails for €25?), is the hallmark of this long-standing eatery. It attracts a lot of be-suited persons from the nearby government ministries (the Ministry of the Interior is just across the road) and law courts. Quietly efficient waiters whisk around the tables, which are spread around several separate dining areas. Prince Felipe, heir to the Spanish throne, and his gal Letizia Ortiz, chose this spot for their wedding banquet in May 2004.

LA BROCHE Map pp262-4   *Creative*

☎ 91 399 34 37; Calle de Miguel Ángel 29-31; meal €80; daily; Metro Chueca

Sergi Arola, a young Catalan acolyte of the world-renowned Ferran Adrià, has made his own splash in this hotel restaurant in the busy uptown area of Madrid. He mixes his ingredients carefully, without necessarily going overboard. Typical is the *butifarra dulce de Figueres con gamba roja y alcachofas de Tudela* (sweet Catalan sausage with red shrimp and artichokes from the northern town of Tudela). The gang from nearby Pricewaterhouse Cooper like to lunch here occasionally, where you can choose a set menu from €65 to €100.

LA VACA ARGENTINA

Map pp262-4   *Argentinian*

☎ 91 559 66 05; Paseo del Pintor Rosales 52; meal €20-25; daily; Metro Argüelles

The 'Argentinian Cow' is a good chain and can mean only one thing: lashings of Argentine meat slabs. Try the *parrillada argentina*, a mixed grill for two at €28. The cowhide wall coverings are a little OTT, but the place is justifiably popular among Madrileño carnivores.

MOMA 56 Map pp262-4   *Fusion*

☎ 91 399 48 73; Calle de José Abascal 56; meal €30-35; daily; Metro Gregorio Marañon

One of *the* places to see and be seen at the moment, Moma 56 is all in one. To the left is Momabar, where you can perch on slippery metallic bar stools or take a table for Basque *pintxos*

Top Five in Chamberí & Argüelles

- La Broche (above)
- Jockey (above)
- Cuenllas (above)
- Dantxari (above)
- El Doble (above)

(tapas). Or head to the right for the split-level Asia Lounge for its self-proclaimed menu of Pan-Asian food. The latter is decent without being the cause for excitement some local critics claim. All serves as a warm-up for the chilled club out back, where the sightseeing is something else.

PIL-PIL BOMBÍN Map pp262-4   *Fish*
☎ 91 548 70 22; Calle de Ferraz 27; meal €20-25;
☺ Tue-Sat & Sun lunch; Metro Ventura Rodríguez
In the Food & Drink chapter (p41) we discuss how much Madrileños like their seafood and the long history of importing salted cod from the distant coast. Here they have successfully made a fetish of *bacalao*. Wander through past the café and take a seat in the cheery, modern restaurant out the back. You can escape the fish with a couple of beef options.

PRADA A TOPE Map pp262-4   *Tapas*
☎ 91 547 80 20; Cuesta de San Vicente 32; meal €20;
☺ daily; Metro Príncipe Pío
This is an atmospheric place for specialities from the El Bierzo region in northwest Castilla y León. They include *cecina* (a kind of beef jerky), *empanada* (a tuna pie) and various *chorizos*. Crowd in around the bar at the entrance or head out the back for a table. It has become a small chain and make all sorts of goodies in El Bierzo, from various transparent liquors through to fried El Bierzo capsicums and chestnuts (with which they make various desserts).

CHEAP EATS
CASA MINGO Map pp262-4   *Asturian*
☎ 91 547 79 18; Paseo de la Florida 34; meal €10-15;
☺ 11am-midnight; Metro Príncipe Pío
This rambling, old Asturian institution is a delight in simplicity. Nothing sophisticated here; the house speciality is chicken and cider. A full roast bird, salad and a bottle of cider is plenty for two. They've been pouring cider in this grand, old establishment since 1888.

EL BRILLANTE Map pp262-4   *bocadillos*
☎ 91 448 19 88; Calle de Eloy Gonzalo 14; bocadillos around €3-5; ☺ 6.30am-12.30am; Metro Quevedo
This is a no-nonsense spot great for post all-nighters or a late-night snack, whether one of its stacked bocadillos or a ración (€6 to €10) of the usual suspects.

RESTAURANTE IBERIA
Map pp262-4   *Tapas & Raciones*
☎ 91 448 14 99; Plaza de Ruiz Jiménez 4; meal €10-15; ☺ 6am-2am; Metro Quevedo
This noisy, no-nonsense bar-restaurant draws squads of taxi drivers like bees to a honey pot. What they say about long-haul truck drivers can probably be said of cab drivers; they know where to go to get a good, simple, inexpensive meal. They are joined by other early-risers for the best *tortilla* and *callos* in town at 6am.

NORTHERN MADRID
With the exception of business folk and football fans, few out-of-towners visit the northern half of Madrid, a combination of business and ministerial district and expensive residential quarters. You might not have too many incentives to wander around in search of monuments but this part of Madrid offers quite a few dining options – after all, they have a ready and cashed-up market to cater for quite aside from tourists.

CALLE 54 Map p261   *Creative*
☎ 90 214 14 12; Calle de la Habana 3; meal €30-60;
☺ 1pm-1am; Metro Nuevos Ministerios
Students of the Basque genius chef Juan Mari Arzak provide a mixed and attractive line-up of food in two separate dining areas. Downstairs in El Bistró you eat all day from 1pm and opt for a pizza (€10) or eat *a la carta*. Upstairs, the Restaurante serves only at night. You might start with *cogollos con langostinos salteados y vinagreta de yogur* (lettuce hearts with sautéed king prawns and a yoghurt vinaigrette) and follow with a *lubina con caldo de carne y manzana* (sea bass in meat stock and apple). Finish up with dessert, a herbal tea or choose from the cigar selection. Calle 54 is a design concept by Valencian Javier Mariscal and boasts a bar, jazz club and cinema (see p161).

CASA BENIGNA Map p260   *Rice & Paella*
☎ 91 413 33 56; Calle de Benigno Soto 9; meal €50;
☺ Mon-Sat; Metro Concha Espina
In a nondescript residential corner of northern Madrid – all apartment blocks and no green open spaces – lurks this pearl. The cooks compose their menu on the basis of what they find at the market that morning, but the place is known above all for offering some of the

best rice dishes in Madrid, including various interpretations of paella.

DE VINIS Map p261 *Mediterranean Creative*
☎ 91 556 40 33; Paseo de la Castellana 123; meal €35;
☺ Mon-Fri & Sat evening Sep-Jul; Metro Cuzco
This may not be in the most romantic location in town, in the heart of *pijolandia* (*pijos* is a somewhat derogatory term for the well lined) but the food is top quality. The menu is as crowded with goodies as the minimalist dining area is bereft of visual stimulation. The steak tartar, accompanied by duck liver and a cream of avocado and pineapple, is a more subtle combination than it might at first sound. You can try class wines by the glass.

EL BODEGÓN
Map p261 *Catalan & Basque*
☎ 91 562 31 37; Calle del Pinar 15; meal €50-60;
☺ Mon-Fri & Sat evening Sep-Jul; Metro Gregorio Marañón
El Bodegón is a Madrid stalwart that never seems to go bad. Although not strictly a Basque restaurant, the northern roots are there, with a mix of Catalan and inventive cuisine thrown in. Service is olde worlde dignified and the wine list a superb mix. An economical approach to dinner is its *menú de degustación* (around €40), in which you sample small portions of several dishes.

EL FOQUE Map p261 *Spanish & Seafood*
☎ 91 519 25 72; Calle de Suero de Quiñones 22; meal €35-45; ☺ Mon-Sat; Metro Cruz del Rayo
Venison and fish are the twin hallmarks in this recently renovated restaurant, lurking just behind the Auditorio Nacional de Música and hence perfect for a post-performance meal. The standout sub-category is *bacalao* (salted cod), which it prepares in some 20 different fashions (€17.50). The *menú de degustación* (€36) is a tempting option.

LA DORADA Map p261 *Seafood*
☎ 91 570 20 04; Calle de Orense 64; meal €35-45;
☺ Mon-Sat; Metro Cuzco
This is the story of a renaissance. Félix Cabeza brought his fish restaurant back to life in 2003 after a long absence from Madrid. He started out running a little joint down in Málaga and first set foot in Madrid in 1980. This is fish land and the key is in simplicity and quality raw materials. The *dorada a la sal* (salted sea bream, €19) is excellent. Prawns, lobster and other seafood delights are prepared to perfection.

LOS ASTURIANOS Map p260 *Asturian*
☎ 91 533 59 47; Calle de Vallehermoso 94; meal €20-25; ☺ Sun-Fri Aug-Jun; Metro Canal
It might not look like much, but this crowded and admittedly worn-looking establishment has its doggedly loyal fans. They don't want designer frills or plush seating. Rather they come for the hearty hill cooking of Asturias, with its *fabadas* (white bean and sausage stews) and *escalopines de venado con salsa de hongos* (a venison fillet in mushroom sauce). The desserts are homemade – try the tangy *tarta de mousse de sidra* (a cider mousse).

Top Five in Northern Madrid
- Zalacaín (p140)
- Príncipe de Viana (below)
- O' Pazo (below)
- Los Asturianos (above)
- La Dorada (below)

O' PAZO Map p261 *Galician Seafood*
☎ 91 553 23 33; Calle de la Reina Mercedes 20; meal €40-45; ☺ Mon-Sat Sep-Jul; Metro Santiago Bernabéu
Madrileños flock here for the quality seafood. A joyful, upscale family atmosphere makes this a welcoming spot to tuck into, say, a dish of *vieiras a la gallega* (scallops). The same people also run Restaurante El Pescador (p135) and the raw materials come through the restaurant-linked Galician fishing outfit All is washed down with fine Albariño, the noblest Galician white.

PRÍNCIPE DE VIANA Map p261 *Basque*
☎ 91 457 15 49; Calle de Manuel de Falla 5; meal €50-70; ☺ Mon-Fri & Sat dinner Sep-Jul; Metro Santiago Bernabéu
Suits closing deals tend to populate the generous lunchtime tables of this Basque bastion, which has been serving up the best in northern cuisine since the 1960s. But that doesn't have to stop you joining in. Along with some fine seafood and meat dishes, they pay particular attention to side orders and vegetables, not always something you can count on in Spanish dining rooms. Well-to-do Madridistas often gather here too, perhaps to keep a watchful eye on the nearby stadium.

SUKOTHAY Map p261 *Japanese & Thai*
☎ 91 598 03 56; Paseo de la Castellana 105; meal €25-40; ☺ Mon-Sat Sep-Jul; Metro Santiago Bernabéu

The mixing of Asian cuisines under the one roof rarely works all that well, but in this bright, modern spot along the city's main boulevard the effort is more than acceptable. You could munch away on sashimi, enjoy an abundant pad thai or turn up on Thursday nights (when it stays open until 2am) for the restaurant's sushi-*cava* nights. For €20 you can enjoy a selection of sushi and wash it down with bubbly.

ZALACAÍN Map p261   *Basque-Navarran*
☎ 91 561 48 40; Calle de Álvarez de Baena; meal €70-90; ☽ Mon-Fri & Sat dinner Sep-Jul; Metro Gregorio Marañón

There is a seamless, quiet efficiency about this classy home of the best in traditional cooking. Everyone who's anyone in Madrid, from the king down, has eaten here since the doors opened in 1973. The *manitas de cerdo rellenas de cordero* (pig's trotters stuffed with lamb) are a house speciality. Precede with a delightful first of *carabineros guisados al coriandro* (small shrimps pan fried with coriander). The wine list is purported to be one of the best in the city. It is certainly extensive (an estimated 35,000 bottles). There are two main dining areas – one facing a garden – and five smaller private ones. Men, don't forget your tie.

CHEAP EATS
IL PASTAIO DEL VECCHIO MULINO
Map p261   *Italian*
☎ 91 554 29 25; Calle de Ríos Rosas 49; meal €15; ☽ Tue-Sat & Sun lunch Sep-Jul; Metro Ríos Rosas

This sparky Italian restaurant keeps locals happy with good-value, simple home cooking. The cooks concentrate on the business of pasta, which is homemade (they sell it in a shop with the same sign a few doors up the road at No 39), prepared al dente and served with an array of tempting sauces.

Drinking &
Nightlife

Drinking & Nightlife

Hemingway said it best: 'Nobody goes to bed in Madrid until they have killed the night' Young and old, chic and dowdy, struggling artist and wealthy businessman, they all head out for a slice of what can justifiably be called the best nightlife in Europe. There's no denying that Madrileños deserve their nickname, *gatos* (cats), for their incurable night prowling and if you have your doubts just check out the terrible 3am traffic jams all over town.

Although you'll find neighbourhood taverns and a dance spot or two in every part of the city, some areas definitely have more *marcha* (action) than others. There are crowds all week long in the Huertas *barrio*, especially along Calle de las Huertas and in and around the Plaza Santa Ana. Chueca is the fun, funky gay district, though it draws partiers of all persuasions, and nearby Malasaña is popular with grunge rockers and the leftover followers of *la movida*. For mega-clubs and a wide variety of bars, head down Gran Vía and the web of small streets winding down toward Calle de Arenal and Calle Mayor.

This section is divided into 'Drinking' and 'Clubs & Discos', though the truth is that the two often overlap. Mid-week you may find a bar atmosphere in a dance club, while on Saturday nights a popular pub may take on a disco feel. Some bars and clubs also have live music, but you'll find the best concert venues listed in the Entertainment chapter (p161).

Finding Out What's On

The nightlife bible is the *Guía del Ocio*, a weekly magazine sold at newsstands for €1. You'll find listings of many clubs and bars as well as a guide to the week's concerts, special events and movies. Although it's all in Spanish, the highlights are given in English at the back. Also check out the monthly *Salir*, also all in Spanish, which has listings and in-depth articles about the Madrid scene. The best gay guide is *Shanguide*, which you can pick up for free in bars around town.

For more on the night's offerings, browse bars in your chosen *barrio*. Flyers, discount tickets and ads for nearby clubs will usually be lying near the entrance, and bar staff or clients may have an inside tip on where the night's best party will be. In Chueca, the place to get in-the-know info is Mamá Inés (p148); most people will be more than happy to point you in the right direction.

DRINKING

Madrileños seem up for a drink most any time of the day or night, and the city happily accommodates with an endless variety of bars, taverns and wine bars. Your options of what to order are every bit as varied as the drinking holes themselves. Beer can be local brand like San Miguel, Cruzcampo or Mahou, or international brews, and it's usually served on tap. Order a *caña* (a small glass of draught beer) if you want something small and cheap (just €1 in some bars) or a *tubo*, a tall thin glass that gives you a bit more.

Only cocktail bars serve Manhattans, Martinis and the like; in other places you'll find mainly whisky, rum, gin and sodas for mixing. Classic clubbing drinks here include gin tonics, *cubatas* (rum with Coke), *maribú piñas* (coconut rum with pineapple juice) and vodka mixed with just about anything.

Find Your Barrio Style

For...
- **University students** Head to Argüelles (p149)
- **Pijos and pijas** Head to Salamanca (p148)
- **Hard-core rockers** Head to Malasaña (p145)
- **The gay scene** Head to Chueca (p145)
- **Guiris (foreigners)** Head to Huertas (opposite)

Early in the night you'll pay as little as €4 for a mixed drink, but as it gets later the prices go up. Bars with good DJs, dancing or live music may not have a cover charge, but the drink prices will shoot up to €8 or more. During the week, closing hours for most bars are from midnight or until 2am, depending on the crowd. Most will stay open until 3am on weekends. If by then you're still wanting more, you'll have to head to a disco (see p148), which often stay open until 6am.

Top Five Spots for Marcha

For...

- **Terrace drinking and lots of English speakers**
  Plaza de Santa Ana (Map pp270-2)
- **A gay-friendly (or just plain friendly) scene**
  Around Plaza de Chueca (Map pp266-7)
- **Eclectic bars and intimate clubs** Around Calle de la Palma (Map pp266-7)
- **Mega-clubs and a young crowd** Around Calle del Arenal (Map pp270-2)
- **Classic bars with tapas, vermouth and flamenco** Around Calle de la Cava Baja (Map pp262-4)

LOS AUSTRIAS & CENTRO

ome of Madrid's oldest taverns line the maze f streets around the Plaza Mayor. Head to he must-visit places we've listed or hunt out our own hole-in-the-wall drinking corner.

CAFÉ DEL NUNCIO Map pp270-2

☎ 91 366 09 06; Calle de Segovia 9; ☽ noon-2am un-Thu, noon-3am Fri & Sat; Metro La Latina
sprawling bar, the Café del Nuncio straggles own a stairway passage to Calle de Segovia. ou can drink on one of several cosy levels inide or, better still in summer, enjoy the outdoor erraza.

TABERNA DE CIEN VINOS Map pp270-2

☎ 91 365 47 04; Calle del Nuncio 17; ☽ 1-3.45pm & 8pm-1.45am Tue-Sat, 1-3.45pm Sun; Metro La Latina
This unpretentious wine bar is the perfect place to order by the glass or by the bottle. The classic décor and friendly service have made it one of the best-known wine bars in town.

SOL, HUERTAS & ATOCHA

The maze of streets around Huertas and the Puerta del Sol is a treasure chest of lively bars and nightspots, and you won't be hard-pressed to find a place to revel in the atmosphere with a drink in hand. A starting point is the Plaza de Santa Ana is the heart of the *barrio*, and the streets branching off the square are full of great nightspots.

CASA ALBERTO Map pp270-2

☎ 91 429 93 56; www.casaalberto.es; Calle de las Huertas 18; ☽ noon-midnight Tue-Thu, noon-1.30am Fri & Sat; Metro Antón Martín
Since 1827 Madrileños have been getting their vermouth from this elegant bar, where the hard stuff is served on tap. Order a *tapa* or two to accompany your drink, or move to the back for a restaurant atmosphere. The place is

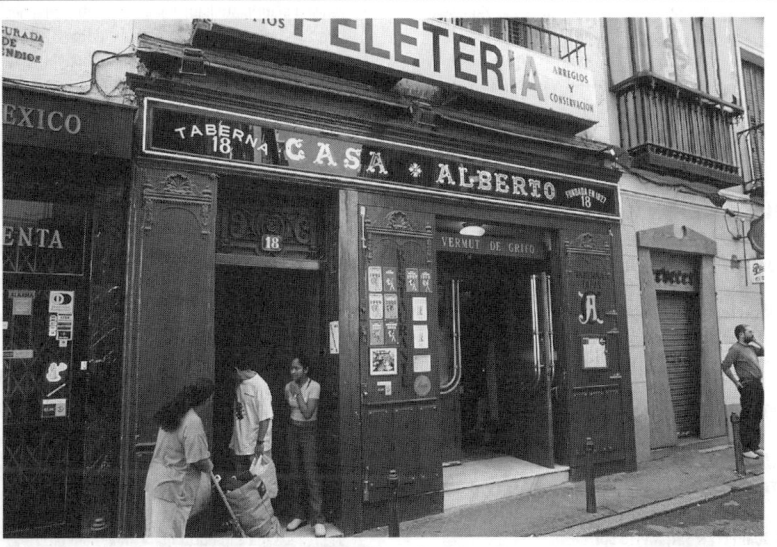

Historic Casa Alberto (above)

especially popular Sundays before lunch, when families and friends go out for the traditional vermouth hour (see boxed text p147).

CERVECERÍA ALEMANA Map pp270-2

☎ 91 429 70 33; Plaza de Santa Ana 6; ☺ 11am-12.30am Sun-Thu, 11am-2am Fri & Sat, closed August; Metro Antón Martín or Sol

If you've only got time to stop at one bar on Plaza Santa Ana, let it be this classic *cervecería*, renowned for its cold, frothy beers and delicious tapas. The *calamares a la romana* (fried calamari) are excellent, and the *tortilla de patatas* (potato omelette) just might be the best in all of Madrid. This was one of Hemingway's haunts, and neither the wood-lined bar nor the bow-tied waiters seem to have changed since his day.

CUEVAS DE SÉSAMO Map pp270-2

☎ 91 429 65 24; Calle del Príncipe 7; ☺ 7pm-2am; Metro Sevilla or Sol

For atmosphere without attitude, head to this wonderful old cellar bar that specialises in sangria and offers live piano music at night. This place is proof that the young crowd doesn't need techno music to have fun.

EL CALLEJÓN Map pp270-2

☎ 91 429 83 97; Calle de Manuel Fernandez y González 5; ☺ 7pm-3am; Metro Antón Martín or Sol

This dark, cosy little flamenco bar is a great place for a late-night *pica pica* (snack) or an intimate drink early in the evening. Music (never live) ranges from jazzy flamenco to fusion to flamenco *puro*, and pictures of flamenco greats line the walls.

LA VENENCIA Map pp270-2

☎ 91 429 73 13; Calle de Echegarary 7; ☺ 1-3.30pm & 7.30pm-1.30am Sun-Thu, 1-3.30pm & 7.30pm-2.30am Fri & Sat; Metro Sol

La Venencia is at best austere and rather dingy, this bar probably won't catch your attention from the street. But it's a *barric* classic, serving up sherry from wooden barrels beside the bar for just €1.35. There's nc music, no flashy decorations, no ambience o' any kind; it's all about you, your *fino* (sherry) and your friends.

MATADOR Map pp270-2

☎ 91 531 89 81; Calle de la Cruz 39; ☺ noon-2am Sun-Thu, noon-2.30am Fri & Sat; Metro Sol

A smoky, dark place with constant flamenco music and a random collection of Spanish memorabilia (boots, guitars, old pots…) hanging from the walls, this bar is popular with a young crowd looking for an unpretentious place for a drink.

TABERNA DE DOLORES Map pp270-2

☎ 91 429 22 43; Plaza de Jesús 4; ☺ 11am-1am Sun-Thu, 11am-2am Fri & Sat; Metro Antón Martín

Old bottles and beer mugs line shelves behind the bar at this Madrid institution, knowr for its blue and white tiled exterior. You car get good house wine and some of Madrid's best beer for €1.50 a pop, though tapas are pricey.

Under the Stars

From April to October, when the evening temperatures in Madrid are balmy and rain is rare, summer *terrazas* (terraces or tables set up outdoors) spring up like mushrooms all over town. Although many of the bars listed here put up *terrazas*, the most popular places to go for a drink under the stars are along the **Paseo de la Castellana** and the **Paseo de los Recoletos** (Map p261), where tables run up and down the sidewalks. The drinks are pricey and the crowd a bit pretentious, but the atmosphere is lively and inviting. Even more pleasant are the *terrazas* that set up in Argüelles, especially those on **Paseo del Pintor Rosales** (Map pp262-4). With parkland on one side and considerably less traffic than Paseo de la Castellana, these places also exercise a little more control over their prices. The **Parque de Berlín**, way up in Chamartín, is another peaceful spot.

Yet there's no need to go so far afield to find *terrazas*; Madrid's squares make perfect locations for outdoor drinking. Several bars on **Plaza de Santa Ana** (Map pp270-2) operate *terrazas*, as do those on squares such as **Plaza del Dos de Mayo** (Map pp266-7) in Malasaña and **Plaza de la Paja** (Map pp270-2) near the Plaza Mayor.

Bottled Up

Perico Chicote (1899–1977) is said to have invented more than a hundred cocktails, which the likes of Hemingway, Sophia Loren, Frank Sinatra and pals all slugged back at one time or another. But the famous barman, founder of the Museo Chicote (p148), was collecting more than just recipes, he was building a huge bottle collection for the museum he kept in the basement. Among his prizes was an 1802 bottle from which Napoleon took a sip and another that Neil Armstrong had taken along to the Moon in 1969. In all, the collection counted more than 10,000 bottles, for which its owner was once offered US$2 million. On his death in 1977, the collection was sold off and changed hands several times. For years the bottles have lain in containers, the possession of an impresario who probably doesn't quite know what to do with them.

VINOTECA BARBECHERA Map pp270-2

☎ 91 420 04 78; direccion@vinotecabarbechera.com; Calle del Príncipe 27; ☾ 10am-2am; Metro Antón Martín or Sol

Perch at the tall tables overlooking the Plaza Santa Ana and enjoy a glass of strong Spanish wine at this chic bar, where the classy crowd (and we do mean crowd) tends to be mature and well dressed. The atmosphere is more casual in summer, when the outdoor terrace is the place to be.

VIVA MADRID Map pp270-2

☎ 91 429 36 40; www.barvivamadrid.com; Calle de Manuel Fernandez y González 7; ☾ 1pm-2am Sun-Thu, 1pm-3am Fri & Sat; Metro Antón Martín or Sol

This wouldn't be a proper guidebook if we didn't include this landmark, a beautifully tiled bar where you can get one of the best *mojitos* in town. There are several service bars over the two crowded levels, and small tables are scattered here and there. There's no defining this mixed crowd, which gathers as much for Viva Madrid's fame as for its friendly atmosphere.

LA LATINA & LAVAPIÉS

This largely working-class area is overflowing with bars, especially around Calle de la Cava Baja and Plaza de la Cebada. Expect these places to be crowded any time, but they're especially popular on Sunday mornings, when young and old alike head out for a little pre-lunch aperitif (see boxed text p147).

BONANNO Map pp270-2

☎ 91 366 68 86; Plaza del Humilladero 4; ☾ noon-2am Sun-Thu, noon-2.30am Fri & Sat; Metro La Latina

Due to the Madrileños genetic aversion to sleep, it can be hard to find a bar with buzz before midnight. Not so in Bonanno, a stylish cocktail bar that has quickly become wildly popular with young professional Madrileños. It gets crowded early, so be prepared to snuggle up close to those around you if you want a spot at the bar.

EL VIAJERO Map pp270-2

☎ 91 366 90 64; Plaza de la Cebada 11; ☾ 1pm-12.30am Tue-Thu & Sun, 1pm-1am Fri & Sat; Metro La Latina

You can get an informal dinner downstairs (tapas €3.50 to €8), but even better is the bar upstairs, a dark, low-key place overlooking the plaza and the glorious Iglesia de San Pedro. In summer we might suggest you head up one floor to the rooftop terrace, where the view is unbeatable.

TABERNA CHICA Map pp270-2

☎ 91 364 53 48; Costanilla de San Pedro 7; ☾ 8pm-2.30am Mon-Thu, 7pm-2.30am Fri, Sat & Sun 12.30pm-2.30am; Metro La Latina

Most of those who come to this narrow little bar are after one thing, the famous Santa Teresa rum that comes served in an extra-large mug. The mood is chill and tables at the front and back are perfect for conversation in the early evening or for a rest if the rum proves too much.

VINOS EL MENTIDERO Map pp270-2

☎ 91 354 64 92; Calle del Almendro 22; ☾ 7pm-2am Mon-Fri, 1pm-2.30am Sat & Sun; Metro La Latina

Get the night started at this fun flamenco bar, where tapas and other goodies are served around the bustling upstairs bar. Downstairs is somewhat more low-key, a place where groups of friends huddle around tall barrels that serve as tables. House wine is just €1.80, and tapas run from €3 to €8.

MALASAÑA & CHUECA

Malasaña and Chueca are two different neighbourhoods with two very different attitudes, especially when it comes to drinking habits. Both are laid-back, lively and sure to offer a good time, but the fact that we've included the two together on the map doesn't erase their quirky peculiarities.

Tempting wine bottles at Vinoteca Barbechera (p145)

Chueca caters to the black-clad and stylish, and is a magnet for Madrid's gay crowd. It goes without saying that most bars here are gay-friendly, but few are strictly gay, and partiers of all preferences have fun here. Malasaña is the stomping ground of grunge kids and leftover *rockeros* from the 1980s. This was the heart of *la movida* movement of the 1980s (see boxed text p150) and the rebellious spirit still lives on in many places here.

ANTIK CAFÉ Map pp266-7
☎ 620 427168; Calle de la Hortaleza 4 & 6;
🕑 10am-3am; Metro Gran Vía
A cross between an old-style gentleman's club and a chic café, this bar-by-night, tearoom-by-day is a dark, smoky place perfect for a drink and some quiet conversation. Head downstairs to the old cellar, a dungeon-like space tastefully decorated in an Asian motif. Gay owned and operated, it draws a sophisticated crowd.

AREIA Map pp266-7
☎ 91 310 03 07; www.areiachillout.com in Spanish;
Calle de la Hortaleza 92; 🕑 noon-3am; Metro Chueca
Take your shoes off and chill on the comfy bed-like couches at this bar, where an Arabian vibe dominates the décor and chill-out music drifts up to the rafters. In the afternoon, get a light lunch, tea, juice or beer (€1.50). At nigh the music takes over, turning this groovy spc into a low-key cocktail lounge with dancin after midnight on weekends.

BAR COCK Map pp266-7
☎ 91 532 28 26; Calle de la Reina 16; 🕑 7pm-3am
Mon-Thu, 7pm-3.30am Fri & Sat; Metro Gran Vía
Although it looks drab from the street, the ele gant Bar Cock (that's cock as in rooster, for a of you with dirty minds, and the lower level i full of drawings and paintings of it) is one c Madrid's classic bars and almost always offer

---

Dancing in the Street

Ever wonder as you wander the streets of Madrid at night what's going on with all those bright young adolescents partying outdoors? They call it the *botellón* (big bottle) and it involves hordes of high schoolers lurching around with huge bottles of beer, bought cheap at supermarkets. They commandeer plazas and street corners, making it hard for neighbours to sleep at night and leaving behind disgusting quantities of trash.

Although the government has banned the *botellón* by making a 'dry law' that decrees drinking in the streets illegal, the practice continues, especially around the Avenida de Brasil, though little by little it's losing popularity.

lively atmosphere. It has the look of an old gentleman's club and is popular with A-listers and a refined older crowd looking for good drinks and funky music.

BODEGA LA ARDOSA Map pp266-7

☎ 91 521 49 79; Calle de Colón 13; ⏰ noon-1.30am; Metro Tribunal or Chueca

The bleeping techno music and lighting contrasts sharply with the tiled walls and traditional look of the bodega, which has old wine bottles and beer cans stacked high behind the wooden bar. A mixed crowd is drawn by the unpretentious attitude and good drinks.

CAFÉ ACUARELA Map pp266-7

☎ 91 522 21 43; Calle de Gravina 10; ⏰ 11am-2am Sun-Thu, 11am-3am Fri & Sat; Metro Chueca

By day an elegant tea room, by night a quiet bar, the Acuarela's dimly-lit salon is a great place for relaxing conversation and evocative eye-catching. Give a wave to the bar's symbol, a huge statue of a nude male angel that guards the doorway.

CAFÉ BELÉN Map pp266-7

☎ 91 308 24 47; Calle de Belén 5; ⏰ 3.30pm-3am; Metro Chueca

With its low, romantic music and dim lighting, the Café Belén is the perfect place when all you want is a nice drink and some nice conversation. It doesn't get any lower key.

CAFÉ PEPE BOTELLA Map pp266-7

☎ 91 522 43 09; Calle de San Andrés 12; ⏰ 11am-2.30am; Metro Bilbao or Tribunal

A quirky spot to start the night, this classy bar has green velvet benches, marble-topped tables and old photos and mirrors covering

the walls. The faded elegance gives the place charm that's made it one of the most popular drinking holes in the *barrio*.

DEL DIEGO Map pp266-7

☎ 91 523 31 06; Calle de la Reina 12; ⏰ 7pm-3am Mon-Thu, 7pm-3.30am Fri & Sat; Metro Gran Vía, Banco de España or Sevilla

Bow-tied waiters stir classic cocktails at the bar while an older, relaxed crowd squashes around the small tables scattered about. Opened by an ex-waiter from Museo del Chicote, this has become something of a Madrid classic. The wall of old liquor and brandy bottles (a pretty sight in itself) was featured in the Spanish film *Amor, Curiosidad, Prozac & Dudas* (Love, Curiosity, Prozac & Doubts).

FINNEGAN'S Map pp266-7

☎ 91 310 05 21; Plaza de las Salesas 9; ⏰ 1pm-2am; Metro Chueca

The bartender claims he knows just about everyone who comes in here, and it's easy to see why. The friendly crowd (mostly regulars) will make it their business to know who you are and what you'd like to drink, so head on in and join the mixed group of Spaniards and expats at the bar.

LA IDA Map pp266-7

☎ 91 522 91 07; Calle de Colón 7; ⏰ 9am-2am Mon-Fri, 11am-2am Sat & Sun; Metro Tribunal or Chueca

Mismatched furniture, arty black-and-white photos, and green walls set the tone at this friendly bar, which draws a surprising number of customers with multiple face piercings. Hopping most nights of the week, this is a good place to meet up with friends, and it's known for having great *mojitos*.

LA PALMERA Map pp266-7

Calle de la Palma 67; ⏰ 9am-2am Tue-Sat; Metro Tribunal

A tiny bar covered in blue and yellow tiles, La Palmera draws an artsy crowd who come to sit at the small wooden tables and nurse a drink or two. The atmosphere is very low-key, though the place is so popular that it's often noisy.

LA VACA AUSTERA Map pp266-7

☎ 91 523 14 87; Calle de la Palma 20; ⏰ 10pm-late Mon-Sat; Metro Tribunal

With its feet still firmly planted in *la movida* atmosphere of the 1980s, this dirty old bar

Relaxing in Cafe Acuarela (p147)

has a warehouse feel and isn't for everyone, but it's a totally unpretentious place to hear alternative rock music.

LA VÍA LACTEA Map pp266-7
☎ 91 446 75 81; Calle de Velarde 18; ✆ 7.30pm-3am; Metro Tribunal

Eyeshadow for boys and girls is the order of the day at this 1980s-style bar, a grungy place that was one of the mainstays of the *movida*. Expect to find a mixed, informal crowd and a good drink selection.

MAMÁ INÉS Map pp266-7
☎ 91 523 23 33; www.mamaines.com in Spanish; Calle de la Hortaleza 22; ✆ 10am-2am Sun-Thu, 10am-3.30am Fri & Sat; Metro Chueca

With its low lights and low music, this café-bar has a romantic air by night and is a popular spot for gay men to meet up before heading out at night. By day you can get breakfast, yummy pastries and all the gossip on where that night's hot spot will be.

MEDINA MAGERIT Map pp266-7
☎ 91 448 34 57; Calle del Divino Pastor 21; ✆ 6.30pm-late; Metro Bilbao

This very cool, laid-back bar plays chill-out music until late and is full of nooks and crannies where you can snuggle in for the night.

Its Art Deco décor is best appreciated early ii the night, when you can stop by for a casua cocktail or a tea.

MUSEO CHICOTE Map pp266-7
☎ 91 532 67 37; Gran Vía 12; ✆ 7.25am-late; Metro Gran Vía

Frequented by film stars and top socialites, th is one of Madrid's classic bars. After midnigh a lounge atmosphere takes over, and couple cuddle on the curved benches while groups o friends chat over drinks and some of the city' best DJs spin. Come earlier in the day for simple drink and a look at photos of celebritie who've passed through.

STOP MADRID Map pp266-7
☎ 91 521 88 87; Calle de la Hortaleza 11; ✆ 12.30-4pm & 6.30pm-2am; Metro Gran Vía

According to the owner, the house specialt is 'a friendly atmosphere', and we couldn' agree more. Squeeze your way through thi old tavern to the bar, where you can get beer or a drink and a plate of tasty Spanish *jamón* (cured ham).

THE QUIET MAN Map pp266-7
☎ 91 523 46 89; Calle de Valverde 44; ✆ 6pm-2am Mon-Thu, 2pm-3.30am Fri-Sun; Metro Tribunal or Chueca

One of the first bars outside Ireland to serve Guinness beer, the Quiet Man is an institutior in Madrid, a spacious, dark bar where you car play darts, have a seat on the refined velvet benches or park yourself at the bar.

SALAMANCA & LAS VENTAS

Madrid's most exclusive neighbourhood. Salamanca is all about gloss and glamour. Don't even think about heading here unless you've dressed the part; that means heels for her and hair gel for him. If the *pijo* (a little snobby) crowds don't win you over, you can always have fun trying to spot the Real Madrid players who hang out here.

INDEPENDENCIA Map pp268-9
☎ 91 781 95 40; Calle de Salustiano Olózaga 11; ✆ 8am-6am Metro Retiro

This is one of those places where you can eat breakfast, then stay on for lunch, coffee, tapas, cocktails and dancing. The bar gets lively around 11pm, when the music is turned up a notch and the crowd (who seem to like the shots of '80s hit TV shows played on the extra-large TV screen) starts moving. Dancing comes later.

L LATERAL Map pp262-4
☎ 91 435 06 04; Calle de Velázquez 57 (other branches at Paseo de la Castellana 132 & Fuencarral 3); ☽ 10am-1am Sun-Thu, until late Fri & Sat; Metro Velázquez or Nuñez de Balboa

It doesn't get much more *pijo* than this chic bar, where wearing hair gel seems to be required for entry. Still, it's a popular place to see and be seen, and the drinks here (accompanied by original tapas) are better than most.

TERRABACUS VINOTECA Map pp262-4
☎ 91 435 37 18; Calle de Lagasca 74; ☽ 1pm-midnight Mon-Sun; Metro Serrano or Velázquez

This stylish wine bar offers more than 60 wines by the glass, and has some 300 more labels you can try by the bottle. If a tasting at the bar isn't enough for you, sign up for their club to get wine news and invites to formal tastings.

THE GEOGRAPHIC CLUB Map pp262-4
☎ 91 578 08 62; Calle de Acalá 141; ☽ 6.30pm-1.30am Sun-Wed, 6.30pm-2am Thu, 5pm-3am Fri & Sat; Metro Retiro

With its elaborate stained-glass windows and mountain explorer theme, this is an atmospheric place for a happy hour drink. Sip at a table on the main floor (like the one built around an old hot-air balloon basket) or head down to the cavern-like pub. There is a restaurant here too.

CHAMBERÍ & ARGÜELLES

Argüelles is popular with university students (the *Zona Universitaria* – University District – is nearby), so you'll find a youngish crowd in many bars here. The hot spots are along the Paseo de Pintor Rosales, where *terrazas* (see boxed text p144) draw crowds on summer evenings, and, in Chamberí, around the Bilbao metro station.

EL CONFIDENCIAL Map pp262-4
Calle de Eduardo Dato 8; ☽ 11pm-5.30am Wed-Sat; Metro Rubén Darío

An upscale *bar de copas*, this place attracts a trendy, well-dressed crowd.

THE TEMPLE Map pp262-4
Plaza Conde Valle Súchil 3; ☽ 8pm-2am; Metro San Bernardo

Walk down the slate steps into this cosy, friendly Irish pub. Wooden choir-stall-like benches give the place a gothic look, and the darkish sitting area in back is perfect for getting lost in a Guinness.

CLUBS & DISCOS

In Madrid, 'night' is a relative term. No matter what their official opening time, don't expect dance clubs to get really going until at least 1am, and some won't even bat an eyelash until 3am. By the time they finally close down at dawn, early risers will already be on their way to work.

To party like the Madrileños and live to tell about it in the morning, remember that pace is everything. Start the night slow and late, with dinner at 10-ish (do be careful with that sleep-inducing Spanish red wine) and the first bar stop around midnight. Take your time with your drinks (bartenders are known for their generous swigs) and by 2am you'll be in the perfect mood to get lost in some dark, pulsating *discoteca*.

Club prices vary wildly, depending on the time of night you enter, the way you're dressed and the number of people inside. Most charge between €8 and €12 to enter, though mega clubs like Palacio Gaviria and swanky places like Moma 56 charge a few euros more. It's often easy to get discounts if you keep your eyes open for the stamped tickets lying in bars about town. You can also get a discount if you arrive early, or if you're a girl (sorry guys).

There's no *barrio* in Madrid without a decent club or disco, but the most popular dance spots are along and around Gran Vía. Classics such as the Palacio Gaviria, Joy Eslava, El Sol, Ohm and Cool are all here. For intimate dancing, head to Chueca or Malasaña, especially the Calle de la Palma, which is lined with quirky clubs.

Top Five Clubs
For...
- **Spotting beautiful people** Moma 56 (p153)
- **House music** Ya'sta (p153)
- **Live shows** Café La Palma (p152)
- **Latin music** El Son (p150)
- **Dancing till dawn** El Sol (p150)

LOS AUSTRIAS & CENTRO

A very mixed crowd heads out to Gran Vía, Calle de Arenal and the narrow streets in between, where most of the city's best-known dance clubs hide. The crowds make this area fairly safe, but it also serves as one of Madrid's major prostitution districts (especially along the Calle de Montcada) and feels seedy late at night.

ANTÍCAFE Map pp270-2

☎ 91 599 41 63; Calle de la Unión 2; ☼ 4pm-2am Sun-Thu, noon-2am Fri & Sat; Metro Ópera

This bar and club doesn't look all that different from dozens of others in the area (kitsch décor, flashy colours, casually cool), but the non-stop events going on here put this 'anti' café a step above the rest. New bands play regularly and there are comedy shows, poetry readings and DJs pumping out everything from Latin jazz to Brazilian or soul. In the afternoons, classic films take the stage.

EL PERRO DE LA PARTE ATRÁS DEL COCHE Map pp266-7

☎ 91 521 03 25; Calle de la Puebla 15; admission free; ☼ 10pm-4am Tue-Sat; Metro Callao

Known simply as 'El Perro' (the Dog), this bohemian bar (see Drinking p140) turns into a light-hearted club late in the evening. DJs like 'The Voodoo Child' grind out house for a few hours, but this is not a late-night stop.

EL SOL Map pp266-7

☎ 91 532 64 90; Calle de los Jardines 3; ☼ Tue-Sat 11.30pm-late; Metro Gran Vía

This ballroom-turned-disco is a great place to end the night. The low-key crowd grooves to a fun mixture of funk, rock and soul music, and there are live concerts most nights (concerts start at 11pm). Although mid-week there's not much going on, it's still a cool place for a drink and a little dancing.

EL SON Map pp270-2

☎ 91 532 32 83; Calle de la Victoria 6; ☼ 7pm-late; Metro Sol

If you're looking for salsa, merengue or som sexy tangos, look no further than El Son. This the top place in town for Latin music, and it very popular with Madrid's South and Centra American population. Live concerts Monda through Thursday keep the place packed a week long.

KATHMANDU Map pp270-2

www.clubkathmandu.com; Calle de los Señores de Luzón 3; admission €7; ☼ midnight-6am Thu-Sat; Metro Sol

Kathmandu claims to be the only club in Spai dedicated to promoting 'black music' in all it forms: funk, soul, hip-hop, acid jazz, breakbea and anything else they feel the whim to play With a very informal, laid-back atmosphere Kathmandu can be a great place to hang ou

LA VIUDA NEGRA Map pp266-7

☎ 91 548 75 29; Calle de Campomanes 6; ☼ 5-9pm Sun & Mon, 9pm-2am Tue & Wed, 9pm-3am Thu-Sat; Metro Ópera

This lounge-like cocktail bar (the Black Widow is minimalist enough for Manhattan and genu inely cool enough to earn its popularity ir Madrid. Eat at the sister restaurant La Viud Blanca next door (p123), then come here fo funky house music until late. On Sunday even ings (5-9pm) the Viudas host 'I Love Sundays a jazzy DJ session.

ARIOS CAFÉ Map pp262-4

☎ 91 547 93 94; Calle de Silva 4; ☺ 9pm-5am;
etro Gran Vía

he tranquil upstairs bar and restaurant, often
ith live music and always serving up tasty
ojitos, gives no sign of the hopping club
ownstairs, where the music goes on until
awn.

ASAPOGA Map pp266-7

☎ 91 532 16 44 & 91 547 57 11; Gran Vía 37;
☺ 6pm-late Tue-Sun, dance club starts late Fri & Sat;
etro Callao

his old baroque music hall is now a cool disco
hat attracts a fashionable, largely gay crowd
n weekends. A hidden stage emerges from
he floor for regular live concerts.

ALACIO GAVIRIA Map pp270-2

☎ 91 526 60 69; Calle del Arenal 9; ☺ 11pm-4am
on-Wed, 11pm-5.30am Thu-Sat, 8.30pm-2am Sun;
etro Sol

n elegant palace converted into one of the
nost popular dance clubs in Madrid, this is
he kind of place where you're guaranteed to
neet the locals, whether you want to or not.
hursdays are international student night; de-
ending on what you're looking for this could
e either a draw or a reason to stay away.

ALA BASH Map pp266-7

☎ 91 541 35 00; Plaza del Callao 4; ☺ midnight-6am
ed-Sun ; Metro Callao

un by the Trip Family of discos, this is a major
layer on Madrid's club scene, and every night
ffers a different atmosphere. Wednesdays
osts the hip-hop **Bash Line**, all-house **Cream**
akes over on Thursdays, sexy, gay-friendly **Ohm**
s on Saturday nights and upbeat **Week-end** fills
he place on Sundays.

UITE Map pp266-7

☎ 91 521 40 31; Calle de la Virgen de los Peligros 4;
☺ 1-5pm & 9pm-3.30am Mon-Sat; Metro Sevilla

his retro bar is currently one of the trendiest
n the area (as a glance at the slickly dressed
nd mainly gay crowd will show). You can stop
y for a drink or get the night started in the
iny club upstairs, where quality house music
eeps things moving.

TEATRO JOY ESLAVA Map pp270-2

☎ 91 366 37 33; www.joy-eslava.com in Spanish;
alle del Arenal 11; ☺ midnight-6am; Metro Sol
r Ópera

A hit with locals, tourists and the occasional
famoso (celebrity), this classic disco claims that
it's opened every single day for the past 20
years. Housed in a 19th-century theatre, Joy
has an endearing scruffy elegance.

HUERTAS & ATOCHA

One of the liveliest *barrios* in Madrid, this
district is given over more to bars and live
music joints than to dance clubs, but stick
around after the pub crawl and you'll definitely find a place to get your groove on.

DUCADOS CAFÉ Map pp270-2

☎ 91 360 00 89; Plaza de Canalejas 3; ☺ noon-2am;
Metro Sevilla

If there's a constant here, it's the promise that
the music, whatever the style, will get you
groovin'. DJs roll through hip-hop, house, funk
and soul but always find a way to keep the
crowd happy. The upstairs bar is open all day
for tapas or snacks, though at night it becomes
a chill bar. Since there's no cover charge, this is
a great place to start the night.

KAPITAL Map p273

☎ 91 420 29 06; Calle de Atocha 125; ☺ until 6am
Thu-Sun; Metro Atocha

Can't make up your mind between salsa and
hip-hop? No problem. Just head to Kapital, a
humongous (no exaggeration) seven-storey
discoteca where every floor offers a different
mood. The crowd is mixed, but early in the
night expect to see a lot of young preppy
types. Don't miss the rooftop club in summer;
the retractable roof gives you a great view of
the night sky. If you want to get the night
started early, head to the evening session from
5.30pm until 11pm, where you can expect to
find lots of teens shaking their thing. On Sundays Kapital becomes 'Kapital Love', drawing
a less touristy crowd that has no intention of
going to work on Monday.

Drinking & Nightlife – Clubs & Discos

MONDO Map pp270-2

www.theroomclub.com in Spanish; Calle de Arlabán 7;
☾ 1am- until late Thu; Metro Sevilla

The Sala Stella's Thursday-night party, Mondo is leading the charge in the recent boom of electro-edged tunes. The rest of the week it's home to one of the original (and best) clubs on Madrid's house circuit, **The Room** (hosted by Sala Stella) which has a great in-house DJ that mixes jazzy, funky house for a devoted crowd of regulars.

PASEO DEL PRADO & EL RETIRO

BABYLON Map pp268-9

☎ 629 066869; Paseo de los Recoletos 11; ☾ 11pm-4am Thu, 10pm-7am Fri & Sat; Metro Serrano

There's no one way to describe this popular club, where every night caters to a different crowd. Thursday night is Reggae Bus Stop. It's a great way to get the night started on the right foot. Fridays it's all about house music, with DJs like Señor Lobo (Mr Wolf) running the show at Toxic & Friends, while Saturdays hot Afro-Latino Music rules at DaJoint.

LA LATINA & LAVAPIÉS

DEEP Map pp262-4

Sala Divino; ☎ 91 470 24 61; Paseo de la Ermita del Santo 48; ☾ midnight-8.30am Fri; Metro Puerta del Ángel

The super-club of the Madrid scene, Deep has changed venues several times over the years but is more popular than ever in its home in Sala Divino. A youngish crowd keeps moving until daybreak and beyond, moving to the mixes of some of the best local and international DJs.

LA FALSA MOLESTIA Map pp270-2

Calle de la Magdalena 30; ☾ 7pm-3am Wed-Sat, 1pm-1am Sun; Metro Antón Martín

The crazy bar staff keeps things lively at this bar and club, where DJs start off weekend nights with quiet 'have a drink and chat' music and end them with an ear-throbbing dance-floor workout. On Saturdays, live vocals, instruments and percussion accompany the DJs tunes.

LA MUSA DE LA LATINA Map pp270-2

☎ 91 354 02 55; Costanilla de San Andres 12; ☾ 9pm-late Thu-Sun; Metro La Latina

La Musa has a divided soul. Upstairs, gorgeous waiting staff serve tasty, fresh food while downstairs a chic bar and club take over. The old cave-like bodega has been outfitted with chic blue-toned lights and fabulous bar area. We only wish there were more room to dance; on a popular night you have to move with your arms pinned to your sides.

MALASAÑA & CHUECA

From the jeans and torn T-shirts of Malasaña's rock 'n' roll joints to the spiffed-up largely gay crowds of Chueca's thumping clubs, these districts offer a great late-night atmosphere for just about anyone's taste.

CAFÉ LA PALMA Map pp266-7

☎ 91 522 50 31; Calle de la Palma 62; ☾ midnight-4am Thu-Sat; Metro Noviciado

It's amazing how much variety the Café la Palma has packed into its labyrinth of rooms. Live shows featuring hot local bands are held at the back, while DJs mix up the front. Some rooms have a café style, while others look like an Arab tea room, pillows on the floor and all. Every night is a little different, so expect to be surprised.

COOL Map pp266-7

☎ 91 542 34 39; ☾ midnight-late Thu-Sat, 9pm-late Sun; Calle Isabel la Católica 6, Metro Santo Domingo

One of the hottest clubs in the city, here you can expect to find gorgeous people, gorgeous clothes and a predictably strict entry policy. The sexy, well-heeled crowd includes a lot of sleek-looking gay men and model-like women.

CORTO MALTES Map pp266-7

☎ 91 531 13 17; Plaza del Dos de Mayo 9; ☾ 7.30pm-3am; Metro Tribunal or Noviciado

This is a great bar and disco with a totally split personality. On weekend nights the downstairs dance floor hosts a long, strong dose of house. Mid-week '80s rock 'n' roll tunes are the norm and drinks are served till late. In summer, one of the best terraces in the *barrio* stretches clear across the Plaza Dos de Mayo.

EL CLANDESTINO Map pp266-7

☎ 91 521 55 63; Calle del Barquillo 34; ☾ 6pm-3am, live concerts 11pm Thu-Sat; Metro Chueca

For a low-key drink and occasional live music, this funky bar is a good bet. A stylish crowd, *mojitos* in hand, grooves to funk and indie rock.

NASTI CLUB Map pp266-7

☎ 91 448 99 13; Calle de San Vicente Ferrer 35;
🕙 11pm-6am Thu-Sat; Metro Tribunal

This popular club has a different atmosphere and a different name) every weekend night. Thursdays is **Fiver**, while the Friday-night **Barbarella** is dedicated to 1980s pop. The night starts off with a live show, and the crowd takes it from there.

NATURE Map pp262-4

Calle Luchana; 🕙 midnight-6am Thu; Metro Bilbao

Truly a one-off in Madrid, Nature is a comeback club that may be the only place in the city to see breakdancers spinning on their heads and showing off their moves. Expect to hear lots of breakbeats and heavy percussion.

PACHÁ Map pp266-7

☎ 91 447 01 28; Calle de Barceló 11; 🕙 12.30-5am Thu-Sat; Metro Tribunal

This mega club is one of the international chain of clubs that earned its fame in Ibiza. Here in Madrid it's mostly frequented by the barely-out-of-school set, but the fun mixture of house, Latin and Spanish music continues to draw dancers of all ages and persuasions. Justin Timberlake did a concert here but don't let that put you off.

PENTA BAR Map pp266-7

☎ 91 447 84 60; www.elpenta.com in Spanish; Calle de la Palma 4; 🕙 9pm-3am; Metro Tribunal

One of the pillars of the *la movida*, this is an informal place where you can get a cheapish drink (€5) and groove to the '80s music you love to hate. The mixed crowd gets going around midnight, especially from Thursdays to Saturdays, when the house DJ keeps the tunes hopping.

SIROCO Map pp266-7

Calle de San Dimás 3; 🕙 midnight-6am Thu-Sat; Metro Noviciados

This funky retro club plays a mix of grooveable styles. Thursdays host The Bongo Club, a refreshing break from the house scene with hip-hop, acid jazz and occasional live acts. Weekends are back to house, but the atmosphere is great and the music top-notch.

SUNRISE Map pp266-7

☎ 91 522 43 17; Calle Barbieri 7; 🕙 until 6am; Metro Chueca

With its bright red walls and perky pop music, this mainly gay spot isn't for serious clubbers,

but it's a fun and friendly place to dance or meet new people.

TUPPERWARE Map pp266-7

☎ 91 446 42 04; Corredera Alta de San Pablo 26;
🕙 9pm-3am Sun-Wed, 9pm-3.30am Thu-Sat; Metro Tribunal

The atmosphere here is the ultimate in kitsch (huge eyeballs stuck to the ceiling, and plastic TVs with action figure dioramas inside are lined up behind the bar…but the atmosphere is fun and friendly. Although Tupperware has been around for a while, DJs are still pumping out a mix of soul, indie rock, and classics from the '60s and '70s.

WHY NOT Map pp266-7

Calle de San Bartolomé 7; 🕙 10.30pm-late; Metro Chueca

Narrow and packed with bodies, gay-friendly Why Not has the look and feel of the inside of a train car. The décor is elegant (carved wooden ceiling, photos of 1950s cinema greats…) but you won't notice because it's full nearly every night of the week. Pop and top 40s music are the standard here, and the dancing crowd is mixed and out to have a good time.

YA'STA Map pp266-7

☎ 651 894200; www.yastaclub.net; Calle de Valverde 10; 🕙 12.30am-until late; Metro Gran Vía

Yet another multi-personalitied club, Ya'sta is a popular place with sounds you won't hear elsewhere. Thursdays host Transgression, an electro session with everything from breakbeat to bleeping electronic trance music. Friday nights get back to basics with Free, dedicated to tribal sounds, and Saturdays are the all-trance Selenium.

SALAMANCA & LAS VENTAS

GARAMOND Map pp268-9

☎ 91 578 19 74; Calle de Claudio Coello 10; 🕙 6pm-3.30am Sun-Thu, 6pm-4.40am Fri &Sat; Metro Retiro

Better look snazzy, 'cause the doormen at this upscale club only let in those who've made an effort. Although it's aimed at a 30-plus crowd, the atmosphere is surprisingly charged and there seem to be enough hormones here to fill a school disco.

MOMA 56 Map pp262-4

☎ 91 395 20 59.; Calle de José Abascal 56; 🕙 midnight-6am Wed-Sat; Metro Gregorio Marañón

Two words: beautiful people. Packed with Prada-toting socialites, small-time celebrities and the owners of the flashy sports cars parked out front, this sleek new club is beyond modern. House music is brought to life by live percussion, and the snazzy atmosphere (red padded walls, red lighting…) is unique in Madrid. Expect to pay a little extra (around €15) for the privilege of being here.

SERRANO 41 Map pp262-4
☎ 91 578 18 65; Calle de Serrano 41; ☺ 10pm-5am Mon-Sat; Metro Serrano
A dance-able mix of R&B, house and Spanish pop have made this disco popular, and its location in the city's most fashionable district has made it a prime place to spot the likes of David Beckham and visiting pop star Robbie Williams. Stay upstairs for a drink, or head down to the lively but otherwise unremarkable dance floor.

CHAMBERÍ & ARGÜELLES
The nearby university campus makes this a popular area with the student crowd, though you'll also find some upscale clubs catering to the equally upscale residents around here.

BARNON BAR CLUB Map pp262-4
☎ 91 447 38 87; Calle de Santa Engracia 17; ☺ 9pm-6am Wed-Sun; Metro Alonso Martínez
Sunday night (midnight to dawn) is Black Sunday, a very cool session where you can hear some great rap and reggae.

CAMPUS BAR
Paseo Juan XXIII 22; ☺ 6pm-6am; Metro Metropolitano
This popular student hangout attracts foreign students like bees to honey with its combo of cheap drinks, Spanish music and theme parties. With the feel of an oversize warehouse the ambience is nothing special, but the mood is light and the crowd friendly.

CHESTERFIELD CLUB Map pp262-4
☎ 91 542 28 17; Calle de Serrano Jover 5; ☺ 2am-7am Fri & Sat; Metro Argüelles
On weekend nights (um, perhaps we'd better make that mornings) the Chesterfield Café becomes a popular club, with resident DJs Javier Chester and David Kem pumping out

some serious house. Wednesdays are student night with theme parties, drinking games and other gimmicks to get you guys to meet each other.

NORTHERN MADRID
IRISH ROVER Map p261
☎ 91 597 48 11; Avenida de Brasil 7; ☺ noon-2.30pm Sun-Thu, noon-5am Fri, 2pm-5am Sat; Metro Santiago Bernabéu
An Irish bar that wouldn't be out of place in Disneyland, the Irish Rover has fake Irish store-fronts and houses lining its walls. Yes, it's kitsch. But the place is always packed with a monied over-30 crowd, and it's a great place to meet new people.

LIVING Map p261
☎ 629 671582; www.living-copas.com in Spanish; Avendia del Brasil 5; ☺ 10pm-late Thu-Sat; Metro Santiago Bernabéu
With its bright décor and its clean-lined look, Living's chic atmosphere goes well with the fashionable, 30-something crowd that hangs out here. Dance and mingle downstairs or head up to a chill lounge where you can talk with a drink in hand.

LOLITA Map p261
☎ 91 344 11 56; www.lolitalounge.net in Spanish; Manuel de Falla 3 (with Paseo de la Castellana 150); ☺ 9pm-4.30am; Metro Santiago Bernabéu or Cuzco
Serving up fashionable cocktails to an equally fashionable crowd, Lolita provides a chic atmosphere for late-night drinks and heads bobbing to '70s-ish lounge music. Occasional special events, like film festivals, fashion shows and theatre performances, keep things lively.

SPACE Map p261
☎ 91 733 35 05; Plaza de la Estación de Chamartín; ☺ midnight-6am Sun; Metro Chamartín
A legend has died. Space, Madrid's mythic Sunday day club (matinal) once threw open its doors Sunday mornings and partied for a dazed and confused crowd until early evening. The party is still just as good – top international DJs ensure that – but the town hall has decreed that dancing before dark isn't good for the city's image, so Space stays shut tight until midnight on Sundays.

Entertainment

Entertainment

Madrid has a lively entertainment calendar, with concerts, festivals and sporting events going on constantly. The year's cultural highlight is the Fiesta de Otoño (p13) when music, theatre and dance fill the city. Summer is generally the slow season, as many performers seem to head off for holidays along with the rest of the country, though this is a great time to catch bullfights and sporting events.

What's On

To find out the current showings at Madrid's theatres, cinemas and concert halls, your best bets are local *ocio* (entertainment) publications. The best and best-known guide is the *Guía del Ocio*, a Spanish-only weekly magazine available for €1 at a news kiosk. Also keep an eye out for the monthly *Salir*, also €1 and in Spanish. The monthly English expat publication *In Madrid* is given out free and has lots of information about what to see and do in town. Find it at some hotels, original-version cinemas and English bookshops. Not as helpful but free and in English are *Vive Madrid* and *En Madrid/What's On*, both available at tourist offices and in some hotels.

The local press is always a good bet, with daily listings of films, concerts and special events. On Fridays pick up *El Mundo's* supplement magazine *Metropoli* for additional information on the week's offerings. Specialised publications, like the free all-flamenco *Alma 100*, available in *tablaos* and flamenco shops, or the free theatre guide *Teatros*, available in local venues, are helpful too.

To get the latest on who Real Madrid is up against or which big-name bullfighters will be in the ring this Sunday, check out daily newspapers and individual teams' websites (listed below). Sports-only dailies like the aptly named *Sport* and *Marca* are wildly popular and will give you the inside scoop on upcoming matches and events, if you read in Spanish that is.

Getting Tickets & Booking From Abroad

There's no excuse for not finding tickets to events on in Madrid. You can buy cinema, theatre, operas or concert tickets *(entradas)* at box offices (see listings in individual sections), at some music stores, by phone, online and even at La Caixa ATMs. Hotels (three stars and up) can usually help with bookings too.

If you're booking from abroad, you can buy tickets at some of the websites listed here or through Caixa Catalunya's Tel-Entrada. Phone numbers that begin with 902 can be dialled from within Spain only.

For details on getting tickets for sporting events, see the Sports, Health & Fitness section (p163).

The city's major ticket vendors are:

Madrid Rock (☎ 91 521 02 39; Gran Vía 25; ☺ 10.30am-3pm & 4.30-8.30pm Mon-Sat; Metro Gran Vía) This music mega store has tickets to most big-name concerts.

FNAC (☎ 91 595 62 00; www.fnac.es in Spanish; Calle de Preciados 28; ☺ 10am-9pm Mon-Sat, noon-9.30pm Sun; Metro Santo Domingo) A multi-floored store selling books, CDs and electronics, it also sells tickets for events throughout Madrid.

El Corte Inglés (☎ 91 379 80 00; www.elcorteingles.es in Spanish; throughout city; ☺ 10am-9pm Mon-Sat) El Corte Inglés has it all, even event tickets.

Servicaixa (☎ 90 233 22 11; www.servicaixa.com in Spanish) You can also get tickets in Servicaixa ATMs .

Caixa Catalunya's Tel-Entrada (☎ 90 210 12 12; if calling from outside Spain ☎ 93 326 29 46) Buy the tickets by phone then pick them up at the box office.

Entradas.com (☎ 90 248 84 88; www.entradas.com in Spanish)

Before you get to Madrid, you can check out the scene online. The *Guia del Ocio*'s site (www.guiadelocio.com) is a virtual version of the publication, and it has some information in English. Also helpful is the extremely complete guide *La Netro* (http://madrid.lanetro .com), with info in Spanish. The Madrid page of www.whatsonwhen.com hits the highlights (in English) of sports and cultural activities. It includes information on getting tickets too. The town hall's website (www.munimadrid.com) has practical details for nearly all the city's theatres and stages.

FLAMENCO

Flamenco didn't start in Madrid, but it was here that the Andalucian art gained a broader following and international attention, and the city has long been a platform for some of flamenco's top dancers, guitarists and singers. Locals say that the offer is not what it was a decade ago, but there are still plenty of flamenco stages to choose from, and overall the quality is as good as you'll find anywhere in the world.

The most accessible flamenco shows are in *tablaos*, small stages that often double as restaurants and are geared toward tourists. Although they're pricey (€25 and up), here you'll see all three elements of the art (dancing, singing and guitar) and you'll probably be sitting close enough to the stage to see the sweat dripping off the dancers. For something more informal, there are numerous flamenco bars and *peñas flamencas* scattered throughout Lavapiés and La Latina. This is where performers hang out, and although shows aren't planned, some spontaneous music may start up after midnight. Festivals are another place to find flamenco; February's Festival Flamenco (p10) is the city's biggest flamenco bash, but flamenco also forms part of other city fiestas that dot Madrid's cultural calendar like the polka dots on frilly flamenco dresses.

You can usually buy same-day tickets at the door, though on a springtime Saturday night or during a holiday weekend you'll want to call ahead to make a reservation. Hotels can sometimes help you find a spot at sold-out shows.

CAFÉ DE CHINITAS Map pp266-7
☎ 91 547 15 02; Calle de Torija 7; admission €32; ⏰ 9pm-2.30am Mon-Sat, show 10.30pm; Metro Santo Domingo

For a high-end flamenco show in an elegant setting, this traditional *tablao* is the perfect choice. It attracts top performers and big crowds, so book in advance.

CANDELA Map pp270-2
☎ 91 467 33 82; Calle del Olmo 2; ⏰ 10pm-2am; Metro Antón Martín

Many of Madrid's young performers hang out at this informal bar, and spontaneous music often breaks out late in the evening. To see Candela at its best, come after 1am and be respectful of the atmosphere.

CARDAMOMO Map pp270-2
☎ 913 69 07 57; www.cardamomo.net in Spanish; Calle de Echegaray 15; admission free; ⏰ 9pm-4am; Metro Sevilla

The place to go if you want to do more than just watch flamenco, here you can dance, clap and even sing along (the crowd is so thick no one will mind you anyway).

Flamenco and flamenco-fusion tunes are played until late, and Wednesday nights there are live shows.

CASA PATAS Map pp270-2
☎ 91 369 04 96; www.casapatas.com; Calle de Cañizares 10; admission about €30; ⏰ noon-5pm & 8pm-3am, shows 10.30pm Mon-Thu, 9pm & midnight Fri & Sat; Metro Antón Martín

One of the top flamenco stages in Madrid, this restaurant and *tablao* is a good place for an introduction to the art. Although it's geared toward tourists, locals stop by too for a glass of the tasty house wine and a soul-filling session of passionate music and dance. They also hold classes here.

CORRAL DE LA MORERÍA Map pp262-4
☎ 91 365 84 46; www.corraldelamoreria.com; Calle de la Morería 17; admission €30; ⏰ 8.30pm-2am, show 10pm; Metro Ópera

For a top-quality show that doesn't take itself too seriously, head to the Corral. The stage area has a rustic feel, and tables are pushed up close to the small stage so that you never feel far from the action.

LAS TABLAS Map pp266-7

☎ 91 542 05 20; Plaza de España 9; admission €12-15; ☽ 7pm- until late, show 10.30pm; Metro España

The newest *tablao* stage in town, Las Tablas has quickly earned a reputation for quality flamenco. Most nights you'll see a classic flamenco show, with plenty of throaty singing and soul-baring dancing, though the venue also hosts fusion concerts featuring jazz or soul musicians.

LOS GABRIELES Map pp270-2

☎ 91 429 62 61; Calle de Echegaray 17; ☽ 1pm-2.30am Sun-Thu, 1pm-3.30am Fri & Sat; Metro Sevilla

Smothered in pretty coloured tile, this is a classic flamenco bar that's drifted from its roots. Although Los Gabrieles operates as a standard *caña* and *copas* place most nights of the week, there are occasional live show performances.

DANCE & BALLET

Spain's dynamic Compañía Nacional de Danza, under director Nacho Duato, performs worldwide and has won accolades for its marvellous technicality and style. The company, made up mostly of international dancers, performs original, contemporary pieces and is considered a main player on the international dance scene.

Madrid is also home to the Ballet Nacional de España, a classical company that's known for its unique mix of ballet and traditional Spanish styles such as flamenco and zarzuela. Both companies perform more often abroad than at home. When in town their works are staged in major venues; check newspapers for listings.

THEATRE

Autumn is the busiest season for Madrileño theatre, but shows worth seeing are going on year-round. Most shows are in Spanish, but those who don't speak the language may still enjoy musicals or zarzuela, Spain's own singing and dancing version of musical theatre. Tickets for all shows start at around €10 and run up to around €50. Most of the time you can get 'day-of' tickets at the box office, but for new, popular or weekend shows you'll need to book ahead. Note that box offices are usually closed Mondays and sometimes Tuesdays, when there are no shows. Other days, they are generally open from about 10am until 1pm and again from 5pm until the start of the night's show.

These theatres are just a handful of those in Madrid. For complete listings pick up local newspapers, *ocio* guides or the free magazine *Teatros*.

CENTRO CULTURAL DE LA VILLA
Map pp268-9

☎ 91 575 60 80; Plaza de Colón; Metro Colón or Serrano

Located under the waterfall at Plaza de Colón, the Centro Cultural stages everything from classical-music concerts to comic theatre, opera and quality flamenco performances.

TEATRO ALBÉNIZ Map p270-2

☎ 91 531 83 11; Calle de la Paz 11; Metro Sol

Usually staging popular Spanish dramas with well-known casts, the Albéniz also hosts the Caja Madrid flamenco festival in late winter and is one of the primary stages of the city's Festival de Otoño.

TEATRO ALFIL Map pp266-7

☎ 91 521 45 41; Calle del Pez 10; Metro Noviciado

Staging a broad range of alternative and experimental theatre, this is a good place to catch up-and-coming Spanish actors and comedians.

TEATRO ARLEQUÍN Map pp266-7

☎ 91 559 43 22; Calle de San Bernardo 5; Metro Santo Domingo

From comedy to conventional theatre, you'll find a good selection of mostly local shows at this intimate theatre off Gran Vía.

TEATRO DE BELLAS ARTES Map pp270-2

☎ 91 532 44 37; Calle del Marqués de Casa Riera 2; Metro Banco de España

Elegant and refined, this theatre leans towards the classics, both national and international.

TEATRO ESPAÑOL Map pp270-2

☎ 91 360 14 80; Calle del Príncipe 25; Metro Sevilla

This is a good choice for mainstream Spanish drama. A theatre has stood on this spot since 1583, when it was known as the Corral del Príncipe. It later became the Teatro del Príncipe and in 1849 was renamed the Teatro Español.

TEATRO PAVÓN Map pp270-2
☎ 91 528 28 19; Calle de los Embajadores 9; Metro La Latino or Tirso de Molina
The home of the National Classical Theatre Company, this theatre nearly always puts on

classical shows by Spanish and European playwrights. Proof that quality never goes out of fashion.

TEATRO COLISEUM Map pp266-7
☎ 91 547 66 12; Gran Vía 78; Metro Plaza de España
One of the larger theatres in the city, here you can expect to see major productions, often of Broadway or West End hits such as, most recently, *Cats*.

Main Hall of Teatro Real (p160)

CLASSICAL MUSIC & OPERA

For all its frenzied partying, Madrid is after all a fairly traditional capital. Tried-and-true classical music takes over most of the city's main stages, and orchestras from throughout Europe perform regularly. Madrid's own Orquesta Sinfónica (www.osm.es) is a splendid orchestra that normally performs (or accompanies) in the Teatro Real.

AUDITORIO NACIONAL DE MÚSICA
Map p261
☎ 91 337 01 00; www.auditorionacional.mcu.es; Calle del Príncipe de Vergara 146; Metro Cruz del Rayo
Resounding to the sounds of classical music, this modern venue offers a varied calendar of classical music led by conductors from all over the world. In season, there are concerts

here almost every day, and you can usually get day-of tickets at the box office.

FUNDACIÓN JUAN MARCH Map pp262-4
☎ 91 435 42 40; www.march.es; Calle de Castelló 77; Metro Nuñez de Balbao
A foundation dedicated to promoting music and culture, the Juan March stages six free

La Zarzuela

What began in the late 17th century as a way to amuse King Felipe IV and his court has become one of Spain's most unique theatre styles. With a light-hearted combination of music and dance, and a focus on everyday people's problems, zarzuelas quickly became popular in the capital and Madrileños' fondness for the genre has only faded slightly since. Although you'll likely have trouble following the storyline (zarzuelas are notoriously full of local references and jokes), seeing a zarzuela gives an entertaining look into local culture. Catch a show at the Teatro de la Zarzuela (below).

concerts each week, each corresponding to a different concert series. Saturdays at noon there are solo concerts, while theme concerts (a series dedicated to a single style or composer) are on Wednesday evenings.

TEATRO DE LA ZARZUELA Map pp270-2
☎ 91 524 54 00; Calle de Jovellanos 4; Metro Banco de España

This 1856 theatre is the premier place to see zarzuela, a very Spanish mix of theatre, music and dance. The theatre also hosts mainstream shows, as well as a smattering of classical music and opera.

TEATRO MONUMENTAL Map pp270-2
☎ 91 429 12 81 or 91 429 81 19; Calle de Atocha 65; Metro Antón Martín

The main concert season runs from October through March, when concerts and occasional operas or zarzuelas show off this modern theatre's fabulous acoustics.

TEATRO REAL Map pp270-2
☎ 91 516 06 06; www.teatro-real.com in Spanish; Plaza de Oriente; Metro Ópera

After spending €100 million-plus on a long rebuilding project, the Teatro Real is as technologically advanced as any venue in Europe and is without a doubt the city's grandest stage. Elaborate operas and occasional ballets are shown in this luxurious theatre, and tickets are among the priciest in town. To see opera or ballet you'll pay as little as €15 for a spot so far away you will need a telescope, to more than €100. You can buy tickets through the theatre's website or through www.entradas.com (see the boxed text p156).

Entertainment – Cinema

CINEMA

Madrileños love to go to the movies, especially on Sunday evenings when just about every *sala* in town is packed. Most people buy tickets at the door, but to ensure a seat for a popular showing it's a good idea to buy ahead of time, either by phone or at a Servicaixa ATM (see the boxed text p156). Regular tickets cost about €5.60, though on the *día de espectador* (spectator's day), which varies according to theatre, there's a discount.

'V.O.' denotes an original version film, and you'll find plenty of them in the capital. On and around Calle de la Princesa are throngs of cinemas, offering Spanish and foreign films in their original versions.

ALPHAVILLE Map pp266-7
☎ 91 559 38 36; Calle de Martín de los Heros 14; Metro Plaza de España

Original-language films from France, the UK, the US and elsewhere, with a penchant for the quirky.

CINE DORÉ Map pp270-2
☎ 91 549 00 11; Calle de Santa Isabel 3; Metro Antón Martín

Home to the Filmoteca Nacional (national film library), this is a wonderful old cinema that shows classics past and present, all in the original language and at the rock bottom price of €1.35. There's also a cheap restaurant and a library (🕐 5-10.30pm) that's open to the public. Four movies are shown nightly, the first one at 5.30pm and the last around 10pm.

CINE IMAX Map p260
☎ 91 467 48 00; Camino de Meneses; Metro Méndez Álvaro

This 3D mega-screen is in the Parque Enrique Tierno Galván, south of Atocha train station. Movies like *Alien Adventure* and *The Human Body* cost €7.

LA ENANA MARRÓN Map pp266-7
☎ 91 308 14 97; www.laenanamarron.org; Travesía de San Mateo 8; Metro Alonso Martínez or Tribunal

A great arty, alternative theatre showing everything from documentaries to animated films, international flicks and oldies.

PRINCESA Map pp266-7
☎ 915 41 41 00; Calle de Princesa 3;
Metro Plaza de España
With a mix of commercial and alternative cinema from Europe and elsewhere, most (but not all) of what's shown here are original-version, subtitled films.

RENOIR Map pp266-7
☎ 91 541 41 00; Calle de Martín de los Heros 12;
Metro Plaza de España
Make a note of this cinema. One thing's for certain, you never know what you'll find here. From documentaries to Asian flicks, there is always something interesting to watch, and there are always original-version films in the mix. Renoir has another branch on Calle de Raimundo Fernández Villaverde 10 (Metro Cuatro Caminos).

LIVE MUSIC
The quality of live shows in Madrid is getting better every year, and there's more variety and more international headliners than ever. Although many bars and clubs (see Drinking & Nightlife, pp141-54) have occasional live shows, the places listed here are known primarily for their concerts. Ticket prices can vary wildly according to the venue and who's performing there. For ticket and reservation information, see the boxed text (p156) at the start of this chapter.

MEGA VENUES
Madrid is a major stop on the European concert tour, and big-name performers from the US, UK and elsewhere make appearances often.

AUDITORIO PARQUE JUAN CARLOS I
Map p260
☎ 91 721 00 79; Avenida de Logroño; Metro Campo de las Naciones
A large auditorium in the midst of the green expanse of the Parque Juan Carlos I, this is a popular venue for big-name concerts. Recent performers include Bjork.

ESTADIO DE LA COMUNIDAD DE MADRID Map p260
☎ 91 720 24 00; Avenida de Arecntales;
Metro Las Musas
Bruce Springsteen and Bon Jovi are just a couple of the rockers who've taken the stage at 'La Peineta' (the stadium's nickname referring to the comb-like shape of the central stage). Truly a mega-venue (the place seats 20,000), there are only a few concerts here each season.

PLAZA DE TOROS MONUMENTAL DE LAS VENTAS Map p260
☎ 91 356 22 00; Calle de Alcalá 237; Metro Ventas
Madrid's main bullring makes a great venue for outdoor concerts. Headliners play here throughout the spring and summer.

JAZZ
Madrid is home to some surprisingly good jazz venues. Calle 54 is the place to be for Latin jazz, and the Café Central has classical and fusion shows every night of the week. You'll pay about €10 to get in most places, but special concerts can run up to €20 or more.

CALLE 54 Map p261
☎ 90 214 14 12 or 91 561 28 32; Paseo de la Habana 3; ⏱ 1pm-late; Metro Nuevos Ministerios or Santiago Bernabeu
Offering soul-satisfying Latin jazz, this wildly popular restaurant (see p138) and bar is responsible for putting Madrid on the European jazz circuit. Partly owned by filmmaker Fernando Trueba, whose movie Calle 54 (see boxed text p163) was its inspiration, it's an upscale (ie pricey) place that attracts a mixed audience of musicians, film stars and locals. Live shows start around 11pm.

> ### Top Five Live Music Venues
> For...
> - **Jazz** Calle 54 (above)
> - **Atmosphere** La Riviera (p163)
> - **Concerts under the stars** Plaza de Toros Monumentas de las Ventas (opposite)
> - **Screaming fans** Sala Caracol (p163)
> - **Folk tunes** Clamores (p162)

All that jazz! Saaha Sokol Band at Calle 54 (p161)

CLAMORES Map pp262-4

☎ 91 445 79 38; Calle de Alburquerque 14; ☽ 6pm-3am Sun-Thu, 6pm-4am Fri & Sat; Metro Bilbao

A jazz café that doesn't mind mixing pop, Brazilian or flamenco, the fusion sounds here always make for an interesting night. A classic on the jazz scene, Clamores' stained walls and the yellowed photographs hanging on them show just how long they've been putting on shows. Live shows begin at 10pm.

CAFÉ CENTRAL Map pp270-2

☎ 91 369 41 43; www.cafecentralmadrid.com; Plaza del Angel 10; ☽ 1.30pm-2.30am Sun-Thu, 1.30pm-3.30am Fri & Sat; Metro Antón Martín or Sol

The Art Deco bar is worth a trip on its own (this is a great spot for an early-evening drink), but the Café Central is most known for jazz. Catch everything from Latin jazz to fusion, tango and classic jazz at the nightly shows, which start at 10pm.

POPULART Map pp270-2

☎ 91 429 84 07; www.populart.es; Calle de las Huertas 22; ☽ 6pm-2.30am Mon-Fri, 6pm-3.30am Fri & Sat; Metro Antón Martín or Sol

One of Madrid's classic jazz clubs, this place offers a low-key atmosphere and top-quality music. The shows start at 11pm, but if you want a seat get here early. There's no cover charge, and drinks cost €7 and up.

ROCK & BEYOND

Many of these concert venues double as clubs, making it possible to start off the night with a great concert and stay on to party until late. Ticket prices vary enormously, but you can expect to pay €10 to €15 for small or relatively unknown bands and up to €50-plus for internationally known groups that occasionally make appearances at these intimate clubs.

ARENA Map pp266-7

☎ 91 547 57 11; Calle de la Princesa 1; ☽ midnight-6am Thu-Sat, 6pm-midnight Sun; Metro Plaza España

Once a classic rock 'n' roll venue, this club has hosted former Guns n' Roses drummer Steve Adler and big-name groups like Love (led by Arthur Lee). Nowadays you're more likely to find alternative shows and, later, a club atmosphere.

GALILEO GALILEI Map p260

☎ 91 534 75 57; Calle de Galileo 100; ☽ 6pm-4.30am; Metro Islas Filipinas

There's no telling what they'll think to stage here next. You'll find everything from ballroom dancing to magic shows to comedy to concerts; it's a quirky mix that ensures a good time.

HONKY TONK Map pp266-7

☎ 91 445 68 86; Calle de Covarrubias 24; ☽ 9.30pm-5.30am; Metro Alonso Martínez

Calle 54

Film director Fernando Trueba, one of *the* names in Spanish cinema, gained a cult following among jazz aficionados after making the 2000 documentary movie *Calle 54*, a passionate and inspiring chronicle of Latin jazz. But Trueba wasn't content with simply recording the genre he loves; he went one step further and created Calle 54 in Madrid, a club where great musicians can bring the vitality of Latin jazz to Spain.

The movie *Calle 54* was shown in major film festivals all over the world and was immediately declared the most important film ever made about the genre (the *Buena Vista Social Club* of Latin jazz). A group of the artists portrayed in the film went on a 'Calle 54' tour, and the movie's soundtrack was nominated for a Grammy. Now, thanks to the support of the legendary artists featured in the film, Trueba has been able to bring a little piece of the movie to Madrid. Located on Paseo de la Habana (Havana Ave), Calle 54 has become a mecca for Latin jazz artists and is solely responsible for putting Madrid on the international Latin Jazz circuit. Greats like Bebo Valdés, Chano Domínguez and Roy Hargrove have taken the stage here, playing for appreciative audiences that often include Trueba's film pals, like Pedro Almodóvar and Penelope Cruz.

Despite the name, this is a great place to see local rock 'n' roll, though many acts have a little country thrown in the mix too. A very mixed crowd packs in this smallish club, so arrive early as the place fills up fast.

LA BOCA DEL LOBO Map pp270-2
☎ 91 523 13 91; Calle de Echegaray 11;
🕑 9.30pm-3am; Metro Sol

Known for offering mostly rock and alternative concerts, The Wolf's Mouth has broadened its horizons recently, adding country and jazz to the line-up. Concerts are held two to three times a week, usually on Wednesdays, Thursdays or Fridays.

LA RIVIERA Map pp262-4
☎ 91 365 24 15; Paseo Bajo de la Virgen del Puerto;
🕑 midnight-6am Tue-Sun; Metro Puerta de Angel

A dance club and concert venue all in one, this Art Deco spot hosts some of the biggest names in rock and electronic music. In summer, the roof is taken away and you can dance under the (smog-covered) stars until early morning.

SALA CARACOL Map pp262-4
☎ 91 527 35 94; Calle de Bernardino Obregón 18;
🕑 8pm-2am; Metro Embajadores

Housed in what seems like an old warehouse, the Sala Caracol (Snail Room) doesn't feel the need to stick to any one style. Hip hop, jazzy flamenco, rock and heavy metal groups have all passed through its stage.

SPORTS, HEALTH & FITNESS

Madrid has plenty to offer sport-a-holics, with top teams in football and basketball, some of the international tennis circuit's best players, and displays of Spain's most dashing *toreros*. Real Madrid is of course the city's most celebrated team and is considered the best football team ever to play the game. With its current superstar line-up including Beckham, Figo, Zidane, Raúl and Ronaldo (all who've either been nominated or named FIFA's world player of the year), there seems to be little doubt that the white jerseys will continue at the top.

Madrileños aren't known as a health-conscious bunch, and workout fever hasn't quite caught on here. That said, there are gyms and health centres (both public and private) scattered throughout the city. Those who'd rather exercise outside will find plenty of jogging, biking or rollerblading options in the parks.

Getting Tickets & Booking from Abroad

You can buy tickets at individual stadiums' box offices or through ticket agents in the city. **Localidades Galicia** (☎ 91 531 27 32 or 62 921 82 91; Plaza del Carmen 1; 🕑 9.30am-1pm & 4.30-7pm Tue-Sat; Metro Sol) is one of the better options, though tickets here will likely be more expensive that those bought direct.

If you're booking from abroad, you can try the numerous websites that hawk tickets. While we can't vouch for their good business practices, we can pass along their Web addresses; you can try www.madrid-tickets.net, www.madrid-tickets.com or www.ticket-finders.com.

WATCHING SPORT
Football

Football (soccer) fans will love Madrid. As the home of the Real Madrid – the team FIFA has declared the all-time greatest team in football – and the first-division Atlético de Madrid, Madrid offers a sports line-up few cities can match. The city's pride in its teams turns into football frenzy during games with rivals like Barça or big teams from the Champions League. See the frenzy first-hand when Real Madrid fans head to the Plaza de Cibeles (see p81) to celebrate the team's victories by cutting off traffic and swarming the statue in the centre of the plaza, sometimes even knocking off bits of it to keep as souvenirs.

TICKETS & RESERVATIONS

Tickets for football matches in Madrid start at around €10 and run up to the rafters for major matches. For some games, tickets can be impossible to get hold of. You can buy tickets directly from the stadiums, either at the box offices or by phone (see individual listings), or from the numerous ticket agents scattered around the city, though the latter tends to be more expensive. One of the best agents is Localidades Galicia (see p163).

ESTADIO SANTIAGO BERNABÉU
Map p261

☎ 91 398 43 00 or 90 232 43 24; www.realmadrid.com; Calle de Concha Espina 1; ⏲ to visit 10.30am-6.30pm except day after game; Metro Lima

Holding 80,000 delirious fans, the Santiago Bernabéu (named after the longtime club president) is a mecca for Madridistas (football fans) worldwide. Those who can't come to a game in the mythic stadium can at least stop by for a tour (adult/child €9/7) and a peek at the trophies exhibit.

ESTADIO VICENTE CALDERÓN
Map p260

☎ 91 366 47 07; www.at-madrid.com in Spanish; Calle de la Virgen del Puerto; Metro Pirámides

The home of first-division team Atlético de Madrid, this stadium isn't as large as Real Madrid's (Vicente Calderón seats fewer than 60,000), but what it lacks in size it makes up for in raw energy. A solid group of devoted fans stuck

Pride of place at Estadio Santiago Bernabéu, home to Real Madrid (p164)

with the club through a few rough years, and now Atlético is back at the top (well, top 10) of division one.

ESTADIO VALLECAS TERESA RIVERO
Map p260

☎ 91 478 22 53; www.rayovallecano.es; Calle de Payaso Fofó; Metro Portazgo

Madrid's third football club is no match for the likes of Real Madrid and Atlético de Madrid, but it's not a bad team and has even spent a few seasons in the top division.

Bullfighting

From the Fiestas de San Isidro (p71) in mid-May until the end of October, Spain's top bullfighters come to swing their capes in Las Ventas bullring. Bullfighters aren't inducted into the upper echelons until they face off with a bull in the capital, and the Sunday afternoon fights here are among the best in all Spain.

The ethical debate about bullfighting is not as loud in Madrid as in other parts of Spain (in Catalonia a law was recently passed forbidding kids under 14 to see the bloody spectacle), but it's not silent. Animal-rights groups argue, not without reason, that the slaughter is cruel, a jabbing, mocking, painful 30 minutes that leaves the bull exhausted and defeated. Yet supporters of this 'art' say that *toros bravos* (wild bulls) live like kings until the day of the slaughter, enjoying freedom that cattle bred for meat only dream about. Both sides have a point, and whether or not you want to see this often-disturbing tradition must be a personal decision.

TICKETS & RESERVATIONS
Tickets are divided into *sol* and *sombra* (sun and shade) seating, the former being considerably cheaper than the latter. Ticket sales for Sunday *corridas* (bullfights) begin on Fridays and are for sale at Las Ventas box office 10am to 2pm and 5pm to 8pm. A few (very few) ticket agencies sell before then, tacking on an extra 20% for their trouble. You can also get tickets at the authorised sales offices on the Calle de la Victoria. For most bullfights, you'll have no problem buying a ticket at the door, but when during the Fiestas de San Isidro or when a popular torero comes to town, book ahead.

The cheapest tickets (€3.60) are for standing-room *sol*, though on a broiling hot summer day it's infinitely more enjoyable to pay the extra €3 for *sombra* tickets, especially since most of the action is directed at the shady seats. The very best seats – on the front row in the shade – will cost you more than €100.

For information on who's in the ring, pay attention to the colourful posters tacked around town. You can also check the daily newspapers or specialist magazines.

PLAZA DE TOROS MONUMENTAL DE LAS VENTAS Map p260

☎ 91 356 22 00; www.las-ventas.com in Spanish; Calle de Alcalá 237; Metro Ventas

One of the largest rings in the bullfighting world, this is the stage for some of Spain's most important confrontations between matadors and *toros* (bulls). A grand *mudéjar* (hispano-moorish) exterior greets you from the street, and, inside, the broad sandy ring provides the stage for the fights.

Basketball

Basketball is quickly gaining a loyal following in Madrid, and while it still has miles to go before it reaches the popularity of football, more and more fans are getting hooked by the sport. Madrid's two teams, Adecco Estudiantes and Real Madrid, play from September through May. The city's basketball stadium, the Palacio de Deportes, burned to the ground in June 2001, and until it's rebuilt the teams have been dribbling in the Palacio Vistalegre and the Pabellón Raimundo Saporta.

TICKETS & RESERVATIONS
Tickets range from about €15 to €50 for regular season games. You can buy Estudiantes tickets through El Corte Inglés (see p163) or at the **Polideportivo Magariños** (☎ 91 562 40 22; Calle de Serrano 127; ◷ 10am-2pm & 4-8pm). Real Madrid tickets go on sale two hours before the game and you can buy them directly at the stadium box office.

ADECCO ESTUDIANTES Map p260

☎ 91 422 07 81 or 91 562 40 22; www.clubestudi antes.com & www.palaciovistalegre.com; Calle de Utebo 1; Metro Vistalegre

The Estudiantes are Madrid's most popular team, and games in this cosy stadium are usually played in front of a packed house. Sitting atop the old Vista Alegre bullring, the Palacio

Statues adorn the exterior of Plaza de Toros Monumental de Las Ventas bullring (p165)

is sometimes used as a concert venue when the team's not playing.

REAL MADRID Map p260

☎ 90 228 17 09; Pabellón Raimundo Saporta, Ciudad Deportiva; Metro Begoña

The Real Madrid basketball team has one of the winningest records in Spanish basketball history. With its excellent record (it has been league champion 28 times in the past 50 years) Real Madrid is a great team to watch live. Getting tickets isn't hard, but getting all the way up here can be a challenge; the stadium is within the club's sprawling 'Ciudad Deportiva' (Sports City) complex.

HEALTH & FITNESS

Swimming

In the sticky heat of Madrid's endless summer, there are few things more satisfying than a dip in a cool pool.

CANAL DE ISABEL II Map p260

☎ 91 533 17 91; www.cyii.es; Avenida Filipinas 54; admission €3.20-3.50; ⏱ 11am-8pm Jun-early Sep; Metro Ríos Rosas or Canal

In summer, splash around in the large outdoor pool. You can also play around on the football field, basketball court or in the weight room.

CASA DEL CAMPO Map p260

☎ 91 463 00 50; Avenida Ángel; pool €3.80; ⏱ 11.30am-9pm summer, 9am-noon & 3-7pm & 9-10pm winter; Metro Lago

It's a bit of a shame but the large, outdoor pools at this sprawling park are open in fine weather only, from May through September. The rest of the year you can splash in the covered pools, but you'll have to be quick about it as the chopped-up opening hours don't give much flexibility.

PISCINA MUNICIPAL BARRIO DEL PILAR Map p260

☎ 91 314 79 43; Calle Monforte de Lemos 13; admission €3.80; ⏱ 10am-8pm summer, 9am-7.45pm Mon-Fri, 10am-7.45pm Sat & Sun winter; Metro Barrio del Pilar

This is a friendly place to take a dip in the refreshing outdoor pool. In summer, you can swim laps indoors.

PISCINA MUNICIPAL PEÑUELAS

Map pp262-4

☎ 91 474 28 08; Calle de Arganda; admission €3.80; ⏱ 11am-9pm Jun-Aug; Metro Acacias, Pirámides or Embajadores

With two gloriously cool pools and a smaller, infants' pool, this outdoor complex in northern Madrid is a popular place for a summer dip, but be warned, it can and does get excessively crowded on summer weekends. Still, it's a sure way to beat the heat.

Tennis
POLIDEPORTIVO VIRGEN DEL PUERTO Map pp262-4
☎ 91 366 28 40; Paseo de la Virgen del Puerto; court rental from €4.90 ☼ 8.30am-8.30pm; Metro Príncipe Pío

If you like rackets, this is the spot for you. Run by the municipal government, this rather modern sports centre near the Puente de Segovia has eight regulation-size tennis courts, eight paddle-ball courts and 12 table-tennis courts.

Skiing
MADRID XANADÚ
☎ 90 226 30 26; www.millsmadridxanadu.com; Calle Puerto de Navacerrada, Arroyomolinos; ☼ 10am-2pm Sun-Thu , 10am-4pm Fri-Sat

That's right, skiing in Madrid. This is the largest covered ski centre in Europe, and you can slide down its snowy slopes all year long. Within the same complex is a mammoth mall, a 15-screen movie theatre, a kart track and a kiddie amusement park. To get here, take bus 529, 531 or 536 from the Méndez Álvaro transportation hub.

Gyms & Fitness Clubs
Public gyms and indoor pools (normally for lap swimming only) are scattered throughout Madrid. They generally charge a modest €3 to €6 for one-day admission. A full listing of Madrid's *polideportivos* (sports centres) and the services they offer is found online at www.imd.es (in Spanish only). If you're looking for swankier sweating options, head to one of Madrid's endless privately owned health centres. You'll pay €9 to €12 for a day's admission, but you'll usually find less-crowded workout rooms.

POLIDEPORTIVO CHAMARTÍN
Map p260
☎ 91 350 12 23; Plaza del Perú; admission €3.80; ☼ 8.30am-9pm Mon-Fri, 10am-8pm Sat & Sun; Metro Pio XXII or Colombia

A large sports centre offering everything from lap pools to badminton courts, volleyball courts and karate classes, this is one of the

city's most complete *polideportivos*, though it's not in the city centre.

POLIDEPORTIVO LA CHOPERA
Map p273
☎ 91 420 11 54; Parque del Buen Retiro; admission €4.50; ☼ 9am-8pm Mon-Fri; Metro Atocha

With a fine new workout centre, several football fields and a tennis court, this sports centre is one of Madrid's oldest and most complete. Sitting in the southwestern corner of El Retiro, it's easily accessible too.

POLIDEPORTIVO LA LATINA Map pp270-2
☎ 91 365 80 31; Plaza de la Cebada; pool adult/child €3.80/2.15; ☼ 8.15am-7pm Mon-Thu, 8.15am-6pm Fri, 10am-8.30pm Sat & Sun; Metro La Latina

One of the most central municipal gyms (and one of the few that has a pool, though it's for indoor lap swimming only) this gym is busy day and night. While not all that new or clean, it offers fairly complete weight and workout rooms.

Yoga
CITY YOGA Map p261
☎ 91 553 47 51; www.city-yoga.com in Spanish; Calle de Artistas 43; ☼ 10.30am-8.30pm Mon-Sat; Metro Cuatro Caminos or Nuevos Ministerios

Bring out the mats and get bendy. This yoga centre is one of the most popular in the city, with a variety of classes suiting all styles and ability levels.

ASHTANGA YOGA Map pp270-2
☎ 91 369 00 33; Calle de Juanelo 13; Metro Tirso de Molino or La Latina

For die-hard ashtanga addicts who can't go a week without their fix, this is the place for you.

Day Spas & Salons
CHI SPA Map pp268-9
☎ 91 578 13 40; www.thechispa.com; Calle del Conde de Aranda 6; ☼ 10am-9pm Mon-Fri, 10am-6pm Sat; Metro Retiro

Wrap up in a robe and slippers and prepare to be pampered. This American-style (so they say) day spa has separate areas for men and women and is one of the city's best. Get a massage (€60 per hour), a facial (€60 to €116), a body peeling (€35) or a plain old manicure (€23) or pedicure (€29), and watch your cares slip away.

HAMMAM MEDINA MAYRIT Map pp270-2

☎ 91 429 90 20; www.medinamayrit.com; Calle de Atocha 14; ⏳ 10am-midnight; Metro Sol

This might just be the most relaxing cultural experience you've ever had. Imitating a trad-iitional Arab bath, this place is a hybrid – a tea room, restaurant and spa where you can soak in warm baths and get massages until midnight.

MASAJES A 1000 Map pp266-7

☎ 91 447 47 77; www.masajesa1000.com; Calle de Carranza 6 (other branches throughout city); ⏳ 8am-midnight; Metro Bilbao

This is the answer to a long day of sightseeing or shopping. Just stop by (no appointments are taken) for a reasonable, professional massage, mani/pedicure, waxing or facial. Other branches have a hair salon too.

Shopping

Shopping

Whether you're looking for quirky cool or designer duds, Madrid is sure to please. The city obviously has its fair share of shopoholics, as stores catering to every whim line central streets

The glitziest shopping district is Salamanca, where all the designer labels show off for drooling window shoppers. This is also the district to find top art, antique and furniture galleries. For artisan goods and typically Spanish items like fans, shawls and even bullfighter suits, explore the maze of streets in Huerta and Los Austrias. Several music shops, selling both mainstream and vintage vinyl, are here too.

Alternative, off-beat fashion is found in Chueca. This lively *barrio* is a magnet for shoe shops; there are a dozen of them along and around Calle Augusto Figueroa. The quirky shops, including the uncontrollable Rastro market, are in La Latina and Lavapiés. Keep an eye out for some of the most unusual storefront displays in the city, including those of Caramelos Paco (a temple to the sweet-toothed) and Corsetería La Latina (featuring the largest bras on the planet).

Bargain hunters flock to the shops during *las rebajas*, the annual winter and summer sales when prices are slashed on just about everything. The winter sales begin around January 7 just after Three Kings' Day, and last well into February. Summer sales begin in early July and last into August.

Some of the most common buys are leather shoes and handbags; Spanish shoe brands like Farrutx, Camper and Jaime Mascaró are popular. Majorica faux pearls and Lladró porcelain are other classic buys. You'll find all these things in shops along Calle de Serrano and Gran Via.

The shopping day starts at about 10am and is almost always broken up by a long lunch from 2pm to 5pm. Shops re-open after lunch and stay busy until 8pm. Almost all stores are closed on Sunday, and many are only open half days on Saturday.

LOS AUSTRIAS & CENTRO

The maze of streets around the Plaza Mayor and extending up toward Gran Via are exploding with original shops. This is the place to find traditional, if sometimes kitschy, Spanish goods, though if you're wanting to buy a cheap flamenco doll or get your name written on a bullfighting poster the abundance of standard souvenir shops will do fine too.

Who's Who of Spanish Designers

Paris, Milan, London…Madrid? Spanish fashion has taken leaps in the past decade and is quickly gaining ground on Europe's traditional capitals of style. Madrid's twice-annual fashion show, Cibeles, showcases the work of top designers from throughout the country. The following are some of Spain's best-known fashion figures.

Amaya Arzuaga Bold colours, harsh lines and totally urban designs for women have made her one of Spain's most famous fashion names.

Armand Basi A classic Spanish designer, his fashions for men and women focus on simple shapes and colours and offer informal elegance.

Antoni Miro A Catalan designer who's renowned throughout Spain and abroad, his clothes are uncomplicated and youthful. He's also got a great range of leather accessories for men.

Agatha Ruiz de la Prada Her bright, fun-loving designs would look good on school children, but they're also surprisingly popular with adults looking to break the fashion mould. Enterprising Agatha has a homeware line and an office supplies line too, all bearing her signature colours and shapes.

Roberto Torreta Romantic yet practical design is Roberto Torreta's trademark. His elegant evening options are flashier but just as popular as his broad selection of workwear.

Market Madness

Flea Markets, fresh markets, crafts markets…bargain hunters will have a field day in Madrid. The city's biggest and best-known market is **El Rastro** (p174), a thriving mass of vendors, buyers and pickpockets. This classic flea market, open Sunday mornings only, is the place to find everything from faux designer purses to 1960s flamenco cassette tapes, with furniture, kitchen appliances and thong underwear thrown in too. Locals say that the selection is not what it used to be, but there are still treasures to be found if you have the patience to dig through the heaps of second-hand goods.

El Rastro owes its name ('The Stain') to the blood that once trickled down these streets from the slaughterhouses that sat uphill. It's been an open-air market for half a millennium and is considered the largest in Europe.

The madness begins at the Plaza de Cascorro, near La Latina metro stop, and worms its way downhill along the Calle de la Ribera de Curtidores and the streets branching off it. The shopping starts at about 8am and lasts until lunchtime (2pm or 3pm), but for many Madrileños the best of El Rastro comes after the stalls have shut down and everyone crowds into nearby bars for an *aperitivo* (appetizer) of vermouth and tapas. Families, friends and die-hard partiers who are still awake from the night before stroll from bar to bar (especially those along the Calle de la Cava Baja), turning the *barrio* into the site of a spontaneous Sunday fiesta. In fine weather, the Plaza de San Andrés attracts a light-hearted bohemian crowd that fills the area with bongo music and dancing.

Although El Rastro takes the prize as Madrid's most colourful market, shoppers will want to check out the city's other bargain haunts too:

Cuesta de Moyano Bookstalls (Calle Claudio Moyano; ⏱ 9am-dusk Mon-Sat, 9am-2pm Sun; Metro Atocha) Second-hand and new books in many languages.

Art Market (Plaza Conde de Barajas; ⏱ 10am-2pm Sun; Metro Sol) For local art and prints of the greats.

Mercadillo Marqués de Viana (El Rastrillo; Calle del Marqués de Viana; ⏱ 9am-2pm Sun; Metro Tetuán) A calmer version of El Rastro.

Mercado de San Miguel (Plaza de San Miguel; ⏱ 9am-2pm & 5-8pm Mon-Sat; Metro Sol) One of the city's best fresh markets.

Mercado de Monedas y Sellos (Plaza Mayor; ⏱ 9am-2pm Sun; Metro Sol) Old coins and stamps.

ADOLFO DOMINGUEZ

Map pp266-7 *Fashion, Clothes & Shoes*
☎ 91 522 65 65; www.adolfodominguez.com in Spanish; Gran Via 11; ⏱ 10am-9pm Mon-Sat, noon-3pm & 6-8pm Sun; Metro Gran Via

It's worth peeking in Spanish designer Adolfo Dominguez's stylish shop just to gawk at the grand chandelier and gorgeous winding staircase inside this historic building.

BANGLADESH Map pp266-7 *Music*

☎ 91 559 50 56; www.bangladeshdiscos.com; Calle de la Costanilla de los Ángeles 5; ⏱ 10.30am-2.30pm & 5-8.30pm Mon-Sat; Metro Ópera or Santo Domingo

The Calle Costanilla de los Ángeles is lined with great CD and music shops. For a wide selection of vinyl, including singles, hard-to-find records and collector's items, head to Bangladesh. If you don't see what you're looking for, just ask the friendly, knowledgeable staff.

CASA DE DIEGO

Map pp270-2 *Jewellery, Perfume & Accessories*
☎ 915 22 66 43; www.casadediego.com; Puerta del Sol 12; ⏱ 9.30am-2pm & 5-8pm Mon-Sat Oct-May, 9.30am-8pm Jun-Sep; Metro Sol

This classic shop has been around since 1858, selling and repairing Spanish fans, shawls, umbrellas and canes. The grumpy old men who wait on you seem like they could have been around for the original shop's opening.

CASA DEL LIBRO Map pp266-7 *Books*

☎ 915 24 19 00; www.casadellibro.com in Spanish; Gran Via 29; ⏱ 9.30am-9.30pm Mon-Sat, 11am-9pm Sun; Metro Gran Via

Spain's answer to Barnes & Noble, this sprawling mega-bookstore has titles on just about

---

Top Five Shopping Streets

For…
- **Glamour** Calle de Salamanca (Map pp268-9)
- **Quirky and kitsch cool** Calle de Fuencarral (Map pp266-7)
- **Traditional Spanish goods** Calle de Hortaleza (Map pp270-2)
- **Utter elegance** Calle de José Ortega y Gasset (Map pp268-9)
- **The weird and wonderful** Calle de Toledo (Map pp270-2)

Top Five One-Stop Shopping Centres

- **ABC Serrano** (p177)
- **Mercado de Fuencarral** (p176)
- **El Corte Inglés** (below)
- **El Jardín de Serrano** (p179)
- **Moda Shopping** (p182)

any topic you can think of. There is a large English and foreign-language literature section, and non-fiction books in English are mixed alongside Spanish titles.

CASA HERNANZ

Map pp270-2   *Fashion, Clothes & Shoes*
☎ 91 366 54 50; Calle de Toledo 18; ☽ 9am-1.30pm & 4.30-8pm Mon-Fri, 10am-2pm Sat; Metro La Latina or Sol
The comfy, rope-soled *alpargatas*, Spain's traditional footwear, are worn by everyone from the King of Spain to the Pope. You can buy your own pair at this humble workshop, where both traditional and more creative styles are sold. You can even get them made to order.

CONVENTO DEL CORPUS CRISTI (LAS CARBONERAS)

Map pp270-2   *Food & Drink*
Plaza del Conde de Miranda 3; ☽ 9.30am-1pm & 4-6.30pm Mon-Sat, 11am-1pm & 4-6.30pm Sun; Metro Ópera, La Latina or Sol
If you're after truly heavenly cookies and sweets, there's no substitute for the nuns of the Convento del Corpus Cristi (Las Carboneras), a closed order that makes and sells moist, rich pastries made with almonds and egg yolks. To the right of the convent's main entrance is a small door with a call button. Ring the nuns, and they'll let you inside, where you'll walk to a small, dark room with a rotating countertop so that the nuns never even see their customers.

EL CORTE INGLÉS

Map pp266-7 *Department & Convenience Stores*
☎ 91 418 88 00; Calle de Preciados 3; ☽ 10am-10pm Mon-Sat; Metro Sol
You could live in El Corte Inglés and have everything you need. Food, furniture, clothes, appliances, toiletries, electronics, books, music…this superstore has it all, though you'll pay a little extra for the convenience of one-stop shopping. Branches are scattered throughout the city.

EL FLAMENCO VIVE Map pp270-2   *Musi*

☎ 91 547 39 17; www.elflamencovive.es in Spanish; Calle del Conde de Lemos 7; ☽ 10.30am-2pm & 5-9pr Mon-Sat; Metro Ópera
This temple to flamenco has it all, from guitar and songbooks to albums, polka-dotted danc ing costumes, shoes, colourful plastic jeweller and literature about flamenco. The know ledgeable staff can point you in the directior of Madrid's best flamenco *tablaos* as well.

JOSÉ RAMÍREZ Map pp270-2   *Musi*

☎ 91 531 42 29; Calle de la Paz 8; ☽ 10am-2pm & 4.30-8pm; Metro Sol
Little wonder he's considered one of Spain' best guitar makers; José Ramírez's guitars have been played by flamenco greats and interna tional musicians (even the Beatles). In the bac of this small shop is a little museum with gui tars dating as far back as 1830.

JUSTO ALGABA Map pp270-2   *Specialist Stor*

☎ 91 523 35 95; Calle de la Paz 4; ☽ 10am-2pm & 5-8pm Mon-Fri, 10am-2pm Sat; Metro Sol
Madrid's *toreros* come here to have their *traj de luces* (suit of lights, the traditional glitterinç bullfighting suit) made. A custom-made sui starts at €2500, but if you just want a souven ask for some of those sexy pink tights (€50).

PETRA'S INTERNATIONAL BOOKSHOP Map pp266-7   *Book*

☎ 91 541 72 91; Calle de Campomanes 13; ☽ 11am- 9pm Mon-Sat, Metro Ópera or Santo Domingo
Here you'll find not only a great selection o books in all major languages, but a lively expa community hosting conversation groups anc activities in English and other languages.

SANTARRUFINA Map pp270-2   *Specialist Stor*

☎ 91 522 23 83; www.santarrufina.com; Calle de la Paz 9; ☽ 10am-2pm & 4.30-8pm Mon-Fri, 10am-2pm Sat; Metro Sol
Churches, priests and monasteries are some o the patrons of this elegant, three-storey shop full of glittering religious items. You'll finc everything from simple rosaries to imposinç statues of saints and even a litter used to carr the Virgin in processions. Head downstairs fo a peek at the gorgeous chapel there.

VIPS

Map pp266-7 *Department & Convenience Store*
☎ 91 559 66 21; Gran Via 43; ☽ 9am-3am; Metro Santo Domingo; branches all over the city

VIPS is one of the few shops open late, and it's about the only spot to get those random items you sometimes need at 3am (snacks, drinks, film, batteries, books etc). There's a bland café too, and while we don't understand why anyone would want to waste their time here when Madrid has thousands of quirky and cool bars, it's very popular with the locals and seems to always be full.

Top Five Spots For Books in English

- Pasajes Librería Internacional (p182)
- Petra's International Bookshop (p172)
- Cuesta de Mayano Bookstalls (p171)
- Casa del Libro (p171)
- El Corte Inglés (p172)

SOL, HUERTAS & ATOCHA

The narrow streets running through this historic quarter are filled with shops selling everything from sweet-smelling pastries to airplane bottles of Spanish brandy. The 'old-time' places rub shoulders with new arrivals selling trendy accessories and fashions, making this a fun area to browse.

CASA MIRA Map pp270-2   *Food & Drink*
☎ 91 429 88 95; Carrera de San Jerónimo 30;
🕑 10am-2pm & 5-9pm Mon-Sat; Metro Sol
A sumptuous, twirling display of goodies in the window draws lots of oohs and ahhs. The real delight is in trying the candied fruits, fat pastries and creamy cakes (all made right here) for yourself. The shop is especially known for its *turrones* (fudge-like Christmas candy).

DISCOS LA METRALLETA
Map pp270-2   *Music*
☎ 91 521 76 95; Plaza del Angel 4; 🕑 10.30am-2.30pm & 5.30-9pm Mon-Sat; Metro Sol or Tirso de Molina
Have fun digging through the old record singles (there are lots of good but forgotten Spanish hits) and hard-to-find CDs. Collector's albums and old movie posters are here too.

GIL
Map pp270-2   *Jewellery, Perfume & Accessories*
☎ 91 521 25 49; Carrera de San Jerónimo 2;
🕑 9.30am-1.30pm & 4.30-8pm Mon-Fri, 9.30am-1.30pm Sat; Metro Sol
Founded in 1880, this historic shop is loaded with fringed, embroidered *mantones* and *mantoncillos* (traditional Spanish shawls) and delicate *mantillas* (Spanish veils). Stepping inside the dark shop, where sales clerks wait behind a long counter to attend to you, is like stepping back in time.

LIBRERÍA DESNIVEL Map pp270-2   *Books*
☎ 902 248848; www.libreriadesnivel.com in Spanish;
Plaza Matute 6; 🕑 10am-2pm & 4.30-8.30pm Mon-Sat; Metro Antón Martín

With its rough wooden floors and pick-axe decoration theme, Desnivel has a very clear focus – mountaineering. Here you'll find beautiful coffee table books, how-to books and plenty of guidebooks about outdoor sports. The perfect stop if you're planning to hike or bike in Spain.

LICORILANDIA Map pp270-2   *Food & Drink*
☎ 91 429 12 57; Calle de León 30; 🕑 9.30am-2pm & 5-8.30pm Mon-Sat; Metro Antón Martín
No need to steal them from an airplane; since 1964 this shop has dedicated itself heart and

Mouthwatering sweets and pastries from Casa Mira (p173)

soul to providing all the miniature bottles of sherry, brandy, whisky and liquor anyone could ever want. Find Torres brandy, Tío Pépe *fino* and Cuban rum in a size that's a cinch to pack.

LUIS MORUECO Map pp270-2 *Antiques*
☎ 91 429 57 57; Calle del Prado 16; 9.30am-1.30pm Mon-Fri; Metro Antón Martín
Specialising in antique Spanish furniture, walking through this elegant shop is like taking a tour of the wealthy Spanish homes of past centuries. Furniture, chandeliers, porcelain and paintings (most anonymous) are gracefully displayed.

MARIA CABELLO Map pp270-2 *Food & Drink*
☎ 91 429 60 88; Calle de Echegaray 19; 9.30am-3pm & 7.30-9pm Mon-Fri, 9.30am-3pm & 6-9.30pm Sat; Metro Sol

The oft-painted wooden shelves and counter of this little corner shop have been here since 1913, when Maria Cabello first began serving the neighbourhood. These days it' devoted exclusively to wines (mostly Span ish) and spirits, and there are some 500 label available.

MÉXICO Map pp270-2 *Specialist Stor*
☎ 91 429 94 76; Calle de las Huertas 20; 9am-2pm & 5-8pm Mon-Fri, 9am-2pm Sat; Metro Tirso de Molina, Antón Martín or Sol
A treasure chest of original old maps, this is a great place to find a unique souvenir of Spair Some 160 folders hold antique, original map of Madrid, Spain and the rest of the worlc You can find everything from a 19th-centur Madrid map (€240) to a 1626 full-colour ma[of Spain (€1500).

LA LATINA & LAVAPIÉS

La Latina and Lavapiés are now home to immigrants of a fascinating array of nationalities and that mix is reflected in the number of ethnic shops. Stroll around and you will fine Asian food markets, Muslim meat shops and stores selling gifts imported from China There is also an abundance of stores selling in bulk; if you see a sign saying 'Venta *e Mayoristas*', it means that they only sell in bulk. This neighbourhood, and especially th Calle de Toledo, is also the place to spot some of Madrid's most creative store-window displays.

Shopping – La Latina & Lavapiés

CARAMELOS PACO
Map pp270-2 *Food & Drink*
☎ 91 365 42 58; Calle de Toledo 53-55; 9.30am-2pm & 5-8.30pm Mon-Fri, 9.30am-2pm & 5.30-8.30pm Sat; Metro La Latina
This place must have more sugar per square inch than any other spot in the city. The showy storefront, packed with colourful candies and sweets, is a sign of what's waiting inside the shop: wall to wall caramels, sugar figurines, giant lollipops and other tempting tooth-rotting goodies.

CERERÍA ORTEGA
Map pp270-2

Antiques & Crafts
☎ 91 365 60 19; Calle de Toledo 43; 9am-1.30pm & 5-8pm Mon-Fri; Metro La Latina
The Ortega family has been in the business of making old-fashioned wax candles here since 1893. The dimly lit little shop smells of warm wax, and you can see the artisan candle makers hard at work in the back.

CORSETERÍA LA LATINA
Map pp270-2 *Fashion, Clothes & Shoe*
☎ 91 365 46 22; Calle de Toledo 49; 10am-1.30pm & 5-8pm Mon-Fri, 10am-1.30pm Sat; Metro La Latina or Tirso de Molina
The impressive two-metre bra in the shop win dow is no sales gimmick; it's real lingerie; as are the other plus-plus size garments here. You may be surprised; some of them are really sexy.

EL RASTRO Map pp270-2 *Marke*
Calle de la Ribera de Curtidores; 8am-2pm Sun; Metro La Latina, Puerta de Toledo or Tirso de Molina
You could easily spend an entire morning inch ing your way down the Calle de la Ribera de Cur tidos and among the maze of streets that host the Rastro flea market every Sunday morning Pick your way through the cheap clothes, imita tion purses, household goods and electronics for sure you'll find a lot of junk, but there migh just be a gem in there too. Shoppers beware: the market is crawling with would-be pickpockets so keep a tight hold on your belongings anc don't keep valuables in easy-to-reach pockets.

Kiddy dreams do come true at the Caramelos Paco (p174)

MALASAÑA & CHUECA

Just can't seem to find the perfect leather collar to go with your studded black miniskirt? No problem. The funky, alternative shops scattered around Chueca and Malasaña will take care of things. This is a great area to find club clothes or fashionable accessories. As a centre of gay life, there are also numerous gay book and speciality shops. Calle de Fuencarral is a good place to start a shopping spree, but Calle de Hortaleza and the small streets around the Plaza de Chueca are a goldmine for original fashions.

A DIFFERENT LIFE
Map pp266-7   *Books*
☎ 91 532 96 52; Calle de Pelayo 30; ⏱ 11am-10pm Mon-Sat; Metro Chueca

This small quirky bookshop sells a variety of gay-oriented books, magazines and videos, as well as fun gifts and music. It also rents videos.

ART DECORATION
Map pp266-7   *Design, Homewares & Gifts*
☎ 91 523 08 41; Calle de Pelayo 31; ⏱ 11am-2.30pm & 5.30-9.30pm Mon-Sat; Metro Chueca

This small furniture and home decor shop is a temple to good taste. Offering a mix of re-stored old furniture and swanky new pieces, the goods on sale range from Asian rugs to leather chaises longues and rich wooden furniture.

CACAO SAMPAKA
Map pp266-7   *Food & Drink*
☎ 91 319 48 40; Calle de Orellana 4; ⏱ 10am-9pm Mon-Fri, 11am-9pm Sat; Metro Alonso Martínez

Chocoholics, this is your dream come true. A sprawling shop dedicated to nothing but rich, dark cocoa. And light sweet cocoa. And cocoa with raspberries. And cocoa with lilacs and roses. And…You get the idea. Chocolate in all its many forms is sold here. Taste some of them at the bar in the back.

CALIGAE
Map pp266-7   *Fashion, Clothes & Shoes*
☎ 91 531 53 43; Calle de Augusto Figueroa 18 & 27; ⏱ 10am-2pm & 5-8.30pm Mon-Fri, 5-8.30pm Sat; Metro Chueca

One of the many great shoe stores on the Calle de Augusto Figueroa, Caligae is actually two shops: a more conservative one selling boots and pumps, and an edgier branch across the street showcasing the verylatest in footwear design.

CUSTO BARCELONA

Map pp266-7 *Fashion, Clothes & Shoes*
☎ 91 360 46 36; www.custo-barcelona.com; Calle de Fuencarral 29; ⏱ 10am-9pm Mon-Fri, 10am-10pm Sat; Metro Gran or Chueca

The now-iconic T-shirts of Barcelona designer Custo Dalmau are artfully displayed in this chic shop. You'll also find funky bags, shoes and clothing for men and women.

DIVINA PROVIDENCIA

Map pp266-7 *Fashion, Clothes & Shoes*
☎ 91 522 02 65; Calle de Fuencarral 45; ⏱ 11am-9pm Mon-Sat; Metro Gran Via or Tribunal

One of many new designers on the Madrid fashion scene, Divina Providencia has fun clothes for women, with strong retro and Asian influences. The label is such a hit that its clothes are regularly spotted on the characters of major Spanish TV series.

ENSANCHEZ

Map pp266-7 *Jewellery, Perfume & Accessories*
☎ 91 319 58 50; Calle de Argensola 12; ⏱ 10am-2pm & 5-8.30pm Mon-Sat; Metro Alonso Martínez

A stylish boutique with an exciting range of original belts, purses and accessories, this is a great place to find special gifts. Many pieces here are handmade, and all are chic and colourful.

GUITARRAS MANUEL RODRIGUEZ

Map pp266-7 *Music*
☎ 91 531 75 84; Calle de Hortaleza 26; ⏱ 10am-1.30pm & 5-8pm Mon-Fri, 10am-1.30pm Sat; Metro Gran Via or Chueca

A family-run business started a century ago, Manuel Rodriguez offers a full range of guitars, from simple models made in the family factory in Toledo to handmade works of art that cost as much as €2500.

HOSS Map pp266-7 *Fashion, Clothes & Shoes*
☎ 91 524 17 28; Calle de Fuencarral 16; ⏱ 10.30am-9pm Mon-Sat; Metro Chueca or Gran Via

Women love the stylish but tailored look of Hoss (short for the brand's full name, 'Homeless'). The collection ranges from cocktail

Funky Converse footwear at Mercado de Fuencarral (p176)

dresses to workwear to jeans and sweaters and there's an emphasis on knits.

LIBERTO

Map pp266-7 *Fashion, Clothes & Shoes*
☎ 91 521 27 51; Calle de Fuencarral 42; ⏱ 10am-9pm Mon-Fri, 11am-9pm Sat; Metro Tribunal, Chueca or Gran Via

With its urban-chic fashions and *discoteca*-worthy loud music, Liberto almost seems like a daytime dance spot. There's bound to be something for everyone. Clothes for men and women range from sexy to grungy cool.

MERCADO DE FUENCARRAL

Map pp266-7 *Shopping Centre*
☎ 91 521 41 52; Calle de Fuencarral 45; ⏱ 11am-9pm Mon-Sat; Metro Tribunal or Chueca

This multi-level shopping centre is a great place to find funky gear for a night out on the town. Selling mostly alternative fashions, here you'll find all the black leather and silver stud you'll ever need.

MULTHISPANO

Map pp266-7 *Fashion, Clothes & Shoes*
☎ 91 532 38 33; Calle de Hortaleza 30; ⏱ 11am-2pm & 5-8.30pm Mon-Fri, 5-8.30pm Sat; Metro Chueca or Gran Via

Multhispano offers light-hearted styles for women, from casual tops to colourful dresses and accessories. This is just one of the countless fashionable boutiques you'll find along the Calle de Hortaleza.

PATRIMONIO COMUNAL OLIVERO

Map pp266-7 *Food & Drink*
☎ 91 308 05 05; Calle de Mejía Lequerica 1;
🕑 10am-2pm & 5-8pm Mon-Fri, 10am-2pm Sat;
Metro Alonso Martínez or Bilbao

Find the finest of olive oils from all over Spain at this simple one-stop shop. Some of the best oils are from Andalucía or the Priorat region of Catalonia, but for a wide sampling why not try the box of 10 mini bottles for just €7.75.

RESERVA & CATA Map pp266-7 *Food & Drink*

☎ 91 319 04 01; www.reservaycata.com; Calle del Conde de Xiquena 13; 🕑 11am-2.30pm & 5.30-8.30pm Mon-Fri, 11am-2.30pm Sat; Metro Colón or Chueca

With a fantastic selection of Spanish wines and a knowledgeable staff that can help you pick out a great one, this is a great place to shop for gifts or tasty souvenirs.

SALAMANCA & LAS VENTAS

Pull out your diamonds, fur coats and stilettos, and join the fashionable shoppers in Madrid's snazziest *barrio*. Don't be afraid to ring the shops' doorbells; it doesn't mean they're closed, just that they want to look you over before letting you in. Although the attitude in some stores can be stand-offish, this is one of the best areas of Madrid to find top-quality goods, whether you're searching for wine and cheese, baby gifts, furniture or fashion.

ABC SERRANO

Map pp262-4 *Shopping Centre*
☎ 91 577 50 31; Calle de Serrano 61; 🕑 10am-9pm Mon-Sat; Metro Serrano

This multi-level shopping mall has shops ranging from trendy Zara to the elegant baby shop Musgo. Restaurants and cafés are scattered about in case all that shopping wears you out.

ALCOLEA Map pp262-4 *Specialist Store*

☎ 91 435 23 47; Calle de Velázquez 12; 🕑 10.30am-2pm & 5.30-9pm Mon-Sat; Metro Velázquez

This sprawling gallery specialises in contemporary Spanish art, and it's a great place to hunt for traditional styles like landscapes, portraits and paintings reflecting the Spanish lifestyle.

AMAYA ARZUAGA

Map pp268-9 *Fashion, Clothes & Shoes*
☎ 91 426 28 15; Calle de Lagasca 50; 🕑 10.30am-8.30pm Mon-Sat; Metro Velázquez

Amaya Arzuaga is one of Spain's top designers, with sexy, bold options. She loves mixing black with bright colours (think 1980s fuchsia and turquoise) and has earned a reputation as one of the most creative designers in Spain today.

ANTONIO MIRO

Map pp262-4 *Fashion, Clothes & Shoes*
☎ 91 426 02 25; www.antoniomiro.com; Calle de Lagasca 65; 🕑 10am-2pm & 4.30-8.30pm Mon-Fri, 10am-8.30pm Sat; Metro Velázquez

Another great Spanish designer, this Catalan is known for his casual looks for men and women, though the accessories line (for men especially) is great too. His clean-lined designs are just bordering on trendy.

ARMAND BASI

Map pp268-9 *Fashion, Clothes & Shoes*
☎ 91 577 79 93; Calle de Claudio Coello 52;
🕑 10.30am-2.30pm & 5-8.30pm Mon-Fri, 10.30am-8.30pm Sat; Metro Serrano

What's in a Name?

Madrid is on a par with any other European capital when it comes to designer shops. You'll find all the top labels here, and the abundance of bejewelled, be-leathered shoppers is proof that business is good. To drool a little, follow our designer route through Salamanca.

Start at the intersection of Calle Serrano and Calle Juan Bravo. Give a nod to Emporio Armani (Calle de Serrano 98) before heading down Serrano to the lusciously elegant jewellers Bulgari (No 49) and Cartier (No 74). Pop into Gucci (No 49) and head left on the elegant Calle José Ortega y Gasset where you'll see Christian Dior (No 6), the Italian leather expert, Furla (No 11), and elegant Kenzo (No 15). If your wallet isn't worn out yet, head on to luxe Luis Viutton (No 17) and weird but wonderful Versace (No 10).

A kind of heaven with fine shops, bars and cafés in the ABC Serrano complex (p177)

With hip, urban designs for men and women, this is the place to find those deliberately cool duds for a night out in the *barrio's* most fashionable bars.

ARTESPAÑA

Map pp268-9   *Design, Homewares & Gifts*
☎ 91 435 02 21; www.artespana.com in Spanish; Calle de la Hermosilla 14; ☽ 10am-8.30pm Mon-Sat; Metro Serrano
Three floors of beautiful furniture and home accents, ranging from classy, dark-leather couches to ultra-modern acrylic chairs. Most things you see come from Spanish designers, but there is a healthy dose of other European design too. Anything can be shipped, so shop away.

BD MADRID

Map pp268-9   *Design, Homewares & Gifts*
☎ 91 435 06 27; bdmadrid@wanadoo.es; Calle de la Villanueva 5; ☽ 9.30am-1.30pm & 4.30-8pm Mon-Fri, 10am-1.30pm & 5-8pm Sat; Metro Retiro
Is it a gallery or is it a shop? A little of both, really. In this ultra-fashionable furniture showroom you can spot the latest from Spanish and international designers along with classics from Spanish greats like Oscar Tusquets and Javier Mariscal. Everything you see is available to order.

BOMBONERÍA SANTA

Map pp268-9   *Food & Drink*
☎ 91 576 86 46; Calle de Serrano 56; ☽ 10am-2pm & 5-8pm Mon-Sat; Metro Serrano
Drool over the exquisite chocolates in this tiny shop, where the boxes are every bit as pretty as the bonbons that fill them. They don't come cheap though – a large box of these yummy chocolates will cost you €120!

CAMPER

Map pp268-9   *Fashion, Clothes & Shoes*
☎ 91 431 43 45; www.camper.es; Calle de Ayala 13; ☽ 10am-8.30pm Mon-Sat; Metro Serrano
The quirky and cool shoe brand that made bowling shoes chic the world over has several shops in Madrid. The brand is made in Mallorca and its colourful, fun designs are all about comfort.

CUARTO DE JUEGOS

Map pp262-4   *For Children*
☎ 91 435 00 99; Calle de Jorge Juan 42; ☽ 10am-2pm & 5-8pm Mon-Fri, 5-8pm Sat; Metro Serrano or Nuñez de Balbao
We're not sure if it's an official rule, but batteries seem to be outlawed at this traditional toy shop, where the kinds of games, puzzles and toys mum and dad used to play with are still

old. It specialises in wooden table games – nd they're not just for kids!

DE VIAJE Map pp268-9 _Books_
☎ 91 577 98 99; www.deviaje.com in Spanish; Calle e Serrano 41; 10am-8pm Mon-Fri, 10.30am-.30pm & 5-8pm Sat; Metro Serrano

A sprawling bookstore dedicated to travel books, here you'll find mountains of literature about Madrid, Spain and the rest of the world. The place doubles as a travel agency, and you can also buy travel gear like backpacks, torches flashlights) and water bottles.

EL JARDIN DE SERRANO
Map pp268-9 _Shopping Centre_
☎ 91 577 00 12; Calle de Goya 6-8; 10am-10pm Mon-Sat; Metro Serrano

Upscale shops and cafés fill this small mall right off Calle Serrano. Pop into Romero for great gifts, Bang & Olufsen for top-end electronics and Lotusse for luxe leather shoes and bags. Rest and recuperate at the Mallorca café downstairs.

EXOTIC Map pp268-9 _Fashion, Clothes & Shoes_
☎ 91 431 89 33; www.delittoecastigo.com; Calle de Villanueva 20; 11am-2.30pm & 5-9pm Mon-Sat; Metro Retiro

Labels like D&G, Valentino and Christian Lacroix rub shoulders at this posh boutique. It's all about fashion here; a video of runway shows flickers on one wall, and the racks are hung with trendy, urban clothes for men and women.

FARRUTX
Map pp268-9 _Fashion, Clothes & Shoes_
☎ 91 577 09 24; Calle de Serrano 7; 10am-2pm & 5-8.30pm Mon-Fri, 10.30am-2pm & 5-8.30pm Sat; Metro Retiro or Serrano

Find exquisite leather shoes and accessories for men and women in this chic boutique. Well made and always fashionable, Mallorca-based Farrutx is arguably Spain's top shoe brand.

HABITAT
Map pp268-9 _Design, Homewares & Gifts_
☎ 91 181 26 00; www.habitat.net; Calle de Hermosilla 18; 10.30am-8.30pm Mon-Sat; Metro Serrano

One of Spain's most popular furniture and home decor stores, Habitat sells the kinds of couches, lamps and bedspreads you'd expect

to see in a Soho flat, but with a preppy twist. Habitat is known for bright colours, clean lines and decent prices.

IMAGINARIUM Map pp268-9 _For Children_
☎ 91 781 33 37; www.imaginarium.es in Spanish; Calle de Claudio Coello 45; 10am-8.30pm Mon-Sat; Metro Serrano

Creative toys, books and games fill this colourful shop, which is focused on things that stimulate kids. The doors, a big one for adults and a mini one for kids, is a sign of what's inside. Careful – you (and the kiddies) will want to stay and play here all day!

JAIME MASCARÓ
Map pp268-9 _Fashion, Clothes & Shoes_
☎ 91 435 00 65; Calle de Hermosilla 22; 10am-8.30pm Mon-Sat; Metro Serrano or Velázquez

This Menorcan label with beautiful leather bags and shoes has surprisingly good prices and is a great place to find unique accessories. The store itself is worth a look too; purses are displayed like art and the minimalist decor screams chic.

LLADRÓ
Map pp268-9 _Design, Homewares & Gifts_
☎ 91 435 51 12; www.lladro.com; Calle de Serrano 68; 10am-8pm Mon-Sat; Metro Serrano

The classic porcelain figures of Lladró have changed little since your mum started collecting them decades ago. Get a little something for a souvenir or gift, or splurge for something really special. A €30,000 scene of a train station, say?

LLUÍS GENERÓ
Map pp262-4 _Fashion, Clothes & Shoes_
☎ 91 426 22 08; Calle de Jorge Juan 43; 10.30am-8.30pm Mon-Fri, 11am-3pm & 5.30-8pm Sat; Metro Velázquez

This Spanish label is known for its funky, colourful, and above all comfortable knits. Find everything from sweaters and scarves to pantsuits and jackets, all in fun shapes and colours.

LOEWE Map pp268-9 _Fashion, Clothes & Shoes_
☎ 91 426 35 88; Calle de Serrano 34; 9.30am-8.30pm Mon-Sat; Metro Serrano

One of the classiest (and most expensive) Spanish labels, Loewe is the place to go for fine leather handbags and shoes and conservative, elegant fashions.

MALLORCA Map pp268-9 *Food & Drink*
☎ 91 577 18 59; Calle de Serrano 6; 🕙 9.30am-9pm; Metro Retiro; branches throughout city

More than just a pastry shop, this is a Madrid institution with branches all over the city. Its cakes, pastries and cookies are among the best you'll find, but you can also get takeaway gourmet dishes perfect for a picnic lunch or surprise dinner guests.

MANTEQUERÍA BRAVO

Map pp268-9 *Food & Drink*
☎ 91 576 76 41; Calle de Ayala 24; 🕙 9.30am-2.30pm & 5.30-8.30pm Mon-Fri, 9.30am-2.30pm Sat; Metro Serrano

A foodie's delight, this busy shop is full of local cheeses, sausages, wines and coffees. Mmm, it makes you hungry just to talk about it.

MEZCLA

Map pp268-9 *Fashion, Clothes & Shoes*
☎ 91 435 42 03; Calle de Claudio Coello 81; 🕙 10am-8.30pm Mon-Fri, 11am-2.30pm Sat; Metro Serrano

A great place to find young, hip fashions by designers like Custo, Ungaru and others. Here you'll spot everything from flirty dresses to chic workwear. (Sorry guys, girl's clothes only.)

OILILY Map pp268-9 *For Children*
☎ 91 577 56 39; Calle de Hermosilla 16; 🕙 10am-8.30pm Mon-Sat; Metro Serrano

If you've always dreamed of having a mini me, bring the kiddies here where mum 'n' tot look-alike clothes are all the rage. The style is pinch-their-cheeks cute, with lots of colour and fun shapes. Find backpacks and school supplies too.

PURIFICACIÓN GARCÍA

Map pp268-9 *Fashion, Clothes & Shoes*
☎ 91 576 72 76; Calle de Serrano 92; 🕙 10am-8.30pm Mon-Sat; Metro Serrano

One of the most successful Spanish designers, Puri offers elegant, mature designs for men and women. With the variety of styles here you could get outfitted for a wedding or a workday.

ROBERTO VERINO

Map pp268-9 *Fashion, Clothes & Shoes*
☎ 91 426 04 75; Calle Serrano 33; 🕙 10am-9pm Mon-Sat; Metro Serrano

Find simple, classy designs for men and women in this popular Spanish designer's shop. There are great suits for him, and tailored jackets for her. A long-time success on the Spanish fashion scene, Roberto Verino is known for his clean lines and for designs that go beyond trends.

SUAREZ

Map pp268-9 *Jewellery, Perfume & Accessories*
☎ 91 578 14 19; Calle de Serrano 62; 🕙 10am-8.30pm Mon-Sat; Metro Serrano

One of the largest and most elegant jewellers of Madrid, this is the place to find watches, engagement rings and special gifts. The atmosphere is formal, but the staff is surprisingly friendly, if a bit stiff.

TARTINE ET CHOCOLAT

Map pp268-9 *For Children*
☎ 91 431 33 57; Calle de Ayala 24; 🕙 10am-2.30pm & 4.30-8.30pm Mon-Sat; Metro Serrano

Yes, the little ones can be as preppy as mummy and daddy, with pin-striped PJs, fur-accented coats and strollers lined with Burberry plaid.

TOUS & TOUS

Map pp268-9 *Jewellery, Perfume & Accessories*
☎ 91 578 17 72; www.tous.es; Calle de Ramon de la Cruz 5; 🕙 10am-8.30pm Mon-Fri; Metro Serrano

Designer Rosa Tous has somehow managed to make the teddy bear one of the most popular insignias of *pija* (snobbish) Spain. The ubiquitous teddy covers bags, scarves and jewellery, and though it really is quite cute the label is finally starting to expand in other, less cuddly directions.

VALENTINA

Map pp262-4 *Fashion, Clothes & Shoes*
☎ 91 4 3113 57; Calle de Villanueva 21; 🕙 10.30am-2pm & 5-8.30pm Mon-Sat; Metro Velázquez

The perfect shop for brides or anyone else looking for sophisticated, special-occasion lingerie, Valentina is all about satin and lace. You can get nightgowns, undergarments and robes made to order.

VINÇON

Map pp262-4 *Design, Homewares & Gifts*
☎ 91 578 05 20; Calle de Castelló 18; 🕙 10am-2pm & 5-8.30pm Mon-Fri, 10am-8.30pm Sat; Metro Príncipe de Vergara

Bet you never knew you needed an automatic parsley cutter or an individual-sized salad spinner. Thank goodness Vinçon did. Designer gadgets and gizmos are this quirky shop's claim to fame, though it also sells trendy lamps and furniture. Even if you're not buying, this is a great place to browse.

CHAMBERÍ & ARGÜELLES

An upscale, largely residential area, this is not one of Madrid's major shopping districts, but there are a few places worth seeking out. If you want to just browse, stroll along major avenues like the Calle de Bravo Murillo, Calle de San Bernardo and the Calle de Fuencarral.

ANTIGÜEDADES HOM

Map pp262-4 *Antiques & Crafts*
☎ 91 594 20 17; Calle de Juan de Austria 31; ☿ 5.30-8.30pm Mon-Fri; Metro Iglesia

Specialising in antique Spanish fans, this tiny shop is a wonderful place to browse or to find a special gift. Delicately painted fans and fans made with bone are some of the things you'll find. It's open afternoons only because the owner spends the morning restoring the fans you see for sale.

BODEGA SANTA CECILIA

Food & Drink
☎ 91 445 52 83; Calle de Blasco de Garay 72-74; ☿ 10am-2pm & 5-8.30pm Mon-Sat; Metro Islas Filipinas

With a warehouse feel and supermarket style, this doesn't seem on first impressions to be one of Madrid's best shops. But don't judge this book by its cover; its enormous collection of Spanish and international wines make it a great stop. It also organises tastings and has information about area wineries.

EL PATIO DE MARTA

Map pp262-4 *Design, Homewares & Gifts*
☎ 91 308 08 02; Calle de Zurbano 25; ☿ 10am-8.30pm Mon-Fri, 10.30am-2pm & 5-8.30pm Sat; Metro Alonso Martínez

Specialising in outdoor furniture, this elegant shop has decorated the balconies of some of Madrid's most luxurious flats. If you've ever wanted to adorn your balcony with plush couches, wooden coffee tables or grand lamps, this is your shop.

HARLEY DAVIDSON MADRID

Map pp262-4 *Specialist Store*
☎ 91 447 17 59; Calle del General Álvarez de Castro 26; ☿ 10am-2pm & 5-8pm Mon-Fri, 10am-2pm Sat; Metro Canal

For the Harley fans who long to connect with like-minded motorcyclists in Madrid, this is the place to go. You can ooh and ahh over the bikes on show, and you'll also find Harley jackets, T-shirts, pins and other simply must have paraphernalia.

LIBRERIA AVIRANETA

Map pp262-4 *Books*
☎ 91 448 43 13; Calle de San Bernardo 128; ☿ 10am-2pm & 4.30-8pm Mon-Fri, 10am-2pm Sat; Metro Quevedo

This independent shop is the way bookstores were meant to be: packed floor to ceilings with enticing books and staffed by knowledgeable people who've actually read much of what's on the shelves. It has especially large travel and kids' sections.

LOU LOU DE PARIS

Map pp262-4 *Jewellery, Perfume & Accessories*
☎ 91 446 53 01; Plaza de Olavide 8; ☿ 11am-2pm & 5-9pm Mon-Sat; Metro Iglesia or Bilbao

This adorable, little shop has original handbags and accessories that look chic and pricey but are surprisingly affordable. The designs here are quirky but sophisticated.

Clothing Sizes
Measurements approximate only, try before you buy

Women's Clothing

Aus/UK	8	10	12	14	16	18
Europe	36	38	40	42	44	46
Japan	5	7	9	11	13	15
USA	6	8	10	12	14	16

Women's Shoes

Aus/USA	5	6	7	8	9	10
Europe	35	36	37	38	39	40
France only	35	36	38	39	40	42
Japan	22	23	24	25	26	27
UK	3½	4½	5½	6½	7½	8½

Men's Clothing

Aus	92	96	100	104	108	112
Europe	46	48	50	52	54	56
Japan	S		M	M		L
UK/USA	35	36	37	38	39	40

Men's Shirts (Collar Sizes)

Aus/Japan	38	39	40	41	42	43
Europe	38	39	40	41	42	43
UK/USA	15	15½	16	16½	17	17½

Men's Shoes

Aus/UK	7	8	9	10	11	12
Europe	41	42	43	44½	46	47
Japan	26	27	27½	28	29	30
USA	7½	8½	9½	10½	11½	12½

MDM

Map pp262-4 *Design, Homewares & Gifts*

☎ 91 444 06 20; Calle de Bravo Murillo 14; ⊗ 9am-9pm Mon-Sat; Metro Quevedo

Full of fun, designer-kitchen gadgets no one really needs, this big, bright store sells everything you never knew you wanted.

PASAJES LIBRERÍA INTERNACIONAL

Map pp266-7 *Books*

☎ 91 310 12 45; www.pasajeslibros.com; Calle de Génova 3; ⊗ 10am-2pm & 5-8pm Mon-Fri; Metro Alonso Martínez

With an entire level dedicated to foreign-language titles, this bookshop has quite a large sections of English, French, German, Italian and Portuguese books. The selection goes far beyond popular fiction: spend tim browsing here and you'll find everything from poetry and classic literature to history, phil osophy and biology.

TEA SHOP Map pp262-4 *Food & Drink*

☎ 91 446 09 34; Calle de Bravo Murillo 9; ⊗ 10am-2pm & 4.30-8.30pm Mon-Fri, 10.30am-2.30pm & 5-8.30pm Sat; Metro Quevedo

It smells heavenly inside this little shop, where dozens of canisters of teas, ranging from peach- to violet- to chocolate-flavoured tea are lined up against the wall. It sells tea pot and other tea accessories too.

NORTHERN MADRID

Filled with more homes, schools and office buildings than shopping streets, northern Madrid, nevertheless, is home to a couple of expat Madrid's favourite places.

MODA SHOPPING

Map p261 *Shopping Centre*

☎ 91 581 15 25; Calle de General Perón 40; ⊗ Mon-Sat 8am-10pm; Metro Santiago Bernabéu

Somehow 'shopping centre' doesn't seem quite the right way to describe Moda. Just off the Paseo de la Castellana, this is a sprawling mall with fashionable shops, restaurants and a few high-quality antique stores. It's a great place to browse on a rainy day.

TASTE OF AMERICA

Map p261 *Food & Drink*

☎ 91 562 16 32; taste@infonegocio.com; Calle de Serrano 149; ⊗ 10am-9pm Mon-Fri, 10.30am-9pm Sat; Metro República Argentina

Aunt Jemima's syrup, Duncan Hines cake frosting, frozen bagels, Goldfish, marshmal lows…You'll find all those oh-so-healthy American brands and more at this food and kitchen-supply shop.

Sleeping

Sleeping

Madrid is packed with hotels and *hostales* of all shapes and sizes, and unless you arriv
during a peak time (Christmas, Easter, holiday weekends, major trade fairs and the like
finding a place to lay your head shouldn't be a problem. Booking ahead is always a goo
idea, though for many budget places it won't be necessary.

The accommodation options start at the bottom of the barrel with informal youth hostels
cheap *pensiones* (guesthouses) and slightly more upscale *hostales* (cheap hotels). Madrid'
budget accommodation is surprisingly nice, with most *hostales* offering private bathroom
and TVs in the rooms.

Moving up the ladder you'll find a great selection of mid-range *hostales* and hotels with
encanto (character), which are often housed in historic buildings and offer personality i
not poshness. For those wanting to be pampered, you won't be disappointed with Madrid'
collection of five-stars.

A room in an upper budget or mid-level *hostal* with its own bathroom and extras suc
as a phone, TV, air conditioning or heating will cost €45 or €50 for a double. The street
around Gran Vía and the Plaza Mayor are full of such places; we've picked just a few of th
best among the throngs on offer. From there, the prices climb right up to the €5000 a nigh
charged at the Ritz for its royal suite. *Hostales* charging less than €50 a night for a doubl
room are listed under 'Cheap Sleeps' headings.

The price of any type of accommodation may vary with the season. Some places hav
separate price structures for high season *(temporada alta)*, mid-season *(temporada media
or low season *(temporada baja)*, all usually displayed on a notice in reception or close by
Hoteliers are not bound by these displayed prices. They are free to charge less, which they
quite often do, or more, which happens fairly rarely. Not all hoteliers consider the same
periods to be high season either.

Accommodation prices in this book are a guide only. Always check room charges before
putting down your bags and remember that prices can and do change with time.

Virtually all accommodation prices are subject to IVA, the Spanish version of value-
added tax, which is 7%. This is often included in the quoted price at cheaper places, but less
often at more expensive ones. To check, ask: '*¿Está incluido el IVA?*' ('Is IVA included?'). In
some cases you will be charged the IVA only if you ask for a receipt.

LOS AUSTRIAS & CENTRO

Stretching from just below the Plaza Mayor up to Gran Vía, this neighbourhood is
home to the bulk of Madrid's historical sites and to some of its most traditional taverns
restaurants and shops. Getting a car in and out can be tricky, but its narrow streets
and lively plazas are excellent places to stroll. You'll find a wide range of hotels here,
from the cheapest of youth hostels to some of the most posh rooms in town. Although
not unsafe, the area has a high concentration of pickpockets, and areas like Calle de la
Montera are popular with prostitutes and their customers, so be especially cautious and
aware at night.

Double or Nothing

In Spain a *habitación doble* (double room) usually indicates a room with two single beds. Cuddly couples
should request a *cama de matrimonio* – literally a
marriage bed – which is usually what the British and
Americans refer to as a queen-sized bed.

HOSTAL ACAPULCO Map pp266-7 *Hostal*
☎ 915 31 19 45; Calle de la Salud 13, 4th fl; s/d/tr/q
€41/51/69/85; Metro Gran Vía
No dusty corners or dingy curtains in this immaculate little *hostal*. Rooms have small balconies
and most overlook a quiet plaza (double-glazed
windows ensure a peaceful night's sleep). Marble floors, newly renovated bathrooms and the

Top Five Sleeps

For...

- **History** Catalonia Moratín (p188)
- **Being chic** Quo (p189)
- **Romance** Hotel AC Santo Mauro (p194)
- **Seeing and being seen** Villa Magna (p193)
- **All-out luxury** Hotel Ritz (p190)

ocation between Gran Vía and the Puerta del Sol make this an excellent option.

ATENEO HOTEL Map pp270-2   *Hotel*
☎ 91 521 20 12; www.ateneohotel.com; Calle de la Montera 22; s €80-95, d €100-135; Metro Sol
Housed in a restored, 18th-century building, this charming hotel offers quiet rooms with attractive parquet floors and private balconies that look onto the busy street below. The spacious work areas in every room include free ADSL Internet access for those toting laptops.

HOSTAL LUIS XV Map pp266-7   *Hostal*
☎ 91 522 13 50; www.hrluisxv.net in Spanish; Calle de la Montera 47, 8th fl; s/d/tr €42/55/70; Metro Gran Vía
Opened at the end of 2003, rooms here are clean and modern, and exterior ones have beautiful views over old Madrid (the sight from triple room No 820 is better than you'll find at any

five-star in the city). All new everything makes this place feel pricier than it is, as do the balconies outside every exterior room. At the time of writing the owners were getting ready to open two other *hostales* in the same building.

HOSTAL MACARENA Map pp270-2   *Hostal*
☎ 91 365 92 21; macarena@silserranos.com; Cava de San Miguel 8; s/d €57/70; Metro Ópera
Set on one of the old, cobblestone streets that runs past the Plaza Mayor, this charming *hostal* is one of the best in the *barrio*. Rooms are quiet and welcoming, decorated in warm colours, and the staff is helpful and friendly.

HOSTAL MADRID Map pp270-2   *Hostal*
☎ 91 522 00 60; www.hostal-madrid.info; Calle de Esparteros 6, 2nd fl; s €50-58, d €70, tr €88; Metro Sol
Rooms here are small and simple, with rustic but attractive decor and fully-equipped bathrooms. The exteriors have small balconies and lots of light, but the quieter interior rooms are dark and make you feel a bit claustrophobic. The *hostal*'s owner also rents out charming apartments (see p196).

HOSTAL ORIENTE Map pp270-2   *Hostal*
☎ 91 548 03 14; Calle del Arenal 23, 1st fl; s €35, d €51-60; Metro Ópera
Near the Teatro Real and the Plaza de Isabel II, this pretty hotel is a good bet. It has been

Built in 1910, the Hotel Ritz oozes old-world luxury (p190)

recently renovated and has tall ceilings, pretty, green bathrooms and attractive rooms that come with all the trimmings (TV, air con, hairdryer etc). The exterior rooms are light-filled and surprisingly quiet. The quieter still interiors are dark and not nearly as pleasant.

HOTEL II CASTILLAS Map pp266-7 *Hotel*
☎ 91 524 97 50; www.hoteldoscastillas.com; Calle de la Abada 7; s €84-110, d €99-125; Metro Sol
Opened in late 2003, this central hotel has casual, smallish rooms with hardwood floors and a pretty beige-and-blue colour motif. The spacious bathroom has some unexpected perks like a heated towel rack and a make-up mirror.

HOTEL ANACO Map pp266-7 *Hotel*
☎ 91 522 46 04; www.anacohotel.com; Calle de las Tres Cruces 3; s/d/tr €78/97/131; Metro Gran Vía
The Anaco seems to have it all: a fair price, a central location, attentive service and attractive decor. Recently renovated, the 39 rooms are stylish (neutral tones with red accents, modern touches like a stainless-steel basin sink, a great work space…) and extremely peaceful, though they look onto a busy street.

HOTEL CLIPPER Map pp266-7 *Hotel*
☎ 91 531 17 00; www.hthotels.com; Calle Chinchilla 6; s €95-140, d €95-170; Metro Santo Domingo
Part of the High Tech hotels chain, the Clipper offers some great perks, like a free ADSL line in all rooms, two computers available for guest use and hydro-massage showers. Rooms are stylish, done in neutral colours, and some top-end rooms even come with their own PC.

HOTEL EMPERADOR Map pp266-7 *Hotel*
☎ 91 540 06 57; www.emperadorhotel.com; Gran Vía 53; s €165, d €220-320; Metro Santo Domingo
The classy lobby has a 1950s Hollywood feel to it, but rooms are up-to-date and well kept, with plush red carpet, large bathrooms and private terraces overlooking Gran Vía. The rooftop pool is a big plus in summer, and year-round you can use the gym, sauna and beauty salon.

HOTEL HH CAMPOMANES
Map pp266-7 *Hotel*
☎ 91 548 85 48; www.hhcampomanes.com; Calle de Campomanes 4; s €77-99, d €87-111; Metro Oriente
One of Madrid's few examples of an urban-chic boutique hotel, the new (built 2002) Campomanes is the ultimate in minimalism, with black walls and red lighting in the lobby.

Rooms are spacious, with high ceilings, simple furniture and well-equipped bathrooms. The owners plan to soon open three more hotel under the brand name Luna.

HOTEL INTUR PALACIO SAN MARTÍN
Map pp266-7 *Hotel*
☎ 91 701 50 00; www.intur.com; Plaza de San Martín 5; s €109-165, d €109-204; Metro Callao; **P**
Set on a picturesque plaza and housed in the former US embassy, this beautiful hotel offer simple luxury. Rooms are spacious and sunny with plush red carpet and enormous beds Room 103 is especially large. The sunlit interior patio is an ideal place for a coffee, even i you're not staying here.

HOTEL NEGRESCO Map pp266-7 *Hotel*
☎ 91 523 86 10; www.partner-hotels.com; Calle de los Mesonero Romanos 12; d €90-120, small discount for single; Metro Callao or Gran Vía
Rooms are small and a little dark, but they're comfortable, with thick carpets, lots of wood accents and a hydro-massage shower. The service is very personal (there are just 19 rooms) and the staff is happy to help you out with travel or activity plans. The location, on a quiet side street nea all the action of the city centre, is excellent.

HOTEL PLAZA MAYOR Map pp270-2 *Hotel*
☎ 91 360 06 06; www.h-plazamayor.com; Calle de Atocha 2; s/d €48/70; Metro Sol or Tirso de Molina
This charming hotel is great value for the neighbourhood. Original elements of the 150-year-old building (like the stone walls or the 1st floor) have been left intact, while the decor itself is modern and stylish. The spacious rooms have all hardwood floors, new ish bathrooms and great views of the city centre.

HOTEL PRECIADOS Map pp266-7 *Hotel*
☎ 91 454 44 00; www.preciadoshotel.com; Calle de Preciados 37; s €120, d €138-150; Metro Callao or Sol; **P**
Near the Puerta del Sol and a busy commercial district, this stylish hotel has comfortable rooms with all the amenities (even a free minibar) and a pretty, historic façade. It's gotten rave reviews with readers for having excellent service and for being all-round good value for money.

HOTEL SANTO DOMINGO
Map pp266-7 *Hotel*
☎ 91 547 98 00; www.bestwestern.es/santodomingo .html in Spanish; Plaza de Santo Domingo 13; s €92-127, d €158-213; Metro Santo Domingo

Top Five Cheap Sleeps

- **Hostal Orly** (p197) For amazing views over central Madrid.
- **Hostal Triana** (p197) For quirky decor and a pretty plaza-side location.
- **Hostal Don Juan** (p193) Antique furniture and original artwork make this place special.
- **Hostal Cruz Sol** (p187) Bright, cheerful and, best of all, it smells nice!
- **Hostal Gran Duque** (p187) Newly renovated, it has all the perks.

Santo Domingo calls itself a 'hotel museum' because of its extensive art and antique-furniture collection, which is scattered around the hotel's public spaces. The bright, inviting rooms don't have original artwork in them, but they are tastefully done in a cheerful yellow, with especially comfortable beds and, on upper floors, a terrace with a view.

HOTEL SENATOR Map pp266-7 *Hotel*
☎ 91 531 41 51; www.senatorhoteles.com; Gran Vía 21; s €95-120, d €115-140; Metro Gran Vía

One of Madrid's best new hotels is housed in a beautifully restored building you can best appreciate from the glass lift (elevator) that zips up its airy central patio. Rooms are sophisticated though not grand, with elegant wallpaper, lusciously thick bedcovers and, on the upper floors, great city views. There's a stylish rooftop pool open in summer.

CHEAP SLEEPS

HOSTAL ALISTE Map pp266-7 *Hostal*
☎ 91 521 59 79; h.aliste@teleline.es; Calle Caballero de Gracia 6, 3rd fl; s/d €35/42; Metro Gran Vía

This well-kept, little *hostal* has cheerful, bright rooms with unfortunate, shimmering-pink bedspreads and curtains. Try to reserve pretty room No 3, which has a balcony and slightly more attractive decor. There's no air con (but fans do come in every room), so be prepared to open the windows in summer.

HOSTAL CRUZ SOL Map pp270-2 *Hostal*
☎ 91 532 71 97; www.hostalcruzsol.com; Plaza Santa Cruz 6, 3rd floor; s/d €38/48; Metro Sol

Set on a small, sunny plaza in the centre, the Cruz Sol is a clean *hostal* that makes a great base for seeing the sights. The newly renovated rooms have yellow walls and bright-coloured bedding, making them especially cheerful.

HOSTAL GRAN DUQUE Map pp266-7 *Hostal*
☎ 91 540 04 13; www.hostalgranduque.com; Calle de Campomanes 6, 3rd fl; s/d/tr €34/49/60; Metro Oriente

The 22 rooms of this quiet *hostal* have just been renovated, making this a good option for the *barrio*. Rooms have wooden floors, a pretty, tiled bath and attractive decor, though the service could be friendlier.

HOSTAL ORLY Map pp266-7 *Hostal*
☎ 91 531 30 12; Calle de la Montera 47, 7th fl; s/d/tr €29/39/51; Metro Gran Vía

In a grand, old, 19th-century building, this quiet *hostal* is excellent value. Rooms are cheerful with tall ceilings and wooden floors, and all windows have thick double glass to block the noise. Request double room No 11, a corner room with lots of light, a charming glassed-in terrace and fabulous views. There is no air con but the bedrooms are equipped with fans.

HOSTAL TRIANA Map pp266-7 *Hostal*
☎ 91 532 68 12; www.hostaltriana.com; Calle de la Salud 13, 1st fl; s/d €35/47; Metro Gran Vía; **P**

Each smallish room of this cheerful *hostal* is different, but all are heavy on pastels and have clean, tiled bathrooms. Exterior rooms look onto the Plaza del Carmen, so if you want more sunlight and a better view, try to book a room on the top floor.

LOS AMIGOS BACKPACKERS' HOSTEL
Map pp270-2 *Hostal*
☎ 915 47 17 07; www.losamigoshostel.com; Calle de Campomanes 6, 4th fl; per bed €15; Metro Oriente

Clean, friendly and English-speaking, this is one of the city's best options if you're truly on a budget. Cheerful, well-kept rooms (yellow bedposts, blue walls, polka dotted curtains…) have four- to 10-bunk beds and free lockers. The communal bathrooms have been recently renovated and look like something from a university dorm suite.

Take a Dip: Top Five Hotel Pools

For...
- **Rooftop views** Hotel Emperador (opposite)
- **The kids** Hotel Senator (above)
- **Spa-style luxury** Hotel AC Santo Mauro (p194)
- **Sunbathing** Hotel Urban (p190)
- **Aeroplane spotting** High Tech Madrid Aeropuerto (p196)

SOL, HUERTAS & ATOCHA

If smoky bars, tile-façaded shops and some of the city's best nightlife are your thing, then this is your *barrio*. Within walking distance to the Plaza Mayor, the Puerta del Sol and the Big Three (the Museo del Prado, Centro de Arte Reina Sofía and Museo Thyssen-Bornemisza) the location is fantastic for those who want to be in the thick of the action. Street noise can be a problem, especially on weekend nights when cars jam the narrow streets and revellers spill from the bars, but interior rooms are normally available for light sleepers.

CATALONIA MORATÍN Map pp270-2 *Hotel*

☎ 91 369 71 71; www.hoteles-catalonia.es; Calle Atocha 23; s/d €136/177; Metro Antón Martín

Opened in 2002 and housed in a meticulously restored, 18th-century palace, this is one of the most charming places to stay in Madrid. The original stone entryway is impressive, but even better is the bright interior patio beyond it. Rooms are the very definition of rustic-chic, with a simple beige-and-red colour scheme, hardwood floors and balconies in every room.

HOSTAL MARTÍN Map pp270-2 *Hostal*

☎ 91 429 95 79; www.hostalmartin.com; Calle de Atocha 43; s €36-58, d €45-70; Metro Antón Martín

This fine *hostal* is luminous and sparklingly clean, with a look you'd expect to see in a two- or three-star hotel. With newly renovated bathrooms and pretty room decor, this is a great value for money. The young, English-speaking owners also run the Hostal Cervelo two floors below, which has a similar style but is not quite as nice. They share one office and one phone number.

HOSTAL SARDINERO Map pp270-2 *Hostal*

☎ 91 429 57 56; Calle del Prado 16, 3rd fl; s/d from €45/60; Metro Sol or Antón Martín

This is one of the area's better *hostales*, with cheerful rooms and tall ceilings. Fine wooden furniture, newly renovated bathrooms and a sparklingly clean look make you feel at home. All rooms have balcony, TV, phone, air con and heating.

HOTEL CORTEZO Map pp270-2 *Hotel*

☎ 913 69 01 01; www.bestwestern.es; Calle Doctor Cortezo 3; s €90-110, d €130; Metro Tirso de Molina

Built in the 1950s but kept up to date, this Best Western hotel is good value for its location near the Puerta del Sol and the Plaza Mayor. Rooms have pretty hardwood floors and elegant decor, though most have two single beds, not big double ones, so lovey-dovey couples should look elsewhere.

HOTEL EL PRADO Map pp270-2 *Hotel*

☎ 91 369 02 34; www.pradohotel.com; Calle del Prado 11; s €74-125, d €115-155; Metro Sol or Antón Martín

The stylish Prado just underwent a full renovation and the new decor and services have given this moderately priced three-star the look and feel of a four-plus. Adding to the charm is the wine theme running throughout; each room is named after a Spanish wine region, and information about that region is hung by the door. Rooms are decorated with an attractive grape motif.

HOTEL INGLÉS Map pp270-2 *Hotel*

☎ 91 429 65 51; fax 91 420 24 23; Calle de Echegaray 8; s €70-80, d €100-120; Metro Sol; P

At the time of publication, the hotel was in the midst of converting its once dingy, dark and overpriced rooms into lovely spaces worthy of a four-star business hotel. Be sure to book one of the new rooms, which boast marbled bathrooms, pretty wooden furniture and fine linens. Don't bother with a room that hasn't been renovated, which will cost the same.

HOTEL LOPE DE VEGA Map p273 *Hotel*

☎ 91 360 00 11; www.hotellopedevega.com; Calle de Lope de Vega 49; s €108-135, d €135-170; Metro Antón Martín

Sitting in the middle of the *barrio de las letras* (literature district), this recently renovated hotel is dedicated to the life and times of Spanish writer Lope de Vega (1562–1635). The stylish rooms, which are decorated in warm colours and have private terraces, are named after the writer's works or those of his contemporaries.

HOTEL MEDIODIA Map p273 *Hotel*

☎ 91 527 30 60; fax 91 530 70 08; Plaza del Emperador Carlos V 8; s/d/tr €54/64/82; Metro Atocha

Just across from the Atocha station, this hotel is perfect if you're arriving on a late train. Rooms aren't luxurious (pressed-wood furniture looks like it could have been bought at a garage sale) but they're attractive and clean. The best rooms look onto the tranquil plaza behind the hotel.

Sleeping – Sol, Huertas & Atocha

HOTEL MIAU Map pp270-2 — *Hotel*

☎ 91 369 71 20; www.hotelmiau.com; Calle del Príncipe 26; s/d incl breakfast €88/98; Metro Sol or Antón Martín

This 20-room boutique hotel overlooks the Plaza Santa Ana and offers light-filled, airy rooms with tall ceilings and stylish neutral decor. Corner room No 13 is lovely, though, like the other rooms, it can be noisy. The owners also run the restaurant next door, and it's a fine place for an informal meal.

HOTEL PARIS Map pp270-2 — *Hotel*

☎ 91 521 64 91; fax 91 531 01 88; Calle de Alcalá 2; s/d incl breakfast €67/87; Metro Sol

Crowned by the emblematic Tio Pepe sign, the 140-year-old hotel is a Madrid classic, exuding kitsch elegance with touches like shimmering gold bedspreads and a decidedly 1960s look. It's impossible to be more central; some rooms look right onto the Puerta del Sol.

HOTEL SUECIA Map pp270-2 — *Hotel*

☎ 91 531 69 00; www.hotelsuecia.com; Calle del Marqués de Casa Riera 4; s/d €115/178

The motto here is 'we just want to be the nicest', and nice they are indeed, with friendly staff and comfortable, if slightly bland, rooms. Set on a quiet side street near the Prado and Gran Vía, the location is unbeatable if you want to be near the action, but not bothered by the bustle.

QUO Map pp270-2 — *Hotel*

☎ 91 532 90 49; www.hotelesquo.com; Calle de Sevilla 4; s/d €143/178

It's one of the few New York–style, boutique hotels in town but Quo sets a new standard for cool. The black-clad staff fit right in with the minimalist look and retro-chic decor. Rooms are predictably modern, with simple but plush furnishings, tall ceilings and huge windows that let light flood in.

REINA VICTORIA Map pp270-2 — *Hotel*

☎ 915 31 45 00; www.trypnet.com; Plaza de Santa Ana 14; s €129-192, d €129-235; Metro Sol or Antón Martín

This elegant hotel is in the perfect spot if you want to be right in the thick of Madrileño life. Rooms are big and bright, with lovely carpets and plush bedding. A room overlooking the lively Plaza de Santa Ana provides unbeatable ambience, but if you need peace and quiet request an interior room.

Hotel Paris (p189)

VILLA REAL Map pp270-2 — *Hotel*

☎ 91 420 37 67; www.derbyhotels.es; Plaza de las Cortes 10; r from €280; Metro Antón Martín

This stylish boutique hotel has mastered the art of combining modern design with classic style. Known for having the largest private collection of ancient Roman mosaics in Europe (they are scattered all about the hotel), the hotel also has an impressive collection of modern art, with a dozen works by Catalan painter Antoni Tàpies hanging in the restaurant, and prints by another Catalan artist, Josep Guinovart, in every room. Antique pieces and sleek modern furniture are brilliantly paired in the rooms, which are warm and inviting, if a bit on the small side.

CHEAP SLEEPS

HOSTAL AGUILAR Map pp270-2 — *Hostal*

☎ 91 429 59 26; www.hostalaguilar.com in Spanish; Carrera de San Jerónimo 32, 2nd fl; s/d/tr €40/47/63; Metro Sol or Sevilla

Although the style of this place seems to have changed little in the past three or four

The New Kids on the Block

Tourism in Madrid is booming, and if you need proof of it just take a look around the central *barrios*, where new hotels are popping up left and right. Traditionally the realm of cheap *hostales* and iffy *pensiones*, areas like Huertas and Chueca are finally getting a sprinkling of three- and four-star hotels promising more variety and competitive prices.

Two new faces to look out for are **Hotel Urban** (☎ 93 366 88 05; www.derbyhotels.es; Carrera de San Jerónimo 34), a chic boutique hotel that was preparing to open at the time of writing, and a new **Vincci Prado Hotel** (Calle del Prado 18; www.vincci hoteles.com in Spanish) that has transformed an entire city block in the Huertas *barrio* and was also nearing completion at the time of writing.

decades, the rooms are large and offer lots of amenities like TV, air con and private balconies. The bubblegum-pink bedspreads and tacky curtains could go, but pluses like the double-glazed, noise-blocking windows and a computer offering Internet access for €3 per hour make the Aguilar a good option.

HOSTAL DULCINEA Map pp270-2 *Hostal*
☎ 91 429 93 09; donato@teleline .es; Calle de Cervantes 19, 2nd fl; s/d/tr €44/48/55; Metro Antón Martín

You'll be warmly welcomed at this friendly *hostal*, where the rooms are simple but clean, and the modern-ish bathrooms leave little to be desired. This is a great place to stay if you're interested in seeing the big three museums as they're all just a short walk away. The Dulcinea's only major shortcoming is noise. Walls are paper thin, and

unless you like knowing intimate details about your neighbours, earplugs are a must.

HOSTAL INTERNACIONAL LA POSADA DE HUERTAS Map pp270-2 *Hostel*
☎ 91 429 35 26; www.posadadehuertas.com in Spanish; Calle de las Huertas 21; beds per person from €16; Metro Sevilla or Antón Martín

This simple youth hostel offers dorm-style rooms with metal beds and lockers. Although the place is clean, with warm blankets and decent (if tiny) bathrooms, it rates a zero on the charm scale.

HOSTAL RESIDENCIA MATUTE
Map pp270-2 *Hostal*
☎ 91 429 55 85; hostalmatute@hostalmatute.com; Plaza Matute 11, 1st fl; s €30-40, d €42-50; Metro Antón Martín

Not the most stylish place around, it's comfortable in a 1970s, guest-bedroom sort of way. Rooms are cheerful and on the large side, and bathrooms are covered in blue tile. Ask for an interior room if street noise bothers you, as these old windows do little to block the noise.

Top Five Most Charming Hotels

Built in old palaces or historic buildings, these hotels offer warmth and personality unmatched by even the most stylish new constructions:

- **Hostal Macarena** (p185)
- **Hostal San Lorenzo** (p192)
- **Hotel Plaza Mayor** (p186)
- **La Residencia de El Viso** (p195)
- **Hotel Orfila** (p195)

PASEO DEL PRADO & EL RETIRO

Once the stomping ground of royalty this part of Madrid has retained its sophisticated air, although the traffic that clogs the streets here does its best to distract from the charm. Nevertheless, this *barrio* is home to some of Madrid's most luxurious hotels (see the boxed text p191) and is ideal if you want to be close to the elegant Parque del Buen Retiro and to cultural monuments such as El Museo del Prado.

HOTEL MORA Map p273 *Hotel*
☎ 91 420 15 69; Paseo del Prado 32; s/d €57/75; Metro Atocha

Near the main museums and a short walk from the centre, this simple hotel offers great value. Rooms are a bit sparse but are spacious and clean, and some overlook the Botanical Gardens. Rooms on the upper floors seem a bit quieter.

HOTEL RITZ Map p273 *Hotel*
☎ 91 701 67 67; www.ritzmadrid.com; Plaza de la Lealtad 5; r from €480; Metro Banco de España

It doesn't get any ritzier than the Ritz, one of the city's oldest and most emblematic hotels. The hotel of choice for all the royal family's guests, rooms here are the last word in old-world luxury, with chandeliers galore ntique furniture and plush carpets made by the Royal Tapestry Factory. Many decor elements are originals from the hotel's creation in 910. The elegant café downstairs is ideal for leisurely coffee or a respite from the busy ity outside.

WESTIN PALACE Map pp270-2   *Hotel*
☎ 91 360 80 00; www.westin.com; Plaza de las Cortes; r from €200; Metro Banco de España or Antón Martín

What else can be said about this century-old Madrid institution? Royals, movie stars and visiting dignitaries have stayed in its plush rooms (the beds are soft as clouds) and dined under its gorgeous 'glass dome'. Even if you can't afford a night here, stop by for a pricey coffee (€6) just to soak in the atmosphere. It also does elegant theme dinners, like the monthly 'opera dinner' with live opera, or the Thursday 'jazz and sushi dinners'.

Loads of atmosphere at historic Westin Palace (p191)

Battle of the Best: Hotel Ritz vs Westin Palace

In the early 20th century, Madrid was a far cry from the cosmopolitan capital we see today. Dirty and poor, it was no match for other European cities like Paris and London, and then-king Alfonso XIII set out an ambitious plan to put his capital on a par. That meant building first-rate hotels, and in 1910 the Ritz, built by Charles Mewes, was inaugurated. Although it was a fine establishment, with just 160 rooms it didn't meet the city's demands for lodging, so two years later the larger Palace Hotel was opened across the plaza.

For decades the two hotels were considered the top in Spain (some people say they still hold the distinction) and were the stages for important meetings as royalty, politicians and international dignitaries were constantly trouping through. The hotels were for the wealthy only, and the Ritz in particular was unashamedly snobby, controlling visitors' dress style and denying entry to those not deemed worthy of the hotel. Even movie stars, artists and bullfighters were turned away for being too 'bohemian'. Meanwhile the Palace was the setting of grand parties and dinners, except for the years of the Civil War when it was used as a hospital.

Although still emblematic, the arrival of other top hotels has forced the Ritz and the Palace to release their exclusive claim on Madrid's illustrious visitors, and the attitudes of both hotels has calmed considerably. These days, their luxurious restaurants and lobbies are open to anyone who wants a slice of the original Madrileño luxury.

LA LATINA & LAVAPIÉS

Just on the edge of the city centre, this colourful, working-class district feels much further off the beaten tourist track than it actually is. You won't find many accommodation options here, but there are a couple worth seeking out.

HOTEL PUERTA DE TOLEDO

Map pp262-4 *Hotel*
☎ 91 474 71 00; www.hotel-puertadetoledo.com; Glorieta Puerta de Toledo 4; s/d €65/108; Metro Puerta de Toledo; P

The façade is as unremarkable as they come, but inside this hotel is friendly and comfortable. You can tell it was built in the 1970s, but recent renovations have given it a fresher look, with plush red carpets and spiffy new bathrooms. There are good city views from upper floors, and several rooms are specially adapted for wheelchairs.

HOTEL REYES CATÓLICOS

Map pp270-2 *Hotel*
☎ 91 365 86 00; www.domus-hoteles.es in Spanish; Calle del Ángel 18; s €74-98, d €68-90; Metro Puerta de Toledo or La Latina

The simple rooms here look out onto a quiet street or to the grand Basilica de San Francisco. With tiled floors, bright decor and lots of natural light, this inviting hotel isn't the most stylish in town but the Hotel Reyes Catolicos by far one of the best options in the neighbourhood.

MALASAÑA & CHUECA

With its youthful energy and *la movida* memories (see p150), this neighbourhood is great for those looking for Madrid's funkier side. Lots of shopping and restaurant offerings make this a fun place to explore by day, while the nonstop nightlife makes it one of the liveliest *barrios* by night. Accommodation offerings here are geared toward budget travellers, so take a peek in Cheap Sleeps (see p193) for more options.

HOSTAL LA ZONA Map pp266-7 *Hostal*
☎ 91 521 99 04; www.hostallazona.com; Calle Valverde 7, 1st fl; d €45-65; Metro Gran Vía

Catering to a gay clientele, the bedrooms here are simple but stylish and very well kept, with exposed-brick walls, marine-blue accents and a fresh look. Particularly pleasing is the spacious room No 203 – it's one of the hostal's best and has a sunny balcony.

HOSTAL SAN LORENZO

Map pp266-7 *Hostal*
☎ 91 521 30 57; www.hostal-lorenzo.com; Calle de Clavel 8; s €45-50, d €55-65, tr €75-90; Metro Gran Vía

On the edge of the busy Chueca district, this charming hotel is a little oasis in the city. On the 1st floor, the original stone walls of this 19th-century building have been left unexposed, adding character you won't find elsewhere. Reformed in 2003, rooms are small but modern, with excellent bathrooms and a pretty, casual style.

PETIT PALACE HOTEL DUCAL

Map pp266-7 *Hotel*
☎ 91 521 10 43; www.hthoteles.com; Calle de Hortaleza 3; s €115-160, d €120-175; Metro Gran Vía

With free computer access and ADSL lines in all rooms, this is the place for those who can't go a day without their high-speed Internet connection. Opened in 2003, rooms here are modern and clean-lined, with wooden floors and perks like a hydro-massage shower.

SIETE ISLAS HOTEL Map pp266-7 *Hotel*
☎ 91 523 46 88; www.hotelsieteislas.com; Calle de Valverde 14-16; s €80-120, d €100-145; Metro Gran Vía

The owners of this 79-room hotel are from the Canary Islands, and their heritage shows in every aspect of the place – from the marine theme in the lobby to the rooms, named after Canarian towns. Rooms are comfortable and stylish, with a generous bathroom and cool beige-and-navy-blue tones throughout.

VILLA DE LA REINA Map pp266-7 *Hotel*
☎ 91 523 91 01; www.h10.es; Gran Vía 22; s €115-175, d €135-190; Metro Gran Vía

Stylish and business focused, rooms here have pretty hardwood floors and a soothing, neutral colour scheme. The hotel is housed in a fine old building that dates to the early 20th century, and on the 1st floor and in common areas original elements like stone pillars and arched doorways have been left intact.

CHEAP SLEEPS

HOSTAL AMERICA Map pp266-7 *Hostal*
☎ 91 522 64 48; fax 91 522 64 47; Calle de Hortaleza 9, 5th fl; s/d/tr/q €35/45/60/75; Metro Gran Vía
Bonnie, this friendly *hostal*'s tiny dog, will greet you with a lick and lead you to the rooms, which are bright and clean, with all-Ikea decor and a pretty, tiled bathroom. There is a sunny common terrace by the lobby that's perfect for having a drink or sunbathing.

HOSTAL ASUNCIÓN Map pp266-7 *Hostal*
☎ 91 308 23 48; www.asuncion-hotel.com; Plaza de Santa Barbara 8, 2nd fl; s/d €36/45; Metro Alonso Martínez
The 17 large rooms here have simple furnishings and a dorm-room style. Bathrooms are small but newly renovated and clean. You can connect to the Internet in the reception area.

HOSTAL BARAJAS Map pp266-7 *Hostal*
☎ 91 532 40 78; www.hostalbarajas.com; Calle de Augusto Figueroa 17, 2nd fl; s/d €38/45; Metro Chueca
Rooms are small (and a little dark) but charming, with wooden floors and grand windows that open onto small balconies. The bathroom obviously has not been renovated in a few years, but it's clean. The best thing about this place is its location right off Calle de Hortaleza and just minutes from the Plaza de Chueca.

HOSTAL DON JUAN Map pp266-7 *Hostal*
☎ 91 522 77 46; Plaza Vazquez de Mella 1, 2nd fl; s/d €34/48; Metro Gran Vía

Apparently someone forgot to tell the owner that *hostales* are supposed to be dank and dirty. This elegant, two-storey *hostal* is filled with art (each room has original works) and antique furniture. Rooms are simple but luminous and attractive, and the bathrooms renovated.

HOSTAL EL CATALAN Map pp266-7 *Hostal*
☎ 91 532 30 17; Calle de Hortaleza 17, 2nd fl; s €27-30, d €42, t €54; Metro Gran Vía
One of the best values in Chueca, this attractive, family-run *hostal* is clean and quiet. The spacious rooms have fresh, tile floors and some have small balconies. Bathrooms look new, though they're a bit small.

HOSTAL MARIA CRISTINA
Map pp266-7 *Hostal*
☎ 91 531 63 00; www.iespana.es/hostalmariacristina; Calle de Fuencarral 20; s/d/tr €32/44/62; Metro Gran Vía
This tidy little *hostal* sits right on a busy commercial street, but the rooms are surprisingly quiet. Charming wooden furniture and lots of light make the place cheerful, and the friendly service makes you feel as though you're staying as a guest in someone's home.

SONSOLES HOSTAL Map pp266-7 *Hostal*
☎ 91 532 75 23; sonsoles@hostalsonsodesa.com; Calle de Fuencarral 18, 2nd fl; Metro Gran Vía
Fake flowers, a fish tank and knick-knacks galore greet you at the lobby of this surprisingly elegant (but often kitschy) *hostal*. Rooms have fine wood furniture and pretty bedcovers. The bathrooms are tiny but sufficient.

SALAMANCA & LAS VENTAS

Within easy strolling distance of both Prada and El Prado, this posh *barrio* is a sophisticated and rather expensive place to stay. Wide boulevards lined with some of Madrid's best shops and restaurants are the main draw. Whereas inexpensive lodgings are few and far between, you'll find several fine upscale hotels.

BAUZÁ Map pp262-4 *Hotel*
☎ 91 435 75 45; www.hotelbauza.com; Calle de Goya 79; s/d €138/198; Metro Goya
Minimalist and modern, the new Bauzá would be right at home in Soho. Neutral colours set a soothing tone, and rooms are bright and airy. The restaurant (equally modern and minimalist) serves excellent food and many light dishes.

HOTEL ADLER Map pp262-4 *Hotel*
☎ 91 426 32 20; www.iova-sa.com; Calle de Velázquez 33; s/d €290/360; Metro Velázquez

Housed in a 19th-century former bank building, the softly lit rooms are romantic and beyond comfortable, with plush furniture, tall ceilings and a classic, sophisticated decor. The city centre is a longish walk (or a quick metro ride) away, but the hotel is in an elegant district in the company of some of Madrid's top shops.

VILLA MAGNA Map pp268-9 *Hotel*
☎ 91 587 12 34; www.madrid.hyatt.com; Paseo de la Castellana 22; s €200-310, d €255-365; Metro Colón or Rubén Darío

The utterly bland façade reveals nothing about the luxury inside the Villa Magna. The mall-like lobby is full of ritzy shops, and the 182 rooms have heavenly, cloud-like beds and all the elegance you'd expect from a place that has catered to a host of international stars such as Tom Cruise, Justin Timberlake and Marilyn Manson. Fresh fruit is placed in every room, and most offer great views of the city.

Top Five Most Chic Hotels

Manhattan, Soho...Madrid? Spain's capital is trying its hand at cool with these swanky boutique hotels:

- **Quo** (p189)
- **Hotel HH Campomanes** (p186)
- **Hotel Miau** (p189)
- **Hotel AC Santo Mauro** (below)
- **Bauzá** (p193)

CHAMBERÍ & ARGÜELLES

Just outside the bustling city centre, this residential area is great for those looking for respite from the crowds of Madrid. The *barrio* has more than its fair share of metro stop so getting around won't be a problem, though you're a good long walk from any of th tourist sights. On the plus side, here you can find cool leafy boulevards, quiet streets an some excellent accommodation options.

GRAN HOTEL CONDE DUQUE

Map pp262-4 *Hotel*

☎ 91 447 70 00; www.hotelcondeduque.es; Plaza del Conde Valle Suchil 5; s €114-151, d €171-246; Metro San Bernardo or Quevedo

Set on a quiet plaza just north of the bustling Bilbao area, this elegant hotel offers good service and a great location. Rooms are spacious and full of the sunlight that fills the plaza, and their provincial-style decor is charming.

GRAN VERSALLES HOTEL

Map pp266-7 *Hotel*

☎ 91 447 57 00; www.hotelgranversalles.es in Spanish; Calle de Covarrubias 4 & 6; s €75-123, d €90-137; Metro Alonso Martín, Iglesia or Bilbao

With all the standard, 4-star perks (satellite TV, hairdryer, Internet access, music system etc),

this hotel offers comfort and quality servic though not much personality. The rooms a smallish but cheerful with lots of colour an large windows.

HOTEL AC SANTO MAURO

Map pp262-4 *Hote*

☎ 91 319 69 00; www.ac-hoteles.com; Calle Zurbano 36; s/d €255/307; Metro Alfonso Martínez

Without a doubt one of Madrid's top hote the Santo Mauro fills three buildings of former palace (one part of the hotel is a con verted stable) and offers discreet elegance an warm service that's meant to make guests fe they're staying in a private home. Rooms hav minimal but comfortable decoration and lo of sunlight. What really sets this hotel apa though are its perks, like the beautiful Ara bian-styled indoor pool, free minibar acces

Madrid's Most Luxurious Rooms

For those unwilling to shell out a few grand for a sleep in the poshest beds Madrid has to offer, we give a sneak peak into the lifestyles of the rich and famous:

Westin Palace, Royal Suite, Room No 423 (€3550) Careful not to scuff the mosaic-ed marble floor on your way to the sauna cabin. This ain't called the Palace for nothing (p191).

Ritz, Royal Suite, Room No 110-115 (€5000) The walls are covered in raw silk, the bed has been slept in by throngs of international dignitaries (not together, we assume) and oh yeah, a personal butler is at your disposal (p190).

Villa Magna, Presidential Suite, Room No 902 (€3000) If you can get past the small security centre at the suite door you'll find a private piano, sauna and an enormous terrace complete with your own hammock for napping (p193).

Hotel Orfila, Deluxe Suite, Room No 31 (€728) Have fun raising and lowering the automatic bed as you sip the Moet champagne that greets you on arrival. Unique furniture, like a 17th-century Dutch table and a gilded mirror valued at €9000, is sure to make you feel special (opposite).

and tons of bathroom amenities foreseeing
every possible need. The hotel's tiny restaurant
is housed in the former palace library, and
shelves full of books stretch to the ceiling
around the diners.

HOTEL ORFILA Map pp268-9 *Hotel*
☎ 91 702 77 72; www.hotelorfila.com in Spanish;
Calle de Orfila 6; s/d €270/331; Metro Alonso Martínez
The former home of the exiled Queen of Bulgaria,
this small 19th-century palace is one of
Madrid's most intimate hotels. Period furniture
and decor from the 18th and 19th centuries fill
the rooms and common areas, making each
corner unique. The staff is discreet but accommodating,
and the breakfast buffet is heavenly.

HOTEL TRAFALGAR Map pp262-4 *Hotel*
☎ 91 445 62 00; www.hotel-trafalgar.com; Calle de
Trafalgar 35; s €76-95, d €109; Metro Bilbao
Attentive service and all the amenities make
this a good-value option for the area. Rooms
are comfortable if rather anonymous, with
shiny wooden floors, cheerful yellow tones
and large windows.

TRYP ALONDRAS Map p261 *Hotel*
☎ 91 447 40 00; www.solmelia.com; Calle de José
Abascal 8; s/d €125/143; Metro Alonso Cano
A standard business hotel, rooms here are
small but elegant, with wooden furniture

*Plaza de Santa Ana from room 23 at Hotel
Miau (p189)*

crowded in and deep colour tones throughout.
All rooms are exteriors looking onto the
busy avenue below; request a room on an
upper floor if you need quiet. Bathrooms are
large with a good selection of amenities.

NORTHERN MADRID
Home to government buildings, towering office complexes and important transportation
hubs such as the Chamartín station and the Nuevos Ministerios metro stop, this is a good
area for those here on business or for those who want a hotel that's easily accessible from
the airport and train stations. Although lacking some of the charm of more central *barrios*,
this is an elegant area with some excellent, high-end hotels.

HESPERÍA CASTELLANA
Map p261 *Hotel*
☎ 91 210 88 88; www.hesperia-madrid.com; Paseo
de la Castellana 57; s/d €310/340; Metro Nuevos
Ministerios
Opened in 2000, the Hespería Madrid has quickly
gained a reputation as being one of the most
stylish hotels in the city. Rooms are luxurious,
with a striking leather headboard, rust-coloured
accents, and touches like Bulgari-brand amenities
and fresh fruit and flowers. The common
areas are worth commenting on as well. The
Scotch bar has Madrid's largest collection of malt
whiskies, and a harpist sets a romantic tone in the
lobby in the evening. Valuable art, both modern
and classic, is scattered throughout the hotel.

HUSA CHAMARTÍN *Hotel*
☎ 91 334 49 00; www.hotelchamartin.com; Calle
de Augustín de Foxá; s €81-111, d €85-130; Metro
Chamartín
A great option if you're arriving late to the
Chamartín train station, this standard business-style
hotel couldn't be any closer to the
station. Rooms are spacious, with pretty, clean
bathrooms and attractive but faded decor.

LA RESIDENCIA DE EL VISO
Map p261 *Hotel*
☎ 91 564 03 70; www.residenciadelviso.com; Calle
del Nervión 8; s €77-103, d €129; Metro Republica
Argentina

A little city oasis, the charming Residencia de El Viso is a quiet, B&B-style hotel with rooms that look rather like a favourite aunt's guest room. Built in the 1930s, common areas have decor elements from the original house (which was once a private residence) like a shady interior patio where lunches are now served.

BEYOND THE CENTRE

If you've got an early morning flight, a hotel by the airport may be just what you need.

HIGH TECH MADRID AEROPUERTO

Hotel

☎ 91 564 59 06; www.hthoteles.com; Calle de Galeón 25; s €100-135, d €120-150; Metro Aeropuerto
Stylish rooms, in-room ADSL connections and free Internet access make this new hotel (opened in 2003) a great bet for business travellers. Located within shouting distance of the airport (naturally the hotel provides free airport transportation) and near the convention centre, it's convenient too. Oh yeah, and there's an outdoor pool worthy of a dip.

LONG-TERM STAYS & APARTHOTELS

If you're planning a longish stay in Madrid or if you're travelling with a family in tow, apartments may be your best bet.

HOSTAL MADRID

Map pp270-2   *Long-term Stays*
☎ 91 522 00 60; www.hostal-madrid.info; Calle de Esparteros 6, 2nd fl; apartment €100; Metro Sol
Each of the 10 apartments owned by the Hostal Madrid (see p185) is different, but they

A Room of Your Own

If you're moving to Madrid and are looking for a place to live, there are several services that can be useful. Websites like www.easyroommate.com and www.easyexpat.com pair up people (often foreigners or students) looking for rooms with those who have rooms to rent. There are also real estate and relocation companies specialising in helping foreign clients; try Re.loc Relocation Service (☎ 91 426 37 91; www.relocspain.com; Calle Juan Bravo 3A) or Solution Relocation Services (☎ 91 550 03 97; www.solucionmad.com; Calle Ferraz 80).

all have kitchens and living areas, and some have terraces. Apartments 52 and 53 have both a closed-in patio and a large, open-air terrace.

APARTHOTELS TRIBUNAL

Map pp266-7   *Apartments*
☎ 91 522 14 55; www.aparthotel-tribunal.com in Spanish; Calle de San Vicente Ferrer; apartments s/d €68/85 or per week from €365; Metro Tribunal; Ⓟ
Here you'll find simple, cheerful apartments with parquet floors, modern decor and small kitchenettes. Larger apartments are available for families or groups.

JARDÍN DE RECOLETOS

Apartments
☎ 91 7811 640; rc@vphoteles.com; Gil de Sanivañes 6; s/d incl breakfast €173/180; Metro
This comfortable spot is an aparthotel (mix of standard hotel and apartment) with large rooms that have a kitchenette, sofa bed and simple but elegant decor. Although rooms are spacious, the maximum number of occupants per room is three. It could be a good holiday option.

Excursions

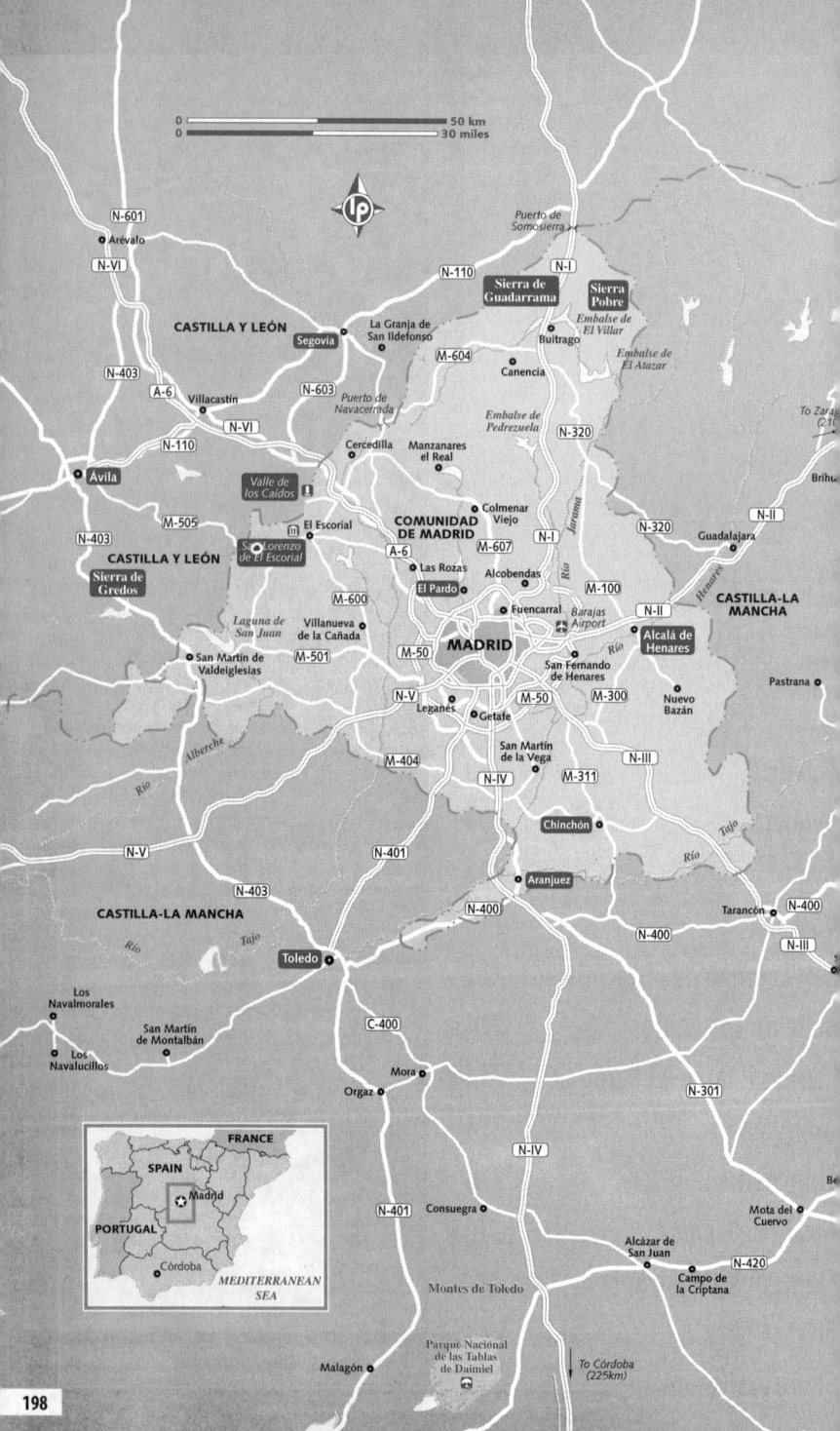

Excursions

When you've marvelled at the Prado, strolled El Retiro, stuffed yourself silly with *cocido a la Madrileña* (a nourishing hearty stew) and stayed out too late in Chueca, maybe it's time for a break in the countryside.

CASTILIAN HEARTLAND

Within an hour's radius of the capital are countless spots worth visiting, each packed with more Spanish charm than the one before it. From the walled cities of Castile to the splendid palaces and parks of El Pardo (p214) and Aranjuez (p214), these are places where Spain's history comes alive.

These trips take you across three regions – Comunidad de Madrid, Castilla–La Mancha and Castilla y León – but most of what you'll experience is the Castilian heartland. This is the land of Don Quixote and windmills, of old stone castles, broad plains and hearty country food.

CULTURE

For an opportunity to experience culture, history and some mighty fine suckling pig, head to towns like Segovia (p203), Ávila (p207) and Toledo (p200). With the high-speed train (AVE) it's possible to go even further afield and land in the Andalucían gem of Córdoba (p210) in under two hours. The fascinating Mezquita de Córdoba has got to be number one on your list of things to do there, but afterward a stroll through the sun-drenched town is a joy.

FOOD

If all you're interested in is the not-so-humble porker served with glistening, crunchy crackling, Chinchón (p216), overflowing with *meson*-style (traditional) restaurants, will suit you fine.

NATURE

If you're aching for a glimpse of nature, follow the well-beaten path into the hills of Sierra de Guadarrama (p217), a favourite Madrileño escape. The Palacio Real de El Pardo (p214) and the pristine pine forest around Valle de los Caídos (p214) are good options for nature lovers too.

SIERRAS

The sierras of Madrid are certainly great spots for walking, exploring small quaint villages and, in winter, snow skiing. Whereas all of these mountainous areas are popular weekend escapes for Madrileños, foreigners are seldom seen in these parts, but it's definitely worth the effort. Manzanares El Real (p217) has an enchanting storybook castle.

Fiestas & Festivals

It's worth planning a trip to coincide with some of the extravagant fiestas going on in towns around Madrid. Here's our pick of the parties:

Corpus Christi, Toledo (June) Several days of festivities culminate in a procession featuring the massive Custodia de Arfe (p202).

Fiesta Mayor, Chinchón (August 12–18) The town's main plaza is turned into a bullring and bullfights are held each morning. Cheer from the surrounding balconies over breakfast and coffee.

Santa Teresa, Ávila (around October 15) In honour of Saint Teresa, who was born in Ávila, the town throws out all stops for days of celebrations and processions.

Semana Santa, Córdoba (Easter week) Elaborate processions, flowers and pointy-headed penitents fill the Andalucian city for one of the year's holiest festivals.

TOLEDO

Standing proudly on a hill above the Río Tajo, Toledo is a bastion of Spain's medieval grandeur. A power long before Madrid was *Madrid*, this was a centre of art, culture and religion throughout the Middle Ages. Jews, Christians and Arabs lived here peacefully for centuries, and the culture they created is one of the most fascinating aspects of Toledo. Although the city centre is now the domain of tourists, souvenir shops and school groups, even they can't mask the old city's glory.

'Toletum', as the Romans called it, was always a strategically important city, and as far back as the 6th century it was the capital of the Visigoth empire. The feuding Visigoths lost the city to Muslim invaders in 711, and from then until the early Middle Ages it was a strong Muslim centre. Alfonso VI wrestled the city back into Christian hands in 1085, and shortly after it was declared 'the seat of the Church' in Spain. This marked the beginning of a golden age that lasted through the Inquisition and into the 16th century, when Felipe II ditched Toledo and its uppity clergy in favour of his new capital, Madrid.

Modern Toledo sprawls to the north, but the old city and the most important sights are stacked atop one another in a crook of the Río Tajo. The hills here make for steep strolls through the centre, and in summer the glaring sun can make walking tiring. For a more relaxing view of the old town, hop on the **Tren Turístico**, a small train that does a 45-minute loop through Toledo and provides a brief but interesting overview of its main sights. The train leaves hourly and tickets are for sale in the Zoco Centro Tourist Office.

Toledo lacks a true centre, however the **Plaza de Zocodover**, at the northeastern end of the old town, is a good place to start a visit. This oddly-shaped plaza once served as an Arab livestock market and later as the main city market, but is now lined with terrace cafés and filled with day trippers.

From here the looming fortress of the **alcázar** is a short walk away, but it's closed indefinitely for restoration. When it reopens (perhaps by 2007) it will gain the collection of Madrid's Museo del Ejército (p76), greatly expanding the army museum already here. This site, the highest in Toledo, was first a Roman military base, then an Arab fortress, and finally a Christian one rebuilt by Alfonso VI in the 11th century. Later Carlos V converted the harsh square block of a building into a royal palace and used it to house his visitors until it was damaged by fire in 1710. The palace burned again in 1810 (thanks to Napoleon) and was nearly destroyed yet again during Spain's Civil War. When Franco ordered it to be rebuilt, he turned it into the military museum of today.

Nearby is the **Catedral**, one of the largest and most opulent in the world. An essentially Gothic creation with a few *mudéjar* afterthoughts, it was built in the 13th century atop an earlier mosque. Toledo's role as the seat of the Church in Spain ensured that the cathedral had a steady stream of patrons, and those moneyed Catholics left their mark with lavish decor throughout.

All the chapels and side rooms are worth peeking into, but the **Capilla de la Torre** (Tower Chapel) in the northwestern corner and the **Sacristía** (Sacristy) are well worth your time. The latter boasts a lovely vaulted ceiling and a small gallery of El Greco's works (see boxed text p202), while the Tower Chapel is the parking place of one of the most

The walled city of Toledo, a bastion of medieval grandeur

TOLEDO

0 ⊏══════════■ 200 m
0 ⊏══════════⊐ 0.1 miles

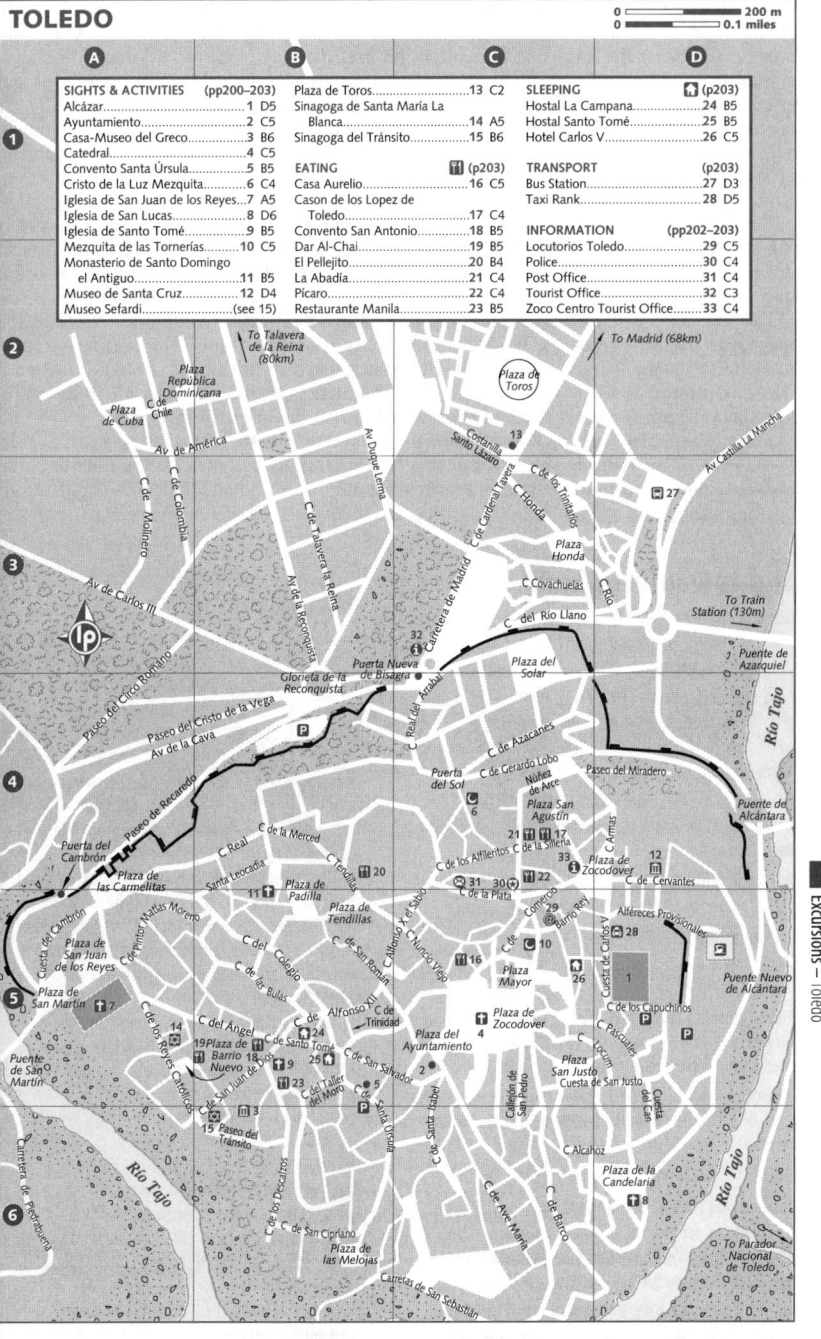

extraordinary monstrances in existence, the 16th-century **Custodia de Arfe**. With 18kg of gold and 183kg of silver, this shimmering mass of metal has a whopping 260 statuettes. Other important sights are the imposing high altar, the Transparente window and the choir stalls.

Southwest of the cathedral is the **Judería** (Jewish Quarter), home of the old city synagogue and the heart of the Greco trail. First stop is the **Iglesia de Santa Tomé**, where one of El Greco's greatest works, *El Entierro del Conde de Orgaz* (The Burial of the Count of Orgaz) hangs. The painting tells the legend of the pious count's funeral in 1323, when St Augustine and St Steven appeared to lay the body in the tomb. The bearded man directly above St Steven (the younger of the golden-robed saints) may be a self-portrait of El Greco.

Keep on El Greco's trail and head downhill to the **Casa-Museo del Greco**. This house is surely not where the painter actually lived but is decorated in the style of the times. Nearly two dozen of El Greco's minor works are housed here along with paintings from others of his day. More of his work is hung in the **Museo de Santa Cruz**, near the Plaza de Zocodover.

Past the Casa-Museo del Greco is the fascinating **Museo Sefardí**, which is housed in the **Sinagoga del Tránsito**, one of the best-preserved relics of Jewish Spain. The curiously mixed name refers to the 'Virgen del Tránsito', the name given to this house of worship when it was consecrated as a Christian church. Breathtakingly beautiful carvings adorn the walls and the museum is a great place to learn about Jewish life in medieval Spain.

For a glimpse of Muslim Toledo, head to the **Cristo de la Luz Mezquita**. During Muslim rule there were 10 mosques in the city, but this one, typical of their style, is the only one that remains. Pay attention to the horseshoe arches, both inside and out, and to the inscriptions on the walls inside.

Sights & Information

Catedral (☎ 92 522 22 41; Calle de Cardenal Cisneros; admission €4.95; ⊙ tourist visits 10.30am-6.30pm Mon-Sat, 2-6pm Sun)

Casa-Museo del Greco (☎ 92 522 40 46; www.mcu .es/museos/index in Spanish; Calle Samuel Leví; admission €2.40; ⊙ 10am-2pm & 4-6pm Mon-Sat, 10am-2pm Sun)

Cristo de la Luz Mezquita (☎ 92 525 41 91; Cuesta de los Carmelitas Descalzos 10; admission €1.50; ⊙ 10am-6pm, to 7pm summer)

Iglesia de Santo Tomé (☎ 92 525 60 98; Plaza del Conde; admission €1.50; ⊙ 10am-5.45pm)

Locutorios Toledo (☎ 92 528 30 43; Plaza de la Magdalena 7; Internet per hr €2.50; ⊙ 11am-2.30pm & 5-10.30pm, closed Thu & Sun morning)

Museo de Santa Cruz (☎ 92 522 10 36; Calle de Cervantes 3; admission free; ⊙ 10am-6.30pm Tue-Sat, 10am-2pm Sun, 10am-2pm & 4-6.30pm Mon)

Post Office (☎ 92 549 04 21; www.correos.es in Spanish; Calle de la Plata 1; ⊙ 8.30am-8.30pm Mon-Fri, 9.30am-2pm Sat)

Police (☎ 091 or 092; Calle de las Cadenas; ⊙ 24 hr)

Sinagoga del Tránsito & Museo Sefardí (☎ 92 522 36 65; www.museosefardi.net in Spanish; Calle Samuel Leví; admission €2.40; ⊙ 10am-2pm & 4-9pm Tue-Sat Mar-Nov, 10am-2pm & 4-6pm Tue-Sat Dec-Feb)

Tourist Office (☎ 92 523 40 30; Plaza del Ayuntamiento 1; ⊙ 10.30am-2.30pm & 4.30-7pm, closed Mon afternoon)

El Greco in Toledo

Born in Crete in 1541, Domenikos Theotokopoulos (El Greco, The Greek) moved to Venice in 1567 to be schooled as a Renaissance artist. Under the influence of masters such as Tintoretto, he learned to express dramatic scenes with few colours, concentrating the observer's interest in the faces of his portraits and leaving the rest in relative obscurity, a characteristic that remained one of his hallmarks. From 1572 he learned from the Mannerists of Rome and the work left behind by Michelangelo.

Theotokopoulos came to Toledo in 1577 hoping to get a job decorating El Escorial although Felipe II rejected him as a court artist. In Toledo, the painter began painting in a style different from anything local artists were producing. He even managed to cultivate a healthy clientele and command good prices.

His rather high opinion of himself and his work, however, did not endear him to all. He had to do without the patronage of the cathedral administrators, who were the first of many clients to haul him to court for his obscenely high fees.

El Greco liked the high life and took rooms in a mansion on the Paseo del Tránsito, where he often hired musicians to accompany his meals.

As Toledo's fortunes declined, so did El Greco's personal finances, and although the works of his final years are among his best, he often found himself unable to pay the rent. He died in 1614, leaving his works scattered about the city, where many have remained to this day.

Excursions – Toledo

Tren Turístico (☎ 92 522 03 00; Plaza de Zocodover; adult/child €3.60/2.15)

Zoco Centro (☎ 92 522 03 00; Calle Sillería 14; 🕐 10.30am-6pm Oct 15-Mar 14, 10.30am-7pm Mar 15-Oct 14)

Eating & Drinking

Casa Aurelio (☎ 92 522 77 16; www.aplinet.com/aurelio in Spanish; Plaza del Ayuntamiento 8; menú €23.75, mains €17-21; 🕐 1-4.30pm & 8-11.30pm, closed Wed) Serves up tasty grilled meats and fresh fish. There is another branch of Casa Aurelio on the Calle Sinagoga.

Cason de los Lopez de Toledo (☎ 92 525 47 74; www.casontoledo.com in Spanish; Calle Sillería 3; mains €18-21) Three establishments in one: a gourmet tapas bar, an upscale restaurant and a pub.

Convento San Antonio (☎ 92 522 40 47; Plaza San Antonio 1; 🕐 11.15am-1.30pm & 4-6pm) The Franciscan nuns here sell their sweet speciality, *corazones de San Antonio* (San Antonio hearts) for €7.50 a box. You can buy other typical cookies and pastries, most of them with a base of almonds and egg yolks.

Dar Al-Chai (☎ 92 522 56 25; Plaza de Barrio Nuevo 5; 🕐 9.30am-11pm Mon-Thu, 9.30am-2.30am Fri, 3pm-2.30am Sat, 3-11pm Sun) An Arab-style tea house with pretty mosaic tables and cushions for those who prefer the floor. Here you can get teas, coffees, alcoholic drinks and pastries.

El Pellejito (☎ 92 522 46 16; Calle Tendillas 14; 🕐 10am-1am Mon-Sat) A tiny, friendly place with a few scattered tables and a worn brick floor, this is a good spot for drinks, tapas and snacks.

La Abadía (☎ 92 525 11 40; Plaza de San Nicolás 3; mains €8-12) Traditional Castilian cooking and a phenomenal wine list. One of the few places in town with a kids' menu (€2.20 to €2.50).

Pícaro (☎ 92 522 13 01; www.picarocafeteatro.com in Spanish; Calle Cadenas 6; 🕐 3pm-3am) Pícaro is most known for its Friday concerts and Sunday belly-dancing sessions, though it's great for a drink any day.

Restaurante Manila (☎ 92 522 20 88; Plaza del Conde 2; menú €9.50) Housed in the former stable of the Palacio de los Condes de Fuensalida, Manila has an enticing lunch menú.

Sleeping

Hostal Santo Tomé (☎ 92 322 17 12; www.hostalsantotome.com; Calle Santo Tomé 13; s €39-48, d €48, tr €60) In this friendly hostel on one of the old town's busiest streets you'll find spacious rooms that smell like the cleaning crew just stopped by.

Hostal La Campana (☎ 92 522 16 62; Calle de la Campana 10-12; s/d €27/45) Fashionable rooms and a pretty sun-room on the top floor make this a great deal.

Hotel Carlos V (☎ 92 522 21 00; www.carlosv.com; Calle Trastamara 1; s €70-74, d €100-108) Rooms at this attractive hotel are simple but stylish, and some have cathedral views.

Parador Nacional de Toledo (☎ 92 522 18 50; www.parador.es; Cerro del Emperador; r from €119) Sitting on a hill outside walled Toledo, the Parador offers a splendid bird's-eye view of the city.

Transport

Distance from Madrid 75km/46 miles
Direction South
Car From Madrid, head south on the N-401 highway, which leads to Toledo. In town, follow the signs to *centro urbano*. Driving time 55 minutes.
Bus The bus makes the 75-minutes trip from Madrid's Estación Sur to Toledo every half hour, starting at 6.30am Monday to Saturday and at 8.30am on Sundays. Some buses are direct and take just one hour. All cost €3.89. Get return information at the bus station in Toledo (☎ 92 522 36 41; Calle de Castilla y la Mancha).
Train Renfe (☎ 90 224 02 02; www.renfe.es; Paseo de la Rosa) sends up to five trains per day to Toledo from Madrid. The trip takes about one hour and 30 minutes and costs €4.95.

SEGOVIA

With its soaring Roman aqueduct, compact historic centre and setting amidst the rolling hills of Castile, Segovia is without doubt one of Spain's most enchanting cities.

Segovia's foundation has been attributed to such lofty personalities as Hercules and the son of Noah, which is wishful thinking at best. What's certain is that the area has been inhabited since ancient times. The first settlers of importance were the Romans, who used Segovia as a military stronghold from which to control the surrounding territory. The city was eventually taken over by the Visigoths and the Moors, but after the Christian reconquest Segovia began to come into its own, building beautiful Romanesque churches and splendid palaces. In the 1500s the Comuneros Revolt, a fight against King Carlos I led by Juan Bravo, brought on economic and social decline, and the city didn't recover until the goddess of tourism arrived in the 1960s.

SEGOVIA

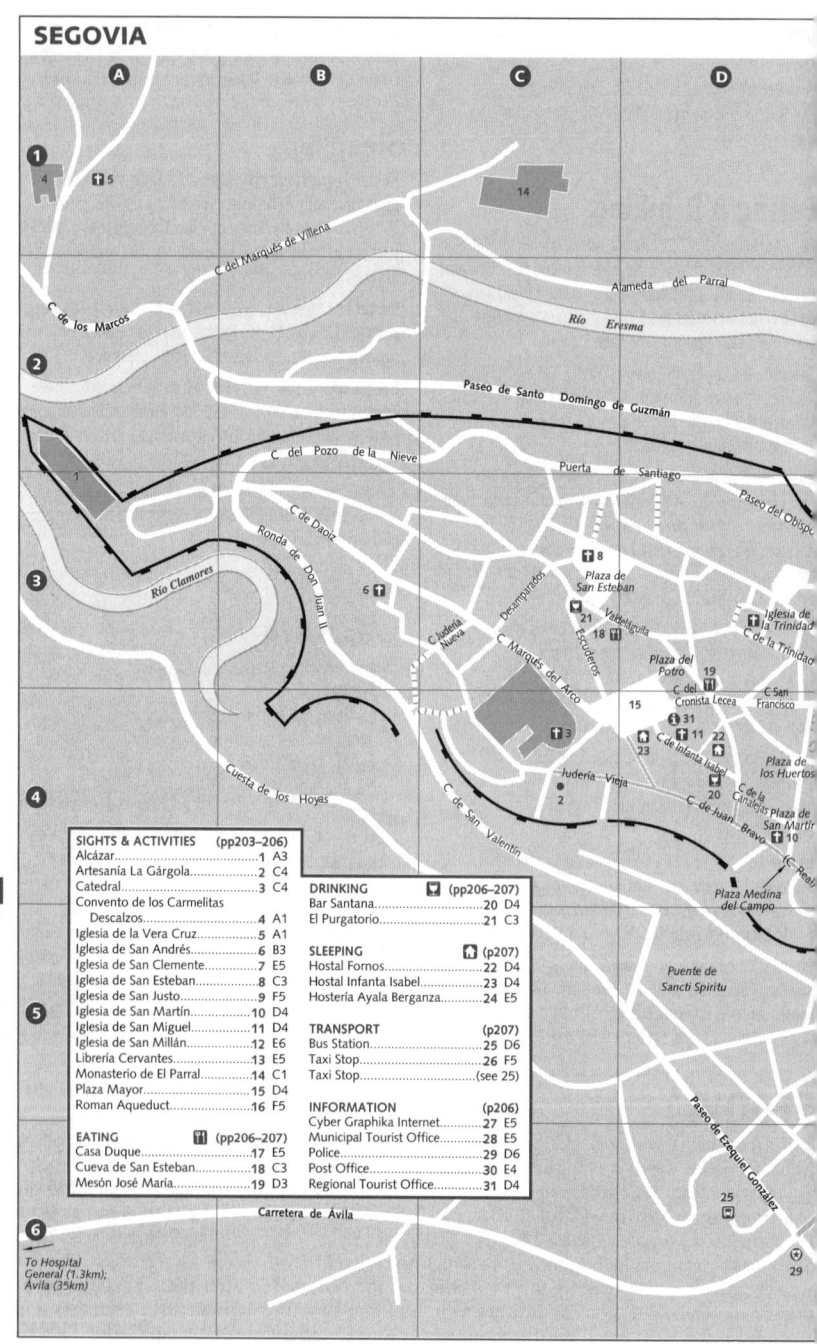

SIGHTS & ACTIVITIES (pp203–206)
Alcázar...1 A3
Artesanía La Gárgola.....................2 C4
Catedral.......................................3 C4
Convento de los Carmelitas
  Descalzos...................................4 A1
Iglesia de la Vera Cruz..................5 A1
Iglesia de San Andrés....................6 B3
Iglesia de San Clemente................7 E5
Iglesia de San Esteban..................8 C3
Iglesia de San Justo......................9 F5
Iglesia de San Martín...................10 D4
Iglesia de San Miguel..................11 D4
Iglesia de San Millán...................12 E6
Librería Cervantes.......................13 E5
Monasterio de El Parral...............14 C1
Plaza Mayor................................15 D4
Roman Aqueduct.........................16 F5

EATING 🍴 (pp206–207)
Casa Duque.................................17 E5
Cueva de San Esteban..................18 C3
Mesón José María........................19 D3

DRINKING 🍷 (pp206–207)
Bar Santana.................................20 D4
El Purgatorio...............................21 C3

SLEEPING 🛏 (p207)
Hostal Fornos..............................22 D4
Hostal Infanta Isabel....................23 D4
Hostería Ayala Berganza...............24 E5

TRANSPORT (p207)
Bus Station..................................25 D6
Taxi Stop.....................................26 F5
Taxi Stop..............................(see 25)

INFORMATION (p206)
Cyber Graphika Internet................27 E5
Municipal Tourist Office...............28 E5
Police...29 D6
Post Office...................................30 E4
Regional Tourist Office.................31 D4

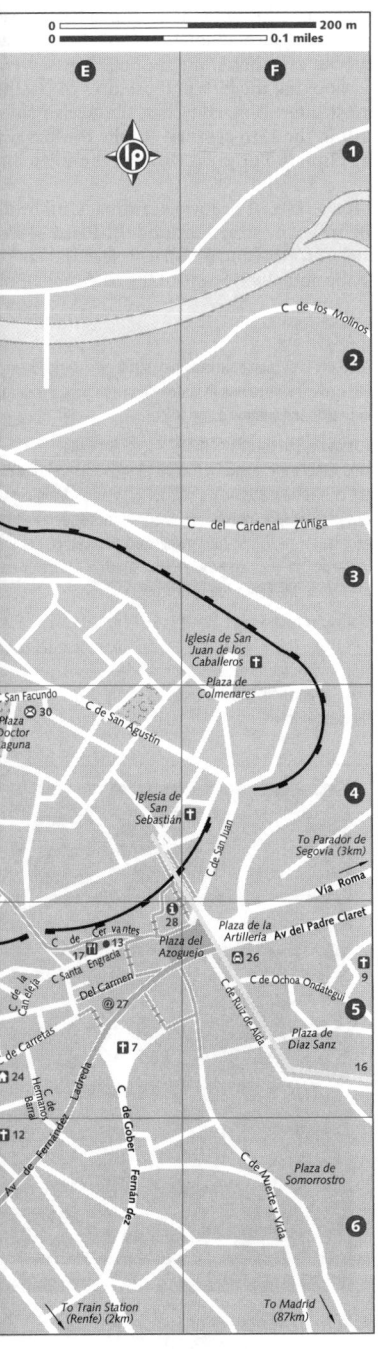

The medieval walled city is in the far western corner of modern Segovia. The **11th-century walls** stretch from the Roman Aqueduct to the *alcázar* on the edge of town, encompassing just about everything worth seeing in a short visit. Two major plazas, the **Plaza del Azoguejo** near the Aqueduct and the **Plaza Mayor** by the cathedral, are the nerve centres of the city. The lively commercial streets **Calle Cervantes** and **Calle Juan Bravo** (together referred to as **'Calle Real'**) serve as the main artery connecting the two plazas. Among the many shops worth browsing here, check out the unusual handmade crafts and souvenirs at **La Gárgola** and the excellent selection of books and maps at the family-run **Librería Cervantes**.

Start your visit at the **Roman Aqueduct**, an 894m-long engineering wonder that looks like an enormous comb plunged into Segovia. It's 28m high and was built without a drop of mortar, just good old Roman know-how. Just as amazing is the fact that it's stayed intact all these years, despite being used and abused by townspeople who built underneath it and siphoned water off it, damaging the structure. Thanks to a major restoration project in the 1990s it may stick around for another couple of millennia.

From here Calle Real climbs into the innards of Segovia, passing the sunny **Plaza de San Martín**, crowned with the lovely 13th-century Romanesque **Iglesia de San Martin**. Take a right turn on the Calle de Isabel Católica to come to the shady **Plaza Mayor**. At the western end the **Catedral** towers over the plaza, resplendent, while the smaller **Iglesia de San Miguel**, where Isabel was crowned Queen of Castile, sits humbly nearby. The church was closed for restoration at the time of writing. Completed in 1577, 50 years after its Romanesque predecessor had been destroyed in the revolt of the Comuneros, the cathedral is one of the most homogenous Gothic churches in Spain. The interior is delicate and refined, with a handful of side chapels, a fine choir stall and stained glass windows from the 1600s. You can visit the cloister and museum, with its fantastic collection of sacred art and 17th-century Belgian tapestries.

From the Plaza Mayor head down Calle del Marqués del Arco to reach the fortified *alcázar*, a fairytale castle perched dramatically on the edge of Segovia. If it looks familiar don't be surprised; Walt Disney supposedly copied Segovia's *alcázar* for Sleeping Beauty's Castle in California's Disneyland.

Excursions – Segovia

205

Roman foundations are buried somewhere underneath this splendour, but what we see today is a reconstruction of a 13th-century structure that burned down in 1862. Inside is an interesting collection of armour and military gear, but even better are the 360-degree views from the *alcázar's* rooftop, which is a balcony overlooking the hills and pastures of Castilla. From here you can make out one of Segovia's most interesting churches, the twelve-sided **Iglesia de la Vera Cruz** (Church of the True Cross), built in the 13th century. A relic of what was said to be the 'true cross' was once housed in the church. For great views of the town and countryside, hike uphill behind the church.

If sightseeing doesn't wear you out, head out for a taste of Segovia's laid-back nightlife. After dark, the action is centred around two main areas: the streets around the Plaza Mayor (especially Calle Escuderos and Calle Infanta Isabel Católica) and a district referred to as 'La Roca', which sits just outside the city walls beside the aqueduct. Some of the best nightspots here are **Bar Santana** and **El Purgatorio**.

Sights & Information

Alcázar (☎ 92 146 07 59; www.alcazardesegovia.com; Plaza de la Reina Victoria Eugenia; admission €3.50; ☾ 10am-6pm Oct-Mar, 10am-7pm Apr-Sep)

Artesenia La Gárgola (☎ 67 074 70 80; Calle Judería Vieja 4; ☾ 11am-2pm & 5-8pm)

Catedral (☎ 92 146 22 05; Plaza de la Catedral; admission €2, free Sun after 1.30pm; ☾ 9.30am-5.30pm)

Cyber Graphika Internet (☎ 92 146 09 66; 1st fl, Avenida Fernández Ladreda 12; per hr €1.80; ☾ 11am-2pm & 3-10pm Mon-Fri, 4-10pm Sat)

Iglesia de la Vera Cruz (☎ 92 143 14 75; Carretera de Zamarramala; admission €1.50; ☾ 10.30am-1.30pm & 3.30-6pm Tue-Sun)

Librería Cervantes (☎ 92 146 24 85; Calle Cervantes 14; ☾ 10am-1.45pm & 4.30-8pm Mon-Sat)

Municipal Tourist Office (☎ 92 146 29 14; www.segovia turismo.es in Spanish; Plaza del Azoguejo 1; ☾ 10am-8pm)

Police (☎ 091; Paseo de Ezequiel González 22; ☾ 24 hr)

Post Office (☎ 92 146 16 16; www.correo.es in Spanish; Plaza Doctor Laguna 5; ☾ 8.30am-8.30pm Mon-Fri, 9am-2pm Sat)

Regional Tourist Office (☎ 92 146 03 34 or 90 220 30 30; www.turismocastillayleon.com; Plaza Mayor; ☾ 9am-2pm & 5-8pm)

Eating & Drinking

Vegetarians beware: you're about to enter the meat-lovers' realm of Segovia, where *cochinillo asado* (roasted suckling pig) and *asado de cordero* (roasted lamb) are the house specialities of just about every restaurant.

Bar Santana (☎ 92 146 35 64; Calle Infanta Isabel 18; ☾ 10.30am-3am, to 4am Fri & Sat) The most popular bar in town, Santana is a friendly rock 'n' roll joint that offers live concerts Tuesday and Thursday nights.

Casa Duque (☎ 92 146 24 87; www.restauranteduque .es; Calle Cervantes 12; mains €5.70-€21, menú €21) The specialty is of course suckling pig, but there is a good range of salads. Downstairs is the informal tavern, where you can get tapas and yummy *cazuelas* (stews).

Cueva de San Esteban (☎ 92 146 09 82; Calle Valdelaguila 15; menú €7.71-€12.15; ☾ 1-11pm) One of the only restaurants in Segovia not pushing suckling pig, this popular spot focuses on seasonal dishes and has an excellent wine list; in 2002 owner Lucio del Campo got the 'Nariz de Oro' (Golden Nose award), which is a prize given in Spain to the year's top sommelier.

El Alcázar Pastelería (☎ 92 146 21 18; Plaza Mayor 13; ☾ 10am-2pm & 4.30-8pm Mon-Fri, 10am-8pm Sat & Sun) Known for its heavenly *Ponches Segovianos* (pastries made of egg yolk and almond) this pastry shop is one of the best in town.

Roman Aqueduct of 166 arches, built in the 1st century AD (p205)

El Purgatorio (Calle Escuderos 26; 1pm-2am Mon-Fri, 5pm-3.30am Sat, 5pm-2am Sun) One of Segovia's best clubs, with a lively bar and non-stop Spanish pop, rock, flamenco and a mostly 20-something crowd.

Mesón José María (92 146 11 11; Calle Cronista Lecea 11; mains €10-20; 10am-1am, to 2am Fri & Sat) The large dining room is the very definition of rustic elegance, and on weekdays it's full of local businessmen and women doing lunch.

Sleeping

Segovia is bursting with charismatic, low-priced accommodation, though it's always a good idea to make a reservation, especially in summer.

Hostal Fornos (92 146 01 98; Calle Infanta Isabel 13; s €32-38, d €45-51) Hand-painted headboards and wall decorations give this tidy little hostel a cheerful air.

Hostería Ayala Berganza (92 146 04 48; www .partner-hotels .com; Calle Carretas 5; r incl breakfast €110-133) Each of the 17 rooms in this restored 15th-century palace are different, though all have tiled floors, beautiful bathrooms and rustic accents.

Hotel Infanta Isabel (92 146 13 00; Plaza Mayor 12; www.hotelinfantaisabel.com; s €50-73, d €74-108) Sitting right on Plaza Mayor, this utterly charming hotel is one of the best in town.

Parador de Segovia (92 144 37 37; www.parador .es; Carretera de Valladolid; r from €119.70; P) The best thing the Parador has to offer are amazing views over old Segovia. Breakfasting in their glass-walled dining room as the sun glitters on the *alcázar* and the cathedral must be one of Segovia's greatest pleasures.

Transport

Distance from Madrid 90km/56 miles
Direction Northwest
Car From Madrid, take the A-6 motorway to the N-603 national highway, which will take you to the city centre. Driving time 1 hour.
Bus (92 142 77 07; Paseo de Ezequiel González) Buses leave every half hour from Madrid's Paseo de la Florida bus stop and arrive in Segovia's central bus station one hour and 15 minutes later. Tickets cost €5.68 .
Train Renfe (90 224 02 02; www.renfe.es) has at least seven trains heading to Segovia from Madrid each day. The trip takes about two hours; tickets cost €5.10.

ÁVILA

Its old town huddled behind pristine medieval walls, Ávila is a remarkable, romantic city perfect for simply strolling and soaking up history. But as one of the highest and windiest cities in Spain it can get chilly, so come prepared. Settled by Celts in 700 BC, it was little more than a rural enclave for centuries. Although the Romans and Muslims passed by, Ávila's population didn't begin to rise until Alfonso VI tried to repopulate the territory after his 1085 victory in Toledo. By the 1500s, Ávila was an economic powerhouse, with an important wool industry, illustrious palaces and new churches popping up left and right.

During this time that the city's most important figure, St Teresa (see boxed text p209), was born. Shortly after her death in 1582, the city's fortunes began a downward spiral that ended in its economic ruin; Ávila has only recently shaken off the slumber of neglect that ensued.

Most of Ávila's must see sights lie within or near the walled city, which is on the far western side of town. Forming part of the wall is the **Catedral**, the heart of the old city. From here the important commercial **Calle de los Reyes Católicos**, which is lined with shops and bars, snakes its way into the busy **Plaza del Mercado Chico**, which has its fair share of restaurants and souvenir shops too. Shoppers should note that at the time of writing, Ávila had no money exchange office, which means that if you arrive on a weekend or after 2pm on weekdays (when banks are closed) you will not be able to exchange money in town. ATMs are open 24 hours.

To get an overview of Ávila and its monuments, hop on the **Murallito Train** which rambles through the narrow streets giving a multilingual audio presentation on the main sights.

A walk along the top of Ávila's splendid **12th-century walls** should head your list of things to do. Offering a unique glimpse into the town's defensive history, more than 1km of wall is open to the public, though it's divided into two sections by the cathedral. Comprised of 2500 turrets – to protect archers – and 88 towers, the walls can be accessed at the **Puerta de San Vicente**, the **Puerta del Alcázar** and the **Puerta del Peso de la Harina**. On some summer nights the town organises 'theatrical visits' to the wall, when actors dressed in period costume recount Ávila's history. Reservations are necessary for these nocturnal visits.

The **Catedral** is embedded into the eastern city walls, forming their central bulwark and providing a telling symbol about the link between cross and sword. Although the main façade hints at the cathedral's 12th-century, Romanesque origins, the church was finished 400 years later in a predominantly Gothic style, making it the first Gothic church in Spain. It boasts rich walnut choir stalls and a long, narrow central nave that makes the soaring ceilings seem all the more majestic. The entry fee includes visits to the cloister, a small museum and the cathedral itself, though the latter is free for those attending services.

Even more beloved by locals than the cathedral is the **Convento de Santa Teresa**, a church built at the birthplace of the 16th-century mystic and ascetic. Teresa joined a Carmelite convent, but when shaken by a vision of hell in 1560 she began the unpopular work of reforming her order, founding convents of Carmelitas Descalzas (Barefoot Carmelite nuns) throughout Spain. This church was built in 1636 and today you can see its simple interior and the gold-smothered chapel that sits atop Teresa's former bedroom, though more interesting are the relics (including a piece of the saint's ring finger!) and the small museum about her life.

After the churches and museums have closed, check out Ávila's cheerful bar scene. There are several good nightlife options just outside the Puerta del Peso de la Harina, along Calle de San Segundo, and on weekend nights a younger crowd heads to the Avenida de Portugal, home to bars such as the Bodeguito de San Segundo and clubs.

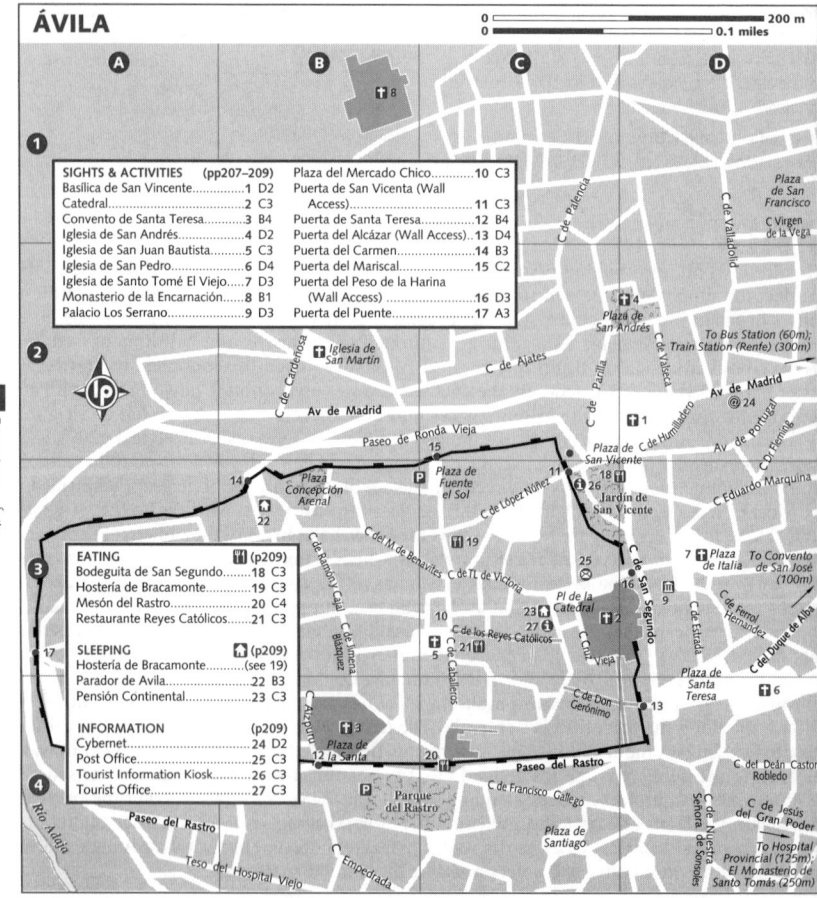

ÁVILA

SIGHTS & ACTIVITIES (pp207–209)
Basílica de San Vincente...............1 D2
Catedral...2 C3
Convento de Santa Teresa............3 B4
Iglesia de San Andrés....................4 D2
Iglesia de San Juan Bautista.........5 C3
Iglesia de San Pedro......................6 D4
Iglesia de Santo Tomé El Viejo.....7 D3
Monasterio de la Encarnación......8 B1
Palacio Los Serrano.......................9 D3
Plaza del Mercado Chico.............10 C3
Puerta de San Vicenta (Wall
    Access)....................................11 C3
Puerta de Santa Teresa................12 B4
Puerta del Alcázar (Wall Access)..13 D4
Puerta del Carmen......................14 B3
Puerta del Mariscal.....................15 C2
Puerta del Peso de la Harina
    (Wall Access)...........................16 D3
Puerta del Puente........................17 A3

EATING   (p209)
Bodeguita de San Segundo........18 C3
Hostería de Bracamonte.............19 C3
Mesón del Rastro........................20 C4
Restaurante Reyes Católicos......21 C3

SLEEPING   (p209)
Hostería de Bracamonte.........(see 19)
Parador de Avila.........................22 B3
Pensión Continental...................23 C3

INFORMATION   (p209)
Cybernet....................................24 D2
Post Office.................................25 C3
Tourist Information Kiosk...........26 C3
Tourist Office............................27 C3

In the Footsteps of Santa Teresa

One of the most important women in the history of the Catholic church, Santa Teresa spent most of her life in Ávila, and you don't have to be here long to feel her enduring presence. From the convent, plaza, and gate that bears her name to the sweet *yemas de Santa Teresa* (gummy cookies made with egg yolk and supposedly invented by the saint) her trail seems to cover every inch of the city.

After a visit to the **Convento de Santa Teresa**, you can pop into the nearby **Iglesia de San Juan Bautista**, where she was baptised. The first convent she founded, **Convento de San José**, is here too, and you can visit its small museum packed with Teresa artefacts and memorabilia. To see a replica of her monastic cell, head to the **Monasterio de la Encarnación** outside the city walls where she lived and worked for 27 years.

Sights & Information

Catedral (☎ 92 021 16 41; Plaza de la Catedral; admission €3; ☺ 10am-5pm Mon-Fri & 12-5pm Sat & Sun Nov-Mar, daily until 7pm Mar-Oct)

Convento & Museum de Santa Teresa (☎ 92 021 10 30; Plaza de la Santa; museum admission €2; ☺ museum 10am-2pm & 4-7pm, relic room 9.30am-1.30pm & 3.30-7pm, church 8.30am-1.30pm & 3.30-8.30pm)

Convento de San José (☎ 92 022 21 27; Calle del Duque de Alba; admission €1; ☺ 10am-1.30pm & 4-7pm)

Cybernet (☎ 92 035 23 52; Avenida de Madrid 25; per hr €2.50; ☺ 11.30am-2.30pm & 4.30pm-1am)

Iglesia de San Juan Bautista (☎ 92 021 11 27; Plaza de la Victoria; admission free; ☺ before & after mass)

Monasterio de la Encarnación (☎ 92 021 12 12; Paseo de la Encarnación; admission €1.30; ☺ 9.30am-1pm & 4-6pm Mon-Fri, 10am-1pm & 4-6pm Sat & Sun)

Murallito train (☎ 60 914 28 40; www.murallito-avila .com in Spanish; Puerta de San Vicente; adult/child €3/2.50; ☺ every 45 min from 11am to dusk)

National Police (☎ 091; Paseo San Roque 34

Municipal Police ☎ 092; Avenida 0Inmaculada 11)

Post Office (☎ 92 031 35 06; Plaza de la Catedral 2; ☺ 8.30am-8.30pm Mon-Fri, 9.30am-2pm Sat)

Tourist Office (☎ 92 021 13 87; www.avilaturismo.com; Plaza de la Catedral 4; ☺ 9am-2pm & 5-8pm Sep 15-Jun, 9am-8pm Sun-Thu, 9am-9pm Fri & Sat Jul-Sep 14)

Walls (☎ 92 021 13 87; admission €3.50; ☺ 11am-5.15pm winter, 10am-7.15pm summer) For days, times and information about theatrical visits on summer nights, ask at the wall ticket offices. Reservations are usually necessary.

Eating

Bodeguito de San Segundo (☎ 92 021 42 47; San Segundo 19; ☺ 11am-1am) For a great selection of Spanish wines and delicious tapas to accompany them.

Restaurante Reyes Católicos (☎ 92 025 56 27; Calle de los Reyes Católicos 6; mains €8-16) A refreshing surprise for those sick of *asado*, this stylish bistro offers a mix of traditional and more imaginative dishes.

Hostería de Bracamonte (☎ 92 025 12 80; Calle Bracamonte 6; mains €8-18; ☺ 1-4pm & 8-11pm Wed-Mon, closed Tue) Tables fill the former stable of this 16th-century palace, providing one of Ávila's most atmospheric spots for a meal. And if you really like the ambience here, you can also stay the night.

Mesón del Rastro (☎ 92 021 12 18; Plaza del Rastro 4; mains €7-14, menú €14) For simple, tasty homestyle cooking, head to this popular spot alongside the city walls.

Sleeping

Hostería de Bracamonte (☎ 92 025 12 80; Calle Bracamonte 6; s €36, d €50-73) Housed in a splendidly restored 16th-century palace, the Bracamonte radiates old-world charm at every turn.

Parador de Avila (☎ 92 021 13 40; www.parador.es; Calle del Marqués de Canales de Chozas 2; r from €97) Tucked beside the Puerta del Carmen, this 16th-century palace is a simply charming place to stay, and best of all it puts you within walking distance of all the old town sites.

Pensión Continental (☎ 92 021 15 02; Plaza de la Catedral 6; s €15, d €26-33, tr €39) This modest pension can hold its head high, with charming (if aged) decor and unbeatable vistas of the cathedral.

Transport

Distance from Madrid 101km/63 miles
Direction West
Car From Madrid, take the A-6 motorway northwest to N-110 west. Driving time one hour.
Bus At least four buses connect Madrid's Estación Sur and Ávila daily. The trip takes one hour 30 minutes and costs €6.30. Contact the bus station (☎ 92 022 01 54; Avenida de Madrid 2) for more information.
Train Renfe (☎ 90 224 02 02; www.renfe.es) sends more than two dozen trains to Ávila every day. The trip takes up to two hours (€5.60) though direct trains take just one hour and 15 minutes and cost €7.15.

CÓRDOBA

With its whitewashed patios, twisted old streets and unreal mixture of Moorish, Christian, Jewish and Roman history, Córdoba is a fascinating city that will leave you hankering for more of its languid, laid-back charm. Although it lies 400km south of Madrid, with the high-speed (AVE) train you can zip down in under two hours.

The Romans founded the colony of 'Corduba' here in the 2nd century BC, and due to its strategic location on the Río Guadalquivir quickly made it the provincial capital. It was an important economic and cultural centre and the birthplace of Roman greats such as

Transport

Distance from Madrid 400km/250 miles
Direction South
Car From Madrid, take the N-IV South, the so-called Andalucía highway, all the way to Córdoba. Driving time four hours.
Bus Four buses make the 4¾-hour trip daily from Madrid's Estación Sur. The trip costs €10.85.
Train Renfe (☎ 90 224 02 02; www.renfe.es) operates the AVE (high-speed) train running 20 times per day between Madrid and Córdoba. The trip lasts about one hour and 40 minutes and cost €48, one way.

Seneca and Lucan. When Moorish invaders took the city in AD 711, they agreed to let locals keep their customs and religious beliefs, and the city flourished with the peaceful coexistence of Christians, Jews and Muslims. When Ferdinand reclaimed the city in the early Middle Ages, its splendour began to fade and it never regained the powerful status it once enjoyed.

Nowhere better illustrates the mixture of Muslim and Christian tradition in Spain than the grand **Mezquita de Córdoba**, at one time the largest temple of worship in the world. Construction on the mosque began in AD 784 on the site of an old Visigoth basilica, though the mammoth masterpiece took another 200 years to finish. Its graceful double arches and pillars (all 1300 of them, of which 850 are still standing) were as splendid then as today.

When Christians took control of the city in 1236, King Ferdinand immediately consecrated the mosque as a church, though he left the structure intact out of appreciation for its beauty. For centuries the original architecture was respected, even while Christians used it as a Cathedral, but in the 16th century a few overzealous church leaders committed architectural sacrilege when they built a Gothic **catedral** in the centre of the mosque. King Carlos I approved the work, but supposedly he deeply regretted giving his support when he saw the irrevocable damage that had been done.

Now, the sight of Christian altars, choir stalls, chapels and statues in the midst of the mosque's original red and white arches is disconcerting but fascinating. In addition to plonking their church in here, the Christians closed off the arches that were intended to let light in from the **Patio de los Naranjos** (Courtyard of the Orange Trees) outside, and the result is decidedly more gloomy than the original. Still, there's no masking the glorious beauty of this place. Pay special attention to the many ornate domes in the ceiling and to the **Sagrarium**, a small room smothered in elaborate paintings.

Southwest of the Mezquita is the **Alcázar de los Reyes Cristianos**, the Castle of the Christian Monarchs. Built in the 13th century as a military base, the Alcázar was remodelled by the Catholic King Ferdinand and Queen Isabella to use as a residence, with lush gardens and ponds. Today you can see little of interest inside the castle, but the garden is worth strolling through.

From here you can cross the **Río Guadalquivir** on the **Puente Romano**, a bridge that has a barely distinguishable Roman base, to reach the **Torre de la Calahorra**, a former defence tower that now houses the **Museo Vivo de Al-Andalus**. There's an interesting exhibit about Córdoba's cultural history and the unique mixture of Christian, Jewish and Islamic culture here. There's also a rather random video about man's origins.

If you feel like pampering yourself and want to learn a little about Arab culture at the same time, visit the **hammam** where you can take a dip in luxurious baths built to look like those used by Córdoba's Muslim community. Or if you have a little more time, head 6km outside town to **Medina Azahara**, the ruins of a 10th-century Muslim palace complex. A guided visit leads you through what's left of the mosque, the ornate gardens and other buildings. Eerily, this splendid creation burned down just 70 years after being built, and it has been in ruins ever since. You can get there on the Autobus Turístico, which makes trips Tuesday through Saturday at 11am leaving from the Avenida Alcázar. Get tickets and information from the tourist office or at hotels.

Excursions – Córdoba

CÓRDOBA

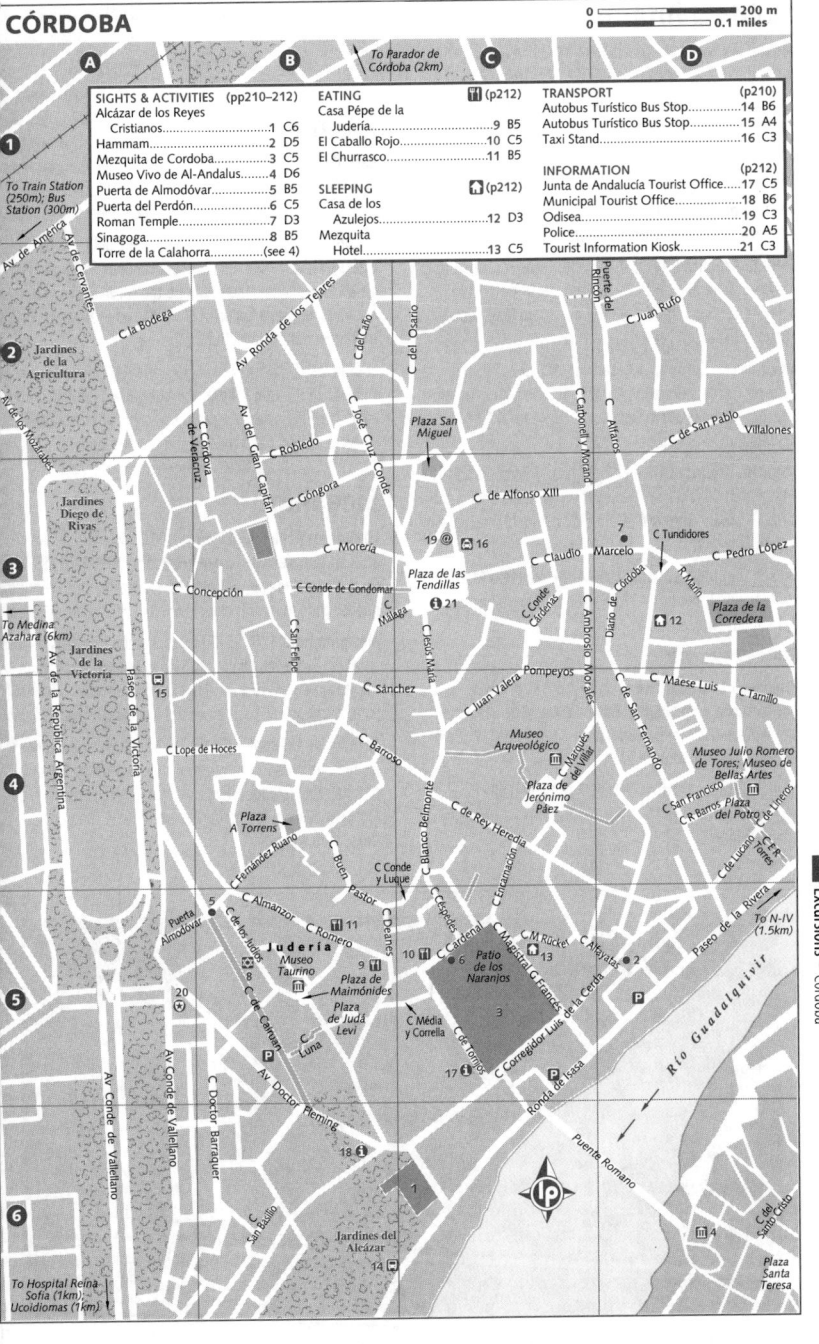

SIGHTS & ACTIVITIES	(pp210–212)
Alcázar de los Reyes	
Cristianos	1 C6
Hammam	2 D5
Mezquita de Cordoba	3 C5
Museo Vivo de Al-Andalus	4 D6
Puerta de Almodóvar	5 B5
Puerta del Perdón	6 C5
Roman Temple	7 D3
Sinagoga	8 B5
Torre de la Calahorra	(see 4)

EATING	🍴 (p212)
Casa Pépe de la	
Judería	9 B5
El Caballo Rojo	10 C5
El Churrasco	11 B5

SLEEPING	🛏 (p212)
Casa de los	
Azulejos	12 D3
Mezquita	
Hotel	13 C5

TRANSPORT	(p210)
Autobus Turístico Bus Stop	14 B6
Autobus Turístico Bus Stop	15 A4
Taxi Stand	16 C3

INFORMATION	(p212)
Junta de Andalucía Tourist Office	17 C5
Municipal Tourist Office	18 B6
Odisea	19 C3
Police	20 A5
Tourist Information Kiosk	21 C3

Sights & Information

Alcázar de los Reyes Cristianos (☎ 95 742 01 51; Campo Santo de los Mártires; admission €2; ☼ 10am-2pm & 4.30-6.30pm Tue-Sat Oct 16-Apr, 10am-2pm & 5.30-7.30pm May-Jun & Sep-Oct 15, 8.30am-2.30pm Jul-Aug, 9.30am-2pm Sun all year)

Córdoba Visión (☎ 95 776 02 41; trips €10-25)

Hammam (☎ 95 748 47 46; Calle del Corregidor; admission €12; ☼ 10am-midnight)

Medina Azahara (☎ 95 732 91 30; Carretera Palma del Río km 5.5; admission €1.50, EU citizens free; ☼ 10am-6.30pm Tue-Sat Sep 16-Apr, 10am-8.30pm May-Sep 15, 10am-2pm Sun all year)

Mezquita de Córdoba & Catedral (☎ 95 747 05 12; Calle de Torrijo; admission €6.25; ☼ 10am-7pm Mon-Fri Mar-Oct, 10am-5.30pm Nov-Apr, 9-10.45am & 1.30-6.30pm Sun)

Municipal Tourist Office (☎ 95 720 17 74 or 90 220 17 74; Calle de Caballerizas Reales 1; www.turismodecordoba.org; ☼ 10am-2pm & 4.30-8pm Nov-Apr, 10am-2pm & 6-9pm May-Oct)

Odisea (Internet Centre; ☎ 95 747 38 10; Plaza Marmól de Bañuelos 1; per hr €1.80; ☼ 10am-11pm Mon-Sat, 4-10.30pm Sun)

Police (☎ 091 or 092)

Provincial Tourist Office (☎ 95 749 16 78; www.turiscordoba.es in Spanish; Calle del Ángel de Saavedra 4; ☼ 9.30am-1.30pm & 5-8pm Mon-Sat Oct-May, 9.30am-1.30pm & 6-9pm Mon-Sat Jun-Sep)

Regional Tourist Office (☎ 95 747 12 35; Calle de Torijos 10; ☼ 9.30am-6pm Mon-Fri, 10am-2pm & 4-6pm Sat, 10am-2pm Sun)

Torre de la Calahorra & Museo Vivo de Al-Andalus (☎ 9 729 39 29; Puente Romano; admission €4; ☼ 10am-6pm Oct-Apr, 10am-2pm & 4.30-8.30pm May-Sep)

Eating

Casa Pépe de la Judería (☎ 95 720 07 44; Calle de Romero 1; menú €18; ☼ 1-4pm & 8.30-11pm) This cosy tavern has some of the best tapas in Córdoba.

El Caballo Rojo (☎ 95 747 53 75; Calle del Cardenal 28; mains €12.50-18.50; ☼ 1-4.30pm & 8pm-midnight) A classic Córdoban restaurant, here the speciality is 'Arabic-Andalus' cuisine, a fusion of Moorish and Spanish cooking that grew out of the cultural mix here.

El Churrasco (☎ 95 729 08 19; Calle de Romero 16; mains €11-25; ☼ 1-4pm & 8pm-midnight) Locals and visitors alike love El Churrasco's traditional style and the local specialities like 'hake cheeks' and roasted lamb.

Sleeping

Casa de los Azulejos (☎ 95 747 00 00; www.casadelosazulejos.com; Calle de Fernando Colón 5; s €69-90, d €83-120) Original wooden ceilings, colourful tile accents and a beautiful interior patio make this one of Córdoba's most unique hotels.

Mezquita Hotel (☎ 95 747 55 85; hotelmezquita@wanadoo.es; Plaza Santa Catalina 1; s €25-48, d €41-69) Across from the Mezquita, this clean-feeling hotel has spacious, if rather bare, rooms and all basic amenities including air conditioning.

Parador de Córdoba (☎ 95 727 59 00; www.parador.es; Avenida de la Arruzafa; r from €113) On a hill to the north of town, the Parador offers lovely city views (especially at night) and is a quiet, elegant place to stay. The pool hits the spot in summer.

Decorations and arches inside the Mezquita de Córdoba (p210)

SAN LORENZO DE EL ESCORIAL

Home to the majestic monastery and palace complex of San Lorenzo de El Escorial, this one-time royal getaway is now a prim little town overflowing with cutesy shops, restaurants and hotels (many of them closed in the off season) catering to throngs of weekending Madrileños. The fresh, cool air has been drawing city dwellers here since the complex was first ordered built by Felipe II in the 16th century.

Several villages were razed to make way for the massive project, which included a monastic centre, a decadent royal palace and a mausoleum for Felipe's parents, Carlos I and Isabel. Architect Juan de Herrera oversaw the project.

The **monastery's** main entrance is on the west. Above the gateway a statue of St Lawrence stands watch, holding a symbolic gridiron, the instrument of his martyrdom (he was roasted alive on one). From here you'll first enter the **Patio de los Reyes** (Patio of the Kings) which houses the statues of the six kings of Judah.

Directly ahead lies the sombre **basilica**. As you enter, look up to the unusual flat vaulting by the choir stalls. Once inside the church proper, turn left to view Benvenuto Cellini's white Carrara marble statue of Christ crucified (1576).

You'll be led through rooms containing tapestries and an El Greco painting, and then downstairs to the northeastern corner of the complex. You pass through the **Museo de Arquitectura** and the **Museo de Pinturaf**. The former covers (in Spanish) the story of how the complex was built, the latter contains a range of 16th- and 17th-century Italian, Spanish and Flemish art.

Head upstairs into a gallery around the eastern part of the complex known as the **Palacio de Felipe II** or **Palacio de los Austrias**. You'll then descend to the 17th-century **Panteón de los Reyes** (the Crypt of Kings), where almost all Spain's monarchs since Carlos I lie interred. Backtracking a little, you find yourself in the **Panteón de los Infantes** (Crypt of the Princesses). Don Juan de Austria, victor over the Turks at the Battle of Lepanto, lies in the fifth vault.

Stairs lead up from the **Patio de los Evangelistas** (Patio of the Gospels) to the **Salas Capitulares** (chapterhouses) in the southeastern corner of the monastery. These bright, airy rooms, whose ceilings are richly frescoed, contain a minor treasure chest of works by El Greco, Titian, Tintoretto, José de Ribera and Hieronymus Bosch (El Bosco to Spaniards).

Stroll around the **Huerta de los Frailes** (Friars Garden), just south of the monastery. In the **Jardín del Príncipe** that leads down to the town of El Escorial (and the train station) is the **Casita del Príncipe**, a little neo-Classical caprice built under Carlos III for his heir. The **Casita de Arriba** (Casa del Infant), another 18th-century neo-Classical gem, is along the road to Ávila.

Sights & Information

Casita de Arriba (☎ 91 890 59 03; admission €3; ☾ daily Jul-Sep, Sat & Sun only Oct-May)

Internet (☎ 91 890 15 33; Plaza de San Lorenzo, Galería Martín; per hr €2; ☾ 11am-10pm Mon-Thu, 11am-11pm Fri-Sun)

Real Monasterio de San Lorenzo (☎ 91 890 59 02; www.patrimonionacional.es; admission €6; ☾ 10am-6pm Apr-Sep, 10am-5pm Oct-Mar, closed Mon) Admission to the basilica is free, and for a small fee you can join a guided tour of the pantheons.

Tourist Office (☎ 91 890 53 13; Calle de Grimalidi 2; ☾ 10am-6pm Mon-Thu, 10am-7pm Fri-Sun)

Eating & Sleeping

La Cueva (☎ 91 890 15 16; www.mesonlacueva.com in Spanish; Calle de San Antón 4; mains €9-18; ☾ closed Mon) A dark place founded in 1768, this is one of the town's classic eateries.

Hotel Parrilla Príncipe (☎ 91 890 16 11; www.inicia .es/de/parillaprincipe; Calle de la Floridablanca 6; s €42-44, d €53-59) Rooms are bare but clean, and some have views of the monastery. The restaurant here – an unpretentious place with great grilled meats – is one of the best in town; a meal will cost you about €30.

Transport

Distance from Madrid 59km/34 miles
Direction Northwest
Car Take the A-6 motorway to the M-600 highway, then follow the signs to El Escorial. Driving time 40 minutes.
Bus Every 15 minutes (every 30 minutes on weekends) Herranz bus company (☎ 91 896 90 28) runs a service to El Escorial from the bus depot outside Madrid's Moncloa station, platform 3. The one-hour trip costs €2.85.
Train A few dozen Renfe (☎ 90 224 02 02; www .renfe.es) C8 cercanías trains make the one-hour trip (€2.10) daily from Madrid to El Escorial.

VALLE DE LOS CAÍDOS

Only a dictator could have conceived of this monstrosity. Franco's memorial to the 'fallen' (well, his fallen) of the civil war – the Valle de los Caídos – is a mammoth stone cross sitting atop a bunker-like basilica dug into the mountainside. The whole cold, stone thing sits in the midst of a pristine pine forest. The scale of the thing is impressive, but when one stops to think that everything here was built by Franco's war prisoners the monuments take on a new meaning.

The turn-off and ticket booth are 9km north of El Escorial. It's another 6km drive to the shrine. There is something spooky about the subterranean basilica and little, artistically, to recommend it. By the altar lies Franco. Coming on or around 20 November (the anniversary of Franco's death) is a curious experience – he still has his nostalgic supporters.

Near the basilica are walking trails, a picnic area and a small restaurant. You can take a funicular up the mountain to the base of the cross, where if the wind doesn't blow you away you can enjoy great views of the surrounding sierra.

Sights & Information

Valle de los Caídos (☎ 91 890 13 98; Carretera 600; admission €5; ⊙ 10am-6pm Apr-Oct, 10am-5pm Nov-Mar)

Funicular (admission €2.50; ⊙ 11am-5.30pm Apr-Oct, 11am-4.30pm Nov-Mar)

Transport

Distance from Madrid 53km/33 miles
Direction Northwest
Car From Madrid take the A-6 north to highway M-600. Driving time 40 minutes.
Bus Herranz (☎ 91 896 90 28) has one bus per day to Valle de los Caídos. It departs at 3.15pm from El Escorial's Plaza de la Virgen de Gracia and returns at 5.30pm. The service runs Tuesday to Sunday and costs €7.80 for the short bus trip and admission to the monument.

PALACIO REAL DE EL PARDO

Built in the 15th century and remodelled in the 17th century, this opulent palace was Franco's favourite residence. It's surrounded by lush gardens, and on Sundays fills with Madrileño families looking for a bit of fresh air and a hearty lunch. Just outside Madrid, it's the nearest of several regal retreats. Of the art displayed inside, the tapestries stand out, particularly those based on cartoons by Goya.

Sights & Information

Palacio Real de El Pardo (☎ 91 376 15 00; www .patrimonionacional.es; Calle de Manuel Alonso; admission €3; ⊙ 10.30am-5pm Mon-Sat & 9.30am-1.30pm Sun Oct-May, 10.30am-6pm Mon-Sat & 9.30am-1.30pm Sun Jun-Sep)

Transport

Distance from Madrid 13km/8 miles
Direction Northwest
Car Take the M-30 highway to the C-601, which leads to El Pardo. Driving time 15 to 20 minutes.
Bus The 601 bus leaves every five to 15 minutes from the bus depot near Moncloa metro station. The trip takes about 25 minutes and costs €1.05.

ARANJUEZ

Modern-day visitors to Aranjuez aren't that different from the royals that established this town as a city escape centuries ago; we're still looking for a breath of fresh air, a stroll among the gardens, and a chance to soak up the opulent art and architecture of the town's palace.

The **Palacio Real** started as one of Felipe II's modest summer palaces but was converted into the current extravaganza by the 18th century. With more than 300 rooms and inspired by the palace at Versailles in France (an ever-popular model with European monarchs), this sprawling box of a palace is filled with a cornucopia of ornamentation. Of all the rulers who spent time here, Carlos III and Isabel II left the greatest mark.

Most of the palace was closed for renovation at the time of writing, but was due to re-pen soon. Taking the obligatory guided tour (in Spanish) gives an interesting look at the alace history and the art that fills it. Afterward, stroll in the lush **gardens**. They're a mix of cal and exotic species that have come along nicely since Spanish botanists and explorers tarted bringing back seeds from all over the world. Within their shady perimeter, which tretches a few kilometres from the palace, you'll find two other man-made attractions. The **asa de Marinos** contains the **Museo de Falúas**, a museum of royal pleasure boats from days gone y. Further away, towards Chinchón, is the **Casa del Labrador**, a tasteless royal jewellery box rammed to the rafters with gold, silver, silk and some second-rate art. It sits in the **Jardín el Príncipe**, an extension of the massive gardens. If you don't want to walk or drive to these asas, you can take the **Chiquitren**, a small tourist train that loops through town and stops at oth houses, allowing you to get off if you choose.

ights & Information

asa de Marinos & Museo de Falúas (☎ 91 891 03 05; dmission €3, bookings essential; ☺ 10am-5.15pm Oct-Mar, 10am-6.15pm Apr-Sep)

asa del Labrador (☎ 91 891 03 05; admission €3, ookings essential; ☺ 10am-5.15pm Oct-Mar, 10am-.15pm Apr-Sep)

hiquitren (☎ 90 208 80 89; train stop near palace ntrance; adult/child €5/3; ☺ 11am-5.30pm Tue-Sun Oct-eb, 10am-8pm Mar-Sep)

alacio Real (☎ 91 891 07 40; admission to palace 3.40, EU citizens free Wed, gardens free; ☺ palace 1am-5.30pm Oct-Mar, 11am-7.30pm Apr-Sep; gardens am-6.30pm Oct-Mar, 8am-8.30pm Apr-Sep)

ourist Office (☎ 91 891 04 27; www.aranjuez.net in panish; Plaza de San Antonio 9; ☺ 10am-6.30pm Nov-pr, May-Oct 10am-8.30pm)

Eating & Sleeping

Casa José (☎ 91 891 14 88; Calle de Abastos 32; mains E8-16; ☺ 9am-midnight Tue-Sat, 9am-4pm Sun) An legant spot, one of the best in town for meats and local Iishes.

Transport

Distance from Madrid South
Direction 50km/31 miles
Car From Madrid take the N-IV south to the M-305, which leads to the city centre.
Bus The AISA bus company (☎ 90 219 87 88; www .aisa-grupo.com in Spanish) sends buses to Aranjuez from Madrid's Estación Sur every 15 minutes. The 30-minute trip costs €3.
Train Renfe (☎ 90 224 02 02; www.renfe.es) *cercanía* trains leave every 15 or 20 minutes from Madrid's Atocha station. The 42-minute trip costs €2.10.

El Rana Verde (☎ 91 801 15 71; Plaza Santiago Rusiñol; mains €8-18; ☺ 9am-midnight) A classic riverside restaurant whose speciality is frogs legs.

Hostal Castilla (☎ 91 891 26 27; www.hostalesaranjuez .com in Spanish; Carretera Andalucía 98; s/d €35/45) Impeccable little rooms with their own bathrooms.

NH Príncipe de la Paz hotel (☎ 91 809 92 22; www .nh-hoteles.com; Calle de San Antonio 22; r from €97) Sleek, modern design and attentive service make this the best hotel in town.

Stunning fountain in Campo del Moro, behind Palacio Real (p214)

CHINCHÓN

A weekend retreat for city-sick Madrileños looking for a slice of country life, Chinchó is a dusty old town that hasn't significantly changed its style in the past 200 years or s That, of course, is its charm. The heart of town is its unique round **Plaza Mayor**, which is line with sagging, tiered balconies and gets converted into a bullring in summer (see boxed tex p199). It's also the stage for a popular passion play shown at Easter. A stroll around th square is pleasant, but even better is feasting in the smorgasbord of traditional **meson-styl restaurants** scattered in and around it.

The few historical monuments here won't detain you long, but you can take a look at th 16th-century **Iglesia de la Asunción** (closed for repairs at the time of writing) that rises above th Plaza Mayor. The late-16th-century Renaissance **Castillo de los Condes** sits out of town abou 1km to the south. The castle was abandoned in the 1700s and was last used as a liquor fac tory. To get an idea of the traditional lifestyle in the area, head to the **Museo Etnológico La Posad**a a well-run museum with old farm equipment, household items and traditional garb.

Chinchón's main sights are usually closed to the public, but the local tourist office has re cently begun a programme allowing sporadic visits. Two sights (usually churches or the castle are open Saturdays and Sundays, on a rotational basis. Ask at the tourist office for details.

Sights & Information

Museo Etnológico La Posada (☎ 91 894 02 07; Calle Morata 5; adult/child €3/2; 🕑 11am-2pm & 4-8pm Mon-Fri, 11am-8pm Sat & Sun, closed Wed)

Police (☎ 629 16 70 70; Plaza Mayor)

Tourist Office (☎ 91 893 53 23; www.ciudad-chinchon.com; Plaza Mayor 6; 🕑 10am-8pm Mon-Fri, 11.30am-8pm Sat & Sun May-Jun & Sep-Oct, to 9pm Jul-Aug, to 7pm Nov-Feb) Small office but very helpful.

Eating

Chinchón is loaded with traditional-style restaurants, but for lighter fare there's nothing better than savouring a few tapas and drinks on the sunny Plaza Mayor.

Mesón Cuevas de a Comendadora (☎ 91 894 09 47; Calle Teniente Ortíz de Zárate; mains €8-16, menú €12; 🕑 closed Wed) The maze of caves that extends underneath the restaurant are worth seeing even if you don't eat here.

Meson Cuevas del Vino (☎ 91 894 02 06; www.cuevasdelvino.com; Calle Benito Hortelano 13; mains €8-22, 🕑 1-5pm & 8pm-midnight, closed Tue) From the huge goatskins used to keep wine in, to the barrels covered in famous signatures, to the atmospheric caves underground, the Meson 'Caves of Wine' is sure to be a memorable eating experience.

Sleeping

Hostal Chinchón (☎ 91 893 53 98; www.hostalchinchon.com; Calle de José Antonio 12; s/d €27/40) Smallish room that are clean but worn around the edges. The highlight of this hostal is the surprise rooftop pool which overlooks the Plaza Mayor.

Parador de Chinchón (☎ 91 894 08 36; www.parador.es Avenida Generalísimo 1; r from €113) The former Convento de Agustinos (Augustine Convent), the Parador is one of the town's most important historical buildings, and it's worth stopping by for a meal or coffee (and a peek around even if you don't plan to stay here.

Transport

Distance from Madrid 45km/28 miles
Direction Southeast
Car Head out of Madrid on the A-4 motorway and exit onto M-404 which makes its way to Chinchón.
Bus La Veloz bus company (☎ 91 409 76 02) has services approximately every hour to Chinchón. The buses leave from a stop on the Plaza Conde de Casal and the 50-minute ride costs €3.

ALCALÁ DE HENARES

With its pretty historical centre, sunny plazas and legendary university, Alcalá de Henares hides a few treasures behind its façade.

The **university** founded in 1486 by Cardinal Cisneros is one of the country's principal seat of learning. A guided tour gives a peek into the *mudéjar* **chapel** and the **Paraninfo** auditorium where the King and Queen of Spain give out the prestigious Premio Cervantes literary award every year.

The town is also dear to Spaniards as the birthplace of the country's literary figurehead, Miguel de Cervantes Saavedra (see p33). The site believed to be Cervantes' birthplace is recreated in the **Museo Casa Natal de Miguel de Cervantes.**

Sights & Information

Iber TK (☎ 91 883 40 24; Calle de San Diego de Alcalá 3; per hr €2; ☻ 10am-2pm & 3-9.30pm Mon-Fri, 10am-2pm & 3-9pm Sat, 3-9pm Sun)

Museo Natal de Miguel de Cervantes (☎ 91 889 96 54; Calle de la Imagen 2; admission free; ☻ 10am-6pm Tue-Sun Jun-Sep, 10am-1.30pm & 4-6.30pm Oct-May)

Tourist Office (☎ 91 881 06 34; Plaza de los Santos Niños; ☻ 10am-2pm & 5-7.30pm Jun-Sep 15, 10am-2pm & 4-6.30pm Sep 16-May)

University (☎ 91 883 43 84; 6 free guided visits per day Mon-Fri, 11 per day Sat & Sun; ☻ 9am-9pm)

Eating & Sleeping

El Ruedo (☎ 91 880 69 19; Calle de los Libreros 38; ☻ 9am-11pm, closed Wed) With a quiet patio for outdoor eating, this is a great place to get informal fare such as salads and mixed plates.

Hostería del Estudiante (☎ 91 888 03 30; Calle de los Colegios 3; menú €24.50; ☻ 1-4pm & 9-11pm) A charming restaurant in the main university building.

Husa El Bedel (☎ 91 889 37 00; www.husa.es; Plaza San Diego 6; s/d €96/108) Perfect location and elegant, spacious rooms.

SIERRA DE GUADARRAMA

To the north of Madrid lies the Sierra de Guadarrama, a popular winter ski destination and the home of several charming towns. In **Manzanares El Real** you can explore the small 15th-century **Castillo de los Mendoza**, a perfectly preserved storybook castle with round towers at its corners and a Gothic interior patio. Nearby is the **Pedriza park**, with trails and freshwater pools.

Cercedilla is a popular base for hikers and mountain bikers. There are several marked trails through the sierra, the main one known as the **Cuerda Larga** or **Cuerda Castellana**. This is a forest track that takes in 55 peaks between the **Puerto de Somosierra** in the north and **Puerto de la Cruz Verde** in the southwest. It would take days to complete the full track, but there are several options for shorter walks. Get more information at the **Centro de Información Valle de la Fuenfría.** Small ski resorts like **Valdesqui** welcome weekend skiers from the city.

Sights & Information

Castillo de los Mendoza (☎ 91 853 00 08; admission incl guided tour €1.80; ☻ 10am-2pm & 3-6pm Tue-Sun Apr-Sep, 10am-5pm Oct-Mar)

Centro de Información Valle de la Fuenfría (☎ 91 852 22 13; Carretera de las Dehesas, 2km outside town of Cercedilla on M-614; ☻ 10am-6pm)

Navacerrada Tourist Information (☎ 91 852 22 02; www.puertonavacerrada.com in Spanish)

Valdesqui Ski Resort (☎ 91 570 12 24; Puerto de Cotos; lift tickets €22-30)

SIERRA POBRE

The 'Poor Sierra' is a toned-down version of its more refined western neighbour, the Sierra de Guadarrama. Popular with hikers and others looking for nature without quite so many creature comforts, the sleepy Sierra Pobre has yet to develop the tourism industry of its neighbours. And that's just why we like it.

Head first to **Buitrago**, the largest town in the area, where you can stroll along part of the old **city walls**. You can also take a peek into the 15th-century *mudéjar* and Romanesque **Iglesia de Santa María del Castillo** and into the small **Picasso Museum**, which contains a few works that the artist gave to his barber, Eugenio Arias.

Tiny hamlets are scattered throughout the rest of the sierra; some, like **Puebla de la Sierra** and **El Atazar**, are pretty walks and are the starting point for winding hill trails.

Sights & Information

Picasso Museum (☎ 91 868 00 56/04; Plaza Picasso; ☽ 11am-1.30pm & 4-6pm Wed-Mon)

Transport

Distance 73km
Direction Northeast
Car Take the N-I highway to Buitrago.
Bus The Continental Auto Company (☎ 91 745 63 00; www.continental-auto.es) has a dozen daily buses connecting Madrid's Plaza de la Castilla with Buitrago (1 hour and 30 minutes; €4.19).

SIERRA DE GREDOS

West of Madrid, the Sierra de Gredos splays out like green fingers, inviting tired city slickers into its hills and valleys. This area, part of which has been declared natural parkland, is popular with rock climbers, but there are plenty of good walking trails for those who want to keep their feet on the ground. Get more information at www.gredos.com or in **Arenas de San Pedro**, one of the larger towns in the area.

In summer, the **Laguna de San Juan**, a massive reservoir, becomes a magnet for water-sports fans, and windsurfers and sailors take to the water in droves. There are a few so-called beaches here; it's not the Mediterranean, but then again it's only 15km away from the city of Madrid.

Sights & Information

Arenas de San Pedro Tourist Information (☎ 92 037 23 68)

Eating & Sleeping

Parador de Gredos (☎ 92 034 80 48; www.parador.es; Carretera Barraco-Béjar km 42; r from €74.40) Spain's very first Parador, this elegant stone hotel overlooks the sierra. The refined restaurant serves tasty local dishes (mains €14 to €25).

Transport

Distance 60–80km
Direction West
Car Take the N-V highway southwest out of Madrid until you come to the N-502, which brings you north to Arenas de San Pedro.
Bus La Supulvedana (☎ 91 530 48 00; www.lasepulvedana.es) buses run from Madrid's Estación Sur to Arenas de San Pedro. The two-hour trip costs €8.18 and there are more than a dozen buses daily. The company Cevesa (☎ 91 539 31 32) makes runs to other points in the Serria de Gredo.

Directory

Directory

The practical information in this chapter is divided into two parts, Transport and Practicalities. Within each section information is presented in strictly alphabetical order.

TRANSPORT

AIR

Madrid is Spain's biggest international transport hub and easy to reach by air from anywhere around the rest of the country, throughout Europe and America.

Many airlines fly directly to Madrid from the rest of Europe. There are some direct intercontinental flights from North and South America too, although some flights from North America involve a change of flight in another major European hub en route.

Look out for budget airline deals. Of the several low-cost airlines now working out of the UK and, increasingly, other European hubs, EasyJet is the main operator into Madrid. These airlines work on a first-come, first-serve basis: the earlier you book a flight the less you pay. As flights fill, the price of a ticket rises. These no-frills airlines skip extras such as in-flight meals (although you can buy snacks).

Within Spain, air travel can be expensive. Iberia, Air Europa and Spanair all have dense networks across the country and, while at times costly, there is no doubt that you can save considerable time by flying from Barcelona and other major cities.

Most airlines, especially budget ones, encourage you to book on their websites. Other useful general sites to search for competitive fares are www.expedia.com, www.opodo.com and www.planesimple.co.uk.

Airlines

Increasingly, airlines have abandoned their shopfront offices in Madrid. You will have to go online, call the following numbers or try a travel agent. Most airlines have information desks at the airports they serve.

Air Berlin (☎ 01805 737800 in Germany, 901 116402 in Spain; www.airberlin.com) German budget airline with flights to Madrid from cities all over Germany via Palma de Mallorca.

Air Europa (☎ 08702 401501 in the UK, 902 401501 in Spain; www.aireuropa.com) Flies to Madrid from London, Paris, Rome, Milan and New York, and from destinations all over Spain.

Basiq Air (☎ 0900 0737 in Holland, 902 114478 in Spain; www.basiqair.com) Low-cost flights from Amsterdam to Madrid.

British Airways (☎ 08708 509850 in the UK, 902 111333 in Spain; www.britishairways.com)

Delta (☎ 800 241 4141 in USA, 901 116946 in Spain; www.delta.com) Flies from New York to Madrid daily.

EasyJet (☎ 08706 000000 in the UK, 902 299992 in Spain; www.easyjet.com) Flies to Madrid from London (Gatwick and Luton), Liverpool and Geneva.

Iberia (☎ 902 400500 in Spain; www.iberia.es; Calle de Velázquez 130; Metro Avenida de América)

Spanair (☎ 902 131415 in Spain; www.spanair.com) Flights from Barcelona and other destinations throughout Spain, as well as some European connections.

Virgin Express (☎ 070 353637 in Belgium, 902 888459 in Spain; www.virgin-express.com) Regular flights from Brussels to Madrid.

Volare (☎ 899 700007 in Italy, 900 810042 in Spain; www.volareweb.com) Flights from Venice to Madrid.

Airports

Madrid's **Barajas airport** (☎ 91 393 60 00, flight information 902 353570; www.aena.es/aero puertos/barajas) lies 13km northeast of the city. Expansion work on the airport will double the number of runways and create a revolutionary new terminal by the end of 2005.

The main airport complex presently contains three terminals: T1, T2 and T3. The first deals mainly with intercontinental and some European flights. T2 handles predominantly domestic and Schengen-area flights with Spanish airlines. T3 is dedicated to Iberia's Puente Aereo (air shuttle) between Madrid and Barcelona, along with what are referred to as 'regional' flights, which can mean domestic as well as short hops to destinations in France or even Italy.

The arrivals halls are on the ground floor and departures are upstairs. Check-in (facturación) is mostly done on the upstairs level. Some airlines also do check-in at the Nuevos Ministerios metro stop and transport interchange in Madrid itself – ask your airline. The service allows you to check your luggage in early, take the metro to the airport unburdened and avoid check-in queues at the airport itself.

The **tourist office** (☎ 91 305 86 56; ☺8am-8pm daily) is on the ground floor in the T1 area. There are ATMs in all terminals. The BBVA and Caja de Madrid banks have branches in T1 and T2. There is a **post office** (☺8.30am-8.30pm Mon-Fri, 9.30am-1pm Sat) in the arrivals lounge of T1. Five international car-rental companies operate desks in the arrivals area of the ground floor of terminals T1 and T2.

There are two **left-luggage offices** (*consignas*; ☺24 hr), one in T1 (near the bus stop and taxi stand) and the other in T2 (near the metro entrance). In either you pay €2.60 for the first 24-hour period (or fraction thereof). Thereafter, it costs €4.55 per day (up until 15 days) in a big locker, or €3.25 in a small one. After 15 days the bag will be moved into storage (€1.30/0.60 per day plus a €32.50 transfer fee). For lost property in the airport call ☎ 91 393 61 19.

The easiest way into town is line 8 of the metro (entrance in T2) to the Nuevos Ministerios transport interchange, which connects with other metro lines and the local overground *cercanías* train service. It operates from 6.05am to 2am. A single ticket costs €1.15 (10-ride Metrobús ticket €5.35).

Alternatively, take the **airport bus** (☎91 406 88 10; €2.50). It arrives/departs from an underground terminus on Plaza de Colón (Map pp268-9). When heading *to* the airport, you could pick it up at a stop next to the Avenida de América metro station to avoid traffic. The bus *is* useful out of metro hours. The first departure from the city and the airport is at 4.45am. The last scheduled service from the airport is 2am, while the 1.30am bus from the city waits at the airport for late flights between 2am and 4.45am. The buses leave every 12 to 15 minutes. Allow about half an hour in average traffic to reach Colón.

Don't want the hassle of public transport? Try **AeroCITY** (☎91 747 75 70; www.aerocity.com; Calle de Marzo 34). It will take you door-to-door from central Madrid to the airport and vice versa. Depending on how many passengers (maximum of seven) book this minibus, the fare can range from €17 to €5.43 per person. It operates 24 hours and you can book by phone or on the Web. There is a supplement for rides after 10pm and on public holidays.

A taxi to/from the centre will cost you around €18 to €20, depending on traffic and where you begin the journey. To the Chamartín train station you might pay about €16, or €20 to Atocha. There are cab ranks outside all three terminals.

Short- and long-term parking is available. A few spots for drop off and pick up are located outside terminal T2. Longer term parking areas (P1 for terminal T1 and P2 for terminals T2 and T3) cost from €1.35 per hour and up to €11.60 for 24 hours. Further away from the terminals and linked by a free shuttle bus is the Parking de Largas Estancias if you plan to leave a vehicle for several days at the airport (€8.50 first day, €7.50 per day second to fifth day, €3.50 per day thereafter).

BICYCLE

Lots of people zip around town on mopeds (*motos*), but brave souls willing to risk life and limb on bicycles are rather thin on the ground (no pun intended). Little has been done to encourage cyclists in Madrid and bike lanes are virtually unheard of.

Hire

Karacol Sports (Map pp262-4; ☎91 539 96 33; Calle de Tortosa 8; Metro Atocha Renfe), rents out road bikes and mountain bikes (with excursions outside Madrid in mind) for €15 per day. There's a refundable deposit of €40 and you also need to leave an original document (passport, driving licence or the like).

Bicycles on Public Transport

You can transport your bicycle on the metro only on weekends and holidays, from 6am to 4pm. You can also take your bike aboard *cercanías* trains from 10am onwards Monday to Friday and all day on weekends.

BUS
Long Distance

Estación Sur de Autobuses (☎91 468 42 00; www.estaciondeautobuses.com; Calle de Méndez Álvaro; Metro Méndez Álvaro), just south of the M-30 ring road, is the city's principal bus station. It serves most destinations to the south and many in other parts of the country. Most bus companies have a ticket office here, even if their buses depart from elsewhere.

The station operates a **consigna** (left-luggage office; ☺6.30am-midnight) near where the buses exit the station. There are cafés, shops, exchange booths, a bank, a police post and direct access to the No 6 metro line and *cercanías* trains to Atocha and Chamartín train stations.

Eurolines (www.eurolines.com), in conjunction with local carriers all over Europe, is the main international carrier. Its website provides links to national operators and it runs services across Europe and to Morocco from the Estación Sur de Autobuses. For information and tickets, contact **Eurolines** (☎ 902 405040; www.eurolines .es). **Internacional** (☎ 902 422242; www.alsa.es) is another international operator.

Several companies operate out of other terminals around the city. Of these, some useful ones are:

ALSA (Map pp262-4; ☎ 902 422242; www.alsa.es; Intercambiador de Avenida de América; Metro Avenida de América) ALSA runs buses to Barcelona via Zaragoza from here, and a host of services to southern Spain from Estación Sur.

AutoRes (Map pp262-4; ☎ 902 020999; www.auto-res .net; Calle de Fernández Shaw 1; Metro Conde de Casal) This company operates buses to Extremadura, western Castilla y León (eg Tordesillas, Salamanca and Zamora) and Valencia via eastern Castilla–La Mancha (eg Cuenca). Also runs buses to Lisbon, Portugal.

Continental-Auto (Map pp262-4; ☎ 91 745 63 00, bookings 902 330400; www.continental-auto.es; Intercambiador de Avenida de América; Metro Avenida de América) Runs north to Burgos, Logroño, Navarra, the País Vasco, Santander, Soria, Alcalá de Henares and Guadalajara. It also runs buses to Toledo from Estación Sur.

Herranz (Map pp262-4; ☎ 91 896 90 28; Moncloa Intercambiador de Autobuses; Metro Moncloa) Buses for San Lorenzo de El Escorial from the bus station below ground level at the Moncloa metro station. The buses leave from platform 3.

La Sepulvedana (Map pp262-4; ☎ 91 530 48 00; www .lasepulvedana.es; Paseo de la Florida 11; Metro Príncipe Pío) Buses to Segovia, La Granja de San Ildefonso and San Rafael (near Cercedilla).

La Veloz (Map pp262-4; ☎ 91 409 76 02; Avenida del Mediterráneo 49; Metro Conde de Casal) Buses to Chinchón.

Madrid

Buses operated by **Empresa Municipal de Transportes de Madrid** (EMT; ☎ 91 406 99 00; www.ctm -madrid.es) travel along most city routes regularly between about 6.30am and 11.30pm.

Twenty night bus routes (*búhos*) operate from midnight to 6am. They run from Puerta del Sol and Plaza de la Cibeles.

The single-deck *piso bajo* buses have no steps inside and in some cases have ramps that can be used by people in wheelchairs. In the long run, EMT plans to make at least 50% of its buses on all routes accessible to the disabled.

Information booths can be found on Puerta del Sol, Plaza de Callao and Plaza de la Cibeles.

MADRID VISIÓN
Backed by the Ayuntamiento, the orange **Madrid Visión buses** (☎ 91 779 18 88; www.madrid vision.es; ⏱ 9.30am-midnight late Jun–late Sep, 10am-7pm late Dec–late Mar, 10am-9pm rest of the year) operate along three routes around the city. For more information, see Organised Tours in the Madrid's Barrios chapter (p64).

CAR & MOTORCYCLE
Driving to Madrid
Madrid is 2622km from Berlin, 2245km from London, 1889km from Milan, 1836km from Paris, 1470km from Geneva, 690km from Barcelona and 610km from Lisbon.

Madrid is the centre point in Spain from which most of the country's major highways radiate out to the coast. The A-I heads north to Burgos and ultimately to Santander (for the UK ferry); the A-2 wends its way northeast to Barcelona and ultimately into France (as the AP-7). The A-4 takes you south to Andalucía, while the A-5 and A-6 respectively take you west towards Portugal via Cáceres and northwest to Galicia. The A-42 goes south to Toledo.

The city is surrounded by: two main ring roads, the outermost M-40 and the inner M-30; an additional partial ring road, the M-45; and the first stages of a still more-distant one, the M-50. The R-5 and R-3, opened in early 2004, are two of a series of planned new approach toll roads. These can all become clogged on Sunday and holiday evenings as Madrileños stream back from vacations and weekend getaways.

Coming from the UK you can put your car on a ferry from Portsmouth to Bilbao with **P&O Ferries** (☎ 08705 202020; www .poportsmouth.com) or from Plymouth or Portsmouth to Santander with **Brittany Ferries** (☎ 08703 665333; www.brittanyferries .co.uk). From Bilbao or Santander you barrel south to the capital. Otherwise, you can opt for a ferry to France or the Channel Tunnel car train, **Eurotunnel** (☎ 08705 353535; www .eurotunnel.com). The latter runs round the clock, with up to four crossings (35 minutes) per hour between Folkestone and Calais in the high season.

Vehicles must be roadworthy, registered and insured (third party at least). Also ask your insurer for a European Accident Statement form, which can simplify matters in the event of an accident. A European breakdown-assistance policy (eg the AA Five Star Service or the RAC Eurocover Motoring Assistance in the UK) is a good investment.

Driving & Parking in Madrid

At first, driving in Madrid can be a little hair-raising. Cars roar down the main boulevards and jostle for position in the grand roundabouts. In the tighter streets of the old centre, quick reflexes are needed to navigate, especially if you have an impatient local on your tail. The streets are dead between about 2pm and 4pm, when people are either eating or snoozing. On the other hand traffic jams can happen in the wee hours of the morning, especially towards the end of the week when the whole city seems to be out and about partying.

Most of central Madrid is governed by the Operación de Regulación de Aparcamiento (ORA) parking system. This means that, apart from designated metered parking areas, loading zones, no-parking areas and the like, all parking positions that appear legitimate are only so for people with yearly permits, or coupons obtainable from tobacconists.

Where meters are in operation you can park for up to two hours (€1.60) in blue areas and up to one hour (€1.30) in green areas. There are also private parking stations all over central Madrid.

If you park in a designated no-parking area, you risk being towed. Double-parking is also risky in this way if you wander far from your vehicle. Should your car disappear, call the **Grúa Municipal** (city towing service; ☎ 91 345 06 66). Getting it back costs €84.14 plus whatever fine you have been given.

Obviously, the parking of motorbikes and scooters is easier. On occasion you'll see spaces marked out especially for bikes.

Rental

The big-name, car-rental agencies have offices all over Madrid. Avis, Europcar, Hertz and Na-tional/Atesa have booths at the airport. Some of them also operate branches at Atocha and Chamartín train stations. The smaller operators often have one reservation phone number and an out-of-the-way office – ask if they can deliver the car to a convenient location. Some addresses include:

Avis (Map pp266-7; ☎ 902 135531, 91 547 20 48; Gran Vía 60; Metro Santo Domingo)

Europcar (Map pp266-7; ☎ 902 105030, 91 541 88 92; Calle de San Leonardo 8; Metro Plaza de España)

Hertz (Map pp266-7; ☎ 902 402405, 91 372 93 00; Edificio de España, Plaza de España; Metro Plaza de España)

Moto Alquiler (Map pp266-7; ☎ 91 542 06 57; Calle del Conde Duque 13; Metro San Bernardo) Motorbike rental. Something like a Honda CB500 will cost you €335 for a Monday to Friday package, and the deposit is €1500 on your credit card.

National/Atesa (Map pp266-7; ☎ 902 100101; 1st fl, Gran Vía 80; Metro Plaza de España)

Pepecar (Map p261; ☎ 807 212121; www.pepecar .com; underground parking area, Plaza de España; Metro Plaza de España) This company specialises in cheap rentals of Mercedes Class A cars and Smarts. It also has outlets near the airport, at Ronda de Atocha 12, near Atocha train station, and Calle de Agustín de Foixa 27, near Chamartín train station. If you book far enough ahead, it can cost you around €12 a day (with 100 free kilometres), plus a credit card handling fee and a €12 cleaning charge.

Sotorent (Map pp262-4; ☎ 91 356 65 78; Avenida de los Toreros 12; Metro Diego de León) It sometimes has some good deals.

WARNING

If you have a rental car in Madrid, take extra care. Groups of delinquents are known to occasionally zero in on them, puncturing tyres and then robbing the drivers when they act to change it. This is reportedly a particular problem on the road from the airport to the centre of town.

TAXI

You can pick up a cab at ranks throughout town or simply flag one down. Flag fall is €1.55 and you should make sure the driver turns the meter on. You pay €0.70 per kilometre (€0.98 between 10pm and 6am). On public holidays you pay €0.98 all day. Several supplementary charges, usually posted up inside the taxi, apply. They include: €4 to/from the airport, €2 from cab ranks at train and bus stations, €2 to/from the Parque Ferial Juan Carlos I and a special €4 charge on Christmas Eve and New Year's Eve. There is no charge for luggage. People with local bank accounts and local mobile phones can pay in some taxis with their mobile phone number using a system called Mobipay.

You can call a cab on ☎ 91 405 12 13; ☎ 91 404 90 00; ☎ 91 445 90 08 or ☎ 91 447 51 80.

Radio-Teléfono Taxi (☎ 91 547 82 00 or 91 547 86 00) runs taxis for the disabled. Generally, if you call any taxi company and ask for a *eurotaxi* you should be sent one adapted for wheelchair users.

A green light on the roof means the taxi is available *(libre)*. Generally a sign to this effect is also placed in the lower passenger side of the windscreen.

METRO & CERCANÍAS

The **metro** (☎ 902 444403; www.metromadrid.es) is a fast, efficient and safe way to navigate Madrid, and generally easier than getting to grips with bus routes. It has 11 colour-coded lines, in addition to the modern southern suburban MetroSur system, and operates from about 6am to 1.30am. You can buy a book of tickets from staffed booths or machines at most stations.

This book contains a colour map of the main central Madrid metro system, as the MetroSur is unlikely to be of interest to visitors. By the time of the Olympics that the city would like to host in 2012, it plans to have 230km of what city authorities proclaim the most modern metro in the world!

Few lines make concessions to the disabled. Many of the new stations are equipped with lifts, but that means that most of the central Madrid stations, among the oldest, are not disabled-friendly.

The short-range *cercanías* regional trains operated by Renfe, the national railways, go as far afield as El Escorial, Alcalá de Henares, Aranjuez and other points in the Comunidad de Madrid. In Madrid itself, they are handy for making a quick, north–south hop between Chamartín and Atocha mainline train stations (with stops at Nuevos Ministerios and in front of the Biblioteca Nacional on Paseo de los Recoletos only). Another line links Chamartín, Atocha and Príncipe Pío stations.

Tickets

Single-journey bus tickets can be obtained on buses or at most tobacconists *(estancos)*. They are not valid on trains. Single-journey metro and *cercanías* tickets are available at stations and tobacconists. The two systems are separate and tickets for one are not valid for the other. In most cases, a single ride throughout the city area costs €1.15 (bus or metro), except on the *cercanías*, which costs €1. A Metrobús ticket valid for 10 rides costs €5.35. It entitles

you to use the buses and metro (but not *cercanías*), and you can share tickets. A similar ticket, MetroSur, is available for use on the new metro network outside the Madrid municipality that takes in such areas as Alcorcón, Getafe, Leganés, Móstoles and Fuenlabrada.

Monthly or season passes *(abonos)* only make sense if you are staying long term and use local transport frequently. You need to get an ID card *(carnet)* from metro stations or tobacconists. Take a passport-sized photo and your passport. A monthly ticket for central Madrid (Zona A) costs €34.55 and is valid for unlimited travel on bus, metro and *cercanías*.

A Tourist Ticket (Abono Turístico), valid for one, two or three days, is also available if you buy the Madrid Card (€28/42/55). See Discount Cards p228.

Fines

The fine for being caught without a ticket on public transport is €18 – in addition to the price of the ticket, of course.

TRAIN

Trains converge on Madrid from major centres all over Spain. A handful of international trains also serve the city. The latter can be a long haul and you may find flying cheaper as well as faster. For information on travelling from the UK contact the **Rail Europe Travel Centre** (☎ 0870 848848; www.raileurope.co.uk; 179 Piccadilly, London W1V 0BA). For travel within Spain you can get information at your nearest train station or travel agent. Alternatively, contact **Renfe** (☎ 902 240202; www.renfe.es).

A host of train types coasts the wide-gauge lines of the Spanish network. A saving of a couple of hours on a faster train can mean a big hike in the fare.

Most long-distance *(largo recorrido)* trains have 1st and 2nd class (known as *preferente* and *turista*). Those running more than 400km are dubbed Grandes Líneas. The oldest and slowest of these are *diurnos* and *estrellas*, the standard interregional trains. The former have become a rarity, but on long overnight hauls you will still encounter the latter. The Tren Regional Diesel (TRD) is a modern diesel train that is used on some faster, shorter-range services.

Faster, more comfortable and expensive are the Talgos (Tren Articulado Ligero Goicoechea Oriol). They make only major stops and have such extras as TVs. The Talgo Pendular is eeker, faster version that picks up speed by eaning into curves. Some of these limited-tops services are denominated InterCity or nterCity Plus.

A classier derivative is the Talgo 200, a Talgo endular that uses the standard-gauge, high-peed Tren de Alta Velocidad Española (AVE) ne between Madrid and Seville on part of he journey to such southern destinations as Málaga, Cádiz and Algeciras.

High-speed Tren de Alta Velocidad Española AVE) services connect Madrid with Seville via lórdoba in the south and Zaragoza, Huesca nd Lleida (and one day Barcelona) in the ortheast. It can reach speeds of 350km/h.

Autoexpreso and Motoexpreso wagons are ometimes attached to long-distance services or the transport, respectively, of cars and mo-orbikes.

A *trenhotel* is a sleeping-car train with up to hree classes: *turista* (for those sitting or in a ouchette); *preferente* (sleeping car) and *gran lase* (sleeping in sheer bloody luxury).

Madrid's Train Stations

wo train stations serve the city. Note that nany trains call in at either one or the other out not both), so check when purchasing ickets. At **Atocha train station** (Map p273; Metro Atocha Renfe), south of the old city centre, there s an information and ticket centre for long-distance services (including the high-speed AVE) in the old station (the part now serving s a tropical garden). In the same area are lug-gage lockers available from 6.30am to 10.20pm €2.40/3/4.50 per day, depending on the size of the locker). Arrivals *(llegadas)* and departures salidas)* appear on big, electronic boards and V screens. Full timetables for long-distance rains are also posted outside the ticket office. Another **information office** (🕑 7am-11pm) near platforms 9 and 10 (look for the 'Atención al Cliente' sign) deals with regional and *cercanías* rains, and property lost on these trains. Tickets or regional trains can be bought at a sepa-ate counter. Timetables for these services are osted all over this part of the station.

At **Chamartín station** (Map p260; Metro Chamartín), information and tickets are avail-ible at the **Centro de Viajes** (🕑 7am-11pm), be-ween platforms 7 and 10. Exchange booths nd ATMs are scattered about the station. ockers are located outside the main station uilding (take the exit opposite platform 18) nd are available between 7am and 11pm €2.40/3/4.50 per day, depending on the size

of the locker). Train timetables are posted. Impending arrivals *(llegadas)* and departures *(salidas)* appear on electronic boards and TV screens. Timetables for specific lines are gener-ally available free of charge.

You can buy tickets at the stations, travel agents and at the **Renfe office** (Map pp266-7; Calle de Alcalá 44; 🕑 9.30am-8pm Mon-Fri; Metro Sevilla).

TRAVEL AGENTS

Some travel agencies which can be worth looking at include:

Abando CTS Viajes (Map pp266-7; ☎ 91 559 31 81; cnr Calle de San Leonardo de Dios & Plaza de España; Metro Plaza de España) Student travel agency.

Asatej Travel Agency (Map pp270-2; ☎ 91 522 96 93; www.almundo.com; Carrera de San Jerónimo 18; Metro Sol) Can organise anything from car rental to trips outside Spain. There's another branch (Map pp262-4; ☎ 91 543 47 61; Calle de Fernando el Católico 60; Metro Argüelles)

Halcón (☎ 902 433000; www.halconviajes.com; Calle de la Princesa 27; Metro Ventura Rodríguez; Gran Vía 39; Metro Callao) A reliable chain with branches all over Madrid.

Juventus Viajes (Map pp266-7; ☎ 91 319 41 35; Calle de Fernando VI 9; Metro Alonso Martínez) Student travel agency.

Viajes Zeppelin (Map pp266-7; ☎ 91 542 51 54; www .zeppelin.com; Plaza de Santo Domingo 2; Metro Santo Domingo) Frequently offers good deals on flights. There's another branch (Map pp262-4; ☎ 91 431 40 36; Calle de la Hermosilla 92; Metro Goya)

PRACTICALITIES

ACCOMMODATION

Sleeping options range from down-and-dirty youth hostels for young party animals, through to grand old luxury hotels and glit-tering designer digs. See the Sleeping chapter earlier in the guide for recommendations. The options are presented by district and in alpha-betical order. The emphasis is on mid-range accommodation, but we have slipped in some of the city's great top range hotels too. Each section ends with a Cheap Sleeps list for those travelling on a tighter budget.

High season is most of the year for most hotels, and when business is good many do not alter their rates significantly during the year. There are slow times. The depths of winter (late November to December, except Christmas, and mid-January to March) can be quieter (although this depends in part on whether or not trade fairs are being held) and hoteliers are often prepared to do deals. When the international scene gets shaky (such as during the Iraq war in 2003), tourism takes a tumble and hoteliers become equally amenable. Many of the top, business-oriented hotels also cut good deals for weekend stays.

For more information on prices, reservations, accommodation websites and so on, turn to the beginning of the Sleeping chapter (p183).

BABY-SITTING
Most of the medium and upper-range hotels in Madrid can organise a baby-sitting service.

BUSINESS
Madrid has imposed itself as the financial as well as political capital of Spain, much to the chagrin of eternal rival Barcelona, once considered the country's economic motor. The kind of comparison people used to draw between the two cities and Rome and Milan (respectively the political and financial capitals of Italy) now seems misplaced. Much of Madrid's business activity takes place in the northern half of the city centre, on and around the Paseo de la Castellana. The biggest trade fairs are held in the complex of the Feria de Madrid, east of the city near the airport.

Opening Hours
Generally, people work Monday to Friday from 8am or 9am to 2pm and then again from 4.30pm or 5pm for another three hours. Shops and travel agencies are usually open these hours on Saturday too, although some may skip the evening session. Big supermarkets and department stores such as El Corte Inglés often stay open all day Monday to Saturday, from about 9am to 10pm. A handful of shops open on Sunday. Many government offices don't bother with afternoon opening any day of the year.

Banks tend to open 8.30am to 2pm Monday to Friday. Some open again from around 4pm to 7pm on Thursday evenings and/or Saturday mornings from around 9am to 1pm. The central post office opens 8.30am to 9.30pm Monday to Saturday. Some branches open 8.30am to 8.30pm Monday to Friday and 9.30am to

1pm Saturday, but most open only 8am to 2pm, Monday to Friday.

Lunchtime is around 2pm to 4pm (although most restaurants are open by 1pm) and dinner from 9pm to midnight and beyond. Many restaurants open earlier for dinner, but few locals would dream of turning up before 9pm.

Doing Business in Madrid
People wishing to make the first moves towards expanding their business into Spain should contact their own country's trade department (such as the DTI in the UK). The commercial department of the Spanish embassy in your own country should also have information – at least on red tape. The trade office of your embassy may be able to help.

The **Cámara Oficial de Comercio e Industria de Madrid** (City Chamber of Commerce; Map pp268-9; ☎ 91 538 35 00; Calle de Alcalá 69; Metro Retiro) offers advisory services on most aspects of doing or setting up business in Madrid, as well as video-conferencing facilities and an accessible business database. The chamber has an **office** (☎ 91 305 88 07) in terminal T (arrivals hall) at Barajas airport. It provides an information service for arriving business people, as well as fax, phone and photocopy facilities and a small meeting area.

Exhibitions & Conferences
The **Oficina de Congresos de Madrid** (Madrid Convention Bureau; Map pp270-2; ☎ 91 588 29 00; www.munimadrid.es/congresos; Patronato de Turismo office, Calle Mayor 69; Metro Ópera) publishes the *Guía de Congresos e Incentivos* (also in a CD-ROM version), in Spanish and English, which can be helpful for those interested in organising meetings or conventions.

Madrid's main trade-fair centre is the **Feria de Madrid** (IFEMA; ☎ 91 722 50 00; www.ifema.es; Parque Ferial Juan Carlos I; Metro Campo de las Naciones) in Campo de las Naciones, one metro stop from the airport. It hosts events throughout the year, from the Fitur tourism fair through to the Arco arts show.

Another important trade-fair centre is the **Palacio de Congresos y Exposiciones** (Map p261; ☎ 91 337 81 00; www.pcm.tourspain.es; Paseo de la Castellana 99; Metro Santiago Bernabéu). The auditorium can seat 2000 and there are smaller meeting rooms, with technical support and secretarial services.

The **Palacio Municipal de Congresos** (☎ 91 722 04 00; www.campodelasnaciones.com; Metro

Campo de las Naciones), also in the Campo de las Naciones area, is yet another conference centre. It has various auditoriums equipped with all the technical facilities you are likely to need (video-conferencing, simultaneous translators and so on).

You can review the month's upcoming trade fairs in the free *En Madrid* booklet available at tourist offices.

The Oficina de Congresos can also help arrange events in such elegant settings as the Círculo de Bellas Artes and the Castillo de Manzanares El Real, north of Madrid.

CHILDREN

One of the great things about Madrid (and Spain in general) is the inclusion of kids in many apparently adult activities. Going out to eat or sipping a beer on a late summer evening at a *terraza* (outdoor café or bar) needn't mean leaving kids with minders. Locals take their kids out all the time and don't worry too much about keeping them up late.

Children may quickly wilt in the face of churches and museums, but you can vary the diet and include ones more likely to capture their attention. At first glance it might seem that Madrid doesn't offer too many kids' options, but this is not really the case.

The interactive elements of the Museo del Libro (p92) are fun and the Museo de Cera (Wax Museum; p88) usually works for young kids.

For young boys especially, the Museo del Ejército (p76), Museo del Ferrocarril (p109) and Museo Naval (p79), respectively the army, railway and navy museums, rarely fail to capture the imagination. A ride in the lift to the top of the Faro (p96) or in the Teleférico (p98) can score points too. Finally, never underestimate the value of parks, in particular the Parque del Buen Retiro (p81), where, on weekends and holidays especially, the kids are bound to love running about. You may catch some marionette theatre there too, or see jugglers and other colourful characters getting around. And of course you could try amusement parks, choosing between the more traditional Parque de Atracciones (p109) or Warner Brothers Movie World (p109), outside the city. For some animal fun, try the Parque Biológico (p108).

In the hot summer months you will doubtless be rewarded by squeals of delight if you take the bairns to one of the city's municipal pools (p163).

For our choice of the top five for kids see the Madrid's Barrios chapter (p62). For general advice on travel with children, grab LP's *Travel with Children*.

CLIMATE

Madrid 'enjoys' a continental climate – scorching in summer, cold in winter and dry. Madrileños sum up their feelings on the subject with the neat phrase *'nueve meses de invierno y tres de infierno'* ('nine months of winter and three of hell'). This is a trifle overstated, but Madrid, at its worst, can be nastily cold and infernally hot.

July is the hottest month, with August running a close second. Average highs hover above 30°C, but the maximum is frequently in excess of 35°C and sometimes nudges 40°C. At 4am you can still be gasping for air. Air-conditioning in your room is a godsend at this time of year.

The coldest months are December and January, when daily average highs are below 10°C. At night it can get close to freezing, although snow in Madrid is a rarity. This may not seem a big deal but, if you bear in mind that many older houses have no central heating and that icy winds frequently blow in off the snow-capped Sierra, you soon realise that a Madrid winter is a short but rather sharp shock to the system. February is oddly often rather pleasant, with blue skies and daytime temperatures reaching the high teens.

The heaviest rainfall (such as it is) comes in spring and autumn, with more than 50mm quite common in October. March can be unpredictable. In Spain they say *'cuando en marzo mayea, en mayo marzea'*. In other words, if you get nice, warm and dry days in March (weather more typical of May), you'll be wiping that grin off your face in May, when the wet spells you missed earlier catch up with you! April too can be capricious. They say *'mes de abril, aguas mil'* – which indicates that it rains a lot in this spring month.

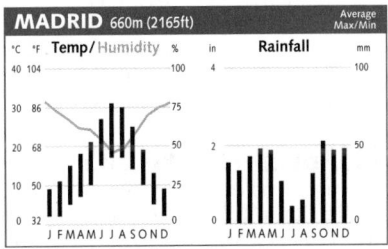

COURSES

Madrid is jammed with language schools of all possible categories, as eager to teach foreigners Spanish as locals other languages.

Non-EU citizens who want to study at a university or language school in Spain should have a study visa. These visas can be obtained from your nearest Spanish embassy or consulate. You will normally require confirmation of your enrolment, payment of fees and proof of adequate funds to support yourself before a visa is issued. The visa will then cover only the period of the enrolment. This type of visa is renewable within Spain but, again, only with confirmation of ongoing enrolment and proof that you are able to support yourself.

Some schools worth investigating include:

Universidad Complutense (Map p260; ☎ 91 394 53 36; www.ucn.es; Secretaria de los Cursos para Extranjeros, Facultade Filologia (Edificio A) Universidad Complutense, Cuidad Universitaria, 28040 Madrid; Metro Ciudad Universitaria) Offers a range of language and cultural courses throughout the year. An intensive semester course of 150 contact hours costs €380.

Escuela Oficial de Idiomas (Map p260; ☎ 91 553 00 88; www.eoidiomas.com; Calle de Jesús Maestro; Metro Canal) Offers courses in Spanish for foreigners (*español para extranjeros*) at most levels. A semester can cost from just €88, but demand means you are not guaranteed a place on application. A little chaotic but inexpensive if you can get in.

International House (Map pp268-9; ☎ 91 310 13 14; www.ihmadrid.es; Calle de Zurbano 8; Metro Alonso Martínez) Intensive courses start at around €340 for two weeks. Staff are happy to organise accommodation with families or in *pensiones*.

CUSTOMS

People entering Spain from outside the EU are allowed to bring in duty-free one bottle of spirits, one bottle of wine, 50mL of perfume and 200 cigarettes. There are no duty-free allowances for travel between EU countries. For duty-paid items bought at normal shops in one EU country and taken into another, the allowances are 90L of wine, 10L of spirits, unlimited quantities of perfume and 800 cigarettes. VAT-free shopping is available in the duty-free shops at airports for people travelling between EU countries.

DISABLED TRAVELLERS

Although some concessions are made to the disabled, the city remains largely an obstacle course. Some hotels and public institutions

have wheelchair access. Metro lines built since the late 1990s generally have elevators for wheelchair access but the older lines are generally ill-equipped. Some of the *pisos bajos* (city buses) also enable wheelchair users to board. The Ayuntamiento de Madrid publishes a *Guía de Accesibilidad* which contains information on disabled access to everything from the city's cinemas through to its public service buildings. It is designed mostly for disabled residents.

Organisations

Accessible Travel & Leisure (☎ 01452-729739; www.accessibletravel.co.uk; Avionics House, Naas Lane, Gloucester GL2 4SN) Claims to be the biggest UK travel agent dealing with travel for the disabled. The company encourages the disabled to travel independently.

Holiday Care (☎ 0845 124 9971; www.holidaycare.org.uk; 2nd fl, Imperial Buildings, Victoria Rd, Horley, Surrey RH6 7PZ) Information on hotels with disabled access, where to hire equipment and tour operators dealing with the disabled.

ONCE (Map pp262-4; ☎ 91 436 53 00; www.once.es; Calle de José Ortega y Gasset 22-24; Metro Núñez de Balboa) The Spanish association for the blind. You may be able to get a hold of a Madrid guide in Braille, although it is not published every year.

Royal Association for Disability & Rehabilitation – RADAR (☎ 020-7250 3222; www.radar.org.uk; Unit 12, City Forum, 250 City Rd, London EC1V 8AS) It publishes *European Holidays & Travel Abroad: A Guide for Disabled People*, which provides a good overview of facilities available to disabled travellers throughout Europe.

DISCOUNT CARDS

The **ISIC** (International Student Identity Card; www.isic.org) and the **Euro<26 card** (for youth under 26; www.euro26.org) are available from most national student organisations and can gain you discounted access to sights.

If you intend to do some intensive sightseeing and travelling on public transport, it might be worth looking at the **Madrid Card** (www.madridcard.com). It includes free entry to 40 museums in and around Madrid, as well as unlimited use of public transport, the Madrid Visión tourist bus, discounts in certain shops and restaurants and a free tour of Habsburg Madrid (los Austrias) on Saturdays. The ticket is available for 1/2/3 days (€28/42/55). It is possible to save €4/5 off the two- and three-day cards respectively by purchasing on the Web. Otherwise, purchase it at the tourist offices on

Plaza Mayor and in Calle del Duque de Medinaceli (see Tourist Information p236), on the Madrid Visión bus and in some tobacconists.

ELECTRICITY

The electric current in Madrid is 220V, 50Hz, as in the rest of continental Europe. Several countries outside Europe (such as the USA and Canada) use 110V, 60Hz, which means that some appliances from those countries may perform poorly. It is always safest to use a transformer. Plugs have two round pins, as in the rest of continental Europe.

EMBASSIES & CONSULATES

Most countries have an embassy or consulate in Madrid. Look them up under *Embajada* in that city's *Paginas Amarillas* (Yellow Pages). They include:

Australia (Map p261; ☎ 91 441 60 25; www.spain .embassy.gov.au; Plaza del Descubridor Diego de Ordás 3; Metro Ríos Rosas)

Canada (Map pp262-4; ☎ 91 423 32 50; www.canada -es.org; Calle de Núñez de Balboa 35; Metro Velázquez)

France (Map pp268-9; ☎ 91 423 89 00; www.amba france-es.org; Calle de Salustiano Olózaga 9; Metro Retiro)

Germany (Map pp268-9; ☎ 91 557 90 00; www.embajada -alemania.es; Calle de Fortuny 8; Metro Rubén Dario)

Ireland (Map pp262-4; ☎ 91 436 40 93; embajadairlanda@terra.es; Paseo de la Castellana 46; Metro Rubén Dario)

New Zealand (Map p273; ☎ 91 523 02 26; nzembmad rid@santandersupernet.com; Plaza de la Lealtad 2; Metro Banco de España)

UK Embassy (Map pp268-9; ☎ 91 700 82 00; www.ukin-spain.com; Calle de Fernando el Santo 16; Metro Colón).

UK Consulate (Map pp268-9; ☎ 91 524 97 00; Paseo de Recoletos 7/9; Metro Colón)

USA (Map pp262-4; ☎ 91 587 22 00; www.embusa.es; Calle de Serrano 75; Metro Núñez de Balboa)

EMERGENCY

It cannot be stressed enough that visitors to Madrid must be on their guard. Petty theft is a problem in the city centre, on some public transport and around most main sights. A little prevention is better than a lot of cure – see Safety p233. Tourists who want to report thefts need to go to the national police. A handy central **police station** (Map pp270-2; ☎ 91 322 10 07; Calle de las Huertas 76; Metro Antón Martín) where they may have an officer who at least speaks English is located in the Huertas area.

Ambulance ☎ 061

EU standard emergency number ☎ 112

Fire Brigade (Bomberos) ☎ 080

Local Police (Policía Municipal) ☎ 092

Military Police (Guardia Civil) ☎ 062

National Police (Policía Nacional) ☎ 091

GAY & LESBIAN TRAVELLERS

The Chueca district of central Madrid has long been the gay focal point of the capital, but it comes more out of the closet all the time. Restaurants, cafés and bars clearly oriented to a gay clientele continue to spread further away from the epicentre, and new book, video and adult-toy shops aimed at gays continue to spring up in and around Chueca. Several gay-friendly hotels operate around here too. Gay travellers will soon feel at home in this vibrant community.

Gay and lesbian sex are both legal in Spain and the age of consent is 16 years, the same as for heterosexuals. A bill proposing the recognition of de facto gay and lesbian couples has been held up for several years in the Cortes by the conservative Partido Popular (PP), which was defeated in the March 2004 general elections. Gays will be watching the new Socialist government keenly in the hope of a more progressive policy.

The former PP-run government of the Comunidad de Madrid did, however, recognise heterosexual de facto couples (seen by many as a first step to the recognition of gay couples).

A couple of informative free magazines are in circulation in gay bookshops and gay and gay-friendly bars. One is the bi-weekly *Shanguide*. It is jammed with listings and contact ads and aimed principally at readers in Madrid and Barcelona. A companion publication is *Shangay Express*, better for articles and a handful of listings and ads. The *Mapa Gaya de Madrid* lists gay bars, discos, saunas and other places of specific gay and lesbian interest in the city. You can pick up a copy in the **Berkana bookstore** (Map pp266-7; ☎ 91 522 55 99; Calle de Hortaleza 64, Chueca). There you'll also find the useful *Punto Guía de España para Gays y Lesbianas*, a countrywide guide for gay and gay-friendly bars, restaurants, hotels and shops around the country.

The monthly *MENsual* (€3.60) is available at newsstands. There is a Web version at www .mensual.com.

Madrid's gay and lesbian pride march is held on the last Saturday in June (p12).

Also check out the following sites on the Web:

Chueca.com (www.chueca.com) You have to become a member of Chueca XL (€18 per year) if you want to access the site's Guía Nocturna for bars and clubs.

Corazon Gay (www.corazongay.com) Gay personals and website search engine.

Esdificil.com (www.esdificil.com) A gay website with listings ranging from bars and restaurants to shops.

Nación Gay (www.naciongay.com) News on the gay community across Spain.

Voz Gay (www.vozgay.com) A Spanish community website with listings for the whole country.

Organisations

Colectivo de Gais y Lesbianas de Madrid (Cogam; Map pp266-7; ☎ 91 522 45 17; www.cogam.org; Calle de Fuencarral 37; Metro Gran Vía) Offers an information office and social centre. It runs an information line (☎ 91 523 00 70) from 5pm to 9pm on Fridays. The Comunidad de Madrid also has an information line (☎ 900 720569 toll free ; 10am-2pm & 5pm-9pm Mon-Fri).

Fundación Triángulo (Map pp262-4; ☎ 91 593 05 40; www.fundaciontriangulo.es; Calle de Eloy Gonzalo 25; Metro Iglesia) Another source of information on gay issues.

HOLIDAYS

When a holiday falls close to a weekend, most people like to make a *puente* (bridge) meaning they take the intervening day off too. On the odd occasion when a couple of holidays fall close, they make an *acueducto* (aqueduct)! For Madrileños, however, the main holiday periods are during summer (July and especially August), Christmas–New Year and Easter. August can be a peculiar time as all Spain largely grinds to a halt – this is a bad time to be trying to do business. While the tourists flock to Spain regardless of the sometimes asphyxiating heat, many locals escape to cooler climes. Not surprisingly, finding accommodation can be more difficult around Christmas and Easter. For information on the city's colourful festivals and other events, see the City Calendar section in the City Life chapter (p10). Here follows a list of Madrid's 14 public holidays:

New Year's Day (Año Nuevo) 1 January – as the clock strikes midnight on New Year's Eve (*noche vieja*) you are expected to eat a grape for each chime.

Epiphany or Three Kings' Day (Epifanía or Día de los Reyes Magos) 6 January – generally known more simply as 'Reyes', this is when children traditionally receive presents (usually, they get little or nothing at Christmas). For more information, see p10.

Good Thursday (Jueves Santo) March/April – this day kicks off the official holiday period known in Spain as *Semana Santa* (Holy Week). Local *cofradías* (lay fraternities) organise religious processions on this day and throughout the Easter period.

Good Friday (Viernes Santo) March/April

Labour Day (Fiesta del Trabajo) 1 May

Fiesta de la Comunidad de Madrid 2 May – commemorates the events of El Dos de Mayo, when Napoleon's troops put down an uprising in Madrid. For more information, see p11.

Fiestas de San Isidro 15 May – this is Madrid's big holiday, when the city celebrates the feast day of its patron saint. For more information, see p11.

Feast of the Assumption (La Asunción) 15 August

Spanish National Day (Día de la Hispanidad) 12 October – a fairly sober occasion.

All Saints' Day (Todos los Santos) 1 November

Día de la Virgen de la Almudena 9 November

Constitution Day (Día de la Constitución) 6 December

Feast of the Immaculate Conception (La Inmaculada Concepción) 8 December

Christmas (Navidad) 25 December

INTERNET ACCESS

Travelling with a portable computer is a great way to stay in touch with life back home, but unless you know what you're doing it's fraught with potential problems. Make sure you have a universal AC adapter, a two-pin plug adapter for Europe and a reputable 'global' modem. Spanish telephone sockets are the US RJ-11 type. Some of the better hotels are set up with Internet connections and sometimes just plugging into the hotel room's phone socket will be sufficient (although frequently this will not work as you have to go through a switchboard). For more information on travelling with a portable computer, see www .teleadapt.com.

Major Internet service providers (ISPs) like **CompuServe** (http://webcenters.compuserve.com) have dial-in nodes in Spain; download a list of the dial-in numbers before you leave home.

Some Spanish internet servers can provide short-term accounts. **Tiscali** (www.tiscali.es) is a reliable one. Another is **Terra** (www.terra.es).

If you intend to rely on cybercafés, for your email you'll need to carry three pieces of information: your incoming (POP or IMAP) mail server name, your account name and your password.

Internet Cafés

Madrid is full of Internet centres. Some offer student rates and also have deals on cards for several hours' use at reduced rates. A handful of options follows:

BBiGG (Map pp270-2; ☎ 91 531 23 64; www.bbigg.com; Calle Mayor 1; €2 per hr; ☻ 9.30am-midnight) Any day of the week you can walk into this modern cybercentre and check email or play games. It also offers fax, phonecards and coffee. It has another branch at Calle de Alcalá 21 (Map pp270-2).

Cervecería El Alamo (Map pp266-7; Calle del Alamo 7; €1.80 per hr; ☻ 8am-2am Mon-Sat) In an odd little bar.

Nevada 2000 (Map pp266-7; ☎ 91 521 20 94; Calle de los Reyes 7; €1.80 per hr; ☻ 8am-1.30am daily) What a funny mixture. Part smoky old café with one-armed bandits and part Internet centre.

Telefónica (Map pp266-7; Gran Vía 30; ☻ 10am-10pm daily; €1.50 per hr) This is the national phone company's phone centre.

WORKCenter (Map pp270-2; ☎ 91 360 13 95; www .workcenter.es; Calle del Príncipe 1; €2 per hr; ☻ 24 hr) You can also get photocopies, scan pictures and buy various stationery items.

LOST PROPERTY

The **Negociado de Objetos Perdidos** (☎ 91 588 43 48; Plaza de Legazpi 7; ☻ 9am-2pm; Metro Legazpi) holds lost property handed in around the city (including the metro and buses). Getting through on the telephone is no easy task. If you leave something in a taxi, you need to call the taxi company concerned. If you lose something on a *cercanías* train, you can check at the information desk at Atocha train station.

MAPS

If you can't get hold of Lonely Planet's *Madrid City Map* try Michelin's *Madrid* map 42 (scale 1:12,000), which comes with a complete street directory. Long-termers seeking more comprehensive map books and atlases are spoiled for choice. A good one is Almax's

Callejero de Madrid, scaled at 1:12,000. The same publisher has another that covers Madrid and the surrounding municipalities, *Atlas de Madrid*.

MEDICAL SERVICES

All foreigners have the same right as Spaniards to free emergency medical treatment in a public hospital. EU citizens are entitled to the full range of health-care services in public hospitals free of charge, but you will need to present your E111 form (enquire at your national health service before leaving home). Even if you have no insurance, you will be treated in an emergency.

Other citizens have to pay for anything other than emergency treatment. Nowadays Most travel insurance policies include medical cover.

For minor health problems, you can try your local pharmacy *(farmacia)*, where pharmaceuticals tend to be sold more freely without prescription than in places such as the USA, Australia or the UK (p232).

Your embassy should be able to refer you to doctors who speak your language. If you have a specific health complaint, obtain the necessary information and referrals for treatment before leaving home.

Some useful numbers and addresses for travellers include:

Anglo-American Medical Unit (Map pp268-9; ☎ 91 435 18 23; Calle del Conde de Aranda 1; ☻ 9am-8pm Mon-Fri; Metro Retiro) A private clinic where staff speak Spanish and English.

Hospital General Gregorio Marañón (Map pp262-4; ☎ 91 586 80 00; Calle del Doctor Esquerdo; Metro Sainz de Baranda) One of the city's main hospitals.

METRIC SYSTEM

Spain uses the metric system. Like other continental Europeans, the Spaniards indicate decimals with commas and thousands with points.

MONEY

As in 11 other EU nations (Austria, Belgium, Finland, France, Germany, Greece, Ireland, Italy, Luxembourg, the Netherlands and Portugal), the euro has been Spain's currency since 2002. By early 2004 it had risen to record levels against other major currencies, especially the US dollar. See also Economy & Costs (p19).

Changing Money

You can change cash or travellers cheques in currencies of the developed world without problems (except, sometimes, queues) at virtually any bank or bureaux de change (usually indicated by the word *cambio*).

Central Madrid abounds with banks, most with ATMs.

Exchange offices (you'll see many around Puerta del Sol and along Gran Vía) are open for longer hours than banks but generally offer poorer rates. Also, keep a sharp eye open for commissions at bureaux de change.

American Express (AmEx; Map pp270-2; ☎ 91 743 77 55, 902 375637; Plaza de las Cortes 2; 🕙 9am-7.30pm Mon-Fri, 9am-2pm Sat; Metro Sevilla) It also has a branch (☎ 91 393 82 15) at Barajas airport.

Credit/Debit Cards

Major cards, such as Visa, MasterCard, Maestro and Cirrus, are accepted throughout Spain. They can be used in many hotels, restaurants and shops. Credit cards can also be used in ATMs displaying the appropriate sign, or (if you have no PIN) you can obtain cash advances over the counter in many banks – MasterCard and Visa cards are among the most widely recognised for such transactions. Check charges with your bank.

If your card is lost, stolen or swallowed by an ATM, you can telephone toll-free to have an immediate stop put on its use. For MasterCard the number in Spain is ☎ 900 971231; for Visa it's ☎ 900 991124; and for Diners Club ☎ 91 701 59 00 or ☎ 901 101011.

AmEx is also widely accepted (although not as commonly as Visa or MasterCard). If you lose your AmEx card, call ☎ 900 994426.

Travellers Cheques

These are a safe way of carrying your money because they can be replaced if lost or stolen. Most banks and exchange offices will cash them. Travelex, AmEx and Visa are widely accepted brands. If you lose your AmEx cheques, call a 24-hour freephone number (☎ 900 994426). For Visa cheques call ☎ 900 948973; for MasterCard cheques call ☎ 900 948971.

Get most of your cheques in fairly large denominations to save on per-cheque commission charges. AmEx exchange offices do not charge commission to exchange travellers cheques (even other brands) or cash equivalent to US$500 or above.

It's vital to keep your initial receipt, along with a record of your cheque numbers and the ones you have used, separate from the cheques themselves.

Take your passport when you go to cash travellers cheques.

NEWSPAPERS & MAGAZINES

There is a wide selection of national daily newspapers from around Europe (including the UK) available at newspaper stands all over central Madrid and at strategic locations like the train and bus stations. The *International Herald Tribune*, *Time*, the *Economist*, *Der Spiegel* and a host of other international magazines are also available.

The free monthly English-language *InMadrid* is a handy newspaper-format publication with articles on the local scene and classifieds that will lead you to English-speaking doctors, dentists, baby-sitters and other useful information. Pick it up in some bars and pubs, language schools, consulates and occasionally in tourist offices.

Spanish Press

The main Spanish dailies can be identified along roughly political lines, with the old-fashioned *ABC* representing the conservative right, *El País* identified with the Partido Socialista Obrero Español (PSOE; Spanish Socialist Workers' Party) and *El Mundo*, a more-radicalised, left-wing paper that prides itself on breaking political scandals. For a good spread of national and international news, *El País* is the pick. It also contains a good central section devoted to the goings-on in Madrid itself. One of the best-selling dailies is *Marca*, devoted exclusively to sport. A recent novelty since late 2003 is th e broadsheet national weekly, *La Estrella*. It is jammed with opinion pieces and analysis, but one wonders how long it can last with only minimal advertising. *El País* contains a central section devoted to what's going on in Madrid and the Comunidad. A free morning daily that you are most likely to find in metro stations in the morning is *20 Minutos en Madrid*. A competitor along similar lines is *Metro*.

PHARMACIES

At least one pharmacy is open 24 hours per day in each district of Madrid. They mostly operate on a rota and details appear daily in *El*

País and other papers. Otherwise you can call ☎ 010. Note that at some late-night pharmacies you have to knock at a small shutter for service. Often they will only fill prescriptions or deal with urgent problems outside normal business hours – this is not the time to buy your shampoo. Pharmacies always open include:

Farmacia del Globo (Map pp270-2; ☎ 91 369 20 00; Plaza de Antón Martín 46; Metro Antón Martín)

Real Farmacia de la Reina Madre (Map pp270-2; ☎ 91 548 00 14; Calle Mayor 59; Metro Ópera)

Farmacia Velázquez 70 (Map pp262-4; ☎ 91 575 60 28; Calle de Veláquez 70; Metro Veláquez)

POST

Correos (☎ 902 197197; www.correos.es), the national postal service, has its **main office** (Map pp268-9; ☎ 91 396 24 43; Plaza de la Cibeles; ◷ 8.30am-9.30pm Mon-Sat; Metro Banco de España) in the ornate Palacio de Comunicaciones. To send big parcels, head for Puerta N on the southern side of the post office on Calle de Montalbán – it even offers a reasonably priced packing service.

Stamps *(sellos)* are sold at most *estancos* (tobacconists' shops with *Tabacos* in yellow letters on a maroon background), as well as post offices.

Postal Rates

A postcard or letter weighing up to 20g costs €0.52 from Spain to other European countries, and €0.77 to the rest of the world. The same would cost €2.71 and €2.96 respectively for registered *(certificado)* mail. Sending such letters *urgente*, which means your mail may arrive two or three days quicker than normal, costs €2.35 and €2.65 respectively. You can send mail both *certificado* and *urgente*.

Sending Mail

Delivery times are erratic but ordinary mail to other Western European countries can take up to a week; to North America up to 10 days; and to Australia or New Zealand up to two weeks.

Receiving Mail

Delivery times are similar to those for outbound mail. All Spanish addresses have five-digit postcodes; using postcodes will help your mail arrive quicker.

Poste restante *(lista de correos)* mail can be addressed to you anywhere in Catalonia that has a post office. It will be delivered to the place's main post office unless another is specified in the address. Take your passport when you pick up mail. A typical *lista de correos* address looks like this:

Jenny JONES
Lista de Correos
28080 Madrid
Spain

AmEx card or travellers cheque holders can use the free client mail-holding service at the AmEx office. Take your passport when you pick up mail. It only accepts standard letters, no packets.

RADIO

The Spanish national network Radio Nacional de España (RNE) has several stations: RNE 1 (88.2 FM in Madrid) has general interest and current affairs programmes; RNE 5 (90.3 FM) concentrates on sport and entertainment; and Radio 3 (93.2 FM) presents a decent range of pop and rock music. For classical music you can tune into Sinfo Radio (104.3 FM). Among the most listened-to rock and pop stations are 40 Principales (93.9 FM), Onda Cero (98 FM) and Cadena 100 (99.5 FM).

You can pick up BBC World Service (www .bbc.co.uk) on, among others, 6195, 9410 and 15,485 kHz (short wave). Voice of America (VOA) can be found on a host of shortwave frequencies, including 6040, 9760 and 15,205 kHz.

SAFETY

There are 50 ways to lose your wallet in Madrid. Every year a contingent of aggrieved readers writes in with tales of woe. Petty crime and theft, with tourists as prey of choice, is a problem in this city and the police can/will do little about it. The moment of most vulnerability is on arrival when visitors are lumbered with luggage and often disoriented. Always keep a close eye on all your belongings. This starts in the airport itself and continues on the transport into the city. Thieves operate on the metro and buses and will be quick to whisk away that small backpack or briefcase left sitting in the aisle.

Tricks abound. They usually involve a team of two or more (sometimes one of them an attractive woman to distract male victims). While one distracts your attention, the other empties your pockets. If approached by strangers offering flowers, offering unsolicited help or simply getting too close to your personal space, wave them away and move on fast. Be aware of jostling on crowded buses and the metro. The list of traps is limited only by the thieves' imagination.

Prevention is better than cure. Where possible, only keep the strictly necessary on your person. Never put anything in your back pocket; small day bags are best worn across your chest. Do not carry around too much cash at any one time. Money belts or pouches worn *under* your clothing are also a good idea. The less you have in your pockets or exposed bags the less you stand to lose if you are done.

You need to keep an eye out for pickpockets and bag snatchers in the most heavily touristed parts of town, especially Plaza Mayor, the Puerta del Sol and the Prado. You need to be aware of your surroundings in the Malasaña, Huertas, Lavapiés and Plaza de Santa Ana areas when bar-hopping. Take particular care in the Rastro flea market.

The Casa de Campo swarms with ladies (and boys) of the night, pimps and junkies. Some of the city's biggest traffic snarls occur here in the wee hours! Parts of the Parque del Oeste are traditionally also given over to prostitution by night. In the city itself, a fairly sad collective of sex workers has traditionally worked Calle de Montera and, more irregularly, the area around Calle de la Luna, near Gran Vía. The prostitutes present no real threat but their clients and pimps can be another story.

As a general rule, dark, empty streets are to be avoided. Luckily, Madrid's most lively nocturnal areas are generally busy with crowds having a good time – and there is definitely safety in numbers. That said, certain bands of young delinquents are becoming more daring and ruthless. Reports of attacks in broad daylight on busy thoroughfares are increasing. Police, aware of the rising tide of theft and violence, seem unable to do anything much about it. Frequently the attackers are minors who are well aware that, even if caught, they will be released within a few hours.

Never leave anything visible in your car and preferably leave nothing at all. Temptation usually leads at least to smashed windows and loss. It happens in broad daylight too, so take this seriously. Foreign and hire cars are especially vulnerable. If you have a foreign or hire car, it might be an idea to leave the glove box open to emphasise there is nothing of value inside.

You can take a few precautions before you even arrive in Madrid. Inscribe your name, address and telephone number *inside* your luggage and take photocopies of the important pages of your passport, travel tickets and other important documents. Keep the copies separate from the originals and, ideally, leave one set of copies with someone at home. These steps will make things easier if you do suffer a loss or theft. Travel insurance against theft and loss is another very good idea.

Don't expect the police to become too agitated over your stories of theft and mishap. It is part of their daily diet. They will, however, take your statement, which you'll need for insurance purposes and to have new passports and other documents issued.

TAXES

Value-added tax (VAT) is known as IVA (EE-ba, *impuesto sobre el valor añadido*). On accommodation and restaurant prices, IVA is 7% and is usually – but not always – included in quoted prices. On retail goods IVA is 16%.

Visitors are entitled to a refund of the 16% IVA on purchases costing more than €90.16 from any shop, if they take the goods out of the EU within three months. Ask the shop for a Cashback refund form showing the price and IVA paid for each item and identifying the vendor and purchaser. Then present the form at the customs booth for IVA refunds when you depart from Spain (or elsewhere from the EU). You will need your passport and a boarding card that shows you are leaving the EU and your luggage (you need to do this before checking in bags). The officer will stamp the invoice and you hand it in at a bank at the departure point for the reimbursement.

A couple of refund offices, including Global Refund, is located in Zona B on the first floor of T1 terminal at Barajas airport.

TELEPHONE

The ubiquitous blue payphones are easy to use for international and domestic calls. They accept coins, phonecards (*tarjetas telefónicas* issued by the national phone company Telefónica and, in some cases, various credit cards. *Tarjetas telefónicas* come in €6 and €12.02 denominations (the latter includes €0.60 free in extra credit) and, like postage stamps, are sold at post offices and tobacconists.

Public phones inside bars and cafés, and phones in hotel rooms, are nearly always a good deal more expensive than street pay phones.

Codes & Dialling

Dial the international access code (00 in most countries), followed by the code for Spain (34) and the full number – including the code, 91, which is an integral part of the number. For example to call the number ☎ 91 455 67 83 in Madrid you need to dial the international access code followed by ☎ 34 91 455 67 83.

The access code for international calls from Spain is 00. To make an international call dial the access code, wait for a new dialling tone, then dial the country code, area code and number you want.

International reverse-charge (collect) calls are simple. Dial ☎ 900 followed by a code for the country you're calling:

Australia	☎ 900 99 00 61
Canada	☎ 900 99 00 15
France	☎ 900 99 00 33
Germany	☎ 900 99 00 49
Ireland	☎ 900 99 03 53
Israel	☎ 900 99 09 72
New Zealand	☎ 900 99 00 64
UK	☎ 900 99 00 44 for BT
	☎ 900 99 09 44 for Cable & Wireless
USA	☎ 900 99 00 11 for AT&T
	☎ 900 99 00 13 for Sprint and various others

You'll get straight through to an operator in the country you're calling. The same numbers can be used with direct-dial calling cards.

If for some reason the above information doesn't work for you, in most places you can get an English-speaking Spanish international operator on ☎ 1008 (for calls within Europe) or ☎ 1005 (rest of the world).

For international directory inquiries dial ☎ 11825. Be warned, a call to this number costs €2!

Within Spain, you must always dial the full area code with the number. All numbers have nine digits and begin with 9. Dial ☎ 1009 to speak to a domestic operator, including for a domestic reverse-charge (collect) call *(llamada por cobro revertido)*. For national directory inquiries dial ☎ 11818.

Mobile phone numbers start with 6. Numbers starting with 900 are national toll-free numbers, while those starting 901 to 905 come with varying conditions. A common one is 902, which is a national standard rate number. In a similar category are numbers starting with 803, 806 and 807.

Mobile Phones

You can buy SIM cards in Spain for your own national mobile phone (provided what you own is a GSM, dual- or tri-band cellular phone) and buy prepaid time. This only works if your national phone hasn't been code blocked, something you might want to find out before leaving home. If you buy a SIM card and find your phone is blocked you won't be able to take it back. You won't want to consider a full contract unless you plan to live in Spain for a good while, and even then the benefits are not always tangible. You need your passport to open any kind of mobile phone account, prepaid or otherwise.

All the Spanish mobile phone companies (Telefónica's MoviStar and Moviline, Vodaphone and Amena) offer prepaid *(prepagado)* accounts for GSM phones (frequency 900 mHz). The SIM card can cost €50 to €60, which includes some prepaid phone time. Phone outlets are scattered across the city. You can then top up in their shops or by buying cards in outlets like tobacconists and newsstands.

US mobile phones generally work on a frequency of 1900 mHz, so for use in Spain, your US handset will have to be tri-band.

You can organise to rent a mobile phone by calling the Madrid-based **Cellphone Rental** (☎ 91 523 21 59; ☎ 656 266844; www.onspanishtime.com/web). In Madrid, delivery and pickup are done personally at a cost of US$20 (US$25 on weekends and holidays). The basic service costs US$30 a week for the phone plus postal costs (except in Madrid). You also pay a US$150 to discourage scarpering with the phone. The whole operation is done on the Web.

Phonecards & Call Centres

Cut-rate phonecards can be good value for international calls. They can be bought from *estancos* (tobacco outlets) and newsstands in central Madrid – compare rates if possible because some are better than others. Private call centres *(locutorios)* specialising in cut-rate overseas calls have popped up all over central Madrid. Before committing yourself you should compare rates – as a rule the phonecards are better value and far more convenient. You can buy them at BBiGG branches and the Telefónica phone and Internet office (see Internet Cafés p231).

TELEVISION

Most TVs receive six or seven channels: two from Spain's state-run Televisión Española (TVE1 and La 2), three independent (Antena 3, Tele 5 and Canal Plus) and the regional Telemadrid station. More than 20 tiny local stations scattered about the Comunidad de Madrid struggle to survive. One you may pick up is Canal 7.

News programmes are generally decent and you can often catch an interesting documentary or film (look out for the English-language classic late at night on La 2). Otherwise, the main fare is a rather nauseating diet of soaps (many from Latin America), endless talk shows and almost vaudevillian variety shows (with plenty of glitz and tits). Canal Plus is a pay channel dedicated mainly to movies: you need a decoder and subscription to see the movies, but anyone can watch the other programmes.

Many private homes and better hotels have satellite TV. Foreign channels you may come across include BBC World (mainly news and travel), CNN, Eurosport, Sky News and the German SAT 1.

TIME

Spain (and hence Madrid) is one hour ahead of GMT/UTC during winter, two hours during the daylight-saving period from the last Sunday in March to the last Sunday in October. Most other Western European countries are on the same time as Spain year round, the major exceptions being the UK, Ireland and Portugal, which are one hour behind. Spaniards use the 24-hour clock for official business (timetables etc), but often in daily conversation switch to the 12-hour version.

When it's noon in Madrid, it's 3am in San Francisco, 6am in New York and Toronto, 11am in London, 9pm in Sydney and 11pm in Auckland. Note that in North America and Australasia, the changeover to/from daylight saving usually differs from the European date by a couple of weeks.

TIPPING

You are not expected to tip on top of restaurant service charges, but it is common to leave a small amount, say €1 per person. If there is no service charge, the customer might consider leaving a 10% tip, but this is by no means obligatory. In bars, Spaniards often leave any small change as a tip, often only €0.05 or €0.10. Tipping taxi drivers is not common practice, but you should tip the porter at higher-class hotels.

TOILETS

Stopping at a bar or café for a quick coffee and then a trip to the toilet is the common solution to those sudden urges at awkward times. Make sure your chosen bar actually has a toilet before committing yourself! Public toilets are a rarity in Madrid.

TOURIST INFORMATION

Several tourist offices operate in Madrid. A useful general information line (if you speak Spanish) worth bearing in mind is ☎ 010, a municipal service dealing with anything from transport to shows in Madrid (call ☎ 91 540 40 10 from other provinces or abroad). For similar help on issues around the Comunidad de Madrid region call ☎ 012. A useful website is the Madrid municipality site (www .munimadrid.es).

Oficina de Turismo (Map pp270-2; ☎ 902 100007, 91 429 49 51; www.comadrid.es/turismo; Calle del Duque de Medinaceli 2; ☻ 9am-7pm Mon-Sat, 9am-3pm Sun; Metro Banco de España) This main tourist office has information on the city and surrounding region and is seconded by branches at: Chamartín train station (☎ 91 315 99 76; ☻ 8am-8pm Mon-Sat, 9am-3pm Sun; Metro Chamartín); Atocha station (☎ 91 528 46 30; ☻ 8am-8pm Mon-Sat, 8am-2pm Sun; Metro Atocha Renfe); Barajas airport (Aeropuerto de Barajas; ☎ 91 305 86 56; ground fl, Terminal T1; ☻ 9am-9pm daily); and the Centro Comercial de la Puerta de Toledo (Map pp262-4; ☎ 91 364 18 76; Ronda de Toledo 1; ☻ 9am-5pm Mon-Fri, 9am-2.30pm Sat; Metro Puerta de Toledo).

Patronato Municipal de Turismo (Map pp270-2; ☎ 91 588 16 36; Plaza Mayor 3; ☻ 10am-8pm Mon-Sat, 10am-3pm Sun; Metro Sol or Ópera) Specialises in the city.

VISAS

Spain is one of 15 member countries of the Schengen Convention, under which all EU member countries (except the UK and Ireland) plus Iceland and Norway have abolished checks at common borders. The other EU countries are Austria, Belgium, Denmark, Finland, France,

Germany, Greece, Italy, Luxembourg, the Netherlands, Portugal and Sweden. Legal residents of one Schengen country do not require a visa for another Schengen country. Citizens of the UK, Ireland and Switzerland are also exempt. Nationals of the 10 countries that entered the EU in May 2004 (Cyprus, Czech Republic, Estonia, Hungary, Latvia, Lithuania, Malta, Poland, Slovak Republic and Slovenia) do not need visas for tourist visits or even to take up residence in Spain and other longer standing EU countries but will not have the full freedom to work enjoyed by other EU citizens for up to seven years. Nationals of many other countries, including Australia, Canada, Israel, Japan, New Zealand and the USA do not require visas for tourist visits of up to 90 days to Spain.

All non-EU nationals entering Spain for any reason other than tourism (such as study or work) should contact a Spanish consulate, as they may need a specific visa.

If you are a citizen of a country not mentioned in this section, check with a Spanish consulate about whether you need a visa. The standard tourist visa issued by Spanish consulates is the Schengen visa (www.eurovisa .info), valid for up to 90 days. A Schengen visa issued by one Schengen country is generally valid for travel in all other Schengen countries. However, individual member countries may impose additional restrictions on certain nationalities. You should check visa regulations with the consulate of each Schengen country that you plan to visit. These visas are not renewable inside Spain and no more than two will be issued in any 12-month period.

WOMEN TRAVELLERS

Women travellers should be ready to ignore stares, catcalls and unnecessary comments, although harassment is much less frequent than you might expect. Think twice about going by yourself down empty city streets at night. It's highly inadvisable for a woman to hitchhike alone – and not a great idea even for two women together.

Organisations

The **Asociación de Asistencia a Mujeres Violadas** (Association for Assistance to Raped Women; Map pp262-4; ☎ 91 574 01 10; Calle de O'Donnell 42; ☯ 10am-2pm & 4pm-7pm Mon-Thu, 10am-4pm Fri; Metro O'Donnell) offers advice and help to rape victims. Only limited English may be spoken.

WORK

Nationals of EU countries, Switzerland, Norway and Iceland are able to work in Spain without a visa, but for stays of more than three months they are supposed to apply within the first month for a *tarjeta de residencia* (residence card). If you are offered a contract, your employer will usually steer you through the labyrinth.

Virtually everyone else is supposed to obtain, from a Spanish consulate in their country of residence, a work permit and, if they plan to stay more than 90 days, a residence visa. These procedures are well nigh impossible unless you have a job contract lined up before you begin them. Quite a few people do work, discreetly, without bothering to tangle with the bureaucracy.

Employment Options

For many people, perhaps the easiest source of work for foreigners is teaching English (or another foreign language), but even with full qualifications, a non-EU citizen will find it difficult to secure a permanent position. Most of the larger, more reputable schools will hire only non-EU citizens who already have work and/or residence permits, but their attitude can become more flexible if demand for teachers is high and they come across someone with particularly good qualifications. In the case of EU citizens, employers generally have no great problem in helping you through the bureaucracy.

Madrid is loaded with 'cowboy outfits' that pay badly and often aren't overly concerned about quality. Still, the only way you'll find out is by hunting around. Schools are listed under *Academias de Idiomas* in the yellow pages.

Sources of information on possible teaching work – school or private – include foreign cultural centres (the British Council, Alliance Française etc), foreign-language bookshops and university notice boards. Many language schools have notice boards where you may find work opportunities, or where you can advertise your own services. Cultural institutes you may want to try include:

British Council (Map pp262-4; ☎ 91 337 35 00; www .britishcouncil.es; Paseo del General Martínez Campos 31; Metro Iglesia)

Alliance Française (Map pp262-4; ☎ 91 435 15 32; Calle de Velázquez 94; Metro Nuñez de Balboa)

Goethe Institut (Map pp268-9; ☎ 91 391 39 44; Calle de Zurbarán 21; Metro Colón)

Translating and interpreting could be an option if you are fluent in Spanish and a language in demand.

Another option might be *au pair* work, organised before you come to Spain. A useful guide is *The Au Pair and Nanny's Guide to Working Abroad*, by Susan Griffith & Sharon Legg. Susan Griffith's *Work Your Way Around the World* is also worth looking at.

University students or recent graduates might be able to set up an internship with companies in Barcelona. For instance, the **Association of International Students for Economics and Commerce** (www.aiesec.org), with branches throughout the world, helps member students find internships in related fields. For information on membership, check out the website.

Language

Language

It's true – anyone can speak another language. Don't worry if you haven't studied language before or that you studied a language at school for years and can't remember any of it. It doesn't even matter if you failed English grammar. After all, that's never affected your ability to speak English! And this is the key to picking up a language in another country. You just need to start speaking.

Learn a few key phrases before you go. Write them on pieces of paper and stick them on the fridge, by the bed or even on the computer – anywhere that you'll see them often.

You'll find that locals appreciate travellers trying their language, no matter how muddled you may think you sound. So don't just stand there, say something! If you want to learn more Spanish than we've included here, pick up a copy of Lonely Planet's comprehensive but user-friendly *Spanish Phrasebook*.

SOCIAL
Meeting People
Hello.
¡Hola!
Goodbye.
¡Adiós!
Please.
Por favor.
Thank you.
(Muchas) Gracias.
Yes.
Sí.
No.
No.
Excuse me.
Perdón.
Sorry!
Perdón/Perdóneme.
Do you speak English?
¿Hablas ingles?
Does anyone speak English?
¿Hay alguien que hable ingles?
Do you understand?
¿Me entiende?
Yes, I understand.
Sí, entiendo.
No, I don't understand.
No, no entiendo.
Pardon?;What?
¿Cómo?

Could you please ...?
¿Puedes ... por favor?
  speak more slowly hablar más despacio
  repeat that   repetir
  write it down   escribirlo

Going Out
What's there to do in the evenings?
¿Qué se puede hacer por las noches?

What's on ...?
¿Qué hay…?
  locally   en la zona
  this weekend   este fin de semana
  today   hoy
  tonight   esta noche

Where are the ...?
¿Dónde hay ... ?
  places to eat   lugares para comer
  nightclubs   discotecas
  pubs   pubs
  gay venues   lugares gay

Is there a local entertainment guide?
¿Hay una guía del ocio de la zona?

PRACTICAL
Question Words
Who?	¿Quién? (sg)
	¿Quiénes? (pl)
What?	¿Qué?
Which?	¿Cuál? (sg)
Which?	¿Cuáles? (pl)
When?	¿Cuándo?
Where?	¿Dónde?
How?	¿Cómo?
How much?	¿Cuantos?
How many?	¿Cuánto?
How much is it?	¿Cuánto cuesta?
Why?	¿Por qué?

Numbers & Amounts

0	cero
1	una/uno
2	dos
3	tres
4	cuatro
5	cinco
6	seis
7	siete
8	ocho
9	nueve
10	diez
11	once
12	doce
13	trece
14	catorce
15	quince
16	dieciséis
17	diecisiete
18	dieciocho
19	diecinueve
20	veinte
21	veintiuno
22	veintidós
30	treinta
31	treinta y uno
32	treinta y dos
40	cuarenta
50	cincuenta
60	sesenta
70	setenta
80	ochenta
90	noventa
100	cien
1000	mil
2000	dos mil

Days

Monday	lunes
Tuesday	martes
Wednesday	miércoles
Thursday	jueves
Friday	viernes
Saturday	sábado
Sunday	domingo

Banking

I'd like to change some money.
Me gustaría cambiar dinero.
I'd like to change a travellers cheque.
Me gustaría cobrar un cheque de viajero.

Where's the nearest ...?
¿Dónde está ... más cercano?
ATM	el cajero automático

foreign exchange office	la oficina de cambio

Do you accept ...?
¿Aceptan ...?
credit cards	tarjetas de crédito
debit cards	tarjetas de débito
travellers cheques	cheques de viajero

Post

Where's the post office?
¿Dónde está correos?

I want to send a/an ...
Quisiera enviar ...
fax	un fax
parcel	un paquete
postcard	una postal

I want to buy a/an ...
Quisiera comprar ...
aerogramme	un aerograma
envelope	un sobre
stamp/stamps	un sello/sellos

Phones & Mobiles

I want to buy a phone card.
Quiero comprar una tarjeta.

I want to make a ...
Quiero hacer ...
call (to ...)	una llamada a ...
reverse-charge/ collect call	una llamada a cobro revertido

Where can I find a/an ...?
¿Dónde se puede encontrar un ...?
I'd like a/an ...
Quisiera un ...
adaptor plug	adaptador
charger for my phone	cargador para mi teléfono
mobile/cell phone for hire	móvil para alquilar
prepaid mobile/ cell phone	móvil pagado por adelantado
SIM card for your network	tarjeta SIM para su red

Internet

Where's the local Internet cafe?
¿Dónde hay un cibercafé cercano?

I'd like to ...
Quisiera ...

| get Internet access | usar el Internet |
| check my email | revisar mi correo electrónico |

Transport

What time does the ... leave?
¿A qué hora sale el ...?

boat	barco
bus	autobús
bus (intercity)	autocar
plane	avión
train	tren

What time's the ... bus?
¿A qué hora es el ... autocar/autobús?

first	primer
last	último
next	próximo

Is this taxi free?
¿Está libre este taxi?
Please put the meter on.
Por favor, ponga el taxímetro
How much is it to ...?
¿Cuánto cuesta ir a ...?
Please take me (to this address).
Por favor, lléveme (a esta dirección).

FOOD

breakfast	desayuno
lunch	comida
dinner	cena
snack	tentempié
to eat	comer
to drink	beber

Can you recommend a ...?
¿Puede recomendar un ...?

bar	bar
cafe	café
coffee bar	cafetería
restaurant	restaurante

Is service/cover charge included in the bill?
¿Il servicio está incluido en la cuenta?

For more detailed information on food and dining out, see 'Eating' on p???.

EMERGENCIES

Help!
¡Socorro!
It's an emergency!
Es una emergencia!
Could you help me please?
¿Me puede ayudar, por favor?
Where's the police station?
¿Dónde está la comisaría?

Call ...!
¡Llame a ...!

the police	la policía
a doctor	un médico
an ambulance	una ambulancia

HEALTH

Where's the nearest ...?
¿Dónde está ... más cercano?

(night) chemist	la farmacia (de guardia)
dentist	el dentista
doctor	el médico
hospital	el hospital

I need a doctor (who speaks English).
Necesito un doctor (que hable inglés).

Symptoms

I have (a/an) ...
Tengo ...

diarrhoea	diarrea
fever	fiebre
headache	dolor de cabeza
pain	dolor

I'm allergic to ...
Soy alérgico ...

antibiotics	a los antibióticos
nuts	las nueces
peanuts	los cacahuetes
penicillin	a la penicilina

Glossary

abierto – open

abono – season pass

acueducto – aqueduct

aduana – customs

albergue juvenil – youth hostel; not to be confused with *hostal*

alcade – mayor

alcázar – Muslim-era fortress

Almoravid – member of a fanatical people of Berber origin and Islamic faith who founded an empire in North Africa that spread over much of Spain in the 11th century

apartado de correos – post-office box

auto de fe – elaborate execution ceremony staged by the Inquisition

autonomía – autonomous community or region. Spain's 50 *provincias* are grouped into 17 of these

autopista – motorway (with tolls)

AVE – Tren de Alta Velocidad Española; high-speed train

ayuntamiento – city or town hall; city or town council

bailaores – flamenco dancers

baño completo – full bathroom, with a toilet, shower and/or bath, and washbasin

barrio – district, quarter (or a town or city)

biblioteca – library

bodega – literally a cellar (especially a wine cellar); also means a winery or a traditional wine bar likely to serve wine from the barrel

bomberos – fire brigade

bota – leather wine or sherry bottle

bottelón – literally 'big bottle'; young adolescents partying outdoors

buzón – postbox

cajero automático – automatic teller machine (ATM)

calle – street

callejón – lane

cama – bed

cambio – change; currency exchange

cantadora(a) – flamenco singer (female)

capilla – chapel

Carnaval – carnival; a period of fancy-dress parades and merrymaking, usually ending on the Tuesday 47 days before Easter Sunday

carnet – identity card

carretera – highway

casco – literally, helmet; often used to refer to the old part of a city

castillo – castle

castizo – literally 'pure', refers to people and things distinctly from Madrid

catedral – cathedral

centro de salud – health centre

cercanías – local trains serving big cities, suburbs and nearby towns; local train network

cerrado – closed

certificado – registered mail

cervecería – beer bar

chato – glass

churrigueresque – ornate style of Baroque architecture named after the brothers Alberto and José Churriguera

comedor – dining room

comunidad – fixed charge for maintenance of rental accommodation

Comunidad de Madrid – Madrid province

condones – condoms, also *preservativos*

consejo – council

consigna – a left-luggage office or lockers

coro – choirstall

correos – post office

corrida (de toros) – bullfight

Cortes – national parliament

cuesta – lane (usually on a hill)

día del espectador – cut-price ticket day at cinemas

diapositiva – slide film

discoteca – nightclyb

documento nacional de identidad (DNI) – national identity card

ducha – shower

embajada – embassy

entrada – entrance; ticket for a performance

estación de autobuses – bus station

estanco – tobacconist shop

farmacia – pharmacy

faro – lighthouse

feria – fair; can refer to trade fairs as well as city, town or village fairs, bullfights or festivals lasting days or weeks

ferrocarril – railway

fiesta – festival, public holiday or party

fin de semana – weekend

flamenco – flamingo; Flemish; flamenco music and dance

fútbol – football (soccer)

gasólea – diesel

gasolinera – service station

gatos – literally 'cats'; colloquial name for Madrileños

gitanos – the Roma people (formerly known as the Gypsies)

glorieta – big roundabout

guiri – foreigner

habitaciones libres – rooms available

hostal – commercial premises providing accommdation in the one- to three-star category; not to be confused with *albergue juvenil*

iglesia – church

infanta – princess

infante – prince

interprovincial – national (call)

IVA – impuesto sobre el valor añadido; or value-added tax

judería – Jewish quarter

largo recorrido – long-distance train
lavabo – washbasin; a polite term for toilet
lavandería – laundrette
librería – bookshop
lista de correos – poste restante
locutorio – telephone centre
luz – electricity

macarras – Madrid's rough but usually likeable lads
Madrileño – a person from Madrid
marcha – action, life, 'the scene'
marisquería – seafood eatery
media-raciones – a serving of tapas, somewhere between the size of tapas and *raciones*
menú del día – fixed-price meal available at lunchtime, sometimes evening too; often just called a *menú*
mercado – market
meseta – the high tableland of central Spain
metropolitana – local (call)
mezquita – mosque
mihrab – prayer niche in a mosque
monasterio – monastery
morería – former Islamic quarter in town
moro – 'Moor' or Muslim, usually in medieval context
moto – moped
movida – a *zona de movida* is an area of town here lively bars and maybe discos are clustered (in Madrid the *movida* refers to the halcyon days of the post-Franco years when the city plunged into an excess of nightlife)
mozarab – Christians who lived in Muslim-ruled Spain; also style of architecture
mudéjar – Muslim living under Christian rule in medieval Spain, also refers to their style of architecture
muralla – city wall
museo – museum

objetos perdidos – lost-and-found office
oficina de turismo – tourist office

Páginas Amarillas – Yellow Pages phone directory
panteón – pantheon (monument to a famous dead person)
parador – state-owned hotel in an historic building or beauty spot
pensión – guesthouse

peques – children, little ones
piscina – swimming pool
plateresco – plateresque, ornate architectural style popular in Spain during the 16th century
plaza mayor – main plaza, square
preservativos – condoms, also *condones*
provincial – (call) within the same province
pueblo – village
puente – bridge

RACE – Real Automóvil Club de Españ; Royal Automobile Club of Spain
ración – meal-sized serve of tapas
rastro – flea market, car-boot (trunk) sale
ronda – ring road

salid – exit or departure
Semana Santa – Holy Week, the week leading up to Eastern Sunday
servicios – toilets
sierra – mountain range
sinagoga – synagogue
sin plomo – lead-free petrol
sol – sun
sombra – shade

tabernas – taverns
taifa – small Muslim kingdom in medieval Spain
tapas – bar snacks traditionally served on a saucer or lid
taquilla – ticket window/office
tarde – afternoon
tarjeta de crédito – credit card
tarjeta de residencia – residence card
tarjeta telefónica – phonecard
temporada alta/media/baja – high, mid or low season
terraza – terrace; often means outdoor tables at a cafe or bar
tetería – teahouse, usually in Middle Eastern style with low seats round low tables
tienda – shop or tent
toro – bull
torreón – tower
turismo – means both tourism and saloon car

urgencia – first-aid station

villa – town

zarzuela – form of Spanish dance and music, usually satirical

Behind the Scenes

THE LONELY PLANET STORY

The story begins with a classic travel adventure: Tony and Maureen Wheeler's 1972 journey across Europe and Asia to Australia. There was no useful information about the overland trail then, so Tony and Maureen published the first Lonely Planet guidebook to meet a growing need.

From a kitchen table, Lonely Planet has grown to become the largest independent travel publisher in the world, with offices in Melbourne (Australia), Oakland (USA), London (UK) and Paris (France).

Today Lonely Planet guidebooks cover the globe. There is an ever-growing list of books and information in a variety of media. Some things haven't changed. The main aim is still to make it possible for adventurous travellers to get out there – to explore and better understand the world.

At Lonely Planet we believe travellers can make a positive contribution to the countries they visit – if they respect their host communities and spend their money wisely.

THIS BOOK

This third edition of Madrid was written by Damien Simonis and Sarah Andrews. Damien also wrote the first two editions. The guide was commissioned in Lonely Planet's London office and produced by:

Commissioning Editor Heather Dickson
Coordinating Editor Margedd Heliosz
Editors & Proofers Carly Hall, Sally Steward & Tom Smallman
Managing Cartographer Mark Griffiths
Coordinating Cartographer Hunor Csutoros
Cartographers Valentina Kremenchutskaya, Sarah Sloane & Bonnie Wintle
Index Margedd Heliosz
Coordinating Layout Designer Laura Jane
Cover Designer Annika Roojun
Project Manager Charles Rawlings-Way
Language Content Coordinator Quentin Frayne

Thanks to Melanie Dankel, Jennifer Garrett, Nic Lehman, Adriana Mammarella, Kate McDonald, Stephanie Pearson & Andrew Weatherill

Cover Puerta de Alcala, Carol & Mike Werner/photolibrary (top); Felipe III statue at Plaza Mayor, San Rostro/photolibrary (bottom); Museo del Prado, Guy Moberly/Lonely Planet Images (back).

Internal photographs by Lonely Planet Images, Richard Nebesky and Guy Moberly except for the following: p103 (#4) Elliot Daniel, p12 Martin Moos, p98 Christopher Groenhout, p200 Bethune Carmichael, p206 Krzysztof Dydynski, p212 Oliver Strewe, p215 Damien Simonis. All images are the copyright of the photographers unless otherwise indicated. Many of the images in this guide are available for licensing from Lonely Planet Images: www.lonelyplanetimages.com

ACKNOWLEDGMENTS

Many thanks to the following for use of their content:
Madrid Metro Map © 2004 Metro de Madrid SA

THANKS
DAMIEN SIMONIS

Muchísimas gracias to all the old crew who came out of the woodwork during my time back in the capital. With these people the line between work and pleasure blurs in the most satisfying way. To them I offer my sincere thanks. In no particular order the following have helped me with research and enjoying myself: Javier Montero, David Ing, Luis Aguilar-Pryde, Pablo García Tobin, Dania Samoul (thanks for the wonderful Syrian nosh!), Olivia Doxsee and Samiti Siv. Co-writer on this edition, Sarah Andrews, also did a great job and helped me out with a few edible suggestions of her own. Never far away is the girl who makes it all worthwhile, Janique - merci infiniment pour tout!

SEND US YOUR FEEDBACK

We love to hear from travellers – your comments keep us on our toes and help make our books better. Our well-travelled team reads every word on what you loved or loathed about this book. Although we cannot reply individually to postal submissions, we always guarantee that your feedback goes straight to the appropriate authors, in time for the next edition. Each person who sends us information is thanked in the next edition – and the most useful submissions are rewarded with a free book.

To send us your updates – and find out about LP events, newsletters and travel news – visit our award-winning website: www.lonelyplanet.com.

Note: We may edit, reproduce and incorporate your comments in Lonely Planet products such as guidebooks, websites and digital products, so let us know if you don't want your comments reproduced or your name acknowledged. For a copy of our privacy policy visit www.lonelyplanet.com/privacy.

SARAH ANDREWS

Researching this guide showed me just how much Madrileños love their city. *Gracias y un abrazo* to Nuria Pardina and Fede Alvarez, who opened so many doors for me. Another huge thanks to Pilar Ballesteros, Carlos Barrio, Ana Maeso, Rafa Ruíz and Ramón Urgarte; the next round is on me! To Andrés Madrigal, Miguel Montañez, Cristina Lobillo and Belén Ramírez, here's to Spanish cuisine without foams. Another appreciative thanks to my dear friend and travelling companion Theresa Coryn, and to local experts Simon Hunter, Clayton Maxwell, Genevieve McCarthy, Gisela Williams, Ed McCullough and the crew at Associated Press. The biggest thanks of all to my wonderful husband Miquel, who helped me in every way both on the road and back at home base.

OUR READERS

Many thanks to the travellers who used the last edition and wrote to us with helpful hints, useful advice and interesting anecdotes. Your names follow:

Annette Blank, Phil Connell, Martin Connolly, Rachel Cowood, Åke Dahllöf, Dimitri van Dijk, Jill Downey, Sysse Engberg, Matthew Fuller, Valerie Giles, Alfonso Gurza, Nuala Heaney, Dorien Jongsma, Agnes Kazmierczak, Winnie Lau, Jose-Angel Martinez, James McInerney, Jenny McMullen, Douglas Cristobal Miller, David Moody Bert Nijs, Rose Pantalone, Sue Pownall, Sue Price, Dawn Sebti, Derek A. Smith, Lesley Smith, Donald Toney Jr, Harry Triggs

Index

Index

253

Index

000 map pages
000 photographs

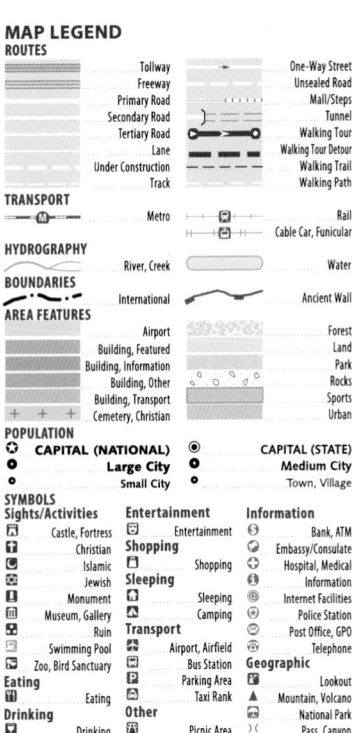

MAP LEGEND

ROUTES

Tollway	One-Way Street
Freeway	Unsealed Road
Primary Road	Mall/Steps
Secondary Road	Tunnel
Tertiary Road	Walking Tour
Lane	Walking Tour Detour
Under Construction	Walking Trail
Track	Walking Path

TRANSPORT

Metro	Rail
	Cable Car, Funicular

HYDROGRAPHY

River, Creek	Water

BOUNDARIES

International	Ancient Wall

AREA FEATURES

Airport	Forest
Building, Featured	Land
Building, Information	Park
Building, Other	Rocks
Building, Transport	Sports
Cemetery, Christian	Urban

POPULATION

CAPITAL (NATIONAL)	**CAPITAL (STATE)**
Large City	**Medium City**
Small City	Town, Village

SYMBOLS

Sights/Activities
- Castle, Fortress
- Christian
- Islamic
- Jewish
- Monument
- Museum, Gallery
- Ruin
- Swimming Pool
- Zoo, Bird Sanctuary

Eating
- Eating

Drinking
- Drinking
- Café

Entertainment
- Entertainment

Shopping
- Shopping

Sleeping
- Sleeping
- Camping

Transport
- Airport, Airfield
- Bus Station
- Parking Area
- Taxi Rank

Other
- Picnic Area
- Wheelchair Access

Information
- Bank, ATM
- Embassy/Consulate
- Hospital, Medical
- Information
- Internet Facilities
- Police Station
- Post Office, GPO
- Telephone

Geographic
- Lookout
- Mountain, Volcano
- National Park
- Pass, Canyon

Map Section

GREATER MADRID

SIGHTS & ACTIVITIES (pp61–110)
Canal de Isabel II..............................1 A3
Estadio Vicente Calderón..................2 A6
Museo de la Ciudad.........................3 C3
Museo Taurino..................................4 D4
Parque Deportivo La Elipa................5 D5
Piscina Municipal Barrio del Pilar......6 B1
Plaza de Toros Monumental de Las
Ventas......................................7 D4
Polideportivo Chamartín...................8 C2
Real Madrid Ciudad Deportiva..........9 C1

EATING (pp119–140)
Casa Benigna..................................10 C3
El Foque..11 C3
Los Asturianos.................................12 A4
Los Timbales...................................13 D4

ENTERTAINMENT (pp149–168)
Auditorio Nacional de Música..........14 C3
Galileo Galilei..................................15 A4

OTHER
Escuela Oficial de Idiomas................16 A3

Avenida Monforte
de Lemos

TETUÁN

See Northern Madrid p261

CHAMARTÍN

Chamartín

To Alcobendas
(8km)

To B
Airport (
Parque
Carlos I

ARAVACA

To Facultad de
Filología (500m)

To Facultad de
Filología (750m)

COMPLEJO AZCA

Avenida de la Reina Victoria

VALLEHERMOSO

ARAPILES

CHAMBERÍ

TRAFALGAR

ARGÜELLES

See Malasaña & Chueca pp265-7

See Salamanca
pp268-9

SALAMANCA

MALASAÑA

CHUECA

RECOLETOS

Príncipe Pío

Gran Vía

CENTRO

SOL

See Centro & Huertas pp270-2

See Paseo del Prado
& El Retiro p273

RETIRO MEDIODÍA

CORTES

Calle de Segovia

JERÓNIMOS

See Central Madrid pp262-4

To Estadie
Come
de Madrid

To Faunia (4

Paseo Imperial

Ronda de Toledo

To Museo del Ferrocarril
(800m); Negociado de
Objetos Perdidos (1.5km);
Palacio Vista Alegre

To Cine Imax
(500m); Estación
de Autobuses (1km)

To Estadio Vallecas
Teresa Rivero

NORTHERN MADRID

CENTRAL MADRID

A   B   C   D

1

Parque del Oeste

Avenida del Arco de la Victoria

Plaza de la Moncloa
Moncloa

Calle de Isaac Peral
Calle de Gaztambide
Calle de Andrés Mellado
Calle de Guzmán el Bueno

To Bodega Santa Cecilia (100m)

ARAPILES

Glorieta del General Alvarez de Castro

Calle de Aloi
Calle de

64

Calle de Santísima Trinidad

Calle de Ruperto Chapí
Calle Hilarión Eslava
Calle de Fernando El Católico

Calle de Blasco de Garay
Calle de Vallehermoso
Calle de Magallanes
Calle de Bravo Murillo

Calle de Viriato

69

Paseo de Moret

Paseo de Camoens

86
91

Calle de Fernando El Católico
Calle de Arapiles

Calle de Feijoo

71

Gloríeta de Quevedo

95
33
79

Calle de Eloy Gonzalo
Calle de Sagunto
Calle de Juan de Austria

Pintor S
60

Calle de Meléndez Valdés
Quevedo
68

Calle de Santa Felic

2

Calle Romero Robledo
Calle Benito Gutiérrez
Calle de Altamirano

ARGÜELLES

Plaza del Conde del Valle de Suchil

Plaza de Olavide

66

TRAFALGAR

Calle de Rodríguez San Pedro

Calle de Cardenal Cisneros
Calle de Palafox
Calle de Luchana

Paseo del Pintor Rosales

37
Argüelles

Calle del Marqués de Urquijo
Calle de Alberto Aguilera

75
50

Calle de San Bernardo
Calle de Carranza

Calle de Fuencarral

42

Bilbao

Malasaña & Chueca pp266-7

Calle de la Princesa

Cementerio de la Florida

88

Calle Buen Suceso
Calle de Quintana

Calle de Santa Cruz de Marcenado

Bilbao

Calle de Sagas

8

Calle de Francisco Jacinto

La Rosaleda

39

Calle de Ferraz

Calle de Tutor
Calle Evaristo San Miguel
Calle de Luisa Fernanda

Ventura Rodríguez

Tribunal

Ali Ma

12
30

Glorieta San Antonio de la Florida

Calle de la Rosaleda
Paseo del Rey

Paseo del Pintor Rosales

32
29
31

Plaza del Marqués Cerralbo

27

Calle de Amaniel

MALASAÑA

Noviciado

Noviciado

3

Paseo de la Florida

Río Manzanares
Paseo del Marqués de Monistrol

84

Parque de la Montaña

Calle de Ferraz

Plaza de España

CH

Chuec

Príncipe Pío
Príncipe Pío

Calle de Irún

Cuesta de San Vicente

Gran Vía

4

CASA DE CAMPO

Glorieta San Vicente

40

Cuesta de San Vicente

Calle de Bailén
Calle de Arriaza

Callao

Santo Domingo

Gran Vía
Gran Vía

Calle de la Montera

Gran Vía

CENTRO

To Swimming Pools; Parque de Atracciones (3km)

Puente del Rey

11

Campo del Moro

Centro & Huertas pp270-1

Opera

Calle del Arenal

Calle de Alcalá

Sevilla

24

Avenida de Portugal

Sol

SOL

Carrera de San Jerónimo

Glorieta de Boccherini

Cuesta de la Vega

16

Calle Mayor

Calle Mayor

Calle de la Cruz

COR

55

Puente de Segovia

Calle de Linneo
Calle Juan Duque
Calle Mazarredo

Calle de Segovia

Ronda de Segovia

Calle de Segovia

Calle de Toledo

Tirso de Molina

Calle de Atocha

Calle de la Magdalena

Antón M

5

Calle Saavedra Fajardo
Paseo del Marqués de Monistrol

Plaza de Gabriel Miró

52

Cuesta de los Ciegos

Carrera de San Francisco

Plaza de la Cebada

Antón Mari

Calle de Pablo Casals

3

La Latina

EL RASTRO

53

Vía Inferior al Paseo Imperial

Gran Vía de San Francisco

Ronda de Segovia

Lavapiés

6

Paseo de la Ermita del Santo
Avenida de Manzanares

Puente de San Isidro

Paseo Imperial

Calle Juan Duque
Calle Alejandro

Glorieta de Puerta de Toledo

78

Puerto de Toledo

Calle de Toledo

Paseo de los Pontones

Plaza de Francisco Morano

Puerta de Toledo

99

Jardín del Rastro

Calle del Concejal Benito Martín

To Piscina Municipal Peñuelas (700m)

Plaza Campillo del Mundo Nuevo

Ronda de Toledo

Paseo de las Acacias

Acacias

9

25
15

Glorieta de Embajadores

Embajadores

Ronda de Valencia

56

Calle de José
Calle de Antonia Armona

Paseo de las Acacias

A **B** **C** **D**

1

Calle de los Mártires de Alcalá
Calle de Santa Cruz de Marcenado
Calle del Acuerdo
Calle de San Bernardo
Calle de Ma
Calle de Monteleón
Calle del Divino

149

🏛 15

Calle de Montserrat

Calle Quiñones
Calle de Daoiz

1
Plaza
Guardias de
Corps

Plaza de las
Comendadoras
77
Calle de San Dimas
48 88

2
Ⓜ Ventura
Rodríguez

Calle de Tutor
Calle Duque de Liria
Calle de los Negros
Calle Manuel
Travesia del Duque
Calle del Conde Duque
Calle del Conde del Limón
Calle de Bernardo López García

65
Calle del Norte
Noviciado
Ⓜ
Calle del Noviciado
Calle de la Palma
Calle de San Vicente
Calle de San Bernardo
Calle de Santa Lucía

de Martín de los Heros
30
Calle Santa María
Micaela
Calle de Venura Rodríguez
Plaza de
Cristino Martos
Calle del Duque Osuna
Calle de San Bernardino
Calle de San Leonardo de Dios
Calle de Juan de Dios
Calle del Ponciano
Calle de Amaniel

3
Calle de Juan Álvarez
Calle de Martín de los Heros
85
Plaza de
Emilio Jiménez
Millas
86
147
Plaza del
Conde de
Toreno
Calle de los Reyes
Travesia de
Pozas
MALASAÑA
Calle de las Minas
Calle del Tesoro
Calle Carlos Plasencia
Calle de la Marqués

94
93
18
148
153
Calle del Maestro Guerero
Calle de los Amigos
159 @
155 @
Calle de Manzana Ⓜ Noviciado
Calle del Álamo

🏛 11
Edificio
de España
151
Plaza de España
Ⓜ

Calle de San Ignacio Loyola
Calle de Antonio
Grilo
Calle de la Cruz Verde
Calle de Andrés Borrego
Calle del Pez
Calle de Pizarro
Calle de la Madera

4
150
97
Calle de los Reyes
Calle del Doctor Cárcado
Calle del General Mitre
Plaza de
Mostenses
Calle Beatas
Calle de San Roq
Calle de la Luna
Calle de la Estrella

Cuesta de San Vicente
Calle de la Flor Baja
Calle del Ricardo
León
Gran Via
Calle García Molinas
Calle del Marqués
de Leganés
Calle de los
Libreros
Plaza de
Santa María
Soledad

92
Calle del Río
Calle del Reloj
Calle Leganitos
Calle Recodo
146
Calle de la Flor Alta
134
Calle de Silva

5
Jardines de Sabatini
Calle del Reloj
Calle del Fomento
Plaza de
la Marina Española
Calle de Isabel la Católica
Calle de San Bernardo
96
Calle de Silva
118
140
68
Plaza de
Santa María
Soledad
Calle de Tudescos
76
2
Calle de Jacometrezo
Ⓜ Callao
157

Calle de Bailén
Calle de Torija
89
Calle de Torija
Calle Guillermo
Rolland
Calle del Fomento
Calle de la Bola
Plaza del
Callao
108

6
Jardines
Cabo Noval
Calle Pavía
47
4
Calle de San Quintín
Plaza de
la Encarnación
117
Calle de Santo Domingo
31
161
139
Calle de Preciados
Santo
Ⓜ Domingo
Calle de Veneras
Calle Tetería
Calle de las
Navas Tolosa
137

16
46
Calle Felipe V
Calle de Arrieta
Plaza de Oriente
38
127
135
Calle de Carlos del Peral
Calle de la Priora Flora
Costanilla Los Ángeles
Calle Concha
26
Calle de Trujillos
Travesia Trujillos
Plaza de
San Martín
5

SALAMANCA

200 m
0.1 miles

(A) **(B)** **(C)** **(D)**

Calle de Almagro
Calle de Zurbarán
Calle de Zurbarán

Calle de Fortuny
65
66
59
46
50

1 Calle de Almagro
Calle de Zurbano
Calle de la Blanca de Navarra
Calle de Monte Esquinza

ALMAGRO

Paseo de la Castellana

Calle del Marqués de Villamagna
Calle de Don Ramón de la Cruz
57
55
4
18
38
26
37

Calle de Fernando el Santo
70
Calle de Ayala

14
67
Calle de Orfila
58
Calle de Zurbano
Calle de Monte Esquinza
Calle de Amador de los Ríos
22
54
39
49
56
34
24

2 Calle de Génova
Calle de García Gutiérrez
Calle de Alcalá Galiano
Paseo de la Castellana
Calle de Serrano

Calle de la Hermosilla
27

Calle de Orellana
Colón
12
Calle del Marqués Zurgena
35
51
43
45
33
44

3 Plaza de la Villa de París
Colón
Plaza de Colón
32
60
6
47
Serrano
40
Serrano

RECOLETOS

Calle del General Castaños
Calle del Marqués de la Ensenada
Jardines de Descubrimiento
Calle de Goya
52

Plaza de las Salesas
8
5
Calle de Lagasca

Calle de Bárbara de Braganza
28
Calle de Jorge Juan

17
7
15

4 Calle del Conde de Xiquena
53
16
Calle del Marqués de Monasterio
Calle de Tamayo y Baus
Recoletos
Calle de Villanueva
36
20

Calle del Almirante
Calle Gil de Santiváñes
41

Calle de Prim
21
29
Calle Cid
Calle de Serrano
61
42
2
Calle Conde de Aranda
30

5 Recoletos
25
Calle Recoletos

JUSTICIA
48
Calle Columela
13

Ministerio del Ejército
69
Calle de Salustiano Olózaga
64
Calle Villalar

Calle Marqués del Duero
Calle Pedro Muñoz Seca
31
63
Plaza de la Independencia
10
Retiro

9
19
Puerta Independencia
Plaza Ma Vill

Banco de España
68
Calle de Alcalá

6 62
Banco de España
Plaza de la Cibeles
Calle Alfonso XI
Calle de Alfonso XII
Calle Valenzuela
Paseo de México
3
11

SALAMANCA

Plaza de Oriente

115

Plaza de Isabel II

Calle del Arenal

CENTRO

Calle Francisco Piquer

Calle de San Martín

Calle Maestro

Travesía de Descalzas

Plaza de Celenque

Calle Preci

32

Calle de Carlos III

33

143

85

16

95

92

Calle del Aren

Jardines de Lepanto

Calle de Vergara

49

31

Calle de la Unión

Calle de Amnistía

Calle Lazo

Calle de las Hileras

Opera

Calle de las Fuentes

Calle de Escalinata

Plaza de San Ginés

Plaza de San Ginés

38

Plaza de Oriente

Plaza de la Armería

25

Plaza de la Armería

Calle de Requena

Calle de Noblejas

Plaza de Ramales

Calle de Santa Clara

Plaza Santiago

Calle de la Independencia

73

124

71

Conde de Lemos

Calle de Santiago

Costanilla Santiago

Calle Ciudad Rodrigo

Plaza del Comandante las Morenas

Plaza Herradores

Calle de los Bordadores

Calle de los Coloreros

Calle Mayor

27

142

138

Calle de Portas

Calle del Ma de Poni

Calle del Factor

Calle de San Nicolás

Calle del Biombo

Plaza del Biombo

17

Juan de Herrera

84

Señores de Luzón

169

Calle del Codo

69

60

Plaza de San Miguel

Plaza Mayor

Calle de San Cristóbal

Calle de Zaragoza

Plaza de Santa Cruz

34

Plaza de la Villa

2

165

Plaza del Duque de Nájera

12

9

Plaza del Conde de Miranda

141

Cava de San Miguel

Calle Gerona

Plaza de la Provincia

150

Calle Mayor

24

19

Calle del Sacramento

Travesía del Sacramento

5

Calle del Cordón

Calle de Pulmonsorio

Calle del Maestro Villa

68

166

Calle Imperial

Calle Lechuga

21

Calle de San Tomás

Calle de Bailén

Calle de la Villa

Calle del Rollo

Plaza de la Cruz Verde

Plaza del Cordón

Plaza Conde

Calle de San Justo

Plaza del Conde de Barajas

Calle de Gomez de Mora

37

118

Calle de Toledo

Plaza del Alamillo

Calle Pelig San Andrés

Calle del Alamillo

Calle de Alfonso VI

Cuesta del Príncipe Anglona

Travesía Nuncio

18

Calle del Nuncio

Calle de la Pasa

Plaza de Puerta Cerrada

Plaza de Segovia Nueva

Calle de la Colegiada

3

Plaza de la Morería

Cuesta de Bailén

42

88

Plaza de la Paja

Costanilla de San Pedro

Calle del Príncipe

93

Calle de Segovia

75

Calle de Almendro

66

Calle de la Cava Baja

Calle de Grafal

Calle de la Cava Baja

64

Tirso de Molina

Plaza de Granado

Calle de Granado

89

96

14

22

74

82

Plaza de San Andrés

Plaza de la Puerta de Moros

Calle de la Cava Baja

36

47

Calle de Cava Alta

70

Calle de la Cava Alta

120

121

Plaza del Duque de Alba

Calle del Duque de Alba

Calle del Mex

Calle de Yeseros

Calle de Redondilla

Calle de Mancebos

Plaza de la Cebada

83

108

59

Plaza de la Cebada

63

116

Calle de San Millán

Plaza de Cascorro

1

Calle de Juanelo

Plaza de las Maldonadas

Calle de la Encomienda

Calle de Don Pedro

Carrera de San Francisco

Calle de las Aguas

Calle de San Isidro Labrador

Calle de Oriente

Calle de Tabernillas

Calle de Humilladero

61

La Latina

La Latina

Calle de Ruda

Calle de las dos Herm

Calle de la Cebada

Calle de la Paloma

Calle de Luciente

Calle del Mediodía Grande

Calle de Sierpe

Calle del Ángel

46

151

Calle de Calatrava

Calle de Águila

Calle del Mediodía Chica

Plaza Genral Vara del Rey

Calle de Santa Ana

Calle de López Silva

Calle de las Amazonas

Calle de Santa Anna

114

EL RASTRO

Calle de Abader

15

125

Calle de San Cayetano

Gran Vía de San Francisco

Calle Mira el Río Alta

Calle de Fray Ceferino González

Calle del Carnero

Calle del Toledo

Calle de Capitan San Martinez

Calle Arganzuela

Cjon Mellizo

Calle Mira el Río Baja

Calle de Carlos Arnches

Calle de Rodas

Calle de Rodas

Calle de la Peña de Francia

Calle del Vendimillo

Calle de Santiago el V

Calle de Águila

Ronda de Segovia

Calle Mira el Sol

CENTRO & HUERTAS (pp270-1)

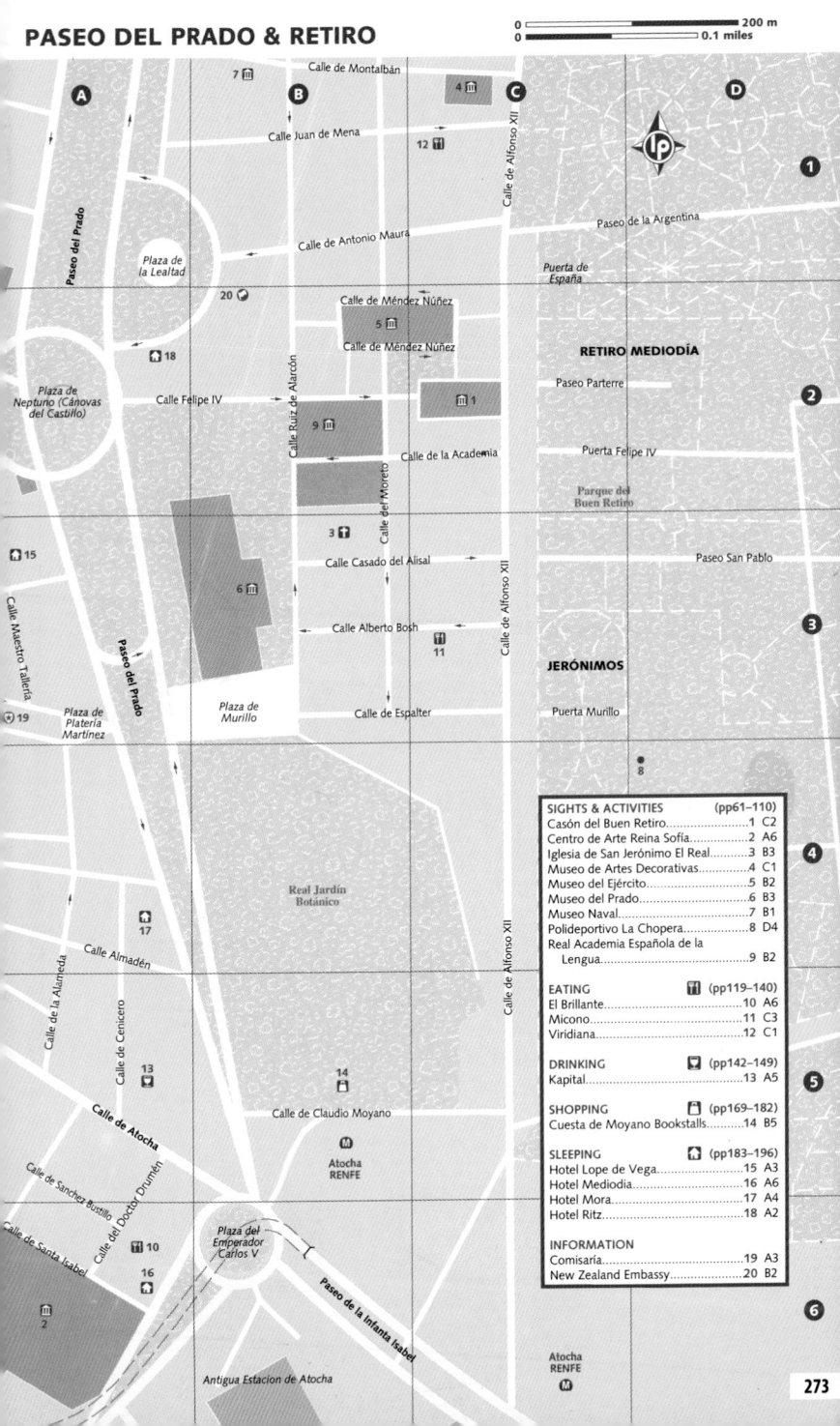

PASEO DEL PRADO & RETIRO

Calle de Montalbán
Calle Juan de Mena
Calle de Antonio Maura

Paseo del Prado

Plaza de
la Lealtad

Paseo de la Argentina

Puerta de
España

RETIRO MEDIODÍA

Calle de Méndez Núñez
Calle de Méndez Núñez

Paseo Parterre

Plaza de
Neptuno (Cánovas
del Castillo)

Calle Felipe IV

Puerta Felipe IV

Calle de la Academia

Calle Ruiz de Alarcón

Parque del
Buen Retiro

Calle del Moreto

Calle Casado del Alisal

Paseo San Pablo

Calle Maestro Tallería

Calle Alberto Bosh

Calle de Alfonso XII

JERÓNIMOS

Paseo del Prado

Plaza de
Platería
Martínez

Plaza de
Murillo

Calle de Espalter

Puerta Murillo

Real Jardín
Botánico

Calle Almadén

Calle de la Alameda

Calle de Cenicero

Calle de Claudio Moyano

Calle de Atocha

Atocha
RENFE

Calle de Sánchez Bustillo

Calle de Doctor Drumén

Calle de Santa Isabel

Plaza del
Emperador
Carlos V

Atocha
RENFE

Paseo de la Infanta Isabel

Antigua Estacion de Atocha

273

METRO MAP

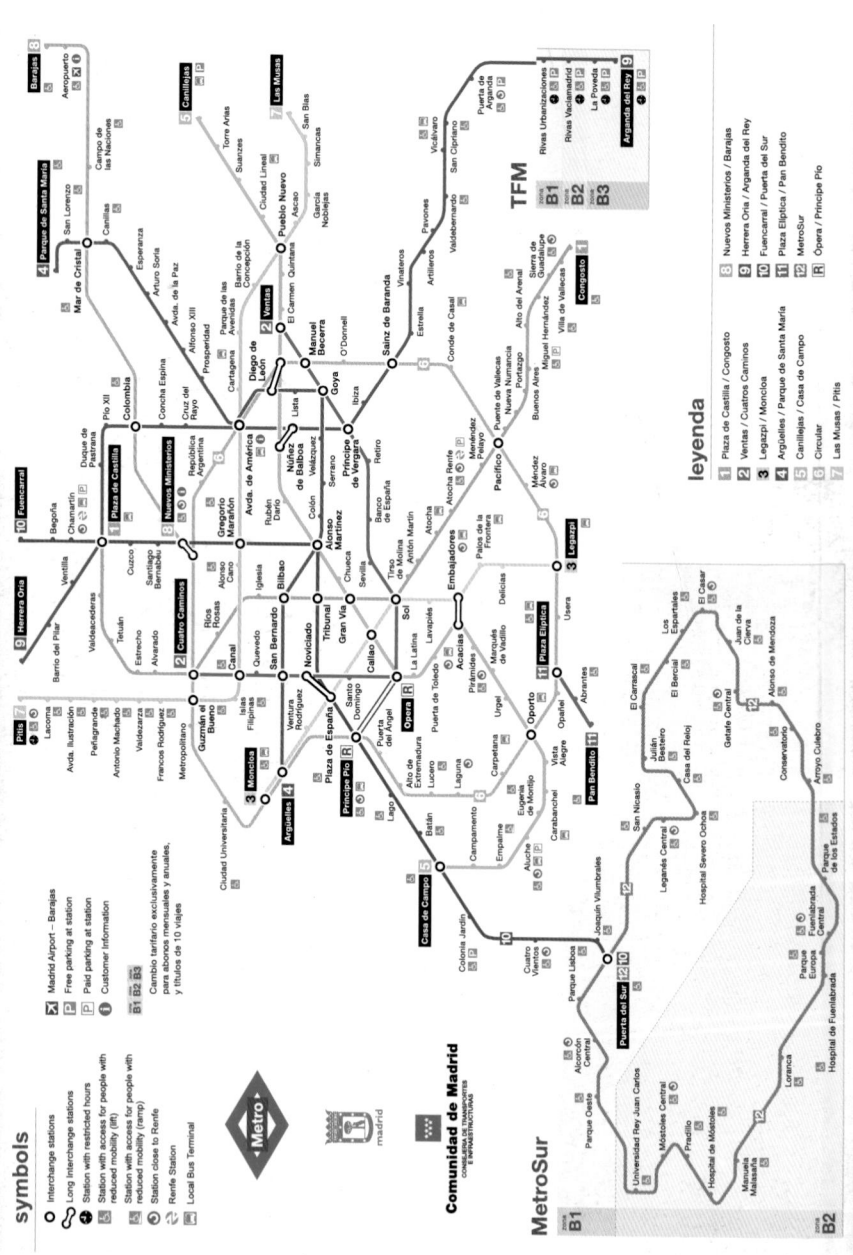

274

Contents – Text

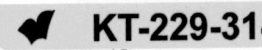

KT-229-314

Contents – Maps

FACTS ABOUT BUDAPEST

COLOUR MAP SECTION   193

MAP LEGEND   back page

METRIC CONVERSION   inside back cover

The Author

Steve Fallon

A native of Boston, Massachusetts, Steve graduated from George-town University with a Bachelor of Science in modern languages and then taught English at the University of Silesia near Katowice in Poland. After working for several years for an American daily newspaper and earning a master's degree in journalism, his fascination with the 'new' Asia led him to Hong Kong, where he lived for over a dozen years, working for a variety of media and running a travel bookshop. Steve lived in Budapest for 2½ years before moving to London in 1994. He has written or contributed to more than two dozen Lonely Planet titles, including the Lonely Planet Journeys title *Home with Alice: A Journey in Gaelic Ireland*, and all editions of *Hungary* and *Budapest*.

FROM THE AUTHOR

Special thanks to Bea Szirti, who helped with the research of the Entertainment and Facts for the Visitor chapters, and to Erzsébet 'Zsóka' Tiszai who assisted with the transport chapters. Péter Lengyel and Balázs Váradi showed me the correct wine roads to follow for the Wines to Hungary section and, once again, Dr Zsuzsa Medgyes of M&G Marketing in Budapest came forward with all those wonderful little details. Many thanks to Dr Mihály Perec and his incomparable choice of restaurants. Tourinform remains the most authoritative and knowledgeable source of information on Budapest; *köszönöm szépen* to staff on both Sütő utca and Vigadó utca. I am indebted to Michael Kovrig for his hospitality; Ildikó Nagy Moran was as welcoming and helpful as always.

Once again, this book is dedicated to Michael Rothschild, *sine quo non*, with love, gratitude and memory.

This Book

Budapest's first edition (August 2000) was also researched and written by Steve Fallon.

FROM THE PUBLISHER

This second edition of *Budapest* was produced in Lonely Planet's Melbourne office and coordinated by Barbara Delissen (editorial), Hunor Csutoros (mapping) and Birgit Jordan (layout design). Editing and proofing assistance was provided by Tegan Murray, Liz Filleul and Katrina Webb. Imogen Franks and Liz Filleul were the commissioning editors, and Bridget Blair the project manager.

Thanks to Quentin Frayne for editing the language chapter, Csanad Csutoros for the climate chart, Jenny Jones for designing the cover, and Simon Bracken for the cover artwork. Photographs were provided by Lonely Planet Images.

Thanks

Many thanks to the travellers who used the last edition and wrote to us with helpful hints, useful advice and interesting anecdotes:

Nick Adlam, Arnon Agmon, Jon Arch, Saara Arvo, Tim Atchison, Kyle Austen, Marilyn Baratto, Steve Barnett, Pierre Bayenet, Szirti Bea, Brenda Bierman, Gerry Bierman, Nina Bjerke, Ron Blair, Vincent Borlaug, Bela Borsos, Anna Bosco, Stephen Boswell, Carolyn Browne, Dylan Browne, Rod George Bryant, Fred Carreon, Guillem Castella, Anthi Charalambous, C W Chen, Line Christensen, Alexander Coley, Catalin Coroama, Jessika Croizat, Sigal Dabach, Frederik Debruyne, Andy Dennis, Kathleen Diamond, Sarah Dillon, James Done, Annick Donkers, David Doughan, Stephen Doughty, Irina Dvorak, Robert Essenyi, Gaynor Evans, Levente Fazekas, Uli Fechner, Anne Fenerty, Vikki Fennell, Rob Ferrara, Bridget Fox, R French, Ricardo Gama, Elise Gatti, Romaima Gatti, Bruce Gibson, Janos Ginstler, John Glen, Sandra Gordon, Meahan Grande, Cicile Griboval, Jerry Gwee, Vanessa Hayes, Catherine Hegyi, Masami Heiser, Wesley Heiser, Mark Henderson, Iris Hendriks, Markus Hjerto, Tom Hughes, Becky Ip, Victor & Agnes Isaacs, Marlyn Jakub, Bill Jancso, Rok Jarc, Helene J Josovitz, Maritta Jumppanen, Sugano Jun, J Kalina, David Katz, Gerald Kellett, Kerry King, Rob Kingston, Ben Korman, Anne-Mari Laiho, Barry Lambert, Hana Leed, Juha Levo, Ralf Liebau, Gerard Lonergon, Nick Lux, Pauline Mahalski, Stephane Makk, Daz Marks, Peter McCulloch, Claire McKee, Joanne Michaels, Dick Middaugh, Lee Gerard Molloy, Thomas Morgan, Tim Morgan, Jason Mote, Grainne Murphy, Susan Nagy, Marjan Nieuwland, Anna Nordmark, Rich Palm, Kathy Prunty, Veronica Quiroz, Rahmin Rabenou, J Reusch, Johan Reyneke, Tony Richmond, Ian Rutt, Emily Sachs, Julie Sadigursky, Rachel Samsonowitz, Adam Schreck, Paul Shenton, Nolan Shulak, Eszter Simonfi, Christine Sontag, Angela Soutar, Mike Stanway, Joanna Stefanska, Anita Steinmann, Samo Štritof, Clare Szilagyi, Bea Szirti, Anne-Lyse Tardivat, Paul Taylor, Valer Tosa, Susan Tripp, Eline van der Werf, Mathieu Vandermissen, Elina Vienamo, Alexander Waanders, Benedict Wabunoha, Deborah Wallace, Duncan Watt, Rebecca Webster, Erika Weidner, Henrik Weston, Luke Wilkinson, David Williams, Ernst Williams, David Woodberry, Ivanka Zemanova, Eric Zimmerman

Foreword

ABOUT LONELY PLANET GUIDEBOOKS

The story begins with a classic travel adventure: Tony and Maureen Wheeler's 1972 journey across Europe and Asia to Australia. There was no useful information about the overland trail then, so Tony and Maureen published the first Lonely Planet guidebook to meet a growing need.

From a kitchen table, Lonely Planet has grown to become the largest independent travel publisher in the world, with offices in Melbourne (Australia), Oakland (USA), London (UK) and Paris (France).

Today Lonely Planet guidebooks cover the globe. There is an ever-growing list of books and information in a variety of media. Some things haven't changed. The main aim is still to make it possible for adventurous travellers to get out there – to explore and better understand the world.

At Lonely Planet we believe travellers can make a positive contribution to the countries they visit – if they respect their host communities and spend their money wisely. Since 1986 a percentage of the income from each book has been donated to aid projects and human rights campaigns, and, more recently, to wildlife conservation.

Although inclusion in a guidebook usually implies a recommendation we cannot list every good place. Exclusion does not necessarily imply criticism. In fact there are a number of reasons why we might exclude a place – sometimes it is simply inappropriate to encourage an influx of travellers.

UPDATES & READER FEEDBACK

Things change – prices go up, schedules change, good places go bad and bad places go bankrupt. Nothing stays the same. So, if you find things better or worse, recently opened or long-since closed, please tell us and help make the next edition even more accurate and useful.

Lonely Planet thoroughly updates each guidebook as often as possible – usually every two years, although for some destinations the gap can be longer. Between editions, up-to-date information is available in our free, monthly email bulletin *Comet* (W www.lonelyplanet.com/newsletters). You can also check out the *Thorn Tree* bulletin board and *Postcards* section of our website, which carry unverified, but fascinating, reports from travellers.

Tell us about it! We genuinely value your feedback. A well-travelled team at Lonely Planet reads and acknowledges every email and letter we receive and ensures that every morsel of information finds its way to the relevant authors, editors and cartographers.

Everyone who writes to us will find their name listed in the next edition of the appropriate guidebook. The very best contributions will be rewarded with a free guidebook.

We may edit, reproduce and incorporate your comments in Lonely Planet products such as guidebooks, websites and digital products, so let us know if you don't want your comments reproduced or your name acknowledged.

How to contact Lonely Planet:
Online: e talk2us@lonelyplanet.com.au, W www.lonelyplanet.com
Australia: Locked Bag 1, Footscray, Victoria 3011
UK: 72-82 Rosebery Ave, London, EC1R 4RW
USA: 150 Linden St, Oakland, CA 94607

Introduction

Budapest is unlike any other city in Eastern Europe. More cosmopolitan than Prague, more romantic than Warsaw and more beautiful than both, Budapest straddles a gentle curve in the Danube, with the Buda Hills to the west and what is essentially the start of the Great Plain to the east. With parks brimming with attractions, museums filled with treasures, pleasure boats sailing up and down the scenic Danube Bend, Turkishera thermal baths belching steam, and a nightlife throbbing till dawn most nights, the Hungarian capital is one the continent's most delightful and fun cities to visit.

Architecturally, Budapest is a gem. Though it may not count as many Gothic and other medieval buildings as, say, Prague, there is enough baroque, neoclassical and Art Nouveau architecture here to satisfy anyone. Overall it has a *fin-de-siècle* feel to it, for it was then, during the industrial boom and the capital's 'golden age' during the last third of the 19th century, that most of what you see today was built. In some places, particularly along the Nagykörút (Big Ring Road) and up broad Andrássy út to the sprawling Városliget (City Park), Budapest's sobriquet – 'the Paris of Central Europe' – is well deserved. Nearly every building has some interesting detail, from Art Nouveau glazed tiles and neoclassical bas-reliefs to bullet holes and shrapnel scorings left over from WWII and the 1956 Uprising.

At times, Budapest's scars are not very well hidden. Over the years, industrial and automobile pollution has exacerbated the decay, but in recent years the rebuilding and renovations have been nothing short of astonishing. Indeed, some people think the city is tidying itself up a bit too quickly. When I first moved to the city in the early 1990s, a local guidebook advised potential visitors to 'hurry up and come before Budapest turns into just another capital of just another nice social-democratic European country' (or words to that effect). 'As if,' I remember thinking in those 'Wild East' days of rapid-fire change and disillusionment. 'As if...'

It's true that in the process of reclaiming its well-deserved title of *világváros* (world-class city) over the past decade, Budapest has taken on all the baggage that such a process usually involves: organised crime, faceless modern architecture, a mobile phone at the ear of every 'suit', an international fast-food outlet at every corner. Yet Budapest remains – and will always stay – Hungarian: exotic, sometimes inscrutable, often passionate, with its feet firmly planted in Europe but with a glance every now and then eastward to the spawning grounds of its people.

Budapest is fabulous at any time, but especially just after dusk in spring and summer when Castle Hill is bathed in a warm yellow light. Stroll along the Duna korzó, the riverside embankment on the Pest side, or across any of the bridges past young couples embracing passionately. It's then that you'll feel the romance of a place that, despite all attempts – from both within and without – to destroy it, has never died.

Budapest is a city that has given me much since our first chance meeting and when I sing a song of this place now it might be in a beautiful and expressive language that I once considered impenetrable, of a people I thought I'd never know, of a sometimes sad but often confident nation whose history seemed too complex ever to comprehend. There's no doubt that the 'Queen of the Danube' will give you just as much as she has me.

Facts about Budapest

HISTORY

Strictly speaking, the story of Budapest begins only in 1873 when hilly, residential Buda and historic Óbuda on the western bank of the Danube (Duna) river merged with flat, industrial Pest on the eastern side to form what was at first called Pest-Buda. But like everything here, it's not that simple.

Early Inhabitants

The Carpathian Basin, in which Hungary lies, has been populated for hundreds of thousands of years. Bone fragments found and exhibited at Vértesszőlős near Tata, some 70km northwest of Budapest, in the 1960s and believed to be half a million years old suggest that Palaeolithic humans were attracted to the area by the warm-water springs and the abundance of mammoth, buffalo and giant reindeer. The capital may have been something of a slow starter, however; the earliest evidence of human settlement in the greater Budapest area is the remains of a Neanderthal hunting camp in the Érd Valley, southwest of the city. Complete with tools, cutters and scrapers, the camp is thought to date back 50,000 years.

During the Ice Age, temperatures in this area rarely exceeded 15°C at the height of summer. During the Neolithic period (around 5000 BC), a warming up of the climate forced much of the indigenous wildlife to migrate northward. The domestication of animals and the first forms of agriculture appeared, as they did in much of Central Europe. The first permanent settlement in this area – on the Buda side near the Danube – dates from between 4600 and 3900 BC. Remains from this culture – bone utensils, fishing nets, even a primitive loom – have been unearthed as far north as Békásmegyer and as far south as Nagytétény.

Indo-European tribes from the Balkans stormed the Carpathian Basin from the south in horse-drawn wheeled carts in about 2000 BC, bringing with them copper tools and weapons. After the introduction of more durable bronze, forts were built and a military elite developed. The remains of several settlements dating from this time have been uncovered on Csepel Island in the Danube.

Over the next millennium, invaders from the west (Illyrians and Thracians) and east (Scythians) brought iron, but the metal was not in common use until the Celts arrived in the area in about the 3rd century BC, settling at Békásmegyer and Óbuda, which they called Ak Ink (Ample Water), and erecting one of their signature *oppida* (fortresses) on Gellért hegy. The Celts introduced glass and crafted some of the fine gold jewellery that can still be seen in the Hungarian National Museum.

Around the beginning of the Christian era, the Romans conquered the area west of the Danube and established the province of Pannonia. Subsequent victories over the Celts extended their domination and the province was divided into Pannonia Superior and Pannonia Inferior. The Romans brought writing, viticulture and stone architecture to the area, and at the end of the 1st century AD established Aquincum, a key military garrison and trading settlement along the Danube in today's Óbuda. Aquincum became the administrative seat of Pannonia Inferior in AD 106 and a fully fledged colony in AD 194. A fortress was built at Contra Aquincum (V Március 15 tér) in Pest and the proconsul's palace on a secure island in the Danube (today's Óbuda Island). Villages nearby, such as Vindonianus (Békásmgyer) and Vicus Basoretensis (Kiscell), were populated by Celts, who were not granted Roman citizenship.

The Great Migrations

The first of the so-called Great Migrations of nomadic peoples from Asia reached the eastern outposts of the Roman Empire in Dacia (now Romania) late in the 2nd century AD. Within two centuries, the Romans were forced to flee Aquincum and abandon the rest of Pannonia by the Huns, whose short-lived empire was established by Attila. Aquincum offered little protection to the civilian population; in the late 430s, the Huns razed it.

Following the death of Attila in 453, Germanic tribes such as the Ostrogoths, Gepids and Longobards (or Lombards) occupied the region for the next century and a half until the Avars, a powerful Turkic people, gained control of the Carpathian Basin in the late 6th century. At first they settled on the Pest plains, but their chieftains soon established their main base at the northern end of Csepel.

The Avars were overcome by Charlemagne in 796 and the area around Budapest and the Danube Bend was incorporated into the Frankish empire. By that time, the Carpathian Basin was virtually unpopulated except for scattered groups of Turkic and Germanic tribes on the plains and Slavs in the northern hills.

The Magyars & the Conquest of the Carpathian Basin

The origin of the Magyars, as the Hungarians call themselves, is a complicated issue, not helped by the similarity (in English) of the words 'Hun' and 'Hungary', which are *not* related. One thing is certain: Magyars belong to the Finno-Ugric group of peoples, who inhabited the forests somewhere between the middle Volga River and the Ural Mountains in western Siberia as early as 4000 BC.

By about 2000 BC, population growth had forced the Finnish-Estonian branch to move westward, ultimately reaching the Baltic Sea. The Ugrians moved from the southeastern slopes of the Urals into the valleys of the region, and switched from hunting and fishing to farming and raising livestock, especially horses. Their equestrian skills proved useful half a millennium later when more climatic changes brought drought, forcing them to move northward onto the steppes.

On the grasslands, the Ugrians turned to nomadic herding. After 500 BC, by which time the use of iron had become common among the tribes, a group moved westward to the area of Bashkiria in Central Asia. Here they lived among Persians and Bulgars and began referring to themselves as Magyars (from the Finno-Ugric words *mon* (to speak) and *er* (man).

After several centuries, another group split away and moved south to the Don River under the control of the Turkic Khazars. Here they lived among different groups under a tribal alliance called *onogur*, or '10 peoples'. This is thought to be the origin of the word 'Hungary' in English and 'Ungarn' in German. The Magyars' last migration before the conquest *(honfoglalás)* of the Carpathian Basin brought them to what modern Hungarians call the Etelköz, the region between the Dnieper and lower Danube rivers above the Black Sea. Nomadic groups of Magyars probably reached the Carpathian Basin as early as the mid-9th century AD, acting as mercenaries for various armies. It is believed that while the men were away during one such campaign in about 889, a fierce people from the Asiatic steppe called the Pechenegs allied themselves with the Bulgars and attacked the Etelköz settlements. When they were attacked again in about 895, seven tribes under the leadership of Árpád – the *gyula* or chief military commander – struck out for the Carpathian Basin. They crossed the Verecke Pass in today's Ukraine some time between 896 and 898.

Within five years some five of the seven tribes settled in the area that is now Budapest and both of the tribes' principal leaders made their base here. Árpád, the military chieftain, established his seat on today's Csepel Island; according to the chronicler Anonymous, his overseer was a Turkic Cuman named Csepel, who gave his name to the island. Árpád's brother, Kurszán, the chief *táltos* (shaman), based himself in Óbuda; Buda and Pest were no more than small villages. On Kurszán's death, Árpád took all power for himself and moved his seat to Óbuda.

The Magyars had met almost no resistance in the Carpathian Basin. Being highly skilled at riding and shooting (a common Christian prayer during the Dark Ages was 'Save us, O Lord, from the arrows of the Hungarians'), they began plundering and pillaging in all directions, taking slaves and amassing booty. Their raids took them as far as Spain, northern Germany and southern Italy, but they were stopped by the German king Otto I at the Battle of Augsburg in 955.

This and subsequent defeats (raids on Byzantium were ended in 970) left the Magyar tribes in disarray and they had to choose between their more powerful neighbours – Byzantium to the south and east or the Holy Roman Empire to the west – to form an alliance. Individual Magyar chieftains began acting independently but, in 973, Prince Géza, Árpád's great-grandson, asked the Holy Roman emperor Otto II to send Catholic missionaries to Hungary. Géza was baptised at his capital, Esztergom, some 46km upriver from Budapest, as was his son Vajk, who took the Christian name Stephen (István). When Géza died, Stephen ruled as prince, but three years later he was crowned 'Christian King' Stephen I, on Christmas Day in 1000, with a crown sent from Rome by Otto's erstwhile tutor, Pope Sylvester II. Hungary the kingdom and Hungary the nation had been born.

King Stephen I & the Árpád Dynasty

Stephen ruthlessly set about consolidating royal authority by expropriating the land of the clan chieftains and establishing a system of counties (megye) protected by fortified castles (vár). Much land was transferred to loyal (mostly Germanic) knights, and the crown began minting coins. Stephen did not find the area of Budapest suitable as a base; instead he made his seat at Székesfehérvár, 66km to the southwest. Esztergom remained the religious centre.

Shrewdly, Stephen sought the support of the church throughout and, to hasten the conversion of the populace, he ordered one in every 10 villages to build a church. He also established 10 episcopates throughout the land. Monasteries staffed by foreign scholars were set up around the country; in Óbuda it was the religious Chapter of Saint Peter. By

---

Kings, Saints, Strong Men & Premiers

The following is a list of the most important monarchs, rulers, dictators and leaders in Hungarian history. Names are given in English, with the Magyar equivalents in brackets. The dates refer to their reign or term of office.

Árpád Dynasty
Árpád 886–907
Géza 972–97
Stephen I (István) 1000–38
Ladislas I (László) 1077–95
Koloman the Bookish (Könyves Kálmán) 1095–1116
Béla III 1172–96
Andrew II (András) 1205–35
Béla IV 1235–70
Ladislas the Cuman (Kun László) 1272–1290
Andrew III (András) 1290–1301

Mixed Dynasties
Charles Robert (Károly Róbert) 1308–42
Louis I the Great (Nagy Lajos) 1342–82
Mary (Mária) 1382–87
Sigismund (Zsigmond) 1387–1437
János Hunyadi (regent) 1446–56
Matthias (Mátyás) Corvinus 1458–90
Vladislav II (Úlászló) 1490–1516
Louis II (Lajos) 1516–26
John Szapolyai (Zápolyai János) 1526–40

Habsburg Dynasty
Ferdinand I (Ferdinánd) 1526–64
Maximilian I (Miksa) 1564–76
Leopold I (Lipót) 1657–1705
Maria Theresa (Mária Terézia) 1740–80
Joseph II (József) 1780–90
Ferdinand V (Ferdinánd) 1835–48
Franz Joseph (Ferenc József) 1848–1916 (of Hungary from 1867)
Charles IV (Károly) 1916–18

Political Leaders
Mihály Károlyi Jan–March 1919
Béla Kun March–Aug 1919
Miklós Horthy (regent) 1920–44
Ferenc Szálasi 1944–45
Mátyás Rákosi 1947–56
János Kádár 1956–88
Károly Grósz 1988–90
József Antall 1990–93
Péter Baross 1993–94
Gyula Horn 1994–98
Viktor Orbán 1998–2002
Péter Medgyessy 2002–

the time of Stephen's death in 1038 (he was canonised less than 50 years later), Hungary was a nascent Christian nation. But pockets of rebellion remained; in 1046 a Venetian-born bishop named Gerard (Gellért in Hungarian), who had been brought to Hungary by Stephen himself, was hurled to his death from a Buda hilltop in a spiked barrel by pagan Hungarians resisting conversion. The hill now bears Gellért's name.

The next two and a half centuries – the reign of the House of Árpád – would further test the new kingdom. The period was one of relentless struggles between rival pretenders to the throne, which weakened the young nation's defences against its powerful neighbours. There was a brief hiatus under King Ladislas I (László; ruled 1077–95), who fended off attacks from Byzantium, and under his successor Koloman the Bookish (Könyves Kálmán), who encouraged literature, art and the writing of chronicles until his death in 1116.

Tension flared again when the Byzantine emperor made a grab for Hungary's provinces in Dalmatia and Croatia, which it had acquired by the early 12th century. But he was stopped by Béla III (ruled 1172–96) who had a permanent residence built at Esztergom (by then an alternative royal seat to Székesfehérvár) but was headquartered at Óbuda. Béla's son, Andrew II (András; ruled 1205–35), however, weakened the crown when he gave in to local barons' demands for more land in order to fund his crusades. This led to the Golden Bull, a kind of Magna Carta signed at Székesfehérvár in 1222, which limited some of the king's powers in favour of the nobility, recognised the 'Hungarian nation' and allowed for a diet, or assembly, of nobles to meet regularly in a meadow in Pest. It was during Andrew's reign that Óbuda grew from just being a centrally located town to a royal and military seat.

When Béla IV (ruled 1235–70) tried to regain the estates that Andrew had forfeited, however, the barons were able to oppose him on equal terms. Fearing Mongol expansion and realising he could not count on local help, Béla looked to the west and brought in German and Slovak settlers. In March 1241, Béla amassed his troops at Óbuda and crossed over into Pest. But his efforts were in vain. The Mongols, who had raced through the country as easily as the Magyars had conquered the Carpathian Basin some 2½ centuries before, attacked from every direction. By the end of the final attack in January 1242, Pest and Óbuda had been burned to the ground and some 100,000 people killed.

To rebuild the nascent royal capital as quickly as possible after the Mongol retreat, Béla again invited Germans and Saxons to settle here. He also ordered what remained of those living in Pest and Óbuda to relocate to Castle Hill and build a fortified town there. Béla proclaimed Buda a municipality by royal charter in 1244 and bestowed civic rights on the citizens of Pest in 1255; another century would go by before Óbuda's citizens won the same rights. By the start of the 14th century, all three had begun to develop into major towns.

But Béla did not always play his cards right. In a bid to appease the lesser nobility, he handed over large tracts of land to the barons. This enhanced their position and bids for more independence even further. At the time of Béla's death in 1270, anarchy ruled. The Árpád line died out with the death of the heirless Andrew III in 1301.

Medieval Budapest

The struggle for the Hungarian throne after the death of Andrew III involved several European dynasties, but it was Charles Robert (Károly Róbert) of the French House of Anjou who finally won out (with the pope's blessing) in 1307 and was crowned at Buda a year later. He didn't stay there long though; until his death in 1342 Charles Robert ruled from a palace he had built for himself on the Danube at Visegrád, 42km to the northwest. Buda would not play a leading role in Hungarian history for another five decades, but after that it would never look back. In the meantime, Pest had started to develop as a town of wealthy and independent burghers; by 1406 it had its own royal charter and full independence from Buda.

Under Charles Robert's son and successor, Louis the Great (Nagy Lajos; ruled 1342–82), the kingdom returned to a policy of conquest. A brilliant military strategist, Louis acquired territory in the Balkans as far as Dalmatia and Romania and, through an alliance, as far north as Poland. But his successes were short-lived and the menace of the Ottoman Turks had begun.

As Louis had sired no sons, one of his daughters, Mary, succeeded him. This was deemed unacceptable by the barons, who rose up against the 'petticoat throne'. Within a short time, Mary's husband, Sigismund (Zsigmond; ruled 1387–1437) of Luxembourg, was crowned king. Sigismund's long reign brought peace at home, and there was a great flowering of Gothic art and architecture. Sigismund enlarged the Royal Palace on Castle Hill, founded a university at Óbuda (1389), oversaw the construction of the first pontoon bridge over the Danube (until then the only way to cross the river was by ferry) and set national standards of measurement, including the 'Buda pound' (490g) for weight and the 'Buda icce' (0.88L) for liquids. But despite these advances and his enthronement as Holy Roman emperor in 1433, he was unable to stop the march of the Turks up through the Balkans.

A Transylvanian general born of a Wallachian (Romanian) father, János Hunyadi began his career at the court of Sigismund. When Vladislav I (Úlászló) of the Polish Jagiellon dynasty was killed fighting the Turks at Varna, Hunyadi was declared regent. His victory over the Turks at Belgrade (Hungarian: Nándorfehérvár) in 1456 checked the Ottoman advance into Hungary for 70 years and assured the coronation of his son Matthias (Mátyás), the greatest ruler of medieval Hungary.

Matthias, called 'the Raven' (Corvinus) from his coat of arms, ruled from 1458 to 1490. Wisely, he maintained a mercenary force of 8000 to 10,000 soldiers through taxation of the nobility, and this 'Black Army' (one of the first standing armies in Europe) conquered Moravia, Bohemia and even parts of Austria. Not only did Matthias Corvinus make Hungary one of Central Europe's leading powers, but under his rule Buda enjoyed something of a golden age and for the first time became the true focus of the nation. His second wife, the Neapolitan Beatrice, brought artisans from Italy who completely rebuilt, extended and fortified the Royal Palace; the beauty and sheer size of the residence astonished visitors and its royal library of more than 2000 codices and incunabula became a major cultural and artistic centre of Renaissance Europe. In 1473 a German named Andreas (András) Hess printed the first book in Hungary at Buda.

But while Matthias busied himself with centralising power for the crown in the capital, he ignored the growing Turkish threat. His successor Vladislav II (Úlászló; ruled 1490–1516) was unable to maintain even royal authority as the members of the diet, which met to approve royal decrees, squandered royal funds, sold off the royal library and expropriated land. In May 1514, what had begun as a crusade organised by the power-hungry archbishop of Esztergom, Tamás Bakócz, turned into uprising against the landlords by peasants who rallied near Pest under their leader, György Dózsa.

The revolt was brutally repressed, some 70,000 peasants were tortured and executed, and Dózsa himself was fried alive on a red-hot iron throne. The retrograde Tripartitum Law that followed in 1522 codified the rights and privileges of the barons and nobles, reduced the peasants to perpetual serfdom and refused them the right to bear arms. By the time Louis II (Lajos) took the throne in 1516 at the tender age of nine, he couldn't rely on either side.

The Battle of Mohács & Turkish Occupation

The defeat of Louis' ragtag army by the Ottoman Turks at Mohács in 1526 is a watershed in Hungarian history. On the battlefield near this small town in Southern Transdanubia, some 195km south of Budapest, a relatively prosperous and independent medieval Hungary died, sending the nation into a tailspin of partition, foreign domination and despair that can still be felt in some respects today.

It would be unfair to put all the blame on the weak and indecisive boy-king Louis or on his commander-in-chief Pál Tomori, the archbishop of Kalocsa. Bickering among the nobility and the brutal crackdown of the Dózsa uprising more than a decade earlier had severely weakened Hungary's military power, and there was virtually nothing left in the royal coffers. By 1526, the Ottoman sultan Suleiman the Magnificent had taken much of the Balkans, including Belgrade, and was poised to march on Buda with a force of some 80,000 men.

Unable – or unwilling – to wait for reinforcements from Transylvania under the command of his rival John Szapolyai (Zápolyai János), Louis rushed from Buda with a motley army of 25,000 men of mixed nationalities to battle the Turks and was soundly thrashed in less than two hours. Along with bishops, nobles and an estimated 20,000 soldiers, the king himself was killed – crushed by his horse while trying to retreat across a stream.

The Turks then turned north, sacking and burning Buda before retreating. John Szapolyai, who had sat out the battle in the castle at Tokaj, was crowned king three months later but, despite grovelling before the Turks, he was never able to exploit the power he had so desperately sought. As would be the case as late as the 20th century, greed, self-interest and ambition had led Hungary to defeat itself.

After the Turks returned and took Buda for good in 1541, Hungary was divided into three parts. The central part, with Buda – Budun to the Turks – as the provincial seat, went to the Turks while parts of Transdanubia and what is now Slovakia were governed by the Austrian House of Habsburg and assisted by the Hungarian nobility based at Bratislava (Hungarian: Pozsony). The principality of Transylvania east of the Tisza River prospered as a vassal state of the Ottoman Empire. This division of the country would remain in place for more than 150 years.

The Turkish occupation was marked by constant fighting among the three divisions: Catholic 'Royal Hungary' was pitted against not only the Turks but the Protestant Transylvanian princes. Although Habsburg Hungary enjoyed something of a cultural renaissance during this period, the Turkish-occupied central part and Buda itself suffered greatly, with many people fleeing the town to Pest, where some churches remained. The Turks did little building in Buda apart from a few bathhouses, dervish monasteries and tombs and city walls; for the most part, they used existing civic buildings for administration and converted churches into mosques. Matthias Church on Castle Hill, for example, was hastily converted into the Büyük Cami, or 'Great Mosque', and the heart of the Royal Palace became a magazine. In 1578 lightning struck and much of the Danube wing was reduced to rubble.

Turkish power began to wane in the 17th century, and with the help of the Polish army, some 45,000 Austrian and Hungarian forces advanced down both banks of the Danube from Štúrovo (Hungarian: Párkány), now in Slovakia, to liberate Buda in 1686. An imperial army under Eugene of Savoy wiped out the last Turkish army in Hungary at the Battle of Zenta (now Senta in Serbia and Montenegro) 11 years later. Peace was signed with the Turks in 1699.

Habsburg Rule

The expulsion of the Turks did not result in a free and independent Hungary. Buda and the rest of the country were under military occupation and governed from Bratislava, and the policies of the Catholic Habsburgs' Counter-Reformation and heavy taxation further alienated the nobility. In 1703 – the very year in which both Buda and Pest regained their privileges as royal free towns – the Transylvanian prince Ferenc Rákóczi II raised an army of *kuruc* (Hungarian mercenaries) against the Habsburgs. The war dragged on for eight years, during which time the rebels 'deposed' the Austrians as rulers of Hungary. But superior imperial forces and lack of funds forced the *kuruc* forces to negotiate a separate peace with Vienna behind Rákóczi's back. The 1703–11 War of Independence had failed, but Rákóczi was the first leader to unite Hungarians against the Habsburgs.

Though the compromise had brought the fighting to an end, Hungary was now a mere province of the Habsburg Empire. Its main cities – Buda, Pest and Óbuda – counted a total of just over 12,000 people. With the ascension of Maria Theresa to the throne in 1740, the Hungarian nobility pledged their 'lives and blood' to her at the diet in Bratislava in exchange for concessions. Thus began the period of enlightened absolutism that would continue under the rule of her son, the 'hatted king' (so-called as he was never crowned in Hungary) Joseph II, who ruled for a decade from 1780. By then the population of Buda and Pest had risen to almost 35,000 – a significant number, even in the sprawling Habsburg Empire.

Under the reigns of Maria Theresa and Joseph, Hungary took great steps forward economically and culturally, though the first real moves toward integration with Austria had also begun. Buda effectively became the German-speaking town of Ofen and the city's first newspaper – in German – was published there in 1730. Pest, fuelled by the grain and livestock trades, began to develop outside the city walls. In 1749 the foundations for a new palace were laid in Buda, the university was moved from Nagyszombat (now Trnava in Slovakia) to Buda in 1777 and seven years later Joseph ordered the government to move from Bratislava to Buda, the nation's new administrative centre.

Joseph's attempts to modernise society by dissolving the all-powerful (and corrupt) religious orders, abolishing serfdom and replacing 'neutral' Latin with German as the official language of state administration (1781–85) were opposed by the Hungarian nobility, and the king rescinded most of these orders on his deathbed.

Dissenting voices could still be heard, and the ideals of the French Revolution of 1789 began to take root in certain intellectual circles in Budapest. In 1795 Ignác Martonovics, a former Franciscan priest, and six other pro-republican Jacobins were beheaded at Vérmező (Blood Meadow) in Buda for plotting against the crown.

By 1800 Pest, with a population of about 30,000, was the nation's most important commercial centre while Buda, with 24,000 people, remained a royal garrison town and developed under the eye of the monarch. But 90% of the national population worked the land, and it was primarily through agriculture that modernisation would come to Hungary.

Liberalism and social reform found their greatest supporters among certain members of the aristocracy in Pest. A prime example was Count István Széchenyi (1791–1860), a true Renaissance man (see the boxed text 'The Greatest Hungarian') who advocated the abolition of serfdom and returned much of his own land to the peasantry, proposed the first permanent link between Buda and Pest (Chain Bridge) and oversaw the regulation of the Danube as much for commerce and irrigation as for safety; the devastating Danube flood of 1838 had taken a heavy toll, with three quarters of the homes in Pest washed away and some 150 people drowned.

The proponents of gradual reform were quickly superseded, however, by a more radical faction demanding more immediate action. The group included such men as Miklós Wesselényi, Ferenc Deák and the poet Ferenc Kölcsey, but the predominant figure was Lajos Kossuth (1802–94). It was this dynamic lawyer and journalist who would lead Hungary to its greatest ever confrontation with the Habsburgs.

The 1848–49 War of Independence

The Habsburg Empire began to weaken as Hungarian nationalism increased early in the 19th century. The Hungarians, suspicious of Napoleon's policies, ignored French appeals to revolt against Vienna, and certain reforms were introduced: the replacement of Latin, the official language of administration, with Magyar; a law allowing serfs alternative means of discharging their feudal obligations of service; and increased Hungarian representation in the Council of State.

The reforms carried out were too limited and too late, however, and the diet became more defiant in its dealings with the crown. At the same time, the wave of revolution

The Greatest Hungarian

The contributions that Count István Széchenyi made to Hungary were enormous and extremely varied. In his seminal 1830 work *Hitel* (meaning 'credit' and based on *hit*, or 'trust'), he advocated sweeping economic reforms and the abolition of serfdom (he himself had distributed the bulk of his property to landless peasants two years earlier). The Chain Bridge, the design of which Széchenyi helped push through Parliament, was the first permanent link between Buda and Pest and for the first time everyone, nobles included, had to pay a toll.

Széchenyi was instrumental in straightening the serpentine Tisza River, which rescued half of Hungary's arable land from flooding and erosion, and his work made the Danube navigable as far as the Iron Gates in Romania. He arranged the financing for Hungary's first railway lines (from Budapest north and east to Vác and Szolnok and west to what is now Wiener Neustadt in Austria) and launched the first steam transport on the Danube and Lake Balaton. A lover of all things English, Széchenyi got the upper classes interested in horse racing with the express purpose of improving breeding stock for farming. A large financial contribution made by Széchenyi led to the establishment of the nation's prestigious Academy of Science.

Széchenyi joined Lajos Batthyány's revolutionary government in 1848, but political squabbling and open conflict with Vienna caused him to lose control and he suffered a nervous breakdown. Despite a decade of convalescence in an asylum, Széchenyi never fully recovered and tragically he took his own life in 1860.

For all his accomplishments, Széchenyi's contemporary and fellow reformer, Lajos Kossuth, called him 'the greatest Hungarian'. This dynamic but troubled visionary retains that accolade to this day.

sweeping Europe spurred on the more radical faction. On 3 March 1848, Kossuth, who had been imprisoned by the Habsburgs at I Táncsics Mihály utca 9 on Castle Hill for three years (1837–40), made a fiery speech in parliament demanding an end to feudalism. On 15 March, a group calling itself the Youth of March led by the poet Sándor Petőfi, who read out his poem *Nemzeti Dal* (National Song) on the steps of the National Museum, took to the streets of Pest with hastily printed copies of their *Twelve Points* to press for radical reforms and even revolution.

The frightened government in Vienna quickly approved plans for a new Hungarian ministry responsible to the diet to be led by the liberal count Lajos Batthyány and to include Deák, Kossuth and Széchenyi. The Habsburgs also reluctantly agreed to abolish serfdom and proclaim equality under the law. But the diet voted to raise a local army and Habsburg patience began to wear thin. In September 1848, Habsburg forces under the governor of Croatia, Josip Jelačić, launched an attack on Hungary and

Batthyány resigned from government. Pest and Buda fell to the Austrian army in the following spring, and the Hungarians hastily formed a national defence commission and moved the government seat from Pest to Debrecen, where Kossuth was elected leader. The parliament declared Hungary's full independence and the 'dethronement' of the Habsburgs for the second time.

The new Habsburg emperor, Franz Joseph (1848–1916), was nothing like his feeble-minded predecessor, Ferdinand V, and quickly took action. He sought the assistance of Russian Tsar Nicholas I, who obliged with 200,000 troops. Support for the revolution was already crumbling, however, particularly in areas of mixed population where the Magyars were seen as oppressors. Weak and outnumbered, the rebel troops had been defeated by July 1849 and martial law declared in Budapest.

A series of brutal reprisals ensued. Summary executions of 'spies' (mostly simple army deserters) took place in the gardens of the National Museum. Batthyány was executed in Pest, 13 of his generals (the so-called

Martyrs of Arad) incarcerated and shot in Romania and Kossuth went into exile in Turkey. (Petőfi had been killed in battle.) Habsburg troops then went around the country systematically blowing up castles and fortifications lest they be used by resurgent rebels. What little of medieval Buda and Pest that had remained after the Turks and the 1703–11 War of Independence was now reduced to rubble.

The Dual Monarchy

Hungary was again merged into the Habsburg Empire as a vanquished province and 'neo-absolutism' was the order of the day. Hungarian war prisoners were forced to build the Citadella atop Gellért hegy to 'defend' the city from further insurrection, but by the time it was ready in 1854 the political climate had changed and the fortress had become obsolete. Passive resistance among Hungarians and disastrous military defeats by Prussia in 1859 and 1866 pushed Franz Joseph to the negotiating table with liberal Hungarians under Deák's leadership.

The result was the Compromise of 1867 (*Ausgleich* in German, which actually means 'balance' or 'reconciliation'), which created the Dual Monarchy of Austria (the empire) and Hungary (the kingdom). It was a federated state of two parliaments and two capitals – Vienna and Budapest (the result of Buda, Pest and Óbuda uniting six years later). Only defence, foreign relations and customs were shared. Hungary was even allowed to raise a small army.

This 'Age of Dualism' would carry on until 1918 and spark an economic, cultural and intellectual rebirth in Budapest – a 'golden age' the likes of which the city has never seen again. In Budapest trade and industry boomed, factories were established and the composers Franz (Ferenc) Liszt and Ferenc Erkel were making beautiful music. The middle class, dominated by Germans and Jews in Pest, burgeoned, and the capital entered into a frenzy of building.

Much of what you see in Budapest today – from the grand boulevards and their Eclectic-style apartment blocks to the Parliament building, State Opera House and Palace of Art – was built at this time. The apex of this *belle époque* was the six-month exhibition in 1896 in City Park celebrating the millennium of the Magyar conquest of the Carpathian Basin. A small replica of Vajdahunyad Castle in Transylvania, but with Gothic, Romanesque and baroque wings and additions to reflect architectural styles from all over the country, was built to house the exhibits (it now houses the Hungarian Agricultural Museum). Some four million visitors from Hungary and abroad were transported to the fairground on Continental Europe's first underground railway (now the M1 or little yellow line). By the turn of the 20th century the population of the 'new' capital jumped from about 280,000 at the time of the Compromise to 750,000, Europe's sixth-largest city.

But all was not well in the capital. The city-based working class had almost no rights – and the situation in the countryside remained almost as dire as it had been in the Middle Ages. Minorities under Hungarian control – Czechs, Slovaks, Croatians and Romanians – were under increased pressure to 'Magyarise' and viewed their new rulers as oppressors. Increasingly they worked to dismember the empire.

WWI & the Republic of Councils

In July 1914, a month to the day after the assassination of Archduke Franz Ferdinand, the heir to the Habsburg throne, by a Bosnian Serb in Sarajevo, Austria-Hungary entered WWI allied with the German Empire. The result was disastrous, with heavy destruction and hundreds of thousands killed on the Russian and Italian fronts. At the Armistice in November 1918 the fate of the Dual Monarchy (and Hungary as a multinational kingdom) was sealed.

A republic under the leadership of Count Mihály Károlyi was set up in Budapest immediately after the war, and the Habsburg monarchy was dethroned for the third and final time. But the fledgling republic would not last long. Widespread destitution, the occupation of Hungary by the Allies, and the success of the Bolshevik Revolution in Russia had radicalised much of the Budapest working class.

In March 1919 a group of Hungarian communists under Béla Kun seized power. The so-called Tanácsköztársaság (Republic of Councils) set out to nationalise industry and private property and build a fairer society, but mass opposition to the regime unleashed a reign of 'red terror' in Budapest and around the country. In August Romanian troops occupied the capital, and Kun and his comrades (including Minister of Culture Béla Lugosi of *Dracula* fame) fled to Vienna. The Romanians camped out at Oktogon, taking whatever they wanted when they wanted it, and left the city in November – just ahead of Admiral Miklós Horthy, the hero of the Battle of Rijeka, mounted on a white stallion and leading 25,000 Hungarian troops into what he called the *bűnös város* (sinful city).

The Horthy Years & WWII

In the nation's first-ever election by secret ballot (March 1920), parliament chose a kingdom as the form of state and – lacking a king – elected as its regent Admiral Miklós Horthy, who would remain in that position until the last year of WWII. The arrangement confused even US President Franklin D Roosevelt in the early days of the war. After being briefed by an aide on the government and leadership of Hungary, he reportedly said: 'Let me see if I understand you right. Hungary is a kingdom without a king run by a regent who's an admiral without a navy?'

Horthy embarked on a 'white terror' – every bit as brutal as the red one of Béla Kun – that attacked Jews, social democrats and communists for their roles in supporting the Republic of Councils. As the regime was consolidated, it showed itself to be extremely rightist and conservative, advocating the status quo and 'traditional values' – family, state, religion. Though the country had the remnants of a parliamentary system, Horthy was all-powerful, and very few reforms were enacted. On the contrary, the lot of the working class and the peasantry worsened.

One thing everyone agreed on was that the return of the territories lost through the Treaty of Trianon (see the boxed text 'A Seven-Letter Word') was essential for national development. Budapest was swollen with ethnic Hungarian refugees from Romania, Czechoslovakia and the Kingdom of Serbs, Croats and Slovenes, unemployment skyrocketed and the economy was at a standstill. Hungary obviously could not count on the victors – France, Britain and the USA – to help recoup its land; instead, it would have to seek help from the fascist governments of Germany and Italy.

Hungary's move to the right intensified throughout the 1930s, though it remained silent when WWII broke out in September 1939. Horthy hoped an alliance would not mean actually having to enter the war but, after recovering northern Transylvania and part of Croatia with Germany's assistance, he was forced to join the Axis in June 1941. The war was as disastrous for Hungary as the 1914–18 one had been, and hundreds of thousands of Hungarian troops died while retreating from Stalingrad, where they'd been used as cannon fodder. Realising too late that his country was again on the losing side, Horthy began negotiating a separate peace with the Allies.

The result was the total occupation of Hungary by the German army in March 1944, with Adolf Eichmann based in the Buda Hills and the Wehrmacht billeted in the Astoria Hotel. Under pressure, Horthy installed Ferenc Szálasi, the deranged leader of the pro-Nazi Arrow Cross Party, as prime minister in October and the regent was deported to Germany. (Horthy would later find exile in Portugal, where he died in 1957. Despite some public outcry, his body was returned to Hungary in September 1993 and reburied in the family plot at Kenderes, east of Szolnok.)

The Arrow Cross Party moved quickly to quash any opposition, and thousands of liberal politicians and labour leaders were arrested. At the same time, its puppet government introduced anti-Jewish legislation similar to that in Germany, and Jews, relatively safe under Horthy, were rounded up into ghettos by Hungarian pro-Nazis. In the summer of 1944, less than a year before the war's end, some 400,000 Jewish men, women and children were deported to

Auschwitz and other labour camps, where they succumbed to disease, starved or were murdered by the German fascists and their savage henchmen. Many of the Jews who did survive owed their lives to Raoul Wallenberg, a Budapest-based Swedish diplomat (see the boxed text 'Raoul Wallenberg, Righteous Gentile' in the Things to See & Do chapter) and the Swiss consul, Carl Lutz.

Budapest now became an international battleground for the first time since the Turkish occupation, and bombs began falling everywhere but particularly on Castle Hill and, in Pest, in Angyalföld and Zugló, where there were munitions factories. The resistance movement drew support from many sides, including the communists, and by Christmas 1944 the Soviet army had surrounded Budapest. When the Germans and Hungarian Nazis rejected a settlement, the siege of the capital began. By the time the German war machine had surrendered in April 1945, three quarters of Budapest's homes, historical buildings and churches had been severely damaged or destroyed. The vindictive Germans even blew up Buda Castle and every bridge spanning the Danube while retreating. Some 20,000 Hungarian soldiers and 25,000 citizens of Budapest had been killed.

The People's Republic

When free parliamentary elections were held in November 1945, the Independent Smallholders' Party received 57% (245 seats) of the vote. But Soviet political officers, backed by the occupying Soviet army, forced three other parties – the Communists, Social Democrats and National Peasants – into a coalition. Limited democracy prevailed, and land-reform laws, sponsored by the communist minister of agriculture, Imre Nagy, were enacted, wiping away the prewar feudal structure. Budapest experienced the worst hyperinflation the world has ever known at this time, with notes worth up to 10,000 trillion pengő issued before the new currency (the forint) was introduced. Still, Independence Bridge, the first of the spans over the Danube to be rebuilt, reopened in 1946.

A Seven-Letter Word

In June 1920, scarcely a year and a half after the Armistice was signed ending WWI, the victorious Allies drew up a postwar settlement under the Treaty of Trianon that enlarged some countries, truncated others and created several 'successor states'. As one of the defeated enemy nations and with large numbers of minorities clamouring for independence within its borders, Hungary stood to lose more than most. And it certainly did. Hungary was reduced to 40% of its historical size and, while it was now largely a uniform, homogeneous nation-state, for millions of ethnic Hungarians in Romania, Yugoslavia and Czechoslovakia, the tables had been turned: they were now in the minority.

'Trianon' became the singularly most hated word in Hungary, and the *diktátum* is often reviled today as if it were imposed on the nation yesterday. Many of the problems it created remain to this day, and it has coloured Hungary's relations with its neighbours to some degree for over four score years.

Within a couple of years, the Communists were ready to take complete control. After a rigged election held under a complicated new electoral law in 1947, they declared their candidate, Mátyás Rákosi, victorious. The Social Democrats were forced to merge with the Communists into the Hungarian Socialist Workers Party.

In 1948 Rákosi, a big fan of Stalin, began a process of nationalisation and unfeasibly fast industrialisation at the expense of agriculture. Peasants were forced into collective farms, and all produce had to be delivered to state warehouses. A network of spies and informers exposed 'class enemies' such as Cardinal József Mindszenty (see the boxed text in the Things to See & Do chapter) to the secret police (the ÁVO, or ÁVH after 1949), who interrogated them at their headquarters at VI Andrássy út 60 (now the House of Terror) in Pest and sent them to trial at the Military Court of Justice on II Fő utca in Buda. Some were executed; many more were sent into internal exile or condemned to labour camps like the notorious one at Recsk in the Mátra Hills. It is estimated that during this period a quarter of the adult population of Budapest faced police or judicial proceedings.

Bitter feuding within the party began, and purges and Stalinesque show trials became the norm. László Rajk, the Communist minister of the interior (which also controlled the ÁVH), was arrested and later executed for 'Titoism'; his successor János Kádár was tortured and jailed. In August 1949, the nation was proclaimed the 'People's Republic of Hungary'. In the years that followed – among the darkest and bleakest in Budapest history – apartment blocks, small businesses and retail outlets in Budapest were expropriated by the state and new cultural and sports facilities, including the Ferenc Puskás Stadium (formerly known as Népstadion, or People's Stadium), were built.

After the death of Stalin in March 1953 and Krushchev's denunciation of him three years later, Rákosi's tenure was up and the terror began to abate. Under pressure from within the party, Rákosi's successor, Ernő Gerő, rehabilitated Rajk posthumously and readmitted Nagy, who had been expelled from the party a year earlier for suggesting reforms. But Gerő was ultimately as much a hardliner as Rákosi had been, and by October 1956 during Rajk's reburial, murmured calls for a real reform of the system – 'Socialism with a human face' – could already be heard.

The 1956 Uprising

The nation's greatest tragedy – an event that for a while shook the world, rocked international communism and pitted Hungarian against Hungarian – began in Budapest on 23 October when some 50,000 university students assembled at II Bem tér in Buda, shouting anti-Soviet slogans and demanding that Nagy be named prime minister. That night a crowd pulled down and sawed into pieces the colossal statue of 'Sztálin' near Hősök tere and shots were fired by ÁVH agents on another group gathering outside the headquarters of Hungarian Radio on VIII Bródy Sándor utca in Pest. In a flash, Budapest was in revolution.

The next day Nagy formed a government while János Kádár was named president of the Hungarian Workers' Party Central Committee. For a short time it appeared that Nagy might be successful in transforming Hungary into a neutral, multiparty state. On 28 October the government offered an amnesty to all those involved in the violence and promised to abolish the ÁVH. On 31 October hundreds of political prisoners were released, and widespread reprisals began against ÁVH agents. The following day Nagy announced that Hungary would leave the Warsaw Pact and proclaim its neutrality.

At this, Soviet tanks and troops crossed into Hungary and within 72 hours began attacking Budapest and other centres. Kádár, who had slipped away from Budapest to join the Russian invaders, was installed as leader.

Fierce street fighting continued for several days – fighting was especially heavy at the Corvin Cinema and the nearby Kilián army barracks on VIII József körút in Pest and II Széna tér in Buda – encouraged by Radio Free Europe broadcasts and disingenuous promises of support from the West, which was embroiled in the Suez Canal crisis at the time. When the fighting was over, 25,000 people were dead. Then the reprisals – the worst in the city's history – began. An estimated 20,000 people were arrested and 2000 – including Nagy and his associates – were executed. Another 250,000 refugees fled to Austria. The government lost what little credibility it had enjoyed and the city many of its most competent and talented citizens. As for the physical scars, look around you in some of the older parts of Pest: the bullet holes and shrapnel damage on the exterior walls still cry out in silent fury.

Hungary under Kádár

The transformation of János Kádár from traitor and most hated man in the land to respected reformer is one of the most astonishing *tours de force* of the 20th century.

After the revolt, the ruling party was reorganised as the Hungarian Socialist Workers' Party, and Kádár, now both party president and premier, launched a programme to liberalise the social and economic structure based on compromise. (His most quoted line was 'Whoever is not against us is with us' – a reversal of the Stalinist adage that 'Those not with us are against us'.) In 1968, he and the economist Rezső Nyers unveiled the New Economic Mechanism (NEM) to introduce elements of a market to the planned economy. But even this proved too daring for many party conservatives. Nyers was ousted and the NEM whittled away.

Kádár managed to survive that power struggle and went on to introduce greater consumerism and market socialism. By the mid-1970s Hungary was light years ahead of any other Soviet bloc country in its standard of living, freedom of movement and opportunities to criticise the government. Budapesters may have had to wait seven years for a Lada car or 12 for a telephone, but most could at least enjoy access to a second house in the countryside and a decent material life. The 'Hungarian model' attracted much Western attention – and investment.

But things began to go sour in the 1980s. The Kádár system of 'goulash socialism', which had seemed 'timeless and everlasting' as one Hungarian writer has put it, was incapable of dealing with such 'unsocialist' problems as unemployment, soaring inflation and the largest per-capita foreign debt in the region. Kádár and the 'old guard' refused to hear talk about party reforms. In June 1987 Károly Grósz took over as premier and in May 1988 Kádár was booted out of the party and forced to retire. He died the following year.

Renewal & Change

A group of reformers – among them Nyers, Imre Pozsgay, Miklós Németh and Gyula Horn – took charge. Party conservatives at first put a lid on real change by demanding a retreat from political liberalisation in exchange for their support of the new regime's economic policies. But the tide had already turned.

Throughout the summer and autumn of 1988, new political parties were formed and old ones revived. In January 1989 Pozsgay, seeing the handwriting on the wall as Mikhail Gorbachev kissed babies and launched his reforms in the Soviet Union, announced that the events of 1956 had been a 'popular insurrection' and not the 'counter-revolution' that the regime had always said it was. Four months later some 250,000 people attended the reburial of Imre Nagy and other victims of 1956 in Budapest. The following month the communists agreed to give up their monopoly on power at their party congress, paving the way for free elections in early 1990. The party also changed its name from the Hungarian Socialist Workers' Party to the Hungarian Socialist Party (MSZP).

In July 1989, again at Pozsgay's instigation, Hungary began to demolish the electrified wire fence separating it from Austria. The move released a wave of East Germans holidaying in Hungary into the West and the opening attracted thousands more. The collapse of the communist regimes around the region was now unstoppable. What Hungarians call *az átkos 40 év* (the accursed 40 years) had come to a withering, almost feeble, end.

The Republic of Hungary Again

On 23 October 1989, the 33rd anniversary of the 1956 Uprising, the nation once again became the Republic of Hungary.

The MSZP's new program advocated social democracy and a free market economy, but this was not enough to shake off the stigma of its four decades of autocratic rule. The 1990 vote was won by the centrist Hungarian Democratic Forum (MDF), which advocated a gradual transition to capitalism. The social-democratic Alliance of Free Democrats (SZDSZ), which had called for much faster change, came second and the socialists trailed far behind. As Gorbachev looked on, Hungary changed political systems with scarcely a murmur, and the last Soviet troops left Hungary in June 1991. Street names in Budapest such as Lenin körút and Marx tér ended up on the stinking rubbish tip of history and monuments to 'glorious workers' and 'esteemed leaders' were packed off to a socialist-realist zoo called Statue Park (see the Things to See & Do chapter for details).

In coalition with two smaller parties – the Independent Smallholders (FKgP) and the Christian Democrats (KDNP) – the

MDF provided Hungary with sound government during its painful transition to a full market economy. Those years saw Hungary's northern (Czechoslovakia) and southern (Yugoslavia) neighbours split apart along ethnic lines. Prime Minister József Antall did little to improve relations with Slovakia, Romania and Yugoslavia by claiming to be the 'emotional and spiritual' prime minister of the large Hungarian minorities in those countries. In mid-1993 the MDF was forced to expel István Csurka, a party vice president, after he made ultra-nationalistic and anti-Semitic statements that tarnished Hungary's image as a bastion of moderation and stability in a volatile region. Antall died after a long fight with cancer in December 1993 and was replaced by Interior Minister Péter Boross.

Despite initial successes in curbing inflation and lowering interest rates, a host of economic problems slowed the pace of development, and the government's laissez-faire policies did not help. Like most people in the region, Hungarians had expected (unrealistically) a much faster improvement in their living standards. Most of them – 76% according to a poll in mid-1993 – were 'very disappointed' with the result.

In the elections of May 1994 the Socialist Party, led by Gyula Horn, won an absolute majority in parliament. This in no way implied a return to the past, and Horn was quick to point out that it was in fact his party that had initiated the whole reform process in the first place. (As foreign minister in 1989 Horn had played a key role in opening the border with Austria.) Árpád Göncz of the SZDSZ was elected for a second five-year term as president of the republic in 1995.

The Road to Europe

After its dire showing in the 1994 elections, the Alliance of Young Democrats (Fidesz), which until 1993 limited membership to those aged under 35 in order to emphasise a past untainted by communism, privilege and corruption, moved to the right and added the extension 'MPP' (Hungarian Civic Party) to its name to attract the support of the burgeoning middle class. In the elections of 1998, on which it campaigned for closer integration with Europe, Fidesz-MPP won government by forming a coalition with the MDF and the agrarian conservative FKgP. The party's youthful leader, Viktor Orbán, was named prime minister.

Despite the astonishing economic growth and other gains made by the coalition government, the electorate grew increasingly hostile to Fidesz-MPP's – and Orbán's – strongly nationalistic rhetoric and perceived arrogance. In April 2002 the largest turnout of voters in Hungarian history unseated the government and returned the MSZP, allied with the SZDSZ, to power under Prime Minister Péter Medgyessy, a free-market advocate who had served as finance minister in the Horn government.

Hungary became a full member of NATO in 1999. In a national referendum held in April 2003, Hungarian voters overwhelmingly approved by just under 88% the nation's entry into the European Union in May 2004. Admission and eventual adoption of the euro – in 2006 at the earliest – will open barrier-free markets for Hungarian goods and services in Western Europe, which already accounts for 80% of the country's trade; increase annual economic growth by as much as 5.5%; make Hungary eligible for US$5.5 billion in EU development aid through 2006; and allow Hungarian citizens to live, work and own property freely within the EU. In June 2000 parliament elected Ferenc Mádl as president of the republic to succeed Göncz.

GEOGRAPHY

Budapest lies in the north-central part of Hungary, some 250km southeast of Vienna. It is by far Hungary's largest city both in terms of population and physical size (525 sq km) and has for its borders Csepel Island in the Danube River to the south, the start of the Danube Bend to the north, the Buda Hills to the west and the start of the Great Plain to the east.

The Danube, the city's traditional artery, is spanned by nine bridges that link hilly, historic Buda with bustling, commercial and very flat Pest.

For detailed information on the city's layout and divisions, see Orientation in the Facts for the Visitor chapter.

CLIMATE

Budapest has a temperate, transitional climate – somewhere between the mild, rainy weather of Transdanubia protected by the Alps to the west and the harsh, variable climate of the flat and open Great Plain to the east.

Spring arrives in early April in Budapest and usually ends in showers. Summer can be very hot and humid. It rains for most of November and doesn't usually get cold until mid-December. Winter is relatively short, often cloudy and damp but sometimes brilliantly sunny. What little snow the city gets usually disappears after a few days.

January is the coldest month (with the temperature averaging -2°C) and August the hottest (21°C). The number of hours of sunshine a year averages just over 2000 – among the highest in Europe; from April to the end of September, you can expect the sun to shine for about 10 hours a day. Mean annual precipitation is about 600mm. The climate chart on this page shows you what to expect and when to expect it.

For information on weather conditions in Budapest, ring the national weather forecast service on ☎ 06-90 304 621 or 06-90 304 611 or visit its website at ⓦ www.met.hu.

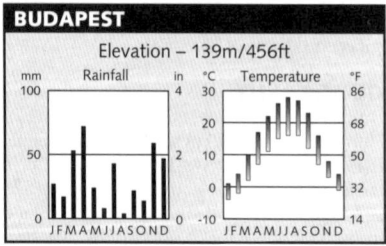

ECOLOGY & ENVIRONMENT

Pollution is a large and costly problem in Budapest. Low-grade coal that continues to fuel some industry and heats homes creates sulphur dioxide and acid rain that threatens the flora and fauna of the Buda Hills to the west and the Börzsöny and Pilis ranges to the north and northwest.

Automobiles manufactured in the former Soviet bloc, especially the two-stroke East German Trabants still seen trawling the streets of the capital, have raised nitrogen oxide levels, reducing the life span of both its citizens and cultural monuments. Waste created by the Soviet military, particularly buried toxic chemicals and routinely dumped jet fuel, threatens the condition of the soil, the ground-water supply, rivers and nearby lakes, as does the overuse of nitrate fertilisers in the hinterland.

There has been a marked improvement in air and water quality in recent years as Hungary attempts to conform to EU environmental standards. Between 1990 and 1997, for example, sulphur dioxide emissions fell by one third and are expected to decrease even further; and from 2004, when EU energy regulations come into force, Hungary will be down to only two coal-fired power stations. At the same time nitrogen oxide levels decreased by one fifth.

FLORA & FAUNA

Budapest and its vicinity counts a total of eight protected areas of national importance. The largest area within the city proper encompasses the Buda Hills, the lungs of the city and a 10,500-hectare protected nature area of dolomite and limestone rocks, steep ravines, rocky grasslands and more than 150 caves. Sashegy (meaning Eagle Hill), a 30-hectare conservation area in south Buda, harbours both cold-resistant and heat-seeking dolomite flora as well as snake-eyed skinks.

The most impressive natural area near the capital, however, is the 60,315-hectare Danube-Ipoly National Park taking in the Börzsöny and Pilis Hills on opposite sides of the Danube to the north and northeast. Among some of the Pilis' botanical attractions are endangered Pannonian fennel and the dolomite flax, with its waxy yellow flowers. The flora and fauna of the Börzsöny Hills is more diverse; some 70 protected plant species and more than 100 bird species have been recorded here.

GOVERNMENT & POLITICS
National Government

Hungary's 1989 constitution provides for a parliamentary system of government. The unicameral assembly sits at Parliament in Budapest and consists of 386 members (32 women at present) chosen for four years in a complex, two-round system that balances direct ('first past the post') and proportional representation. The youngest MP is currently 25, the oldest 92. The head of state, the president, is elected by the house for five years. The prime minister is head of government.

The political parties with seats in the National Assembly at present are the ruling socialist MSZP (Hungarian Socialist Party) in coalition with the liberal SZDSZ (Alliance of Free Democrats) with 198 seats and the centre-rightist Fidesz-MPP (Alliance of Young Democrats-Hungarian Civic Party) and the conservative MDF (Hungarian Democratic Forum) making up the opposition (188 seats). Other parties are the agrarian conservative FKgP (Independent Smallholders' Party), the family-values orientated KDNP (Christian Democratic People's Party) and the xenophobic and ultra-nationalist MIÉP (Hungarian Justice and Life Party).

Local Government

Budapest is governed by a municipal council (*fővárosi önkormánzat*), whose 66 members are elected to four-year terms and whose leader is the city mayor (*főpolgármester*). The current mayor, the youthful SZDSZ liberal Gábor Demszky, handily won his fourth term in office in October 2002 after his party and its coalition partners, the MSZP socialists, received almost 60% of the popular vote. The runner up was Pál Schmitt, backed by the opposition Fidesz-MPP and MDF coalition, who received just under 36% of the vote.

ECONOMY

Hungary, with Budapest as its economic centre, has the third largest (after Poland and the Czech Republic) but most developed economy in Eastern Europe and will join the EU in May 2004.

Memories of the transition from a state-controlled economy to capitalism have dimmed as inflation and unemployment levels approach those of Western Europe. Hungary's 3.5% growth in gross domestic product is among the highest in Europe as consumers increase purchases of household appliances, cars and televisions made in the country. By comparison, the average growth rate in EU countries is less than half.

Hungary is not well endowed with natural resources but this has proved a blessing, for it means the country isn't saddled with the number of rusting industrial plants processing iron or coal that still plague Poland and neighbouring Slovakia. Instead, manufacturing and brainpower have led to jobs that have reduced unemployment to 5% in Budapest (just 6% nationwide) and inflation to 4.7% (from 31% in 1995), figures that helped the country in its bid to join the EU in May 2004.

Foreign companies have pumped more than US$20 billion in direct investment into the country since 1989, the highest level of all the former communist countries. Royal Philips Electronics, Europe's largest producer of consumer electronics products, and automobile manufacturer General Motors have helped boost the economy with exports from the Hungarian factories. About 80% of exports wind up in EU countries, with Austria and Germany taking the lion's share.

Foreign companies have set up in Hungary because the workforce is considered flexible, skilled, highly educated and, well, cheap. The average monthly salary in Hungary at the time of writing was 135,000Ft (about 81,000Ft net), with the new minimum wage set at 50,000Ft (35,000Ft to 40,000Ft net). The American Chamber of Commerce in Budapest figures that office operations in the Hungarian capital cost about one third less than in Western European cities.

Still, wages for some professions have risen sharply, as the government boosted salaries and pensions during an election year. Teachers and doctors, for instance, saw their pay hiked by 50% in 2002. Further increases at that rate are unlikely as the government seeks to keep inflation in check in order to stick to targets set for joining the EU.

POPULATION & PEOPLE

With just under two million inhabitants, Budapest is home to almost one fifth of the national population. Most are Magyars, an Asiatic people of obscure origins who do not speak an Indo-European language and make up the vast majority of Hungary's 10.2 million people.

No exact breakdown exists, but the ethnic make-up in the capital reflects the national one. Ethnic Magyars make up 97.7% of Hungary's population. Minorities include Roma (1.5% to 2.5% of the population), Germans (0.3%) and Slovaks, Croatians and Serbs and Romanians (0.1% each).

Life expectancy is very low by European standards: about 67 years for men and just over 76 for women. The nation also has one of Europe's lowest rates of natural population increase – 9.32 per 1000 population, with a population growth of -0.32%.

The population density of Budapest is 3380 people per sq km against a national average of 110 per sq km.

EDUCATION

Hungary is a well-educated society with a literacy rate of 98%. School is compulsory until the age of 16. About 63% of the population have attained secondary degrees.

The education system generally follows the German model. Nursery school (*óvoda*; ages from about three to six) is followed by primary or elementary school (*általános iskola*) to age 14. Secondary education lasts four years and can be either in grammar (*gimnázium*) or vocational (trade) schools (*szakközépiskola or szakiskola*). About 30% of those aged over 18 have secondary-school certificates. College and university matriculation is very competitive and decided by matriculation exams (*érettségi vizsgák*) at the age of 18. About 10% of the population holds university degrees, a quarter of which are in engineering and economics.

Most of Hungary's most prestigious universities are based in Budapest, including the Loránd Eötvös University of Science (ELTE), which was founded in 1635 and moved to Budapest in 1777 from what is now Trnava (Hungarian: Nagyszombat) in Slovakia; the 200-year-old Semmelweis University of Medicine (SOTE); the Budapest Technical & Economic Sciences University (BME) established in 1782; and the Budapest University of Economic Sciences (known

The Roma

The origins of the Gypsies (Hungarian: *cigány*), who call themselves the Roma (singular Rom) and speak Romany, a language closely related to several still spoken in northern India, remain a mystery. It is generally accepted, however, that they began migrating to Persia from India sometime in the 10th century and had reached the Balkans by the 14th century. They have been in Hungary for at least 500 years, and their numbers today are estimated at anywhere between 125,000 and a quarter of a million people.

Though traditionally a travelling people, in modern times the Roma have by and large settled down in Hungary and worked as smiths and tinkers, livestock and horse traders, and as musicians (see Music & Dance under Arts). As a group, however, they are chronically underemployed and have been the hardest hit by economic recession. Statistically, Roma families are twice the size of *gadje*, or 'non-Roma' ones.

Unsettled people have always been persecuted in one form or another by those who stay put, and Hungarian Roma are no exception. They are widely despised and are frequently the scapegoats for everything that goes wrong, from the rise in petty theft and prostitution to the loss of jobs. Though their rights are inscribed in the 1989 constitution along with other ethnic minorities, their housing ranks among the worst in the nation, police are regularly accused of harassing them and, more than any other group, they fear a revival of right-wing nationalism. You will probably be shocked at what even educated, cosmopolitan Hungarians say about Roma and their way of life.

as 'Közgáz'). Budapest-based and English-language Central European University (CEU), founded in 1991 by philanthropist George Soros, has gained an international reputation for itself in just over a decade.

Hungary has an international reputation in certain areas of specialised education. A unique method of music education with preliminary emphasis on voice instruction devised by composer Zoltán Kodály (1882–1967) is widespread. The Pető Institute in Budapest has a very high success rate in teaching children with cerebral palsy to walk.

SCIENCE

Hungary's contributions to the sciences and related fields have been far greater than its present size and population would suggest. Albert Szent-Györgyi (1893–1986) won the Nobel Prize for Medicine or Physiology in 1937 for his discovery of vitamin C, Georg von Békésy (1899–1972) the same prize in 1961 for his research on the inner ear and Eugene Paul Wigner (1902–95) received a Nobel Prize in 1963 for his research in nuclear physics. Both Edward Teller (1908–) and Leo Szilárd (1898–1964) worked on the so-called Manhattan Project, which led to the development of the atomic bomb, under Italian-American Nobel Prize–winning physicist Enrico Fermi (1901–54).

ARTS

The arts in Budapest have been both stunted and spurred on by the pivotal events in the nation's story. King Stephen's conversion to Catholicism brought Romanesque and Gothic art and architecture, while the Turkish occupation nipped most of Budapest's Renaissance in the bud. The Habsburgs opened the doors to baroque influences. The arts thrived under the Dual Monarchy, then through truncation and even under fascism. The early days of communism brought socialist-realist art celebrating wheat sheaves and muscle-bound steel-workers to a less-than-impressed populace, but much money was spent on music and 'correct art' such as classical theatre. All in all, it's not surprising that the works of writers and artists have tended to reflect the struggle against oppression.

While the artistic, cultural and literary hypertrophy of Budapest is indisputable, it would be foolish to ignore folk art when discussing urban (and urbane) fine arts here. The two have been inextricably linked for several centuries and have greatly influenced one another. The music of Béla Bartók and the ceramic sculptures of Margit Kovács are deeply rooted in traditional Hungarian culture. Even the architecture of the Secession (see the special section 'Fin-de-Siècle Architecture' in this chapter) incorporated many folk elements. The best place in Budapest to see this type of art is the Ethnography Museum on V Kossuth Lajos tér 12 (see the Things to See & Do chapter).

Music & Dance

Hungary has made many contributions to the music world, but one person stands head and shoulders above all: Franz – or Ferenc – Liszt. Liszt (1811–86), who established the Academy of Music in Budapest and lived in a four-room, 1st-floor apartment on VI Vörösmarty utca from 1881 until his death. Liszt liked to describe himself as 'part Gypsy', and some of his works, notably *Hungarian Rhapsodies*, echo traditional Roma music.

Ferenc Erkel (1810–93), who taught at the Academy of Music (1879–86) and was the State Opera House's first musical director, is the father of Hungarian opera. Two of his works – the stirringly nationalistic *Bánk Bán*, based on József Katona's play of that name, and *László Hunyadi* – are standards at the State Opera House. Erkel also composed the music for the Hungarian national anthem.

Béla Bartók (1881–1945) and Zoltán Kodály (1882–1967), both long-term residents of Budapest (their former residences are now museums – see the Things to See & Do chapter) made the first systematic study of Hungarian folk music, travelling and recording throughout the Magyar linguistic region in 1906. Both integrated some of their findings into their own compositions – Bartók in *Bluebeard's Castle*, for example, and Kodály in his *Peacock Variations*.

Rubik Cubes, Biros, Vitamin C & Zsa Zsa

It is not enough to be Hungarian – one must also have talent.
Slogan hanging in a Toronto employment office in the early 1960s

The contributions made by Hungarians in any number of fields – from films and toys to science and fine art – both at home and abroad have been enormous, especially when you consider the nation's size and relatively small population. The following is a list of people whom you may not have known were Hungarian or of Hungarian ancestry.

Biro, Leslie (Bíró László; 1899–1985) Inventor of the ballpoint pen (1938)

Brassaï (Halász Gyula; 1899–1984) French poet, draftsman, sculptor and photographer, known for his dramatic night-time photographs of Paris

Capa, Robert (Friedmann Endre; 1913–54) One of the greatest war photographers and photo-journalists of the 20th century

Cukor, George (Cukor György; 1899–1983) Legendary American film producer/director (eg, *The Philadelphia Story*, 1940)

Curtis, Tony (Bernard Schwartz; 1925–) Evergreen American actor (eg, *Spartacus*, 1960)

Eszterhas, Joe (1944–) American scriptwriter (eg, *Basic Instinct, Showgirls*)

Gabor, Eva (1921–95) American actress chiefly remembered for her starring role as a New York City socialite making her comical life on a farm in the 1960s TV series *Green Acres*; younger sister of Zsa Zsa

Gabor, Zsa Zsa (? –) Ageless-ish American starlet of grade BBB films and older sister of Eva

Houdini, Harry (Weisz Erich; 1874–1926) American magician and celebrated escape artist

Howard, Leslie (Steiner László; 1893–1943) Quintessential English actor most famous for his role in *Gone with the Wind* (1939)

Koestler, Arthur (1905–83) British novelist *(Darkness at Noon, The Gladiators)*

Lauder, Estée (1910?–) American fragrance and cosmetics baroness

Liszt, Franz (Liszt Ferenc; 1811–86) Piano virtuoso and composer

Lugosi, Béla (Blasko Béla; 1884–1956) The film world's only real Dracula – and Minister of Culture under the Béla Kun regime (see the History section)

Rubik, Ernő (1944–) Inventor of the hottest toy of the 1980 Christmas season – an infuriating plastic cube with 54 small squares that when twisted out of its original arrangement has 43 quintillion variations

Soros, George (Soros György; 1930–) Billionaire financier and philanthropist

Szent-Györgyi, Dr Albert (1893–1986) Nobel Prize-winning biochemist who discovered vitamin C

Vasarely, Victor (Vásárhelyi Győző; 1908–97) French painter of geometric abstractions and the 'Father of Op Art'

Wilder, Billy (Wilder Samuel; 1906–2002) American film director and producer (*Some Like It Hot*, 1959)

Away from classical music, it is important to distinguish between 'Gypsy music' and real Hungarian folk music. Gypsy music as it is known and heard in Hungarian restaurants from Budapest to Boston is urban schmaltz and based on recruiting tunes called *verbunkos* played during the Rákóczi independence wars. At least two fiddles, a bass and a cymbalom (a curious stringed instrument played with sticks) are *de rigueur*.

Hungarian folk musicians play violins, zithers, hurdy-gurdies, bagpipes and lutes on a five-tone diatonic scale. There are lots of different performers, but watch out especially for Muzsikás, the incomparable Marta Sebestyén and the group Ghymes, who play the doleful and haunting music of the Csángó, pockets of Hungarians living in eastern Transylvania and Moldavia.

To confuse matters even further, real Roma music does not use instruments but is sung as a cappella (though sometimes it is backed with percussion and even guitar). The best modern Roma group is Kalyi Jag (Black Fire) from northeastern Hungary, led by Gusztav Várga.

The *táncház* (literally 'dance house'; see Folk & Traditional Music in the Entertainment chapter) is an excellent place to hear Hungarian folk music and even to learn to dance.

There are two ballet companies based in Budapest though the best in the country is the Győr Ballet from Western Transdanubia. For modern dance, however, Budapest is *the* place (see Dance in the Entertainment chapter for details). There are several symphony orchestras based in the capital, including the National Philharmonic, the Budapest Festival Orchestra and the Hungarian Radio Orchestra.

Literature

Sándor Petőfi (1823–49), who led the Youth of March through the streets of Pest in 1848, is Hungary's most celebrated and accessible poet, and a line from his work *National Song* became the rallying cry for the 1848–49 War of Independence, in which Petőfi fought and died. A deeply philosophical play called *The Tragedy of Man* by his colleague, Imre Madách (1823–64), published a decade after Hungary's defeat in the War of Independence, is still considered to be the country's greatest classical drama. Madách did not participate in the war due to illness but was imprisoned in Pest for assisting Lajos Kossuth's secretary in 1852.

The defeat in 1849 led many writers to look to romanticism for inspiration and solace: heroes, winners and knights in shining armour. Petőfi's comrade-in-arms, János Arany (1817–82), whose name is synonymous with impeccable Hungarian and who edited two Pest literary journals in the 1860s, wrote epic poetry *(Toldi Trilogy)* and ballads.

Another friend of Petőfi, the prolific novelist Mór Jókai (1825–1904), who divided his time between his villa in XII Költő utca in Buda and his summer retreat at Balatonfüred on Lake Balaton, wrote of heroism and honesty in such wonderful works as *The Man with the Golden Touch* and *Black Diamonds*. This 'Hungarian Dickens' still enjoys widespread popularity. Another perennial favourite, Kálmán Mikszáth (1847–1910), wrote satirical tales like *St Peter's Umbrella* in which he poked fun at the declining gentry. Apparently the former US president Theodore Roosevelt enjoyed the latter work so much that he insisted on visiting the ageing novelist, by then an MP, in Budapest during a European tour in 1910.

Zsigmond Móricz (1879–1942), one of the co-founders of the influential literary magazine *Nyugat* (West; 1908) was a very different type of writer. His works, very much in the tradition of the French naturalist Émile Zola (1840–1902), examined the harsh reality of peasant life in late-19th-century Hungary. His contemporary, Mihály Babits (1883–1941), poet and the editor of *Nyugat*, made the rejuvenation of Hungarian literature his lifelong work.

Two other important names of this period are the poet and short-story writer Dezső Kosztolányi (1885-1936), who met his lifelong friend Babits at university in Pest, and the novelist Gyula Krúdy (1878–1933), who lived in Óbuda and liked the bone marrow on toast as served at the Kéhli restaurant (see the Places to Eat chapter) so much that he included a description of it in his *The Adventures of Sindbad*.

Two 20th-century poets are unsurpassed in Hungarian letters. Endre Ady (1877–1919), who is sometimes described as a successor to Petőfi, was a reformer who ruthlessly attacked the complacency and materialism of Hungary at that time, provoking a storm of protest from right-wing nationalists. He died in his flat on V Veres Pálné utca in Pest at age 42.

The work of the socialist poet Attila József (1905–1937), who was raised in the slums of Ferencváros, expressed the alienation felt by individuals in the modern age; *By the Danube* is brilliant even in English translation.

Among Hungary's most important contemporary writers are György Konrád (1933–), Péter Nádas (1942–), Péter Esterházy (1950–) and Imre Kertész (1930–). Konrád's *A Feast in the Garden* (1985) is an almost autobiographical account of the fate of the Jewish community in a small eastern Hungarian town. *A Book of Memoirs* by Nádas concerns the decline of communism in the style of Thomas Mann. In his *The End of a Family Story*, he uses a child narrator as a filter for the adult experience of 1950s communist Hungary. Esterházy's *Harmonia Cælestis* (2000) is a partly autobiographical novel that paints a favourable portrait of the protagonist's father. His recent *Revised Edition* (2002) is based on documents revealing his father to have been a government informer during the communist regime.

In 2002 novelist and Auschwitz survivor Kertész was awarded the Nobel Prize for Literature, the first time Hungary has gained that distinction. Of his seven novels, only two – *Fateless* (1975) and *Kaddish for a Child Not Born* (1997) – have been translated into English, though that will almost certainly change over the next few years.

Painting & Architecture

You won't find as much Romanesque and Gothic art and architecture in Budapest as you will in Prague – the Mongols, Turks and Habsburgs destroyed most of it – but the Royal Palace incorporates many Gothic features and the sedile (niches with seats) in the Castle District, most notably on I Úri utca and I Országház utca, are pure Gothic. The chapels in the Inner Town Parish Church have some fine Gothic and Renaissance tabernacles, and you can't miss the Renaissance stonework, the Gothic wooden sculptures and panel paintings and late-Gothic triptychs at the Hungarian National Gallery.

Baroque abounds in Budapest; you'll see architectural examples of it everywhere. The Church of St Anne on I Batthyány tér in Buda and the Óbuda Parish Church on III Flórián tér are fine examples of ecclesiastical baroque while the Citadella on Gellért hegy in Buda and the municipal council office on V Városház utca in Pest are baroque in its civic or secular form.

Distinctly Hungarian art and architecture didn't come into its own until the mid-19th century when Mihály Pollack, József Hild and Miklós Ybl began changing the face of Budapest. The romantic nationalist school of heroic paintings, best exemplified by Bertalan Székely (1835–1910), who painted much of the interior of Matthias Church, and Gyula Benczúr (1844–1920), gratefully gave way to the realism of Mihály Munkácsy (1844–1900), who was given a state funeral in Hősök tere. But the greatest painters from this period were Kosztka Tivadar Csontváry (1853–1919) and József Rippl-Rónai (1861–1927), both habitués of the Café Japán (see the boxed text 'My Café, My Castle' in the Places to Eat chapter), whose works are on display at the Hungarian National Gallery.

The 20th-century painter Victor Vasarely (1908–97), the so-called father of op art, has his own museum in Óbuda, as does the contemporary sculptor Imre Varga.

The romantic Eclectic and Secessionist styles of architects like Ödön Lechner (Museum of Applied Art, former Postal Savings Bank) and the Hungarian Art Nouveau of Aladár Arkay (Városligeti Calvinist Church) brought unique architecture to Hungary at the end of the 19th century and the start of the 20th (see the special section '*Fin-de-Siècle* Architecture' in this chapter).

Postwar architecture in Hungary is almost completely forgettable. One exception is the work of Imre Makovecz, who has developed his own 'organic' style (not always popular locally) using unusual materials like tree trunks and turf. His work can be found everywhere in provincial Hungary but it's not so common in Budapest. Two fine examples are the office building at VIII Szentkirályi utca 18 and the spectacular funerary chapel with its reverse vaulted ceiling at Farkasréti Cemetery in district XII.

Cinema

The scarcity of government grants has limited the production of quality Hungarian films in recent years, but a handful of good (and even great) ones still get produced every year. For classics, look out for anything by Oscar-winning István Szabó *(Sweet Emma, Dear Böbe, The Taste of Sunshine)*, Miklós Jancsó *(Outlaws)* and Péter Bacsó *(The Witness, Live Show)*.

Other favourites are *Simon Mágus*, the epic tale of two magicians and a young woman in Paris directed by Ildikó Enyedi and many of the films of comic director Péter Timár. Timár's *Csinibaba* is a satirical look at life – and film-production quality – during the communist regime. *Zimmer Feri*, set on Lake Balaton, pits a young practical joker against a bunch of loud German tourists; the typo in the title is deliberate. His *6:3* takes viewers back to 1953 to that glorious moment when Hungary defeated England in football by that score away at Wembley (see Spectator Sports in the Entertainment chapter). Gábor Herendi's *Valami Amerika* (Something America) is the comic tale of a filmmaking team trying to profit from an expatriate Hungarian who is pretending to be a rich producer.

SOCIETY & CONDUCT
Social Life

In general Hungarians – and people from Budapest in particular – are not uninhibited like the extroverted Romanians or sentimental Slavs who will laugh or cry at the drop of a hat (or a drink). They are reserved, somewhat formal people. Forget the impassioned, devil-may-care Gypsy-fiddling stereotype – it doesn't exist and probably never did. The national anthem calls Hungarians 'a people torn by fate' and the overall mood is one of *honfibú* (literally 'patriotic sorrow', but really a penchant for the blues with a sufficient amount of hope to keep most people going).

This mood certainly predates communism. To illustrate what she calls the 'dark streak in the Hungarian temperament', the late US foreign correspondent Flora Lewis recounts a story from the 1930s in *Europe: A Tapestry of Nations*. 'It was said,' she writes, 'that a song called *Gloomy Sunday* so deeply moved otherwise normal people (in Budapest) that whenever it was played, they would rush to commit suicide by jumping off a Danube bridge.' The song has been covered in English by several artists, including Billie Holiday and Sinéad O'Connor. Boy, is it a downer...

Hungarians are almost always extremely polite in social interaction, and the language can be very courtly – even when doing business with the butcher or having your hair cut. The standard greeting for a man to a woman (or youngsters to their elders, regardless of the sex) is *Csókolom* ('I kiss it' – 'it' being the hand, of course). People of all ages – even close friends – shake hands profusely when meeting up.

But while all this gentility certainly oils the wheels that turn a sometimes difficult society, it can be used to keep 'outsiders' (foreigners and other Hungarians) at a distance. Perhaps as an extension of this desire to keep everything running as smoothly as possible, Hungarians are always extremely helpful in an emergency – be it an accident, a pick-pocketing or simply helping someone who's lost their way.

Like Spaniards, Poles and many others with a Catholic background, Hungarians celebrate name days rather than birthdays. Name days are usually the Catholic feast day of their patron saint, but 'less holy' names have a date too. Most Hungarian calendars list them.

Drinking is an important part of social life in a country that has produced wine and fruit brandies for thousands of years. Consumption is high; only France and Germany drink more alcohol per capita. Alcoholism in Budapest is not as visible to the outsider as it is, say, in Warsaw, but it's there nonetheless; official figures suggest that as many as 900,000 people – almost 9% of the national population – are fully fledged alcoholics, but some experts say that between 40% and 50% of all males drink 'problematically'. Cirrhosis of the liver is the third most common cause of death here.

Hungarians let their hair – and most of their clothes – down in summer at lake and riverside resorts; going topless is almost the norm for women even in Budapest's parks. In warm weather you'll see more public displays of affection on the streets than perhaps anywhere else in the world. It's all very romantic, but beware: in the remoter corners of Budapest's parks and on Margaret Island you may stumble upon more passionate displays (which always seems to embarrass the stumbler more than the active participants).

Last Name First

Following a practice unknown outside Asia, Hungarians reverse their names in all uses, and their 'last' name (or surname) *always* comes first. For example, John Smith is never János Kovács to Hungarians but Kovács János, while Elizabeth Taylor is Szabó Erzsébet and Francis Flour is Liszt Ferenc.

Most titles also follow: Mr John Smith is Kovács János úr. Many women follow the practice of taking their husband's full name. If Elizabeth were married to John, she might be Kovács Jánosné (Mrs John Smith) or, increasingly popular among professional women, Kovácsné Szabó Erzsébet.

To avoid confusion, all Hungarian names in this guide are written in the usual Western manner – Christian name first – including the names of museums, theatres etc if they are translated into English. Budapest's Arany János színház is Hungarian; it's the János Arany Theatre in English. Addresses are always written in Hungarian as they appear on street signs: Kossuth Lajos utca, Rákóczi Ferenc tér etc.

Treatment of Animals

Hungarians as a whole are extremely fond of animals and Budapest has scores of *állatdíszhal bolt*, pet shops selling everything from puppies and hamsters to tropical fish. Budapesters are especially fond of dogs (you can't miss the mop-like *puli*, the sleek *vizsla* or the giant white *komondor* breeds indigenous to Hungary), and people of all ages go gaga over a particularly friendly or attractive one. I should know; I was at the other end of the lead for 2½ years with a pair of them.

RELIGION

Throughout history, religion here has often been a question of expediency. Under King Stephen I, Catholicism won the battle for dominance over Orthodoxy and, while the majority of Hungarians were quite happily Protestant by the end of the 16th century, many donned a new mantle during the Catholic Counter-Reformation under the Habsburgs. During the Turkish occupation in the 16th and 17th centuries, thousands of Hungarians converted to Islam – though not always willingly.

As a result, Hungarians tend to have a more pragmatic approach to religion than most of their neighbours, and little of the bigotry. It has even been suggested that this generally sceptical view of matters of faith has led to Hungarians' high rate of success in science and mathematics. You'll never see Christian churches in Budapest full, even on important holy days. On the other hand, the Jewish community in the capital has seen a great revitalisation in recent years.

Of those Hungarians declaring religious affiliation, about 68% say they are Roman Catholic, 21% Reformed (Calvinist) Protestant and nearly 6% Evangelical (Lutheran) Protestant. There are also small Greek Catholic (Uniate) and Orthodox congregations. Hungary's Jews number about 100,000, down from a prewar population of almost eight times that number. Some 400,000 died during deportation under the fascist Arrow Cross Party in 1944 or were murdered in Nazi concentration camps. Many others emigrated after the 1956 Uprising.

Budapest

Steve Fallon

LONELY PLANET PUBLICATIONS
Melbourne • Oakland • London • Paris

Budapest
2nd edition – August 2003
First published – August 2000

Published by
Lonely Planet Publications Pty Ltd ABN 36 005 607 983
90 Maribyrnong St, Footscray, Victoria 3011, Australia

Lonely Planet offices
Australia Locked Bag 1, Footscray, Victoria 3011
USA 150 Linden St, Oakland, CA 94607
UK 72-82 Rosebery Ave, London, EC1R 4RW
France 1 rue du Dahomey, 75011 Paris

Photographs
Many of the images in this guide are available for licensing from
Lonely Planet Images.
w www.lonelyplanetimages.com

Front cover photograph
The interior of the neo-Renaissance Hungarian State Opera House
(Stuart Wasserman)

ISBN 1 86450 356 4

text & maps © Lonely Planet Publications Pty Ltd 2003
photos © photographers as indicated 2003

Printed through Colorcraft Ltd, Hong Kong
Printed in China

JONATHAN SMITH

JONATHAN SMITH

MARTIN MOOS

DAVID GREEDY

DAVID GREEDY

Title Page: Roof of the Geology Instititute (Photograph by David Greedy)

Top: The Elephant House at the City Zoo

Centre Left: A typical Secessionist wall decoration

Centre Right: Stained-glass skylight at the Applied Arts Museum

Bottom Left: The gates of the Geology Institute

Bottom Right: Art Nouveau lamp on display in the Applied Arts Museum

FIN-DE-SIÈCLE ARCHITECTURE

Art Nouveau architecture and its Viennese variant, Secessionism, abound in Budapest, and examples can be seen throughout the city. Its sinuous curves, flowing, asymmetrical forms, and colourful Zsolnay tiles and other decorative elements stand out like beacons in a sea of refined and elegant baroque and mannered, geometric neoclassical buildings. It is not uncommon to hear visitors to the city gasp in surprise as they round a corner and spot yet another splendid example.

Some people (myself included) go out of their way for another glimpse of such 'hidden' favourites near City Park as the **Geology Institute** *(Map 3; XIV Stefánia út 14)* designed by Ödön Lechner in 1899 and Sándor Baumgarten's **National Institute for the Blind** *(Map 3; XIV Ajtósi Dürer sor 39)* dating from 1904 or the **Philanthia** *(Map 6; V Váci utca 9)*, a flower shop with an exquisite Art Nouveau interior (Kálmán Albert Körössy, 1906) in the Inner Town. It is almost as if we are afraid that these delightful structures – built at a time when all was right with the world in affluent, cosmopolitan Budapest – will wither and disappear unless they are regularly drenched in admiring glances.

Art Nouveau was both an architectural style and an art form that flourished in Europe and the USA from about 1890 to 1910. It began in Britain as the Arts and Crafts Movement founded by William Morris (1834–96), which stressed the importance of manual processes over machines and attempted to create a new organic style in direct opposition to the imitative banalities spawned by the Industrial Revolution. It soon spread to Europe, where it took on distinctly local and/or national characteristics. In France it became known as Art Nouveau or Style 1900, in Germany as Jugendstil and in Italy as Stile Liberty.

In Vienna a group of artists called the Secessionists lent its name to the more geometric local style of Art Nouveau architecture: Sezessionstil (Hungarian: szecesszió). In Budapest, the use of traditional facades with allegorical and historical figures and scenes, folk motifs and Zsolnay ceramics and other local materials led to an eclectic style. Though working within an Art Nouveau/Secessionist framework, this style emerged as something that was uniquely Hungarian.

Fashion and styles changed as whimsically and rapidly at the start of the 20th century as they do a century later, and by the end of the first decade Art Nouveau and its variations were considered limited, passé, even tacky. Fortunately for the good citizens of Budapest and us, the economic and political torpor of the prewar period and the 40-year 'big sleep' after WWII left many Art Nouveau/Secessionist buildings here beaten but standing – many more, in fact, than remain in such important Art Nouveau/Jugendstil centres as Paris, Brussels and Vienna. Some have got (or are getting) face-lifts and are being used for different purposes, including the gem-like **Gresham Palace**

Inset: Geological elements engraved into glass panels inside the Geology Institute (Photograph by David Greedy)

(Map 6; V Roosevelt tér 5-6), designed by Zsigmond Quittner (1907) and recently converted into the five-star Four Seasons Hotel.

The first Hungarian architect to look to Art Nouveau for inspiration was Frigyes Spiegel, and his exotic and symbolic ornamentation (birds, shells, flowers, fish etc) can still be seen on the **Lindenbaum apartment houses** *(Map 5; VI Izabella utca 94),* though just barely. For a better idea of how the principles of the new style were applied with a distinctly Magyar twist (sometimes called Magyaros style), have a look at some of the large civic buildings designed by the master of this style, Ödön Lechner (1845–1914).

The most ambitious of Lechner's works in the capital is undoubtedly the **Applied Arts Museum** *(Map 3; IX Üllői út 33-37).* Purpose-built as a museum and completed in time for the millenary exhibition in 1896, it was faced and roofed in a variety of Zsolnay ceramic tiles, and its turrets, domes and ornamental figures lend it an 'Eastern' or 'Indian' feel. However his crowning glory is the sumptuous former **Postal Savings Bank** *(Map 5; V Hold utca 4),* a Secessionist extravaganza of floral mosaics, folk motifs and ceramic figures just off Szabadság tér in Lipótváros and dating from 1901. The bull's head atop the central tower symbolises the nomadic past of the Magyars while the ceramic bees scurrying up the semi-pillars towards their hives represent organisation, industry and economy.

The **Liszt Academy of Music** *(Map 5; VI Liszt Ferenc tér 8),* designed by Kálmán Giergl and Flóris Korb in 1907, is not so interesting for its exterior as for its decorative elements within. There's a dazzling Art Nouveau mosaic called *Art Is the Source of Life* by Aladár Kőrösfői Kriesch, a leader of the seminal Gödöllő Artists' Colony, and some fine stained glass by master craftsman Miksa Róth. Also note the grid of laurel leaves below the ceiling, which mimics the ironwork dome of the Secession Building (1897–1908) in Vienna, and the large sapphire-blue Zsolnay ball finials on the stair balusters.

Other buildings worth a detour are the former **Török Bank House** *(Map 6; V Szervita tér 3),* designed by Henrik Böhm and Ármin Hegedűs in 1906 and sporting a wonderful Secessionist mosaic by Róth in the upper gable called *Patrona Hungariae* and depicting Hungary surrounded by great Hungarians of the past; Ármin Hegedűs' **primary school** *(Map 5; VII Dob utca 85),* with its mosaics depicting contemporary children's games built in the same year; and the **Calvinist church** *(Map 3; VII Városligeti fasor 7),* a stunning example of late Art Nouveau architecture by Aladár Arkay (1913) with carved wooden gates, stained glass and ceramic tiles on the facade. **Bedő House** *(Map 5; V Honvéd utca 3),* an apartment block by Emil Vidor and completed in 1903, is one of the most intact Art Nouveau structures in the city. It contains some lovely interior features and the exterior (ironwork gate, majolica flowers) has been renovated.

The Art Nouveau/Secessionist style was hardly restricted to public buildings in Budapest, and the affluent districts to the west of City Park are happy hunting grounds for some of the best examples of private residences built in this style. Many of these structures were funded by wealthy industrialists and merchants who demanded that the architects include a personal statement beyond just the pattern in vogue at the time. The cream-coloured **Egger Villa** *(Map 3; VII Városligeti fasor 24)*, designed by Emil Vidor in 1902, is among the purest – and most extravagant – examples of Art Nouveau in the city. Across the road the green **Vidor Villa** *(Map 3; VII Városligeti fasor 33)* with the curious turret was designed by Vidor for his father in 1905 and incorporates any number of European styles in vogue at the time, including French Art Nouveau and Japanese-style motifs. It is now a college. Other interesting buildings in this area are **Lédere Mansion** *(Map 5; VI Bajza utca 42)*, a block with lovely stained glass and grillwork built by Zoltán Bálint and Lajos Jámbor in 1902, and **Sonnenberg Mansion** *(Map 3; VI Munkácsy Mihály utca 23)* designed by Albert Körössy and completed the following year.

One of the joys of exploring the 'Queen of the Danube' is that you'll find elements of Art Nouveau and Secessionism in the oddest places, not just in grandiose public buildings or ostentatious residences; keep your eyes open and you'll spot bits and pieces everywhere. The **City Zoo's main entrance** *(XIV Állatkerti út 6-12)* and the **Elephant House**, designed by Kornél Neuschloss-Knüsli et al in 1912 and festooned with ceramic animal heads, are extravagant examples influenced by the Moorish architecture in vogue in Europe at the time. The **Gellért Hotel** *(Map 7; XI Szent Gellért tér 1)*, designed by Ármin Hegedűs in 1909 and completed in 1918, contains examples of late Art Nouveau, notably the thermal spa with its enormous arched glass entrance hall and Zsolnay ceramic fountains in the bathing pools. And embellishment in the new style was not just reserved for the living. The **Schmidl family tomb** designed by Béla Lajta in 1903 in the Jewish section of the **New Municipal Cemetery** *(Új köztemető; Map 1; X Kozma utca)*

Right: The National Institute for the Blind

JONATHAN SMITH

Facts for the Visitor

WHEN TO GO

Every season has its attractions – and its limitations – in Budapest. Though it can be pretty wet April and May, spring is just glorious here. The summer is warm, sunny and unusually long but, as elsewhere in Europe, Budapest comes to a grinding halt in August, which Hungarians traditionally call 'the cucumber-growing season' because that's about the only thing happening.

Nowadays, though, lots more festivals, including the mammoth Pepsi Sziget Music Festival (see Special Events), are being scheduled during that month.

Autumn is beautiful, particularly in the Buda Hills. Winter can be wonderful, with bright blue skies, a light dusting of snow on church spires, ice floes in the Danube and ice skating in City Park. But it can also be cold and bleak, with museums and other tourist sights closed or their hours sharply curtailed.

For more information, see Climate in the Facts about Budapest chapter.

ORIENTATION

Budapest is a large, sprawling city but, with few exceptions (the Buda Hills, City Park and some excursions), the areas beyond the Nagykörút (literally the 'big ring road') in Pest and west of Moszkva tér in Buda are residential or industrial and of little interest to visitors. It is a well laid-out city, so much so that it is almost difficult to get lost here.

If you look at a map of the city you'll see that two ring roads – Nagykörút (the big one) and the semicircular Kiskörút (the 'little ring road') – link three of the bridges across the Danube and essentially define central Pest. The Nagykörút consists of the contiguous Szent István körút, Teréz körút, Erzsébet körút, József körút and Ferenc körút. The Kiskörút comprises Károly körút, Múzeum körút and Vámház körút. Important boulevards such as Bajcsy-Zsilinszky út, leafy Andrássy út, Rákóczi út and Üllői út fan out from these ring roads, creating large squares and circles.

Buda is dominated by Castle and Gellért Hills; the main square is Moszkva tér. Important roads on this side are Margit körút (the only part of either ring road to cross the river), Fő utca and Attila út on either side of Castle Hill, and Hegyalja út and Bartók Béla út running west and southwest.

Budapest is divided into 23 kerület, or districts, which usually also have traditional names such as Lipótváros (Leopold Town) in district XIII or Víziváros (Watertown) in district I. The Roman numeral appearing before each street address signifies the district.

Many visitors will arrive at one of the three train stations: Keleti (Eastern) and Nyugati (Western) in Pest and Déli (Southern) in Buda; see Train in the Getting There & Away chapter for details. All three stations are on one of the three metro lines, which converge at Deák Ferenc tér, a busy square a few minutes' walk northeast of the Inner Town (Belváros).

MAPS

Lonely Planet's Budapest City Map covers the more popular parts of town in detail.

The best folding maps of the city are Cartographia's Budapest 1:20,000 (550Ft) and 1:28,000 (450Ft) . If you plan to explore the city thoroughly, the Budapest Atlas, also from Cartographia, is indispensable. It comes in two scales: 1:25,000 (1900Ft) and the larger format 1:20,000 (2900Ft). There is also a 1:25,000 pocket atlas of just the Inner Town available for 900Ft.

Many bookshops, including **Libri Könyv-palota** (Map 5; ☎ 267 4844; VII Rákóczi út 12; metro M2 Astoria; open 10am-7.30pm Mon-Fri, 10am-3pm Sat), stock a wide variety of maps. **Cartographia** (Map 5; ☎ 312 6001; VI Bajcsy-Zsilinszky út 37; metro M3 Arany János utca; open 9am-5pm Mon-Wed, 9am-6.30pm Thur, 9am-3.30pm Fri) has its own outlet in Budapest, but it's not self-service, which can be annoying. Better bets include **Térképkirály** (Map King; Map 6;

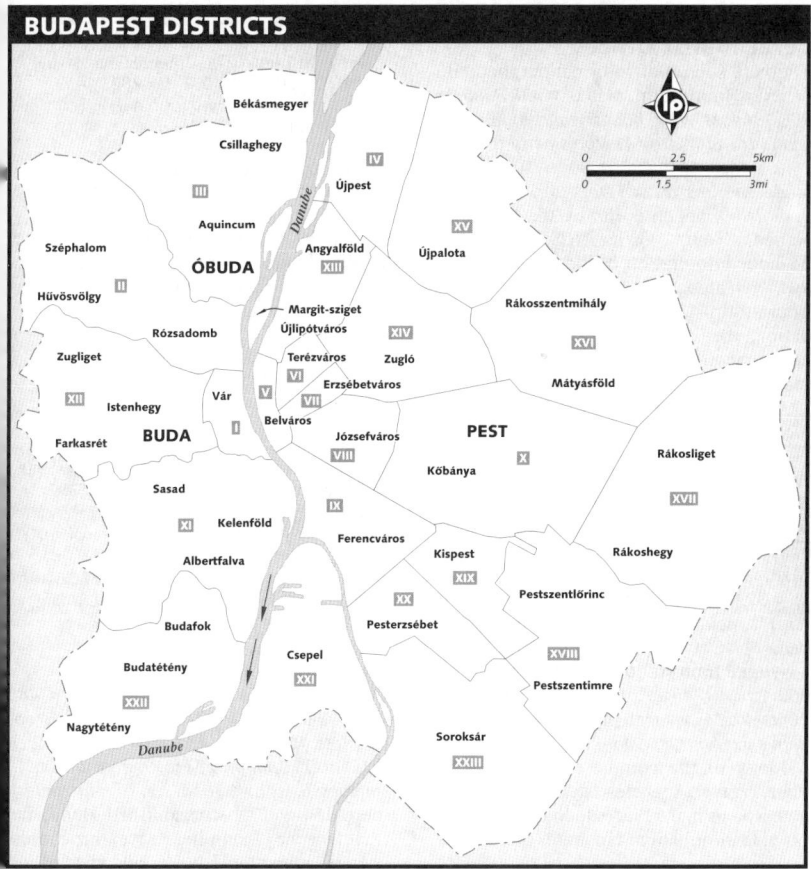

BUDAPEST DISTRICTS

Békásmegyer

Csillaghegy

IV

Újpest

III

Aquincum

Danube

XV

Széphalom

Angyalföld

XIII

Újpalota

ÓBUDA

Hüvösvölgy

II

Margit-sziget

Rákosszentmihály

Újlipótváros

Rózsadomb

XIV

XVI

Zugliget

Terézváros

Zugló

VI

Mátyásföld

Vár

V

Erzsébetváros

XII

Istenhegy

VII

Belváros

I

Farkasrét

BUDA

Józsefváros

PEST

Rákosliget

VIII

Kőbánya

X

Sasad

Rákoshegy

XI

Kelenföld

IX

XVII

Albertfalva

Ferencváros

Kispest

Rákoshegy

XIX

Pestszentlőrinc

XX

Budafok

Pesterzsébet

XVIII

Budatétény

Csepel

Pestszentimre

XXI

XXII

Nagytétény

Danube

Soroksár

XXIII

☎ 266 0561; V Sas utca 1; metro M1/2/3 Deák Ferenc tér; open 10am-5pm Mon-Fri) and the small **Párisi Udvari Könyvesbolt** (Párisi Udvar Bookshop; Map 6; ☎ 235 0379; V Petőfi Sándor utca 2; metro M3 Ferenciek tere; open 9am-7pm Mon-Fri, 10am-2pm Sat) in the Párisi Udvar.

RESPONSIBLE TOURISM

Budapest already has enough cars clogging its avenues and side streets. Not only does the ensuing air pollution damage people's health, it also ruins historic buildings and monuments – sometimes irrevocably. Do us

all a favour: leave your car behind and resist the temptation to rent one unless you're touring farther afield into the countryside (see the Excursions chapter). Instead, bring or rent a bike (see Cycling under Activities in the Things to See & Do chapter), enjoy the city on foot (Budapest is an eminently walkable city) and/or use the public transport system – it's safe, extremely efficient and very cheap.

For further tips on how you can reduce your impact on the environment, contact the **Friends of Nature Bicycle Touring Association** (TTE; ☎ 316 5867; II Bem rakpart 51).

TOURIST OFFICES
Local Tourist Offices

The best source of information about Budapest is **Tourinform** *(Map 6; ☎ 438 8080, fax 356 1964;* **w** *www.hungarytourism.hu; V Vigadó utca 6; metro M1 Vörösmarty tér; open 24hr • Map 6;* ☎ *438 8080; V Sütő utca 2; metro M1/2/3 Deák Ferenc tér; open 8am-8pm daily)*, which is run by the Hungarian National Tourist Office (HNTO). It has a **24-hour information hotline** *(☎ 06-80 660 044, from abroad ☎ 36-60 55 00 44)*. Though Tourinform staff can't book you accommodation, they'll send you somewhere that does and will help with anything else – from maps to where to find vegetarian food.

Another option for tourist information is the **Budapest Tourist Office** *(BTO; fax 266 7477;* **w** *www.budapestinfo.hu)*, with a **Castle Hill branch** *(Map 4;* ☎ *488 0453, fax 488 0474; I Szentháromság tér; bus No 16 or Várbusz; open 8am-8pm daily Apr-Oct, 9am-6pm daily Nov-Mar)* in a kiosk opposite Saint Matthias Church; a **central Pest branch** *(Map 5;* ☎ *322 4098, fax 342 9390; VI Liszt Ferenc tér 11; metro M1 Oktogon; open 8am-8pm daily Apr-Oct, 9am-6pm daily Nov-Mar)* and a **Nyugati train station branch** *(Map 5;* ☎/fax *302 8580; Nyugati pályaudvar, platform No 10; metro M3 Nyugati pályaudvar; open 8am-8pm daily Apr-Oct, 9am-6pm daily Nov-Mar)*.

Many of the commercial outfits listed under Travel Agencies later and under Private Rooms in the Places to Stay chapter also provide information, brochures and maps.

Tourist Offices Abroad

The HNTO has offices in some 19 countries, including the following:

Austria *(*☎ *01-585 20 1213, fax 585 20 1214,* **e** *htvienna@hungarytourism.hu) Opernring 5/2, A-1010 Vienna*
Czech Republic *(*☎ *02-2109 0135, fax 2109 0139,* **e** *htpragaue@hungarytourism.hu) Rumunská 22, 22537 Prague 2*
France *(*☎ *01 53 70 67 17, fax 01 47 04 83 57,* **e** *htparis@hungarytourism.hu) 140 ave Victor Hugo, 75116 Paris*
Germany *(*☎ *030-243 146 0, fax 243 146 13,* **e** *htberlin@hungarytourism.hu) Karl Liebknecht Strasse 34, D-10178 Berlin*

Netherlands *(*☎ *070-320 9092, fax 327 2833,* **e** *htdenhaga@hungarytourism.hu) Laan van Nieuw Oost Indië 271, 2593 BS The Hague*
UK *(*☎/fax *020-7823 1032, fax 7823 1459,* **e** *htlondon@hungarytourism.hu) 46 Eaton Place, London SW1X 8AL*
USA *(*☎ *212-355 0240, fax 207 4103,* **e** *htnewyork@hungarytourism.hu) 33rd floor, 150 East 58th St, New York, NY 10155-3398*

In countries without an HNTO office, contact Malév Hungarian Airlines, which has offices or associated agencies in some 40 countries worldwide, including the following:

Australia *(*☎ *02-9244 2111, fax 9290 3306;* **e** *wassyd@worldaviation.com.au) World Aviation Systems, 403 George St, Sydney, NSW 2000*
Canada *(*☎ *416-944 0093, fax 944 0095;* **e** *toronto@malev.hu) 175 Bloor St East, Suite 909 South Tower, Toronto, ON M4W 3R8*
Ireland *(*☎ *1-844 4303, fax 278 8142;* **e** *dublin@malev.hu) Pace International, 101/3 Collinstown House, Dublin Airport*
New Zealand *(*☎ *09-379 4455, fax 377 5648) World Aviation Systems, Trustbank Building, 6/F, 229 Queen St, Auckland 1*

TRAVEL AGENCIES

The main office of **Ibusz** *(Map 6;* ☎ *485 2723, 485 2767;* **w** *www.ibusz.hu; V Ferenciek tere 10; metro M3 Ferenciek tere; open 8.15am-5.30pm Mon-Fri, 9am-1pm Sat in summer; 8.15am-4.30pm Mon-Fri in winter)*, the oldest and most established Hungarian travel agency, supplies travel brochures, changes money and books all types of accommodation. The nearby **Ibusz branch** *(Map 6;* ☎ *322 7214; VII Dob utca 1; metro M2 Astoria)* is good for booking train tickets.

Express *(Map 6;* ☎ *317 8600;* **e** *express@axelero.hu; V Semmelweis utca 1-3; metro M2 Astoria; open 8am-6pm Mon-Fri, 9am-1pm Sat)*, traditionally for students and young travellers, can organise budget accommodation in Budapest, particularly at hostels and colleges, while the **Express branch** *(Map 5,* ☎ *311 6418; V Zoltán utca 10; metro M2 Kossuth Lajos tér; open 8.30am-4.30pm Mon-Thur, 8.30am-4pm Fri)* books international and domestic trains and Eurolines buses, and sells cheap airline tickets.

An excellent one-stop shop for all your outbound needs (air tickets, package tours etc) is the massive **Vista Travel Center** *(Map 6; ☎ 429 9999, 429 9760; ⓦ www.vista.hu; VI Andrássy út 1; metro M1 Bajcsy-Zsilinszky út; open 9am-6.30pm Mon-Fri, 9am-2.30pm Sat)*. The **Vista Visitor Center** *(Map 6; ☎ 429 9950; VI Paulay Ede utca; metro M1 Bajcsy-Zsilinszky út; open 9am-8pm Mon-Fri, 10am-6pm Sat)* handles all the incoming stuff – tourist information, study and ecological tours in Hungary, room bookings, organised tours etc. There's a popular café and Internet centre here too.

The **Wasteels agency** *(Map 3; ☎ 210 2802, 343 3492; VIII Kerepesi út 2-6; metro M2 Keleti pályaudvar; open 8am-7pm Mon-Fri, 8am-1pm Sat)* at the top of platform No 9 in Keleti train station sells BIJ (Billet International de Jeunesse; youth train fare for those under 26) tickets. You must have an ISIC or IYTC card (see Documents later), available at Express or Vista for 1100Ft, in order to get the discounted fare.

Another helpful agency is **Cooptourist** *(Map 5; ☎ 312 1017, 332 6387; Kossuth Lajos tér 13-15; metro M2 Kossuth Lajos tér; open 8am-4pm Mon & Tues, Thur & Fri, 8am-5pm Wed)*, with a **Buda branch** *(Map 7; ☎ 466 5349, 209 6667; XI Bartók Béla út 4; tram No 47 or 49; open 9am-5pm Mon-Sat)*.

DOCUMENTS
Passport
Everyone needs a valid passport or, for citizens of 11 European countries (Austria, Belgium, Croatia, France, Germany, Italy, Liechtenstein, Luxembourg, Slovenia, Spain and Switzerland), a national identification card, to enter Hungary. It's a good idea (though not a requirement) to carry your passport or other identification at all times.

Visas
Citizens of virtually all European countries, the USA, Canada, Israel, Japan and New Zealand do not require visas to visit Hungary for stays of up to 90 days. UK citizens do not need a visa for a stay of up to six months. Nationals of Australia, and at the moment South Africa, still require visas.

Check current visa requirements at a consulate, any HNTO or Malév office or on the website of the **Foreign Affairs Ministry** *(ⓦ www.kum.hu, www.mfa.gov.hu)* as requirements often change without notice.

Visas are issued at Hungarian consulates or missions, most international highway border crossings (see the boxed text 'Major Border Crossings' in the Getting There & Away chapter), Ferihegy airport and the International Ferry Pier in Budapest. They are rarely issued on international buses and *never* on trains. Be sure to retain the separate entry and exit forms issued with the visa that is stamped in your passport.

Single-entry tourist visas are issued at Hungarian consulates or missions in the applicant's country of residence upon receipt of US$40 (or equivalent) and three photos; it costs US$65 at a mission outside the country of residence or at the border. A double-entry tourist visa costs US$75/100, and you must have five photos. A multiple-entry visa is US$180/200. Express service (visa issued on the spot as opposed to overnight) costs US$15 extra. Single- and double-entry visas are valid for six months prior to use. Multiple entries are good for a year.

Be sure to get a tourist visa rather than a transit visa; the latter – available for both single (US$38/50), double (US$65/90) and multiple (US$150/180) entries – is only good for a stay of 48 hours. You must enter and leave through different border crossings and already hold a visa (if required) for the next country you visit.

Tourist visas can only be extended in emergencies (eg, medical ones; 3000Ft) and must be extended at the central police station *(rendőrkapitányság)* of any city or town 15 days before the original one expires. It's no longer an option to go to a neighbouring country such as Austria or Slovakia and then re-enter. As of January 2002, tourist visas now allow visitors to stay for 90 days within a six-month period only.

You are supposed to register with the local police if staying in one place for more than 30 days, and your hotel, hostel, camp site or private room booked through an agency will do this for you. In other situations – if you're staying with friends or relatives, for example – you or the head of household has to take care of this within 72 hours. Don't worry if you haven't got round to it; it's a hangover from the old regime, and enforcement is pretty lax. Address registration forms for foreigners (*lakcímbejelentő lap külföldiek részére*) are available at main post offices.

Travel Insurance

A travel insurance policy to cover theft, loss and medical problems is a good idea. Some policies offer lower and higher medical-expense options; the higher ones are chiefly for countries such as the USA, which have extremely high medical costs. There is a wide variety of policies available, so check the small print.

Some policies specifically exclude 'dangerous activities', which can include scuba diving, motorcycling and even trekking. A locally acquired motorcycle licence is not valid under some policies.

You may prefer a policy which pays doctors or hospitals directly rather than you having to pay on the spot and claim later. If you have to claim later, make sure you keep all documentation. Some policies ask you to call back (reverse charges) to a centre in your home country, where an immediate assessment of your problem is made.

Check that the policy covers ambulances or an emergency flight home.

Driving Licence & Permits

If you don't hold a European driving licence and plan to drive in Budapest, obtain an International Driving Permit (IDP) from your local automobile association before you leave – you'll need a passport photo and a valid local licence. It is usually inexpensive and valid for one year only. Remember: An IDP is not valid unless accompanied by your original driver's licence.

Hostel Cards

A hostel card is not particularly useful in Budapest as no hostel here requires you to be a Hostelling International (or associated) member. Having said that, a hostel card will sometimes get you a 10% discount on quoted rates. Express (see Travel Agencies earlier) issues Hungarian Youth Hostel Association cards to Hungarian citizens and residents for 1600Ft, which includes a 400Ft Matáv Barangoló (Roaming) phonecard.

Student, Youth & Teacher Cards

The International Student Identity Card (ISIC; w www.isic.org), a plastic ID-style card with a photo, provides bona fide student discounts on some forms of transport and cheap admission to museums and other sights. If you're aged under 26 but not a student, you can apply for an International Youth Travel Card (IYTC) issued by the Federation of International Youth Travel Organisations (FIYTO), which gives the same discounts as the ISIC. Teachers can apply for the International Teacher Identity Card (ITIC). Express sells all these cards for 1100Ft each.

Seniors Cards

Many attractions offer reduced-price admission for people over 60 or 65 (sometimes as low as 55 for women), but this is usually just for Hungarian *nyugdíjasok* (pensioners) holding national ID cards. Indeed, Hungarian citizens over 65 travel for free on MÁV trains.

Discount Cards

The **Budapest Card** (☎ 266 0479; w www .budapestinfo.hu) offers free admission to most museums and galleries in town and unlimited travel on all forms of public transport. It also gives discounts on organised tours, at thermal baths and at selected shops and restaurants. A card valid for 48/72 hours costs 3700/4500Ft. The card is sold at Tourinform offices and travel agencies, hotels, and train, bus and main metro stations.

Those planning on doing extensive travelling elsewhere in the country might consider the **Hungary Card** (☎ 266 3741; w www .hungarycard.hu), which gives free admission to many museums nationwide, 50% discount on all railway return fares and some bus and boat travel, as well as other museums and attractions, up to 25% off selected accommodation and 20% off the price of the Budapest Card. The card is valid for 13 months and costs 6888Ft.

Copies

All important documents (passport data and visa pages, credit cards, travel insurance policy, air/bus/train tickets, driving licence etc) should be photocopied before you leave home. Leave one copy behind with someone and keep another with you, separate from the originals.

There is another option for storing details of your vital travel documents before you leave – ekno's online Travel Vault. Storing details of your important documents in the vault is safer than carrying photocopies. It's the best option if you travel in a city like Budapest where Internet access is so easily available; your password-protected travel vault is accessible online at any time. You can create your own travel vault free of charge at **w** www.ekno.lonelyplanet.com.

EMBASSIES & CONSULATES
Hungarian Embassies & Consulates

Almost all of the Hungarian missions listed below have information posted on the Web at **w** www.kum.hu and **w** www.mfa.gov.hu.

Australia (☎ 02-6282 2555) 17 Beale Crescent, Deakin, ACT 2600
Consulate in Sydney: (☎ 02-9328 7859) Suite 405, Edgecliff Centre, 203–233 New South Head Rd, Edgecliff, NSW 2027
Austria (☎ 01-537 80300) Bankgasse 4–6, 1010 Vienna
Canada (☎ 613-230 9614) 299 Waverley St, Ottawa, ON K2P 0V9
Consulate in Toronto: (☎ 416-923 8981) Suite 1115, 121 Bloor St East, Toronto, ON M4W 3M5
Croatia (☎ 01-489 0900) Krlezin gvozd 11/a, 10000 Zagreb
Germany (☎ 030-203 100) Unter den Linden 76, 10117 Berlin
Consulate in Munich: (☎ 089-911 032) Vollmannstrasse 2, 81927 Munich
Ireland (☎ 01-661 2902) 2 Fitzwilliam Place, Dublin 2
Romania (☎ 01-311 0062) Strada Jean-Louis Calderon 63–65, Bucharest 70202

Serbia and Montenegro (☎ 011-444 0472) ul Ivana Milutinovica 74, Belgrade 11000
Slovakia (☎ 02-544 30541) ul Sedlárska 3, 81425 Bratislava
Slovenia (☎ 01-512 1882) Konrada Babnika ulica 5, 1210 Ljubljana-Sentvid
South Africa (☎ 012-430 3030) 959 Arcadia St, Hatfield, 0083 Pretoria
UK (☎ 020-7235 5218) 35 Eaton Place, London SW1X 8BY
Consulate in London: (☎ 020-7235 2664) 35/b Eaton Place, London SW1X 8BY
Ukraine (☎ 044-212 4134) ul Rejtarskaja 33, Kiev 01034
USA (☎ 202-362 6730) 3910 Shoemaker St NW, Washington, DC 20008
Consulate in Los Angeles: (☎ 310-473 9344) Suite 410, 11766 Wilshire Blvd, Los Angeles, CA 90025
Consulate in New York: (☎ 212-752 0661) 223 East 52nd St, New York, NY 10022

Embassies & Consulates in Budapest

Selected countries with representation in Budapest include those below – the hours indicate when consular or chancellery services are available:

Australia (Map 3; ☎ 457 9777) XII Királyhágó tér 8–9. Open 9am to noon Monday to Friday
Austria (Map 3; ☎ 352 9613) VI Benczúr utca 16. Open 9am to 11am Monday to Friday
Canada (Map 1; ☎ 392 3360) XII Budakeszi út 32. Open 8.30am to 11am and 2pm to 3.30pm Monday to Thursday
Croatia (Map 3; ☎ 354 1315) VI Munkácsy Mihály utca 15. Open 1pm to 3pm Monday, Tuesday, Thursday and Friday
Germany (Map 4; ☎ 488 3500) I Úri utca 64–66. Open 9am to noon Monday to Friday
Ireland (Map 5; ☎ 302 9600) V Szabadság tér 7–9. Open 9.30am to 12.30pm and 2.30pm to 4.30pm Monday to Friday
Romania (Map 3; ☎ 352 0271) XIV Thököly út 72. Open 8.30am to noon Monday to Friday
Serbia and Montenegro (Map 3; ☎ 322 9838) VI Dózsa György út 92/b. Open 9am to 1pm Monday to Friday
Slovakia (Map 3; ☎ 460 9010) XIV Stefánia út 22–24. Open 8am to noon Monday to Friday
Slovenia (Map 1; ☎ 438 5600) II Cseppkő utca 68. Open 9am to noon Monday to Friday
South Africa (Map 1; ☎ 392 0999) II Gárdonyi Géza út 17. Open 9am to 12.30pm Monday to Fri

FACTS FOR THE VISITOR

UK (Map 6; ☎ 266 2888) V Harmincad utca 6.
Open 9.30am to 12.30pm and 2.30pm to
4.30pm Monday to Friday

Ukraine (Map 1; ☎ 355 2443) XII Nógrádi utca
8. Open 9am to 12pm Monday to Wednesday
and Friday by appointment only

USA (Map 5; ☎ 475 4400) V Szabadság tér 12.
Open 1pm to 4.30pm Monday to Friday

CUSTOMS

You can bring the usual personal effects with
you as well as 200 cigarettes, 1L of wine or
champagne and 1L of spirits.

When leaving Budapest, you are not supposed to take out valuable antiques without a
special permit (see the boxed text 'Permission Granted' in the Shopping chapter). You
must declare the import/export of any amount
of cash exceeding the sum of 1,000,000Ft.

MONEY
Currency

The Hungarian forint (Ft) was once divided
into 100 fillér, worthless little aluminium
coins that have now been withdrawn from
circulation. (*Filléres* actually means 'cheap'
or 'inexpensive' in Hungarian.) There are
coins of one, two, five, 10, 20, 50 and 100Ft.
Notes come in seven denominations: 200,
500, 1000, 2000, 5000, 10,000 and 20,000Ft.

The green 200Ft features the 14th-
century King Charles Robert and his castle
at Diósgyőr near Miskolc. Ferenc Rákóczi
II, the hero of the independence wars, and
Sárospatak Castle are on the burgundy-
coloured 500Ft note.

The 1000Ft note is blue and bears a portrait of King Matthias Corvinus, with Hercules Well at Visegrád Castle on the verso.
The 17th-century prince of Transylvania,
Gábor Bethlen, is on his own on one side of
the 2000Ft bill and meeting with advisers
on the other.

The 'greatest Hungarian', Count István
Széchenyi, and his family home at
Nagycenk are on the purple 5000Ft note.
The 10,000Ft bears a likeness of King
Stephen, with an Esztergom scene appear-
ing on the other side. The 20,000Ft note,
currently the highest denomination, has
Ferenc Deák, the architect of the 1867

Compromise, on the recto and the erstwhile
House of Commons in Pest (now the Italian
Institute of Culture on VIII Bródy Sándor
utca) on the verso.

Exchange Rates

Exchange rates at the time of going to press
were:

country	unit		forint
Australia	A$1	=	137Ft
Canada	C$1	=	153Ft
Euro zone	€1	=	245Ft
Japan	¥100	=	185Ft
New Zealand	NZ$1	=	123Ft
UK	UK£1	=	355Ft
USA	US$1	=	222Ft

Exchanging Money

Cash & Travellers Cheques Nothing
beats cash for convenience – or risk. It's
always prudent to carry a little foreign cash,
though, in euros or US dollars, in case you
can't find an automatic teller machine
(ATM) nearby or there's no bank or travel
office open to cash your travellers cheques.
You can always change cash at a hotel.

ATMs There are ATMs all around the city,
including in the train and bus stations, and
quite a few foreign-currency exchange machines too, including ones at V Károly körút
20 (Map 6) and at the K&H Bank at V Váci
utca 40 (Map 6). The best ATMs to use are
the Euronet ones as they dispense cash in
units of 5000Ft. OTP ATMs give out
20,000Ft notes, which are tough to change.

Credit Cards The use of credit cards is
gaining ground in Budapest, especially Visa,
MasterCard and American Express. You'll
be able to use them at upmarket restaurants,
shops, hotels, car-rental firms, travel agencies and petrol stations, but not at museums,
supermarkets or train and bus stations.

Many banks, including K&H and Posta-
bank (represented at most large post offices
in the city), give cash advances on major
credit cards. You can do the same with an
AmEx card at **American Express** *(Map 6;*
☎ 235 4330; V Deák Ferenc utca 10; metro

M1/2/3 Deák Ferenc tér; open 9am-5.30pm Mon-Fri, 9am-2pm Sat). Citibank cardholders should go to **Citibank** *(Map 6; ☎ 458 2351, 266 9895; V Vörösmarty tér 4; open 8am-5pm Mon-Fri)*.

International Transfers Having money wired to Budapest through **Western Union Money Transfer** *(☎ 266 4995; open 7am-midnight daily)* or American Express is fast and fairly straightforward; for AmEx (see Credit Cards earlier) you don't need to be a card-holder, but the sender does. The procedure takes less than 30 minutes. You should know the sender's full name, the exact amount and the reference number. You'll be given the amount in US-dollar travellers cheques or forint. The sender pays the service fee (about US$40 for US$500 sent, US$60 for US$1000).

Moneychangers You can exchange cash and travellers cheques – American Express, Visa and Thomas Cook are the most recognisable brands here – at most banks and post offices. Banks and bureaux de change generally don't take a commission, but exchange rates can vary; private agencies are always the most expensive.

The national savings bank, Országos Takarékpénztár (OTP), has offices everywhere, including an **OTP central Pest branch** *(Map 6; V Nádor utca 6; metro M1 Vörösmarty tér, bus No 15; open 7.45am-5pm Mon, 7.45am-4pm Tues-Fri)*. It offers among the best exchange rates for cash and travellers cheques, but get here at least an hour before closing to ensure the bureau de change counter is still open. **K&H bank** *(Map 6; V Váci utca 40; metro M3 Ferenciek tere; open 8am-5pm Mon, 8am-4pm Tues-Thur, 8am-3pm Fri)* often offers good rates too.

The **Tribus Non-stop Hotel Service** *(Map 6; ☎ 318 3925, 318 4848; w www.tribus.hu; V Apáczai Csere János utca 1; metro M3 Ferenciek tere)* near the Budapest Marriott Hotel is a 24-hour facility with exchange. Another good bet is Ibusz; most other travel agents usually take a commission of 1% to 2%. Shops never accept travellers cheques in Budapest.

American Express (see Credit Cards earlier) changes its own travellers cheques without commission, but its rates are poor. Its commission on converting US-dollar travellers cheques into cash dollars is 7%.

Whatever you do, avoid the big commercial bureaux de change, such as Interchange in Vörösmarty tér or on Castle Hill. Some deduct exorbitant 10% commissions while others have huge signs reading 'no commission' and advertise a rate – omitting the fact that you have to change the equivalent of US$1000 or more to get it or receive 10% below the bank rate.

Though the forint is now a totally convertible currency, you should avoid changing too much as it will be difficult exchanging forint beyond the borders of Hungary and its immediate neighbours.

Black Market It's senseless to make use of the black market to change money. The advantage – 5% on the outside – is not worth the bother. In any case, it's illegal and you are almost certain to be ripped off.

Security

Overall Budapest is a safe city, but pickpocketing can be a problem (see Dangers & Annoyances later in this chapter). Don't carry more money than you need, and keep your credit cards, passport and other documents in a concealed pouch or in a hotel safe or safe-deposit box. Always keep some spare travellers cheques or cash in a safe place for an emergency.

Lonely Planet has received numerous reports of unscrupulous waiters, shop assistants and even an airport official making hi-tech duplicates of credit- or debit-card information with a machine and then using the information illegally to make purchases or get cash. If your card leaves your possession for an uncomfortably long time, consider having it cancelled.

Costs

Prices may have risen somewhat over the past few years, but Budapest remains a bargain destination for foreign travellers for food, lodging and transport. If you stay in private rooms, eat at medium-priced restaurants and travel on public transport, you should get by on US$30 daily without scrimping. Those staying at hostels, dormitories or camp sites, and eating at food stalls or self-catering, will cut costs substantially.

Because of the changing value of the forint, many hotels quote their rates in euros, as does MÁV, the national rail company. In such cases, we have followed suit.

Tipping & Bargaining

Hungary is a very tip-conscious society and virtually everyone in Budapest routinely tips waiters, hairdressers and taxi drivers. Doctors and dentists accept 'gratitude money' (see Health later in this chapter), and even petrol station and thermal spa attendants expect something. If you were less than impressed with the service at the restaurant, the joyride in the taxi, or the way someone cut your hair, leave next to nothing or nothing at all. He or she will get the message loud and clear.

The way you tip in restaurants is unusual. You never leave the money on the table – this is considered both rude and stupid in Hungary – but tell the waiter how much you're paying in total. If the bill is 2700Ft, you're paying with a 5000Ft note and you think the waiter deserves an extra 10% or so, first, ask if service is included (some restaurants in Budapest add it to the bill automatically, which makes tipping unnecessary). If it isn't, say you're paying 3000Ft and you want 2000Ft back.

Though you'll never be able to bargain in shops, you may haggle in flea markets or with individuals selling folk crafts. But even this is not as commonplace as it is in other Eastern Europe capitals.

Taxes & Refunds

ÁFA, a value-added tax of just under 11% to 25%, covers the purchase of all new goods and services in Hungary. It's usually included in the quoted price, but not always, so it pays to check. Visitors are generally not exempt, but they can claim refunds for total purchases of more than 50,000Ft on one receipt as long as they take the goods out of the country within 90 days. The ÁFA

receipts (available from the shops where you made the purchases) should be stamped by customs at the border, and the claim has to be made within 183 days of exporting the goods. The 25% ÁFA on rental cars does not apply to nonresidents paying with foreign currency or credit card.

Budapest-based **Global Refund Hungary** (☎/fax 468 2965, fax 468 2966; **w** www .globalrefund.com; XIV Zászlós utca 54) can help you with refunds, for a fee.

Like most other municipalities in Hungary, Budapest levies a tourist tax on most forms of accommodation of about 3%. This may or may not be included in the rate you are quoted.

POST & COMMUNICATIONS

The Hungarian Postal Service (Magyar Posta) has improved greatly in recent years; perhaps its jaunty logo of a stylised St Stephen's Crown has helped kick-start it into the 21st century. But post offices in Budapest are usually still crowded, service is slow and staff generally speak Hungarian only.

Postal Rates

Sending letters within Budapest costs 33Ft, while for the rest of Hungary and neighbouring countries it's 38Ft (add 96/200Ft if you want to send it registered/express). Postcards within the country and to neighbouring countries cost 30Ft to send.

Airmail letters within Europe cost 150/240Ft for up to 20/50g and 160/260Ft for the rest of the world. Postcards cost 100Ft and 110Ft respectively.

Sending & Receiving Mail

To beat the crowds at the post office, ask at kiosks, newsagents or stationery shops if they sell stamps (bélyeg). If you must deal with the post office, you'll be relieved to learn that most people are there to pay electric, gas and telephone bills or parking fines. To get in and out with a minimum of fuss, look for the window marked with the symbol of an envelope. Make sure the destination of your letter is written clearly, and simply hand it over to the clerk, who will apply the stamps for you, postmark it and send it on its way.

If you are sending a parcel, look for the sign *'Csomagfeladás'* or *'Csomagfelvétel'*. Packages sent domestically cost 360/400/480Ft for up to 2/5/10kg. Packages going abroad must not weigh more than 2kg or else you'll face a Kafkaesque nightmare of permits and queues; try to send small ones. You can send up to 2kg in one box for 2840Ft to Europe and 3150Ft to the rest of the world. Up to 5kg of books and other printed matter can be sent to the same destinations for 4250Ft and 6000Ft respectively.

Hungarian addresses start with the name of the recipient, followed on the next line by the postal code and city or town and then the street name and number. The postal code consists of four digits. The first indicates the city or town ('1' is Budapest), the second and third the *kerület* (district) and the last the neighbourhood.

The **main post office** *(Map 6; V Petőfi Sándor utca 13-15 or V Városház utca 18; metro 1/2/3 Deák Ferenc tér; open 8am-8pm Mon-Fri, 8am-2pm Sun)* is a few minutes' walk from Deák Ferenc tér and the Tourinform branch office. This is where you buy stamps, mail letters, send packages and faxes and pick up poste restante. For the last, look for the sign *postán maradó küldemények* over the counter and make sure you have identification. Since the family name *always* comes first in Hungarian usage, have the sender underline your last name, as letters are often misfiled under foreigners' first names.

If you have an AmEx credit card or their travellers cheques, you can have your mail sent to **American Express** *(Deák Ferenc utca 10, 1052 Budapest)*, where it will be held for one month free of charge.

Two other convenient post offices with extended hours are the **Nyugati station post office** *(Map 5; VI Teréz körút 51-53; metro M3 Nyugati pályaudvar; open 7am-9pm Mon-Sat, 8am-8pm Sun)* and the **Keleti station post office** *(Map 3; VIII Kerepesi út 2-6; metro M2 Keleti pályaudvar; open 7am-9pm Mon-Sat)*.

Telephone

You can make both domestic and international calls from all public telephones in Budapest, which are usually in good working order. They work with both coins and phonecards, though the latter are now far more common. Phonecards (800/1800Ft) are available from post offices, newsagents, hotels and petrol stations. Telephone boxes with a black and white arrow and red target on the door and the word *'Visszahívható'* display a telephone number, so you can be phoned back. The phone boxes just inside the front door of the main post office (see earlier) are relatively quiet.

All localities in Hungary have a two-digit telephone area code, except for Budapest, which has just a '1'. To make a local call, pick up the receiver and listen for the neutral and continuous dial tone, then dial the phone number (seven digits in Budapest, six in the provinces). For an intercity call within Hungary, dial ☎ 06 and wait for the second, more musical, tone. Then dial the area code and phone number. You must *always* dial ☎ 06 when ringing a mobile telephone, area codes of which are ☎ 06-20 (Pannon), ☎ 06-30 and ☎ 06-60 (Westel) and ☎ 06-70 (Vodafone). Cheaper or toll-free blue and green numbers start with ☎ 06-40 and ☎ 06-80 respectively.

The procedure for making an international call is the same except that you dial ☎ 00, wait for the second dial tone, then dial the country code, the area code and the number. International phone charges from a public/private phone are: 131/90Ft per minute to neighbouring countries and 136/94Ft to Europe, North America, Australia, New Zealand and East Asia. Other rates include 447/307Ft to Southeast Asia, Middle East and South America; 524/360Ft to Africa, South Asia and the Caribbean; 633/435Ft to the Pacific and parts of Asia and Africa. The country code for Hungary is ☎ 36.

Lonely Planet's ekno global communication service provides low-cost international calls – though for local calls you're usually better off with a local phonecard. Ekno also offers free messaging services, email, travel information and an online travel vault, where you can securely store all your important documents. You can join online at **w** www.ekno.lonelyplanet.com, where you'll find the local-access numbers for the 24-hour customer-service centre. Once you've joined, always check the ekno website for the latest access numbers for each country and updates on new features.

You can get straight through to an operator in your home country by dialling the appropriate Country Direct number from a public phone, but you need a coin or phonecard for the initial connection. Some of the services listed below are very expensive, although they will still be cheaper than a normal phonecall from a hotel room.

Australia	☎ 06-800 11573/720
Australia (Telstra)	☎ 06-800 06111
Britain	☎ 06-800 04411
Britain (BT)	☎ 06-800 04413
Canada	☎ 06-800 01211/2
New Zealand	☎ 06-800 06411
South Africa	☎ 06-800 02711
USA (AT&T)	☎ 06-800 01111
USA (MCI)	☎ 06-800 01411
USA (Sprint)	☎ 06-800 01877

A much better deal is the Barangoló card (3000Ft) from **Matáv** (☎ 06-80 495 949, 06-80 424 424; W www.matav.hu), which will lower the per-minute costs to certain countries substantially: 70Ft to Austria, Germany, the USA and Canada and 75Ft to Italy, France and the UK.

Telephone numbers you may find useful include:

Domestic operator (English spoken)	☎ 198
International operator (English spoken)	☎ 199
Time/speaking clock (in Hungarian)	☎ 180
Wake-up service (in Hungarian)	☎ 193

For emergency numbers, see Emergencies later in this chapter.

Fax

You can send faxes from the main post office as well as most Internet cafés for 150/500Ft per page within/outside Hungary. It is also possible to make calls and send or receive faxes at hotel business centres like the one at the **Kempinski Hotel Corvinus** (Map 6; ☎ 429 3777; V Erzsébet tér 7-8; metro M1/2/3 Deák Ferenc tér).

Email & Internet Access

Hungary has taken to the Internet in a big way and most businesses, including hotels and hostels, have websites. The number of Internet cafés has grown exponentially in the past few years.

Internet Service Providers Well-trafficked ISPs in Budapest include **Axelero** (☎ 06-80 420 042; W www.axelero.hu), **Datanet** (☎ 452 4444; W www.datanet.hu, Hungarian only) and **Nextra** (☎ 484 8100; W www.nextra.hu).

Internet Cafés Budapest has more than a dozen Internet cafés, but the smaller ones can get crowded in the early evening. Many of the year-round hostels and almost all hotels (see the Places to Stay chapter) in Budapest now offer Internet access (usually from 20Ft per minute). If the place you're staying at doesn't have it or you just feel like checking your mail on the trot, the following are among the more central Internet cafés:

Ami Internet Coffee (Map 6; ☎ 267 1644, W www.amicoffee.hu) V Váci utca 40; metro M3 Ferenciek tere. Open 9am to 2am daily. This very central place has 50 terminals and charges 200/400/700Ft for up to 15/30/60 minutes. Five/10 hours costs 3250/6400Ft.

Budapest Net Internet Café (Map 6; ☎ 328 0292, W www.budapestnet.hu, Hungarian only) V Kecskeméti utca 5; metro M3 Kálvin tér. Open 10am to 10pm daily. With more than 50 terminals, this place attracts students from the nearby ELTE university in droves. It charges 150/350/700Ft for up to 10/30/60 minutes (2400/4600Ft for five/10 hours).

Libri Könyvpalota (Map 5; ☎ 267 4844) VII Rákóczi út 12; metro M2 Astoria. Open 10am to 7.30pm Monday to Friday and 10am to 3pm Saturday. Budapest's biggest bookshop has nine terminals on the 1st floor that cost 250/400Ft for 30/60 minutes' access.

Matáv Telepont Internet Kávézó (Map 6; ☎ 485 6612) V Petőfi Sándor utca 17–19; metro M1/2/3 Deák Ferenc tér. Open 9am to 8pm Monday to Friday and 10am to 3pm Saturday. This smallish Internet centre with eight terminals is run by the national telecommunications company and charges 300/500Ft for 30/60 minutes. A 10-hour pass is 4000Ft.

Narancs (Map 5; ☎ 413 6733) VII Akácfa utca; metro M2 Blaha Lujza tér. Open 10am to midnight daily. This small but charming French-run café charges 150/400Ft for 10/60 minutes online. An hour costs only 300Ft from 10am to noon and 10pm to midnight.

Mystery Bar (Map 5; ☎ 312 1436; **w** home.tvnet .hu/~mystery1, Hungarian only) V Nagysándor József utca 3; metro M3 Arany János. Open noon to 4am Monday to Friday and 6pm to 4am Saturday and Sunday. This neighbourhood gay bar (see Gay & Lesbian Venues in the Entertainment chapter) is just the ticket for boyz who want to log on and get off. Connection costs 300/500Ft for 30/60 minutes.

Netvillage (Map 6; ☎ 266 8425) Millennium Centre, V Váci utca 19-21; metro M1 Vörösmarty tér. Open 9am to 9pm Monday to Friday and 10am to 6pm Saturday and Sunday. This very central café in a shopping mall in the heart of turista-land has 40 terminals and charges 150/400/800Ft for 10/30/60 minutes.

Private Link (Map 3; ☎ 334 2057; **w** www.private -link.hu) VIII József körút 52. Open 24 hours, this is Budapest's largest and most comfortable Internet café and the only one open round the clock (700/1310/3000/55000/10,000Ft for 1/2/5/10/20 hours).

Vista Internet Café (Map 6; ☎ 429 9952, 269 6032, fax 429 9951; **e** icafe@vista.hu) VI Paulay Ede utca 7; metro M1/2/3 Deák Ferenc tér. Open 10am to 10pm Monday to Friday and 10am to 8pm Saturday. This café at the Vista Visitor Centre (see Travel Agencies earlier) charges 11/660Ft per minute/hour.

DIGITAL RESOURCES

The World Wide Web is a rich resource for travellers. You can research your trip, hunt down bargain air fares, book hotels, check on weather conditions or chat with locals and other travellers about the best places to visit – or avoid.

There's no better place to start your Web explorations than the Lonely Planet website (**w** www.lonelyplanet.com). Here you'll find succinct summaries on travelling to most places on earth, postcards from other travellers and the Thorn Tree bulletin board, where you can ask questions before you go or dispense advice when you get back. You can also find travel news, and the subwwway section links you to the most useful travel resources elsewhere on the Web.

The best overall site for Budapest is the BTO website at **w** www.budapestinfo.hu, though you might also try **w** www.visitors guide.hu. Budapest Week Online (**w** www .budapestweek.com) has events, music and movie listings. Budapest Sun Online (**w** www .budapestsun.com) is similar but also has local news, interviews and features. Tourinform's informative website (**w** www.hungary tourism.hu) has reams of information on the capital as well as the rest of the country.

For information on hotels, try **w** www .hotelshungary.com, **w** www.hotelsinfo.hu, **w** www.holidayhungary.com or **w** www .szallasinfo.hu. **w** www.alfaapartments.com is good for short-term flat rentals. Check out **w** www.youthhostels.hu for hostel accommodation and **w** www.camping.hu for camp sites.

The weekly news magazine *HVG* (see Newspapers & Magazines later) gives summaries of its lead stories in English on its website (**w** www.hvg.hu).

The Yellow Pages telephone directory can be found at **w** www.aranyoldalak.hu (Hungarian only).

BOOKS

There's no shortage of books on Budapest and things Hungarian – from travel guides and histories to accounts of personal journeys and cookery books. Once regarded as one of the city's biggest bargains, books have become more expensive, though haven't reached Western prices yet.

Lonely Planet

Hungary takes a detailed look at the country, for those wanting to explore well beyond the capital. *Eastern Europe, Central Europe* and *Europe on a shoestring* all contain chapters on Hungary, including sections on Budapest. *Eastern Europe Phrasebook* contains sections of useful words and expressions in Hungarian.

Specialised Guidebooks

If you want a very personal look at one man's home town – without much practical help, though – pick up a copy of *Budapest: A Critical Guide* by András Török. It's basically five walking tours and a lot of esoteric ruminations written by a 'thinking dandy' born and raised in the capital.

Another good walking guide from a very solid historical (at times almost academic) perspective is *Budapest: A Cultural Guide* by Michael Jacobs.

Budapest Architectural Guide, edited by Zsuzsa Lőrinczi and Mihály Vargha, is the most serious guide to Budapest's 20th-century architecture. This bilingual guide takes a close look at almost 300 buildings from 1896 to the present.

Get *Budapest in Detail*, edited by Zsuzsa Lőrinczi, if it's applied art that interests you. This spectacularly illustrated volume looks at tiles, mosaics, ironwork and stained glass in and on buildings throughout the capital.

Jewish Budapest: Monuments, Rites, History, by Kinga Frojimovics et al, is an exhaustive study on Judaism writ on the cityscape of Budapest.

Travel

Travellers writing diary accounts tend to give Hungary and Budapest cursory treatment as they make tracks for 'more exotic' Romania or points beyond, but there are some exceptions.

In describing his 1933 walk through Hungary en route to Constantinople, Patrick Leigh Fermor wrote the classic account of Hungary, *Between the Woods and the Water*.

Published in 1840, *The City of the Magyar* by Julia Pardoe is one of the best sources for contemporary views of early-19th-century Hungary. Unfortunately, you'll only find this three-volume set (almost an entire volume is devoted to Budapest) in a library or antiquarian bookshop.

Stealing from a Deep Place by Brian Hall is sensitive but never cloying. The author describes his tempered love affair with the still communist Budapest of the 1980s.

History & Politics

For a close look at *fin-de-siècle* Budapest, pick up a copy of *Budapest 1900: A Historical Portrait of a City and its Culture* by John Lukacs, an illustrated social history of the capital at the height of its glory.

Now in its second edition, *Budapest Then & Now* by Imre Móra is a collection of essays that offers some esoteric bits of information on the capital.

A Concise History of Hungary by Miklós Molnár is the book to read if you find Sugar's tome (see below) too daunting.

A Cultural History of Hungary: From the Beginnings to the 18th Century and *A Cultural History of Hungary: In the 19th & 20th Centuries* by László Kósa offer an easy (and illustrated) introduction from earliest times to the end of the last century.

A Golden Age: Art & Society in Hungary 1896-1914, edited by Gyöngyi Éri and Zsuzsa Jobbágyi, is a glossy book that covers the late 19th and early 20th centuries, when Budapest was at its apogee.

A History of Hungary, edited by Peter F Sugar, is arguably the best single-volume history of Hungary in English, written by 20 scholars (14 of them Hungarians) and edited by one of the most incisive historians of Central and Eastern Europe.

An Illustrated History of Budapest by Géza Buzinkay is an oversized and illustrated 'easy entry' to the complicated history of the Hungarian capital.

We the People by Timothy Garton Ash and *The Rebirth of History: Eastern Europe in the Age of Democracy* by Misha Glenny are still classic and insightful interpretations of what led to the collapse of Communism in 1989.

General

Culinaria Hungary by Aniko Gegely et al is a lavish, 320-page tome on all things involving Hungarian food, from soup to nuts and more.

Celebrated restaurateur Lang offers a comprehensive history of Magyar cooking and an examination of its regional differences in *George Lang's Cuisine of Hungary*.

Homage to the Eighth District by Giorgio and Nicola Pressburger, twin brothers who emigrated to Italy in 1956, is a poignant account of life in what was a Jewish working-class section of Budapest during and after WWII .

Hungarian Ethnography and Folklore by Iván Balassa and Gyula Ortutay is a real gem. It is an 800-page opus that weighs in at 3kg and leaves no question on traditional culture unanswered. It's out of print but can still be found in some Budapest bookshops and on the Web. Highly recommended.

Hungary & the Hungarians: The Keywords (A Concise Dictionary of Facts, Beliefs, Customs, Usage & Myths) by István Bart is a quirky book that will guide you from ABC (a kind of greengrocers under the old regime) to Zsolnay.

Memoir of Hungary: 1944-1948, by Sándor Márai, describes remembrances of the playwright and celebrated author of *Embers* who fled Budapest in 1948 to escape communist persecution.

Under the Frog by Tibor Fischer is an amusing account of a basketball team's antics in the Hungary of the early 1950s.

NEWSPAPERS & MAGAZINES

As in most European capitals, printed news has strong political affiliations in Budapest. The two main exceptions are the highly respected news magazine *Heti Világgazdaság* (World Economy Weekly), better known as *HVG*, and the former Communist Party mouthpiece *Népszabadság* (People's Freedom), which is now completely independent (though socialist-oriented) and has the highest circulation of any paid newspaper. (The daily commuter freebie *Metro* counts more readers, however.)

Budapest has two English-language weeklies: the tabloid *Budapest Sun* (298Ft), with a useful *Style* arts and entertainment supplement, and the *Budapest Business Journal* (550Ft; see Doing Business later in this chapter). *The Hungarian Spectator* (100Ft), an unsuccessful mix of the two, appears twice a month.

Another useful English-language periodical is the erudite *Hungarian Quarterly* (950Ft), which examines a wide variety of issues in great depth and is a valuable source of current Hungarian thinking in translation.

English-language Western newspapers available on the day of publication at many large kiosks, newsagents and hotels include the *International Herald Tribune*, the European edition of the *Wall Street Journal*, the

Financial Times and the weekly *Guardian International*.

The best place in Budapest for foreign-language newspapers and magazines is **World Press House** *(Világsajtó Háza; Map 6; V Városház utca 3-5; metro M3 Ferenciek tere; open 7am-7pm Mon-Fri, 7am-6pm Sat, 8am-4pm Sun)*. Other reliable places to find them are the small **Kempinski Hotel Corvinus bookshop** *(Map 6; V Erzsébet tér 7-8; metro M1/2/3 Deák Ferenc tér)*; the **outdoor kiosk** *(Map 6; V Deák Ferenc utca; metro M1 Vörösmarty tér)* as you enter Vörösmarty tér; and the **Hírker newsstand** *(Map 5)* in the subway below Nyugati tér.

RADIO & TV

With the sale of the state-owned TV2, Magyar Televízió (MTV) controls only one channel (M1), though there are public channels (M2 and Duna TV) and a host of cable and satellite ones (eg, RTL Klub and Magyar ATV) broadcasting everything from game and talk shows to Pokémon, all in – or dubbed into – Hungarian. Most larger hotels and pensions in Budapest have satellite TV, mainly in German, but sometimes Sky News, CNN, Eurosport and BBC News in English.

Hungarian Radio has three stations, named after Lajos Kossuth (jazz and news; 98.6 AM), Sándor Petőfi (1960s to '80s music and news; 94.8 FM) and Béla Bartók (classical music and news; 105.3 FM). Est.fm (98.6 FM) is a popular alternative-music station while Rádió © (88.8 FM) is excellent for Roma music, as well as jazz, Latino and North African sounds. Budapest Rádió is on 88.1 FM and 91.9 FM.

VIDEO SYSTEMS

If you want to record or buy video tapes to play back home, you won't get the picture if the image registration systems are different. Like most of Europe and Australia, Hungary uses PAL, which is incompatible with the North American and Japanese NTSC system or the SECAM system used in France.

PHOTOGRAPHY & VIDEO

All major brands of film are readily available in Budapest, and you can have your film developed in one hour at many locations in Budapest, including any of the dozen or so **Fotex outlets** *(W www.fotexnet.hu, Hungarian only)* including a **district VII branch** *(Map 6; ☎ 202 2400; VII Rákóczi út 2; open 8am-9pm Mon-Fri, 9am-7pm Sat, 10am-7pm Sun)* opposite the East-West Business Centre and a **district V branch** *(Map 5; ☎ 301 0053; V Szent István körút 9).*

Film prices vary but generally 24 exposures of 100 ASA Kodacolor II, Agfa or Fujifilm costs 999Ft, and 36 exposures 1290Ft. Ektachrome 100 costs 1790Ft for 36 exposures. Developing film is 1099Ft a roll; for the prints themselves, you choose the size and pay accordingly (eg, 10cm x 15cm prints cost 89Ft each). Developing a 40-exposure reel of Kodak 400 APS film costs from 2800Ft; slide film costs 1099Ft to process. Video tape such as TDK EHG 30/45 minutes costs 990/1310Ft.

TIME

Budapest lies in the Central European time zone. Winter time is GMT plus one hour and in summer it's GMT plus two hours. Clocks are advanced at 2am on the last Sunday in March and set back at the same time on the last Sunday in October.

Without taking daylight-saving times into account, when it's noon in Budapest, it's:

11pm in Auckland
1pm in Bucharest
11am in London
2pm in Moscow
6am in New York
noon in Paris
3am in San Francisco
9pm in Sydney
8pm in Tokyo

To make sure that you arrive on time for a film, play or concert, see the boxed text 'A Complicated Time' in the Entertainment chapter.

ELECTRICITY

The electric current in Budapest is 220V, 50Hz AC. Plugs are the European type with two round pins.

WEIGHTS & MEASURES

The metric system (see the conversion table on the back flap of this book) is in use here. In supermarkets and outdoor markets, fresh food is sold by weight or by piece *(darab)*. When ordering by weight, you specify by kilos or *deka* (decagrams – 50dg is equal to 0.5kg or a little more than 1lb).

Beer at a *söröző* (pub) is served in a *pohár* (0.3L) or a *korsó* (0.4L or 0.5L). Wine in an old-fashioned *borozó* (wine bar) is ladled out by the *deci* (decilitre, 0.1L), but in more modern places it comes by the undefined *pohár* (glass).

LAUNDRY

Most hostels and camp sites have some sort of laundry facilities; expect to pay from 500Ft to 1000Ft per load. Commercial laundries *(patyolat)* are fairly common in Budapest. You can elect to have your laundry done in six hours or one, two or three days – and pay accordingly (from 1500Ft). About the only self-service laundrette in town is **Irisz Szalon** *(Map 6; ☎ 317 2092; V Városház utca 3-5; metro M3 Ferenciek tere; open 7am-7pm Mon-Fri, 7am-1pm Sat).*

In general, dry-cleaning is of a low standard except at big international hotels such as the **Budapest Marriott Hotel** *(Map 6; ☎ 266 7000; V Apáczai Csere János utca 4; open 7am-6pm Mon-Fri).* That said, the **Top Clean chain** *(☎ 227 1500 • Map 5; ☎ 312 5418; V Arany János utca 34; metro Arany János utca; open 7am-6.30pm Mon-Fri, 8am-1pm Sat • Map 5; ☎ 238 0388; VI Váci út 3; metro Nyugati pályaudvar; open 7am-6.30pm Mon-Fri, 8am-1pm Sat)* does a fairly reliable and affordable job on both dry-cleaning and laundry and has some 30 locations around Budapest, including a district V branch and a West End City Centre branch.

TOILETS

Public toilets in Budapest are invariably staffed by an old *néné* (auntie), who mops the floor continuously, hands out sheets of grade AAA sandpaper as toilet tissue and has seen it all before. The usual charge is 50Ft a go, and even restaurants and cafés sometimes charge their patrons.

LEFT LUGGAGE

There's a left-luggage office downstairs at **Népliget bus station** *(open 6am-9pm daily; 150Ft per piece per day)* and one at **Népstadion bus station** *(open 6am-6pm daily)* as well. The left-luggage offices at the train stations include those at **Keleti** *(open 24hr)* next to platform No 6; **Nyugati** *(open 5am-midnight)* beside platform No 10; and **Déli** *(open 3.30am-11.30pm)* next to platform No 1. They charge 200/400Ft per day for a normal/large piece. There's also a left-luggage office at **Ferihegy Terminal 2B** *(open 24hr)*, which charges 250/600/800Ft for 1/3/6 hours and 1000/5000Ft per day/week per piece.

HEALTH

Budapest poses no health risks and the water is perfectly safe. Mosquitoes can be a real scourge around pools, ponds and the Danube in summer, so be armed with insect repellent *(rovarírtó)*. One insect that can bring on more than just an itch, though, is the forest tick *(kullancs)*, which burrows under the skin causing inflammation and even encephalitis. It has become a common problem in parts of Central and Eastern Europe, especially eastern Austria, Germany, the Czech Republic and Hungary. You might consider getting an FSME (meningo-encephalitis) vaccination if you plan to do extensive hiking between May and September in the Buda Hills or in other parts of Hungary such as Transdanubia or the Northern Uplands.

Foreigners are entitled to first-aid and ambulance services only when they have suffered an accident and require immediate medical attention; follow-up treatment and medicine must be paid for. Treatment at a public outpatient clinic *(rendelő intézet)* costs little, but doctors working privately will charge more and expect 'gratitude money' (ie, a tip). Very roughly, a consultation in a Hungarian doctor's surgery *(orvosi rendelő)* costs from 5000Ft while a home visit is 10,000Ft.

Medical Services

Consultations and treatment are much more expensive in the Western-style clinics.

American Clinics *(Map 3; ☎ 224 9090; [W] www.americanclinics.com; I Hattyú utca 14, 5th floor; metro M2 Moszkva tér; open 8.30am-7pm Mon-Thur, 8.30am-6pm Fri, 8.30am-noon Sat, 10am-2pm Sun)* is a flash private medical clinic and can help you in an emergency (24-hour service), but it's not cheap: a basic consultation costs 28,600Ft.

Dental Services

Dental work is usually of a high standard and cheap by Western European standards (at least the Austrians seem to think so, judging from the numbers who regularly cross the border to have their teeth cleaned or fixed). Some dentists advertise in the English-language press in Budapest.

S.O.S Dental Service *(Map 6; ☎ 267 9602, 269 6010; VI Király utca 14; metro M1/2/3 Deák Ferenc tér; open 24hr)* charges 2000Ft for a consultation, 5000Ft to 6000Ft for extractions and from 6000Ft to 10,000Ft for fillings.

Pharmacies

Each of Budapest's 23 districts has a rotating all-night pharmacy; a sign on the door of any pharmacy will help you locate the closest 24-hour one. Pharmacies with extended hours include:

Csillag Gyógyszertár (Map 5; ☎ 314 3695) VIII Rákóczi út 39; metro Blaha Lujza tér. Open 7.30am-9pm Mon-Fri, 7.30am-2pm Sat

Déli Gyógyszertár (Map 3; ☎ 355 4727) XII Alkotás utca 1/b; metro M2 Déli pályaudvar. Open 8am-8pm Mon-Fri, 8am-2pm Sat

Teréz Patika (Map 5; ☎ 311 4439) VI Teréz körút 41; metro Nyugati pályaudvar. Open 8am-8pm Mon-Fri, 8am-5pm Sat, 8am-1pm Sun

HIV/AIDS Organisations

The numbers of registered AIDS cases and those who are HIV-positive are relatively low (below 800 nationwide) though local epidemiologists estimate the actual number of those infected with HIV to be 3500 to 4000. That number could multiply substantially as Budapest claims its less-than-distinctive title of 'sex-industry capital of Eastern and Central Europe'.

Two AIDS lines operate in the capital: a 24-hour **AIDS information line** (☎ *338 4555*) and a **help line** (☎ *338 2419; operating 8am-3pm Mon-Thur, 8am-1pm Fri*), with some English spoken.

SOCIAL GRACES

If you're invited to someone's home, bring a bunch of flowers (available in profusion all year and very inexpensive) or a bottle of good local wine. You can talk about anything, but money is a touchy subject. Traditionally, the discussion or manifestation of wealth – wearing flashy jewellery, for example – was considered gauche here (as it was throughout Eastern Europe). Nowadays no-one thinks they have enough money, and those still in the low-paying public sector are often jealous of people who have made the leap to better jobs in the private sector. Your salary – piddling as you may think it is back home – will astonish many Hungarians.

WOMEN TRAVELLERS

Hungarian men can be sexist in their thinking, but women in Budapest do not suffer any particular form of harassment (though domestic violence and rape get little media coverage). Most men – even drunks – are effusively polite with women. Women may not be made to feel especially welcome when eating or drinking alone, but it's really no different from many other countries in Europe.

For assistance and/or information ring the **Women's Line** (*Nővonal;* ☎ *06-80 505 101*) or **Women for Women against Violence** (*NANE;* ☎ *267 4900*), which operates from 6pm to 10pm daily.

GAY & LESBIAN TRAVELLERS

For up-to-date information on venues, events, parties etc, pick up the freebie pamphlet *Na Végre!* (At Last!) at gay venues in Budapest or contact them directly (ⓔ navegre@hotmail .com). Useful websites include ⓦ www.gay guide.net/europe/hungary/budapest, ⓦ mas program.freeweb.hu, ⓦ english.gay.hu and ⓦ www.pride.hu.

For one-to-one information and/or assistance, ring the **Gay Switchboard** (☎ *351 2015, 06-30 932 3334; open 4pm-8pm Mon-Fri*) or

Háttér Gay & Lesbian Association (☎ *329 3380; open 6pm-11pm daily*).

Several gay associations organise outings, including: **Vándor Mások** (*Rambling Others;* ⓦ *www.gay.hu/vandormasok/en/index.html*), with hikes around Budapest and two- or three-day trips to other parts of Hungary; **Mozdulj ki!** (*Get Out!;* ⓦ *www.gay.hu/van dormasok/en/mozduljki.html*), with monthly hikes into the Buda Hills; and **GayGuide.Net Budapest** (☎ *06-30 932 3334;* ⓦ *www.gay guide.net/europe/hungary/budapest*), with a night and day gay tour of Budapest.

See also Gay & Lesbian Venues in the Entertainment chapter for information.

The age of consent for gays and lesbians is 18 years against 14 years for heterosexual couples.

DISABLED TRAVELLERS

Budapest has a very long way to go before it becomes truly accessible to the disabled. Wheelchair ramps, toilets fitted for the disabled and inward-opening doors are few and far between, though audible traffic signals for the blind are becoming increasingly commonplace and the higher-denominated forint notes have markings in Braille.

For more information, contact the **Hungarian Disabled Association** (*MEOSZ;* ☎ *388 5529, 388 2387;* ⓔ *meosz@matavnet.hu; III San Marco utca 76; open 8am-4pm Mon-Fri*) in Óbuda.

SENIOR TRAVELLERS

Seniors are sometimes entitled to discounts on things such as public transport and museum admission fees, provided they show proof of their age. However these are usually only for citizens of Hungary. See Seniors Cards under Documents earlier in the chapter for more information.

BUDAPEST FOR CHILDREN

Successful travel with young children requires planning and effort. Don't try to overdo things; packing too much into the time available can cause problems. Make sure the activities include the kids as well –balance that morning at the Museum of Fine Arts with an afternoon at the nearby

Grand Circus or a performance at the puppet theatre. Include children in the trip planning; if they've helped to work out where you will be going, they'll be much more interested when they get there. Lonely Planet's *Travel with Children* is a good resource.

Most car-rental firms in Budapest have children's safety seats for hire at a nominal cost (from 500Ft a day), but it is essential that you book them in advance. The same goes for highchairs and cots (cribs); they're standard in many restaurants and hotels but numbers are limited.

The **Municipal Great Circus** *(Fővárosi Nagycirkusz; Map 3; ☎ 343 8300, 343 6002; XIV Állatkerti körút 7; metro M1 Széchenyi fürdő; adult 800-1200Ft, child 600-1000Ft)* has performances at 3pm and 7pm on Wednesday and Friday, at 3pm on Thursday, at 10.30am, 3pm and 7pm on Saturday and at 10am and 3.30pm on Sunday from mid-April to August. Although the matinées are occasionally booked out by school groups, there's almost always space in the evening.

The **Budapest Puppet Theatre** *(Budapesti Bábszínház; Map 5; ☎ 342 2702; w www.budapest-babszinhaz.hu, Hungarian only; VI Andrássy út 69; metro M1 Vörösmarty utca; tickets 350-580Ft)*, which doesn't really require fluency in Hungarian, presents shows designed for children during the day and programmes for adults occasionally in the evening.

Funfair Park *(Vidám Park; ☎ 343 9810, 343 0993; w www.vidampark.hu; XIV Állatkerti körút 14-16; metro M1 Széchenyi fürdő; admission 200Ft, rides 100-500Ft; 11am-7pm Mon-Fri, 10am-10pm Sat, 10am-8pm Sun May & June; open 10am-8pm Mon-Fri & Sun, 10am-10pm Sat July & Aug; noon-7pm Mon-Fri, 10am-7.30pm Sat & Sun Apr & Sept; noon-6pm Mon-Fri, 10am-7pm Sat & Sun Mar & Oct)* is a 150-year-old amusement park on 2½ hectares next to the circus (see earlier). There's a couple of dozen new rides, including the heart-stopping Ikarus Space Needle and the Looping Star roller coaster, go-karts, dodgem cars and a carousel built in 1906 and protected as a monument.

The **Palace of Wonders** *(Csodák Palotája; Map 3; ☎ 350 6131; XIII Váci út 19; metro M3 Lehel tér; adult/child 550/500Ft; open 9am-5pm Tues-Fri, 10am-6pm Sat & Sun Jan–mid-April; 9am-5pm Mon-Fri, 10am-6pm Sat & Sun mid-Apr–Dec)* is an interactive playhouse for children of all ages.

The **Planetarium** *(Map 7; ☎ 263 1811, 265 0725; X Népliget; metro M3 Népliget; admission 595Ft; shows 9.30am, 11am, 1pm, 2.30pm & 4pm Tues-Sun)* might be combined with a visit to the Laser Theatre (see Rock & Pop in the Entertainment chapter) next door.

LIBRARIES

Libraries in Budapest with foreign-language books and periodicals include the following:

America House Library (Amerika Ház Könyvtár; Map 3; ☎ 343 0148 ext 4435) XIV Ajtósi Dürer sor 19–21. Open 9am to 6pm Monday, Tuesday and Thursday, noon to 6pm Wednesday, and 9am to 5pm Friday. This library is on the campus of Loránd Eötvös Science University, or ELTE, just below the university's English-language library. America House will issue a library card valid for a year for around 4000Ft.

British Council (Map 3; ☎ 478 4741, w www.britishcouncil.hu) VI Benczúr utca 26; metro M1 Bajza utca. Open 11am to 7pm Monday to Friday August to mid-May; 11am to 8pm Monday to Friday, 9am to 1pm Saturday mid-May to July. British Council charges 2500Ft for a one-year membership, allowing the card holder to borrow books, audio cassettes and magazines (videos cost extra).

National Foreign Language Library (Országos Idegennyelvű Könyvtár; Map 6; ☎ 318 2772/3688) V Molnár utca 11; metro M3 Ferenciek tere. Open 10am to 8pm Monday, Tuesday, Thursday and Friday, noon to 8pm Wednesday. You can join for about 1000Ft a year, but you'll need a Hungarian address and identification to do so.

National Széchenyi Library (Országos Széchenyi Könyvtár; Map 4; ☎ 224 3700, e inform@oszk.hu) Royal Palace, Wing F. Open 1pm to 9pm Monday, 9am to 9pm Tuesday to Friday, 9am to 5pm Saturday. This library allows members (annual adult/student 3000/1500Ft, daily 400/200Ft) to do research, peruse the general stacks and read the large collection of foreign newspapers and magazines.

CULTURAL CENTRES

Cultural centres in Budapest include the following – hours vary according to the department (library, media centre, gallery etc) and what's on:

British Council (Map 3; ☎ 478 4741, 478 4779, Ⓦ www.britishcouncil.hu) VI Benczúr utca 26; metro M1 Bajza utca. Open 9am to 1pm and 2pm to 5pm Monday to Friday
French Institute (Map 4; ☎ 489 4200, Ⓦ www.inst-france.hu) I Fő utca 17; bus No 86, tram No 19. Open 8am to 9pm Monday to Friday, 8.30am to 1.30pm Saturday
Goethe Institute (Map 5; ☎ 374 4070, Ⓦ www.goethe.de) VI Andrássy út 24; metro M1 Opera. Open 9am to 7pm Monday to Friday
Italian Institute of Culture (Map 6; ☎ 483 2040, Ⓦ www.datanet.hu/iic) VIII Bródy Sándor utca 8; metro M3 Kálvin tér, tram No 47 or 49. Open 10am to 1pm and 4pm to 6pm Monday to Thursday, 10am to 1pm Friday

DANGERS & ANNOYANCES

No parts of Budapest are 'off-limits' to visitors, although some locals now avoid Margaret Island after dark, and both residents and visitors give the dodgier parts of the 8th and 9th districts (areas of prostitution) a wide berth.

As elsewhere while travelling, you are most vulnerable to pickpockets, taxi louts, car thieves and scammers. To avoid having your car ripped off, follow the usual security procedures: don't park it in a darkened street, make sure the burglar alarm is armed, have a steering-wheel lock in place and leave nothing of value inside.

Pickpocketing is most common in markets, the Castle District, Váci utca and Hősök tere, and on certain popular buses (eg, No 7) and trams (Nos 2, 4, 6, 47 and 49).

Scams involving attractive young women known as *konzumlányok* (consume girls), gullible guys, expensive drinks in nightclubs and a frog-marching to the nearest ATM by gorillas in residence have been all the rage in Budapest for several years now, and we frequently receive letters from male readers complaining they've been ripped off. Guys, please: if it seems too good to be true, it is. Trust us and the mirror; such vanity has cost

hapless victims hundreds and even thousands of dollars. A list of these rip-off cafés and restaurants (they change all the time) is available at tourist offices and the US embassy, which circulates the information to hotels and hostels. The police will not (and actually cannot) be of much help in these matters. Caveat emptor.

Taking a taxi in Budapest can be an expensive and even an unpleasant experience. Never hail a cab on the street; call one from a phone – private, mobile or public – and give the number (almost always posted somewhere in the phone box) to the dispatcher. For more information, see Taxi in the Getting Around chapter.

It is not unknown for waiters to try to rip you off once they see you are a foreigner. They may try to bring you an unordered dish or make a 'mistake' when tallying the bill. If you think there's a discrepancy, ask for the menu and check the bill carefully. If you've been taken for more than 15% or 20% of the bill, call for the manager. Otherwise just don't leave a tip (see Tipping & Bargaining earlier in this chapter).

If you've left something on any form of public transport contact the **BKV lost and found office** *(Map 5; ☎ 267 5299; VII Akácfa utca 18; metro M2 Blaha Lujza tér; open 7am-3pm Mon-Thur, 7am-2pm Fri).*

EMERGENCIES

In an emergency, the following are the most important numbers:

central emergency number (English spoken)	☎ 112
ambulance	☎ 104
fire	☎ 105 (or ☎ 321 6216)
police	☎ 107
English-language crime hotline	☎ 438 8000
24-hour car assistance	☎ 188 (or ☎ 345 1800)

LEGAL MATTERS

If you need to report a crime or a lost or stolen passport or credit card, call the central emergency number (☎ 112), the police (☎ 107) or the English-language crime hotline (☎ 438 8000). Any crime must then be reported at the police station of the district you're in. In central Pest that would be the **District V Police Station** *(Map 5; ☎ 302 5935; V Szalay utca 11-13)*. If possible, bring along a Hungarian speaker. In the high season, police officers pair up with university students, who act as translators, and patrol the busiest areas.

The main **city and national police station** *(Map 2; XIII Teve utca)* is housed in a futuristic landmark building near the Árpád híd metro station.

There is virtually a 100% ban on alcohol when you are driving here, and this rule is *very* strictly enforced. Do not think you will get away with even a few glasses of wine at lunch; if found to have even 0.001% of alcohol in the blood, you will be fined up to 30,000Ft. If the level is high, you will be arrested and your license almost certainly taken away. In the event of an accident, the drinking party is automatically regarded as guilty.

BUSINESS HOURS

With rare exceptions, the opening hours *(nyitvatartás)* of any concern are posted on the front door. *Nyitva* means 'open' while *zárva* is 'closed'.

Grocery stores and supermarkets open from about 7am to 6pm or 7pm on weekdays, and department stores generally from 10am to 6pm. Most shops stay open until 8pm on Thursday, but on Saturday they usually close at 1pm. Many private retail shops close early on Friday and throughout most of August.

Most neighbourhoods have a 'nonstop' – a convenience store open until very late or even round the clock – that sells basic food items, bottled drinks and cigarettes. Many of the hyper-supermarkets around Budapest open on Sunday.

Banking hours vary but are usually 8am to about 4pm Monday to Thursday and to 1pm on Friday. The main post office in any Budapest district is open from 8am to 7pm or 8pm weekdays and till noon or even 2pm on Saturday. Branch offices close much earlier – usually at 4pm – and are never open at the weekend.

PUBLIC HOLIDAYS

Hungary currently celebrates 10 public holidays *(ünnep)* every year, and these are the following:

New Year's Day 1 January
1848 Revolution/National Day 15 March
Easter Monday March/April
International Labour Day 1 May
Whit Monday May/June
St Stephen's/Constitution Day 20 August
1956 Remembrance/Republic Day 23 October
All Saints' Day 1 November
Christmas holidays 25–26 December

SPECIAL EVENTS

Countless festivals and events are held in and around Budapest each year; look out for the tourist board's annual brochure *Events in Hungary from January to December* for a complete listing. Among the most important annual events, month by month, are the following:

January
New Year Opera Gala Held at the Pesti Vigadó on 1 January

February
Opera Ball Held at the Opera House

March
Budapest Spring Festival Held at venues throughout the capital

April
Spring Running Carnival Marathon between Budapest and Visegrád
World Dance Festival Held at venues throughout the capital

May
Ancient Music Festival Held at the Liszt Academy of Music and churches around Budapest

June
Budapest Búcsú A festival of rock and pop music that originally marked the departure of the last Soviet soldier from Hungarian soil
Danube Folklore Carnival Pan-Hungarian international carnival held in Vörösmarty tér and on Margaret Island
Ferencváros Summer Festival Held in late June and July

FACTS FOR THE VISITOR

July

Pepsi Sziget Music Festival Europe's largest outdoor music festival held on Óbuda Hajógyár Island late July to early August

August

BudaFest Summer Opera & Ballet Festival Held at the Opera House

Hungarian Formula-1 Grand Prix Held in the Hungaroring at Mogyoród, 24km northeast of the capital

September

Budapest Marathon Race up and down the Danube River and across its bridges

European Heritage Days Doors open to buildings and other sites around the city normally closed to the public

International Wine & Champagne Festival Held in the Castle District

October

Budapest Autumn Festival Held at venues throughout the city until early November

December

New Year's Gala & Ball Held at the Opera House on 31 December

DOING BUSINESS

The main source of information in English for businesspeople in Budapest is the *Budapest Business Journal (BBJ;* ☎ *374 3344;* **W** *www.bbj.hu; 550Ft)*, an almost archival publication of financial news and business stories that's been around for over a decade. Other useful publications include: the feature-orientated *Business Hungary* (900Ft), published by the American Chamber of Commerce; the *Central European Business Weekly* (**W** www.ceebiz.com); and *Business & Economy Invest in Hungary* (600Ft).

On the Internet, the BBJ's **Hungary A.M. service** (**e** *circulation@bbj.hu)* offers a daily synopsis of news and business stories from Budapest's top dailies by subscription.

For national news and a myriad of excellent links on everything from business to culture, visit **W** www.insidehungary.com or subscribe to **Hungary Around the Clock** (☎ *351 7142;* **e** *info@hatc.hu).*

Important addresses and/or useful sources of information include the following:

American Chamber of Commerce in Hungary (Map 6; ☎ 266 9880, **W** www.amcham.hu) V Deák Ferenc utca 10, 4/F; metro M1 Vörösmarty tér

British Chamber of Commerce in Hungary (Map 5; ☎ 302 5200, **W** www.bcch.com) V Bank utca 6, 2/F; metro M3 Arany János utca

Budapest Chamber of Commerce & Industry (Budapesti Kereskedelmi és Iparkamra; Map 4; ☎ 488 2000, **W** www.bkik.hu) I Krisztina körút 99; tram No 18

Canadian Chamber of Commerce (Map 5; ☎ 239 8169, fax 239 8170, **e** ccch@webreklam.hu) · XIII Nyugati tér 4; metro M3 Nyugati pályaudvar

Economy Ministry (Gazdasági Minisztérium; Map 5; ☎ 374 2700, **W** www.gm.hu) V Honvéd utca 13–15; metro M2 Kossuth Lajos tér

Finance Ministry (Pénzügy Minisztérium; Map 6; ☎ 318 2066, fax 318 2570, **W** www.meh.hu) V József nádor tér 2–4; metro M1 Vörösmarty tér

Hungarian Chamber of Commerce & Industry (Magyar Kereskedelmi és Iparkamra; Map 5; ☎ 474 5100, **W** www.mkik.hu) V Kossuth Lajos tér 6–8; metro M2 Kossuth Lajos tér

For photocopying, digital printing and computer services like scanning, visit one of eight outlets of **Copy General** (**W** *www.copygeneral .hu)*, including the **district V branch** (Map 5; ☎ *302 3206; V Kálmán Imre utca 22; metro M3 Nyugati pályaudvar; open 24hr).* A similar (and aptly named) place nearby is **CopyCat** (Map 5; ☎ *332 2563;* **e** *alko.copt@copycat.hu; V Alkotmány utca 18; metro M3 Nyugati pályaudvar; open 7am-10pm daily).*

All the major courier companies are represented here including **DHL** (☎ *06-40 454 545;* **W** *www.dhl.hu)*, **UPS** (☎ *06-40 262 000;* **W** *www.ups.com*), and **Federal Express** (☎ *216 3606;* **e** *royalexp@axelero.hu).*

WORK

Travellers on tourist visas in Budapest are not supposed to accept employment, but many end up teaching, doing a little writing for the English-language press or even working for foreign firms without permits. Check the English-language telephone book or advertisements for English-language schools in the *Budapest Sun*, which also has job listings, but pay is generally pretty low. You can do much better teaching privately (2000Ft to 4000Ft per 45-minute 'hour', depending on your experience).

Obtaining a work permit *(munkavállalási engedély)* involves a Byzantine paper chase. You'll need a letter of support from your prospective employer, copies of your birth certificate, your academic record officially translated into Hungarian (about 3000Ft per page) and results of a recent medical examination (including a test for exposure to HIV, costing about 4000Ft). The employer then has to submit these to the local labour centre *(munkaügyi központ)*, and you *must* return to your country of residence and apply for the work permit (which will cost about US$40 or equivalent) at the Hungarian embassy or consulate there.

When you return to Budapest, you have 15 days to gather all the documents required to apply for a one-year renewable residence permit *(tartózkodási engedély;* 8000Ft) through the main police station *(főkapitányság)* in your district or city.

Getting There & Away

AIR

Malév Hungarian Airlines *(MA; ☎ 235 3888; w www.malev.hu)*, the national carrier, flies nonstop to Budapest's **Ferihegy International Airport** *(☎ 296 9696)* from North America, the Middle East and almost three dozen cities in Continental Europe and the British Isles. It links up with flights from Asia and Australasia at some of its European gateways (eg, Paris, Frankfurt or Helsinki for Hong Kong, and London, Frankfurt or Rome for Sydney).

Malév flights and those of its 10 code-share partners arrive and depart from Ferihegy's **Terminal 2A** *(departures info ☎ 296 7000, arrivals info ☎ 296 8000)*. All other international airlines use **Terminal 2B** *(departures info ☎ 296 5882, arrivals info ☎ 296 5052)*. The old **Terminal 1**, about 5km to the west, is now used only for cargo and by air-taxi companies (see Other Parts of Hungary in this section for listings).

Departure Tax

An air passenger duty *(illeték)* of between 8000Ft and 10,000Ft is levied on all air tickets written in Hungary. The one exception is JFK International Airport in New York, which attracts a tax of 20,000Ft. This duty is almost always incorporated in the quoted fare. There are no other departure or port taxes.

Other Parts of Hungary

There are no scheduled flights within Hungary. The cost of domestic air taxis is prohibitive (eg, from 140,000Ft for up to three people from Budapest to Szeged and back), and the trips can take almost as long as the train when you add the time required to get to and from the airports. Several better-known firms with offices in Budapest are **Indicator Aviation** *(☎ 202 6284; w www.indicator.hu; XII Városmajor utca 30)*; **Farnair Hungary** *(☎ 347 6040; w www.farnair.com; XIX Üllői út 200)*; and **Avia Express** *(☎ 296 7092, 296 7791, fax 296 7891; Ferihegy Terminal 1)*.

Warning

The information in this chapter is particularly vulnerable to change: Prices for international travel are volatile, routes are introduced and cancelled, schedules change, special deals come and go, and rules and visa requirements are amended. You should check directly with the airline or a travel agent to make sure you understand how a fare (and ticket you may buy) works and be aware of the security requirements for international travel.

The upshot of this is that you should get opinions, quotes and advice from as many airlines and travel agents as possible before you part with your hard-earned cash. The details given in this chapter should be regarded as pointers and are not a substitute for your own careful, up-to-date research.

Continental Europe & the UK

Malév flies nonstop to Budapest from Amsterdam, Athens, Berlin, Brussels, Bucharest, Copenhagen, Dublin, Düsseldorf, Frankfurt, Hamburg, Helsinki, Istanbul, Kiev, Larnaca, London, Madrid, Milan, Moscow, Munich, Paris, Prague, Rome, Sarajevo, Skopje, Sofia, Stockholm, Stuttgart, Thessaloníki, Tirana, Vienna, Warsaw, Zagreb and Zürich.

Other airlines serving Budapest from European gateways include:

Aeroflot (SU) Moscow
Aerosvit Airlines (VV) Kiev
Air France (AF) Paris
Air Malta (KM) Malta
Air Ukraine (6U) Kiev
Alitalia (AZ) Rome, Milan
British Airways (BA) London
Carpatair (V3) Cluj-Napoca
Crossair (LX) Zürich
CSA Czech Airlines (OK) Prague
EgyptAir (MS) Cairo
Finnair (AY) Helsinki
KLM Royal Dutch Airlines (KL) Amsterdam
LOT Polish Airlines (LO) Warsaw
Pulkovo Aviation (Z8) St Petersburg

Tarom Romanian Airlines (RO) Bucharest
Turkish Airlines (TK) Istanbul

At the time of writing, **British Airways** (☎ 0845 773 3377; W *www.britishairways.co .uk*) was offering basic return excursion tickets with fixed dates (and heavy penalties if you changed them) from London to Budapest for UK£239 and £279, depending on whether travel was on a weekend or midweek respectively; the fares were £10 less if you booked online. Of course, you can always fly to Prague on the budget airline **Go** (☎ 0845 605 4321; W *www.go-fly.com*) for around UK£100 and then cover the last leg by bus or train.

From Budapest, most destinations in Europe on Malév cost from 63,000Ft to 80,000Ft return, including Warsaw and Prague (63,000Ft each) and Moscow and London (both 75,000Ft). You may find cheaper tickets through discount travel agencies; at the time of writing, Budapest-based **Ázsia Travel** (☎ 318 0505, fax 317 6013; V *Városház utca 16*) had a return to London for 57,000Ft and one to Paris for just under 40,000Ft.

The USA & Canada
Malév runs a daily service nonstop to/from New York (JFK Airport), though you can also fly direct with KLM or via Amsterdam with Northwest Airlines and Malév. Malév also has a flight nonstop to/from Toronto four times a week. Air Canada and Malév fly to/from Montreal via Paris (Charles de Gaulle Airport). From New York with Malév, the standard return fare hovers around US$850 though a discount one with the usual restrictions costs about US$515.

From Budapest with Malév, a return fare to New York starts at about 129,000Ft though a discount one can go as low as 85,000Ft.

Australia & New Zealand
The easiest way to get to Hungary from Australia is to fly Qantas from Sydney or Melbourne direct to London Heathrow and get on a Malév or British Airways flight to Budapest. Another option is Sydney to Frankfurt and then Malév to Budapest. Air New Zealand flies daily to London Heathrow and

connects with a nonstop Malév flight to Budapest. Return low-season fares from Sydney and Melbourne range from A$1865 to A$2300. Fares from Auckland and Wellington are NZ$2299 to NZ$2599. A standard return flight to Sydney or Melbourne from Budapest costs 336,000Ft, but official discounted special deals are available direct from the airline from time to time.

Africa & the Middle East
Malév flies nonstop six times a week (daily in summer) to/from Tel Aviv while El Al has a service three or four times a week, depending on the season. Malév serves Cairo three times a week (four departures daily in summer) while EgyptAir has twice-weekly nonstop flights. Malév also flies nonstop twice a week to both Beirut and Tripoli. Tunisair flies a nonstop charter once a week to Budapest.

Representative return fares include those from Tel Aviv US$400, Cairo US$310, Beirut US$350, Tripoli US$345 and Tunis US$530.

Asia
Malév hooks up with a number of other carriers serving destinations in Asia, including Colombo (with Sri Lankan Airlines via Zürich or Paris), Hong Kong (with Cathay Pacific via Frankfurt or Paris, or with Finnair via Helsinki), Taipei (with China Airlines via Amsterdam or Frankfurt) and Bangkok (with Finnair via Helsinki, or with China Airlines via Amsterdam).

A return Budapest–Bangkok ticket should cost from 157,000Ft to 163,000Ft, though you might find a discounted one for as low as 149,000Ft. Expect to pay 240,000Ft from Budapest to Bangkok via London on British Airways and from 210,000Ft to Hong Kong.

Airline Offices
The main **Malév ticket office** (Map 6; ☎ 235 3534, 235 3417; W *www.malev.hu*; V *Dorottya utca 2; open 8.30am-5.30pm Mon-Wed & Fri, 8.30am-6pm Thur*) is near Vörösmarty tér. In addition Malév has ticket-issuing desks at Ferihegy's **Terminal 2A** (☎ 296 7211) and at **Terminal 2B** (☎ 296 5767).

GETTING THERE & AWAY

Other major carriers and their locations and contact numbers include:

Aeroflot (☎ 318 5892) V Váci utca 4
Air Canada (☎ 317 9109) V Ferenciek tere 10
Air France (☎ 318 0441) V Kristóf tér 6
Alitalia (☎ 483 2170) V Bajcsy-Zsilinszky út 12
Austrian Airlines (☎ 327 9080) V Régiposta utca 5
Balkan Airlines (☎ 317 1818) V Párizsi utca 7
British Airways (☎ 411 5555) VIII Rákóczi út 1–3, East-West Business Centre
CSA Czech Airlines (☎ 318 3175) V Vörösmarty tér 2
Finnair (☎ 317 4022) V Bajcsy-Zsilinszky út 12
KLM Royal Dutch Airlines (☎ 373 7737) VIII Rákóczi út 1–3, East-West Business Centre
LOT Polish Airlines (☎ 317 2444) V Vigadó tér 3
Lufthansa (☎ 266 4511) V Váci utca 19–21
SAS (☎ 266 2633) V Bajcsy-Zsilinszky út 12
Swiss International Air Lines/Crossair (☎ 328 5000) V Kristóf tér 7–8
Tarom Romanian Airlines (☎ 317 2307) V Apáczai Csere János utca 4
Turkish Airlines (☎ 266 4269) V Apáczai Csere János utca 4

BUS

All international buses and some (though not all) domestic ones to/from southern and western Hungary now arrive at and depart from the new **Népliget bus station** (*Map 7; ☎ 264 3939; IX Üllői út 131; metro M3 Népliget*) in Pest. The **international ticket office** (*open 6am-6pm Mon-Fri, 6am-4pm Sat & Sun*) is upstairs. **Eurolines** (*☎ 219 8080, 219 8000; w www.eurolines.com*) is represented here, as is its Hungarian associate **Volánbusz** (*☎ 485 216, 485 2100; w www.volanbusz.hu, Hungarian only*). There's a **left-luggage office** (*open 6am-9pm daily; per piece per day 150Ft*) downstairs.

Népstadion bus station (*Map 3; ☎ 252 4498, 251 0125; XIV Hungária körút 48-52; metro M2 Népstadion*) serves cities and towns to the east of the capital. Things were in a state of flux at the time of research while the adjacent Budapest Sportcsarnok, destroyed by fire in 1999, was being rebuilt, but you should find the **ticket office** (*open 6am-6pm Mon-Fri, 6am-noon Sat & Sun*) as well as the **left-luggage office** (*open 6am-6pm daily*) here.

The **Árpád híd bus station** (*Map 2; ☎ 329 1450; XIII Róbert Károly körút; metro M3 Árpád híd; ticket office open 7am-4pm Mon-Fri*), on the Pest side of Árpád Bridge, is the place to catch buses for the Danube Bend and parts of the Northern Uplands (Balassagyarmat, Szécsény, Salgótarján etc).

Széna tér bus station (*Map 3; ☎ 201 3688; I Széna tér 1/a; metro M2 Moszkva tér*) in Buda handles some traffic to and from the Pilis Hills and towns northwest of the capital, with a half-dozen departures to Esztergom as an alternative to the Árpád híd bus station.

Western Europe

From Népliget station there's a bus on Monday, Wednesday, Friday and Saturday year-round to Amsterdam (1435km, 19 hours) via Frankfurt and Düsseldorf and carrying on to Rotterdam (1510km, 21½ hours) costing 24,900/37,900Ft one way/return, with a 10% discount for those under 26 or over 60 years of age. From early June to late September the Amsterdam bus runs on Thursday and Sunday too and in July and early August it goes daily at slightly higher rates: 25,900/39,900Ft. In summer this bus fills up quickly, so try to book ahead.

The Budapest–Amsterdam bus goes through Austria, eliminating the need for a Czech or Slovakian visa. In Amsterdam tickets are sold by **Eurolines Nederland** (*☎ 020-560 8788; Rokin 10*), and at **Amstel bus station** (*☎ 020-560 8788; Julianaplein 5*). In Budapest you can buy them at the Népliget bus station.

Buses to London (1755km, 26 hours) via Brussels and Lille depart on Monday, Wednesday, Thursday and Sunday (32,900/47,900Ft). From May to late October the bus also runs on Friday, from late June to September on Saturday and from July to mid-October on Tuesday. In London check with **Eurolines** (*☎ 0870 514 3219; 52 Grosvenor Gardens SW1*)

Other Eurolines services between Budapest and Western European cities, with high-season (mid-June to mid-September) one-way/return fares quoted, include the following.

Athens
19,000/32,000Ft; 16 hours (1560km) via Thessaloníki (same price); three weekly year-round

Berlin
19,900/33,900Ft; 15 hours (915km) via Prague, continuing on to Hamburg (22,900/ 37,900Ft); three weekly year-round, five weekly from early June to late September

Paris
27,900/42,900Ft; 22 hours (1525km) via Strasbourg (25,900/40,900Ft); two to three weekly from April to late October

Rome
23,500/37,900Ft; 15 hours (1330km) via Bologna (16,900/27,500Ft) and Florence (18,900/30,500Ft), continuing on to Naples (25,500/39,500Ft); four weekly year-round, five to six weekly from early April to late October to Rome, two weekly year-round to Naples

Venice
13,500/22,500Ft; 13½ hours (770km) via Graz (8400/13,500Ft); three weekly year-round, five to six weekly from mid-May to early October

Vienna
6390/9390Ft; 3½ hours (254km) via Győr (4400/6400Ft); three buses daily (four on Saturday)

Czech Republic, Slovakia & Poland

From Népliget station there are buses to Bratislava (Pozsony in Hungarian; 3100/ 4900Ft, four hours, 213km) daily and to Prague (8900/14,500Ft, 10½ hours, 640km) three times weekly year-round. Extra overnight buses to Prague run on Sunday and Monday from July to mid-September, leaving Budapest at 7pm and arriving at 5.30am. Buses also leave on Saturday year-round for Kraków (6900/10,900Ft, 11 hours, 491km) via Zakopane (5600/8900Ft).

Romania

There are regularly scheduled buses on Saturday year-round from Budapest to Arad (4000/5700Ft, seven hours, 282km) and to Timişoara (Temesvár in Hungarian; 4900/ 6900Ft, eight hours, 334km).

Croatia & Serbia and Montenegro

From late June to early September a bus leaves Népliget for Pula (9900/15,800Ft, 14½ hours, 775km) every Friday travelling

through Rijeka (7900/12,600Ft) and Poreč (9300/14,900Ft). There's a daily service year-round to Belgrade (4100/6800Ft, nine hours, 422km) and another bus to Subotica (Szabadka in Hungarian; 3300/5300Ft, 4½ hours, 224km).

TRAIN

Magyar Államvasutak *(MÁV;* w *www.mav .hu)*, which translates as Hungarian State Railways, links up with the European rail network in all directions, running trains as far as London (via Cologne and Brussels), Paris (via Frankfurt), Stockholm (via Hamburg and Copenhagen), Moscow, Rome and Istanbul (via Belgrade).

The international trains listed below are expresses, and many – if not all – require seat reservations. On long hauls, sleepers are almost always available in both 1st and 2nd class, and couchettes are available in 2nd class. Not all express trains have dining or even buffet cars; make sure you bring along some snacks and drinks as vendors can be few and far between. Most Hungarian trains are hardly what you would call luxurious but they are generally clean and always very punctual.

In Budapest, most international trains arrive and depart from **Keleti station** *(Map 3;* ☎ *313 6835; VIII Kerepesi út 2-6)*; trains to certain destinations in Romania and Germany leave from **Nyugati station** *(Map 5;* ☎ *349 0115; VI Nyugati tér)*, while **Déli station** *(Map 3;* ☎ *355 8657; I Krisztina körút 37/a)* handles trains to/from Zagreb and Rijeka in Croatia. But these are not hard-and-fast rules, so always make sure you check which station the train leaves from when you buy a ticket. For 24-hour information on international train services call ☎ 461 5500 in Budapest.

To reduce confusion, specify your train by the name listed under the following sections or on the posted schedule when requesting information or buying a ticket. You can buy tickets at the three international train stations in Budapest, but it's easier at the **MÁV central ticket office** *(Map 5;* ☎ *461 5500, 461 5400;* w *www.mav.hu; VI Andrássy út 35; open 9am-6pm Mon-Fri Apr-Sept, 9am-5pm Mon-Fri Oct-Mar)*. They accept credit cards.

If you just want to get across the border, local trains are cheaper than international expresses, especially if you're on a one-way trip. Concession fares between cities of the former socialist countries are only available on return tickets.

As elsewhere in Europe, timetables for both domestic and international trains and buses use the 24-hour system. Remember that 0.05 means five minutes past midnight (or 12.05am) while 12.05 is five minutes after noon (12.05pm).

On many (though not all) bus and train timetables, Hungarian names are used for cities and towns in neighbouring countries. Many of these are in what once was Hungarian territory and the names are used by the Hungarian-speaking minorities who live there. You should at least be familiar with the more important ones (eg, Pozsony for Bratislava, Kolozsvár for Cluj-Napoca, Bécs for Vienna) to help decipher bus and some train timetables. See the Alternative Place Names appendix in the back of this book for reference.

Tickets & Fares

There are big discounts on return fares from Hungary to most of the former socialist countries: 30% to Bulgaria, the Czech Republic and Poland; 40% to Serbia and Montenegro and the Baltic states; 50% to Belarus, Russia and the Ukraine; up to 65% to Slovakia and Slovenia and up to 75% to Romania. Also, there's a 40% concession on return fares from Budapest to six selected cities: Prague and Brno in the Czech Republic, and Warsaw, Kraków, Katowice and Gdynia in Poland. Sample 2nd-class return fares include Prague €56, Moscow €103 and Warsaw €71.

For tickets to Western Europe you'll pay the same as everywhere else unless you're aged under 26 and qualify for the 30% to 50% BIJ (Billet International de Jeunesse) discount. If you do qualify, ask at MÁV, Express or **Wasteels** (☎ 210 2802; open 8am-7pm Mon-Fri, 8am-1pm Sat) in Keleti train station.

The following are sample 2nd-class return fares from Budapest: Amsterdam €212;

Berlin €126 (via Prague) and €198 (via Vienna); London €352; Munich €91; Rome €172 (via Ljubljana); Vienna €41. There's a 30% discounted return fare to Vienna of 7150Ft if you come back to Budapest within four days. Three daily EuroCity (EC) trains to Vienna and points beyond charge a supplement (650Ft to 1500Ft). The 1st-class seats are around 50% more expensive than seats in 2nd class, depending on the destination.

International seat reservation costs vary according to the destination (eg, €6.60 to Prague, €10.60 to Warsaw). Fines are levied on passengers without tickets (400Ft plus full single fare) or seat reservations (1000Ft plus reservation fee) on trains where they are mandatory.

Costs for sleepers depend on the destination, but a two-berth 2nd-class sleeper to Berlin/Prague/Venice/Moscow costs 5350/5250/5350/7000Ft per person per night; a single always costs at least double the price. A 2nd-class couchette in a compartment for six people costs from 1800Ft on the *Transbalkan* to Romania and Greece, to 5500Ft on the *Kálmán Imre* to Munich. Tickets are valid for 60 days from purchase and stopovers are permitted.

Budapest is no longer the bargain basement that it once was for tickets on the Trans-Siberian or the Trans-Mongolian Railways. In fact, MÁV will only write you a ticket to Moscow; you have to buy the onward ticket from there. Of course, if you are coming back to Budapest from Moscow you get a 50% discount.

When pricing train tickets from Western Europe remember that airfares (especially those out of London) usually beat surface alternatives (especially trains) hands down in terms of cost. For example, a low-season return airfare from London to Budapest is available through discount travel agents for around or under UK£200. By comparison, a two-month return ticket by rail to Budapest available from **Rail Europe** (☎ 0870 584 8848; w www.raileurope.com) costs UK£397 for adults, though the fare drops to UK£356 if the ticket is purchased a month in advance.

Western Europe

Seven trains a day link Vienna with Budapest (three hours, 273km) via Hegyeshalom and Győr. Most depart from Vienna's Westbahnhof, including the *Arrabona*, the EuroCity *Bartók Béla* and the EuroNight *Kálmán Imre* from Munich (7½ hours, 742km) via Salzburg (six hours, 589km), the EC *Liszt Ferenc* from Cologne (11 hours, 1247km) via Frankfurt (10 hours, 1026km), the *Dacia Express* to Bucharest (15½ hours, 874km), and the InterCity *Avala* to Belgrade (10 hours, 647km). The early morning EC *Lehár* departs from Vienna's Südbahnhof. None require seat reservations, although they're highly recommended in summer.

Up to nine trains leave Vienna's Südbahnhof every day for Sopron (1¼ hours, 76km) via Ebenfurth; as many as 10 daily also serve Sopron from Wiener Neustadt (easily accessible from Vienna). Some five milk trains daily make the four-hour, 136km trip from Graz to Szombathely.

The EC *Hungária* travels from Berlin (Zoo and Ostbahnhof stations) to Budapest (12½ hours, 1002km) via Dresden, Prague and Bratislava. The express *Spree-Donau Kurier* arrives from Berlin via Nuremberg.

Czech Republic, Slovakia & Poland

In addition to the EC *Hungária*, Budapest can be reached from Prague (seven hours, 611km) on the EC *Comenius*, the IC *Csárdás*, the *Slovan* and the *Pannónia Express*, which then carries on to Bucharest. The *Amicus* runs directly from Bratislava (three hours, 215km) every day.

Each day the EC *Polonia* and the *Báthory* leave Warsaw for Budapest (12 hours, 802km) passing through Bratislava or Štúrovo and Katowice. The *Cracovia* runs from Kraków to Budapest (10½ hours, 598km) via Košice. From Miskolc in northern Hungary, you can pick up the *Karpaty* to Warsaw via Kraków and Košice.

Another train, the *Rákóczi*, links Budapest with Košice and Bratislava. The *Bem* connects Budapest with Szczecin (17 hours, 1019km) in northwestern Poland via Wrocław and Poznań.

Three local trains daily cover the 90km from Košice to Miskolc (two hours). The 2km hop from Sátoraljaújhely in Hungary to Slovenské Nové Mesto (two daily) is only a four-minute ride by train.

Ukraine & Russia

From Moscow to Budapest (42 hours, 2106km) there's only the *Tisza Express*, which travels via Kiev and Lvov in the Ukraine. Most nationalities require a transit visa to travel through the Ukraine.

Romania

From Bucharest to Budapest (14 hours, 874km) you can choose from among six trains: the EC *Traianus*, the *Dacia Express*, the *Ovidius*, the EN *Ister*, the *Muntenia* and the *Pannonia*. All go via Arad (5½ hours, 253km) and some require seat reservations. The *Karpaty* links Miskolc and Bucharest.

There are two daily connections from Cluj-Napoca to Budapest (eight hours, 402km) via Oradea: the *Ady Endre* and the *Corona*. The *Partium* links Budapest with Oradea only. All three trains require a seat reservation.

There are two local trains daily connecting Baia Mare in northern Romania with Bucharest (8¾ hours, 285km) via Satu Mare and Debrecen.

Bulgaria and Serbia & Montenegro

The *Transbalkan*, which originates in Thessaloníki in Greece and travels through Bucharest, links Sofia with Budapest (25 hours, 1366km). Trains between Budapest and Belgrade (seven hours, 374km) via Subotica include the *Beograd*, the *Ivo Andrić* and the IC *Avala*.

You must reserve your seats on some of these trains.

Two local trains daily make the 1¾-hour, 45km journey between Subotica (in Serbia and Montenegro) and Szeged (in Hungary).

Croatia, Slovenia & Bosnia-Hercegovina

You can get to Budapest from Zagreb (seven hours, 386km) on two trains that pass through

Siófok on Lake Balaton's southern shore: the *Maestral*, which originates in Split and the *Venezia Express*, which goes to Budapest from Venice via Ljubljana (10 hours, 504km). Two other trains from Ljubljana are the IC *Citadella* and the IC *Dráva*, which also originates in Venice. The IC *Kvarner* links Budapest with Rijeka (nine hours, 591km) via Siófok on Lake Balaton and Zagreb. The no-name train linking Sarajevo with Budapest (616km) takes 14 hours and goes via Pécs.

CAR & MOTORCYCLE

Of the 60-odd border road crossings Hungary maintains with its neighbours, about a third (mostly in the north and northeast) are restricted to local citizens on both sides of the border (or, in the case of Austria, Hungarian and EU citizens).

See the boxed text for a list of major border crossings that are open to all motorists round the clock. For the latest information, check out Tourinform's website (**w** www.hungarytourism.hu).

WALKING & HITCHING

To save the cost of an international ticket, or just for fun, you may consider walking across the frontier into or out of Hungary. But many border guards frown on this practice, particularly in Romania, Serbia and Montenegro and the Ukraine; try hitching a ride instead.

If you're heading north, there are three crossings to/from Slovakia where you shouldn't have any problems. Bridges link Esztergom with Štúrovo and Komárom with Komárno. At Sátoraljaújhely, northeast of Miskolc, there's a highway border crossing over the Ronyva River which links the centre of town with Slovenské Nové Mesto.

To get to/from Romania, the easiest place to cross on foot is at the Nagylak/Nădlac border between Szeged and Arad (border open 7am-7pm daily). There are six local trains daily from the train station at Újszeged across the Tisza River from Szeged proper to Nagylak (47km, 1¼ hours) near the border. After crossing into Romania you must walk, cycle or hitch for

3km to Nădlac, where you can connect with a local train to Arad (52km, 1½ hours).

If you're bound for Slovenia, take one of up to 11 trains daily from Zalaegerszeg to Rédics (49km, 1½ hours), which is only a couple of kilometres from the main highway border crossing from Hungary into Slovenia. From the border it's a 5km walk south to the Lendava bus station, where you can catch a bus to Maribor (92km, 1¾ hours) or to Ljubljana (212km, four hours).

Ride Sharing

Kenguru *(Map 5; ☎ 266 5837, 483 0105; **w** www.kenguru.hu; VIII Kőfaragó utca 15; open 8am-6pm Mon-Fri, 10am-2pm Sat & Sun)* matches up drivers and riders for a fee – mostly to points abroad. Approximate one-way fares include Amsterdam 13,800Ft, London 15,200Ft, Munich 7300Ft, Paris 14,400Ft, Prague 5400Ft and Vienna 2800Ft.

BICYCLE

Cyclists may have problems crossing Hungarian border stations connected to main roads since bicycles are banned on motorways and national highways with single-digit route numbers.

See Cycling under Activities in the Things to See & Do chapter for more details on cycling in and around Budapest.

BOAT

A hydrofoil service on the Danube between Budapest and Vienna (5½ hours, 282km) with the possibility of disembarking at Bratislava (on request) operates daily from April to early November, with an extra sailing in August. Adult one-way/return fares for Vienna are €65/89 and for Bratislava €59/83. Students with ISIC cards pay €51/75, and children under six go free. Taking along a bicycle costs €16 extra each way.

In Budapest, ferries arrive and depart from the **International Ferry Pier** *(Nemzetközi hajóállomás; Map 6)* on V Belgrád rakpart, between Erzsébet and Szabadság Bridges on the Pest side. In Vienna, the boat docks at the Reichsbrücke pier near Mexikoplatz.

In April and from September to early November there's a daily sailing at 9am from

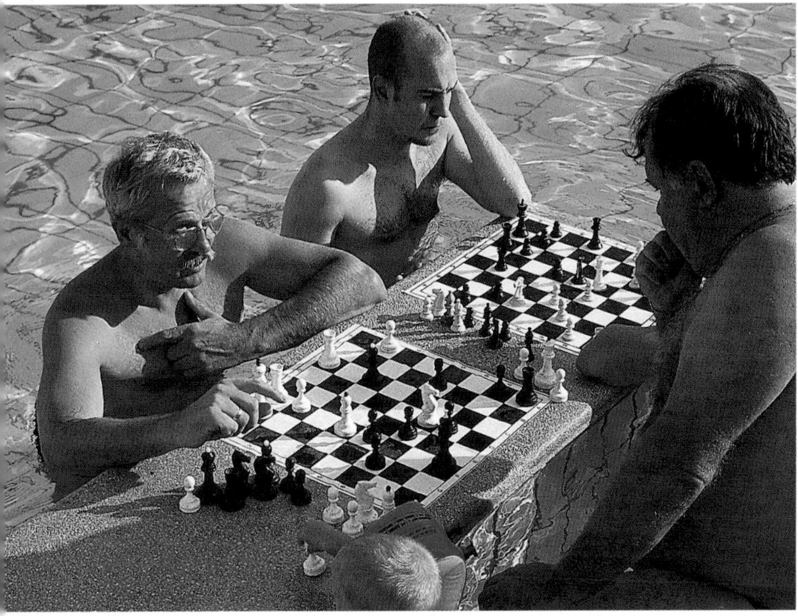

MARTIN MOOS

Playing chess at Széchenyi Baths

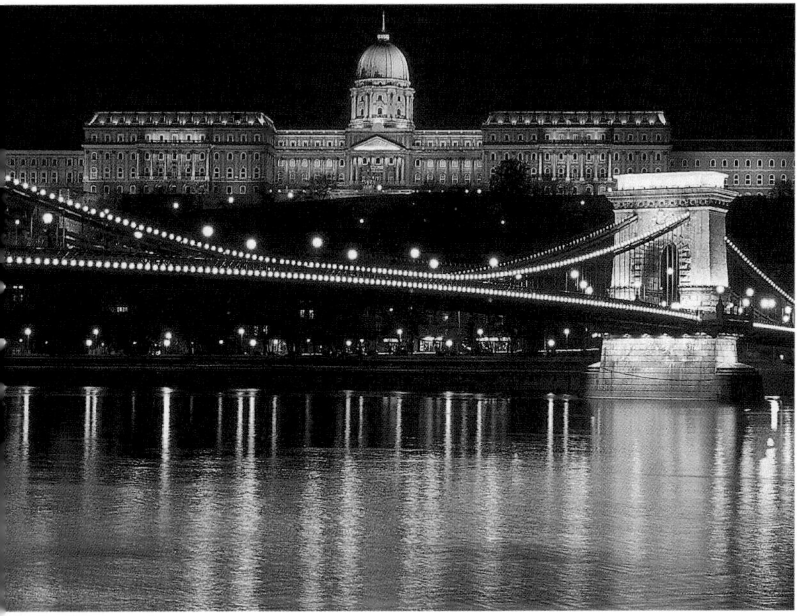

JONATHAN SMITH

Széchenyi Chain Bridge and Royal Palace

Dome of Parliament building

Chimneys, Geology Institute

Gül Baba's tomb

Váci utca

Major Border Crossings

The following is a list of border crossings between Hungary and its neighbouring countries (beginning in Austria and moving clockwise) that are open to motorists all year. The Hungarian checkpoint appears in the first column followed by the foreign checkpoint (or closest town) in the second column, with references to cities or big towns nearby (where applicable) inserted in brackets.

Hungary	Austria
Rábafüzes (5km north of Szentgotthárd)	Heiligenkreuz
Bucsu (13km west of Szombathely)	Schachendorf
Kőszeg	Rattersdorf
Kópháza (11km north of Sopron)	Deutschkreutz
Sopron (7km northwest of the city)	Klingenbach
Hegyeshalom (51km northwest of Győr)	Nickelsdorf

Hungary	Slovakia
Rajka (18km northwest of Mosonmagyaróvár)	Rusovce
Vámosszabadi (13km north of Győr)	Medvedov
Komárom	Komárno
Esztergom	Štúrovo
Hont (40km north of Vác)	Šahy
Balassagyarmat	Slovenské Darmoty
Somoskőújfalu (8km north of Salgótarján)	Šiatorska Vukovina (9km from Filakovo)
Bánréve (43km northwest of Miskolc)	Král
Tornyosnémeti (60km northeast of Miskolc)	Milhost
Sátoraljaújhely	Slovenské Nové Mesto

Hungary	Ukraine
Záhony (23km north of Kisvárda)	Čop (23km south of Užgorod)
Beregsurány (21km northeast of Vásárosnamény)	Berehove
Tiszabecs (27km northeast of Fehérgyarmat)	Vilok

Hungary	Romania
Csengersima (40km southeast of Mátészalka)	Petea (11km northwest of Satu Mare)
Nyírábrány (30km east of Debrecen)	Valea lui Mihai
Ártánd (25km southeast of Berettyóújfalu)	Borş (14km northwest of Oradea)
Méhkerék (24km north of Gyula)	Salonta
Gyula	Varşand (66km north of Arad)
Battonya (45km southeast of Orosháza)	Turnu
Nagylak (52km west of Szeged)	Nădlac (54km west of Arad)

Hungary	Serbia & Montenegro
Rözske (16km southwest of Szeged)	Horgoš (30km northeast of Subotica)
Tompa (30km south of Kiskunhalas)	Kelebija (11km northwest of Subotica)
Hercegszántó (32km south of Baja)	Bački Breg (28km northwest of Sombor)

Hungary	Croatia
Udvar (12km south of Mohács)	Kneževo
Drávaszabolcs (9km south of Harkány)	Donji Miholjac (49km northwest of Osijek)
Barcs (32km southwest of Szigetvár)	Terezino Polje
Berzence (24km west of Nagyatád)	Gola
Letenye (26km west of Nagykanizsa)	Goričan

Hungary	Slovenia
Rédics (9km southwest of Lenti)	Dolga Vas
Bajánsenye (60km west of Zalaegerszeg)	Hodoš

GETTING THERE & AWAY

both Budapest and Vienna. From May to August the boats leave both cities at 8am. In August an additional one departs from both cities at 1pm daily.

For information and tickets, contact **Mahart PassNave** *(Map 6; ☎ 484 4010, 318 1704; ⓦ www.maharttours.com; V Belgrád rakpart; 8am-4pm Mon-Fri)* in Budapest and **Mahart PassNave Wien** *(☎ 01-72 92 161, 72 92 162; Handelskai 265/3/517)* in Vienna.

ORGANISED TOURS

A number of travel agencies, including Vista and Ibusz (see Travel Agencies in the Facts for the Visitor chapter) as well as Cityrama and Program Centrum (see Organised Tours in the Getting Around chapter), offer both excursions and special interest guided tours (horse riding, cycling, bird-watching, Jewish culture etc) to every corner of Hungary.

A 4½-hour tour by boat and bus to Szentendre or by bus only to Gödöllő with Cityrama costs 10,000Ft (half-price for children under 12) while a 10-hour tour of the Danube Bend by coach and boat with stops at Szentendre, Visegrád and Esztergom is 16,000Ft. Cityrama also offers day trips to Lake Balaton (Balatonfüred, Tihany and the southern shore) and Herend (nine hours) as well as to Lajosmizse on the Southern Plain (eight hours) for 17,000Ft each. Program Centrum offers similar tours at almost the same prices as well as an eight-hour trip to Bugac in Kiskunság National Park and a nine-hour tour of the Eger wine region (19,000Ft each). Vista tours of the countryside start at 9750Ft.

Getting Around

THE AIRPORT

Budapest's **Ferihegy International Airport**
(☎ 296 9696), 24km southeast of the city
centre, has two modern terminals side by
side and within easy walking distance of
one another. For information on which airlines use which terminal, see Air in the Getting There & Away chapter. Terminal 2B
has an OTP bank and ATM, car rental and
hotel booking desks, a **post office** (open
8am-4pm Mon-Fri) and a **left-luggage office**
(open 24hr; 250/600/800Ft per 1/2/6 hrs,
1000/5000Ft per day/week).

TO/FROM THE AIRPORT

The **Airport Minibus Service** (☎ 296 8555,
fax 296 8993) ferries passengers in eight-seat vans from the airport directly to their
hotel, hostel or residence. The fare is
1800/3300Ft one way/return, and tickets are
available at a clearly marked desk in the arrival halls. You need to book your journey
to the airport 24 hours in advance, but remember that with all the pick-ups en route
this can be a nerve-wracking way to go if
you're running late.

The cheapest – but most time-consuming –
method to get into town is to take the **airport
bus** (look for the stop marked 'BKV Plusz
Reptér Busz' on the pavement between Terminals 2A and 2B), which terminates in
Kőbánya-Kispest metro station. From there
take the blue metro line (M3) into the centre.
The total cost is 190Ft.

If you want to take a taxi, call one of the
companies listed under Taxi later in this
chapter with a mobile or from a public phone
at arrivals (dispatchers speak English). **Tele 5**
(☎ 355 5555) has a flat fare of 2800Ft to or
from the airport from Pest (3200Ft to or from
Buda). Its taxis are waiting for calls just down
the road.

PUBLIC TRANSPORT

Budapest has an ageing but safe, efficient
and very inexpensive public transport system that will never have you waiting more

than five or 10 minutes for any conveyance.
There are five types of vehicles in use:
metro trains on three city lines, green HÉV
trains on four suburban lines, blue buses,
yellow trams and red trolleybuses. All are
run by **BKV** (Budapest Transport Company;
☎ 342 2335, 06-80 406 688; w www.bkv.hu).

The invaluable Budapesti Közlekedési
Térkép (Budapest Transport Map) detailing
all is available for a nominal fee at most
metro ticket booths.

Fares & Travel Passes

To ride the metro, trams, trolleybuses,
buses and the HÉV (as far as the city limits,
which is the Békásmegyer stop to the north)
you must have a valid ticket, which you can
buy at kiosks, newsstands or metro entrances. Children up to the age of six travel
free when accompanied by an adult. Bicycles can only be transported on the HÉV.

The basic fare for all forms of transport
is 106Ft (1000/1910Ft for a block of 10/20
tickets), allowing you to travel as far as you
like on the same metro, bus, trolleybus or
tram line without changing. A ticket allowing unlimited stations with one change
within 1½ hours costs 190Ft.

On the metro exclusively, the 106Ft base
fare drops to 75Ft if you are just going three
stops within 30 minutes. For 120Ft you can
travel five stops and transfer at Deák Ferenc
tér to another metro line within one hour.
Unlimited stations travelled with one
change within one hour costs 175Ft.

You must always travel in one continuous direction on any ticket; return trips are
not allowed. Tickets have to be validated in
machines at metro entrances and aboard
other vehicles – inspectors will fine you for
not validating your ticket.

Life will most likely be much simpler if
you buy a travel pass. Passes are valid on all
trams, buses, trolleybuses, HÉV (within the
city limits) and metro lines, and you don't
have to worry about validating your ticket
each time you get on. The most central places

to buy them are the **Deák Ferenc tér metro station ticket office** (*Map 6; open 6am-8pm daily*) and the **Nyugati metro station ticket office** (*Map 5; open 6am-8pm daily*).

A one-day pass is poor value at 850Ft, but the three-day pass (*touristajegy*, or tourist ticket) for 1700Ft and seven-day pass (*hetijegy*, or one week) for 2100Ft are worthwhile for most people. You'll need a photo for the fortnightly (2650Ft) and monthly (4050Ft) passes. All but the monthly travel passes are valid from midnight to midnight, so buy them in advance and specify the date(s) you want. The monthly pass is valid from the first day of the month until (generously) the fifth day of the following one.

Travelling 'black' (ie, without a valid ticket or pass) is risky: due to increased surveillance (especially in the metro), there's an excellent chance you'll get caught. (Note: tickets are *always* checked on the HÉV.) The on-the-spot fine is 1600Ft, which rises to 4000Ft if you pay later at the **BKV office** (*Map 5; ☎ 461 6800; VII Akácfa utca 22; open 6am-8pm Mon-Fri, 8am-2pm Sat*), and 8000Ft after 30 days. If you forget your travel pass (with photo) but can produce it at the BKV office within eight days, you'll be fined just 450Ft.

Of course, it's your decision, but remember how cheap BKV is to use. If you do get caught, do us all a favour: shut up and pay up. The inspectors – and your fellow passengers – hear the same boring (and usually false) stories every day of the year.

Metro

Budapest has three underground metro lines, which converge (only) at Deák Ferenc tér: the little yellow (or Millennium) line (M1) from Vörösmarty tér to Mexikói út in Pest; the red line (M2) from Déli train station in Buda to Örs vezér tere in Pest; and the blue line (M3) from Újpest-Központ to Kőbánya-Kispest in Pest. A possible source of confusion on the yellow line is that one stop is called Vörösmarty tér and another is Vörösmarty utca. The HÉV above-ground suburban railway, which runs north from Batthyány tér in Buda via Óbuda and Aquincum to Szentendre, south to Ráckeve and east and northeast to Gödöllő, is almost like a fourth metro line.

The metro is the fastest – but obviously the least scenic – way to go. All three lines run from 4.30am and begin their last journey at 11.10pm. After that a network of night buses (see the following) picks up the mantle.

Bus, Tram & Trolleybus

An extensive system of trams, trolleybuses and buses serve greater Budapest, and you'll seldom wait more than a few minutes for any of them. On certain bus lines the same number bus may have a black or a red number. In this case, the red-numbered bus is the express, which makes limited stops and is, of course, faster.

Daytime public transport in Budapest runs from about 4am to between 9pm and 11.30pm, depending on the line. From 11.30pm to 4am some 17 night buses (marked with an 'É' after the designated number) operate every 10 to 60 minutes, again depending on the line.

Buses and trams are much of a muchness, though the latter are often faster and generally more pleasant for sightseeing. Trolleybuses go along cross streets in central Pest and are of little use to most visitors – with the exception of those to City and Népliget Parks.

The most important tram lines (always marked with red lines on a Budapest map, while a broken red line is a trolleybus) are the following:

Nos 2 and 2/a Scenic trams that travel along the Pest side of the Danube as far as Jászai Mari tér

Nos 4 and 6 These are extremely useful trams that start at Fehérvári út and Móricz Zsigmond körtér, respectively, in district XI of south Buda and follow the entire length of the Big Ring Road in Pest before terminating at Moszkva tér in Buda

No 18 Runs from southern Buda along Bartók Béla út through the Tabán to Moszkva tér

No 19 Covers part of the same route but then runs along the Buda side of the Danube to Batthyány tér

Nos 47 and 49 Links Deák Ferenc tér in Pest with points in southern Buda via the Little Ring Road

No 61 Buda tram connecting Móricz Zsigmond körtér with Déli station and Moszkva tér

Some buses (always shown with blue lines on Budapest maps) you may find useful include:

Black No 4 Runs from northern Pest via Hösök tere to Deák Ferenc tér (the red No 4 follows the same route but crosses over Chain Bridge into central Buda)

No 6É night bus Follows the tram No 6 route along the Big Ring Road

No 7 Cuts across a large swathe of central Pest from Bosnyák tér and down Rákóczi út before crossing Elizabeth Bridge to Kelenföld station in southern Buda

No 14É night bus Follows the blue metro line above ground

No 86 Runs the length of Buda from Kosztolányi Dezső tér to Óbuda

No 105 Goes from Deák Ferenc tér to Apor Vilmos tér in central Buda

CAR & MOTORCYCLE

Though it's not so bad at night, driving in Budapest during the day can be a nightmare: roadworks reduce traffic to a snail's crawl, there are more serious accidents than fender-benders and parking spots are difficult to find. The public transport system is good and cheap. Try to use it.

Foreign drivers' licences are valid for one year after entering Hungary. Third-party liability insurance is compulsory. If your car is registered in the EU, it is assumed you already have it. Other motorists must show a Green Card or will have to buy insurance at the border.

Road Rules

You must drive on the right-hand side of the road. Speed limits for cars and motorbikes are consistent throughout Hungary and strictly enforced: 50km/h in built-up areas (from the town sign as you enter to the same sign with a red line through it as you leave); 80km/h on secondary and tertiary roads; 100km/h on most highways/dual carriageways; and 120km/h on motorways. Exceeding the limit will earn you a fine of between 5000Ft and 30,000Ft, which must be paid by postal cheque or at any post office.

The use of seat belts in the front (and in the back – if fitted – outside built-up areas) is compulsory in Hungary, but this rule is often ignored. Motorcyclists must wear helmets, a law strictly enforced. Another law taken very seriously indeed is the one requiring *all* drivers to use their headlights throughout the day outside built-up areas. Motorcyclists must use headlights at all times everywhere. Using a mobile phone while driving is prohibited in Hungary.

Drink-driving is taken very seriously in Hungary, where there is a 100% ban on alcohol for anyone taking the wheel (see Legal Matters in the Facts for the Visitor chapter). **Soför Szervíz** (☎ 06-30 934 9824) in Budapest will send a staff member to meet you and drive your car home should you decide to drink. Prices vary but range from 1400Ft to 3700Ft. They operate from 8pm to 4am, and it takes about an hour for the driver to arrive on Friday or Saturday evening and during rush hour.

All accidents should be reported to the police (☎ 107) immediately. Several insurance companies handle auto liability, and minor claims can be settled without complications. Any claim on insurance policies bought in Hungary can also be made to **Hungária Biztosító** (Map 4; ☎ 301 6565; I Dísz tér 4-5) in Budapest. It is one of the largest insurance companies in Hungary and deals with foreigners on a regular basis.

For information on traffic and public road conditions nationwide, contact **Útinform** (☎ 322 2238, 322 7643; www.kozut.hu). In the capital ring **Főinform** (☎ 317 1173).

Motoring Organisations

The so-called **Yellow Angels** (Sárga Angyal; 24hr nationwide ☎ 188, in Budapest ☎ 345 1744) of the **Hungarian Automobile Club** (Magyar Autóklub; Map 3; ☎ 212 2821; II Rómer Flóris 4/a) do basic car repairs free of charge in the event of a breakdown if you belong to an affiliated organisation such as AAA in the USA or AA in the UK. Towing, however, is still very expensive even with these reciprocal memberships.

Petrol

Petrol (benzin) of 91 octane and unleaded (ólommentes) of 95 and 98 octane is available everywhere and costs 219/222/231Ft per litre respectively. Most stations also have diesel fuel *(gázolaj)* costing 203Ft per litre. Payment by credit card is now standard at Hungarian petrol stations.

Parking

In Budapest parking now costs between 80Ft and 180FT on the street (8am to 6pm Monday to Friday, 8am to noon Saturday). There are 24-hour covered car parks charging around 100Ft an hour in V Szervita tér and V Aranykéz utca 4–6 in the Inner Town, and at VII Nyár utca 20. If you're trying to trace a towed vehicle, call ☎ 383 0700 or ☎ 383 0770. It's going to cost you just under 8500Ft to set your vehicle free though, plus a charge of 500Ft a day for storage.

Rental

In general, you must be at least 21 years old and have had your licence for a year or longer to rent a car. Drivers under 25 sometimes have to pay a surcharge. All the big international firms have offices in Budapest, and there are scores of local companies throughout the country, but don't expect many bargains. An Opel Corsa from **Avis** *(Map 6; ☎ 318 4158, fax 318 4859; V Szervita tér 8)*, for example, costs €35/215 per day/week plus €0.35 per kilometre and €23 collision damage waiver (CDW) and theft protection insurance. The same car with unlimited kilometres and insurance costs from €131 per day or €146 for a weekend. The 25% ÁFA (value-added tax) doesn't apply to nonresidents paying with foreign currency or credit card.

One of the cheapest outfits for renting cars is **Inka Rent a Car** *(Map 7; ☎ 456 4666, fax 456 4699; e mail@inkarent.hu; IX Könyves Kálmán körút; open 8am-7pm Mon-Sat, 8am-2pm Sun)*. One of their Opel Corsas costs €20 a day plus €0.20 per kilometre (or €250 a week with up to 800km a day included). Though more expensive than Inka, **Americana Rent-a-Car** *(Map 3; ☎ 350 2542, fax 320 8287; w www.americana.matav.hu; XIII Dózsa György út 65)* in the Ibis Volga hotel is reliable. Another good bet is **Fox Autorent** *(Map 7; ☎ 382 9004; w www.fox-autorent.com; XI Vegyész utca 24-28)*, which charges €46 per

---

A Street by Any Other Name

After WWII most streets, squares and parks were renamed after people, dates or political groups that have since become anathema to an independent and democratic Hungary. From April 1989 names were changed at a frantic pace and with a determination that some people felt was almost obsessive; Cartographia's *Budapest Atlas* lists almost 400 street name changes in the capital alone. Sometimes it has just been a case of returning a street or square to its original (perhaps medieval) name – from Lenin útja, say, to Szent korona útja (Street of the Holy Crown). Other times the name is new.

The new (or original) names are now in place after more than a decade, the old street signs with a red 'X' drawn across them have all but disappeared and virtually no one refers to Ferenciek tere (Square of the Franciscans), for example, as Felszabadulás tér (Liberation Square), which honoured the Soviet Army's role in liberating Budapest in WWII.

---

day (€230 per week) for a Fiat Seicento and €69/420 for a Suzuki Swift, kilometres and insurance included.

TAXI

Taxis remain a Budapest bugbear after all these years, but with such an excellent public transport network available, you won't really have to use them very much. We've heard from many readers who were grossly overcharged and even threatened by taxi drivers in Budapest, so taking a taxi in this city should be approached with caution. However, the reputable firms listed in this section have caught on to the concept of customer service and they now take complaints quite seriously.

Watch out for taxis with no name on the door and only a removable taxi light box on the roof: these are just guys with cars and will most likely rip you off. Never *ever* get into a cab that does not have a yellow licence plate, an identification badge displayed on the dashboard (as required by law), the logo of one of the reputable taxi firms on the side doors and a table of fares posted prominently.

Not all taxi meters are set at the same rates, and some are much more expensive than others, but there are price ceilings within which cab companies are free to manoeuvre. From 6am to 10pm the highest flag-fall fee that can be legally charged is 200Ft; the per-kilometre charge is 200Ft and the waiting fee 50Ft per minute. From 10pm to 6am the fees are 280/280/70Ft.

Budapest residents – local or foreign – rarely flag down taxis in the street. They almost always ring for them, and fares are actually cheaper if you book. Make sure you know the number of the landline phone you're calling from as that's how they establish your address (though you can, of course, call from a mobile phone too). Dispatchers usually speak English.

The following are the telephone numbers of reliable taxi firms in Budapest:

Buda	☎ 233 3333
City	☎ 211 1111
Est Taxi	☎ 244 4444
Fő	☎ 222 2222
Rádió	☎ 377 7777
Tele 5	☎ 355 5555

BICYCLE

More and more cyclists can be seen on the streets and avenues of Budapest these days taking advantage of the excellent network of bike paths. The main roads in the city might be a bit too busy and nerve-wracking to allow enjoyable cycling, but the side streets are fine and there are some areas (City Park, Margaret Island etc) where biking is ideal. See Cycling under Activities in the Things to See & Do chapter for ideas on where to cycle and information on where to rent bikes.

BOAT

Between May and mid-September **BKV passenger ferries** (☎ 369 1359; w www.ship-bp .hu, Hungarian only) depart from IX Boráros tér (Map 7) beside Petőfi Bridge up to five times a day Friday to Sunday and head for III Rómaifürdő and Pünkösdfürdő in Óbuda, a one-hour trip with many stops along the way. Tickets (adult/child 500/400Ft from end to end or 400/200Ft from intermediate stops) are sold on board. The ferry stop closest to the Castle District is I Batthyány tér, and V Petőfi tér is not far from Vörösmarty tér, a convenient place to pick up the boat on the Pest side.

See Boat in the Organised Tours section later in this chapter for information about river cruises.

ORGANISED TOURS
Bus

Many travel agencies, including **Cityrama** (Map 5; ☎ 302 4382; w www.cityrama.hu; V Báthory utca 22) and **Program Centrum** (Map 6; ☎ 317 7767; w www.programcentrum.hu; V Erzsébet tér) at the Hotel Le Meridien, offer three-hour city tours with three stops from 6000/3000Ft per adult/child under 12. They also have excursions farther afield to the Danube Bend, Lake Balaton, the Southern Plain and the Eger wine region (see Organised Tours in the Getting There & Away chapter).

Budatours (Map 6; ☎ 353 0558, 374 7070; w www.budatours.hu; VI Andrássy út 2) runs eight bus tours daily in both open and covered coaches in July and August (between two and three daily the rest of the year) from V Andrássy út 3. It's a two-hour nonstop tour with taped commentary in 16 different languages and costs 5300/2700Ft per adult/child under 16. **Queenybus** (Map 1; ☎ 247 7159, fax 309 0395; XI Törökbálinti út 28) has buses departing three times daily (10am, 11am and 2.20pm) from St Stephen's Basilica, V Bajcsy-Zsilinszky út, for three-hour city tours (6000/4000/3000Ft per adult/student/child).

Boat

From late April to September **Mahart PassNave** (Map 6; ☎ 484 4013, 318 1223; V Belgrád rakpart) has half-hour cruises on the Danube at noon and 7.30pm daily for 1200/600Ft per adult/child under 10. In April the noon cruise operates on Saturday and holidays only, and from mid-June to August the evening program begins at 8.15pm and includes music and dance (1800/900Ft). Other, more expensive, cruises also operate on the river, including **Legenda** *(☎ 266 4190, fax 317 2203;* **w** *www .legenda.hu)*, which runs tours by day (3400/1600Ft) and night (4000Ft) with taped commentary in up to 30 languages. The night lights of the city rising to Buda Castle, Parliament, Gellért-hegy and the Citadella make the evening trip far more attractive than the afternoon one. Mahart also has a two-hour folk evening cruise (8900Ft) at 8pm Wednesday and Saturday from May to September and **Kulturinfo** *(☎ 06-20 332 9116)* runs an operetta ship cruise from 8am to 10pm on Monday, Friday and Sunday from April to September.

Walking

Highly recommended is **Absolute Walking Tours** *(☎ 06-30 211 8861;* **w** *www.budapes tours.com)*, offering a 3½-hour guided promenade through City Park, central Pest and Castle Hill. Tours (3500/3000Ft per adult/student and under-26) depart at 9.30am and 1.30pm daily from the steps of the yellow Calvinist church on Deák Ferenc tér and at 10am and 2pm daily from the steps of the Műcsarnok art gallery in Hősök tere from mid-May to September. During the rest of the year they leave from the Calvinist church on Deák Ferenc tér at 10.30am and the Műcsarnok at 11am only, with tours curtailed over Christmas and in January. They've got some cracker specialist tours, including the Hammer & Sickle Tour.

Castle Walks *(☎ 488 0453)*, sponsored by the Tourism Office of Budapest, will lead you through the winding ways and tortuous tales of the historic Castle District starting from Matthias Church for 2400Ft. Tours leave at 11am and 3.30pm daily from late June to mid-September and on Saturday and Sunday only from late April to late June and late September to late October.

More personal are **Paul Street Tours** *(☎ 06-20 958 2545;* **e** *kfaurest@hotmail.com)*, which cover the Castle District (30 minutes), less-explored areas of Pest such as the Jewish Quarter and Andrássy út (two hours), the Little Ring Road, the parks and gardens of Budapest, shopping etc, with lots of anecdotal background information on architecture and social history, especially life in and around the *udvar* (courtyards) of *fin-de-siècle* Pest. Tours are available year-round in English or Hungarian and cost around €25 per hour for up to 15 people.

Specialised Focusing on Budapest's Jewish heritage, **Hungária Koncert** *(☎ 317 2754, 317 1377)* has a 2½-hour tour available at 10.30am and 1.30pm most weekdays year-round and at 11.30am on Sunday. The tour includes a visit to the Great and Orthodox Synagogues, the Jewish museum, a walking tour of the ghetto and a nonkosher snack for 5600/5100Ft per adult/student (4900/4300Ft without the snack) including transport to the Great Synagogue. Tickets are available from locations throughout the city, including the **Duna Palota** *(Map 6; V Zrínyi utca)* and at the entrance to the Great Synagogue. **Chosen Tours** *(☎ 355 2202;* **w** *www.wittmann-tours .com)* offers a similar programme at 10am Sunday to Friday.

Cycling

Yellow Zebra Bikes *(☎ 06-30 399 7093;* **e** *yellowzebrabikes@yahoo.com)*, run by the same people behind Absolute Walking Tours, has cycling tours of Budapest by day at 11.30am May to October and by night at 8pm on Sunday, Tuesday and Thursday from June to September. Tours cost 4000/3500Ft per adult/student and under-26, include the bike and a drink, and depart from the yellow Calvinist church on Deák Ferenc tér.

Things to See & Do

HIGHLIGHTS

Though it's a matter of taste and interest, the highlights in the boxed text on this page list what could be considered the top sights and activities in Budapest; several of them should be included on every traveller's itinerary. For those with more time or an interest in seeing the city in greater depth, there are a dozen walking tours to follow.

WALKING TOURS

Budapest is a city made for walking and there are sights around every corner – from a brightly tiled gem of an Art Nouveau building to peasant women up from the countryside hawking their home-made *barack lekvár* (apricot jam) or colourful embroidery at the markets.

The following tours can easily be done individually or in tandem with the preceding or following ones; the highlights listed here can be found along the way. Don't worry about doing every tour or even finishing one; linger as long as you like in a museum or market that takes your fancy, do a little shopping or even visit one of the city's fine thermal spas along the way.

Budapest's museums and other important sights are listed in alphabetical order and described in detail after this section for those who just want to visit a handful of sights and/or are not into walking.

Walking Tour 1: Castle Hill

Castle Hill (Várhegy), a 1km-long limestone plateau towering 170m above the Danube, contains Budapest's most important medieval monuments and museums and is a Unesco World Heritage Site. It is the premier sight in the capital, and with its grand views and so many things to see, you should start your touring here. Castle Hill sits on a 28km network of caves formed by thermal springs. The caves were used by the Turks for military purposes, as air-raid shelters during WWII and as a secret military installation during the Cold War.

Budapest Highlights

- The view from Fishermen's Bastion on Castle Hill

- A night at the Hungarian State Opera House

- A soak at any of the city's celebrated thermal baths, especially the Gellért, Rudas or Széchenyi

- The two icons of Hungarian nationhood: the Crown of St Stephen in the Parliament building and the saint-king's mortal remains in the Basilica of St Stephen

- The period furniture and bric-a-brac inside the Applied Arts Museum and the Secessionist features on the outside

- The wonderfully restored Great Market Hall (Nagycsarnok) or the more traditional markets at VIII Rákóczi tér and XIII Lehel tér

---

All the sights listed in this section can be found on Map 4.

The walled Castle area consists of two distinct parts: the Old Town (Vár), where commoners lived in the Middle Ages (the current owners of the coveted burgher houses here are no longer so common) and the Royal Palace (Budavári palota), the original site of the castle built by Béla IV in the 13th century.

The easiest way to get to Castle Hill (on the Buda side of town) from Pest is to take bus No 16 from Deák Ferenc tér to Dísz tér, midway between the Old Town and the Royal Palace. Much more fun, though, is to take a stroll across Chain Bridge and board the **Sikló** (*uphill/downhill adult 450/250Ft, child aged 2-10 350/250Ft; open 7.30am-10pm daily*), a funicular railway built in 1870 that ascends from Clark Ádám tér to Szent György tér near the Royal Palace in only two minutes. The funicular does not run on the first and third Monday of each month.

Alternatively, you can walk up the Király lépcső, the 'Royal Steps' that lead from Hunyadi János út north-west of Clark Ádám tér, or the wide staircase that goes to the southern end of the Royal Palace from Szarvas tér.

Another option is to take metro M2 to Moszkva tér, cross the footbridge above the square and walk up Várfok utca to Vienna Gate. A minibus with a logo of a castle and labelled 'Várbusz' or 'Dísz tér' follows the same route from the start of Várfok utca.

The best way to see the **Old Town** is to stroll along the four medieval streets that run parallel (more or less) to one another; three of them converge on Szentháromság tér. Poke your head into the attractive little courtyards (an acceptable activity) and visit the odd museum, but be selective; it would take you at least two full days to see everything here. A brief tour of the Old Town in one of the horse-drawn hackney cabs (*fiáker*) standing in Szentháromság tér roughly from March to November will cost 1500Ft per person.

You can start your tour by climbing to the top of **Vienna Gate** (Bécsi kapu), rebuilt in 1936 to mark the 250th anniversary of the retaking of the castle from the Turks. It's always open. It's not all that huge, but when children in Budapest are loquacious or noisy, their parents tell them: 'Your mouth is as big as the Vienna Gate!' The large building to the west with the superb majolica tile roof contains the **National Archives** (Országos Levéltár; built in 1920). Across the square, which was a weekend market in the Middle Ages, a **Lutheran church** with the words 'A Mighty Fortress is Our God' written in Hungarian marks the start of Táncsics Mihály utca. On the west side of Bécsi kapu tér there's an attractive group of burger houses; No 7 has medallions of classical poets and philosophers, No 8 a curious round corner window.

Táncsics Mihály utca is a narrow street of little houses painted in lively hues and adorned with statues. Most have plaques with the word *műemlék* (memorial) attesting to their historical associations. The house at Táncsics Mihály utca 9, for example, cites that Lajos Kossuth was imprisoned here 'for his homeland' from 1837 to 1840. In the

entrances to many of the courtyards, you'll notice lots of **sedilia** – stone niches dating as far back as the 13th century. Some historians think they were used as merchant stalls, while others believe servants cooled their heels here while their masters (or mistresses) paid a visit to the occupant.

The **medieval Jewish prayer house** (*I Táncsics Mihály utca 26*), dating partly from the 14th century, contains a small museum. Across the road to the southeast is the **Museum of Music History** (*I Táncsics Mihály utca 7*) in an 18th-century palace. Concerts are sometimes held in the Kodály Hall here. The controversial **Budapest Hilton Hotel** (*I Hess András tér 1*), which incorporates parts of a 14th-century Dominican church and a baroque Jesuit college, is farther south. Have a look at the little red hedgehog in the relief above the doorway at the house on Hess András tér 3, which was an inn in the 14th century.

If you walk north from Hess András tér along Fortuna utca, another street of decorated houses, you'll soon reach one of Budapest's most interesting small museums: the **Commerce and Catering Museum** (*I Fortuna utca 4*). This street leads back into Bécsi kapu tér, but if you continue west along Petermann bíró utca you'll reach Kapisztrán tér. This square was named after John Capistranus (1386–1456), a charismatic Franciscan monk who raised an entire army for János Hunyadi in his campaign against the Turks. He was canonised in 1724 and is known as St John of Capistrano.

The large white building to the north of the square houses the **Military History Museum**. Around the corner, along the so-called **Anjou Bastion** (Anjou bástya), with displays detailing the development of the cannon, lies the turban-topped grave of Pasha Abdi Arnaut Abdurrahman (1615–86), the last Turkish Grand Vizier of Budapest, who was killed here on the day Buda was liberated. 'He was a heroic foe,' reads the tablet, 'may he rest in peace.'

The large steeple on the south side of Kapisztrán tér, visible for kilometres to the west of Castle Hill, is the **Mary Magdalene Tower** (*Magdolna torony; I Kapisztrán tér*), the reconstructed spire of an 18th-century church. The church, once reserved for Hungarian-speakers in this district (German-speakers worshipped at Matthias Church), was used as a mosque during the Turkish occupation and was destroyed in an air raid in 1944. Normally visitors are allowed to climb the steps to the top, but the tower was under renovation at the time of writing.

From Kapisztrán tér, walk south on Országház utca, being careful not to miss the sedile in the entrance to No 9 and the medieval houses painted white, tangerine and lime at Nos 18, 20 and 22.

Úri utca, the next parallel street to the west, has some interesting courtyards, especially No 19 with a sundial and what looks like a tomb. There are more Gothic sedilia at Nos 32 and 40; if the gates are locked there's a peephole to look through. The **Telephony Museum** (I Úri utca 49) is housed in an old Clarist monastery. At No 9 of the same street is the entrance to the **Buda Castle Labyrinth**.

Tree-lined Tóth Árpád sétány, the next 'street' (or walkway) over, follows the west wall from the Anjou Bastion to Dísz tér and has some great views of the Buda Hills. Toward the southern end you'll see a mounted **statue of András Hadik** (cnr I Úri utca & Szentháromság utca), a Hussar field marshal in the wars against the Turks. If you're wondering – and I know you are – why the steed's brass testicles are so shiny, well, it's a student tradition in Budapest to give them a stroke before taking an exam. Szentháromság utca leads east into the square of the same name.

In the centre of the square there's a **statue of the Holy Trinity** (Szentháromság szobor), another one of the 'plague pillars' put up by grateful (and healthy) Buda citizens in the early 18th century. Szentháromság tér is dominated by the Old Town's two most famous sights: Matthias Church and Fishermen's Bastion just beyond it. If you'd like to break now there's a chance for a crash course on viticulture at the **House of Hungarian Wines** (I Szentháromság tér 6).

Parts of **Matthias Church** (Mátyás templom; ☎ 489 0717; W www.matyas-templom .hu; I Szentháromság tér 2; adult/student or child 300/150, with guide 600/300Ft; open 9am-5pm Mon-Fri, 9am-1pm Sat, 1pm-5pm Sun) – so named because the 15th-century Renaissance king Matthias Corvinus married Beatrix here in 1474 – date back some 500 years, notably the carvings above the southern entrance. But basically the church is a neo-Gothic creation designed by architect Frigyes Schulek in 1896. The church has a colourful tile roof and a lovely tower; the interior is remarkable for its stained-glass windows, frescoes and wall decorations by the Romantic painters Károly Lotz and Bertalan Székely. They also did the wall decorations, an unusual mixture of folk, Art Nouveau and Turkish designs. There are organ concerts in the church on certain evenings (see Classical Music in the Entertainment chapter), continuing a tradition that began in 1867 when Franz Liszt's *Hungarian Coronation Mass* was first played here for the coronation of Franz Joseph and Elizabeth as king and queen of Hungary. Steps to the right of the main altar lead to the crypt. The entrance to the **Matthias Church Collection of Ecclesiastical Art** is straight ahead as you enter the church.

Fishermen's Bastion (Halászbástya; adult/ child 250/120Ft; open 8.30am-11pm daily) is another neo-Gothic masquerade that most visitors (and Hungarians) believe to be much older. Built as a viewing platform in 1905 by Schulek, the bastion's name was taken from the guild of fishermen responsible for defending this stretch of the wall in the Middle Ages. The seven gleaming white turrets represent the Magyar tribes who entered the Carpathian Basin in the late 9th century. In front of the bastion is an ornate equestrian **statue of St Stephen** by Alajos Stróbl. The bastion can be explored for free at night, when it is much more romantic.

The **Golden Eagle Pharmacy** (I Tárnok utca 18), a short distance to the southwest and just before Dísz tér, probably looks exactly the way it did in Buda Castle in the 16th century, though it was moved to its present site 100 years later. Today it houses a museum.

From Dísz tér, walk south along Színház utca to Szent György tér. Along the way you'll pass the bombed-out **Ministry of Defence** on the right, a casualty of WWII and during the Cold War NATO's supposed nuclear target for Budapest. Farther south and on the left is the **National Dance Theatre** *(Nemzeti Táncszínház; I Színház utca 1-3)*, built in 1736 as a Carmelite church and monastery, and then the recently restored **Sándor Palace** (Sándor palota), which may become the residence of the president.

From Szent György tér, you can enter the Royal Palace via one of two gates. **Corvinus Gate**, with its big black raven symbolising King Matthias Corvinus, is southwest of the square. To the southeast is an ornamental gateway dating from 1903 that leads to the **Habsburg Steps**. Flanking the steps is an enormous **statue of the turul** (1905), an eagle-like totem of the ancient Magyars (see the boxed text 'Blame it on the Bird') honoured as an ancestor of the Magyars.

The former Royal Palace has been burned, bombed, razed, rebuilt and redesigned at least half a dozen times over the past seven centuries. Béla IV established a royal residence here in the mid-13th century and subsequent kings either rebuilt their own or added on to them. The palace was destroyed in the battle to rout the Turks in 1686; the Habsburgs rebuilt it but spent very little time here. What you see today clinging to the southern end of Castle Hill is an 18th- and early-20th-century amalgam reconstructed after the last war, when it was bombed to bits. Today the palace contains not royal residences but museums – three of them – and the National Széchenyi Library.

The first part of the palace (Wing A) houses the **Ludwig Museum of Contemporary Art**. In the middle of the square facing the entrance, a Hortobágy *csikós* (cowboy) in full regalia breaks a mighty *bábolna* steed, a sculpture that won international recognition for its creator, György Vastagh, at the Paris World Exhibitions of 1900 and 1901.

To reach one of two entrances to the Hungarian National Gallery, walk under the little archway south of Wing B to the square facing the Danube for Wing C or walk under the massive archway protected by four snarling lions to Wing D. Those choosing the former will enter what was once the palace terrace and gardens. Just in front of Wing C stands a **statue of Eugene of Savoy**

(1663–1736), who wiped out the last Turkish army in Hungary at the Battle of Zenta in 1697. Designed by József Róna 200 years later, it is considered to be the finest equestrian statue in the capital.

Either route you take, you'll pass the large, Romantic-style **Matthias Fountain** (Mátyás kút), which portrays the young King Matthias Corvinus in hunting garb. To his right below is Szép Ilona (Beautiful Helen), a protagonist of a Romantic ballad by the poet Mihály Vörösmarty. Apparently the poor girl fell in love with the dashing 'hunter' and, upon learning his true identity and feeling unworthy, she died of a broken heart. The rather smug-looking fellow with the shiny foot below to the left is Galeotto Marzio, an Italian chronicler at Matthias' court. The middle of the king's three dogs was blown up during the war; canine-loving Hungarians – and they all are – quickly had an exact copy made.

If you want to bail out of the tour and leave Castle Hill now, there's a lift (elevator) to the right of the Lion Court archway that will take you down to Dózsa György tér and the bus stop (No 16) for Pest. The hallway leading to the lift has old maps and engravings of the palace, and there is an ATM here – a rare breed in the Castle District – on the left side as you enter.

The **Hungarian National Gallery** spreads out through Wings B, C and D and is devoted almost exclusively to Hungarian art from the early Middle Ages onward, though there are a few German artists represented. In Wing F of the palace on the west side of Lion Court is the **National Széchenyi Library**, which contains codices and manuscripts, a large collection of foreign newspapers and a copy of everything published in Hungary or the Hungarian language. It was founded by Count Ferenc Széchenyi (1754–1820), father of István Széchenyi (see the boxed text 'The Greatest Hungarian' in the Facts about Budapest chapter) who endowed it with 15,000 books and 2000 manuscripts. You can peruse the shelves and read the large collection of foreign newspapers by buying a day or annual membership; see Libraries in the Facts for the Visitor chapter for details. The **Budapest History Museum** is in Wing E.

You can walk through the history museum and exit through the rear doors without buying a ticket. Have a look around the castle walls and enter the palace gardens. **Ferdinand Gate** under the conical **Mace Tower** will bring you to a set of steps. These descend to Szarvas tér in the Tabán district via the **Turkish cemetery** dating from that decisive battle in 1686.

Walking Tour 2: Gellért hegy & the Tabán

Gellért hegy, a 235m rocky hill southeast of Castle Hill, is crowned with a fortress of sorts and the Independence Monument, Budapest's unofficial symbol. From Gellért hegy, you can't beat the views of the Royal Palace or the Danube and its fine bridges, and Jubilee Park on the south side is an ideal spot for a picnic. The Tabán, the leafy area between the two hills and stretching northwest as far as Déli train station, is associated with the Serbs, who settled here after fleeing from the Turks in the early 18th century.

Blame it on the Bird

The ancient Magyars were strong believers in magic and celestial intervention, and the *táltos* (shaman) enjoyed an elevated position in their society. Certain animals (eg, bears, stags and wolves) were totemic, and it was taboo to mention them directly by name. Thus the wolf was 'the long-tailed one' and the stag the 'large-antlered one'. In other cases the original Magyar word for an animal deemed sacred was replaced with a foreign loan word: *medve* for 'bear' comes from the Slavic *medved*.

No other totemic animal is better known to modern Hungarians than the *turul*, an eagle or hawk-like bird that had supposedly impregnated Emese, Árpád's grandmother. That legend can be viewed in many ways: as an attempt to foster a sense of common origin and group identity in the ethnically heterogeneous population of the time; as an effort to bestow a sacred origin on the House of Árpád and its rule; or just as a nice story – not entirely unlike the Virgin Mary begotten with child by the Holy Spirit anthropomorphosed as a dove.

Later it became known for its restaurants and wine gardens – a kind of Budapest Montmartre – but most of them burned to the ground at the turn of the 20th century. Today Gellért hegy and the Tabán are given over to private homes, parks and three thermal spas that make good use of the hot springs gushing from deep below Gellért hegy.

If you're starting the tour from Castle Hill, exit via **Ferdinand Gate** *(Map 4)* and walk south from Szarvas tér to **Elizabeth Bridge** *(Map 3 & Map 4)*, the big white span rebuilt after the war (see the boxed text 'The Bridges of Budapest'). To the west and looking down on the bridge from Gellért hegy is a **St Gellért Monument** *(Map 4)*, complete with waterfall. St Gellért was an Italian missionary invited to Hungary by King Stephen. The monument marks the spot where the bishop was hurled to his death in a spiked barrel in 1046 by pagan Hungarians resisting conversion. The stairs lead to the top of Gellért hegy. Though bus No 27 runs almost to the top of the hill from Móricz Zsigmond körtér *(Map 7)*, we'll begin at Szent Gellért tér, which is accessible from Pest on bus No 7 or tram Nos 47 and 49 and from the Buda side on bus No 86 and tram Nos 18 and 19.

Bartók Béla út runs southwest from the square and leads to Móricz Zsigmond körtér, a busy 'circular square' or circus. Nearby, on Műegyetem rakpart along the river before Petőfi Bridge, stands **Budapest Technical and Economic Sciences University** *(Budapesti Műszaki és Gazdaságtudományi Egyetem; Map 7)*, whose students were among the first to march during the Uprising on 23 October 1956.

Szent Gellért tér faces **Independence Bridge** *(Map 3)*, which opened for the millenary exhibition in 1896 (see the boxed text 'The Bridges of Budapest'). The square is dominated by the **Gellért Hotel** *(Map 7)*, an Art Nouveau pile (1918) and the city's favourite old-world caravanserai. If you don't want to fork out the €100-plus a night to sleep here (as every celebrity in the world seems to have, judging from the guest book), you can take the waters in the impressive spa or use the indoor and outdoor

The Bridges of Budapest

The bridges of Budapest, both landmarks and delightful vantage points over the Danube, are stitches that have bound Buda and Pest together since well before the two were linked politically. There are a total of nine spans, including two railroad bridges, but those in the very centre stand head and shoulders above the rest. All were left in ruins by the retreating Nazis in January 1945 but have since been rebuilt.

Margaret Bridge (Margit híd) introduces the Big Ring Road to the joys of Buda. It is unique in that it doglegs like a circumflex in order to stand at right angles to the Danube at its confluence at the southern tip of Margaret Island. It was originally built by French engineer Ernest Gouin in 1876; the branch leading to the island was added in 1901.

The twin-towered bridge to the south, the city's oldest and arguably its most beautiful, is the **Széchenyi Chain Bridge** (Széchenyi lánchíd), which is named in honour of its initiator, István Széchenyi (see the boxed text 'The Greatest Hungarian' in the Facts about Budapest chapter). It was actually built by Scotsman Adam Clark and, when it opened in 1849, Chain Bridge was unique for two reasons: it was the first permanent link between Buda and Pest, and the nobility – previously exempt from all taxation – had to pay a toll like everybody else to use it.

Elizabeth Bridge (Erzsébet híd) is the gleaming white, though rather generic, suspension bridge farther downstream. It enjoys a special place in the hearts of many Budapesters, though, as it was the first newly designed bridge to reopen after WWII (1964). (The original span, erected in 1903, was too badly damaged to rebuild.) Boasting a higher arch than the others, it offers dramatic views of both Castle and Gellért Hills and, of course, the more attractive bridges to the north and south.

Independence Bridge (Szabadság híd) is a *fin-de-siècle* cantilevered span that opened for the millenary exhibition in 1896. Each post of the bridge, which was originally named after Habsburg Emperor Franz Joseph, is topped by a mythical *turul* bird ready to take flight. It was rebuilt in the same style in 1946.

swimming pools (see the special section 'Taking the Waters' in this chapter).

Directly north on the small hill above the hotel is the **Cliff Chapel** (*Sziklakápolna; Map 3;* ☎ *385 1529; open 9am-9pm daily*), which was built into a cave in 1926. It was the seat of the Pauline order until 1951 when the priests were arrested and imprisoned by the communists and the cave sealed off. It was reopened in 1992 and re-consecrated; the main altar with a symbolic fish is made partly of Zsolnay porcelain (porcelain made in Pécs in southern Hungary). Behind the church is the monastery, with its neo-Gothic turrets visible from Szabadság Bridge. The chapel is closed to the public when Mass is being said.

From the chapel, follow a small path called Verejték utca (meaning Perspiration Street) and Dezső Szabó sétány, a walkway named after the controversial writer killed in the last days of WWII. You'll pass a funny bust of this large and rather angry-looking man along the way as you ascend through what once were vineyards and are now the lawns and gardens of **Jubilee Park** (Jubileum park).

Another route to follow from Gellért tér is along Kelenhegyi út. At No 12–14 is the interesting Art Nouveau **studio building** (*műteremház; Map 7*), which was built in 1903 and has enormous rooms with high ceilings in which huge socialist-realist monuments were once constructed and now modern art is made again. Continue up Kelenhegyi út and turn north on Minerva utca. No 3a/b, the **Swedish embassy** (*Map 3*) during the war, is where the diplomat Raoul Wallenberg, assisted by the lesser-known (but equally heroic) diplomats Carl-Ivan Danielsson (1880–1963) and Per Anger (1913–2002), saved the lives of thousands of Hungarian Jews (see the boxed text 'Raoul Wallenberg, Righteous Gentile' later in this chapter). The flight of steps at the end rejoins Verejték utca.

Towering above you is the **Citadella** *(Map 3; admission 300Ft; open 8am-10pm daily)*, a fortress that never did battle. Built by the Habsburgs after the 1848–49 War of Independence to 'defend' the city from further insurrection, by the time it was ready in 1854 the political climate had changed and the Citadella had become obsolete. It was given to the city in the 1890s and parts of it were symbolically blown to pieces. There's not much inside the Citadella today except for some big guns and dusty displays in the central courtyard, a hotel/hostel (see the Places to Stay chapter), a restaurant and club and a pleasant outdoor café.

To the east along Citadella sétány stands the **Independence Monument** *(Szabadság szobor; Map 3)*, the lovely lady with the palm frond proclaiming freedom throughout the city. It was erected in 1947 in tribute to the Soviet soldiers who died liberating Budapest in 1945, but the victims' names in Cyrillic letters on the plinth and the statues of the Soviet soldiers were removed in 1992. Today the monument is dedicated to 'Those who gave up their lives for Hungary's independence, freedom and prosperity'. In fact, the independence monument had been designed by the politically 'flexible' sculptor Zsigmond Kisfaludi Strobl for the ultra-right government of Admiral Miklós Horthy. After the war, when pro-communist monuments were in short supply, Kisfaludi Strobl passed it off as a memorial to the Soviets.

If you walk west for a few minutes along Citadella sétány north of the fortress, you'll come to what is the best vantage point in Budapest. The trail below leads northward to the St Gellért statue and waterfall mentioned earlier. Across the street is another of the area's three thermal spas, the **Rudas Baths** *(Rudas gyógyfürdő; Map 6; Döbrentei tér 9)* – and the most Turkish of them, with octagonal pool, domed cupola with coloured glass and massive columns. If you don't like getting wet you can try a 'drinking cure' by visiting the **pump room** *(ivócsarnok; Map 6; open 11am-6pm Mon, Wed & Fri, 7am-2pm Tues & Thur)*, which is below the western

end of Elizabeth Bridge and within sight of the Rudas Baths. A half-litre/litre of the hot smelly water – meant to cure whatever ails you – is just 15/25Ft.

To the north of the bridge and through the underpass is a **statue of Elizabeth** *(Map 6)*, the Habsburg empress and Hungarian queen and the consort of Franz Joseph much beloved by Hungarians because, among other things, she learned to speak Hungarian. Sissi, as she was affectionately known, was assassinated by an Italian anarchist in Geneva in 1898.

As you walk north along Döbrentei utca, have a look at the plaques at No 15. These mark the water level on the Danube during two devastating floods in 1775 and 1838 (the latter vividly described by Julia Pardoe in *The City of the Magyar*; see Books in the Facts for the Visitor chapter). What's most interesting about them is that they are in Hungarian, German and Serbian, attesting to the mixed population that once lived here. The **Tabán Parish Church** *(Tabáni plébániatemplom; Map 4; Szarvas tér)*, which you enter from Hegedűs köz, dates from the early 18th century. A short distance to the northwest is the **Semmelweis Museum of Medical History** *(Map 4; I Apród utca 1-3)*, named in honour of the 19th-century physician who discovered the cause of life-threatening childbirth fever.

To the east of the museum is a lovely renovated building with a fountain known as the **Castle Garden Kiosk** *(Várkert kioszk; Map 4; I Ybl Miklós tér 2-6)*. Once a pump house for Castle Hill, it was designed by Ybl in 1879 and is now a casino. The dilapidated steps and archways across the road, the **Castle Bazaar** *(Várbazár; Map 4)*, once functioned as a pleasure park with shops that were later used as art studios.

Return to Szarvas tér and turn right on Attila út. In the park across the road you'll see a yellow block with a domed roof; this is the **Rác Bath** *(Rác gyógyfürdő; Map 4)*. It's an Ybl design on the outside and a Turkish delight within. The Rác was under renovation at the time of writing and its future unclear.

There's not a heck of a lot to see along Attila út (though the neighbourhood seems to figure in Hungarian literature pretty often). The lift at the bottom of the National Széchenyi Library on Dózsa György tér can whisk you back up to Castle Hill, but if you carry on you will see the entrance to the **Alagút** (Map 4), the tunnel under Castle Hill that links Chain Bridge with Attila, and is a main thoroughfare of Buda.

The large park at the northern end of Attila út is **Vérmező** (Map 3), the 'Blood Field' where Ignác Martonovics and six other pro-republican intellectuals were beheaded in 1795 for plotting against the Habsburgs. **Déli train station** (Map 3), an eyesore completed in 1977, is across the Vérmező to the west.

Walking Tour 3: Víziváros

Víziváros (Watertown) is the narrow area between the Danube and Castle Hill that widens as it approaches Óbuda to the north and Rózsadomb (Rose Hill) to the northwest, spreading as far west as Moszkva tér, one of Buda's main transport hubs. In the Middle Ages, those involved in trades, crafts and fishing – the commoners who couldn't make the socio-economic ascent to the Old Town on Castle Hill – lived here. Under the Turks many of the district's churches were used as mosques, and baths were built, one of which is still functioning. Today Víziváros is the heart of urban Buda.

Víziváros actually begins at Ybl Miklós tér, but the best place to begin a stroll is at **Clark Ádám tér** (Map 4). You can reach it on foot from the metro M2 Batthyány tér stop by walking south along the river or via tram No 19, which links it with Szent Gellért tér. Bus No 16 from Deák Ferenc tér stops here on its way to/from Castle Hill.

The square – a circle, really – is named after the Scottish engineer who supervised the building of the **Széchenyi Chain Bridge** (Map 4), leading from the square (see the boxed text 'The Bridges of Budapest'), and who designed the **tunnel** (alagút; Map 4) under Castle Hill, which took eight months to carve out of the limestone. The curious sculpture hidden in the bushes to the south that looks like a elongated doughnut is the **0km stone** (Map 4); all Hungarian roads to and from the capital are measured from this point.

Fő utca is the 'Main Street' running through Víziváros and dates from Roman times. **Kapiszory House** (Kapisztory ház; Map 4; I Fő utca 20), with the corner turret opposite the French Institute, has interesting Chinese reliefs above and below the windows. It houses Le Jardin de Paris (see the Places to Eat chapter). At the former **Capuchin church** (Map 4; I Fő utca 30-32), used as a mosque during the Turkish occupation, you can see the remains of Islamic-style ogee-arched doors and windows on the south side. Around the corner there's the seal of King Matthias Corvinus – a raven and a ring – and the little square under renovation and expansion is called **Corvin tér** (Map 4). The Eclectic building on the north side is the **Buda Concert Hall** (Budai Vigadó; Map 4; Corvin tér 8), much less grand than its counterpart in Pest. The **Iron Stump** (Vastuskó; Map 4; cnr I Vám utca & Iskola utca) to the north is the odd-looking tree trunk into which itinerant artisans and merchants would drive a nail to mark their visit.

Batthyány tér (Map 3), a short distance to the northeast, is the centre of Víziváros and the best place to snap a picture of the Parliament building across the river. In the centre of this rather shabby space is the entrance to both metro M2 and the HÉV suburban line to Szentendre.

On the southern side of Batthyány tér is **St Anne's Church** (Szent Ana templom; Map 4; I Batthyány tér 7) whose completion in 1805 was the culmination of more than six decades' work because of the interruption caused by floods and an earthquake. It has one of the loveliest baroque interiors of any church in Budapest. The attached building at No 7 was an inn until 1724, then the church presbytery and now a fine café. Batthyány tér was called Upper Market Square in the Middle Ages, but the market hall (1902) to the west now contains just a Spar supermarket and discount department store. Have a look at the double courtyard at No 4, which housed an elegant inn in the 18th century. The house at No 3 has friezes showing people at work during the four seasons; (from left to right) spring, summer, winter, autumn.

A couple of streets north is **Nagy Imre tér**, with the enormous former **Military Court of Justice** (Map 3; II Fő utca 70-78) on the northern side. Here Imre Nagy and others were tried and sentenced to death in 1958 (see The 1956 Uprising in the Facts about Budapest chapter). It was also the site of the notorious Fő utca prison where many lesser mortals (but victims nonetheless) were incarcerated and tortured.

The **Király Baths** (Király gyógyfürdő; Map 3; Fő utca 82-86), parts of which date from 1580 (note the hexagonal Turkish domes), is one block north (see the special section 'Taking the Waters' later in this chapter). Next to it and across pedestrianised Ganz utca is the Greek Catholic **St Florian Chapel** (Szent Flórián kápolna; Map 3; II Fő utca 88-90), built in 1760 and dedicated to the patron saint of firefighters. The whole chapel was raised more than a metre in the 1930s after earlier flooding had washed up dirt and silt. Opposite is the modern and rather attractive **Foreign Ministry building** (Map 3).

Fő utca ends at **Bem József tér** (Map 3), named after the Polish general Josef Bem (1794–1850) who fought on the Hungarian side in the 1848-49 War of Independence. In 1956 students from the Technical University rallied in front of the statue of him here at the start of the Uprising. Bem József utca leads westward from the square, past the **Foundry Museum** (Map 3; III Bem József utca 20) and joins Margit körút, Buda's only share of the Nagykörút (Big Ring Road). If you were to follow it southwest for 700m or so, you'd reach **Széna tér**. This square saw some of the heaviest fighting in Buda during the 1956 Uprising; today it is the site of **Mammut I & II** (Map 3), central Budapest's biggest double shopping malls.

Moszkva tér (Map 3), the large square to the southwest, is an important centre for transport connections (including the M2 Moszkva tér metro station). Behind it is the new **Millennium Park** (Millenáris Park; Map 3; II Kis Rókus utca), one of the more successful urban redevelopment projects on either side of the Danube in recent years. It is a large landscaped complex behind the Mammut shopping malls consisting of fountains, ponds, little bridges, a theatre and the **Millennium Exhibition Hall** (Millenáris Kiállítócsarnok; Map 3; ☎ 438 5335; II Kis Rókus utca; adult/student or child 1000/500Ft), which hosts some unusual cultural exhibits.

Back at Bem tér, Fő utca turns into **Frankel Leó út**, a tree-lined street of pricey antique shops. If you cross Margit körút and continue north, you'll reach Gül Baba utca on the left. This steep, narrow lane leads to the renovated **tomb of Gül Baba** (Map 3), named after a Muslim holy man who died in 1548. Farther north along Frankel Leó út is the **Lukács Bath** (Lukács gyógyfürdő; Map 3; II Frankel Leó út 25-29), which caters to an older crowd desperate to prolong their lives (see the special section 'Taking the Waters' in this chapter). A short distance north and tucked away in an apartment block is the **Újlak Synagogue** (Újlaki zsinagóga; Map 3; II Frankel Leó út 49), built in 1888 on the site of an older prayer house. It is the only functioning synagogue left on the Buda side.

Walking Tour 4: Óbuda & Aquincum

Ó means ancient in Hungarian; as its name suggests, Óbuda is the oldest part of Buda. The Romans established Aquincum, a key military garrison and civilian town north of here at the end of the 1st century AD and it became the seat of the Roman province of Pannonia Inferior in 106 AD. When the Magyars arrived, they named it Buda, which became Óbuda when the Royal Palace was built on Castle Hill and turned into the real centre. Like the Tabán area to the south, Óbuda today is only a shadow of its former self.

Most visitors on their way to Szentendre are put off by what they see of Óbuda from the highway or the HÉV commuter train. Prefabricated housing blocks seem to go on forever, and the Árpád Bridge flyover splits the heart of the district (Flórián tér) in two. But behind all this are some of the most important Roman ruins in Hungary, noteworthy museums and small, quiet neighbourhoods that still recall fin-de-siècle Óbuda.

The sights listed here can be found on Map 2.

Flórián tér is the historic centre of Óbuda. You can reach it on the HÉV commuter train (Árpád híd stop) from Batthyány tér, which is on the M2 metro line, or bus No 86 from many points along the Danube on the Buda side. If you're up near City Park (Városliget) in Pest, walk southeast to the intersection of Hungária körút and Thököly út and catch the No 1 tram, which avoids Buda and crosses Árpád Bridge into Óbuda.

Archaeology buffs taking the No 86 bus to Flórián tér should descend at Nagyszombat utca (for HÉV passengers, it's the Tímár utca stop), about 800m south of Flórián tér on Pacsirtamező utca, to explore the **Roman Military Amphitheatre** (Római katonai amfiteátrum) built in the 2nd century for the garrisons. It could accommodate up to 15,000 spectators and was larger than the Coliseum in Rome. The rest of the military camp extended north to Flórián tér.

If you walk west along Nagyszombat utca and then north on Bécsi út (the old road to Vienna) from here, you'll reach the **Kiscelli Museum**, one of Budapest's 'forgotten' museums and a personal favourite.

The yellow baroque **Óbuda Parish Church** (Óbudai plébániatemplom; III 168 Lajos utca), built in 1749, dominates the easternmost side of Flórián tér. There's a massive rococo pulpit inside. To the south, the large neoclassical building beside the Corinthia Aquincum Hotel is the former **Óbuda Synagogue** (Óbudai zsinagóga; III Lajos utca 163), dating from 1821. It now houses sound studios of Hungarian Television (MTV). Directly opposite is the **Budapest Gallery Exhibition House** (III Lajos utca 158).

In the subway below Flórián tér are Roman objects that have been discovered in the area (many of them, sadly, vandalised and tagged in graffiti), including the **Bath Museum** (Fürdő Múzeum; ☎ 250 1650; adult/child 100/50Ft; open 10am-6pm Tues-Sun May-Sept, 10am-5pm Tues-Sun 15-30 Apr & October), which may or may not be 'resting' at the moment. Still more Roman ruins, including a reconstructed temple, can be found in the park outside. The so-called **Hercules Villa** (Meggyfa utca 19-21) is northwest of Flórián tér.

Two squares northeast of Flórián tér and through the labyrinthine subway are Óbuda's most important museums. In the former Zichy Mansion is the **Vasarely Museum** (III Szentlélek tér 6) devoted to the works of the 'father of op art', Victor Vasarely. In the back of the same building facing the courtyard (enter at Fő tér 1) is the **Kassák Museum** of early-20th-century avant-garde art.

Fő tér is a restored square of baroque houses, public buildings and restaurants. Walking northeast from the square, you'll see a group of odd metal sculptures of rather worried-looking women in the middle of the road. It is the work of the prolific Imre Varga, who seems to have sat on both sides of the fence politically for decades – sculpting Béla Kun and Lenin as easily as he did St Stephen, St Elizabeth and Imre Nagy. The **Imre Varga Exhibition House** (III Laktanya utca 7) is in a charming townhouse nearby.

The HÉV or bus Nos 34 and 43 from Szentlélek tér head north for a few stops to **Aquincum**, the most complete Roman civilian town in Hungary and now an indoor and outdoor museum. A **Roman aqueduct** used to pass this way from a nearby spring, and remains have been preserved in the central reservation (median strip) of the highway alongside the HÉV railway line. The prosperous town's heyday was in the 2nd and 3rd centuries, lasting until the Huns and assorted other hordes came and ruined everything.

Aquincum had paved streets and fairly sumptuous single-storey houses with courtyards, fountains and mosaic floors as well as sophisticated drainage and heating systems. Not all of this is easily apparent today as you walk among the ruins, but you can see their outlines as well as those of the big public baths, market, an early Christian church and a temple dedicated to Mithras, the chief deity of a religion that once rivalled Christianity in its number of believers (see the boxed text 'Mithras & the Great Sacrifice'). The **Aquincum Museum** (Szentendrei út 139) tries to put it all in perspective.

Across Szentendrei út to the northwest is the **Roman Civilian Amphitheatre** (Római polgári amfiteátrum), about half the size of the one reserved for the garrison (see earlier). Much is left to the imagination, but you can still see the small cubicles where lions were kept and the 'Gate of Death' to the west through which slain gladiators were carried.

North of Aquincum are the outer suburbs of **Rómaifürdő** and **Csillaghegy**, both of them on the HÉV line. The holiday area of Rómaifürdő (Roman Bath) has an open-air thermal pool in a big park, Budapest's largest camping ground and a collection of popular food kiosks and drink bars along the riverfront. The swimming pool and 'beach' in Csillaghegy is one of the most popular in the city. To reach them from the HÉV stop, walk west along Ürömi út for a few minutes to Pusztakúti út.

Mithras & the Great Sacrifice

Mithraism, the worship of the god Mithras, originated in Persia. As Roman rule extended into Asia, the religion became extremely popular with traders, imperial slaves and mercenaries of the Roman army and spread rapidly throughout the empire in the 2nd and 3rd centuries AD. It was the principal rival of Christianity until Constantine came to the throne in the 4th century.

Mithraism was a mysterious religion with devotees sworn to secrecy. What little is known of Mithras – the god of the sun, justice and social contract – has been deduced from reliefs and icons found in sanctuaries and temples like the one at Aquincum. Most of these portray Mithras clad in a Persian-style cap and tunic, sacrificing a white bull. From the bull's blood and semen sprout grain, grapes and living creatures. The bull is then transformed into the god Soma, the moon, and time is born.

Mithraism and Christianity were close competitors partly because of the striking similarity in many of their rituals. Both involve the birth of a deity on 25 December, shepherds, death and resurrection and a form of baptism. Devotees knelt when they worshipped and a common meal – a 'communion' of bread and water – was a regular feature of both liturgies.

Walking Tour 5: Margaret Island

Neither Buda nor Pest though part of district XIII, 2.5km-long Margaret Island (Margit sziget) in the middle of the Danube was always the domain of one religious order or another until the Turks arrived and turned what was then called the Island of Rabbits into – appropriately enough – a harem, from which all 'infidels' were barred. It's been a public park open to everyone since the mid-19th century.

With its large swimming complex, thermal spa, gardens and shaded walkways, the island is a lovely place to escape the city on a hot afternoon. You can walk anywhere – on the paths, the shoreline, the grass – but don't try to camp: that's strictly *tilos* (forbidden). If you follow the shoreline in winter, you'll see thermal water gushing from beneath the island into the river.

Cross over to Margaret Island from Pest or Buda via tram No 4 or 6. Bus No 26 covers the length of the island as it makes the run between Nyugati train station and Árpád Bridge. Cars are allowed on Margaret Island from Árpád Bridge only as far as the two big hotels at the northeastern end; the rest is reserved for pedestrians, cyclists and horse-drawn carriages.

You can walk the length of Margaret Island in one direction and return on bus No 26. Or you can rent a bicycle from one of several kiosks, including **Sétacikli** *(Map 3; ☎ 06-30 966 6453; three-speed per half-hour/hour/day 400/600/1200Ft, pedal coach for 3/5 people per hour 1800/2800Ft; open 10am-dusk Mar-Oct)*, which is on the west side just before the athletic stadium as you walk north from Margaret Bridge, and **Bringóvár** *(Map 2; ☎ 329 2073, 329 2746; mountain bike per half-hour/hour 560/920Ft, pedal coach for 4 1380/2180Ft, inline skates 820/1380Ft; open 8am-dusk year-round)* at the refreshment stand near the Japanese Garden in the north of the island.

A twirl around the island in one of the **horse-drawn coaches** *(Map 2)* stationed just south of the Bringóvár bike-rental stand costs 1000Ft per person.

In the flower-bed roundabout at the southern end of the island, the **Centennial**

THINGS TO SEE & DO

Monument *(Centenariumi emlékmű; Map 3)*, unveiled in 1973, marks the union of Buda, Pest and Óbuda 100 years before. Three decades ago was an entirely different era in Budapest, and the sculptor filled the strange cone with all sorts of socialist and nationalist symbols. They remain – as if contained in a time capsule that's been cracked open.

Margaret Island boasts two popular swimming pools on its west side. The first is the indoor/outdoor **National Sports Pool** *(Nemzeti Sportuszoda; Map 3)*, officially named after the Olympic swimming champion Alfréd Hajós, who won the 100m and 1200m races at the first modern Olympiad in 1896 and actually built the place. Farther north is the recently renovated **Palatinus** *(Map 2)*, a large complex of outdoor pools, huge water slides and grassy strands. It's an absolute madhouse on a hot summer afternoon but a good place to watch Hungarians at play. If you want to take all your clothes off, there are single-sex sunbathing decks on the roof of the main building (see the special section 'Taking the Waters').

Just before you reach the Palatinus and almost in the exact geographical centre of the island, you'll pass the ruins of a **Franciscan church and monastery** *(Ferences templom és kolostor; Map 3)* – no more than a tower and a wall dating from the late 13th century. The Habsburg archduke Joseph built a summer residence here when he inherited the island in 1867. It was later converted into a hotel that ran until 1949.

The **water tower** *(víztorony; Map 2)*, erected in 1911 in the central north part of the island, rises 66m above an **open-air theatre** *(szabadtéri színpad; ☎ 239 0920)*, which is used for opera, plays and concerts in summer. The tower now houses the **Lookout Gallery** *(Kilátó Galéria; ☎ 340 4520; adult/child 350/200Ft; open 11am-7pm daily May-Oct)*, which contains some interesting folkcraft and contemporary art on the ground floor. But the main reason for entering is to climb the 153 steps for a stunning 360° view of the island, Buda and Pest from the cupola terrace.

Due east is the former **Dominican convent** *(Domonkos kolostor; Map 2)* built by Béla IV whose scribes played an important role in the

continuation of Hungarian scholarship. Its most famous resident was Béla's daughter, St Margaret of Hungary (1242–71). As the story goes, the king promised to commit his daughter to a life of devotion in a nunnery if the Mongols were driven from the land. They were and she was – at nine years of age. Still, she seemed to enjoy it – if we're to believe the *Lives of the Saints* – especially the mortification-of-the-flesh parts. St Margaret, only canonised in 1943, commands something of a cult following in Hungary. A red-marble sepulchre cover surrounded by a wrought-iron grille marks her original resting place, and there's a much visited shrine with ex-votives nearby.

A short distance north is the reconstructed Romanesque **Premonstratensian Church** *(Premontre templom; Map 2)*, dedicated to St Michael and originally dating back to the 12th century. Its 15th-century bell is real enough, though; it mysteriously appeared one night in 1914 under the roots of a walnut tree that had been knocked over in a storm. It was probably buried there by monks at the time of the Turkish invasion.

The Romans used the thermal springs in the northeastern part of the island both as drinking water and therapy and so do modern Magyars. **Margitszigeti Krisztályvíz** *(Margaret Island Crystal Water; Map 3)*, one of the more popular brands of mineral water in Hungary, is sourced and bottled here, and the **thermal spa** *(Map 2)* at the Danubius Thermal Hotel Margitsziget (see the special section 'Taking the Waters' in this chapter) to the northeast is one of the cleanest, most modern in Budapest.

The attractive **Japanese Garden** *(Japánkert; Map 2)*, at the northwestern end of the island, has koi, carp and lily pads in its ponds, a small wooden bridge and a waterfall. The raised gazebo to the north is called the **Musical Fountain** *(Zenélőkút; Map 2)*, a replica of one in Transylvania. A tape plays chimes and tinny snatches of a march on the hour.

Walking Tour 6: Szent István körút & Bajcsy-Zsilinszky út

This relatively brief walk crosses over into Pest and follows Szent István körút, the northernmost stretch of the Big Ring Road, to Nyugati tér and then south to central Deák Ferenc tér. You can reach Jászai Mari tér, the start of this walk, via tram No 4 or 6 from either side of the river or simply by walking over the bridge from Margaret Island. If you're coming from the Inner Town in Pest, hop on the waterfront tram No 2 to its terminus.

Two buildings of very different styles and functions face Jászai Mari tér *(Map 5)*, which is split in two by the foot of Margaret Bridge. To the north is an elegant block of flats called **Palatinus House** *(Map 5; XIII Pozsonyi út 2)*, built in 1912. The modern building south of the square is nicknamed the White House *(Map 5; V Széchenyi rakpart 19)*, the former headquarters of the Central Committee of the Hungarian Socialist Workers' Party. It now contains the offices of ministers of Parliament.

The area north of Szent István körút is known as Újlipótváros *(New Leopold Town; Map 3 & Map 5)* so as to distinguish it from Lipótváros in the Northern Inner Town. (Archduke Leopold was the grandson of Habsburg Empress Maria Theresa.) It is a wonderful neighbourhood with tree-lined streets, boutiques and a few cafés and is vaguely reminiscent of uptown Manhattan. The area was upper middle class and Jewish before the war, and many of the 'safe houses' organised by the Swedish diplomat Raoul Wallenberg and others during WWII were here (see the boxed text 'Raoul Wallenberg, Righteous Gentile'). A street named after this heroic man, two blocks to the north, bears a commemorative plaque. A **statue of Wallenberg** *(Map 3)* doing battle with a snake (evil) entitled *Kígyóölő* (Serpent Slayer) was erected in **Szent István Park** *(Map 3)* in 1999, replacing one created by sculptor Pál Pátzay that was mysteriously removed the night before its unveiling in 1948. West of the park and facing the river is a rarity for Budapest: a row of **Bauhaus apartments**. They may not look like much today after decades of bad copies, but they were the bee's knees when they were built in the late 1920s.

Szent István körút is an interesting street to stroll along; as elsewhere on the Big Ring Road, most of the Eclectic-style buildings, decorated with Atlases, reliefs and other details, were erected in the last part of the 19th century. Don't hesitate to explore the inner courtyards here and farther on – if Dublin is celebrated for its doors and London for its squares, Budapest is known for its lovely *udvar*.

This stretch of the boulevard is also good for shopping. The **Szőnyi Antikvárium** *(Map 5; V Szent István körút 3)*, a second-hand and antiquarian bookshop, is excellent for browsing – it has old prints and maps in the chest of drawers at the back. Falk Miksa utca, the next street on the right and running south, is loaded with pricey antique shops. You can get an idea of what Hungarians are off-loading these days from the second-hand **BÁV shop** *(V Szent István körút 3)* at the corner.

The attractive little theatre roughly in the middle of this section of the Big Ring Road is the **Comedy Theatre** *(Vígszínház; Map 5; ☎ 329 2340; XIII Szent István körút 14)*, a popular venue for comedies and musicals. When it was built in 1896, the new theatre's location was criticised for being too far out of the city.

You might recognise the large iron and glass structure on Nyugati tér (known as Marx tér until 1989) if you arrived by train. It's the **Nyugati train station** *(Nyugati pályaudvar; Map 5)* built in 1877 by the Paris-based Eiffel Company. In the early 1970s a train actually crashed through the enormous glass screen on the main facade when its brakes failed, coming to rest at the tram line. The old restaurant room to the right now houses one of the world's most elegant McDonald's.

If you look north up Váci út from Nyugati tér, beyond the new **West End City Centre** shopping mall, you may catch sight of the twin spires of the **Lehel church** *(Map 3)*, a 60-year-old copy of the 13th-century Romanesque church (now in ruins) at Zsambék, 33km west of Budapest. The monstrosity that is the **Lehel Csarnok** market (see Self-Catering under Places to Eat – Pest) is next to it.

From Nyugati tér, walk south on Bajcsy-Zsilinszky út for about 800m to **St Stephen's**

Basilica *(Szent István bazilika; Map 6; ☎ 311 0839; V Szent István tér; metro M2 Arany János utca; open 9am-7pm Mon-Sat, 1pm-4.30pm Sun)*. This neoclassical cathedral was built over the course of half a century and not completed until 1905. Much of the interruption had to do with the fiasco in 1868 when the dome collapsed during a storm, and the structure had to be demolished and built from the ground up. No one was killed but it certainly must have frightened the horses. The basilica is rather dark and gloomy inside – disappointing for the city's largest and most important Catholic church – but take the lift or walk (370 steps!) to the top of the **dome** *(☎ 403 5370; adult/student or child 500/400Ft; open 10am-5pm daily Apr, May, Sept & Oct; 10am-6pm daily June-Aug)*, which offers one of the best views in the city.

To the right as you enter the basilica is a small **treasury** *(kincstár; open 10am-5pm daily Apr-Sept, 10am-4pm daily Oct-Mar)* of ecclesiastical objects. Behind the main altar and to the left is the basilica's major drawing card: the **Holy Right Chapel** *(Szent Jobb Kápolna; open 9am-4.30pm Mon-Sat, 1am-4.30pm Sun May-Sept, 10am-4pm Mon-Sat, 1am-4.30pm Sun Oct-Apr)*. It contains the Holy Right (also known as the Holy Dexter), the mummified right hand of St Stephen. It was returned to Hungary by Habsburg Empress Maria Theresa in 1771 after it was discovered in a monastery in Bosnia. Like the Crown of St Stephen, it too was snatched by the bad guys after WWII but was soon, er, handed back. To view the relic you have to put a 100Ft coin into a little machine to light up the glass casket containing the Holy Right. At nigh on to 1000 years of age, it is – unsurprisingly – *not* a pretty sight.

Bajcsy-Zsilinszky út ends at Deák Ferenc tér, a busy square and the only place where the three metro lines converge. In the subway below near the entrance to the metro is the **Underground Railway Museum**.

In the early part of the 20th century, big foreign insurance companies built their offices at Deák Ferenc tér, with some huge ones still standing. **Madách Imre út**, running east from Károly körút (Little Ring Road), was originally designed to be as large and

grand a boulevard as nearby Andrássy út. But WWII nipped that plan in the bud, and it now ends abruptly and rather self-consciously after just two blocks. Much of **Erzsébet tér** is now given over to a park since the international bus station was moved to Népliget and the new National Theatre opened its doors along the Danube in Ferencváros and not here, as originally planned.

Walking Tour 7: Northern Inner Town

This district, also called Lipótváros (Leopold Town), is full of offices, government ministries, 19th-century apartment blocks and grand squares.

From Deák Ferenc tér metro stop, walk northwest through Erzsébet tér and west on József Attila utca toward the Danube. **Roosevelt tér** *(Map 6)*, named in 1947 after the long-serving (1933–45) American president, is at the foot of Chain Bridge and offers among the best views of Castle Hill. You can also reach it on tram No 2 or 2/a.

On the south side of this large square is a **statue of Ferenc Deák** *(Map 6)*, the Hungarian minister largely responsible for the Compromise of 1867, which brought about the Dual Monarchy of Austria and Hungary. The statues on the west side are of an Austrian and a Hungarian child holding hands in peaceful bliss. The Magyar kid's hair is tousled and he is naked; the Osztrák is demurely covered by a bit of the patrician's robe, his hair neatly coifed.

The Art Nouveau building with the gold tiles to the east is the **Gresham Palace** *(Map 6; V Roosevelt tér 5-6)*, built by an English insurance company in 1907 (see the special section 'Fin-de-Siècle Architecture'). It recently opened as a five-star hotel after a protracted renovation. The **Hungarian Academy of Sciences** *(Magyar Tudományos Akadémia; Map 6; V Roosevelt tér 9)*, founded by Count István Széchenyi, is at the northern end of the square.

Szabadság tér *(Independence Square, Map 5)*, one of the largest squares in the city, is a few minutes' walk to the northeast of Roosevelt tér. It has one of Budapest's few remaining monuments to the Soviets in

Raoul Wallenberg, Righteous Gentile

Of all the 'righteous gentiles' honoured by Jews around the world, the most revered is Raoul Wallenberg, the Swedish diplomat and businessman who rescued as many as 35,000 Hungarian Jews during WWII.

Wallenberg, who came from a long line of bankers and diplomats, began working in 1936 for a trading firm whose president was a Hungarian Jew. In July 1944 the Swedish Foreign Ministry, at the request of Jewish and refugee organisations in the USA, sent the 32-year-old Wallenberg on a rescue mission to Budapest as an attaché to the embassy there. By that time, almost half a million Jews in Hungary had been sent to Nazi death camps.

Wallenberg immediately began issuing Swedish safe-conduct passes (called 'Wallenberg passports') and set up a series of 'safe houses' flying the flag of Sweden and other neutral countries where Jews could seek asylum. He even followed German 'death marches' and deportation trains, distributing food and clothing and actually pulling some 500 people off the cars along the way.

When the Soviet army entered Budapest in January 1945, Wallenberg went to Debrecen to report to the provisional government but was arrested for espionage and sent to Moscow. In the early 1950s, responding to reports that Wallenberg had been seen alive in a labour camp, the Soviet Union announced that he had in fact died of a heart attack in 1947. Several reports over the next two decades suggested Wallenberg was still alive, but none were ever confirmed. Many believe Wallenberg was executed by the Soviets, who suspected him of spying for the USA.

the centre; in 2002 the square was closed to traffic when the remains of Soviet soldiers were discovered during excavations to build an underground car park.

On the east side of the square is the **US Embassy** *(Map 5; V Szabadság tér 12)*, where Cardinal József Mindszenty took refuge for 15 years until leaving for Vienna in 1971 (see the boxed text 'Cardinal Mindszenty'). The embassy backs onto Hold utca (Moon St), which, until 1990, was named Rosenberg házaspár utca (Rosenberg Couple St) after the American husband and wife Julius and Ethel Rosenberg who were executed as Communist spies in the USA in 1953. (Research now suggests that's exactly what they were.)

On that street you'll find the sensational former **Postal Savings Bank** *(Map 5; V Hold utca 4)*, a Secessionist extravaganza built by Ödön Lechner in 1901 (see the special section 'Fin-de-Siècle Architecture'). It is now part of the **National Bank** of Hungary *(Magyar Nemzeti Bank; Map 5; Szabadság tér 8)* around the corner, which has reliefs that illustrate trade and commerce through history: Arab camel traders, African rug merchants, Chinese tea salesmen – and the inevitable solicitor witnessing contracts.

The large white and yellow building on the west side of the square housed the Budapest Stock Exchange when it was built in 1906. It is now the **headquarters of Hungarian Television**, MTV *(Magyar Televízió Cégbíróság; Map 5; V Szabadság tér 17)*.

Northwest of Szabadság tér is **Kossuth Lajos tér**, which is a stop on the M2 metro line and the site of Budapest's most photographed building: **Parliament**. This is where the national government sits, and visitors are allowed into a few rooms throughout the year. It is also the home of the Crown of St Stephen and other priceless bits and bobs (see the listing under Museums & Other Attractions later in this chapter). The Parliament building is a blend of many architectural styles – neo-Gothic, neo-Romanesque, neo-baroque (to name just three) – and in sum works very well. Unfortunately what was spent on the design wasn't matched in the building materials. The ornate structure was surfaced with a porous form of limestone that does not resist pollution very well at all. Renovations began almost immediately after it opened and will continue until the building crumbles.

Opposite Parliament is the **Ethnography Museum** *(Map 5; V Kossuth Lajos tér 12)*, Hungary's largest and most important folk collection. The building itself, designed in 1893 to house the Supreme Court, is worth a look, especially the massive central hall with its marble columns and ceiling fresco of *Justice* by Károly Lotz.

Southeast of Kossuth Lajos tér is a **statue of Imre Nagy** *(Map 5; V Vértanúk tere)*, the reformist Communist prime minister executed in 1958 for his role in the Uprising two years before. It was unveiled to great ceremony in the summer of 1996.

Walking Tour 8: Inner Town

The Inner Town (Belváros in Hungarian) is the heart of Pest and contains the most valuable commercial real estate in the city, but it retains something of a split personality. North of Ferenciek tere is the 'have' side with the flashiest boutiques, the biggest hotels, some expensive restaurants and the lion's share of tourists. You'll often hear more German, Italian and English spoken here than Hungarian. Until recently the south was the 'have not' side – studenty, quieter and much more local. Now it, too, has been reserved for pedestrians, and is full of trendy clubs, pubs, cafés and restaurants.

All the sights in this section can be found on Map 6.

You can decide which part of the Belváros you want to explore first; we'll start with the latter. Busy Ferenciek tere, which divides the Inner Town at Szabadsajtó út (Free Press Avenue), is on the M3 metro line and can be reached by bus No 7 from Buda or points east in Pest. To get here from the end of the last tour, take tram No 2 along the Danube and get off at Elizabeth Bridge.

The centre of this part of the Inner Town is **Egyetem tér** *(University Square)*, a five-minute walk south along Károly Mihály utca from Ferenciek tere. The square's name refers to the branch of the prestigious **Loránd Eötvös Science University** *(ELTE; V Egyetem tér 1-3)*. Next to the university building to the west is the **University Church**, a lovely baroque structure built in 1748. Over the altar inside is a copy of the **Black Madonna of Czecstochowa** so revered in Poland. The church is often full of young people – presumably those who haven't tickled András Hadik's horse on Castle Hill (see Walking Tour 1).

Leafy Kecskeméti utca runs southeast from the square to **Kálvin tér**. At the end of it, near the Korona hotel, there's a plaque marking the location of the **Kecskemét Gate** *(Kecskeméti kapu)*, part of the medieval city

Cardinal Mindszenty

Born József Pehm in the village of Csehimindszent, near Szombathely, in 1892, Mindszenty was politically active from the time of his ordination in 1915. Imprisoned under the short-lived regime of communist Béla Kun in 1919 and again when the fascist Iron Cross came to power in 1944, Mindszenty was made archbishop of Esztergom (and thus primate of Hungary) in 1945 and cardinal the following year.

When the new cardinal refused to secularise Hungary's Roman Catholic schools under the new communist regime in 1948, he was arrested, tortured and sentenced to life imprisonment for treason. Released during the 1956 Uprising, Mindszenty took refuge in the US Embassy on Szabadság tér when the communists returned to power. There he would remain until 1971.

As relations between the Kádár regime and the Holy See began to thaw in the late 1960s, the Vatican made several requests for the cardinal to leave Hungary, which he refused. Following the intervention of US President Richard Nixon, Mindszenty went to Vienna, where he continued to criticise the Vatican's relations with the regime in Hungary. He retired in 1974 and died the following year. But as he had vowed not to return to Hungary until the last Soviet soldier had left, Mindszenty's remains were not returned until May 1991 – actually several weeks before the pivotal date.

wall that was pulled down in the 1700s. Semi-pedestrianised **Ráday utca**, which leads south from Kálvin tér and is full of cafés, clubs and restaurants, is where university students entertain themselves these days.

Just north of Egyetem tér, the **Petőfi Literary Museum** *(V Károlyi Mihály utca 16)* in the sublime (and newly renovated) Károly Palace (Károlyi Palota) has rooms devoted to Sándor Petőfi, Endre Ady, Mór Jókai, Attila József and other greats of Hungarian literature. The building to the north with the multicoloured tile dome is the **University Library** *(Egyetemi könyvtár; V Ferenciek tere 10)*.

Southwest of Egyetem tér, at the corner of Szerb utca and Veres Pálné utca, stands the **Serbian Orthodox church** *(Szerb ortodox templom; V Szerb utca 2-4)* built by Serbs fleeing the Turks in the 17th century. The iconostasis is worth a look though the church is normally open only during divine liturgy.

There are a couple of interesting sights along **Veres Pálné utca**, which runs north to south just to the west of Egyetem tér. The building at No 19 has bronze reliefs above the 2nd floor illustrating various stages of building in the capital. At the corner of the next street, **Papnövelde utca**, the stairwells of the enormous elementary school building at No 4–10 (Kálmán Reichl, 1913) is topped with little doric temples on either side of the roof symbolising culture and learning. A few steps north is **Szivárvány köz** (Rainbow Alley), one of the narrowest and shortest streets in Budapest.

The best way to see the posher side of the Inner Town is to walk up pedestrian **Váci utca**, the capital's premier – and most expensive – shopping street, with designer clothes, antique-jewellery shops, pubs and some bookshops for browsing. This was the total length of Pest in the Middle Ages. To gain access from Ferenciek tere, walk through **Párisi Udvar** *(Parisian Court; V Ferenciek tere 5)*, a gem of a Parisian-style arcade built in 1909, out onto tiny Kigyó utca. Váci utca is immediately to the west.

Make a little detour by turning east on Haris köz – once a privately owned street – and continue across Petőfi Sándor utca to Kamermayer Károly tér, a lovely little square with antique shops and boutiques, an old umbrella maker, artsy cafés and, in the centre, a statue of Károly Kamermayer, united Budapest's first mayor.

On the southeastern corner of the square is the green **Pest county hall** *(Pest Megyei Önkormánzat Hivatal; V Városház utca 7)* – the city of Budapest is in the county of Pest – a large neoclassical building with three courtyards that you can walk through during office hours. North of the square is the 18th-century **municipal council office** *(Fővárosi Önkormánzat Hivatal; V Városház utca 9-11)*, or city hall, a rambling red and yellow structure that is the largest baroque building in the city.

Szervita tér is at the northwestern end of Városház utca. Naturally there's the requisite baroque church (Szervita templom; 1732), but much more interesting are the buildings to the west. You'd probably never guess, but Rózsavölgyi House, an apartment block at No 5, was built in 1912, a wonderful example of early Modernism. Next door is the former **Török Bank House** *(Török Bánkház; V Szervita tér 3)*; look up to the gable to see its marvellous mosaic (see the special section 'Fin-de-Siècle Architecture'). You can return to Váci utca via Régiposta utca.

Many of the buildings on Váci utca are worth a closer look, but as it's a narrow street you'll have to crane your neck or walk into one of the side lanes for a better view. **Thonet House** *(V Váci utca 11/a)* is another masterpiece built by Ödön Lechner (1890), and a flower shop called **Philanthia** *(V Váci utca 9)* has an original Art Nouveau interior. The **Polgár Gallery** *(V Váci utca 11/b)* next door, in a building dating from 1912, has recently undergone a spectacular renovation and contains a stained glass domed ceiling. To the west, at Régiposta utca 13, there's a relief of an old postal coach by the ceramist Margit Kovács of Szentendre. The souvenir shop here always displays items of the same colour in its front window; originally the various shades of the same hue represented crafts from a particular region.

At the top of Váci utca, across from Kristóf tér with the little Fishergirl Well, is a brick outline of the foundations of the Vác

Gate (Váci kapu), part of the old city wall. The street leads into **Vörösmarty tér**, a large square of smart shops, galleries, airline offices, cafés and an outdoor market of stalls selling tourist schlock, and artists who will draw your portrait or caricature. Suitable for framing (maybe).

In the centre is a statue of the 19th-century poet after whom Vörösmarty tér was named. It is made of Italian marble and is protected in winter by a bizarre plastic 'iceberg' that kids love sliding on. The first – or last – stop of the little yellow metro line (M1) is also in the square, and at the northern end is **Gerbeaud**, Budapest's most famous café and cake shop.

The despised modern building on the west side of Vörösmarty tér (No 1) contains a music shop and Vigadó Ticket Office for concerts in the city. South of it is the sumptuous **Bank Palace** (Bank Palota; V Deák Ferenc utca 5), built in 1915 and now housing the Budapest Stock Exchange.

The **Pesti Vigadó** (V Vigadó tér 1), the Romantic-style concert hall built in 1865 but badly damaged during the war, faces the river on Vigadó tér to the west of Vörösmarty tér. But before proceeding, have a look (if open) in the foyer at Vigadó utca 6, which has one of those strange conveyances called Pater Noster lifts (see the boxed text 'Lift Us This Day').

A pleasant way to return to Ferenciek tere is along the **Duna korzó**, the riverside 'Danube Embankment' between Chain and and Elizabeth Bridges and above Belgrád rakpart. It's full of cafés, musicians and handicraft stalls by day and hookers and hustlers by night. The promenade leads into **Petőfi tér**, named after the poet of the 1848–49 War of Independence and the scene of political rallies (both legal and illegal) over subsequent years. **Március 15 tér**, which marks the date of the outbreak of the revolution, abuts it to the south.

On the east side of Március 15 tér, sitting uncomfortably close to the Elizabeth Bridge flyover, is the **Inner Town parish church** (Belvárosi plébániatemplom; V Március 15 tér 2), where a Romanesque church was first built in the 12th century within a Roman

fortress. You can see a few bits of the fort, Contra Aquincum, in the square to the north. The church was rebuilt in the 14th and 18th centuries, and you can easily spot Gothic, Renaissance, baroque and even Turkish elements both inside and out. Two of the side chapels have 16th-century Renaissance tabernacles and the fifth one on the right is pure Gothic. There's a mihrab (Muslim prayer nook) in the chancel from the time when the Turks used the church as a mosque.

Behind the church is the arts faculty of ELTE. The two grand buildings flanking the western end of Ferenciek tere on both sides of Szabadsajtó út are the so-called Klotild Palaces built in 1902. They contain apartments on the upper floors, shops at street level and, in the northern one, the **Budapest Exhibition Hall** (Budapest Kiállítóterem; V Szabadsajtó út 5; adult/child 150/50Ft; open 10am-6pm Tues-Sun).

Walking Tour 9: Andrássy út & City Park

This is a rather long tour starting at Deák Ferenc tér and following the most attractive boulevard in Budapest into the city's most

Lift Us This Day

One of the strangest public conveyances you'll ever encounter can still be found in a few office and government buildings in Budapest. They're the *körfogó* (rotator) lifts or elevators, nicknamed 'Pater Nosters' for their supposed resemblance to a large rosary. A Pater Noster is essentially a rotating series of individual cubicles that runs continuously. You don't push a button and wait for a door to open; you hop on just as a cubicle reaches the floor level and you jump out – quickly – when you reach your desired floor. If you were wondering what happens at the top, stay on and find out. Don't worry – you'll live. The lift simply descends to the ground floor in darkness to begin its next revolution again. The most central Pater Nosters – that you may or may not be able to ride – are in the buildings at V Vigadó utca 6 next to the 24-hour Tourinform office and at V Vörösmarty tér 1.

attractive park. The yellow metro (M1) runs just beneath Andrássy út from Deák Ferenc tér to City Park (Városliget), so if you begin to lose your stamina, just go down and jump on.

Join Andrássy út some 200m north of Deák Ferenc tér as it splits away from Bajcsy-Zsilinszky út. This section of Andrássy út is lined with plane trees – cool and pleasant on a warm day. Your first port of call might be the **Postal Museum** (Map 6; VI Andrássy út 3) if for no other reason than to admire its lovely staircase.

The neo-Renaissance **Hungarian State Opera House** (Map 5; VI Andrássy út 22) on the left was designed by Miklós Ybl in 1884 and can be visited on a tour (see the listing under the Museums & Other Attractions section later in this chapter).

The building across from the Opera House, the so-called **Drechsler House** (Map 6; VI Andrássy út 25), was designed by Art Nouveau master builder Ödön Lechner in 1882. Until recently it housed the Hungarian State Dance Institute but is now being redeveloped as a hotel and café. For something even more magical, walk down Dalszínház utca to the **New Theatre** (Új Színház; Map 6; ☎ 351 1406; VI Paulay Ede utca 35), a Secessionist gem embellished with monkey faces, globes and geometric designs. It opened as the Parisiana music hall in 1909.

The old-world **Művész café** (Map 5; V Andrássy út 29) is one block up (see Traditional Cafés under Places to Eat – Pest). The next cross street is Nagymező utca, 'the Broadway of Budapest', counting a number of theatres, including the **Thália** (Map 5; ☎ 331 0500; VI Nagymező utca 22-24), lovingly restored in 1997. The **House of Hungarian Photographers** (Map 5; VI Nagymező utca 20) has excellent exhibitions.

The **Fashion House** (Divatcsarnok; Map 5; VI Andrássy út 39), the fanciest emporium in town when it opened as the Grande Parisienne (Párisi Nagyáruház) in 1912, contains the ornate **Ceremonial Hall** (Díszterem) on the mezzanine floor, a room positively dripping with gilt, marquetry and frescoes by Károly Lotz. It is currently being redeveloped so may be closed when you pass by.

Andrássy út meets the Big Ring Road at **Oktogon**, a busy intersection full of fast-food places, shops, honking cars and pedestrians. Teréz körút runs to the northwest and for 250m to the southeast where it then becomes Erzsébet körút.

Beyond Oktogon, Andrássy út is lined with very grand buildings, housing such institutions as the **Budapest Puppet Theatre** (Bábszínház; Map 5; VI Andrássy út 69), the **Academy of Fine Arts** (Magyar Képzőművészeti Egyetem; Map 5; VI Andrássy út 71) and MÁV headquarters (V Andrássy út 73). The former secret police building, which now houses the **House of Terror** (Map 5; VI Andrássy út 60), has a ghastly history, for it was here that many activists of whatever political side was out of fashion before and after WWII were taken for interrogation and torture (including Cardinal Mindszenty; see boxed text 'Cardinal Mindszenty'). The walls were apparently double thickness to mute the screams. A plaque on the outside of this house of shame reads in part: 'We cannot forget the horror of terror, and the victims will always be remembered.' The **Franz Liszt Memorial Museum** (Map 5; VI Vörösmarty utca 35) is diagonally opposite.

The next square (more accurately a circus) is **Kodály körönd**, one of the most beautiful in the city, with the facades of the four neo-Renaissance townhouses slated for a massive face-lift at long, long last. The **Zoltán Kodály Memorial Museum** (Map 5; VI Kodály körönd 1), where the great composer lived for 43 years, is on the southeast side.

The last stretch of Andrássy út and the surrounding neighbourhoods are packed with stunning old mansions that are among the most desirable addresses in the city. It's no surprise to see that embassies, ministries, multinationals and even political parties (eg, FIDESZ-MPP at VI Lendvay utca 28) have moved in.

The **Ferenc Hopp Museum of East Asian Art** (Map 3; VI Andrássy út 103) is in the former villa of its eponymous collector and benefactor. More of the collection is on display at the nearby **György Ráth Museum** (Map 3; VI Városligeti fasor 12), a few minutes' walk southwest.

Andrássy út ends at **Hősök tere** (Heroes' Square), which in effect forms the entrance to City Park. The city's most flamboyant monument and two of its best exhibition spaces are here.

The **Millenary Monument** *(Ezeréves emlékmű; Map 3)*, a 36m pillar backed by colonnades to the right and left, defines Hősök tere. About to take off from the top of the pillar is the Angel Gabriel, who is holding the Hungarian crown and a cross. At the base are Árpád and the six other Magyar chieftains who occupied the Carpathian Basin in the late 9th century. Beneath the column is the nation's most solemn memorial – an empty coffin beneath a stone tile, representing one of the unknown insurgents from the 1956 Uprising.

The 14 statues in the colonnades behind are of rulers and statesmen – from King Stephen on the left to Lajos Kossuth on the right. The reliefs below show a significant scene in each man's life. The four allegorical figures atop are (from left to right): Work & Prosperity, War, Peace and Knowledge & Glory.

On the northern side of Hősök tere is the **Museum of Fine Arts** *(Map 3)*, which contains an outstanding collection of foreign works. To the south is the ornate **Palace of Art** *(Műcsarnok; Map 3)* built around the time of the millenary exhibition in 1896 and renovated a century later. It is used for temporary (usually modern) art exhibits. South of the hall, along the parade grounds of Dózsa György út, stood the 25m statue of Josef Stalin, pulled down by demonstrators on the first night of the 1956 Uprising.

City Park *(Városliget; Map 3)* is Pest's green lung, an open space measuring almost a square kilometre that hosted most of the events during Hungary's 1000th anniversary celebrations in 1896. It's not so cut and dry but in general museums lie to the south of Kós Károly sétány while activities of a less cerebral nature – including the **Municipal Great Circus** and **Funfair Park** (see Budapest for Children in the Facts for the Visitor chapter), **Széchenyi Baths** (see the special section 'Taking the Waters' at the end of this chapter) and the **City Zoo and Botanical Garden** (see Museums & Other Attractions at the end of this chapter) – are to the north.

The large castle on the little island in the lake southeast of Hősök tere is **Vajdahunyad Castle** *(Vajdahunyad vára; Map 3)*, partly modelled after a fortress in Transylvania, but with Gothic, Romanesque and baroque wings and additions to reflect architectural styles from all over Hungary. The castle was erected as a temporary canvas structure for the millenary exhibition in 1896 but proved so popular that the same architect was commissioned to build it in stone. The stunning baroque wing, incorporating designs from castles and mansions around the country, now houses the **Hungarian Agricultural Museum**.

The little church opposite the castle is called **Ják Chapel** *(Jáki kápolna; Map 3)*, but only its intricate portal is copied from the 13th-century Abbey Church in Ják in Western Transdanubia. The statue of the hooded scribe south of the chapel is that of **Anonymous**, the unknown chronicler at the court of King Béla III who wrote a history of the early Magyars. Writers (both real and aspirant) touch his pen for inspiration.

In the park south of the lake, Americans will spot a familiar face. The **statue of George Washington** *(Map 3; Washington György sétány)* was erected by Hungarian Americans in 1906.

OK, so it doesn't sound like a crowd-pleaser, but the **Transport Museum** *(Map 3, XIV Városligeti körút 11)* in the park to the southeast is one of the most enjoyable in Budapest and great for children. The museum's air and space-travel collection is housed in the **Aviation Museum** *(Map 3; XIV Zichy Mihály utca 14)* in the **Petőfi Csarnok**, a large hall nearby, better known for its rock and pop concerts (see the Entertainment chapter).

Walking Tour 10: Oktogon to Blaha Lujza tér

The Big Ring Road slices district VII (also called Erzsébetváros or Elizabeth Town) in half between these two busy squares. The eastern side is a rather poor area, with little of interest to travellers except the Keleti train station on Baross tér. The western side, bounded by the Little Ring Road, has always been predominantly Jewish, and this was the ghetto where Jews were forced to live behind wooden fences when the Nazis occupied Hungary in 1944. From an estimated 800,000 people nationwide before the war, the Jewish population has dwindled to about 80,000 through wartime executions, deportations and emigration.

Oktogon is on the M1 metro line, Blaha Lujza tér on the M2. This area also be reached via tram Nos 4 and 6 from both Buda and the rest of Pest.

The **Liszt Academy of Music** (Liszt Zeneakadémia; Map 5; ☎ 342 0179; VI Liszt Ferenc tér 8), one block southeast of Oktogon, was built in 1907. It attracts students from all over the world and is one of the top venues in Budapest for concerts. The interior, with large and small concert halls richly embellished with Zsolnay porcelain and frescoes, is worth a look even if you're not attending a performance. But there are always cheap tickets available to something – perhaps a recital or an early Saturday morning rehearsal (see the Entertainment chapter for details).

If you walk west on Király utca you'll pass a lovely neo-Gothic house at No 47 built in 1847 and, diagonally opposite, the **Church of St Teresa** (Szent Teréz templom; Map 6; 1811) with a massive neoclassical altar and chandelier. Due south is the **Stamp Museum** (Map 5; VII Hársfa utca 47). **Klauzál tér** (Map 5), the heart of the old Jewish Quarter, is a couple of streets to the west down Dob utca.

The square and surrounding streets retain a feeling of prewar Budapest. Signs of a continued Jewish presence are still evident – in a kosher bakery at Kazinczy utca 28, the Kővári delicatessen at Kazinczy utca 41, the Frölich cake shop and café, which has old Jewish favourites, at Dob utca 22, a kosher wine shop at Klauzál tér 16 and a wig shop at Kazinczy utca 32.

There are about half a dozen synagogues and prayer houses in the district, and these were originally reserved for different sects and ethnic groups: conservatives, the orthodox, Poles, Sephardics etc. The **Orthodox Synagogue** (Ortodox zsinagóga; Map 6; VII Kazinczy utca 29-31), which can also be accessed from Dob utca 35, was built in 1913 for Budapest's orthodox community and the Moorish **Rumbach Sebestyén utca Synagogue** (Rumbach Sebestyén utcai zsinagóga; Map 6; VII Rumbach Sebestyén utca 11) in 1872 by Austrian Secessionist architect Otto Wagner for the conservatives.

But none compares with the **Great Synagogue** (Nagy zsinagóga; Map 6; VII Dohány utca 2-8), which is the largest Jewish house of worship in the world outside New York and can seat 3000 of the faithful. Built in 1859 with Romantic and Moorish elements, the copper-domed synagogue was renovated with funds raised by the Hungarian government and a New York-based charity headed by actor Tony Curtis, whose parents emigrated from Hungary in the 1920s. The organ, dating from 1859, has been completely rebuilt and concerts are held here in summer.

In an annexe of the synagogue is the **Jewish Museum** (Map 6; VII Dohány utca 2). Outside the annexe a plaque notes that Theodore Herzl, the father of modern Zionism, was born at this site in 1860.

The **Holocaust Memorial** (Map 6; VII Wesselényi utca), on the northern side of the synagogue and facing Rumbach Sebestyén utca, stands over the mass graves of those murdered by the Nazis in 1944–45. On the leaves of the metal 'tree of life' are the family names of some of the 400,000 victims. Nearby, in front of Dob utca 12, there's an unusual antifascist **monument to Carl Lutz** (Map 6), a Swiss consul who, like Raoul Wallenberg, provided Jews with false papers in 1944. It portrays an angel on high sending down a long bolt of cloth to a victim. The **Hungarian Electrotechnology Museum** (Map 6; VII Kazinczy utca 21), a personal favourite, is a short distance to the northeast.

Rákóczi út, a busy shopping street, leads to **Blaha Lujza tér**, named after a leading 19th-century stage actress. The subway below the square is one of the liveliest in the city, with hustlers, beggars, peasants selling their wares, musicians and, of course, pickpockets. The 18th-century **St Rókus Chapel** (Szent Rókus kápolna; Rákóczi út 27/a) is a cool oasis away from all the chaos.

Just north of the square is the Art Nouveau **New York Palace** *(New York Palota; VII Erzsébet körút 9-11)* erstwhile home of the celebrated **New York Café**, scene of many a literary gathering over the years (see the boxed text 'My Café, My Castle' in the Places to Eat chapter). It is currently being developed, sadly, as a hotel.

Rákóczi út ends at Baross tér and the **Keleti train station** *(Keleti pályaudvar; Map 3)*. It was built in 1884 and renovated a century later. The city's 'other' opera house, the ugly **Erkel Theatre** *(Erkel Színház; Map 3; ☎ 333 0540; VIII Köztársaság tér 30; metro M3 Keleti pályaudvar, bus No 7 or 7/a)* is southwest of the train station. From the outside, you'd never guess it was built in 1911. On the same square is the **former Communist Party headquarters** *(Map 3; VIII Köztársaság tér 26-27)* from which members of the secret police were dragged and shot by demonstrators on 30 October 1956.

About 500m southeast of Keleti station is the entrance to **Kerepesi Cemetery** *(Kerepesi temető; Map 3; ☎ 333 9125; VIII Fiumei út 16; tram 24; open 8am-7pm daily)*. Budapest's Highgate or Père Lachaise is also called the National Graveyard (Nemzeti Sírkert) and was established in 1847. The flower shop at the entrance sometimes has maps for sale, but you can strike out on your own, looking at the graves of creative and courageous men and women whose names have now been given to streets, squares and bridges around the city.

Some of the mausoleums are worthy of a Pharaoh, especially those of statesmen and national heroes like Lajos Kossuth, Ferenc Deák and Lajos Batthyány. Other tombs are quite moving (eg, those of Lujza Blaha and Endre Ady). Plot 21 contains the graves of many who died in the 1956 Uprising. Near the huge mausoleum for party honchos, which is topped with the words 'I lived for Communism, for the people', is the simple grave of János Kádár, who died in 1989, and his wife Mária Tamáska.

If you're really into necropolises, you can reach the huge **New Municipal Cemetery** *(Új köztemető; Map 1; X Kozma utca; tram 28)* on the far eastern side of town via tram No 28 from Blaha Lujza tér. It would be just another huge city cemetery if Imre Nagy, prime minister during the 1956 Uprising, and 2000 others hadn't been buried here in unmarked graves (plot Nos 300–301) after executions in the late 1940s and 1950s.

Today, the area has been turned into a moving **National Pantheon**, which stipulates that 'Only with a Hungarian soul can you pass through the gate.' We always don ours before visiting. The posts with Transylvanian-style notches mark the graves of some of the victims. The area is about a 30-minute walk from the entrance; walk eastward on the main road till you reach the end (and a yellow building), then head north. There are some signs pointing the way to '300, 301 parcela'. At peak periods you can take a microbus marked *temető járat* around the cemetery or hire a taxi at the gate.

Walking Tour 11: Blaha Lujza tér to Petőfi Bridge

From Blaha Lujza tér, the Big Ring Road runs through district VIII, also called Józsefváros (Joseph Town). The west side transforms itself from a neighbourhood of lovely 19th-century townhouses and villas around the Little Ring Road to a large student quarter. East of the boulevard is the rough-and-tumble district so poignantly described in the Pressburger brothers' *Homage to the Eighth District*. Dilapidated entrances give way to dark and foreboding courtyards with few traces left of the dignified comfort enjoyed by the bourgeois residents in the early part of the 20th century. Much of the fighting in October 1956 took place in this district. This area is best served by tram Nos 4 & 6.

Rákóczi tér *(Map 3)*, the only real square right on the Big Ring Road, is as good a place as any to get a feel for this area. It is the site of a busy **market hall** *(vásárcsarnok; Map 3; VIII Rákóczi tér 8)*, erected in 1897 and renovated in the early 1990s after a fire.

Across the boulevard, Bródy Sándor utca runs west from Gutenberg tér (with a lovely Art Nouveau building at No 4) to the old headquarters of **Hungarian Radio** *(Magyar Rádió; Map 5; VIII Bródy Sándor utca 5-7)*, where shots were first fired on 23 October

1956. Beyond it is the **Hungarian National Museum** *(Map 6; VIII Múzeum körút 14-16)*. You may enjoy walking around the museum gardens, laid out in 1856. The column to the left of the museum entrance once stood at the Forum in Rome. Have a look at some of the villas and public buildings at Pollack Mihály tér behind the museum and the white wrought-iron gate in the centre.

You can wander back to the Big Ring Road through any of the small streets. If you follow Baross utca eastward from Kálvin tér, drop into the **Ervin Szabó Library** *(VIII Reviczky utca 3; Map 5; open 10am-8pm Mon-Fri, 10am-4pm Sat)*, built in 1887 and exquisitely renovated over the past two years. With its gypsum ornaments, gold tracery and enormous chandeliers, you'll never see another public reading room like it. Enter from Reviczky utca 1.

Farther east, across the Big Ring Road, the old **Telephone Exchange building** *(Map 3; VIII Horváth Mihály tér 18)*, built in 1910, has reliefs of classical figures using the then newfangled invention, the telephone. The Art Deco **Corvin Film Palace** *(Corvin Filmpalota; Map 3; VIII Corvin köz 1)*, at the southern end of Kisfaludy utca in the middle of a square flanked by Regency-like houses, has been restored to its former glory.

Opposite is Hungary's answer to London's Victoria & Albert: the **Applied Arts Museum** *(Map 3; IX Üllői út 33-37)*. In fact, the London museum was the inspiration when this museum was founded in 1864. The building, designed by Ödön Lechner and decorated with Zsolnay ceramic tiles (see the special section '*Fin-de-Siècle* Architecture') was completed for the millenary exhibition but was badly damaged during WWII and again in 1956. Two metro stops to the southeast is the ambitious **Hungarian Natural History Museum** *(Map 7; VIII Ludovika tér 6)*.

The neighbourhood south of Üllői út is Ferencváros (Francis Town), home of the city's most popular football team, Ferencvárosi Torna Club (FTC), and many of its rougher supporters dressed in green and white. Most of the area was washed away in the Great Flood of 1838.

The area to the west toward the Little Ring Road is dominated by the **Budapest Economics University** *(Budapesti Közgazdaságtodományos Egyetem; Map 3; IX Fővám tér)* and is full of hostels, little clubs and inexpensive places to eat. Pop into the university (entrance on the west side facing the river) for a look at its beautiful central courtyard and glass atrium. Next door is the imposing **Great Market Hall** *(Nagycsarnok; Map 6; IX Fővám tér)*. It was built for the millenary exhibition and reopened in 1996 after a major face-lift. It is now the nicest covered market in the city.

The long-awaited **National Theatre** *(Nemzeti Színház; Map 7; ☎ 476 6800; w www.nemzetiszinhaz.hu; IX Bajor Gizi park 1; tram No 2 or 2/a)* in southwestern Ferencváros and by the Danube, opened in March 2002 and its detractors have not ceased braying since. The design, by architect Mária Siklós, is supposedly 'Eclectic' to mirror other great Budapest buildings of that style (eg, the Gellért Hotel, Gresham Palace, Parliament). But in reality it is a jumble of classical and folk motifs, porticoes, balconies and columns on the outside that just does not work. As one local wag put it: 'It looks like a cross between a five-star hotel and Ceauşescu's House of the People'. Guided tours (☎ 476 6866) of the theatre lasting 30 minutes leave hourly from 11am to 3pm on Saturday and Sunday.

Walking Tour 12: Buda Hills

With 'peaks' reaching over 500m, a comprehensive system of trails and no lack of unusual transport, the Buda Hills are the city's true playground and a welcome respite from hot, dusty Pest in summer. If you're walking, take along a copy of Cartographia's 1:30,000 *A Budai hegység* map (No 6; 650Ft) to complement the trail markers. Aside from the Béla Bartók Memorial House, there are few sights, though you might want to poke your head in one of the trio of caves here (see Caving in the Activities section).

All the sights and attractions in this section can be found on or arrowed off Map 1.

With all the unusual transport options, heading for the hills is more than half the fun. From the Moszkva tér metro station on the M2 line in Buda, walk westward along Szilágyi Erzsébet fasor for 10 minutes (or take tram No 18 or bus No 56 for two stops) to the circular high-rise Hotel Budapest at No 47. Directly opposite is the terminus of the **Cog Railway** (Fogaskerekű; ☎ 355 4167; admission one BKV ticket; open 5am-11pm daily). Built in 1874, the cog climbs for 3.5km to **Széchenyi-hegy** (427m), one of the prettiest residential areas in the city.

At Széchenyi-hegy, you can stop for a picnic in the pretty park south of the station or board the narrow-gauge **Children's Railway** (Gyermekvasút; ☎ 395 5429, 397 5394; adult/child 150/50Ft; open 10am-5pm Mon-Fri, 9.45am-5.30pm Sat & Sun mid-Mar–late Oct; 10am-4pm Tues-Fri, 10am-5pm Sat & Sun late Oct–mid-Mar), two minutes to the south on Hegyhát út. The railway was built in 1951 by Pioneers (socialist Scouts) and is staffed entirely by schoolchildren aged 10 to 14 – the engineer excepted. The little train chugs along for 12km, terminating at **Hűvös-völgy** (Chilly Valley). There are walks fanning out from any of the stops along the way, or you can return to Moszkva tér on tram No 56 from Hűvös-völgy. The train operates about once an hour.

A more interesting way down from the hills, though, is to get off at **János-hegy**, the fourth stop on the Children's Railway and the highest point (527m) in the hills. The **Elizabeth Lookout** (Erzsébet kilátó), a tower built on the summit in 1910, has excellent views of the city, and there are some good walks. About 700m due east of the station is the **chair lift** (libegő; ☎ 394 3764; adult 300/150Ft; open 9.30am-6pm daily mid-May–mid-Sept, 9.30am-4pm mid-Sept–mid-May, closed on 2nd & 4th Mon of each month), which will take you down to Zugligeti út. From here bus No 158 returns to Moszkva tér.

Hármashatár-hegy (Three Border Hill) is less crowded even in peak season and is a great spot for a picnic, hiking or watching the gliders push off from the hillside. The view is 360° and worth the trip alone. There's also a lovely restaurant here with a large open terrace. You can reach this hill by taking bus No 86 or tram No 17 in Buda to III Kolosy tér, from where bus No 65 goes

to the Fenyőgyöngy restaurant on Szépvölgyi út at the base of Hármashatárhegyi út.

The museum close by is the **Béla Bartók Memorial House** (II Csalán út 29), which is also on the No 29 bus route. The house was the composer's residence from 1932 to 1940 before he emigrated to the USA.

MUSEUMS & OTHER ATTRACTIONS

The museums and some of the sights mentioned on the 12 walking tours, as well as ones not appearing on any of them, are listed alphabetically (by their English names) and described in detail below.

Applied Arts Museum

This museum (Iparművészeti Múzeum; Map 3; ☎ 456 5100; IX Üllői út 33-37; metro M3 Ferenc körút; adult/child 500/250Ft; open 10am-6pm Tues-Sun mid-Mar–Oct, 10am-4pm Tues-Sun Nov–mid-Mar), whose galleries surround a central hall of white marble supposedly modelled on the Alhambra in southern Spain, contain a wonderful array of Hungarian furniture dating from the 18th and 19th centuries, Art Nouveau and Secessionist artefacts and objects related to the history of trades and crafts (glass making, bookbinding, gold-smithing, leatherwork etc). Don't miss the painted 18th-century coffered ceiling in the room with the old printing presses, or the stained-glass skylight in the entrance hall.

Aquincum Museum

In the centre of what remains of this Roman civilian settlement, the Aquincum Museum (Aquincumi Múzeum; Map 2; ☎ 368 4260 or 250 1650; III Szentendrei út 139; HÉV Aquincum; grounds adult/student or child 400/150Ft, grounds & museum adult/student or child/family 700/300/1200Ft; grounds/museum open 9am/10am-6pm Tues-Sun May-Sept, 9am/10am-5pm Tues-Sun 15-30 Apr & October) is Hungary's largest collection of Roman finds. Most of the big sculptures and stone sarcophagi are outside to the left of the museum or behind it along a covered walkway. Keep

[Continued on page 100]

Taking the Waters

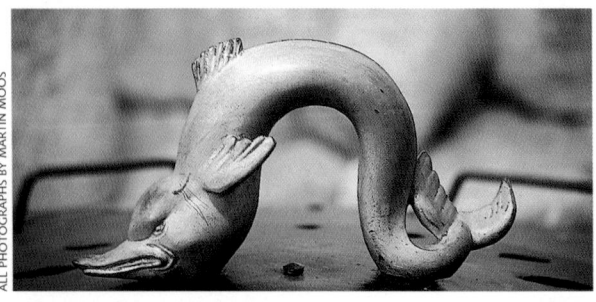

Title Page: Gellért Bath (Photograph by Martin Moos)

Top: Széchenyi Baths

Centre: Art Nouveau dome of the Gellért Bath

Bottom: Dolphin motif Király Baths

TAKING THE WATERS

Budapest lies on the geological fault separating the Buda Hills from the Great Plain, and more than 30,000 cubic metres of warm to scalding (21° to 76°C) mineral water gush forth daily from 118 thermal springs. As a result, the city is a major spa centre and 'taking the waters' at one of the many baths or spa-swimming pools is a real Budapest experience. Some of the baths date from Turkish times, others are Art Nouveau wonders, while a few more are spic-and-span modern establishments.

All baths and pools in Budapest have cabins or lockers. Find one, get changed in it (or beside it) and call the attendant. He or she will lock the door with your clothes inside, write the time on a chalkboard on the door and hand you a numbered tag to tie on your costume. Note: In order to prevent theft lest you lose or misplace the tag, the number is not the same as the one on the locker, so commit the *locker* number to memory.

While bathing suits are *de rigueur* at swimming pools (excluding nudist areas), some bathhouses require you to wear a bathing suit while others do not. For peace of mind, take one just in case. Most bathhouses and pools hire out bathing suits and towels (500Ft) if you don't have your own.

THERMAL BATHS

Generally, entry to the baths *(gyógyfürdő)* allows you to stay for two hours on weekdays and 1½ hours at weekends, though this rule is not always enforced. Most of the baths offer a full range of serious medical treatments as well as services like massage (1100/2000Ft for 15/30 minutes) and pedicure (1200Ft). Specify what you want when buying your ticket. In some of Budapest's baths you will be given a number and will have to wait until it is called or appears on the electronic board.

Though some of the local spas and baths may look a little rough around the edges, they are clean and the water is changed continuously. You might consider taking along a pair of plastic sandals or flip-flops, however.

Some of the baths become gay venues on male-only days – especially the Király and, to a lesser extent, the Gellért. Not much actually goes on except for some intensive cruising, but those not into it may feel uncomfortable.

Gellért (Map 7; ☎ 466 6166; XI Kelenhegyi út; admission 1600Ft; tram No 18, 19, 47 or 49; open 6am-7pm Mon-Fri, 6am-5pm Sat & Sun May-Sept; 6am-7pm Mon-Fri, 6am-2pm Sat & Sun Oct-April). Soaking in this Art Nouveau palace, open to both men and women in separate sections, has been likened to taking a bath in a cathedral. The pools maintain a constant temperature of 44°C and a large outdoor pool is open from April to September.

Inset: Art Nouveau dome of the Gellért Baths (Photograph by Martin Moos)

Király (Map 3; ☎ 202 3688, 201 4392; II Fő utca 84; bus No 60 or 86; admission 1000Ft; open to men 9am-8pm Tues, Thur & Sat, to women 9am-8pm Mon, Wed & Fri). The four pools here are genuine Turkish baths erected in 1570 and have a wonderful skylit central dome.

Lukács (Map 3; ☎ 326 1695; II Frankel Leó út 25-29; tram No 17, bus No 60 or 86; 3/4 hours 600/800Ft; open 6am-7pm Mon-Fri, 6am-1pm Sat & Sun). This sprawling 19th-century establishment popular with an older crowd has everything from thermal and mud baths to a swimming pool. The thermal baths are open to both men and women in separate sections; the mud and weight baths (1500Ft) are open to men on Tuesday, Thursday and Saturday and women on Monday, Wednesday and Friday.

Rudas (Map 6; ☎ 356 1322, 356 1010; I Döbrentei tér 9; tram No 18 or 19, bus No 7 or 86; admission 1000Ft; open to men only 6am-8pm Mon-Fri, 6am-1pm Sat & Sun). This is the most Turkish of all the baths in Budapest, built in 1566, with an octagonal pool, domed cupola with coloured glass and massive columns.

Széchenyi (Map 3; ☎ 363 3210, 321 0310; XIV Állatkerti körút 11; metro M1 Széchenyi fürdő; admission thermal baths and pool before/after 3pm 1500/ 900Ft; open 6am-7pm daily May-Sept; 6am-7pm Mon-Fri, 6am-5pm Sat & Sun Oct-Apr). This bath in City Park is unusual for three reasons: its immense size (nine indoor and outdoor pools); its bright, clean look; and its water temperatures, which really are what the wall plaques say they are. It is open both to men and women in separate sections, and the entrance fee is actually a kind of deposit; you get back 900/600/300Ft if you leave within two/three/ four hours before 3pm and 600/300Ft if you exit within two/three hours after 3pm. Just make sure you hold on to your receipts.

Thermal (Map 2; ☎ 452 6237; XIII Margit-sziget; bus No 26; Mon-Fri/Sat & Sun 4000/5000Ft; open 6.30am-9.30pm daily). This thermal bath, in the Danubius Thermal Hotel on leafy Margaret Island, is the most upmarket (and expensive) bath in town. It is open to men and women in separate sections.

SWIMMING POOLS

Hungarians are keen swimmers and Budapest boasts dozens of indoor and outdoor pools *(uszoda)*. They're always excellent places to get in a few laps (if indoor), cool off on a hot summer's day (if outdoor) or watch all the posers strut their stuff (both).

Many pools require the use of a bathing cap, so bring your own or wear the plastic one provided or sold for a nominal fee.

The following is a list of the best outdoor and indoor pools in the city. The former are usually open from May to September unless specified otherwise. Addresses for the swimming pools attached to the thermal baths can be found in the previous Thermal Baths section.

Csillaghegy (Map 2; ☎ 250 1533; III Pusztakúti út 3; HÉV Csillaghegy; adult/child 2-12 1000/900Ft; outdoor pools open 7am-7pm daily May-Sept, indoor pools open 6am-7pm Mon-Fri, 6am-4pm Sat, 6am-1pm Sun Oct-Apr). There's a nudist section on the southern slope that's popular in summer.

Dagály (Map 2; ☎ 452 4500, 320 2203; XIII Népfürdő utca 36; metro M3 Árpád híd, tram No 1; with/without cabin 1100/1000Ft; outdoor pools open 6am-7pm daily May-Sept, indoor pools open 6am-7pm Mon-Fri, 6am-5pm Sat & Sun Oct-Apr). This huge complex has a total of 12 pools, with plenty of grass and shade.

Gellért (admission to swimming pool & thermal baths with locker/cabin 2000/2400Ft, 1700Ft after 5pm daily May-Sept; after 5pm Mon-Fri & after 2pm Sat & Sun Oct-Apr; open 6am-7pm daily May-Sept, 6am-7pm Mon-Fri, 6am-5pm Sat & Sun Oct-April). The indoor pools are the most beautiful in Budapest; the outdoor pools have a wave machine and nicely landscaped gardens.

Alfréd Hajós (Map 3; ☎ 340 4946, 349 2357; XIII Margit-sziget; bus No 26; winter/summer 330/550Ft; outdoor pools open 6am-7pm daily May-Sept, indoor pools open 6am-7pm Mon-Fri, 6am-5pm Sat & Sun Oct-Apr). The pools, one indoor and two outdoor, form the National Sports Swimming Pool where Olympic teams train.

Hélia (Map 3; ☎ 452 5800; XIII Kárpát utca 62-64; metro M3 Dózsa György út, trolleybus No 79; admission 4200Ft; open 7am-10pm daily). This ultra-modern spa and swimming pool in four-star Danubius Hélia Hotel boasts three pools, sauna and steam room and a health-food bar.

Béla Komjádi (Map 3; ☎ 335 2097; II Árpád fejedelem útja; tram No 17, bus No 60 or 86; winter/summer 330/500Ft; open 6am-9pm Mon-Sat, 6am-7pm Sun) This very serious pool has widely varying opening hours depending on the time of year and day of the week.

Lukács (open 6am-7pm daily May-Sept; 6am-7pm Mon-Fri, 6am-5pm Sat & Sun Oct-Apr). Like the attached spa, this pool attracts an older crowd.

Palatinus (Map 2; ☎ 340 4505; XIII Margit-sziget; bus No 26). The largest series of pools in the capital, with a total of seven plus a wave pool, was being extensively renovated at time of research but promises to be better then ever. There are same-sex roof decks for nude sunbathing.

Rómaifürdő (Map 2; ☎ 388 9740; III Rozgonyi Piroska utca 2; HÉV Rómaifürdő, bus No 34; adult/child 2-12 1000/900Ft, 900Ft for all after 5pm Mon-Fri). The outdoor cold-water thermal pools here are in a leafy area north of Óbuda.

Rudas (adult/child 2-12 700/600Ft; open 6am-6pm Mon-Fri, 6am-1pm Sat & Sun). These pools, close to the river, were built by the Turks in 1566 and retain a strong Turkish atmosphere.

Széchenyi The enormous and renovated pools of the Széchenyi baths, the largest medicinal bath extant in Europe, contain thermal water and are thus open year round. (See earlier.)

Thermal Admission to the Thermal bath (see earlier) on Margaret Island includes the swimming pool.

Bottom: Swimmers in one of the Lukács baths

MARTIN MOOS

[Continued from page 96]

an eye open for the replica of a 3rd-century portable organ (and the mosaic illustrating how it was played), pottery moulds and floor mosaics from the governor's palace across the river on Óbuda Island. A new exhibition space focuses on Roman weaving, dying and dress and there's now a mock-up of a Roman bath. English-language tours (3000Ft per group) are available by arrangement.

Aviation Museum

This part of the Transport Museum's collection (Repülési Múzeum; Map 3; ☎ 363 4016; XIV Zichy Mihály utca 14; metro M1 Széchenyi fürdő, trolleybus No 72; adult/child 200/70Ft; open 10am-5pm Tues-Sun mid-May–mid-Oct) is housed in Petőfi Csarnok in City Park. It contains passenger planes and gliders as well as the space capsule in which Hungary's first astronaut travelled.

Béla Bartók Memorial House

North of Szilágyi Erzsébet fasor but still very much in the Buda Hills, this (Bartók Béla Emlékház; Map 1; ☎ 394 2100; II Csalán út 29; bus No 29; adult/child 300/150Ft; open 10am-5pm Tues-Sun) is where the great composer resided from 1932 until 1940 when he emigrated to the USA. Among other things on display is the old Edison recorder (complete with wax cylinders) he used to record Hungarian folk music in Transylvania, as well as furniture and other objects he collected. Concerts are held in the music hall most Friday evenings at 6pm and occasionally outside in the garden in summer.

Buda Castle Labyrinth

The labyrinth (Budavári Labirintus; Map 4; ☎ 212 0207; I Úri utca 9; bus No 16; adult/student or child 1000/800Ft; open 9.30am-7.30pm daily), a 1200m-long cave system some 16m under the Castle District, looks at how the caves have been used – from prehistoric times to the 20th century. The entry fees are extortionate by Hungarian standards, but it's all good fun and a relief from the heat and the crowds above on a hot summer's day.

Budapest Gallery Exhibition House

Some of the most interesting avant-garde exhibitions in town are hosted at the Budapest Gallery Exhibition House (Budapest Galéria Kiállítóháza; Map 2; ☎ 388 6771; III Lajos utca 158; HÉV Árpád híd, bus No 86; adult/child 150/50Ft; open 10am-5.30pm Tues-Sun). It also has a standing exhibit of works by Pál Pátzay, whose sculptures can be seen throughout the city (eg, the fountain on Tárnok utca in the Castle District and the Serpent Slayer in honour of Raoul Wallenberg in Szent István Park).

Budapest History Museum (Castle Museum)

The Budapest History Museum (Budapesti Történeti Múzeum; Map 4; ☎ 225 7815, 375 7533; Royal Palace, Wing E; bus No 16; adult/student or child/family 600/300/1000Ft; open 10am-6pm daily mid-May–mid-Sept, 10am-6pm Wed-Mon Mar–mid-May & mid-Sept–Oct, 10am-4pm Wed-Mon Nov-Feb), also known as the Castle Museum (Vár Múzeum), traces the 2000 years of the city on three floors of jumbled exhibits. Restored palace rooms dating from the 15th century can be entered from the basement, which contains an exhibit on the Royal Palace in medieval Buda.

Three vaulted halls, one with a magnificent door frame in red marble bearing the seal of Queen Beatrice and tiles with a raven and a ring (the seal of her husband King Matthias Corvinus), lead to the **Gothic Hall**, the **Royal Cellar** and the 14th-century **Tower Chapel**.

On the ground floor is an exhibit entitled 'Budapest in the Middle Ages' as well as Gothic statues of courtiers, squires and saints discovered in 1974 during excavations and now kept in a temperature-controlled room. The exhibit on the 1st floor – 'Budapest in Modern Times' – traces the history of the city from the expulsion of the Turks in 1686 to the collapse of communism.

City Zoo & Botanical Garden

The large zoo and Botanical Garden (Városi Állatkert és Növénykert; Map 3; ☎ 363 3797, 364 0109; XIV Állatkerti út 6-12; trolleybus

72, 75 or 79; adult/student/child/family 900/750/650/2800Ft; open 9am-7pm daily May-Aug, 9am-6pm daily Apr & Sept, 9am-5pm daily Mar & Oct, 9am-4pm daily Nov-Feb), a five-minute walk to the northeast of Hősök tere along Állatkerti út, has a good collection of animals (big cats, rhinos, hippopotamuses), but some visitors come here just to look at the Secessionist animal houses built in the early part of the 20th century, such as the Elephant House with pachyderm heads in beetle-green Zsolnay ceramic and the Palm House erected by the Eiffel Company of Paris.

Commerce and Catering Museum

The catering section of this museum (Kereskedelmi és Vendéglátóipari Múzeum; Map 4; ☎ 375 6249; I Fortuna utca 4; bus No 16; adult/student or child 200/100Ft; open 10am-5pm Wed-Fri, 10am-6pm Sat & Sun), to the left as you enter the archway, contains an entire 19th-century cake shop in one of its three rooms, complete with a pastry kitchen. There are moulds for every occasion, a marble-lined icebox and an antique ice-cream maker. Much is made of those great confectioners Emil Gerbeaud of cukrászda (café) fame and József Dobos, who gave his name to Dobos torta, a layered chocolate and cream cake with a caramelised brown sugar top.

The commerce collection traces retail trade in the capital. Along with electric toys and advertisements that still work, there's an exhibit on the hyperinflation that Hungary suffered after WWII when a basket of money would buy no more than four eggs. Before you leave, check the great old pub sign of a satyr and foaming mug of brew in the courtyard out the back.

Dreher Brewery

Budapest's – and Hungary's – largest beer maker Dreher Brewery (Dreher Sörgyárak; Map 1; ☎ 432 9850, 432 9700 ext 9623; W www.dreher.hu, Hungarian only; X Jászberényi utca 7-11; metro M3 Örs vezér tere then bus No 85; museum/museum & film/museum, film & tasting 200/400/1200Ft) has now set up the Dreher Beer Museum (Dreher Sörmúzeum) in its honour. A film about beer

making and a generous tasting session are also available.

Ethnography Museum

Visitors are offered an easy introduction to traditional Hungarian life here (Néprajzi Múzeum; Map 5; ☎ 473 2400; W www.hem.hu; V Kossuth Lajos tér 12; metro M2 Kossuth Lajos tér; adult/child/family 500/250/900Ft; open 10am-6pm Tues-Sun Mar-Oct, 10am-5pm Tues-Sun Nov-Feb), with thousands of displays in a dozen rooms on the 1st floor. The mock-ups of peasant houses from the Őrség and Sárköz regions of Transdanubia are pretty well done, and there are some excellent rotating exhibits. On the 2nd floor, another permanent display deals with the other peoples of Europe and farther afield. The special exhibits here are usually excellent.

Foundry Museum

This museum (Öntödei Múzeum; Map 3; ☎ 202 5011; II Bem József utca 20; metro M2 Moszkva tér, tram No 4 or 6; adult/child 200/100Ft; open 9am-4pm Tues-Sun) is housed in the Ganz Machine Works foundry that was in use until the 1960s, and the massive ladles and cranes still stand, anxiously awaiting use.

The exhibits – cast-iron stoves, bells, street furniture – are a lot more interesting than they sound.

Golden Eagle Pharmacy Museum

The Golden Eagle Pharmacy Museum (Arany Sas Patikamúzeum; Map 4; ☎ 375 9772; I Tárnok utca 18; bus No 16; adult/student or child 100/50Ft; open 10.30am-6pm Tues-Sun Mar-Oct, 10.30am-3.30pm Tues-Sun Nov-Feb), a branch of the Semmelweis Museum of Medical History just north of Dísz tér, contains an unusual mixture of displays, including a miniature of Christ as a pharmacist, the mock-up of an alchemist's lab and a small 'spice rack' used by 17th-century travellers for their daily fixes of herbs and other elixirs.

Gül Baba's Tomb

This reconstructed tomb (Gül Baba türbéje; Map 3; ☎ 355 8764; II Mecset utca 14; HÉV

THINGS TO SEE & DO

Margit híd, tram No 4, 6 or 17; adult/student or child 300/150Ft; open 10am-6pm daily May-Sept, 10am-4pm Tues-Sun Oct) contains the remains of Gül Baba, an Ottoman Dervish who took part in the capture of Buda in 1541 and is known in Hungary as the 'Father of Roses'. To reach it from Török utca, which runs parallel to Frankel Leó út, walk west along steep Gül Baba utca to the set of steps just past No 16; this will lead you to a small octagonal building and a lookout tower. You can also get here from Mecset utca. The tomb is a pilgrimage place for Muslims, and you must remove your shoes.

Hercules Villa

Hercules Villa *(Herkules villa; Map 2; ☎ 250 1650; III Meggyfa utca 19-21; HÉV Filatorigát; adult/child 100/50Ft; open 10am-6pm Tues-Sun May-Sept, 10am-5pm Tues-Sun late Apr & October)*, in the middle of a vast housing estate northwest of Fő tér, is the name given to some reconstructed Roman ruins. The name is derived from the astonishing 3rd-century floor mosaics of Hercules' exploits found in what was a Roman villa.

Ferenc Hopp Museum of East Asian Art

This museum *(Hopp Ferenc Kelet-ázsiai Művészeti Múzeum; Map 3; ☎ 322 8476; VI Andrássy út 103; metro M1 Bajza utca; adult/student or child 300/150Ft; open 10am-6pm Tues-Sun)* was founded in 1919, and has a good collection of Indonesian *wayang* puppets, Indian statuary and lamaist sculpture and scroll paintings from Tibet. There's an 18th-century Chinese moon gate in the back garden, but the lion's share of Japanese and Chinese art is on display at the György Ráth Museum (see later in this section).

House of Hungarian Photographers

The House of Hungarian Photographers *(Magyar Fotográfusok Háza; Map 5; ☎ 473 2666; VI Nagymező utca 20; metro M1 Opera; adult/child 300/100Ft; open 2pm-7pm Mon-Fri, 11am-7pm Sat & Sun)* is an extraordinary venue in the city's theatre district with top-class photography exhibitions.

House of Hungarian Wines

The chance of a crash course in Hungarian viticulture is offered here *(Magyar Borok Háza; Map 4; ☎ 212 1030; W www.kertnet.hu /mbh; I Szentháromság tér 6; bus No 16; tasting 3500Ft; open noon-8pm daily)*, in the heart of the Castle District. But with over 700 wines on display from Hungary's 22 wine regions and up to 70 to try, 'crash' may soon become the operative word.

House of Terror

Budapest's newest museum, the House of Terror *(Terrorháza; Map 5; ☎ 374 2600; W www.terrorhaza.hu; Andrássy út 60; metro M1 Vörösmarty utca; adult/student or child 1000/500Ft; open 10am-6pm Tues-Sun)*, in what was once the headquarters of the dreaded ÁVH secret police, focuses on the crimes and atrocities committed by Hungary's fascist and Stalinist regimes. Although well received (expect a long wait to get in), it's a rather superficial look at totalitarian rule in Hungary and needs to be expanded. The tank in the central courtyard is a jarring introduction, however, and the wall of victims' photos speaks volumes. The exhibit bears remarkable similarity to the Topographie des Terrors (Topography of Terror) one in Berlin, which opened in the former headquarters of the SS and Gestapo in 1990.

Hungarian Agricultural Museum

In the stunningly beautiful baroque wing of Vajdahunyad Castle, the Hungarian Agricultural Museum *(Magyar Mezőgazdasági Múzeum; Map 3; ☎ 363 1117, 363 1873; XIV Vajdahunyad sétány; metro M1 Hősök tere; adult/child 400/200Ft; open 10am-5pm Tues-Fri & Sun, 10am-6pm Sat mid-Feb–mid-Nov; 10am-4pm Tues-Fri, 10am-5pm Sat & Sun mid-Nov–mid-Feb)* is Europe's largest agricultural collection, with several permanent exhibits on cattle, pig and poultry breeding, winemaking, forestry, hunting and fishing. After a visit here there's not much you won't know about Hungarian fruit production, cereals, wool, poultry and pig slaughtering – if that's the kind of thing you want.

Hungarian Electrotechnology Museum

This (Magyar Elektrotechnikai Múzeum; Map 6; ☎ 322 0472; VII Kazinczy utca 21; metro M2 Astoria; admission free; open 11am-5pm Tues-Sat) doesn't sound like everyone's cup of tea, but the staff are very enthusiastic and some of the exhibits are unusual enough for a visit. Its collection of electricity-consumption meters, one of the largest in the world, is not very inspiring, though it has one that was installed in the apartment of 'Rákosi Mátyás elvtárs' (Comrade Mátyás Rákosi), the Communist Party secretary, on his 60th birthday in 1952.

The staff will also show you how the alarm system of the barbed-wire fence between Hungary and Austria once worked, and there's an exhibit on the nesting platforms that the electric company kindly builds for storks throughout the country so they won't try to nest on the wires and electrocute themselves.

Hungarian National Gallery

The Hungarian National Gallery (Magyar Nemzeti Galéria; Map 4; ☎ 375 7533, 375 8584; Royal Palace, Wings B, C & D; bus No 16; adult/student or child 600/300Ft, audio-guide 1250Ft; open 10am-6pm Tues-Sun Mar-Nov, 10am-4pm Tues-Sun Dec-Feb) is an overwhelmingly large collection and traces the development of Hungarian art from the 10th century to the present day. The largest collections include medieval and Renaissance stonework, Gothic wooden sculptures and panel paintings, late-Gothic winged altars, late-Renaissance and baroque art. On no account should you miss the restored altar of St John the Baptist from Kisszebes (now in Romania) and the 16th-century painted wooden ceiling in the next room.

The museum also has an important collection of Hungarian paintings and sculptures from the 19th and 20th centuries. You won't recognise many names, but keep an eye open for works by the Romantic painters József Borsos, Gyula Benczúr and Mihály Munkácsy and the impressionists Jenő Gyárfás and Pál Merse Szinyei. Personal favourites include the harrowing depictions of war and the dispossessed by László Mednyánszky, the sublime portraits by József Rippl-Rónai, the mammoth canvases by Tivadar Csontváry and the paintings of carnivals by the modern artist Vilmos Aba-Novák.

Hungarian National Museum

This 200-year-old museum (Magyar Nemzeti Múzeum; Map 6; ☎ 317 7806, 327 7768; VIII Múzeum körút 14-16; metro M3 Kálvin tér, tram No 47 or 49; adult/student or child 600/300Ft; open 10am-6pm Tues-Sun mid-Apr–mid-Oct, 10am-5pm Tues-Sun mid-Oct–mid-Apr) contains the nation's most important collection of historical relics in a large neoclassical building purpose-built in 1847. Exhibits trace the history of the Carpathian Basin from earliest times, of the Magyar people to 1849 and of Hungary in the 19th and 20th centuries in 16 comprehensive rooms. Look out for the enormous 3rd-century Roman mosaic from Balácapuszta, near Veszprém, at the foot of the central staircase, the crimson silk royal coronation robe stitched for King Stephen by nuns at in 1031, the reconstructed 3rd-century Roman villa from Pannonia, the treasury room with pre-Conquest gold jewellery, a second treasury room with later gold objects (including the 11th-century Monomachus crown), the Turkish tent, the stunning baroque library and Beethoven's Broadwood piano.

Hungarian Natural History Museum

There are lots of hands-on interactive displays here (Magyar Természettudományi Múzeum; Map 7; ☎ 333 0655; W www.nhmus .hu, Hungarian only; VIII Ludovika tér 6; metro M3 Nagyvárad tér; adult/senior or child 400/200Ft, open 10am-6pm Wed-Mon Apr-Sept, 10am-5pm Oct-Mar). The geological park in front of the museum is well designed and there's an interesting exhibit focusing on both the natural resources of the Carpathian Basin and the flora and fauna of Hungarian legends and tales.

Hungarian Railway History Park

Train-spotters will be in raptures here (Magyar Vasúttörténeti Park; Map 2; ☎ 428 0180;

THINGS TO SEE & DO

w *www.lokopark.hu; XIV Tatai út 95; bus No 30 or red No 20; adult/child 800/200Ft; open 10am-6pm Tues-Sun Apr-Oct, 10am-3pm Tues-Sun Nov-Mar)*, with more than 100 locomotives (most of them still working) and an exhibition on the history of the railroad in Hungary. From April to October a vintage diesel train leaves Nyugati train station for the park once an hour from 9.45am to 3.45pm and returns hourly from 11.15am to 5.15pm.

Hungarian State Opera House

The neo-Renaissance Opera House *(Magyar Állami Operaház; Map 5; ☎ 332 8197; VI Andrássy út 22; metro M1 Opera; adult/student 1500/900Ft; 1-hour guided tours in English 3pm and 4pm daily)* is among Budapest's most beautiful buildings. The interior is especially lovely; if you cannot attend a concert or an opera, at least join one of the guided tours, which includes a brief musical performance. Tickets are available from the office on the east side of the building facing Hajós utca.

Jewish Museum

The Jewish Museum *(Zsidó Múzeum; Map 6; ☎ 342 8949; VII Dohány utca 2; metro M2 Astoria; synagogue and museum adult/student or child 600/200Ft; open 10am-5pm Mon-Thur, 10am-3pm Fri, 10am-2pm Sun Apr-Oct; 10am-3pm Mon-Thur, 10am-2pm Fri, 10am-2pm Sun Nov-Mar)* contains objects related to religious and everyday life and an interesting hand-written book of the local Burial Society from the 18th century. The Holocaust Memorial Room – dark and sombre – relates the events of 1944–45, including the infamous mass murder of doctors and patients at a hospital on Maros utca. There are English-language tours available hourly from 10.30am to 3.30pm Monday to Thursday and 10.30am to 12.30pm Friday and Sunday.

Kassák Museum

In the back of the same building as the Vasarely Museum but facing the inner courtyard, is the Kassák Museum *(Map 2; ☎ 368 7021; III Fő tér 1; HÉV Árpád híd, bus No 86; adult/child 150/100Ft; open 10am-6pm Tues-Sun)*, a six-room art gallery with some real gems of early-20th-century avant-garde art as well as the complete works of the artist and writer Lajos Kassák (1887–1967).

Kiscelli Museum & Municipal Gallery

The Kiscelli museum *(Map 2; ☎ 388 8560; III Kiscelli utca 108; tram No 17, bus No 60; adult/child 400/200Ft; open 10am-6pm Tues-Sun Apr-Oct, 10am-3.30pm Tues-Sun Nov-Mar)*, housed in an 18th-century monastery that was badly damaged in WWII and again in 1956, attempts to tell the story of Budapest since liberation from the Turks from the human side. The museum counts among its best exhibits a complete 19th-century apothecary moved here from Kálvin tér and rooms furnished in Empire, Biedermeier and Art Nouveau furniture and bric-a-brac. The Municipal Gallery (Fővárosi Képtár) is upstairs, with its impressive art collection (József Rippl-Rónai, Lajos Tihanyi, István Csók, Béla Czóbel etc). The former **monastery chapel** attached to the museum is an impressive space used for temporary exhibits.

Zoltán Kodály Memorial Museum

In the flat where the great composer Kodály lived from 1924 until his death in 1967 is the Zoltán Kodály Memorial Museum *(Kodály Zoltán Emlékmúzeum; Map 5; ☎ 352 7106; Kodály körönd 1; metro M1 Kodály körönd; adult/senior or child 200/100Ft; open 10am-4pm Wed, 10am-6pm Thur-Sat, 10am-2pm Sun)*, containing four rooms of furniture, furnishings and other personal items; one room is devoted to Kodály's manuscripts.

Franz Liszt Memorial Museum

This museum *(Liszt Ferenc Emlékmúzeum; Map 5; ☎ 322 9804; w www.lisztmuseum.hu; VI Vörösmarty utca 35; metro M1 Vörösmarty utca; adult/student or child 300/150Ft; open 10am-6pm Mon-Fri, 9am-5pm Sat)* is in the house where the great composer had a 1st-floor apartment from 1881 until his death in 1886. Its four rooms are filled with his pianos (including a tiny glass one), composer's table, portraits and personal effects.

Ludwig Museum of Contemporary Art

The Ludwig Museum of Contemporary Art (Ludwig Kortárs Művészeti Múzeum; Map 4; ☎ 375 9175; w www.ludwigmuseum.hu; Royal Palace, Wing A; bus No 16; adult/student or child 400/300Ft; open 10am-6pm Tues-Sun) surveys American pop art as well as works by Russian, German and French contemporary artists over the past 50 years. There are also Hungarian contemporary works from the 1990s. The temporary exhibits are often better than the permanent collection.

Matthias Church Collection of Ecclesiastical Art

The collection (Mátyás Templom Egyházművészeti Gyűteménye; Map 4; ☎ 355 5657; I Szentháromság tér 2; bus No 16; admission 300Ft; open 9am-5pm Mon-Fri, 9am-1pm Sat, 1pm-5pm Sun) contains ornate monstrances, reliquaries, chalices and other church plate as well as a copy of the Coronation Jewels. You'll get some interesting views of the chancel from high up in the Royal Oratory.

Medieval Jewish Prayer House

With parts dating from the 14th century, this medieval Jewish prayer house (középkori zsidó imaház; Map 4; ☎ 225 7815; I Táncsics Mihály utca 26; bus No 16; adult/student or child 300/100Ft; open 10am-6pm Tues-Sun May-Oct) contains documents and items linked to the Jewish community of Buda as well as Gothic stone carvings and tomb stones from the Great Synagogue in Pest.

Military History Museum

Loaded with weaponry from before the Turkish conquest, the Museum of Military History (Hadtörténeti Múzeum; Map 4; ☎ 356 9522; I Tóth Árpád sétány 40; bus No 16; adult/student or child 250/80Ft; open 10am-6pm Tues-Sun Apr-Sept, 10am-4pm Tues-Sun Oct-Mar) also does a good job with uniforms, medals, flags and battle-themed fine art. Exhibits focus on the 15th-century fall of Buda Castle, the 1848–49 War of Independence, the Hungarian Royal Army under Admiral Miklós Horthy and the 1956 Uprising.

Museum of Fine Arts

The city's outstanding collection of foreign art works is housed here (Szépművészeti Múzeum; Map 3; ☎ 363 2675; XIV Hősök tere; metro M1 Hősök tere; adult/student or child 700/350Ft; open 10am-5.30pm Tues-Sun), in a renovated building dating from 1906. The Old Masters collection is the most complete, with thousands of works from the Dutch and Flemish, Spanish, Italian, German, French and British schools between the 13th and 18th centuries, including seven paintings by El Greco. Other sections include Egyptian and Graeco-Roman artefacts and 19th- and 20th-century paintings, watercolours, graphics and sculptures, including some important impressionist works. Free tours of key galleries are available in English at 11am Tuesday to Friday.

Museum of Music History

Housed in an 18th-century palace with a lovely courtyard, this Museum of Music History (Zenetörténeti Múzeum; Map 4; ☎ 214 6770; I Táncsics Mihály utca 7; bus No 16; adult/child 400/200Ft; open 10am-6pm Tues-Sun Mar–mid-Nov) traces the development of music and musical instruments in Hungary from the 18th century till today. The violin maker's workbench and the unusual 18th-century sextet table are particularly interesting. The paintings on loan from the Museum of Fine Arts all have musical themes. A special room upstairs is devoted to the work of Béla Bartók, with lots of scores.

Nagytétény Castle Museum

In a baroque mansion in deepest south Buda, the Nagytétény Castle Museum (Nagytétényi Kastélymúzeum; Map 1; ☎ 207 5462; XXII Kastélypark utca 9-11; bus No 3 from Móricz Zsigmond körtér; adult/child 300/150Ft; open 10am-6pm Tues-Sun Mar-Oct, 10am-4pm Tues-Sun Nov-Feb), contains an exhibition from the Applied Arts Museum tracing the development of European furniture – from the Gothic to Biedermeier. From June to September there's an exhibition of fans titled 'The Breeze of Vanity'.

National Geological Museum

This museum *(Országos Földtani Múzeum; Map 3; XIV Stefánia út 14; trolleybus 75; adult/child 150/100Ft; open Fri-Sun 10am-4pm)* would only be of interest to experts but it's an easy way to see some of the interior of Ödön Lechner's fabulous Geology Institute (see the special section '*Fin-de-Siècle* Architecture') built in 1899.

Palace of Art

The city's largest exhibition hall *(Mű-csarnok; Map 3; ☎ 460 7000, 363 2671; W www.mucsarnok.hu; XIV Dózsa György út 37; metro M1 Hősök tere; adult/student or child 600/300Ft; open noon-6pm Tues, 10am-6pm Wed-Fri & Sun, 10am-1pm Sat)* hosts temporary exhibits of works by Hungarian and foreign artists in fine and applied art, photography and design. Concerts are sometimes staged here as well.

Parliament

The eclectic Parliament *(Országház; Map 5; ☎ 441 4904; V Kossuth Lajos tér 1-3, Gate X; metro M2 Kossuth Lajos tér; adult/student or child 1700/800Ft; English language tours at 10am, 12pm and 2pm daily)*, designed by Imre Steindl and completed in 1902, has almost 700 sumptuously decorated rooms but you'll only get to see three in the North Wing: the main staircase and Domed Hall,

where the Crown of St Stephen, the nation's most important national icon, is on display along with the ceremonial sword, orb and the oldest object among the coronation regalia, the 10th-century Persian-made sceptre with a crystal head depicting a lion; the Loge Hall; and the Congress Hall, where the House of Lords of the one-time bicameral assembly sat until 1944.

Petőfi Literary Museum

Focusing on the work of Sándor Petőfi, this museum *(Petőfi Irodalmi Múzeum; Map 6; ☎ 317 3611; V Károlyi Mihály utca 16; metro M3 Ferenciek tere; adult/child 250/100Ft; open 10am-6pm Tues-Sun)* also has rooms and exhibits devoted to Endre Ady, Mór Jókai and Attila József – among other Hungarian writers. But even these great authors' works are not all that easy to obtain in (or translate into) English and probably won't mean much to most travellers. The neoclassical building (1840) also houses a centre for contemporary literature, library, concert/lecture hall and terrace.

Postal Museum

The museum *(Postamúzeum; Map 6; ☎ 269 6838, 268 1997; VI Andrássy út 3; metro M1 Bajcsy-Zsilinszky út; adult/senior or child 100/50Ft; open 10am-6pm Tues-Sun)* exhibits the contents of original 19th-century

The Crown of St Stephen

Legend tells us that it was Asztrik, the first abbot of the Benedictine monastery at Pannonhalma in Western Transdanubia, who presented a crown to Stephen as a gift from Pope Sylvester II around the year 1000, thus legitimising the new king's rule and assuring his loyalty to Rome over Constantinople. It's a nice story but has nothing to do with the object on display in the Parliament building. That two-part crown with its characteristic bent cross, pendants hanging on either side and enamelled plaques of the Apostles dates from the 12th century. Regardless, the Crown of St Stephen has become the very symbol of the Hungarian nation.

The crown has disappeared several times over the centuries, only to reappear later. During the Mongol invasions of the 13th century, the crown was dropped while being transported to a safe-house, giving it that slightly jaunty, skewed look. More recently, in 1945, Hungarian fascists fleeing the Soviet army took it to Austria. Eventually the crown fell into the hands of the US Army, which transferred it to Fort Knox in Kentucky. In January 1978 the crown was returned to Hungary with great ceremony – and relief. Because legal judgements had always been handed down 'in the name of St Stephen's Crown' it was considered a living symbol and had thus been 'kidnapped'.

post offices – old uniforms and coaches, those curved big brass horns etc – that probably won't do much for you. But the museum is housed in the seven-room apartment of a wealthy late-19th-century businessman and is among the best-preserved in the city. Even the communal staircase and hallway are richly decorated with fantastic murals and worth a peek.

György Ráth Museum

Housed in an incredibly beautiful Art Nouveau residence, the György Ráth Museum (Ráth György Múzeum; Map 3; ☎ 342 3916; VI Városligeti fasor 12; metro M1 Bajza utca; adult/student or child 300/150Ft; open 10am-6pm Tues-Sun) contains most of the Chinese and Japanese collection of ceramics and porcelain, textiles and sculptures belonging to the Ferenc Hopp Museum of East Asian Art (see earlier listing). To reach it from there walk south on Bajza utca and then west.

Semmelweis Museum of Medical History

This museum (Semmelweis Orvostörténeti Múzeum; Map 4; ☎ 375 3533; I Apród utca 1-3; bus No 86, tram No 19; adult/child 150/70Ft; open 10.30am-5.30pm Tues-Sun Mar-Oct, 10.30am-3.30pm Tues-Sun Nov-Feb) traces the history of medicine from Graeco-Roman times through medical tools and implements and photographs, and yet another antique pharmacy makes an appearance. Ignác Semmelweis (1818–65), the 'saviour of mothers' who discovered the cause of puerperal fever, was born in this house.

Stamp Museum

The Stamp Museum (Bélyegmúzeum; Map 5; ☎ 341 5526; VII Hársfa utca 47; metro M1 Oktogon, tram No 4 or 6; adult/child 100/50Ft; open 10am-6pm Tues-Sun Apr-Oct, 10am-4pm Tues-Sun Nov-Mar) contains some 300,000 stamps from around the world, every Hungarian first-day cover issued and a 4000-volume library on the subject.

Statue Park

Home to three dozen busts, statues and plaques of Lenin, Marx, Béla Kun and 'heroic' workers that have ended up on trash heaps in other former socialist countries, Statue Park (Szoborpark; Map 1; ☎ 424 7500, fax 337 5050; W www.szoborpark.hu; XXII Szabadkai út & Balatoni út; adult/student or child 300/200Ft; open 10am-dusk daily Mar-Nov, 10am-dusk Sat & Sun Dec-Feb) is a truly mind-blowing place. Ogle at the socialist realism and try to imagine that at least four of these monstrous monuments were erected as recently as the late 1980s; many were still in place when I moved to Budapest in early 1992. The museum shop sells fabulously kitsch communist memorabilia – statues, pins, CDs of revolutionary songs – as well as a worthwhile guidebook in English (600Ft). To get here take tram No 19 or 49 (or a red-numbered bus No 7 from Ferenciek tere in Pest) to the terminus at XI Etele tér. From there catch a yellow Volán bus from stand No 2 or 3 to Diósd-Érd. They leave every 15 minutes and the trip takes 20 minutes. From June to August a direct bus (1250Ft, including admission to the park) leaves from in front of the Hotel Le Meridien (Map 6) at V Erzsébet tér 9–10 at 9am, 10am and 11am and again at 3pm, 4pm and 5pm.

Telephony Museum

This museum (Telefónia Múzeum; ☎ 201 8188; I Úri utca 49; bus No 16; adult/child 100/50Ft; open 10am-4pm Tues-Sun) documents the history of the telephone in Hungary since 1881, when the world's first switchboard – a 7A1 Rotary still working and the centrepiece of the exhibition – was set up here. Other exhibits pay tribute to Tivadár Puskás, a Hungarian associate of Thomas Edison, and of the latter's fleeting visit to Budapest in 1891.

Transport Museum

In an old and new wing, the Transport Museum (Közlekedési Múzeum; Map 3; ☎ 363 2658; XIV Városligeti körút 11; metro M1 Széchenyi fürdő, trolleybus No 72; adult/child 350/150Ft; open 10am-5pm Tues-Fri, 10am-6pm Sat & Sun May-Sept; open 10am-4pm Tues-Fri, 10am-5pm Sat & Sun Oct-Apr) contains scale models of ancient trains (some of which run), classic late-19th-century automobiles and lots of those old wooden bicycles called 'bone-shakers'. There are a few hands-on exhibits and lots of show-and-tell from the attendants. Outside are pieces from the original Danube bridges that were retrieved after the bombings of WWII and a café in an old MÁV coach. The Aviation Museum (see earlier in this section) is a short distance to the northwest.

Tropicarium

This *(Map 1; ☎ 424 3050; XXII Nagytétényi út 37-45; bus No 3 from Móricz Zsigmond körtér; adult/child 1300/600Ft; open 10am-8pm daily)* is a vast aquarium and indoor tropical rainforest at the Campona shopping centre in south Buda. The best time to visit is Wednesday or Saturday afternoon; that's when the half-dozen sharks get fed.

Underground Railway Museum

In the pedestrian subway beneath V Deák Ferenc tér, the Underground Railway Museum *(Földalatti Vasúti Múzeum; Map 6; ☎ 461 6500; metro M1/2/3 Deák Ferenc tér; adult/child 110/80Ft or 1 metro ticket; open 10am-5pm Tues-Sun)* traces the history of the capital's three underground lines and plans for the future. Much emphasis is put on the little yellow metro (Continental Europe's first underground railway) which opened for the millenary celebrations in 1896 and was completely renovated for the millecentenary 100 years later. The best thing in the tiny museum are the two old coaches with curved wooden benches. The track they're sitting on and the platform were actually part of the system until diversions were made in 1973.

Imre Varga Exhibition House

As part of the Budapest Gallery, the Imre Varga Exhibition House *(Varga Imre kiállítóháza; Map 2; ☎ 250 0274; III Laktanya utca 7; HÉV Árpád híd, bus No 86; adult/child 250/100Ft; open 10am-6pm Tues-Sun)* includes sculptures, statues, medals and drawings by Hungary's foremost sculptors.

Vasarely Museum

Housed in the crumbling Zichy Mansion, this museum *(Map 2; ☎ 250 1540; III Szentlélek tér 6; HÉV Árpád híd, bus No 86; adult/child 200/50Ft; open 10am-5.30pm Tues-Sun)* contains the works of Victor Vasarely (or Vásárhelyi Győző before he emigrated to Paris in 1930), the 'Father of Op Art'. The works, especially ones like *Dirac* and *Tlinko-F*, are excellent and fun to watch as they swell and move around the canvas. On the 1st floor are some of the unusual advertisements Vasarely did for French firms before the war.

ACTIVITIES

For information on Budapest's thermal baths and swimming pools, see the see the special section 'Taking the Waters' in this chapter.

Cycling

Parts of Budapest – including City Park, Népliget, Margaret, Óbudai and Csepel Islands and the Buda Hills – are excellent places for cycling. At present bike paths in the city total about 300km, including one along Andrássy út. There are places to rent bicycles on Margaret Island (see Walking Tour 5: Margaret Island earlier for details) and in City Park. **Rent-a-Bike** *(☎ 06-30 922 3113, 06-30 971 0941; 2000/3000Ft for 6/12 hours; open 9am-8pm daily)* has bikes available from several locations in Pest, including a stand opposite V Váci utca 30 (Map 6). **Yellow Zebra Bikes** (see Cycling under Organised Tours in the Getting Around chapter) rents out bikes for 3000/5000Ft for 1/2 days; it's 2000Ft for each subsequent day. The agency **Starting Point** (see Private Rooms in the Places to Stay chapter) rents out bikes for 2400Ft a day.

The **Friends of the City Cycling Group** *(VBB; Map 6; ☎ 318 0933; w www.vbb.hu; V Curia utca 3; open 5pm-8pm Thur)* has the useful four-sheet *Budapesti bringás térkép* (Budapest Map for Bikers; 980Ft). Frigoria publishes a number of useful guides and maps, including one called *Kerékparral Budapest környékén* (By Bike in Budapest; 1890Ft) that takes in the surrounding areas and describes 30 different routes. Both publications are available in most bookshops.

Bicycles can be transported on the HÉV, all Mahart boats and the Cog Railway but *not* on the metro, buses or trams.

Skating

Bringóvár on Margaret Island (see Walking Tour 5) rents out inline skates for 820/1320Ft per 30 minutes/hour. **Görzenál Roller Skating Park** (*Görzenál Görkocsolya Park; Map 2; ☎ 250 4800; III Árpád fejedelem útja 125; admission 300/500Ft weekdays/weekends*) is an indoor rink in Óbuda. They rent skates for 300Ft.

In winter a huge outdoor **ice-skating rink** (*műjégpálya; Map 3; ☎ 364 0013; XIV Olof Palme sétány 5; admission Mon-Fri/Sat & Sun 250/500Ft; open 9am-1pm & 4pm-8pm Mon-Fri, 10am-2pm & 4pm-8pm Sat & Sun*) operates on the edge of the lake in City Park.

Horse Riding

Recommended riding schools in Budapest are the **Hajógyári-sziget Lovarda** (*Map 2; ☎/fax 457 1025; III Obudai hajógyári-sziget; HÉV Árpád-híd*) where riding costs 1300/2000Ft for 25/45 minutes (no cross-country riding possible on the island) and the **Petneházy Lovascentrum** (*Map 1; ☎ 397 5048; w www.petnehazy-lovascentrum.hu; II Feketefej utca 2-4; bus No 63; open 9am-8pm Fri-Sun*) at Adyliget near Hűvös-völgy. The latter offers beginner's lessons (2500Ft per 25 minutes), paddock practice (3000Ft per hour), trail riding (4500Ft per hour) and carriage rides (10,000Ft for 25 minutes for 10 people). It's risky – particularly in the high season – to show up at a riding centre without a booking.

The non-profit **Hungarian Equestrian Tourism Association** (*MLTSZ; Map 6; ☎ 456 0444; w www.equi.hu; IX Ráday utca 8*) can provide you with a list of recommended riding schools. **Pegazus Tours** (*Map 6; ☎ 317 1644, fax 266 2827; e orycsilla@pegazus.hu; V Ferenciek tere 5*) organises riding tours of between three days and a week (€290 to €850) in Transdanubia, the Great Plain and around Lake Balaton.

Boating

The best place for canoeing and kayaking in Budapest is on the Danube at Romai-part; take the HÉV suburban line to Rómaifürdő and walk east towards the river. Two reliable places to rent kayaks (1000Ft per day) or canoes (1300Ft per day) are the **Óbuda Sport Club** (*ÓSE; Map 2; ☎ 240 3353; III Rozgonyi Piroska utca 28; open 7am-7pm daily*) and **KSH** (*Map 2; ☎ 368 8967; III Királyok útja 31; open 8am-6pm daily mid-Apr–mid-Oct*). You'll probably find a boat available if just you go to either place, but it's always safer to book ahead.

Caving

Budapest has a number of caves, two of which are open for walk-through guided tours in Hungarian and another when pre-booked. **Pálvölgy Cave** (*Pálvölgyi-barlang; Map 2; ☎ 325 9505; II Szépvölgyi út 162; bus No 65 from Kolosy tér in Óbuda; adult/student or child 450/350Ft; hourly tours 10am-4pm Tues-Sun*), the third-largest in Hungary, is noted for its stalactites and bats. Be advised that the tour involves climbing some 400 steps and a ladder so it may not be suitable for children.

A more beautiful cave, with stalactites, stalagmites and weird grape-like formations, is **Szemlőhegy Cave** (*Szemlőhegyi-barlang; Map 2; ☎ 325 6001; II Pusztaszeri út 35; bus No 29 from III Kolosy tér; adult/student or child 400/300Ft; open 10am-3pm Mon & Wed-Fri, 10am-4pm Sat & Sun*), about a kilometre southeast of Pálvölgy Cave.

More adventurous caving possibilities can be booked through the adventure sports department of the Vista Visitor Centre (see Travel Agencies in the Facts for the Visitor chapter) as well as many of the hostels listed in the Places to Stay chapter. Some offer 2½-hour excursions to **Mátyáshegy Cave** (*Mátyáshegyi-barlang; Map 2*) opposite Pálvölgy; they're at 11am on Tuesday and Thursday and at 5pm on Monday, Wednesday and Friday for 2800Ft.

Tennis & Squash

There are some three dozen tennis clubs in Budapest usually charging between 1500Ft and 3500Ft per hour for use of their courts (clay and/or green set). Among the best are the **Városmajor Tennis Academy** (*Map 1; ☎ 202 5337; XII Városmajor utca 63-69; bus No 28*), **Szépvölgyi Tennis Centre** (*Szépvölgyi Tenisz Centrum; Map 2; ☎ 388 1591; III*

THINGS TO SEE & DO

Virág Benedek utca 39-41; bus No 65 from Kolosy tér in Óbuda) and **Vasas Tennis Stadium** *(Vasas Teniszstadion; Map 1; ☎ 355 7650; II Pasaréti út 11-13; bus No 5).* You will also find courts at Margitsziget Hotel (see the Places to Stay chapter) on Margaret Island, open 7am to 10pm April to October (800-2200Ft per hour).

For squash (1700-36000Ft per hour), book a court at any of the following: **A&TSA Fitness Club** *(Map 4; ☎ 488 7220; I Pálya utca 9; bus No 105; 7am-11pm Mon-Fri, 9am-9pm Sat & Sun)*; **Arnold Gym** *(Map 2; ☎ 250 4052; III Szépvölgyi út 15; HÉV Szépvölgyi út)*; **City Squash** *(Map 3; ☎ 325 0082; II Marczibányi tér 13; open 7am-midnight)*; and **Top Squash** *(Map 3; ☎ 345 8193; Lövőház utca 2-6; metro M2 Moszkva tér, tram No 4 or 6; open 7am-11pm Mon-Fri, 8am-10pm Sat & Sun).*

Fitness

A daily ticket to the thermal bath and pools at the **Danubius Thermal Hotel** (see the special section 'Taking the Waters' in this chapter) includes use of the fitness room and machines.

Astoria Fitness Centre *(Map 5; ☎ 343 1140; V Dohány utca 32; metro M2 Astoria, trolleybus 74; adult/student with ISIC card 1200/900Ft; open 6.30am-11pm Mon-Fri, 8.30am-9pm Sat & Sun)* has fitness machines, sauna and aerobics classes every hour.

LANGUAGE COURSES

Schools teaching Hungarian to foreigners have proliferated in Budapest recently, but they vary greatly in quality, approach and success rates. You should establish whether your teacher has a degree in the Hungarian language and whether they have ever taught foreigners. You should be following a text or at least a comprehensive series of photocopies produced by your teacher. Remember also that you'll never get anywhere by simply sitting in class and not studying at home or practising with native speakers. Expect to pay 1000Ft per hour in a classroom with six to 12 students, 2000Ft in one with three to six, and 3000Ft to 3800Ft for a private lesson.

The granddaddy of all Hungarian language schools is the **Debrecen Summer University** *(Debreceni Nyári Egyetem; ☎/fax 52-489 117; W www.nyariegyetem.hu; Egyetem tér 1)* in Hungary's second largest city, Debrecen. They organise intensive two-week (€350) and four-week (€ 640) courses in July and August and 80-hour, two-week advanced courses in winter there but now there is also **Budapest branch** *(Map 5; ☎/fax 320 5751; Jászai Mari tér 6; tram No 4 or 6)* with regular and intensive courses lasting three (60 hours)/six (120 hours) weeks for €240/470. The emphasis is not just on language but the whole Magyar picture: art, history, culture, literature.

Other reliable schools in the capital for either classroom study or one-to-one instruction include:

Hungarian Language School (Map 3; ☎ 351 1191, fax 351 1193; W www.hls.hu; VI Rippl-Rónai utca 4)

InterClub Hungarian Language School (Map 7; ☎ 279 0831, fax 365 2535; W www.interclub .hu; XI Bertalan Lajos utca 17)

International House (Map 3; ☎ 212 4010, fax 316 2491; W www.ih.hu; II Bimbó út 7)

Places to Stay

Accommodation in Budapest runs the gamut from hostels in converted flats and private rooms in concrete housing estates to luxury pensions in the Buda Hills and five-star properties charging well over €200 a night for a double. The low season for hotels runs roughly from mid-October or November to March (not including the Christmas/New Year holidays). The high season is the rest of the year – a lengthy seven months or so – when prices can increase substantially. Almost without exception the rate quoted for hostel and hotel accommodation includes breakfast. If you're driving, parking at many of the central Pest hotels will be difficult.

Because of the changing value of the forint, many hotels quote their rates in euros. In such cases, we have followed suit.

PLACES TO STAY – BUDGET
Camping

Buda In a leafy park north of the city, **Római Camping** (Map 2; ☎ 388 7167, fax 250 0426; III Szentendrei út 189; HÉV Rómaifürdő; per person/tent site/campervan/caravan 990/1990/2200/3300Ft, 2-bed cabins 3600-6000Ft; camp site open year-round, cabins mid-Apr–mid-Oct) is Budapest's largest site, with room for 2500 happy (or otherwise) campers and 58 cabins. The Rómaifürdő station is almost opposite the camping ground. Use of the adjacent strand and swimming pool is included.

Niche Camping (Map 1; ☎ 200 8346; XII Zugligeti út 101; bus No 158 from Moszkva tér; 2-person tent site 2900-3000Ft, caravan 3950-4400Ft, 2/4-person bungalow 4000/6000Ft, car 700Ft; open year-round) is a small site in the Buda Hills at the bottom station of the chair lift.

Pest Hardly attractive, **Haller Camping** (Map 7; ☎ 215 5741 or 215 4775, fax 218 7909; IX Haller utca 27; metro M3 Nagyvárad tér, tram No 24; camp sites per person/tent/car from 400/1800/300Ft; open June–mid-Sept) is about the most central site you'll find to

pitch a tent, in the back garden of a cultural centre in urban Pest.

Metro Tennis Camping (Map 1; ☎ 406 5584, fax 405 1050; XVI Csömöri utca 156; red-numbered bus No 130, bus No 31; camp sites per person 900-1400Ft, tent 450-700Ft, caravan 800-1200Ft, car 450-600Ft, double room 5000-7500Ft; open June–mid-Sept), in far-flung Rákosszentmihály northeast of the centre, has space for 50 tents and caravans alongside a sporting field.

Hostels

Hostel beds are available year-round in Budapest, but during the university summer holidays (generally mid-June or July to August) the numbers increase exponentially. During this time, private outfits rent vacant dormitories from the universities and turn them into hostels. Competition is fierce and there are several rival hostel operators, so you can afford to shop around a bit.

Dormitory accommodation in both year-round and summer hostels averages ranges from 1700Ft to 3300Ft; expect to pay from 2800Ft to 4700Ft for doubles (book these in advance). High season usually means April to October. Hostel, student and youth cards are not required at any hostel in Budapest, but they'll often get you a discount of up to 10%; make sure to ask beforehand. Prices almost always include breakfast; it's 350Ft to 400Ft otherwise.

Year-round hostels generally have laundry facilities (about 1000Ft per load), a fully equipped kitchen, storage lockers, TV lounge, no curfew and computers for accessing the Internet (usually from 20Ft per minute).

Travellers' Youth Hostels-Mellow Mood (☎ 413 2062, 215 0660; W www.hostels.hu, W www.backpackers.hu;), which is affiliated with Hostelling International (HI), runs two year-round and six summer hostels. Staff at its three booths in Keleti train station (☎ 343 0748; open 7.30am-11pm daily July-Aug, 7.30am-9pm daily rest of year), in the international ticket hall, at the Tourinform office and under the large clock near platform No 9, make bookings and may arrange to transport you there. You can also go directly to either of their two year-round hostels – Marco Polo or Diáksport (see Year-Round Hostels – Pest).

Express is the best travel agency to approach for hostel information (see Travel Agencies in the Facts for the Visitor chapter).

Year-Round Hostels – Buda The colourful **Back Pack Guesthouse** *(Map 7; ☎ 385 8946;* W *www.backpackbudapest.hu; XI Takács Menyhért utca 33; black-numbered bus No 7 or 7A from Keleti station, tram No 49 from central Pest, tram No 19 from I Batthyány tér; dorm beds 1800-2300Ft, doubles 2800Ft per person)* has 50 beds and a friendly, much-travelled manager. There are dormitories with between five and 11 beds and one small double, a lovely garden and very laid-back clientele. It's in south Buda and not central but transport is reliable.

Citadella Hotel *(Map 3; ☎ 466 5794;* W *www.citadella.hu; XI Citadella sétány; bus No 27 from XI Móricz Zsigmond körtér; dorm beds 2200Ft)* in the fortress atop Gellért hegy has a room with 14 beds as well as hotel rooms (see Hotels – Buda). The dorms are usually booked by groups a week ahead – call in advance for a reservation. Also, this area is something of a tourist trap and you may feel more like a prisoner than a prince or princess; if you're travelling alone try something more central.

Martos Hostel (see Summer Hostels – Buda), in addition to the 200 beds on offer in summer, has another 20 beds in student accommodation available year round.

Year-Round Hostels – Pest With 22 beds, **Aquarium Youth Hostel** *(Map 3; ☎ 322 0502, 344 6143;* e *aquarium@budapesthostel.com; VII Alsóerdősor utca 12, 2/F; metro M2 Keleti pályaudvar; dorms with 4-8 beds 2500Ft, doubles 8000Ft)* is 250m west of Keleti metro station but a second choice after most of the other hostels in this section.

Best Hostel *(Map 5; ☎ 332 4934;* e *bestyh@ mail.datanet.hu; VI Podmaniczky utca 27, 1/F;*

metro M3 Nyugati pályaudvar; dorm beds 2800Ft, doubles/quads 4000/3400Ft per person), with accommodation in rather rickety bunk beds, has big, airy and relatively quiet rooms. It can organise caving excursions in the Buda Hills.

Caterina Hostel *(Map 5; ☎ 342 0804, fax 352 6147;* e *caterina@mail.inext.hu; VI Andrássy út 47, 3/F; metro M1 Oktogon; dorm beds 2500Ft, singles/doubles 3500/7000Ft)*, run by an affable English-speaking woman, has 32 beds and is within spitting distance of all the pubs and bars on Liszt Ferenc tér.

Cosy Guest House *(Map 5; ☎ 321 7420, 321 4623;* e *cozygh@yahoo.com; VII Wesselényi utca 41, 3/F; metro M2 Blaha Lujza tér; dorm beds 1800Ft)* is a less-than-salubrious, 21-bed hostel.. The dorm room counts an unhealthy 12 beds.

Diáksport Hostel *(Map 3; ☎ 340 8585, 413 2062;* W *www.hostels.hu or* W *www .backpackers.hu; XIII Dózsa György út 152; metro M3 Dózsa György út; 6-bed dorms 3300Ft, singles & doubles with bath 4600Ft per person, doubles/triples & quads with shared bath from 3600/3500Ft per person)* is the Travellers' Youth Hostels-Mellow Mood group's original year-round flagship property. The 131-bed hostel is a bit far from the action but compensates by having its own 24-hour pub called the Travellers' Bar. This is definitely a party place, so go elsewhere if you've come to Budapest to sleep. Breakfast is not included.

Hostel Marco Polo *(Map 5; ☎ 413 2555;* W *www.marcopolohostel.com; VII Nyár utca 6; metro M2 Blaha Lujza tér; bed in 12-bed dorm low/high season €17/19, singles €46/ 51, doubles/triples/quads per person low season €31/26/22, high season €34/29/24)* is the same group's more central (and expensive) year-round place. This swish, powder-blue, 47-room place is almost like a mid-range hotel, with telephones in the rooms, a lovely courtyard and a great bar with cheap drinks and a restaurant (set meals 1000Ft, open 10am-10pm). Even the five spotless 12-bed dorm rooms (one reserved for women only) are 'private', with beds separated by lockers and curtains. Breakfast is included in the price.

Central Pest from Gellért hegy

Speed skaters in City Park

Budapest trams

DAVID GREEDY

Statue Park

JONATHAN SMITH

Margaret Island

MARTIN MOOS

Matthias Church

Museum Castle Guest House (Map 5; ☎ 318 9508 or 266 8879; e museumgh@ freemail.C3.hu; VIII Mikszáth Kálmán tér 4, 1/F; metro M3 Kálvin tér; dorm beds 2500Ft) is a poky but creatively decorated and friendly place, with six to nine dorm beds in three rooms. Its free Internet access, location on a lovely square and proximity to the nightlife of VIII Krúdy utca and IX Ráday utca are all pluses.

Red Bus Hostel (Map 6; ☎/fax 266 0136; e redbusbudapest@hotmail.com; V Semmelweis utca 14, 1/F; metro M2 Astoria; dorm beds 2700Ft, singles winter/summer 6000/7000Ft, doubles 7000Ft) is a very central, well-managed place, with 28 beds in large, airy and spotlessly clean rooms cobbled from two flats, a modern kitchen and exceptionally friendly management. It's for those looking for peace and quiet – not a party.

Station Guesthouse (Map 3; ☎ 221 8864; w www.stationguesthouse.hu; XIV Mexikói út 36/b; metro M1 Mexikói út, red-numbered bus No 7 from Keleti station, Zugló train station; 14/8-bed dorms 1700/2400Ft, doubles & triples/quads per person 3200/2700Ft) is a tad off the beaten track but has a great atmosphere. It's a real party place with a 24-hour bar, pool table, occasional live entertainment and between 42 and 56 beds, depending on the season. HI card–holders get 200Ft off the above prices and rates drop by 100Ft a night from the second to sixth night of stay.

Yellow Submarine Youth Hostel (Map 5; ☎/fax 331 9896; w www.yellowsubmarine hostel.com; VI Teréz körút 56, 3/F; metro M3 Nyugati pályaudvar; dorm beds 2500Ft, doubles/quads 3750/2800Ft per person), with 44 beds, has lots of facilities and high ceilings but overlooks one of Pest's busiest boulevards and there's no lift. We've heard complaints about no one responding to calls (both by telephone and in person) in the evening.

Summer Hostels – Buda The Travellers' Youth Hostels-Mellow Mood group (see Hostels earlier for central contact numbers and website) has four hostels open to individual travellers in Buda. All are open 24 hours a day and you can check in any time,

but you must check out by 9am or pay for another night.

Hostel Bakfark (Map 3; II Bakfark Bálint utca 1-3; metro M2 Moszkva tér, tram No 4 or 6; 4/6-bed dorms 3500/3300Ft; open early June–Aug) is in a solid brick pile near Moszkva tér and below Castle Hill.

Hostel Hill (Map 7; XI Ménesi út 5; tram No 18, 19, 47 or 49, bus No 7 or 7/a; apartments for 2-4 with shower 4700Ft per person; open July–early Sept), on the way up leafy Gellért hegy, is a comfortable 120-bed place, despite the faceless, institutional look of the building. There's a sports ground here and a swimming pool (admission 600Ft) as well as a cheap canteen.

Hostel Schönherz (Map 7; XI Irinyi József utca 42; tram No 4 or 6; rooms with 4-6 beds 4600Ft, doubles 4200Ft per person; open July & Aug), in an 18-storey block with 600 beds, has rooms with two, three or four beds (all with shower). There's a cheap büfé (snack bar) open from 7am to 4pm.

Hostel Universitas (Map 7; XI Irinyi József utca 9-11; tram No 4 or 6; doubles 2400Ft per person; open July & Aug), with 500 beds, is close to the Schönherz and much more basic, with just wash basins in the room and shared showers in the hallway. This place has a real party atmosphere.

Universum (☎ 275 7046, fax 344 5368; e universumhostels@axelero.hu) is the other major player in the competitive world of Budapest summer hostels. This chain has three hostels in the vicinity of the Technical University (tram No 18, 19, 47 or 49, bus No 7 or 7/a) in Buda. All have fridges in the rooms, safes and washer-dryers.

Hostel Landler (Map 7; ☎ 463 3621; XI Bartók Béla út 17; dorms for 3-4 3600Ft, doubles 3900Ft per person), at the foot of Gellért hegy with 280 beds, has basic rooms with wash basins and shared showers for two to four people.

Hostel Rózsa (Map 7; ☎ 463 4250; XI Bercsényi utca 28-30; doubles 2900Ft per person), with 222 beds, has doubles only with wash basins and shared showers.

Hostel Vásárhelyi (Map 7; ☎ 463 4326; XI Kruspér utca 2-4; triples & quads per person 4200Ft, doubles 4500Ft), with a total of 500

PLACES TO STAY

beds, has rooms with the same number of beds as the Landler, but all have private showers.

Martos Hostel *(Map 7; ☎ 209 4883, fax 463 3650;* e *reception@hotel.martos.bme.hu; XI Sztoczek József utca 5-7; tram No 4 or 6; singles 3500FT, doubles/triples/quads per person 2200Ft)* has 200 beds available in summer, in addition to another 20 on offer year-round. It's independent, reasonably well located, near the Danube and a few minutes' walk from Petőfi Bridge. There are also doubles with shower and toilet (8000Ft) and small apartments with four beds (14,000Ft).

Summer Hostels – Pest The Travellers' Youth Hostels-Mellow Mood group counts two hostels in Pest that operate in July and August only.

Hostel Bánki *(Map 5; VI Podmaniczky utca 8; metro M3 Nyugati pályaudvar; 8-bed dorms 3300Ft, doubles/quads with shared shower 3800/3500Ft per person, doubles with shower per person 4200Ft)*, the more central and smaller (80 beds) of the two hostels, is a short walk from Nyugati train station.

Hostel Kinizsi *(Map 7; IX Kinizsi utca 2-6; metro M3 Ferenc körút; dorm beds 3500Ft)*, close to the Danube and the IX Ráday utca nightlife strip, has basic rooms with two and four beds (total 190 beds) in a modern, six-storey student residence.

Hostel Apáczai *(Map 6; ☎ 267 0311; V Papnövelde utca 4-6; metro M3 Ferenciek tere; dorms with 6-8/3-5 beds 3300/3600Ft, doubles 4300Ft per person)* is the Universum group's only summer hostel in Pest. With 160 beds, it's in a great area just off Egyetem tér, another neighbourhood absolutely in the thick of things.

Summer Hostels – Margaret Island Overlooking the Danube on leafy Margaret Island is the **Sirály Hostel** *(Map 3; ☎ 329 3952, fax 422 0331; XIII Margit-sziget; tram No 4 or 6; bus No 26; dorm beds for 1st/sub-sequent nights 1900/1700Ft; open May-Oct)*. It has three very basic rooms with 12 beds in each and a large rooftop terrace for sitting outdoors by the river.

Private Rooms

Private rooms in Budapest generally cost from 3600Ft to 5000Ft for a single room, 5000Ft to 7000Ft for a double and 8000Ft to 15,000Ft for a small apartment, with a 30% supplement if you stay less than four nights. To get a room in the centre of town, you may have to try several offices. There are lots of rooms, and even in July and August you'll be able to find something. You'll probably need an indexed city map to find the block where your room is located, though.

Individuals on the streets outside the train stations and some travel agencies may offer you a private room, but their prices are usually higher than those asked by the agencies, and there is no quality control. They vary considerably and cases of travellers being promised an idyllic room in the centre of town, only to be taken to a dreary, cramped flat in some distant suburb are not unknown. On the other hand, we've received dozens of letters extolling the virtues of the landlords who readers have dealt with directly in this way. You really have to use your own judgement here. Until you suss out the pitfalls, you're probably better off getting a room from an agency.

Tourinform in Budapest does not arrange private accommodation, but will send you to a travel agency such as the ones listed below.

Among the best places to try for private rooms are **Ibusz** and **Vista** (see Travel Agencies in the Facts for the Visitor chapter). Other good places are **To-Ma** *(Map 6; ☎ 353 0819;* w *www.tomatour.hu; V Október 6 utca 22; metro M1/2/3 Deák Ferenc tér; open 9am-noon & 1pm-8pm Mon-Fri, 9am-5pm Sat-Sun)*, with extended opening hours; **U Tours** *(Map 3; ☎ 303 9818;* w *www.utours.hu; VII Kerepesi út 2-4; metro M3 Keleti pályaudvar, open 7am-7pm daily May-Sept, 9am-5pm Oct-Mar)* at the end of platform No 6 in Keleti station; and **Starting Point** *(Map 6, ☎ 266 5563, 06-30 972 6383;* e *starting point@mailbox.hu; V Szabadsajtó utca 6, metro M3 Ferenciek tere; open 9am-9pm daily July-Oct, 9am-7pm daily Nov-June)*, with private rooms, apartments and even bicycles for rent.

After hours, try **Tribus Non-stop Hotel Service** *(Map 6; ☎ 266 8942, 318 5776; W www.tribus.hu; V Apáczai Csere János utca 1; metro M1 Vörösmarty tér; open 24 hours)* near the Budapest Marriott Hotel. It books all types of accommodation and changes travellers cheques round the clock.

Pensions & Guesthouses

Budapest has scores of *panziók*, but most of them are in the outskirts of Pest or in the Buda Hills and not very convenient unless you have your own (motorised) transport. Pensions are popular with Germans and Austrians who like the homey atmosphere and the better breakfasts. Often pensions can cost as much as a moderate hotel, although there are some worthwhile exceptions.

Buda A pension just north of Moszkva tér, **Büro Panzió** *(Map 3; ☎ 212 2929, fax 212 2928; e buro-panzio@axelero.hu; II Dékán utca 3; metro M2 Moszkva tér; singles/ doubles with shower 9000/13,500Ft)* looks basic from the outside but its 10 rooms are comfortable and have TVs and telephones.

Papillon Hotel *(Map 3; ☎ 212 4750, fax 212 4003; e rozsahegy@axelero.hu; II Rózsahegy utca 3/b; singles 6000-8800Ft, doubles 8000-11,500Ft)*, one of Buda's best-kept accommodation secrets, has 20 rooms with bath. Prices depend on the season.

San Marco Pension *(Map 2; ☎/fax 388 9997; e saiban@elender.hu; III San Marco utca 6; tram No 17; singles/doubles 11,000/ 12,000Ft)* is a small, family-run and very friendly place in Óbuda. It has five spic-and-span rooms on the 2nd floor (three with private bath), a pleasant courtyard out back and air-conditioning.

Pest Beside a large church just off Thököly út, **Dominik Panzió** *(Map 3; ☎ 460 9428; fax 343 7655; e dominikpanzio@axelero.hu; XIV Cházár András utca 3; bus No 7; singles/ doubles €26/31 Apr-Oct, €21/27 Nov-Mar)* is just two stops northeast of Keleti train station by bus. The 36 rooms come with shared bath. It also has a five-person apartment for €66/61. This friendly pension is a convenient place to stay for a few nights.

Garibaldi Guesthouse & Apartments *(Map 5; ☎ 302 3457, fax 302 3456; e garibaldi guest@hotmail.com; V Garibaldi utca 5, 5/F; metro M2 Kossuth Lajos tér; singles/doubles 5000/7000Ft)*, arguably the most welcoming guesthouse in Budapest, has five rooms with shared bathrooms and kitchen in a flat just around the corner from Parliament and a number of other rooms and self-contained flats with all facilities in the same building costing from €20 to €45 per person.

Leó Panzió *(Map 6; ☎ 266 9041, fax 266 9042; e panzioleo@mail.datanet.hu; V Kossuth Lajos utca 2/a, 2/F; metro M3 Ferenciek tere; singles €45-66, doubles €69-82, triples €88-108)* is excellent value for its location and immaculate 14 rooms. They all have double-glazing, minibar and television.

Hotels

A budget (ie, one- or two-star) hotel room in Budapest will cost more than a private room – roughly 7500Ft to 13,500Ft (€30 to €55) for a double – though the management won't mind if you stay only one night.

Buda The **Citadella Hotel** *(Map 3; ☎ 466 5794; W www.citadella.hu; XI Citadella sétány; bus No 27 from XI Móricz Zsigmond körtér; doubles with/without bath from €50/55)* has 12 big, clean, dark-wood rooms, though we've heard complaints about the noisy dance club called *Barfly* below.

Junior Griff Hotel *(Map 7; ☎ 203 2398, fax 203 1255; e reserve@hotelgriffjunior .hunguesthotels.hu; XI Bartók Béla út 152; tram No 19 or 49, red-numbered bus No 7; singles/doubles/quads with wash basin €35/47-57/70, singles/doubles with shower €40/53-66)*, with 71 basic rooms at rock-bottom prices in a low-rise office block, is next to the much larger and pricier Griff Hotel (see under Buda in the Places to Stay – Mid-Range section).

Tusculanum Hotel *(Map 2; ☎ 388 7673, fax 368 7773; e tusculanum@axelero.hu; III Záhony utca 10; HÉV Aquincum; singles/ doubles/triples €25/30/35)*, off Szentendrei út in Óbuda, gets low marks for location and the groups it packs in, but you can't beat the price for a room with bath. It has 82 rooms.

PLACES TO STAY

Pest The 116-room **Flandria Hotel** *(Map 2; ☎ 350 3181, fax 320 8853; ⓦ www.hotel flandria.hu, Hungarian only; XIII Szegedi út 27; bus No 4; singles/doubles/triples/quads 5100/6300/8600/9800Ft, singles & doubles with shower from 9500Ft)* is close to Góliát Hotel (see next) and of a similar standard but not as nice.

Góliát Hotel *(Map 3; ☎ 350 1456, fax 349 4985; ⓔ hotelgoliat@gerandhotels.hu; XIII Kerekes utca 12-20; bus No 4; singles/doubles/triples/quads 5200/6200/6700/7700Ft)*, in Angyalföld northeast of the Inner Town and Lehel market, has 135 basic rooms with between one and four beds.

Medosz Hotel *(Map 5; ☎ 374 3000, fax 332 4316; VI Jókai tér 9; metro M1 Oktogon; singles/doubles/triples 10,000/13,000/15.5000Ft)*, one of the most central cheap places in Pest, is just opposite the restaurants and bars of Liszt Ferenc tér. The 70 rooms are well worn but have private bath and satellite TV; the best ones are in the main block, not in the labyrinthine wings.

Metro Hotel *(Map 5; ☎ 329 3830, fax 329 2049; XIII Kádár utca 7; metro M3 Nyugati pályaudvar; singles/doubles/triples 10,900/13,900/16,900Ft)*, operated by a branch of BKV (Budapest Transport Company), is a much divier place but very central, with 15 rooms. Hungarian citizens pay between 30% and 40% less.

Radio Inn *(Map 3; ☎ 342 8347, fax 322 8284; ⓔ radioinn@elender.hu; VI Benczúr utca 19; metro M1 Bajza utca; singles €43-48, doubles €48-65)*, just off leafy Andrássy út, is a real find, with 33 large suites with bath, kitchen and bed (or beds).

Rila Hotel *(Map 7; ☎ 216 1621, fax 215 5184; ⓔ info@hotelrila.com; IX Fehér Holló utca 2; metro M3 Nagyvárad tér, tram No 24; singles/doubles with wash basin 7700/10,200Ft, with shower 10,900/13,400Ft)*, owned by the Universum hostel group, is a 28-room, former workers' hostel that has been spruced up into quite a nice (if far-flung) and bright little property.

Margaret Island In the middle of Margaret Island, **Margitsziget Hotel** *(Map 3; ☎ 329 2949, fax 340 4846; ⓔ hotelmargitsziget@* axelero.hu; XIII Margit-sziget; bus No 26; singles €43-48, doubles €43-56)* is good value and almost feels like a budget resort, with free use of tennis courts, swimming pool and sauna. It has suites for four to six people costing €18 to €23 per person, depending on the season.

PLACES TO STAY – MID-RANGE

Budapest is not as well endowed with accommodation choices in the middle price range as it is with budget and top-end places. Expect to pay 13,500Ft to 25,000Ft (€55 to €81) for a double, depending on the season.

Buda

Beatrix Panzió *(Map 1; ☎ 275 0550, fax 394 3730; ⓔ beatrix@pronet.hu; II Széher út 3; bus No 29; singles/doubles €55/60)*, up in the Buda Hills but easily accessible by bus, is an attractive 15-room pension in a leafy neighbourhood with a lovely garden.

Burg Hotel *(Map 4; ☎ 212 0269, fax 212 3970; ⓔ hotel.burg@mail.datanet.hu; I Szentháromság tér 7-8; bus No 16, Várbusz; singles €73-97, doubles €85-109, suites for 2 €103-127)* is a new, 26-room hotel with all the mod cons in the Castle District just opposite Matthias Church.

Griff Hotel *(Map 7; ☎ 204 0046, fax 204 0062; ⓔ reserve@hotelgriff.hunguesthotels.hu; XI Bartók Béla út 152; tram No 19 or 49, red-numbered bus No 7; singles €45-63, doubles €57-80, triples €71-98)* is a boxy, 108-room in south Buda. Location keeps its rates low; it might be far from the action but transport is reliable.

Kulturinnov Hotel *(Map 4; ☎ 355 0122, fax 375 1886; ⓔ mka3@axelero.hu; I Szentháromság tér 6; bus No 16, Várbusz; singles €35-65, doubles €55-80, triples €70-110)*, a 16-room hotel in the former Finance Ministry, can't be beaten for location and price in the Castle District. Chandeliers and a sprawling marble staircase greet you on entry and the halls often host art exhibitions and concerts. The rooms, though clean and with private baths, are not so nice.

Normafa Hotel *(☎ 395 6505; ⓦ www .normafahotel.com; XII Eötvös út 52-54; bus No 21, cog railway; singles/doubles €77/85)*, on an expanse of lawn up in the Buda Hills, is a newish place with 63 rooms, an indoor swimming pool and sauna.

Ventura Hotel *(Map 7; ☎ 208 1232, fax 208 1234;* e *hotelventura@gerandhotels.hu; XI Fehérvári út 179; tram No 47 or 18; singles/doubles/triples €58/74/93)* is all faux Art Deco in various shades of blue, green and purple. It is primarily a business hotel and boasts 148 rooms and a modern gym.

Pest

Hotel Baross Panzió *(Map 3; ☎ 461 3010, fax 343 2770;* e *info@budapestpensions.hu; VII Baross tér 15, 5/F; metro M3 Keleti pályaudvar; singles/doubles/triples/quads low season €55/65/75/85, high season €75/85/95/105)* has yet to establish its true identity but is a comfortable, 29-room caravanserai owned by the Travellers' Youth Hostels-Mellow Mood group (see Hostels earlier in this chapter) and conveniently located across from Keleti train station.

Carmen Mini Hotel *(Map 6; ☎ 352 0798, fax 318 3865;* e *carmen@axelero.hu; Károly körút 5/b; 2/F; metro M1/2/3 Deák Ferenc tér; singles/doubles €50/60)* is very close to Deák Ferenc tér, and has nine large and spotless rooms all protected from the noise of the Little Ring Road by double glazing.

City Panzió *(*w *www.taverna.hu)* group of pensions (small hotels in reality) counts three central properties in Pest. All of them charge about the same rates: singles/doubles/triples/ suite for two low season €51/69/87/99, high season €69/92/117/128. **City Panzió Mátyás** *(Map 6; ☎ 338 4711, fax 317 9086;* e *matyas@taverna.hu; Március 15 tér 7-8; metro M3 Ferenciek tere)*, with 80 rooms, is arguably the least desirable, with lots of package tourists and a noisy (if central) location near Elizabeth Bridge. **City Panzió Pilvax** *(Map 6; ☎ 266 7660, fax 317 6396;* e *pilvax@ taverna.hu; Pilvax köz 1-3; metro M3 Ferenciek tere)*, with 32 rooms, couldn't't be more central; you'll roll out of bed onto Váci utca. **City Panzió Ring** *(Map 5; ☎ 340 5450, fax 340 4884;* e *ring@taverna.hu; XIII Szent István körút 22; metro M3 Nyugati pályaudvar)*, with 39 rooms, is in a wonderful old building in leafy Újlipótváros.

Délibáb Hotel *(Map 3; ☎ 342 9301, fax 342 8153; VI Délibáb utca 35; metro M1 Hősök tere; singles €51-66, doubles €59-76)* with 34 rooms, is housed in what was once a Jewish orphanage across from Hősök tere and City Park.

Emke Hotel *(Map 5; ☎ 478 3050, fax 478 3055;* e *emke@pannoniahotels.hu; VII Akácfa utca 1-3; metro M2 Blaha Lujza tér; singles/doubles/triples €66/80/110)*, with 74 rooms, is a tarted-up older hotel a minute from central Blaha Lujza tér.

Fortuna Hotel *(Map 7; ☎ 215 0660, fax 217 0666;* e *hotelfortuna@reservation.hu; IX Gyáli út 3/b; metro M3 Nagyvárad tér; singles 12,000-15,000Ft, doubles 14,000-17,000Ft)*, with 30 rooms, is another property owned by the ever-expanding Travellers' Youth Hostels-Mellow Mood group. It's not in the best part of Budapest but it's quiet and the huge Taiwan restaurant (see Chinese under Pest in the Places to Eat chapter) is just below it.

Oriental Hotel *(Map 2; ☎ 239 2399, fax 239 2268;* e *hoteloriental@euroweb.hu; XIII Fáy utca 61; tram No 14; singles/doubles/triples €50/60/90)* is the place to choose should the untouristed Angyalföld district of northern Pest and the Chinese market attract. The 96-room hotel has a decent Chinese restaurant and there are others nearby.

Pedagógus Hotel *(Map 3; ☎ 322 0821, fax 322 9019;* e *pedhotel@axelero.hu; VI Benczúr utca 35; metro M1 Bajza utca; singles/doubles/triples/suites for 2 low season €50/64/78/82, high season €67/84/98/102)* is a moderately priced, 62-room guesthouse in a block behind the more expensive Hotel Benczúr (see Pest under Places to Stay – Top End).

Platánus Hotel *(Map 7; ☎ 333 6505, fax 210 4386;* e *reserve@hotelplatanus.hunguest hotels.hu; VIII Könyves Kálmán körút 44; metro M3 Népliget; singles/doubles/triples/suites for 2 low season €61/81/99/90, high season €81/99/110/90)*, with 128 rooms, is moderately priced in the low season, but room prices jump in summer. It has a fitness centre with a well-equipped gym, sauna and aerobics room (open 8am to 10pm Monday to Friday, noon to 5pm Saturday and Sunday) and is a short distance from the Népliget international bus station.

PLACES TO STAY

Sissi Hotel *(Map 7; ☎ 215 0082;* w *www .hotelsissi.hu; IX Angyal utca 33; metro M3 Ferenc körút; singles €67-90, doubles €78-100)* is a 44-room, pension-like place with both nicer and cheaper rooms than the Corvin Hotel (see Places to Stay – Top End) next door.

Thomas Hotel *(Map 7; ☎ 218 5505, fax 218 5506;* e *thurzo@westel900.net; IX Liliom utca 44; metro M3 Ferenc körút; singles/ doubles €61/82)*, with 45 rooms, multinational flags, mirrored frontage and primary colours is a real bargain for its location in up-and-coming Ferencváros.

Gay Hotels A very central place to stay is **Connection Guest House** *(Map 6; ☎ 267 7104, fax 352 1703;* e *guesthouse@connectionbt.hu; VII Király utca 41; metro M1 Opera; singles €33-50, doubles €78)*, a gay pension above a leafy courtyard that attracts a young crowd of boyz on the go.

K.M. Saga Guest Residence *(Map 3; ☎ 217 1934, fax 215 6883; IX Lónyay utca 17, 3/F; metro M3 Kálvin tér, tram No 47 or 49; singles €41-68, doubles €54-81)* has five themed rooms (the Hunter, Mozart, Suite, Bust and OTT Baroque), 19th-century furnishings and a wonderfully welcoming Hungarian-American owner. Gay travellers may want to visit Budapest just to stay here. Two rooms share a bath. **K.M. Saga II** *(Map 6; ☎/fax same; IX Vámház körút 11, 6/F; metro M3 Kálvin tér, tram No 47 or 49)*, its branch, is more modern but less atmospheric and has three rooms with private bath and shared kitchen at the same rates.

Kosher Hotels Budapest's only kosher hotel., with 78 rooms, is **King's Hotel** *(Map 5; ☎ 352 7675, fax 352 7617; VII Nagy Diófa utca 25-27; metro M2 Blaha Lujza tér; singles/ doubles/triples low season €40/50/75, summer €50/70/90)*. Its *lemehadrin* (strictly) kosher restaurant (see Places to Eat – Pest) is supervised by the chief rabbi of Budapest.

PLACES TO STAY – TOP END

Double room rates at top-end hotels range from about 21,000Ft to 37,000Ft (€85 to €150).

Buda

Carlton Hotel *(Map 4; ☎ 224 0999, fax 224 0990;* e *carltonhotel@axelero.hu; I Apor Péter utca 3; bus No 86; singles/doubles/triples low season €75/85/100, summer €90/105/126)*, the erstwhile Alba Hotel with a facelift and extra star, is a spotless 95-room hotel in a quiet cul-de-sac in Víziváros.

Orion Hotel *(Map 4; ☎ 356 8583, fax 375 5418;* e *orionhot@axelero.hu; I Döbrentei utca 13; tram No 18 or 19, bus No 7 or 7/a; singles €54-82, doubles €75-105, triples €94-123)*, hidden away in the Tabán district, is a cosy, 30-room hotel with a relaxed atmosphere and within walking distance of the castle.

Victoria Hotel *(Map 4; ☎ 457 8080, fax 457 8088;* e *victoria@victoria.hu; I Bem rakpart 11; tram No 19, bus No 86; singles/ doubles/triples low season €74/79/109, summer €97/102/143)* has 27 rooms with larger-than-life views of Parliament and the Danube and gets high marks for friendly service and facilities. It's very good value for a four-star hotel.

Pest

Andrássy Hotel *(Map 3; ☎ 462 2100;* w *www .andrassyhotel.com; VI Andrássy út 111; metro M1 Hősök tere; standard singles & doubles €100-145, deluxe €175-250, suites €210-400)* has 70 stunning rooms (most with balconies) in a listed building. It's a lovely place but the address sounds posher than it is; enter from VI Munkácsy Mihály utca 5-7.

Hotel Art *(Map 6; ☎ 266 2166, fax 266 2170;* e *hotelart@matav.hu; V Király Pál utca 12; metro M3 Kálvin tér; singles/doubles €80/102)*, with 32 rooms, has Art Deco touches (including pink façade), a fitness centre and sauna and a very central location.

Benczúr Hotel *(Map 3; ☎ 342 7971, fax 342 1558;* e *hotel.benczur@hotelbenczur.hu; VI Benczúr utca 35; metro M1 Bajza utca; singles €65-87, doubles 79-107)* is a reconditioned, rather soulless place with 93 serviceable rooms just off Andrássy út.

Club Hotel Ambra *(Map 6; ☎ 321 1538; fax 321 1540;* e *ambrahotel@axelero.hu; VII Kisdiófa utca 13; metro M1 Opera; singles €65-75, doubles €85-95; triples/quads €105/115)* doesn't look like much on the outside, but its 21 air-conditioned rooms and suites are spacious and nicely furnished in a modern, streamlined way. There's a sauna and Jacuzzi.

Corvin Hotel (Map 7; ☎ 218 6566, fax 218 6562; e corvin@mail.datanet.hu; IX Angyal utca 31; metro M3 Ferenc körút; singles/doubles/triples €80/100/120), close to the Danube, has 40 very comfortable rooms with all the mod cons.

Astoria Hotel (Map 6; ☎ 484 3200; w www .danubiusgroup.com/astoria; V Kossuth Lajos utca 19-21; metro M2 Astoria; singles €82-108, doubles €107-141, suites €152-190), with 131 rooms, is so established it has a metro station named after it. It's a constant favourite with business travellers because of its location.

Erzsébet Hotel (Map 6; ☎ 328 5700; w www.danubiusgroup.com/erzsebet; V Károlyi Mihály utca 11-15; metro M2 Ferenciek tere; singles/doubles €103/130), with 123 rooms, was one of Budapest's first smaller hotels and is still renowned for its personal service.

Hotel Fiesta (Map 6; ☎ 266 6021; w www.hotelfiesta.hu; VI Király utca 20; metro M1/2/3 Deák Ferenc tér; singles €74-93, doubles €93-119, triples/quads €112-122) is a positive stunner of a new boutique hotel, with 112 tastefully furnished rooms and a vaulted wine cellar restaurant minutes from Budapest's main square.

Ibis Centrum Hotel (Map 6; ☎ 215 8585, fax 215 8787; e h2078@accor-hotels.com; IX Ráday utca 6; metro M3 Kálvin tér; singles/doubles €78/85 low season, €99/106 high season) may not be the most atmospheric hotel in town, but the price is right for the location at the start of the Ráday utca pedestrianised nightlife area. It has 126 rooms, an in-house garage and a lovely rooftop garden.

Liget Hotel (Map 3; ☎ 269 5300, fax 269 5329; e hotel@liget.hu; VI Dózsa György út 106; metro M1 Hősök tere; singles €90-140, doubles €112-140) faces leafy City Park, part of the zoo and a very busy road. Its an oddly shaped peach-coloured building, but the Liget's 139 rooms are comfortable and service here is excellent. The hotel also rents bicycles to its guests for €10 a day.

Mercure Nemzeti (Map 5; ☎ 477 2000, fax 477 2001; e h1686@accor-hotels.com; VIII József körút 4; metro M2 Blaha Lujza tér; singles/doubles €80-105, doubles €85-115), with 76 rooms, has a beautifully renovated Art Nouveau exterior and fabulous common rooms, including a dining room with a skylight of stained glass. The neighbourhood is centrally located but noisy and less than salubrious.

PLACES TO STAY – LUXURY
A double room in a luxury hotel will cost a minimum of €150. From there the sky's the limit.

Buda
Art'otel Budapest (Map 4; ☎ 487 9487; w www.parkplazaww.com; I Bem rakpart 16-19; tram No 19, bus No 86; singles/doubles from €198/218, suites from €298) is a new luxury hotel with 165 rooms along the Danube in Buda that would not look out of place in London or New York.

Danubius Gellért Hotel (Map 7; ☎ 385 2200; w www.danubiusgroup.com/gellert; XI Szent Gellért tér 1; tram No 18, 19, 47 or 49; singles €115-150, doubles €190-235, suites €270-300), Budapest's grande dame of hotels, is a 234-room, old-world, four-star hotel with loads more personality than most. The gorgeous thermal baths are free for guests, but with the exception of the terrace restaurant on the Kelenhegyi út side, its other facilities are forgettable. Prices depend on which way your room faces and what sort of bathroom it has. Lower-level rooms facing the river can be noisy.

Budapest Hilton (Map 4; ☎ 488 6600, w www.hilton.com; I Hess András tér 1; bus No 16, Várbusz; singles/doubles from €210/240), perched above the Danube on Castle Hill, was built carefully in and around a 14th-century church and baroque college (though it still has its detractors). It has 321 rooms, great views and some good facilities, including the medieval Faust Wine Cellar serving a good range of Hungarian vintages.

Park Hotel Flamenco (Map 7; ☎ 372 2000; w www.danubiusgroup.com/flamenco; XI Tas vezér utca 7; tram No 19 or 49; singles

€99-140, doubles €127-160, suites €203-215), a rambling 358-room place, has little to recommend itself (faceless rectangular block, smallish rooms) except for its leafy location overlooking a park and Buda's 'Bottomless Lake' (Feneketlen-tó) and excellent gym and fitness centre.

Pest

Hilton West End (Map 5; ☎ 288 5500; W www.hilton.com; VI Váci út 1-3; metro M3 Nyugati pályaudvar; singles €195-276, doubles €215-296, suites €245-398), the chain's more central, 230-room property, abuts the massive West End City Centre shopping mall and offers every type of facility and food and beverage outlet imaginable. Rates are 30% less at the weekend (Friday to Monday).

K+K Hotel Opera (Map 5; ☎ 269 0222; W www.kkhotels.com; VI Révay utca 24; metro M1 Opera; singles/doubles/triples €149/180/225, suites €290) is a 205-room Austrian-owned place with all the amenities you'd expect for the price. If you plan to attend a lot of performances at the State Opera House, you won't find any top-class hotel closer than this.

Kempinski Hotel Corvinus (Map 6; ☎ 429 3777; W www.kempinski-budapest.com; V Erzsébet tér 7-8; metro M1/2/3 Deák Ferenc tér; singles €300-410, doubles €340-450, suites from €500) is Budapest's (and Hungary's) most expensive hotel. Essentially for business travellers on hefty expense accounts, the hotel has European service, American efficiency and Hungarian charm. If you want to have and show face, stay here.

Le Meridien Budapest (Map 6; ☎ 429 5500; W www.lemeridien-budapest.com; V Erzsébet tér 9-10; metro M1/2/3 Deák Ferenc tér; singles €235-385, doubles €275-425, suites from €360), Budapest's newest luxury hotel, has 218 rooms and public areas furnished in over-the-top Louis XIV brocade and French polished furniture. It's next door to the Kempinski.

Radisson SAS Béke Hotel (Map 5; ☎ 301 1600; W www.radissonsas.com; VI Teréz körút 43; metro M3 Nyugati pályaudvar; singles & doubles €140-170, suites €340), though another chain hotel, has several pluses, including a very central location on the Big Ring Road, a lovely Eclectic building dating from 1914, 247 large rooms and suites and great health facilities, including a swimming pool in the basement.

Margaret Island

Danubius Grand Hotel Margitsziget (Map 2; ☎ 452 6200; W www.danubiusgroup.com /grandhotel; XIII Margit-sziget; bus No 26; singles €136-176, doubles €168-208, suites €254), built in 1873 on Margaret Island, is a posh and tranquil hotel with 164 rooms and all the mod cons, and is connected to the Thermal spa via an under-ground corridor. Of course it isn't cheap: rates depend on the season and the not-so-spectacular view of the Danube and Pest.

Danubius Thermal Hotel Margitsziget (Map 2; ☎ 452 6200; W www.danubiusgroup .com/thermalhotel; XIII Margit-sziget; bus No 26; singles €136-176, doubles €168-208, suites 254), a 206-room 1970s concrete block due north, is not as nice as its sister hotel, the Grand, but is sitting atop all the spa facilities.

LONG-TERM RENTALS
Finding a Flat

After the changes of 1989, many families in Budapest were given the opportunity to buy – at very low rates – the flats they had been renting from the state since the 1950s. As a result, Budapest is full of fully paid-up flats waiting to be let.

Your best source of information is the daily classifieds-only newspaper *Expressz* (85Ft) available at newsstands everywhere, or the monthly property magazines *Képes Ingatlan* (197Ft), *Ingatlan Magazin* (168Ft) or *Otthon Expo* (178Ft). Since the ads are always in Hungarian – and the landlord is likely to be monolingual – you'll have to get a native speaker to help you. It's also a way to keep prices down; foreigners always pay more.

Rental prices vary according to the district; the most expensive areas are districts II and XII in Buda, the cheapest districts are VIII (Józsefváros) and XIV (Zugló) in Pest. Expect to pay at least 2000Ft per sq m in the leafy, sought-after neighbourhoods in Buda. In Pest a flat in central district V will cost from 1500Ft to 2000Ft per sq metre, from 1000Ft to 1500Ft in districts VI or VII. The diplomatic quarter west of City Park will cost as much as districts II and XII in Buda.

Serviced Apartments

Budapest is chock-a-block with serviced apartments, apartment hotels and flats and studios rented out by individuals. They all have private bathrooms and kitchens.

The staff at Caterina Hostel (see Year-Round Hostels – Pest) can organise apartments for two people for from 10,000Ft a night. Another great deal are the self-contained flats and rooms at the Garibaldi Guesthouse & Apartments (see Pensions & Guesthouses under Places to Stay – Budget).

Charles Hotel & Apartment (Map 4; ☎ 212 9169; W www.charleshotel.hu; I Hegyalja út 23; bus No 8 or 112; standard singles €44-48, doubles €52-64, triples €64-80, executive singles €64-72, doubles €72-84, triples €92-104, apartments €72-125), on the Buda side, has 70 'studios' (larger-than-average rooms) with tiny kitchens, and two-room apartments.

Garzonház (Map 3; ☎/fax 224 9061; e emghrt@mail.datanet.hu; I Batthyány utca 49; metro M2 Moszkva tér, tram No 4 or 6; studios from €70-80, 1/2-bedroom portents from €110/130) is a 24-unit place in Buda with serviced apartments and studios with garage. The minimum stay here is one week, and the per-night rates quoted above drop substantially if your stay is longer than one month.

Millennium Court (Map 6; ☎ 235 1800; W www.execapartments.com/buder; V Pesti Barnabás utca 4; metro M3 Ferenciek tere; studios & 1-bedroom apartments €89-129, 2-bedroom apartments €140-174) in Pest, has 108 serviced studio apartments measuring about 60 sq m, one-bed apartments of 32 to 64 sq m and two-bedroom ones of 57 to 87 sq m. Minimum stay is eight nights and, again, rates quoted here drop after a stay of one month.

Peter's Apartments (Map 3; ☎ 06-30 940 0252, fax 359 6015; e sutipeti@westel900.net, XIII Victor Hugó utca 25-27; metro M3 Lehel tér, bus No 15; apartments for 2-3 people €32-62) offers real bargains 40 apartments of about 20 sq m in a basic but clean building dating from the socialist era. Some have air-conditioning and balcony; all have television. Prices are negotiable, especially during the low season and at weekends.

Starlight Suiten Hotel (Map 6; ☎ 484 3700; W www.starlighthotels.com; V Mérleg utca 6; metro M1 Vörösmarty tér, bus No 15; single/double suites €127/157), a new and very luxurious suite hotel with 54 units, is primarily aimed at the German and Austrian business markets. There are no kitchens; suites have microwave ovens only.

Sydney Apartment Hotel (Map 3; ☎ 236 8800; W www.sydneyaparthotel.hu; XIII Hegedüs Gyula utca 52-54; bus No 133; studio €145, 1-bedroom apartment €155-170, 2-bedroom apartment €235-255), with 97 units, is another very upmarket property (especially for this part of town) with a gorgeous courtyard garden, marble finishings throughout and classical music in the lobby. Special rates are available at the weekend and after a month's stay.

PLACES TO STAY

Places to Eat

FOOD

Much has been written about Hungarian food – some of it silly, much of it downright false. It's true that Hungarian cuisine has had many outside influences and that it makes great use of paprika. But that spice is pretty mild stuff; a taco with salsa or chicken vindaloo from the corner takeaway will taste a lot more 'fiery' to you. Paprika in its many varieties is used predominantly with sour cream or in *rántás*, a heavy roux of pork lard and flour added to cooked vegetables. Most meat dishes – and Hungarians eat an astonishing amount of meat – are breaded and fried or baked.

Budapest's reputation as a food centre dates partly from the 19th century and partly from the communist era. In the heady days following the advent of the Dual Monarchy and right up to WWII, food became a passion among well-to-do city folk, and writers and poets sang its praises. This was the 'gilded age' of the famous chef Károly Gundel, the confectioner József Dobos and the Gypsy violinists Jancsi Rigo and Gyula Benczi, an age when nothing was too extravagant. The world took note and Hungarian-style restaurants sprouted up in cities around the world – including a 'Café Budapest' in Boston, Massachusetts – complete with imported Gypsy bands and staff who sounded like Béla Lugosi and Zsa Zsa Gabor.

After the war, Budapest's gastronomic reputation lived on, most notably because food elsewhere in the other capitals of Eastern Europe was virtually inedible, if available (think Warsaw, circa 1975). Hungarian food was, as one observer noted, 'a bright spot in a culinary black hole'. But most of the best chefs, including Gundel himself, had voted with their feet and left the country in the 1950s, and restaurants were put under state control. The reputation and the reality of food had diverged.

Although inexpensive by Western standards and served in huge portions, Hungarian food today remains heavy and, frankly, often unhealthy. Meat, sour cream and fat abound and, except in season, *saláta* (salad) usually means a plate of pickled beets, pickled cabbage and pickled peppers. There are some bright spots in Budapest, though. A fair few vegetarian restaurants (or ones at least halfway there) have opened up, and ethnic food – from Middle Eastern and Italian to fast-food Thai and Chinese – is very popular. And even Hungarian food itself is undergoing a long-awaited transformation at many middle-level and upmarket restaurants; many Budapesters have tried 'New Hungarian' cuisine and seem to like it – judging from the heavy bookings at the establishments serving it.

Meals

Hungarians are not big breakfast eaters at home, preferring a cup of tea or coffee with an unadorned bread roll – they say that Hungarians will 'eat bread with bread' – at the kitchen table or on the way to work. Lunch, eaten at 1pm, is traditionally the main meal in the countryside and can consist of two or three courses, but this is no longer the case for working people in Budapest. Dinner – supper, really – is less substantial when eaten at home, often just sliced meats, cheese and some pickled vegetables.

Dishes & Cooking Methods

The most famous traditional meal is *gulyás* (or *gulyásleves*), a thick beef soup cooked with onions and potatoes and usually eaten as a main course. *Pörkölt* (stew) is closer to what we call 'goulash' abroad; the addition of sour cream and paprika makes the dish, whatever it may contain, *paprikás*.

Many dishes are seasoned with paprika, which appears on restaurant tables as a condiment beside the salt and pepper shakers. It's quite a mild spice and is used predominantly with sour cream or in *rántás*. Things stuffed *(töltött)* with meat and rice, such as cabbage or peppers, are cooked in *rántás*, tomato sauce or sour cream. *Lecsó* is a tasty stewed sauce of peppers, tomatoes and onions served with meat.

Another Hungarian favourite is fisherman's soup *(halászlé)*, a rich mixture of several kinds of poached freshwater fish, tomatoes, green peppers and paprika. It's a meal in itself.

Pork, beef, turkey and chicken are the most common meats and can be breaded and fried or baked. Chicken and goose legs and turkey breasts – though not much else of the birds – make it on to most menus as does beef in some form. Freshwater fish from Lake Balaton, such as the indigenous *fogas* (pike-perch), is plentiful, but quite expensive and often overcooked. Lamb and mutton are very rarely eaten here.

Vegetarian Food

In restaurants, vegetarians can usually order fried mushroom caps *(gombafejek rántva)*, pasta dishes with cheese like *túrós csusza* and *sztrapacska*, or plain little dumplings *(galuszka)*. Salad as it's usually known around the world is called *vitamin saláta* here and usually available when in season; everything else is *savanyúság* (literally 'sourness') or pickled things. Boiled vegetables *(zöldség)* are 'English-style' or *angolos zöldség*. The traditional way of preparing vegetables is called *főzelék*, where they're fried or boiled and then mixed into a roux with cream.

Other vegetarian dishes include *rántott sajt* (fried cheese), *gomba leves* (mushroom soup), *gyümölcs leves* (fruit soup) and *sajtos kenyér* (sliced bread with soft cheese). *Bableves* (bean soup) usually contains meat. Pancakes *(palacsinta)* may be savoury and made with cheese *(sajt)* or mushrooms *(gomba)* or sweet and prepared with nuts *(dió)* or poppy seeds *(mák)*.

Lángos, a deep-fried dough with various toppings, is a cheap meatless snack sold on streets throughout the land.

Eating Out

Types of Eateries It's useful to know the names of the types of eateries in Budapest though distinctions can sometimes be blurred.

An *étterem* is a restaurant with a large selection, including international dishes. A *vendéglő* or *kisvendéglő* is smaller and is supposed to serve inexpensive regional dishes or 'home cooking', but the name is now 'cute' enough for a lot of large places to use it. An *étkezde* is like a *vendéglő* but cheaper, smaller and often with counter seating. The term *csárda* originally signified a country inn with a rustic atmosphere, Gypsy music and hearty local dishes. Now any place that strings dry paprikas on the wall is a *csárda*. Most restaurants offer a good-value set menu *(menü)* of two or three courses at lunch. Most Budapest restaurants are open till 11pm or midnight, but it's best to arrive by 9pm or 10pm. It is advisable to book tables at medium-priced to expensive restaurants.

A *bisztró* is a much cheaper sit-down place that is usually *önkiszolgáló* (self-service). A *büfé* is cheaper still with a very limited menu. Here you eat while standing at counters.

Some traditional butcher shops *(hentesáru bolt)* still have a *büfé* attached selling boiled or fried *kolbász* (sausage), *wirsli* (frankfurters), roast chicken, bread and pickles. Point to what you want; the staff will weigh it all and hand you a slip of paper with the price. You usually pay at the *pénztar* (cashier) and hand the stamped receipt back to the staff for your food. Food stalls, known as *Laci konyha* (Larry's kitchen) or *pecsenyesütő* (roast oven), sell the same sorts of things, as well as fish when located beside lakes or rivers. At these last places you pay for everything, including mustard for your *kolbász*, and eat with your hands.

A *kávéház* is a 'coffee house' or café (see boxed text 'My Café, My Castle' in this chapter); a *kávézó* is more like a coffee bar. An *eszpresszó* is a rather more simple coffee house and usually sells alcoholic drinks and light snacks as well. A *cukrászda* is a shop or café selling cakes, pastries and ice cream. In recent years, the teahouse *(teaház)* has made a big splash in Budapest.

Menus Restaurant menus are often translated into German and sometimes into English – with mixed degrees of success. The main categories on a menu are *előételek* (appetisers), *levesek* (soups), *saláták* (salads), *készételek* (ready-made dishes that are just heated up), *frissensültek* (dishes made to order), *halételek* or *halak* (fish dishes), *szárnyasok* (poultry dishes), *köretek* (side dishes), *édességek* or *tészták* (desserts) and *sajtok* (cheese). For more details, see the boxed text 'Menu Reader'.

A main course in a restaurant usually comes with some sort of starch and a little garnish of pickles. Vegetables and salads must be ordered separately. A typical menu will have up to 10 pork and beef dishes, a couple of fish ones and usually only one poultry dish.

Costs Very roughly, a two-course sit-down meal for one person with a glass of wine or beer for under 2000Ft in Budapest is 'cheap', while a 'moderate' meal will cost up to 4000Ft. There's a pretty big jump to an 'expensive' meal (4000Ft to 7000Ft), and 'very expensive' is anything above that.

It is not unknown for waiters to try to rip you off once they see you are a foreigner. They may try to bring you an unordered dish or make a 'mistake' when tallying the bill. If you think there's a discrepancy, ask for the menu and check the bill carefully. The most common ruse is to bring you the most expensive beer or wine when you order a draught or a glass. Ask the price before you order. If you've been taken for more than 15% or 20% of the bill, call for the manager. Otherwise just don't leave a tip (see Tipping & Bargaining in the Facts for the Visitor chapter).

DRINKS
Nonalcoholic Drinks
Most international soft drink brands are available in Budapest, but mineral water seems to be the most popular libation for teetotallers in pubs and bars. Fruit juice is usually canned or boxed fruit 'drink' with lots of sugar added.

Budapesters drink a tremendous amount of coffee *(kávé)* – as a single black *(fekete)*, a double *(dupla)* or with milk *(tejes kávé)*. Most cafés now serve some variation of

cappuccino. Decaffeinated coffee is *koffeinmentes kávé*.

Black tea *(tea*, pronounced **tay**-ah) has never been popular with Hungarians (many consider it to be something to be drunk when sick) though teahouses have become the bee's knees in the trendier neighbourhoods of Budapest in recent years. In fact, it can often be difficult to find 'English' tea in small grocery stores, though you'll always be able to choose from a wide range of herbal teas and fruit tisanes. Tea is almost never drunk with milk but with lemon or honey.

Alcoholic Drinks
Places in which to sample the local vintage or brew include a *borozó*, an establishment (usually a dive) serving wine; a *pince*, which can be a beer or a wine cellar; and a *söröző*, a pub with draught beer *(csapolt sör)* on tap.

Wine Wine has been produced in Hungary for thousands of years, and you'll find it available by the glass or bottle everywhere. See the boxed text 'The Wines of Hungary' for tips on what to drink, where and with what.

Brandy & Liqueur An alcoholic drink that is as Hungarian as wine is *pálinka*, a strong brandy distilled from a variety of fruits but most commonly from plums or, even better, apricots. There are many different types and qualities but the best are Óbarack, the double-distilled 'Old Apricot' and Zwack's Fütyülős Barack.

Hungarian liqueurs are usually unbearably sweet and taste artificial, though the Zwack brand is reliable. Zwack also produces Unicum, a bitter aperitif that has been around since 1790. The Austrian emperor Joseph II christened the liqueur when he tasted it and supposedly exclaimed *Das ist ein Unikum!* (This is a unique drink!). It remains an acquired taste for most non-Magyars.

Beer Hungary produces a number of its own beers for national distribution (eg, Dreher and Kőbanyai, both bottled in Budapest), though some are usually found only near where they are brewed such as Kanizsai in Nagykanizsa and Szalon in

Menu Reader

The following is a sample menu as it would appear in many restaurants in Budapest. It's far from complete, but it gives a good idea of what to expect. For more food and ordering words, see the Language chapter at the back of this book.

Előételek – Appetisers
hortobágyi palacsinta – meat-filled pancakes with paprika sauce
libamáj pástétom – goose-liver pâté
rántott gombafejek – breaded, fried mushrooms

Levesek – Soups
bableves – bean soup
csontleves – consommé
gombaleves – mushroom soup
jókai bableves – bean soup with meat
meggyleves – cold sour-cherry soup (in summer)
újházi tyúkhúsleves – chicken broth with noodles

Saláták – Salads
cékla saláta – pickled beetroot salad
ecetes almapaprika – pickled peppers
paradicsom saláta – tomato salad
uborka saláta – sliced pickled-cucumber salad
vegyes saláta – mixed salad of pickles
vitamin saláta – seasonal mixed salad

Zöldség – Vegetables
gomba – mushrooms
káposzta – cabbage
karfiol – cauliflower
sárgarépa – carrots
spárga – asparagus
spenót – spinach
zöldbab – string (green) beans
zöldborsó – peas

Köretek –Side Dishes
főzelék – Hungarian-style vegetables
galuska – dumplings
rizi-bizi – rice with peas
sült hasábburgonya – chips (French fries)

Készételek – Ready-Made Dishes
csirke paprikás – chicken paprika
gulyás – beef goulash soup
halászlé – spicy fish soup
pörkölt – stew (many types)
töltött paprika/káposzta – stuffed peppers/ cabbage

Frissensültek –Dishes Made to Order
borjú bécsiszelet – Wiener schnitzel
brassói aprópecsenye – braised pork Braşov-style
cigánypecsenye – roast pork Gypsy-style
csülök – smoked pork knuckle
fogas – Balaton pike-perch
hagymás rostélyos – beef sirloin fried with onions
rántott hátszínszelet – breaded, fried rump steak
rántott ponty – breaded, fried carp
rántott pulykamell – breaded, fried turkey breast
sertésborda – pork chop
sült csirkecomb – roast chicken thigh
sült libacomb – roast goose leg
sült libamáj – fried goose liver

Édességek or Tészták – Desserts
dobos torta – multilayered 'Dobos' chocolate and cream cake with caramelised brown sugar top
Gundel palacsinta – 'Gundel' flambéed pancake with chocolate and nuts
rétes – strudel
somlói galuska – Somló-style sponge cake with chocolate and whipped cream

Gyümölcs – Fruit
alma – apple
banán – banana
cseresznye – cherries
eper – strawberries
körte – pear
málna – raspberries
meggy – sour cherries
narancs – orange
őszibarack – peach
sárgabarack – apricot
szilva – plum
szőlő – grapes

Cooking Methods
főtt or *főve* – boiled
főzelék – frying or boiling vegetables, then mixing into a roux with cream
füstölt – smoked
párolt – steamed
pirított – braised
rántva or *rántott* – breaded and fried
roston – grilled
sült or *sütve* – fried or roast

Pécs. Bottled Austrian and German beer such as Gösser, Holstein and Zipfer – either imported or brewed in Hungary under licence – are readily available, as are Czech imports like Pilsner Urquell, Budweiser and Staropramen. Locally brewed and imported beer is almost always lager, though occasionally you'll come across Dreher stout.

PLACES TO EAT – BUDA
Hungarian

Aranyszarvas (Golden Stag; Map 4; ☎ 375 6451; I Szarvas tér 1; mains 1800-2500Ft; open noon-11pm daily) is set in an old 18th-century inn at the foot of Castle Hill and serves – what else? – game dishes. The outside terrace is lovely in summer.

Kacsa (Map 3; ☎ 201 9992; II Fő utca 75; starters 1200-3300Ft, mains 2500-5400Ft; open noon-3pm & 6pm-1am Mon-Fri, 6pm-1am Sat & Sun) is the place for duck (which is what its name means) but not exclusively so. It's a fairly elegant place, with piano music in the evening.

Kéhli (Map 2; ☎ 250 4241; III Mókus utca 22; mains 1580-3580Ft; open 5pm-midnight Mon-Fri, noon-midnight Sat & Sun), a rustic but stylish place in Óbuda, has the best traditional Hungarian food in town. In fact one of Hungary's best-loved writers, the novelist Gyula Krúdy (1878–1933), moonlighted here as a restaurant critic and enjoyed bone marrow on toast (better than it sounds) so much he included it in one of his novels.

Kisbuda Gyöngye (Map 2; ☎ 368 6402, 368 9246; III Kenyeres utca 34; starters 720-1980Ft; mains 1780-4980Ft, set menus 5900-6300Ft; open noon-midnight Mon-Sat) is a favourite traditional but elegant Hungarian restaurant in Óbuda; the antique-strewn dining room and attentive service manage to create a fin-de-siècle atmosphere. Try the excellent goose liver dishes and more pedestrian things like csirke paprikás (chicken paprika).

Náncsi Néni (Auntie Nancy; Map 1; ☎ 397 2742; II Ördögárok út 80; mains 1360-1950Ft; open noon-11pm daily), more expensive than Szép Ilona, is a perennial favourite with Hungarians and expats alike. In autumn and winter go for the game; in summer, it's the seafood and the garden seating that attract.

Szép Ilona (Map 1; ☎ 275 1392; II Budakeszi út 1-3; 2-course meal about 2000Ft; open 11am-10pm daily), in the Buda Hills and opposite Remíz (see International later in this section), is the place to come for heavy, indigenous Hungarian and other dishes at very modest prices.

Új Sípos Halászkert (New Piper Fish Garden; Map 2; ☎ 388 8745; III Fő tér 6; starters 1200-1900Ft, mains 2400-2800Ft; open noon-midnight daily) wouldn't be a destination in itself, but if you're in Óbuda and want to sit out on its most beautiful square, this is the choice. Try the halászlé (fish soup; 790Ft to 990Ft).

Vadrózsa (Map 3; ☎ 326 5817; II Pentelei Molnár utca 15; mains from 3000Ft; open noon-4pm & 7pm-midnight daily), in a beautiful neo-Renaissance villa on Rózsa-domb, remains one the swishest (and expensive) restaurants in Buda. It's filled with roses, antiques and soft piano music, and there's no menu – you choose off the cart of raw ingredients and specify the style.

International

Hemingway (Map 7; ☎ 381 0522; XI Kosztolányi Dezső tér 2; starters 650-1550Ft, mains 1400-3800Ft; open noon-midnight daily), in a fabulous location in a small park overlooking Feneketlen-tó (Bottomless Lake), has a varied and ever-changing menu and a wonderful terrace.

Rivalda (Map 4; ☎ 489 0236; I Színház utca 5-9; starters 1050-1800Ft, mains 2900-5200Ft; open 11.30am-11.30pm daily) is an international café-restaurant in an old Carmelite convent next to the National Dance Theatre. With a thespian theme and garden courtyard, it is the place to choose if you are going to splash out in Castle District.

Remíz (Map 1; ☎ 275 1396; II Budakeszi út 5; 2-course meal about 3500Ft; open 9am-1am daily), next to an old tram depot (remíz) in the Buda Hills, remains excellent for its food (try the grilled dishes, especially the ribs), prices and verdant garden terrace.

French & Belgian

Le Jardin de Paris (Map 4; ☎ 201 0047; II Fő utca 20; starters 750-1950Ft, mains 1760-3500Ft; noon-midnight daily) is a regular haunt of staff from the French Institute across the road, who should know their *cuisine française*. The back garden ablaze in fairy lights is a delight in summer.

Pater Marcus Belgian Abbey *(Map 4; ☎ 212 1612; I Apor Péter utca 1; starters 890-1450Ft; mains 1090-2750Ft; open noon-midnight daily)*, 50m from Chain Bridge, is short on monks but heavy on mussels, frites and lots of flavoured beers.

Italian
Marcello *(Map 7; ☎ 466 6231; XI Bartók Béla út 40; salad bar 480-780Ft, pizza & pasta 720-850Ft; open noon-10pm Mon-Sat)*, non-smoking and popular with students from the nearby university, offers reliable Italian fare at affordable prices.

Marxim *(Map 3; ☎ 316 0231; II Kis Rókus utca 23; pizza 490-1130Ft, pasta 420-740Ft; open noon-1am Mon-Thur, noon-2am Fri & Sat, 6pm-1am Sun)*, a short walk from the Mammut shopping malls on Széna tér, is a hangout for teens who have added a layer of their own graffiti to the communist memorabilia. Okay, we all know Stalin *szuksz*, but it's still a curiosity for those who appreciate the Gulag, Lenin and Red October pizzas and the campy Stalinist decor.

Villa Doria *(Map 4; ☎ 225 3233; I Döbrentei utca 9; starters 650-3000Ft, pasta 1200-1800Ft, mains 2800-4100Ft; open noon-11pm Tues-Sun)*, a flash new restaurant in a mid-18th-century townhouse below Castle Hill, has everything from simple pasta and pizza (1100Ft to 1800Ft) to complex seafood and veal dishes.

Asian
Fuji Japán *(Map 1; ☎ 325 7111; II Csatárka utca 54/b; from 3500Ft per person; open noon-11pm daily)*, above Rózsadomb (the poshest area of Budapest) on the corner of Zöldlomb utca and Zöldkert utca (bus 29 from III Kolosy tér in Óbuda), is a long way to schlep for sushi, sashimi and sukiyaki, but it's the most authentic in town.

Maharaja *(Map 2; ☎ 250 7544; III Bécsi út 89-91; starters 350-990Ft, mains 1190-1890Ft; open noon-11pm Tues-Sun)*, in Óbuda, was Budapest's very first Indian restaurant. It specialises in northern Indian dishes and does some mean samosas.

Mongolian Barbecue *(Map 3; ☎ 353 6363; XII Márvány utca 19/a; buffet before/after 5pm 1990/3690Ft; open noon-5pm & 6pm-midnight daily)* is another one of those all-you-can-eat pseudo-Asian places that includes as much beer and wine as you can sink too.

Seoul House *(Map 4; ☎ 201 9607; I Fő utca 8; mains 1700-2200Ft; open noon-3pm & 6pm-11pm Mon-Sat)* serves excellent Korean food from *bulkoki* and *galbi* grills to *bibimbab* rice and *kimchi*.

Late Night & Nonstop
Nagyi Palacsintázója *(Granny's Palacsinta Place; Map 3; ☎ 201 8605, 212 4866; I Hattyú utca 16; menus 568-888Ft; open 24h • Map 4; ☎ 212 4866; I Batthyány tér 5; menus 568-888Ft; open 24h)* serves Hungarian pancakes – both savoury (148Ft to 248Ft) and sweet (78Ft to 248Ft) – throughout the day.

Traditional Cafés
The majority of traditional cafés are in Pest, but Buda can lay claim to several good examples.

Ruszwurm *(Map 4; ☎ 375 5284; I Szentháromság utca 7; open 10am-7pm daily)* is the perfect place for coffee and cakes in the Castle District, though it can get pretty crowded at the weekend.

Angelika *(Map 4; ☎ 212 3784; I Batthyány tér 7; open 9am-midnight daily)* is another charming café, this time attached to a church, with a lovely terrace overlooking the Danube.

Caffè Déryné *(Map 4; ☎ 212 3864; I Krisztina tér 3; open 8am-10pm Mon-Fri, 8am-9pm Sat, 9am-9pm Sun)* is as untouristed a traditional café as you'll find in Buda. It's famed for both its cakes and ice cream.

Modern Cafés & Teahouses
Café Miró *(Map 4; ☎ 375 5458; I Úri utca 30; open 9am-midnight)*, a personal favourite in touristy Castle District, has Med-coloured walls and furniture, snacks and light meals and local artwork and photography on the walls.

The Wines of Hungary

Wine has been produced in Hungary for thousands of years, and it remains very important here both economically and socially. You'll find it available by the glass or bottle everywhere in Budapest – at *borozók* (wine bars, but very basic affairs, almost like 'wine pubs'), food stalls, restaurants, supermarkets and 24-hour grocery stores – at very reasonable prices. If you're seriously into wine, visit the speciality shops listed in the Shopping chapter.

Before WWII Hungarian wine was much in demand throughout Europe, but with the advent of socialism and mass-production, foreign wine enthusiasts were generally disappointed by the Hungarian product. Most of what wasn't consumed at home went to the Soviet Union where, frankly, they were happy to drink anything. This and state control offered little incentive to upgrade antiquated standards of wine-making and to apply modern methods to traditional grape varieties.

All of that is changing – and fast. Small to medium-sized upscale family-owned wineries such as Tiffán, Bock, Szeremley, Thummerer Szepsy and Demeter are now producing very fine wines indeed. Joint ventures with foreign vintners are helping to restructure the industry. All in all, wine production is arguably the most exciting business in Hungary right now

When choosing a Hungarian wine, look for the words *minőségi bor* (quality wine) or *különleges minőségű bor* (premium quality wine), Hungary's version of *appellation controlée*. Generally speaking, vintage *(évjárat)* is not as important here as it is in France and Germany, and the quality of a label can sometimes vary widely from bottle to bottle.

The first word of the name on a label indicates where the wine comes from while the second is the grape variety (eg, Villányi Kékfrankos) or the type or brand of wine (eg, Tokaji Aszú, Szekszárdi Bikavér). Other important words you'll see are *édes* (sweet), *fehér* (white), *félédes* (semi-sweet), *félszáraz* (semi-dry or medium), *pezsgő* (sparkling wine), *száraz* (dry) and *vörös* (red).

Hungary counts 22 distinct wine-growing areas, which range in size from tiny Somló in Western Transdanubia to the vast vineyards of the Kunság on the Southern Plain.

Of course it's all a matter of taste, but the most distinctive red wines come from Villány and Szekszárd in Southern Transdanubia and the best whites are produced around Lake Balaton and in Somló. However, the reds from Eger and sweet whites from Tokaj are much better known abroad.

Tokaj

The volcanic soil, sunny climate and protective mountain barrier of the Tokaj region in the Northern Uplands make it ideal for growing grapes and making wine. French King Louis XIV famously called Tokaj 'the wine of kings and the king of wines', while Voltaire wrote that 'this wine could only be given by the boundlessly good God'.

Tokaj dessert wines are rated according to the number – from three to six – of *puttony* (butts, or baskets for picking) of sweet Aszú grapes added to the base wines. These are grapes infected with 'noble rot', a mould called *botrytis cinera* that almost turns them into raisins on the vine.

Tokaj also produces less-sweet wines, including dry Szamorodni (an excellent aperitif) and sweet Szamorodni, which is not unlike an Italian *vin santo*. Of the four grape varieties gown here, Furmint and Hárslevelű (Linden Leaf) are the driest.

Eger

This lovely city flanked by two of the Northern Uplands' most beautiful ranges of hills is the home of the celebrated Egri Bikavér (Eger Bull's Blood). By law, Hungarian winemakers must spell out the blend on the label; the sole exception is Bikavér, though it is usually Kékfrankos (Blaufränkisch) mixed with other reds, sometimes including Kadarka.

Eger also produces Pinot Noir and some think Vilmos Thummerer's variety is on a par with the *premiers crus* of Burgundy. Thummerer's 1999 Vili Papa Cuvée (Granddad Bill's Cuvée) is a monumental

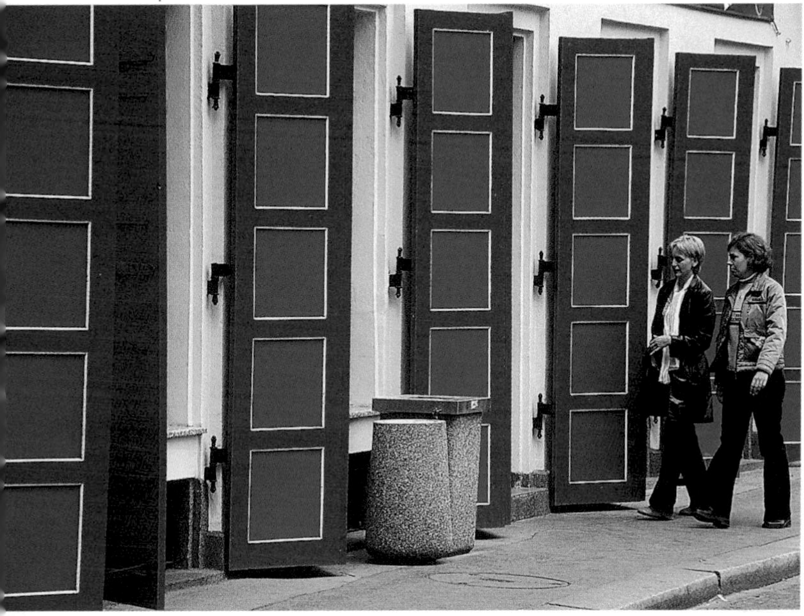
Centrál Kávéház

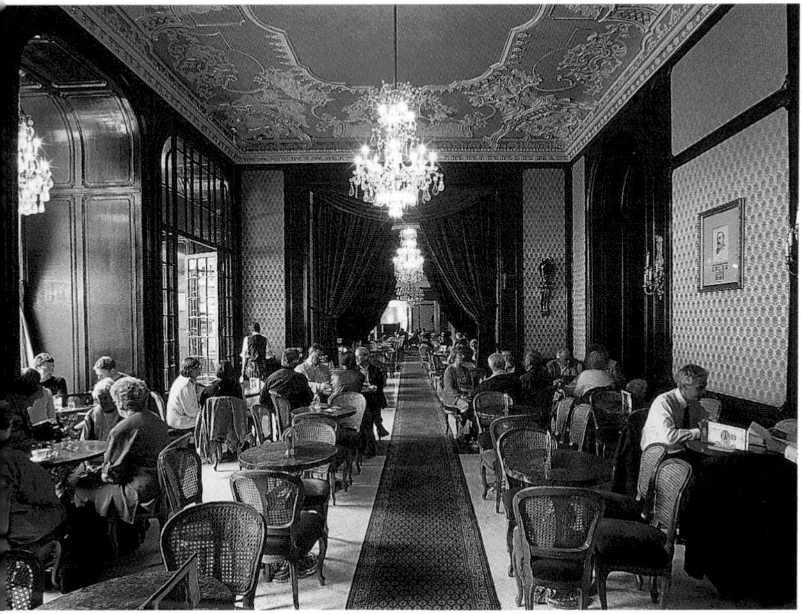
Café Gerbeaud

BOTH PHOTOGRAPHS BY MARTIN MOOS

Entrance to the New Theatre

Süss Fél Nap

Thália Theatre

Performance Hall, Liszt Academy of Music

Performance at the Capella Café

The Wines of Hungary

wine aged in new wood with fleshy fruit flavours. You'll also find several decent whites here, including Leányka (Little Girl), Olaszrizling (Italian Riesling) and Hárslevelű from Debrő.

Villány

Villány, in Hungary's southernmost and warmest region, is one of the country's principal producers of wine, noted especially for its red Kékoportó (Blauer Portugieser), Cabernet Franc, Cabernet Sauvignon and Merlot wines. They are almost always big-bodied Bordeaux-style wines and high in tannin. Many are *barrique* wines – those aged in new oak barrels that are then discarded or passed on to other wineries – and remain a favourite of Hungarian yuppies, who like the 'big', recognisable flavours.

Szekszárd

Mild winters and warm, dry summers combined with favourable loess soil help Szekszárd in Southern Transdanubia to produce some of the best red wines in Hungary. They are not like the big-bodied reds of Villány but softer, less complex, with a distinctive paprika flavour and easy to drink. In general they are much better value.

The premier grape here is Kadarka, a late-ripening and vulnerable variety that is produced in limited quantities. Kadarka originated in the Balkans and is a traditional ingredient in making Szekszárd Bikavér, a wine that is usually associated with Eger. In fact, many wine aficionados in Hungary prefer the Szekszárd variety of Bull's Blood.

Badacsony

The Badacsony region is named after the 400m-high basalt massif that rises like a bread loaf from the Tapolca Basin along the northwestern shore of Lake Balaton. Wine has been produced here for centuries, and the region's Olaszrizling is arguably the best dry white wine for everyday drinking to be had in Hungary.

Olaszrizling, a straw-blond Welschriesling high in acid, is drunk young – in fact, the younger, the better. The area's volcanic soil gives the unique Kéknyelű (Blue Stalk) wine its distinctive mineral taste; it is a blunt, complex and age-worthy tipple wine of very low yield.

Somló

The entire region of Somló is a single volcanic dome, and the soil (basalt talus and volcanic tuff) helps to produce wine that is mineral-tasting, almost flinty. The region can boast two great and indigenous varieties: Hárslevelű and Juhfark (Sheep's Tail); the latter takes its name from the shape of its grape cluster. Firm acids give 'spine' to this wine, and it is best when five years old.

Wine & Food

The pairing of food with wine is as great an obsession in Hungary as it is elsewhere. Everyone agrees that sweets like strudel *(rétes)* go very well indeed with a Tokaji Aszú but what is less appreciated is the wonderful synergy that this wine enjoys with savoury foods like *foie gras* and such cheeses as Roquefort, Stilton and Gorgonzola. A bone-dry Olaszrizling from Badacsony is a superb accompaniment to any fish dish, but especially to the *fogas* (pike-perch) indigenous to nearby Lake Balaton. Villány Sauvignon Blanc is an excellent accompaniment to goat's cheese.

It would be a shame to 'waste' a big wine on traditional but simple Hungarian dishes like *gulyás* or *pörkölt*; save it for a more complex or sophisticated meat dish. Instead, try Kékfrankos or Szekszárd Kadarka. Cream-based dishes stand up well to late-harvest Furmint, and pork dishes are nice with new Furmint or Kékfrankos. Try Hárslevelű with poultry.

Demmer's (Map 3; ☎ 345 4150; II Fény utca 1; open 10.30am-8pm daily • Map 5; ☎ 302 5674; VI Podmaniczky utca 14; open 11am-8pm Mon-Sat, noon-8pm Sun), a cosy little teahouse next to the Mammut I shopping mall, is the place to come in Buda if you're serious about your cuppa cha.

Café Gusto (Map 3; ☎ 316 3970; II Frankel Leó út 12; open 10am-10pm Mon-Sat) is a fun little café with outside seating along a leafy street lined with antique shops. Interesting clientele.

Fast Food & Cheap Meals

Fortuna Önkiszolgáló (Map 4; ☎ 375 2401; I Hess András tér 4; about 600Ft per person; open 11.30am-2.30pm Mon-Fri), a self-service place above the Fortuna restaurant, has cheap and quick weekday lunches in the Castle District.

Gasztró Hús-Hentesáru (Map 3; ☎ 212 4159; II Margit körút 2; open 7am-6pm Mon, 6am-7pm Tues-Fri, 6am-1pm Sat), opposite the first stop of tram Nos 4 and 6 on the west side of Margaret Bridge, is a traditional butcher shop serving cooked sausages and roast chicken.

Il Treno (Map 3; ☎ 356 4251, XII Alkotás utca 15; pizzas 850-1310Ft, set menu 690Ft; open 11am-midnight Sun-Thur, 11am-1am Fri & Sat), with pizzas and a cheap set menu, is a popular place near Déli station.

Íz-É Faloda (Map 3; ☎ 345 4130; II Lövőház utca 12; soups 180-450Ft, mains 320-590Ft; open 11am-6pm Mon-Fri, 11am-4pm Sat) is a clean, modern and very cheap self-service place in the Fény utca market next to the Mammut shopping mall with excellent főzelék dishes (180Ft to 260Ft).

Self-Catering

Budapest counts some 20 markets though the lion's share of them are in Pest.

Fény utcai piac (Fény utca market; Map 3; II Fény utca, open 6am-6pm Mon-Fri, 6am-2pm Sat), one of the largest in Buda, is just next to the Mammut shopping mall.

Kolosy téri sütőde (Kolosy tér Bakery; Map 2; ☎ 368 6571; III Szépvölgyi út 5; open 6am-8pm Mon-Fri, 6am-5pm Sat, 8am-4pm Sun) in Óbuda is the best takeaway bakery in the

city, according to many local people. The scent of baking bread is the best, for certain.

There are 24-hour **nonstop shops** selling everything from cheese and cold cuts to cigarettes and beer all over Buda, including ones at I Attila utca 57 (Map 4) and I Alkotás utca 27 (Map 3).

PLACES TO EAT – PEST
Hungarian

Bagolyvár (Map 3; ☎ 468 0217; XIV Állatkerti út 2; starters 450-740Ft, mains 1180-2380Ft, set menu 3050Ft; open noon-11pm) attracts the Budapest cognoscenti who leave its sister restaurant, Gundel, to the expense-account brigade and head next door to the 'Owl's Castle'. Its reworked classics make it a winner.

Borvendéglő 1894 (Map 3; ☎ 468 4044; XIV Állatkerti út 2; starters 990-1600Ft, mains 1600-2100Ft; open noon-11pm Tues-Sat, noon-6pm Sun), the younger – and prettier – child in the Gundel family, is a new cellar restaurant with an emphasis on wine. Both main meals and borkorcsolyák (wine snacks) are available.

Firkász (Scribbler; Map 3; ☎ 450 1118; Tátra utca 18; mains 950-2050Ft; open noon-midnight Sun-Thur, noon-2am Fri & Sat), popular with local hacks, is a new retro Hungarian restaurant with newspaper decor, good home cooking and a great wine list. Would that they were all like this.

Kalocsa (Map 5; ☎ 318 0091; VIII Baross utca 10; starters 690-1290Ft, mains 890-1350Ft; open noon-10pm Mon-Sat), just south of the National Museum and named for the centre of paprika production, offers rustic and slightly kitsch decor and moderately priced Magyar home cooking.

Károlyi (Map 6; ☎ 328 0240; V Károlyi Mihály utca 16; starters 920-1450Ft, mains 1450-2800Ft; open noon-midnight daily) beckons not so much for the food (though it is decent enough) but for its location in the newly renovated Károly Palace (Károlyi Palota) near ELTE university.

Kárpátia (Map 6; ☎ 317 3596; V Ferenciek tere 7-8; 2000-3000Ft per person; open restaurant noon-3pm & 6pm-11pm, pub 11am-11pm daily), a veritable palace of fin-de-siècle decor dating back 120 years, serves Hungarian and Transylvanian specialities in both its restaurant and cheaper pub. This is *the* place to hear authentic Gypsy music.

Móri Borozó *(Map 3; ☎ 349 8390; XIII Pozsonyi út 37; mains 500-750Ft; open 10am-8pm Mon-Thur, 10am-3pm Fri)* is a simple wine bar and restaurant a short walk north of Szent István körút that has arguably some of the best home-cooked Hungarian food in Budapest.

Művész Bohém *(Map 5; ☎ 339 8008; XIII Vígszínház utca 5; starters 450-1500Ft, mains 750-1700Ft; open 11am-11pm daily)*, with antique furniture, photos of Magyar stars of stage and screen bedecking the walls, and a pianist softly tickling the ivories in the background, is the perfect place for a romantic Hungarian meal. It's just behind the Comedy Theatre.

Múzeum *(Map 6; ☎ 338 4221, 267 0375; VIII Múzeum körút 12; starters 1200-3500Ft, mains 1700-4100Ft; open noon-midnight Mon-Sat)* is the place to come if you want to dine in style. It's a café-restaurant that is still going strong after more than a century at the same location near the National Museum.

Pesti Vendéglő *(Map 6; ☎ 266 3227; VI Paulay Ede utca 5; starters 320-740Ft, mains 890-1450Ft; open 11am-11pm daily)*, a popular, family-run place conveniently located near the Vista Visitor Centre, offers a lighter take on standard Hungarian food.

Pozsonyi Kisvendéglő *(Map 3; ☎ 329 2911; XIII Radnóti Miklós utca 38; starters 200-380Ft, mains 620-980Ft; open 9am-midnight Mon-Fri, 10am-midnight Sat & Sun)* is the ultimate local experience: gargantuan portions of standard Hungarian favourites, rock-bottom prices and waitresses in lace-up Hungo boots.

Premier *(Map 3; ☎ 342 1768; VI Andrássy út 101; starters 950-2600Ft, mains 1900-3300Ft; open noon-11pm Mon-Sat, noon-4pm Sun)*, in the hallowed halls of the Hungarian Journalists' Association and far enough from the House of Terror for our comfort, attracts a motley crew of media types with its Hungarian comfort food.

Rosenstein *(Map 3; ☎ 313 4196; VIII Mosonyi utca 3; starters 350-1400Ft, mains 980-3600Ft; open noon-11pm Mon-Sat)* is an odd fish: a classy place with super service in the dark (and rather mean) streets of district VIII just south of Keleti train station.

Stex Alfred *(Map 3; ☎ 318 5716; VIII József körút 55-57; starters 410-1290Ft, mains 710-1980Ft; open 8am-6am daily)* is a big, noisy place that's open almost 24 hours. The extensive menu includes soups, sandwiches, pasta, fish and meat dishes as well as vegetarian selections (250-590Ft), and it transforms into a lively bar late at night. Best of all there's breakfast (320-860Ft).

Vörös és Fehér *(Red & White; Map 5; ☎ 413 1545; VI Andrássy út 41; 2-course meal about 3000Ft; open 11am-midnight daily)* is all about wine – Hungarian to be precise – and here you can order from the top of the shelf by the 0.1L to sip and compare. The menu is brief but complete enough, with dishes very much in the shadow of the wine.

International

Baraka *(Map 6; ☎ 483 1355; V Magyar utca 12-14; starters 650-1150Ft; mains 1250-2350Ft; open noon-3pm & 6pm-11pm Mon-Fri, 6pm-11pm Sat)* has fusion food in modern upbeat surrounds.

Chapter One *(Map 5; ☎ 473 0123; V Nádor utca 29; starters 1200-1800Ft, mains 1650-3400Ft; open 9am-midnight Mon-Sat, 10am-4pm Sun)*, with art both on its walls and plates, is the place to come if you want both light and airy surrounds and nourishment. Breakfasts (350-700Ft) are inspired.

Café Kör *(Map 6; ☎ 311 0053; V Sas utca 17; salads 650-1320Ft, mains 1450-2980Ft; open 10am-10pm Mon-Sat)* near St Stephen's Basilica in Pest, is a great place for a light meal at any time, including breakfast (550Ft). Salads, desserts and daily specials are very good, though you should book.

Cosmo *(Map 6; ☎ 266 4747, 266 6818; 1st floor, V Kristóf tér 7-8; starters 990-2250Ft, mains 1990-3870Ft; open noon-3pm & 5pm-11pm Mon-Sat, 5pm-11pm Sun)*, a postmodern, minimalist restaurant in the Inner Town, is the place to hop to if you really want to be in the thick of things hip.

Marquis de Salade *(Map 5; ☎ 302 4086; VI Hajós utca 43; salads 750-1500Ft, mains*

PLACES TO EAT

1100-2800Ft; open 12am-midnight daily) is a serious hybrid, with dishes from as far apart as Russia and Japan, Greece and Azerbaijan. There's lots of quality vegetarian choices too in this attractively decorated place.

Resti Kocsma *(Map 6; ☎ 266 6210; V Deák Ferenc utca 2; dishes 620-1500Ft; open noon-5am Mon-Sat)*, on the south side of the Pesti Vigadó, is to Pest what Marxim (see Italian under Places to Eat – Buda) is to Buda. The difference is that here the menu is international (mostly Central and Eastern European) and in a different class altogether.

Soul Café *(Map 6; ☎ 217 6986; IX Ráday utca 11-13; mains 1200-2300Ft; open noon-1am daily)*, one of the better choices along a street heaving with restaurants and cafés, has inventive Continental food and decor.

Robinson *(Map 3; ☎ 422 0222; XIV Városligeti tó; starters 1200-2100Ft, mains 1650-2600Ft; open noon-4pm & 6pm-midnight daily)* in City Park is *the* place to secure a table on the lakeside terrace on a warm summer's evening. There are starters like sliced goose liver and home-made venison pâté; mains like *fogas* (Balaton pike-perch), grilled tuna and smoked duck breast cooked on lava stones.

French

La Fontaine *(Map 6; ☎ 317 3715; V Mérleg utca 10; mains 1050-2860Ft, menu 4990Ft; open noon-3pm & 6.45pm-11.15pm Mon-Fri, 6.45pm-11.15pm Sat)* is a Parisian-style 'café théâtre', with more of the former than the latter. The relatively simple brasserie food is good, especially the leg of lamb.

Képíró *(Map 6; ☎ 266 0430; V Képíró utca 3; soups 1150Ft, starters 2000Ft, mains 2400Ft; open noon-3pm & 6pm-midnight daily)*, the 'Picture Writer', is one of the more stylishly appointed eateries in town. The food is French classical, the service seamless and there is a good selection of vegetarian dishes.

Lou Lou *(Map 6; ☎ 312 4505; V Vigyázó Ferenc utca 4; mains 1850-3600Ft; open noon-3pm & 7pm-11pm Mon-Fri, 7pm-11pm Sat)* is one of the most popular places with expatriate *Français* in Pest. It's a lovely bistro with excellent daily specials.

Mokka *(Map 6; ☎ 328 0081; V Sas utca 4; 2-course meal about 7000Ft; open 9am-1am Mon-Fri, 6pm-1am Sat, 11am-1am Sun)*, serving *la cuisine évolutive* (eg, New Age French leaning toward the Maghreb), has a menu for which you'll need a map to read but the great space, décor and wine list make up for the confusion.

Zazie *(Map 6; ☎ 321 2405; VII Klauzál tér 2; starters 800-2600Ft, mains 1800-2500Ft, lunch menu 1700Ft; open noon-midnight daily)*, the new kid on the block in the Jewish quarter, serves earthy Provençal fare in a setting reminiscent of a rustic farmhouse.

Italian & Mediterranean

Articsóka *(Map 5; ☎ 302 7757; VI Zichy Jenő utca 17; starters 990-1800Ft, pizza & pasta 370-1150Ft, mains 1900-2600Ft; open 11am-midnight daily)* has great decor, an atrium and roof-top terrace and OK food that is more Hungo-Med than Italian (but heading in that general direction). The atmosphere wins the trophy here.

Fausto's *(Map 5; ☎ 269 6806; VIII Dohány utca 5; pasta 1800-2800Ft, mains 2600-5400Ft; open noon-3pm, 7pm-11pm Mon-Sat)* is still the most upmarket Italian restaurant in town with excellent (though pricey) pasta dishes, daily specials and desserts. There's lots of choices for vegetarians.

Happy Bank *(Map 5; ☎ 210 0373; V Bank utca 3; dishes 680-1020Ft; open 11am-9pm Mon-Fri)* is a great place for an inexpensive lunch or early supper of home-made pasta and gnocchi.

Krizia *(Map 5; ☎ 331 8711; VI Mozsár utca 12; mains 950-2600Ft; open noon-3pm & 6.30pm-11.30pm)* is a Mediterranean basement restaurant with rustic appeal and well prepared dishes. Pity about the service.

Okay Italia *(Map 5; ☎ 349 2991; XIII Szent István körút 20; pizzas & pasta 1090-1640Ft, mains 1390-2480Ft; open 11am-11.30pm daily)* is a perennially popular Italian-run place with a nearby **branch** *(Map 5; ☎ 332 6960; V Nyugati tér 6)*, serving just pasta and pizza at the same prices.

Papageno *(Map 6; ☎ 485 0161; V Semmelweis utca 19; mains 1290-2550Ft; open 11.30am-midnight Mon-Fri, 5.30pm-midnight*

Sat) has a relatively brief menu of Med classics and is most popular at lunch.

Pink Cadillac (Map 3; ☎ 216 1412; IX Ráday utca 22; pizzas 655-1055Ft; open 11am-12.30am Sun-Thur, 11am-1am Fri & Sat), more of an upbeat 1950s diner than a pizzeria, still reigns supreme on IX Ráday utca after all this time. If you don't like the surrounds, have it delivered to Paris, Texas (that's a pub next door – not some one-horse town in the Lone Star State; see Pubs & Bars in the Entertainment chapter).

Sole d'Italia (Map 6; ☎ 337 9638; V Molnár utca 15; pasta & pizza 370-1150Ft, mains 990-1800Ft; open noon-midnight daily) has super-friendly service, good, inexpensive pizzas and pastas and – wait for it – some of the cleanest toilets in town.

Trattoria Toscana (Map 6; ☎ 327 0045; V Belgrád rakpart 15; mains 1090-2800Ft; open noon-midnight daily), by the Danube, serves as authentic Italian (rather than Tuscan) food as you are going to find in Hungary.

Greek

Pireus Taverna (Map 6; ☎ 266 0292; V Fővám tér 2-3; starters 450-1290Ft, open noon-midnight), overlooking a leafy square and the Great Market Hall, serves reasonably priced and authentic Greek fare. There are regular live music performances and on Friday there's Greek dancing.

Taverna Dionysos (Map 6; ☎ 318 1222; V Belgrád rakpart 16; mains 1290-2490Ft; open noon-midnight daily), all faux Greek columns and a blue and white colour scheme, packs in diners on its three floors.

Spanish & Latin American

La Bodega (Map 5; ☎ 267 5048; VII Wesselényi utca 35; salads 700-1350Ft, mains 1200-2200Ft; open noon-midnight Mon-Fri, 6pm-midnight Sat & Sun) is a bright and airy place serving Latin American and Spanish specialities.

La Tasca (Map 5; ☎ 351 1289; VII Csengery utca 24; starters 530-1950Ft, mains 1290-2590Ft; open noon-11pm daily) is a bit off the beaten track but the paella (2440Ft) and flamenco music in this cellar restaurant are worth the trip.

American & Mexican

Chicago Rib Shack (Map 5; ☎ 302 3112; V Szent István körút 13; mains 990-1900Ft; open noon-1am daily) is a spacious eatery serving barbecued chicken, corn on the cob and ribs, ribs and more ribs (950/1590Ft for a half/whole cage). It is expat city and conveniently located next to the Trocadero (see Clubs in the Entertainment chapter).

Iguana (Map 5; ☎ 331 4352; Zoltán utca 16; starters 590-750Ft; mains 1080-1890Ft; open 11.30am-12.30am daily) serves decent enough Mexican food (not a difficult task in these parts) but it's hard to say whether the pull is the chicken and prawn fajitas, the enchiladas and burritos or the frenetic, boozy 'we-party-every-night' atmosphere.

Leroy's Country Pub (Map 3; ☎ 340 3316; XIII Visegrádi utca 50/a; mains 1580-3980Ft; open noon-midnight daily), a small and very popular place, is the best choice for steaks (2510Ft), spare ribs (1580Ft) and fajitas (3980Ft) in upmarket surrounds.

Jewish & Kosher

Carmel Pince (Map 6; ☎ 342 4585; VII Kazinczy utca 31; starters 600-2200Ft, mains 1600-2800Ft; open noon-11pm daily) is decidedly not kosher – signs outside will warn you of that fact in six living languages – but the Ashkenazic specialities like gefilte fish (700Ft), matzo-ball soup (750Ft) and cholent are almost like Aunt Pearl used to make.

Hanna (Map 6; ☎ 342 1072; VII Dob utca 35; lunch about 2500Ft per person; open 11.30am-3pm Sun-Fri), housed in an old school behind the Orthodox Synagogue, serves very, very basic kosher fare at lunch only. Expect to pay (in advance) 1000Ft more at the high holidays.

King's (Map 5; ☎ 352 7675; VII Nagy Diófa utca 25-27; 2000-3000Ft per person; open noon-10pm daily), in King's Hotel (see the Places to Stay chapter), is as soulless a kosher eatery as any though the food is not half bad. Pay in advance for Sabbath and holiday meals.

Kinor David (David's Harp; Map 5; ☎ 352 1341; VII Wesselényi utca 18; starters 800-1200Ft, mains 2500-3500Ft; open 11am-11pm Mon-Fri & Sun, 11am-3pm Sat), run by the Lubavitchers and Budapest's newest kosher restaurant, is no great shakes but at least it serves two meals a day and is open later. You have to order and pay in advance for Friday dinner and Saturday lunch.

Middle Eastern

Al-Amir *(Map 6; ☎ 352 1422, VII Király utca 17; mezze 300-600, mains 950-1800Ft; open noon-11pm daily)* is arguably the most authentic Middle Eastern (in this case, Syrian) place in town and light years from the gyros and falafel places listed under Fast Food & Cheap Meals later in the chapter. Mind you, they also have a window selling takeaway gyros (400Ft) and falafels (350Ft).

Shiraz *(Map 3; ☎ 218 0881; IX Mátyás utca 22; mains 1350-1950Ft; open noon-midnight daily)* is a 'Persian' restaurant with carpets and hookahs loaded with apple, peach and strawberry tobacco (990Ft) to lure in the punters. You can also go to their **takeaway window** *(Map 3; ☎ 217 4547; IX Ráday utca 21)* around the corner with gyros (460-550Ft).

Chinese

Kilenc Sárkány *(Nine Dragons; Map 3; ☎ 342 7120; XIV Dózsa György út 56; starters 200-590Ft, mains 735-1450Ft; open 11.30am-11.30pm daily)* just south of City Park, is a large, flashy and relatively authentic Chinese restaurant.

Víg *(Map 5; ☎ 351 8530; VI Liszt Ferenc tér 7; mains 790-2180Ft; open 11.30am-11.30pm daily)* won't win any culinary awards but it's central and just the ticket should you need a fix of rice or noodles after a concert at the Liszt Academy of Music.

Taiwan *(Map 7; ☎ 215 1236; IX Gyáli út 3/b; mains 725-1200Ft; open noon-midnight daily)*, in the same building as the Fortuna hotel (see the Places to Stay chapter) in south Ferencváros, may seem a long way to go for a bit of rice but it's the only place I know of in Budapest that has dim sum.

Xi Hu *(West Lake; Map 6; ☎ 337 5697; Nádor utca 5; mains 950-3300Ft; open noon-11pm daily)*, a decent Chinese eatery in the centre, is popular with staff of the nearby Central European University. There's a cheap weekday lunch for under 500Ft.

Japanese

Arigato *(Map 5; ☎ 353 3549; VI Teréz körút 23; mains 1180-2800Ft; open noon-11pm Mon-Sat)* has an inexpensive sushi lunch menu and plenty of other choices but eating alongside a car showroom – a Suzuki one at that – may not be everyone's idea of a Budapest experience.

Sushi An *(Map 6; ☎ 317 4239; V Harmincad utca 4; sushi 600-1800Ft, sets 2700-3900Ft; open noon-3.30pm & 5pm-10pm daily)*, next door to the British embassy, is the best place in Pest for sushi and sashimi.

Thai

Bangkok House *(Map 6; ☎ 266 0584; V Só utca 3; soups & Thai salads 550-2150Ft, mains 1450-3350Ft; open noon-11pm daily)* has kitsch Asianesque decor, acceptable Thai and Laotian dishes and Indonesian waiters. Didn't fool us.

Indian

Bombay Palace *(Map 5; ☎ 332 8363; VI Andrássy út 44; curries & tandoori dishes 1700-2850Ft; open noon-2.45pm & 6pm-11pm daily)* is a flashy place just opposite VI Liszt Ferenc tér and the best place for Indian food in Budapest.

Shalimar *(Map 5; ☎ 352 0297; VII Dob utca 50; starters 520-690Ft, mains 1330-2890Ft; open noon-4pm & 6pm-midnight daily)* serves tandoor, tikka and seek kebab dishes that taste like they've come via southern Hungary (there's paprika in there somewhere) rather than India but it's a cheaper and less flash alternative to the Bombay Palace.

Vegetarian

BioPont *(Map 5; ☎ 266 4601; VIII Krúdy utca 7; soups 220Ft, dishes 550-770Ft; open 10am-10pm Mon-Fri, noon-10pm Sat, noon-5pm Sun)*, in the Darshan Udvar complex (see Entertainment chapter), is a pleasant place for a meatless meal, with all dishes available in half-portions for half the price.

Falafel Faloda *(Map 5; ☎ 267 9567; VI Paulay Ede utca 53; large/small sandwiches 450/270Ft, salads 420-1050Ft; open 10am-8pm Mon-Fri, 10am-6pm Sat)* is an inexpensive place to nosh Israeli-style in which you pay a fixed price to stuff a piece of pita bread or fill a plastic container from a great assortment of salads.

Gandhi (Map 6; ☎ 269 1625; V Vigyázó Ferenc utca 4; dishes 980-1690Ft; open noon-10pm Mon-Sat), in a cellar near Chain Bridge, serves up a daily Sun and Moon plate set menu as well as wholesome salads, soups and desserts.

Vegetarium (Map 6; ☎ 484 0848; V Cukor utca 3; soups & starters 420-850Ft, mains 750-1300Ft, lunch menu 540Ft; open 11.30am-10pm Mon-Sat), a basement restaurant just off Egyetem tér, serves vegetarian food of the old style (rather unappetising) but there are lots of choices for vegans here.

Wabisabi (Map 5; ☎ 412 0427; XIII Visegrádi utca 2; mains 1080-1480Ft; open 9am-11pm Mon-Sat) has wonderful Asian-inspired vegan dishes in a clean and fresh environment.

Late Night & Nonstop

Soho Palacsintabár (Map 5; VI Nagymező utca 21; pancakes 178-210Ft; open 10am-2am Mon-Fri, noon-2am Sat, noon-11pm Sun) can provide you with a fix of Hungarian-style pancakes till the wee hours.

Grill 99 (Map 5; ☎ 352 1150; VIII Dohány utca 52; soups 160-420Ft, mains 460-780Ft; open 24h) is a popular place for late, late meals or early, early post-club breakfast (about 250Ft).

Traditional Cafés

Auguszt (Map 6; ☎ 337 6379; V Kossuth Lajos utca 14-16; open 10am-6pm Mon-Fri), tucked away in a courtyard off one of Pest's major thoroughfares, is a wonderful place for a tête-à-tête or a slice of something sweet (or both).

Centrál Kávéház (Map 6; ☎ 266 4572; V Károlyi Mihály utca 9; starters & snacks 1690-3490Ft, mains 1990-3590Ft; open 8am-1am Mon-Sat, 8am-midnight Sun) is a recently reopened grande dame jostling to reclaim her title as the place to sit and look intellectual. It serves meals as well as fine coffee and cakes.

Gerbeaud (Map 6; ☎ 429 9000; V Vörösmarty tér 7; open 9am-9pm daily) is the most famous of the famous cafés in Budapest – bar none. Founded in 1858, it has been a fashionable meeting place for the city's elite,

on the west side of Pest's busiest square, since 1870. A visit is mandatory. Set lunches of two/three courses are 2900/3500Ft.

Lukács (Map 5; ☎ 302 8747; VI Andrássy út 70; open 9am-8pm Mon-Fri, 10am-8pm Sat & Sun) is once again dressed up in the finest of divine decadence – all mirrors and gold and soft piano music (with a no-smoking section too) – after a major renovation.

Művész (Map 5; ☎ 352 1337; VI Andrássy út 29; open 9am-11pm daily), almost opposite the State Opera House, is a more interesting place to people-watch than most Pest cafés, though its cakes are not what they used to be, with the exception of the almás torta (apple cake).

Szalai (Map 5; ☎ 269 3210; V Balassi Bálint utca 7; open 9am-7pm Wed-Sun), a humble little cake shop in the northern Inner Town, probably has the best cherry strudel in the capital.

Modern Cafés

Leafy VI Liszt Ferenc tér is surrounded by hip cafés. If they're not playing music in situ, you can catch strains from musicians practising in the Liszt Academy of Music at the southern end of the square.

Café Vian (Map 5; ☎ 268 1154; VI Liszt Ferenc tér 9; open 9am-midnight daily) remains the anchor tenant on the sunny side of 'the tér' and the court of Pest's arty aristocracy.

Fortuca (Map 5; ☎ 413 1612; VI Liszt Ferenc tér 10; pizzas & pasta 990-1290Ft; open 11am-1am daily) is the new kid on the block and recommended. Be advised that it's always crowded, though, and service can be slow.

Incognito (Map 5; ☎ 342 1471; VI Liszt Ferenc tér 3; open 10am-midnight Mon-Fri, 12.30pm-midnight Sat & Sun) was the first café on the square, and it's still going strong.

Két Szerecsen (Two Moors; Map 5; ☎ 343 1984; VI Nagymező utca 14; mains 800-2000Ft; open 8am-1am Sun-Thur, 11am-1am Fri & Sat), not on the square but close enough, serves both main meals and decent breakfasts (from 600Ft).

The cafés along pedestrian IX Ráday utca offer less hip but better drip.

Coquan's (Map 3; ☎ 215 2444; IX Ráday utca 15; open 7.30am-7pm Mon-Fri, 9am-5pm

PLACES TO EAT

My Café, My Castle

Café life has a longer (and arguably more colourful) history in Budapest than in any other city in Europe. The Turks introduced coffee here in the early 16th century, and the coffee house was an essential part of the social scene in Budapest long before it had even made an appearance in Vienna and Paris. The heyday for cafés here, however, was in the final decades of the Austro-Hungarian Empire, when the city counted upwards of 600 of them.

Budapest cafés were a lot more than just places to drink coffee 'black like the devil, hot like hell and sweet like a kiss'. In them, momentous events were plotted or occurred, great alliances formed and rivalries spawned, *chefs d'œuvres* written or sketched. To the English aphorism about the sanctity of one's house, the great writer Dezső Kosztolányi had a reply in his essay *Budapest, City of Cafés*: 'Az én kávéházam, az én váram' (My café is my castle).

The Budapest café of the 19th century embodied the progressive liberal ideal that people of all races and classes could mingle under one roof, and acted as an incubator for Magyar culture. Combining the neighbourliness of a local pub, the bonhomie of a gentlemen's club and the intellectual activity of an open university, coffee houses were places to relax, gamble, work, network, do business and debate.

Or start a revolution... On the morning of 15 March 1848, the future novelist Mór Jókai stood on a table on the Pilvax Café in the Inner Town to proclaim the demands of the Hungarian nation. The so-called Youth of March then took over a printing shop two streets away to print copies of their *Twelve Points* (see The 1848–49 War of Independence under History in the Facts about Budapest chapter) and marched to the National Museum. The rest, as they say, is history.

Different cafés catered to different groups. Actors preferred the Pannónia and businessmen the Orczy while cartoonists frequented the Lánchíd and stockbrokers the Lloyd. But the two most important in terms of the city's cultural life were the Japán and the New York.

The Café Japán at VI Andrássy út 45 – now ironically the Writers' Bookshop – was a favourite haunt of artists and architects and attracted the likes of Kosztka Tivadar Csontváry, József Rippl-Rónai, Pál Merse Szinyei and Ödön Lechner. The New York Café (VII Erzsébet körút 9–11), which opened in 1894 and quickly became the city's most celebrated literary café, hosted virtually every Hungarian writer of note at one time or another – from Kosztolányi and Endre Ady to Gyula Krúdy and Ferenc Molnár. The last, playwright-in-residence at the Comedy Theatre, famously threw the key to the New York into the Danube the night the café opened so that it would never close. And that's just what it did, remaining open round the clock 365 days a year for decades.

But all good things must come to an end, and the depression of the 1930s, WWII and the dreary days of communism conspired against grand old cafés in favour of the cheap (but seldom cheerful) *eszpresszó*. By 1989 and the return of the Republic of Hungary only about a dozen remained and since then even the New York, where the influential literary magazine *2000* was edited right up into the 1990s, has been shut down to make room for another five-star hotel.

Nowadays you're more likely to find young Budapesters drinking a beer or a glass of wine at one of the new breed of cafés – all polished chrome, neon lighting and straight lines – that have mushroomed in VI Liszt Ferenc tér and IX Ráday utca sipping *kávé* in the Centrál or Gerbeaud cafés. It's true – the café is very much alive in Budapest. It has just reinvented itself, that's all.

Sat & Sun • Map 5; ☎ 266 9936; V Nádor utca 5; open 8am-7pm Mon-Fri, 9am-5pm Sat), with a long list of cakes, bagels, and the best brews in Budapest.

Castro Bisztró *(Map 7; ☎ 217 0269; IX Ráday utca 35; dishes 520-1100Ft; open 10am-midnight Mon-Thurs, 10am-1am Fri, 2pm-1am Sat, 2pm-midnight Sun)* is an eclectic place with a mixed clientele, Serbian dishes and chilli on the menu and screens for logging on to the Internet (99Ft for 10 minutes).

Budapest Blue Café *(Map 5; ☎ 266 0084; VIII Somogyi Béla utca 8; salads & sandwiches 350-1100Ft; open 8am-midnight Mon-Fri, 9am-midnight Sat & Sun)* is a bright and friendly oasis in the less-than-salubrious swamp that is the Blaha Lujza tér area.

Teahouses

1000 Tea *(Map 6; ☎ 337 8217; V Váci utca 65; open noon-9pm Mon-Sat, 3pm-8pm Sun)*, in a small courtyard off lower Váci utca, is the place to go if you want to sip a soothing blend made by tea-serious staff and lounge on pillows in a Japanese-style tearoom. You can also sit and sip on the tea chests in the courtyard.

CD Fű Teázó *(Map 6; ☎ 317 5094; V Szerb utca 15; open 1pm-10pm Mon, 1pm-11pm Tues-Fri, 3pm-11pm Sat, 5pm-10pm Sun)* is a popular underground (in every sense) teahouse in a big old cellar whose name means 'CD Grass Teahouse'. Count on both (and enter from V Fejér György utca).

Mozaik *(Map 6; ☎ 327 0078; VI Király utca 18; open 10am-10.30pm daily)* is an eclectic (note the mosaic of a satyr outside) rarity among Budapest teahouses: non–New Age music played and smoking permitted.

Teaház a Vörös Oroszlánhoz *(Teahouse at Sign of the Red Lion; Map 5; ☎ 269 0579; VI Jókai tér 8; open 11am-11pm Mon-Sat, 3pm-11pm Sun)* is a funky (and quite serious) teahouse just north of VI Liszt Ferenc tér with a **branch** *(Map 6; ☎ 215 2101; IX Ráday utca 9; open 11am-11pm Mon-Sat, 3pm-11pm Sun)*.

Fast Food & Cheap Meals

American fast-food places (such as McDonalds – the one at VI Teréz körút 19 near Oktogon (Map 6) is open nearly 24 hours a day) and the very cheap local Paprika chain abound in Budapest (Oktogon is full of them), but old-style self-service restaurants, the mainstay of both white- and blue-collar workers in the old regime are fast disappearing.

Pick Ház *(Map 5; ☎ 331 7783; V Kossuth Lajos tér 9; open 6am-7pm Mon-Fri)*, next to the M2 Kossuth Lajos tér metro station, is a salami showroom and has a self-service eatery upstairs. The **Central European**

University cafeteria *(Map 5; ☎ 327 3000; V Nádor utca 9; dishes 210-695Ft; open 11.30am-4pm Mon-Fri)* is good value and the surrounds are upbeat. **Fakanál** *(Wooden Spoon; Map 6; ☎ 217 7860; IX Fővám tér; soups 550-690Ft, mains 950-2180Ft; open 10am-5pm Mon-Fri, 10am-2pm Sat)*, on the upper level of the Great Market Hall (see Self-Catering later), is a self-service restaurant with budget, ready-made dishes.

More interesting for local colour and better value in the long run are the wonderful little restaurants called *étkezde* – canteens not unlike British 'cafs' – that serve simple dishes that change every day. A meal should easily cost under 1000Ft. Some of the best ones are given here.

Frici Papa Kifőzdéje *(Papa Frank's Canteen; Map 5; ☎ 351 0197; VI Király utca 55; soups 200-370Ft, mains 250-460Ft; open 11am-9pm Mon-Sat)* is larger than most and more modern. **Kádár** *(Map 5; ☎ 321 3622; VII Klauzál tér 9; soups 300Ft, mains 450-820Ft; open 11.30am-3.30pm Mon-Fri)* is in the former Jewish district. **Kisharang** *(Map 6; ☎ 269 3861; V Október 6 utca 17; soups 145-240Ft, mains 400-750Ft; open 11am-8pm Mon-Fri, 11.30am-4.30pm Sat & Sun)* is close to the Central European University. **Mini Étkezde** *(Map 5; ☎ 312 8648; VII Dob utca 45; soups 220-380Ft, mains 420-750Ft; open 11am-3.30pm daily)* is the littlest one.

If you're craving for a Western-style sandwich, there are two good options.

Durcin *(Map 6; ☎ 267 9624; VI Bajcsy-Zsilinszky út 7; sandwiches 90-120Ft; open 8am-6pm Mon-Fri, 9am-1pm Sat • Map 6; ☎ 332 9348; V Október 6 utca 15; open 8am-5pm Mon-Fri, 9am-1pm Sat)* is the place to go for bite-sized open-face and very cheap sandwiches.

Marie Kristensen Sandwich Bar *(Map 6; ☎ 218 1673; IX Ráday utca 7; sandwiches 220-550Ft; open 8am-9pm Mon-Fri, 11am-8pm Sat)* has a large selection and does salads (from 490Ft) too.

Pizza Along with Okay Italia (see Italian & Mediterranean under Places to Eat – Pest) there are several pizzerias on this side of the river.

Don Pepe *(Map 5; ☎ 332 2954; VI Nyugati tér 8; pizzas 380-980Ft; open noon-6am daily)* is just OK but open till the very wee hours.

Pompeii *(Map 5; ☎ 351 8738; VII Liszt Ferenc tér 3; pizzas 650-1100Ft; open noon-1am daily)* is convenient for a bit of blotter in the heart of 'the tér' café and publand.

San Marzano *(Map 5; ☎ 413 6589; VI Andrássy út 41; pizzas 890-1490Ft, pasta 990-1290Ft; lunch menu 910Ft; open 10am-midnight daily)* is the place if you like things, well, familiar. It's part of the UK-based Pizza Express chain and looks it, acts it.

Middle Eastern Great any time but especially for a late-night snack or post-club bit of blotter, is **Három Testvér** *(Three Brothers; Map 5; ☎ 342 2377; VII Erzsébet körút 17; salads 250-300Ft; gyros & kebabs 390-700Ft; open 9am-3am daily • Map 5; ☎ 06-30 201 1661, XIII Szent István körút 22 • Map 5; ☎ 363 6646; VI Teréz körút 23).*

Semiramis *(Map 5; ☎ 311 7627; V Alkotmány utca 20; dishes 1150-1400Ft; open noon-9pm Mon-Sat)* is the old Middle Eastern standby (Hungo-Syrian this time) and still has some of the most authentic fare around. Seating is on two levels.

Szeráj *(Map 5; ☎ 311 6690; XIII Szent István körút 13; mains 350-800Ft; open 9am-4am daily)* is a very inexpensive self-service place for Turkish kebabs, with some 10 on offer, open very late.

Chinese Fast-food places *(gyors kinai büfé)* serving uninspired but cheap rice and noodle dishes are everywhere in Budapest. Central ones include **Arany Folyó** *(Golden River; Map 5; ☎ 344 4218; VII Akácfa utca 9/a; dishes from 450Ft; open 10.30am-8pm Mon-Fri);* and **Nagy Fal** *(Great Wall; Map 6; ☎ 353 4021; V Nádor utca 20; dishes from 400Ft; open 9.30am-10pm Mon-Fri, 10.30am-10pm Sat & Sun).*

Self-Catering

Budapest counts some 20 large food markets, most of them in Pest. Markets are usually open from 6am or 6.30am to 6pm weekdays and till 2pm on Saturday. Monday is always very quiet (if the market is open at all).

Great Market Hall *(Nagycsarnok; Map 6; IX Fővám tér; open 6am-6pm Mon-Fri, 6am-2pm Sat)* is Budapest's biggest market, though it has become a bit of a tourist trap since it was renovated for the millecentenary in 1996. Still, plenty of locals head there for fruit and vegetables, deli items, fish and meat. There are good food stalls on the upper level.

Lehel Csarnok *(Map 3; XIII Lehel tér; open 6am-6pm Mon-Fri, 6am-2pm Sat, 6am-1pm Sun)* is one of Pest's more interesting traditional markets recently rehoused in a modern, boat-like, bad-taste structure that has to be seen to be believed. It was designed by László Rajk, son of the Communist minister of the interior executed for 'Titoism' in 1949. This is his revenge apparently.

Among other colourful **food markets** in Pest are the ones on **VIII Rákóczi tér 8** *(Map 3; open 6am-4pm Mon, 6am-6pm Tues-Fri, 6am-1pm Sat)* and **V Hold utca** *(Map 5; open 6am-6pm Mon-Fri, 6am-2pm Sat)* near V Szabadság tér.

Large supermarkets are everywhere in Pest, including: **Match** *(Map 5; VIII Rákóczi út; open 6am-9pm Mon-Fri, 7am-8pm Sat, 7am-4pm Sun)* facing Blaha Lujza tér; **Smatch** *(Map 5; VI Andrássy út 30; open 7am-8pm Mon-Fri, 7am-6pm Sat)* at the corner with VI Nagymező utca; and **Kaiser's** *(Map 5; VI Nyugati tér 1-2; open 7am-8pm Mon-Sat, 7am-3pm Sun)* opposite Nyugati train station. **Rothschild** *(Map 5; XIII Szent István körút 4; open 6am-8pm Mon-Fri, 7am-4pm Sat, 9am-5pm Sun • Map 5; VI Teréz körút 17-19; open 7am-8pm Mon-Fri, 7am-4pm Sat, 7am-5pm Sun)* is another chain, with a good supply of kosher products. Hypermarket chains are a fairly recent development; the UK supermarket chain, **Tesco** *(Map 3; XIV Pillangó utca),* for example, has an enormous outlet northeast of Ferenc Puskás Stadium.

Nagy Tamás *(Big Tom; Map 6; V Gerlóczy utca 3; open 10am-6pm Mon-Fri, 9am-1pm Sat),* Budapest's best cheese shop, sells over 200 varieties of Hungarian and imported cheeses; ask for the Hungarian goat's cheese made by an eccentric theatre critic.

Mézes Kuckó *(Honey Nook; Map 5; XIII Jászai Mari tér 4/b; open 10am-6pm Mon-Fri, 9am-1pm Sat)* is the place to go if you've got the urge for something sweet; their nut and honey cookies (100Ft for 100g) are to die for.

Butterfly *(Map 5; VI Teréz körút 20; 70Ft per scoop; open 10am-6pm Mon-Fri, 10am-3pm Sat)* –and *not* the pastry shop next door called Vajassütemények boltja – is the place in Pest for ice cream. **Spaghetti Ice** *(Map 6; VI Andrássy út 14; 100Ft per scoop; open*

9am-midnight daily), which sells a pasta-like gelato, has its own fans too.

Nonstop shops open very late or even 24 hours in Pest include the ones at the Nyugati train station (Map 5) next to track No 13; VI Nagymező utca 50 (Map 5); VIII Baross tér 3 (Map 3) near Keleti train station; and VIII Üllői út 2-4 (Map 6).

PLACES TO EAT

Entertainment

For a city of its size, Budapest has a huge choice of things to do and places to go after dark – from opera and folk dancing to jazz and meat-market clubs. It's almost never difficult getting tickets or getting in; the hard part is deciding what to do.

LISTINGS

One of the best sources of information for what's on in the city is the weekly freebie *PestiEst* (w www.est.hu, Hungarian only), published every Thursday but available from Wednesday evening at bars, cinemas and fast-food joints, and popular with party people. Also useful is the more thorough weekly – with everything from clubs and films to art exhibits and classical music – *Pesti Műsor* (Budapest Program; w www .pestimusor.hu, Hungarian only), also called *PM Program Magazin*, available at newsstands every Thursday for 99Ft.

Other freebies include the vastly inferior (though English-language) *Look*, also published on Thursday, and the bilingual publications *Programme in Ungarn/Hungary* and its scaled-down monthly version for the capital, *Budapest Panorama*. The free *Koncert Kalendárium*, published once a month (bimonthly in summer), has more serious offerings: concerts, opera, dance etc. The weekly *Budapest Sun* (see Newspapers & Magazines in the Facts for the Visitor chapter) and the bimonthly *Budapest in Your Pocket* (750Ft) also list events and concerts.

For a list of websites with entertainment listings, see Internet Resources in the Facts for the Visitor chapter.

BOOKING AGENCIES

Ticket Express (*information* ☎ 312 0000, *bookings* ☎ 06-30 303 0999; w www.tex.hu • Map 6; VI Andrássy út 18; metro M1 Opera; open 9.30am-6.30pm Mon-Fri, 9am-1pm Sat • Map 5; MCD Zeneáruház, VIII József körút 50; tram No 4 or 6; open 9.30am-6.30pm Mon-Fri, 9am-1pm Sat) is the largest ticket-office network in the city with half a dozen outlets.

Vigadó Ticket Office (*Vigadó Jegyiroda; Map 6;* ☎ *327 4322; V Vörösmarty tér 1; metro M1 Vörösmarty tér; open 9am-7pm Mon-Fri, 10am-5pm Sat*) is another office with tickets for all types of concerts, dance performances and theatre.

Central Ticket Office (*Központi Jegyiroda; Map 6;* ☎ *267 9737, 318 1920; VI Andrássy út 15; metro M1 Opera; open 10am-6pm Mon-Fri*) is the busiest theatrical ticket agency, with tickets to plays and other events at theatres around Budapest (including the new National Theatre). Go to the **National Philharmonic Ticket Office** (*Országos Filharmónia Jegyiroda; Map 6;* ☎ *318 0281; V Mérleg utca 10; metro M1/2/3 Deák Ferenc tér, bus No 15; open 10am-5.30pm Mon-Thur, 10am-5pm Fri*) for tickets to the philharmonic and other classical concerts.

Music Mix (*Map 6;* ☎ *266 7070, 317 7736;* w *www.tex.hu; V Kecskeméti utca 8; metro M3 Kálvin tér; open 10am-6pm Mon-Fri*) has tickets to special events such as rock-music spectaculars and big-ticket concerts by foreign superstars.

Pocok Media (*Map 6;* ☎ *266 0314;* e *pocokmedia@nextra.hu; open 9am-8pm Mon-Fri, 10am-6pm Sat*) in the **Vista Visitor Center** (*VI Paulay Ede utca; metro M1/2/3 Deák Ferenc tér*) is a small but comprehensive booking service, with tickets to everything from concerts and theatre to sporting events.

To buy theatre, opera and Formula-1 tickets from abroad contact **InterTicket** (☎ *266 0000, fax 311 9017;* w *www.interticket.com;* e *interticket@interticket.hu*), which sells tickets by credit card (plus 1350Ft surcharge) only by phone, fax or email. You can collect your tickets on site 30 minutes before the performance.

PUBS & BARS

Budapest (and particularly Pest) is loaded with pubs and bars and there are enough to satisfy all tastes. In summer, outdoor venues such as Zöld Pardon and pubs and bars with terraces (eg, those in VI Liszt Ferenc tér and along VI Andrássy út, IX Ráday utca and the Danube) empty out even the otherwise most popular indoor venues. There are even discos *en plein air* in season.

Buda

Oscar's American Bar *(Map 3; ☎ 212 8017; I Ostrom utca 14; metro M2 Moszkva tér; open 5pm-2am Sun-Thur, 5pm-4am Fri & Sat)*, with film memorabilia on the wood-panelled walls and leather director's chairs on the floor, serves powerful cocktails (some 150, in fact) that are perfect on a warm summer night.

Erzsébet híd Eszpresszó *(Map 4; ☎ 214 2785; I Döbrentei tér 1; tram No 19; open 10am-10.30pm daily)*, if you're in the mood for something simpler, is a wonderful old dive with a large terrace and view of Elizabeth Bridge. The terrace is jammed in warmer months. Most people call it Platán in honour of the big plane tree in front.

Kisrabló *(Map 7; ☎ 209 1588; XI Zenta utca 3; tram No 18, 19, 47 or 49; open 11am-2am Mon-Sat, noon-midnight Sun)* is an evergreen student pub close to the university and to many of the hostels mentioned in the Places to Stay chapter.

Rolling Rock Café *(Map 2; ☎ 368 2298; III Bécsi út 53-55; HÉV Szépvölgyi út; 9am-1am Mon-Thur, 9am-2am Fri, 9am-4am Sat, noon-midnight Sun)* is a pub where the trendies of Óbuda (not necessarily a contradiction in terms) gather for some of that peculiar American brew in the little green bottles. There's a 'nostalgia disco' on Saturdays from 11pm with music from the 1970s, '80s and – egad! – '90s.

Poco Loco *(Map 3; ☎ 326 1357; II Harcsa utca 1; tram No 17; open noon-2am daily)*, at the corner of Harcsa utca and Frankel Leó út, is a seamier place (and more interesting for that), with live music some nights.

Pest

Inevitably the capital has a number of 'Irish' pubs on offer; if you're into these McDonald's of drinking venues head for **Becketts** *(Map 5; ☎ 311 1035; V Bajcsy-Zsilinszky út 72; metro M3 Nyugati pályaudvar; open 10am-1am Sun-Thur, 10am-3am Fri & Sat)*, the best

of the lot, with decent breakfasts (550Ft to 1250Ft), or the **Irish Cat** *(Map 6; ☎ 266 4085; V Múzeum körút 41; metro M3 Kálvin tér; open 11am-2am Mon-Thur, 11am-4am Fri & Sat, 5pm-2am Sun)*, which has Guinness and Kilkenny on tap, over-tattooed and pierced waiters and dancing in the narrow spaces between tables at the weekend. Yet another Irish pub is **Columbus** *(Map 6; ☎ 266 9013; tram No 2 or 2/a; open noon-midnight or 1am daily)* – and we thought Chris was Italian – which sits on a boat moored in the Danube opposite the Inter-Continental hotel.

Those who prefer their pubs in the style more common east of the Irish Sea should head for **Morrison's Music Pub** *(Map 6; ☎ 269 4060; VI Révay utca 25; metro M1 Opera; open 9pm-4am Mon-Sat)*, with its self-conscious red telephone booth and a spacious dance floor.

Cactus Juice *(Map 5; ☎ 302 2116; VI Jókai tér 5; metro M1 Oktogon; open 11am-2am Mon-Thur, 11am-4am Fri & Sat, 4pm-2am Sun)* is supposed to be 'American rustic' but it's really Wild West out of Central Casting. The Juice is a good place to sip and sup with no distractions except at weekends, when there's dancing.

For cocktails and friendly service, **Bar Martinez** *(Map 6; ☎ 266 7226; V Dohány utca 1; metro M2 Astoria; open 5pm-midnight daily)* is the Pest equivalent of Oscar's in Buda.

Mojito *(Map 6; ☎ 215 4569; IX Ráday utca 5; metro M3 Kálvin tér; open 11am-2am daily)*, with its entrance on Török Pál utca, is at the start of the 'Ráday Soho' nightlife strip and specialises in the eponymous Cuban cocktail (mint, lime and rum) as well as Brazilian *caipirinhas*, cocktails made from Brazilian *cachaça*, a sugar cane–based alcohol, lime juice, sugar cane syrup and shaved ice.

Portside *(Map 5; ☎ 351 8405; VII Dohány utca 7; metro M2 Astoria; open noon-1am Mon-Thur, noon-4am Fri, 4pm-4am Sat, 4pm-1am Sun)*, quite the opposite of Cactus Juice, absolutely packs in a yuppie mingle-and-meat crowd nightly. There's a DJ and dancing from 10pm Thursday to Saturday. It has an open-air sister bar called **Partside** *(Map 7; ☎ 463 0423; XI Vízpart utca 3; HÉV Lágymányosi híd, bus No 103; open noon-4am*

ENTERTAINMENT

daily) on the banks of the Danube in Buda south of Lágymányosi Bridge.

Garage Café *(Map 6; ☎ 302 6473; V Arany János utca 9; tram No 2 or 2/a, bus No 15; open 11am-2am Mon-Fri, 5pm-2am Sat)* is a popular lunch place by day and a watering hole by night with a good wine selection.

Paris, Texas *(Map 3; ☎ 218 0570; IX Ráday utca 22; metro M3 Kálvin tér; open 10am-2am Mon-Fri, 4pm-2am Sat & Sun)* has a coffee-house feel to it with old sepia-tinted photos on the walls and pool tables downstairs. Nurse a cocktail here and order a pizza from **Pink Cadillac** (see Pest in the Places to Eat chapter) next door.

Darshan Udvar *(Map 5; ☎ 266 5541; VIII Krúdy utca 7; tram No 4 or 6; open 10.30am-1am Mon-Wed, 10.30am-2am Thur & Fri, noon-2am Sat, 6pm-midnight Sun)* is a cavernous complex of two bars, a restaurant and a courtyard terrace vegetarian café (see Vegetarian under Pest in the Places to Eat chapter) with decor that combines Euro-techno with Eastern flair. **Darshan Café** *(Map 5; ☎ 266 7797; VIII Krúdy utca 8; tram No 4 or 6; open 8am-midnight Mon-Fri, noon-midnight Sat, 4pm-midnight Sun; 4pm-midnight daily July & Aug)*, much smaller than Darshan Udvar, is just opposite. **Darshan Cafeeling** *(Map 6; ☎ 266 0391; V Veres Pálné utca 7; metro M3 Ferenciek tere; open 11am-1am daily)*, with similar over-the-top decor, hippy-trippy clientele and (ca)feeling, makes up the Darshan trinity.

Champs Sport Bar *(Map 6; ☎ 413 1655; VII Dohány utca 20; metro M2 Astoria; open noon-2am daily)*, owned by five Olympic medallists (swimmer, runners, pentathlon), is the place for sportspeople and the vicarious. Two huge screens and 35 TVs fill the walls and tables so you can choose what you want to watch and when. Champs packs them in during big matches and events, and there's a wide choice of low-fat 'fitness meals' along with the less healthy favourites of armchair athletes.

A less flashy place (and the name says it all) is the distressed-looking **Szimpla** *(Map 5; ☎ 342 1034; VII Kertész utca 46; tram No 4 or 6; open noon-2am Mon-Fri, 4pm-2am Sat & Sun)*, a hop, skip and a jump south of Liszt Ferenc tér. Its newer (and more stylish) sister **Extra Caffè** *(Map 6; ☎ 342 1034; V Királyi Pál utca 6; metro M3 Kálvin tér; open 9am-5am daily)* has a dance floor downstairs, large armchairs upstairs and good (not popular) music. A similar place is **Pótkulcs** *(Spare Key; Map 5; ☎ 269 1050; VI Csengery utca 65/b; metro M3 Nyugati pályaudvar; open 1pm-1am)*.

Szent Jupát Söröző *(Map 6; ☎ 342 6074; VII Kazinczy utca 55; metro M1 Opera; open 6pm-2am Mon-Sat)*, with no sign above the door, is universally known as 'Wichmann' after its owner/waiter and nine times canoeing world champion Tamás Wichmann (check out his photo and memorabilia on the wall). Wichmann is quite a louche place, with a real Hungarian *kocsma* (pub – but sleazier) feel to it that attracts students and actors.

Cha Cha Cha *(Map 6; ☎ 215 0545; metro M3 Kálvin tér; open 8am-3am Mon-Thur, 10am-4am Fri & Sat)*, in the underpass/subway at the Kálvin tér metro near the Üllői út and Ráday utca exit, is a campy/groovy café-bar with zebra- and leopard-print armchairs, a *very* – and we're talking *Star Wars* here – mixed crowd and bopping from the start of the 'artists' weekend' (Thursday).

CLUBS

Like everywhere else, clubs in Budapest don't really get off the ground until well after Cinderella's coach has turned into a pumpkin. Most have a cover of between 500Ft and 1000Ft, though women sometimes get in for free.

If you're looking for a big, international-style disco in the centre of Pest, head for **Bank Music Club** *(Map 5; ☎ 414 5025, 302 1142; VI Teréz körút 55; open 9pm-5am Thur-Sat)*, in the south wing of Nyugati train station next to McDonald's, which has funk, Latino, hip-hop and concerts on the 1st floor and international hit music on the 2nd. There's a huge dance floor, trippy lights, a glass staircase and lots of young bloods reeking of cologne and on the prowl.

Another, even Euro-cheesier place is **E-Klub** *(Map 7; ☎ 263 1614; X Népliget; metro M3 Népliget; open 9pm-5am Tues summer only, 9pm-5am Fri, 10pm-5am Sat)* in Népliget, with multiple rooms and music styles and a sociological cross section of Budapest party goers. A similar place to try is the **M4 Music Club** *(Map 5; ☎ 322 0006; VII Dohány utca 22; metro M2 Astoria; open 6pm-5am daily)*, a particularly smoky place named after the illusory 4th metro line, with both DJs (soul, funk, junkhouse) and live music.

Farther afield **Dokk Backstage** *(Map 2; ☎ 457 1023; III Óbudai Hajógyári-sziget 122; HÉV Filatorigát; open noon-midnight Mon-Thur, noon-6am Fri, 6pm-4am Sat)*, one of the perennials in Budapest's ever-changing club scene, is a restaurant during the week and a cavernous club with mostly funky music at the weekend. It's in a converted warehouse on an island in the Danube. Dokk attracts the city's well-heeled crowds and is at its hottest, grinding-est best on a Friday night (concerts from 9pm or 10pm). Take a taxi, or it's an easy walk from the HÉV stop.

Közgáz Pince Klub *(Map 3; ☎ 215 4359, 218 6855; IX Fővám tér 8; tram No 47 or 49; open 9pm-3am Mon, 9pm-5am Tues-Sat)*, with few frills and cheap covers, is the pick-up venue of choice for many a student. There's plenty of room to dance. Another student-oriented place is the techno-free **Ráday Klub** *(Map 7; ☎ 218 7466; IX Ráday utca 43-45; bus No 15, tram No 4 or 6; open 9pm-4.30am Fri & Sat)*.

Trocadero *(Map 5; ☎ 311 4691; VI Szent István körút 15; tram No 4 or 6; open 9pm-2am Tues-Thur, 9pm-5am Fri & Sat)* attracts one of the most diverse crowds in Budapest with its great canned Latin, salsa, reggae and soul nights. The best parties are at weekends. **Picasso Point** *(Map 5; ☎ 312 1727; VI Hajós utca 31; metro M3 Arany János utca; open 11am-midnight Mon & Tues, 11am-2am Wed, 11am-4am Thur & Fri, 4pm-4am Sat, 4pm-midnight Sun)*, a stalwart of the Budapest entertainment scene, is a good place to bop.

Kaméleon *(Map 3; ☎ 345 8547; Mammut II, II Lövőház utca 2-6; metro Moszkva tér; open 5pm-midnight Sun-Thur, 5pm-3am Fri & Sat)*, on the top floor of a massive Buda shopping mall, has a wonderful roof terrace and Latin dance classes during the week.

Cellar club **Süss Fél Nap** *(Map 5; ☎ 302 3799, 374 3329; V Honvéd utca 40; tram No 4 or 6; open 5pm-dawn daily)* attracts a student crowd and hosts student bands; it's a lot of fun and less expensive than many of the other clubs.

Sark Café *(Map 5; ☎ 06-30 282 9625; VII Klauzál tér 14; tram No 4 or 6; open 9am-3am Mon-Thur, 9am-5am Fri-Sun)*, a brand-new place on three floors with a big dance floor downstairs, attracts a hip rather than cool crowd.

Rigoletto *(Map 5; ☎ 237 0666; XIII Visegrádi utca 9; metro M3 Nyugati pályaudvar, tram No 4 or 6; open 4pm-2am Tues, 4pm-3am Wed, 4pm-4am Thur-Sat)*, north of Szent István körútis, is a Gothic-inspired club and watering hole with stone arches and lots of wrought iron. There's live music Tuesday to Thursday, and DJs spinning funk, soul and disco on Friday and Saturday.

One place attracting arty (ie, less booze, more smoke) types and their hangers-on is **Trafó Bár Tangó** *(Map 7; ☎ 456 2049; IX Liliom utca 41; metro M3 Ferenc körút; open 6pm-4am daily)* in the basement of the Trafó House of Contemporary Arts (see Dance later in this chapter). With DJs and Latin music (Fridays) after 10pm, this is a great place to meet people.

When everything else slows down, **Piaf** *(Map 5; ☎ 312 3823; VI Nagymező utca 25; metro M3 Arany János utca, trolleybus No 70 or 78; open 10pm-6am daily)* is the place to go for dancing and action well into the new day. Skip the piano bar and head downstairs for the smoky dance cavern; there are some great characters here.

A wonderful spot to chill out along the banks of the Danube is **Zöld Pardon** *(Map 7; w www.zp.hu; tram No 4 or 6)*, an outdoor dancing and drinking venue on the Buda side of Petőfi Bridge. The 'world's longest summer festival' runs from 9am to 6am daily from late April to mid-September. Concerts begin at 8pm and then DJs take over till dawn.

On the northern side of Petőfi Bridge but still in Buda, **Café del Rio** *(Map 7; ☎ 06-70 240 4412; tram No 4 or 6)* is another open-air venue but even more relaxed than Zöld Pardon. The outdoor **Rudas Romkert** *(Map 6; ☎ 06-20 344 3155; I Döbrentei tér 9; tram No 18 or 19)*, alongside the Rudas thermal

ENTERTAINMENT

bath on the Danube in Buda, gets positively packed on summer evenings.

West Balkán *(Map 7; ☎ 371 1807; XI Kopaszi gát; HÉV Lágymányosi híd; open 5pm-dawn late Apr–mid-Sept)* is another great open-air bar next to a backwater of the Danube on the Buda side. There are concerts and dancing to some of the best alternative DJs in town, often from the now defunct (and much-missed) Tilos Rádió (Forbidden Radio). Free trishaws driven by students in summer will transport you from Petőfi Bridge across a wasteland of concrete buildings and cement hills to the venue.

GAY & LESBIAN VENUES

What a difference a decade makes! With only a couple of sleazy speakeasies just over 10 years ago, Budapest can now claim to be Central Europe's gayest city. For useful websites and other information, see Gay & Lesbian Travellers in the Facts for the Visitor chapter.

Budapest's flagship gay club is **Angel** *(Map 3; ☎ 351 6490; VII Szövetség utca 33; metro M2 Blaha Lujza tér, bus No 7 or 7/a; open 10pm-5am Fri-Sun)*, which is sometimes called by its Hungarian name, Angyal. It welcomes girls on Friday and Sunday, and there are drag shows on those days at 11.45pm.

Capella Café *(Map 6; ☎ 318 6231; V Belgrád rakpart 23; tram No 2 or 2/a; open 10pm-5am Wed-Sat)* and its new extension **Limo Café** *(Map 6; ☎ 266 5455; V Belgrád rakpart 9; open noon-5am Sun-Thur, noon-6am Fri & Sat)*, a few doors down, are twin clubs frequented by gays, lesbians and fellow travellers. Limo hosts some really bad – in the real sense of the word – nudge-nudge, wink-wink drag shows at 11pm and 1am nightly. They are repeated at midnight and 2am from Wednesday to Saturday at Capella.

Club Bohemian Desire *(Map 5; w www.clubbohemian.hu; VI Ó utca 51; metro M1 Oktogon; open 10pm-3am Wed-Sat)*, more gay-friendly than out-and-out queer, has a multilevel dance floor and shows at 1am at the weekend. **Gay.Pont** *(Map 3; ☎ 06-20 517 5727; Margit körút 50-52, enter from Erőd utca; tram No 4 or 6; open 7pm-4am Wed-Sat)* is the only gay bar in Buda. It has DJs,

often from Tilos Rádió, as well as alternative and underground music.

Chaos Music Pub *(Map 5; ☎ 344 4884; VII Dohány utca 38; bus No 7 or 7/a; open 9pm-4am Sun-Thur, 9pm-5am Fri & Sat)*, a cellar bar that is all stainless steel and silver bricks, has a small dance floor and DJ, but is more of a pub than a club. There's a gallery at street level just to let you know this pub has a serious side too.

Mystery Bar *(Map 5; ☎ 312 1436; V Nagysándor József utca 3; metro M3 Arany János utca; open noon-4am Mon-Fri, 6pm-4am Sat & Sun)*, a neighbourhood-style gay bar recently remodelled with draped muslin and Greek statuary, attracts so few clients these days that part of it is now an Internet café (see Email & Internet Access in the Facts for the Visitor chapter).

Darling Bar *(Map 6; ☎ 267 3315; V Szép utca 1; open 7pm-4am daily)* is a seriously skeezy venue known for trade (mostly Romanian).

Angel, Chaos and Darling all have darkrooms, and for those seriously OFB (out for business) head to **Action Bar** *(Map 6; ☎ 266 9148; V Magyar utca 42; open 9pm-4am daily)*, where the name says it all. Take the usual precautions and have a ball. Strippers and dancers make appearances every night from midnight till 3am.

Budapest's thermal baths (see the special section 'Taking the Waters' in the Things to See & Do chapter) are not gay venues as such, though the **Király Baths** attract a lot of gays (especially on Friday afternoons) as do the **Gellért** and **Rudas Baths** on Sunday mornings. At the **Széchenyi Baths** and the **Palatinus pool** the areas reserved for male nude sunbathing are visited mainly by gays.

Two other outdoor nudist areas popular with gays are a bit farther out. **Csillaghegy Pools** *(Csillaghegyi Strandfürdő; Map 2; ☎ 250 1533; II Pusztakúti út 3; HÉV Csillaghegy)* has a nudist section on the southern slope of the hill. North from there, **Omszki-tó** *(HÉV Budakalász)* is a lake in Budakalász just outside the city limits and a 20- to 30-minute walk from the HÉV station. Remember you'll need to buy a supplementary ticket for the HÉV if you're carrying a BKV travel pass.

The city's first exclusively gay sauna is **Magnum Sauna & Gym** (Map 3; ☎ 267 2532; VIII Csepreghy utca 2; metro M3 Ferenc körút; under-26 590-1190Ft, over-26 900-1590Ft; open 1pm-1am Sun-Thur, 1pm-4am Fri & Sat), a 400-sq-metre place with all the usual facilities and amenities.

If you prefer to meet friends *en plein air*, the Danube Embankment walkway between Elizabeth and Chain Bridges in Pest is notoriously cruisy after dark (visit at own risk) and full of hustlers from Romania and Ukraine along with the home-grown variety. The park on the Buda side of Margaret Bridge is the same.

The only real lesbian venue is **Café Eklektika** (Map 6; ☎ 266 3054; V Semmelweis utca 21; open noon-midnight Mon-Fri, 5pm-midnight Sat & Sun), even though it attracts a mixed crowd. There are occasional jazz concerts here. Morrison's Music Pub hosts a get-together for lesbians every second Sunday.

ROCK & POP

The 12,500-seat Budapest Sportcsarnok near Ferenc Puskás Stadium, the venue of choice for big-ticket foreign and local performers, has recently reopened after having been destroyed by fire in December 1999. A smaller but popular venue is **Kisstadion** (Map 3; ☎ 251 1222; XIV Szabó József utca 1; bus No 7 or 67) was where the likes of Jamiroquai and others warbled.

Petőfi Csarnok (Map 3; ☎ 251 7266, 363 3730; W www.petoficsarnok.hu; XIV Zichy Mihály út 14; metro M1 Széchenyi fürdő, trolleybus No 72 or 74), the city's main youth centre, is in City Park and *the* place for smaller rock concerts as the hall is small enough to get really close to the performers.

Almássy tér Recreation Centre (Almássy téri Szabadidő Központ; Map 3; ☎ 342 0387, 352 1572; W www.almassy.hu, Hungarian only; VII Almássy tér 6; trolleybus 74) is a venue for just about anything that's in and/or interesting.

Wigwam Rock Club (Map 7; ☎ 208 5569; XI Fehérvári út 202; tram No 41 or 47; open 8pm-5am daily), one of the best of its kind in Hungary, hosts some big-name Hungarian bands on Saturday (800Ft).

Jailhouse (Map 7; ☎ 06-30 989 4905, 218 1368; IX Tűzoltó utca 22; metro M3 Ferenc körút; open 6pm-midnight Sun-Wed, 10pm-5am Thur-Sat) is a tiny venue with punk decor, a friendly atmosphere and live music.

Laser Theatre (Lézer Színház; Map 7; ☎ 263 0871, 263 1811; X Népliget; metro M3 Népliget; adult/student 1690/1190Ft, 3D 600Ft extra; open 7.30pm Mon-Sat, closed June), at the Planetarium in Népliget, has a mixed bag of video (some 3D) concerts with laser and canned music featuring the likes of Madonna, Pink Floyd, Queen, Mike Oldfield and performances of Carmina Burana.

You simply can't miss a **Cinetrip Water-Movie** (Cinetrip Vízi-Mozi; Map 6; ☎ 266 0314; W www.cinetrip.net, Hungarian only; admission 3200-4000Ft) event at the Rudas Baths (see the special section 'Taking the Waters' in the Things to See & Do chapter) and other party venues if one is taking place during your visit. These events combine partying and dancing with music (a mix of ambient, hip-hop, nuskool and techno by local and international DJs), film and bathing, and are just short of being all-out orgies. They are held monthly or bimonthly (usually from 9pm to 3.30am Saturday); schedules are available at tourist offices and other venues around town. Book through **Pocok Media** (Map 6; ☎ 266 0314; e pocokmedia@nextra .hu; open 9am-8pm Mon-Fri, 10am-6pm Sat) at the Vista Visitor Centre or through **I&I Records** (☎ 339 2906; cnr XIII Kádár utca & Visegrádi utca; metro M3 Nyugati pályaudvar).

JAZZ & BLUES

Jazz Garden (Map 6; ☎ 266 7364; V Veres Pálné utca 44/a; tram No 47 or 49; open noon-1am daily) is a sophisticated venue with odd decor: a faux cellar 'garden' with street lamps and a night 'sky' bedecked with blinking stars. Book a table (starters 970Ft to 1650Ft, mains 1640Ft to 2390Ft); music starts at 8.30pm.

New Orleans Music Club (Map 5; ☎ 354 1130; W www.neworleans.hu; VI Lovag utca 5; trolleybus No 72 or 73, tram No 4 or 6; open 6pm-late), an upscale jazz supper club (starters 950Ft to 1500Ft, mains 1200Ft to

2650Ft), has live jazz and blues at 9pm Tuesday to Saturday and is *the* Budapest jazz club to attract international acts.

Hades (*Map 5; ☎ 352 1503; VI Vörösmarty utca 31; metro M1 Vörösmarty utca; open noon-midnight Mon-Fri, 5pm-midnight Sat*) calls itself (shudder) a 'jazztaurant', but most people go as much for the food as the low-key jazz.

Old Man's Music Pub (*Map 5; ☎ 322 7645; VII Akácfa utca 13; metro M2 Blaha Lujza tér; open 3pm-4am daily*) pulls in the best live blues and jazz acts in town; shows are from 9pm to 11pm. A dinner reservation (soups 400Ft to 800Ft, mains 1800Ft to 2950Ft, pizzas 1100Ft to 1900Ft) is usually required to score a table, though you can stand and watch from the bar. The dance floor really gets going after the live music ends.

Fat Mo's Music Club (*Map 6; ☎ 267 3199; V Nyáry Pál utca 11; metro M3 Ferenciek tere, bus No 15; open noon-2am Mon & Tues, noon-3am Wed, noon-4am Thur & Fri, 6pm-4am Sat, 6pm-2am Sun*), with a speakeasy Prohibition theme and enough beer and booze to get Bonnie and Clyde shot again, has live jazz and country from 9pm Sunday to Tuesday before the bar gets too packed for anything but schmoozin' and cruisin'. DJs take over from midnight Wednesday to Saturday.

FOLK & TRADITIONAL MUSIC

Authentic *táncház*, literally 'dance house' but really folk-music workshops, are held at various locations throughout the week but less frequently in summer. Times and venues change as frequently as theme nights do at London clubs. Make sure you consult *Pesti-Est* or *Pesti Műsor* (see Listings earlier in this chapter) before you set out or consult the website of the Dance House Guild (w www .tanchaz.hu) or w www.folkinfo.net for the latest updates.

Venues in Buda include: **Fonó Buda Music House** (*Fonó Budai Zeneház; Map 7; ☎ 206 5300; w www.fono.hu; XI Sztregova utca 3; tram No 41 or 47*), with programmes at 8pm Wednesday and 7pm on the 1st and 2nd Friday of the month (the popular folk group Muzsikás also plays here every odd

Tuesday); the **Folklór Centrum** in the **Municipal Cultural House** (*Fővárosi Művelődési Háza; Map 7; ☎ 203 3868; XI Fehérvári út 47; tram No 41 or 47*), with music every Friday at 7.30pm or 8pm; and the **Marczibányi tér Cultural Centre** (*Marczibányi téri Művelődési Központ; Map 3; ☎ 212 2820; w www.marczi .hu, Hungarian only; II Marczibányi tér 5/a; tram No 4, 6 or 49*), where Muzsikás jams at 8pm on each odd Thursday a month, the group Tatros plays at 8pm each Wednesday and Ghymes, a group specialising in Csángó music, can also be heard from time to time. This is also a good venue for world music.

In Pest there's the wonderful **Kalamajka Táncház** at the **Aranytíz Youth Centre** (*Aranytíz Ifjúsági Centrum; Map 6; ☎ 317 5928; V Molnár utca 9; tram No 2 or 2/a*), with programmes from 7pm on Monday and Wednesday and 8.30pm on Saturday (the last arguably being the best in town).

Throughout most of the year the Hungarian State Folk Ensemble's Gypsy Orchestra stages rather touristy performances at the **Budai Vigadó** (*Map 4; I Corvin tér 8; bus No 86, tram No 19*) at 8pm on Friday. Tickets cost 7200/6600Ft per adult/student. Contact **Hungaria Koncert** (*☎ 317 2754, 201 5928; w www.ticket.info.hu*) for information and bookings.

CLASSICAL MUSIC

The *Koncert Kalendárium* (see Listings earlier in this chapter) highlights all concerts in Budapest each month, and most nights you'll have several to choose from. Budapest's main concert halls are the stunning **Liszt Academy of Music** (*Liszt Zeneakadémia; Map 5; ☎ 342 0179; VI Liszt Ferenc tér 8; metro M1 Oktogon; tickets 600-5000Ft*) in Pest and the modern **Budapest Congress Centre** (*Budapesti Kongresszusi Központ; Map 3; ☎ 372 5700, 372 5429; XII Jagelló út 1-3; bus No 8 or 112*) in Buda. The **Pesti Vigadó** (*Map 6; ☎ 318 9903; V Vigadó tér 2; metro M1 Vörösmarty tér, tram No 2 or 2/a*) and the **Duna Palota** (*Map 6; ☎ 317 2790; V Zrínyi utca 5; bus No 15*) have light classical music and touristy musical revues in summer. A less flashy but very serious venue is the **Óbuda Society** (*Óbudai Társaskör; Map 2; ☎ 250*

Just Folk

It is important to distinguish between 'Gypsy music' and real Hungarian folk music. Gypsy music as it is known and heard in Hungarian restaurants from Budapest to Boston is urban schmaltz and based on recruiting tunes called *verbunkos* played during the Rákóczi independence war. At least two fiddles, a bass and a cymbalom (a curious stringed instrument played with sticks) are *de rigueur*. If you want to hear this saccharine *csárdás* music, almost any hotel restaurant in Budapest can oblige, or you can buy a tape or CD by Sándor Lakatos or his son Déki.

Hungarian folk musicians play violins, zithers, hurdy-gurdies, bagpipes and lutes on a five-tone diatonic scale. There are lots of different performers, but watch out especially for Muzsikás and the incomparable Marta Sebestyén. Anyone playing the haunting music of the Csángó (which refers to pockets of Hungarians living in eastern Transylvania and Moldavia) is a good bet.

To confuse matters even further, real Roma music does not use instruments but is sung a cappella (though it's sometimes backed with guitar and percussion); a very good tape of Hungarian Roma folk songs is *Magyarországi Cigány Népdalok*, produced by Hungaroton. The best modern Roma group is Kalyi Jag (Black Fire), which comes from northeastern Hungary and is led by Gusztav Várga.

The *táncház* (dance house) is an excellent place to hear Hungarian folk music and even learn to dance. It's all good fun and they're easy to find in Budapest, where the dance house revival began.

0288; **w** *www.obudaitarsaskor.hu; III Kis Korona utca 7; HÉV Timár utca, tram No 1).*

There are many museums and other places where chamber music is played, but those with the best atmosphere are the **Old Music Academy** (*Régi Zeneakadémia; Map 5; ☎ 322 9804; VI Vörösmarty utca 35; metro M1 Vörösmarty utca),* where the Franz Liszt Memorial Museum is housed; the **Béla Bartók Memorial House** (*Bartók Béla Emlékház; Map 1; ☎ 394 2100; II Csalán utca 29; bus No 29);* the **Ethnography Museum** (*Néprajzi Múzeum; Map 5; ☎ 473 2400; V Kossuth Lajos tér 12; metro M2 Kossuth tér);* and the **Museum of Music History** (*Zenetörténeti Múzeum; Map 4; ☎ 214 6770; I Táncsics Mihály utca 7; bus No 16 or Várbusz).*

Organ recitals are best heard in the city's churches, including **Matthias Church** (*Map 4; I Szentháromság tér 2; bus No 16 or Várbusz),* on various days but most frequently on Sunday evening, and **St Anne's Church** (*Map 3; I Batthyány tér 7; metro M2 Batthyány tér)* on some Tuesday and Sunday evenings; both churches are in Buda. In Pest, excellent venues include **St Stephen's Basilica** (*Map 6; V Szent István tér 1; metro M1 Bajcsy-Zsilinszky út)* and the **Deák Ferenc tér Calvinist Church** (*Map 6; V Deák Ferenc tér 4; metro M1/2/3 Deák Ferenc tér).*

OPERA

The beautiful **Hungarian State Opera House** (*Map 5; ☎ 332 7914, 331 2550; **w** www.opera.hu; VI Andrássy út 22; metro M1 Opera; tickets 300-6900Ft)* should be visited at least once – both to see a production and admire the incredibly rich decoration inside. Performances usually start at 7pm. The **ticket office** (*☎ 353 0170; open 11am-7pm Mon-Sat, 4pm-7pm Sun)* is in the main lobby. If there is a morning performance (usually at 11am) the ticket office opens at 10am.

Erkel Theatre (*Map 3; ☎ 333 0540; VIII Köztársaság tér 30; metro M2 Keleti pályaudvar, bus No 7 or 7/a; tickets 500-4500Ft; ticket office open 11am-7pm Tues-Fri, 11am-3pm Sat, 10am-1pm & 4pm-7pm Sun),* Budapest's modern (and ugly) second opera house, is southwest of Keleti train station. Tickets are sold just inside the main door.

Budapest Operetta Theatre (*Budapesti Operettszínház; Map 5; ☎ 269 3870; **w** www .operettszinhaz.hu; VI Nagymező utca 17; metro M1 Opera)* presents operettas – always a riot, especially campy ones like the *Queen of the Csárdás* by Imre Kálmán. The **ticket office** (*☎ 269 0118; VI Nagymező utca 19; open 10am-6pm Mon-Thur, 10am-5pm Fri)* is next door to the theatre.

DANCE

Budapest's two so-so ballet companies perform at the Opera House and the Erkel Theatre. If the Győr Ballet from Western Transdanubia is performing in town, however, jump at the chance of a ticket. It's Hungary's best classical dance troupe.

For modern-dance fans, the capital has several good options. The best stage on which to see it is the **Trafó House of Contemporary Arts** (Trafó Kortárs Művészetek Háza; Map 7; ☎ 456 2045, 215 1600; w www .trafo.hu; IX Liliom utca 41; metro M3 Ferenc körút), which presents the cream of the crop, including a good pull of international acts. Everyone got their start at the **MU Színház** (Map 7; ☎ 466 4627, 209 4014; w www.mu .hu, Hungarian only; XI Kőrösy József utca 17; tram No 4), where the cutting edge of modern dance can be enjoyed in Budapest.

Trafó and **Kamra** (Chamber; Map 6; ☎ 318 2487; V Ferenciek tere 4; metro M3 Ferenciek tere), the studio theatre of the József Katona Theatre, sometimes host Yvette Bozsik's contemporary dance ensemble. Watch for their performances.

Central Europe Dance Theatre (Közép-Európa Táncszínház; Map 3; ☎ 342 7163; w www .cedt.hu; VII Bethlen Gábor tér 3; trolleybus No 74 or 78) has some fine contemporary dance performances. The **National Dance Theatre** (Nemzeti Táncszínház; Map 4; ☎ 201 4407, 375 8649; w www.nemzetitancszinhaz.hu; I Színház utca 1-3) usually hosts the Honvéd Ensemble, one of the city's best folk troupes and now experimenting with modern choreography as well.

As for folk dancing, many people attend táncház evenings (see Folk & Traditional Music earlier in this chapter) to learn the folk dances that go with the music, and you can become part of the programme as well instead of merely watching others perform.

From May to mid-October and on Saturday and/or Sunday only the rest of the year, the 30 dancers of the Hungarian State Folk Ensemble (Állami Népi Együttes) perform at the **Budai Vigadó** (Map 4; I Corvin tér 8; bus no 86, tram No 19) in Buda on Tuesday, Thursday and Sunday. On Saturday the Rajkó Folk Ensemble (Rajkó Népi Együttes)

stages folk-dance performances at the **Budapest Puppet Theatre** (Bábszínház; Map 5; VI Andrássy út 69; metro M1 Vörösmarty utca) and the Duna Folk Ensemble (Duna Népi Együttes) dances at the **Duna Palota** just off Roosevelt tér in Pest on Monday and Wednesday. The 1½-hour programmes begin at 8pm, and tickets cost 5600/5100Ft per adult/student. Contact Hungaria Koncert (☎ 317 2754, 201 5928; w www.ticket.info.hu) for information and bookings.

CINEMAS

A couple of dozen movie houses (mozi) show English-language films with Hungarian subtitles. Consult the listings in the Budapest Sun newspaper, PestiEst or Pesti Műsor (see Listings earlier in this chapter). Tickets cost between 350Ft and 950Ft depending on the time and day of the week.

Be aware that many foreign films are dubbed into Hungarian, so try asking the ticket seller if the film retains the original soundtrack and has Hungarian subtitles (feliratos) or is dubbed (szinkronizált or magyarul beszélő). The latter is often abbreviated as 'mb' in listings.

The **Corvin Film Palace** (Corvin Filmpalota; Map 3; ☎ 459 5050; VIII Corvin köz 1; metro M3 Ferenc körút) saw a lot of action during the 1956 Uprising and led a revolution of a different sort four decades later – the introduction of state-of-the-art sound systems and comfortable seating. But it shows mostly commercial American blockbusters nowadays. Another newly tarted-up film palace is the Art-Deco/neo-Moorish **Uránia National Cinema** (Uránia Nemzeti Filmszínház; Map 5; ☎ 486 3400; VIII Rákóczi út 21; bus No 7 or 7/a).

The **Örökmozgó Film Museum Cinema** (Örökmozgó Filmmúzeum; Map 5; ☎ 342 2167; VII Erzsébet körút 39; tram No 4 or 6), part of the Hungarian Film Institute, shows an excellent assortment of foreign classic films in their original languages.

Művész (Map 5; ☎ 332 6726; VI Teréz körút 30; metro M1 Oktogon, tram No 4 or 6) shows artsy and cult films while **Puskin** (Map 6; ☎ 429 6080; V Kossuth Lajos utca 18; bus No 7 or 7/a) has a mix of art and popular releases.

Szindbád (Map 5; ☎ 349 2773; XIII Szent István körút 16; tram No 4 or 6) shows good Hungarian and foreign films with subtitles but sometimes on a video projector, which makes for a less pleasurable night out at the movies.

THEATRE

The **Merlin Theatre** (Map 6; ☎ 318 9338, 266 4632; W merlin.szinhaz.hu/merlin; V Gerlóczy utca 4; metro M1/2/3 Deák Ferenc tér, tram No 47 or 49; tickets 1000-1800Ft) in Pest stages numerous plays in English, often put on by the Merlin's Atlantis Company and the local Madhouse troupe. Tickets should always be booked in advance. The **Kolibri Pince** (Map 5; ☎ 311 0870, 351 3348; VI Andrássy út 77; metro M1 Vörösmarty utca), with its entrance round the corner at VI Rózsa utca 65, has a sporadic schedule of amateur and experimental theatre in English that true theatregoers would enjoy.

The **International Buda Stage** (IBS; Map 1; ☎ 391 2525; II Tárogató út 2-4; tram No 56, bus No 29), a more recent arrival but farther afield in Buda, is another theatre with performances in English.

The new **National Theatre** (Nemzeti Színház; Map 7; ☎ 476 6800; W www.nemzetiszin haz.hu; IX Bajor Gizi park 1; tram No 2 or 2/a; tickets 1500-3500Ft) is the place to go if you want to brave a play in Hungarian or just check out the bizarre and very controversial architecture (see Walking Tour 11: Blaha Lujza tér to Petőfi Bridge). The **József Katona Theatre** (Katona József Színház; Map 6; ☎ 318 3725; W www.szinhaz.hu/katona; V

A Complicated Time

An important note on the complicated way Hungarians tell time: 7.30 is 'half eight' (fél nyolc óra) and the 24-hour system is often used in giving times of movies, concerts etc. So a film at 7.30pm could appear on a listing as 'f8', 'f20', '-½ 8' or '-½ 20'. A quarter to the hour has a -¾ in front (thus '-¾ 8' means 7.45) while quarter past is -¼ of the next hour (eg, '-¼ 9' means 8.15).

Petőfi Sándor utca 6; metro M3 Ferenciek tere) and its studio theatre, **Kamra** (see Dance earlier) have among the best troupes in the country.

You won't have to understand Hungarian to enjoy what's going on at the **Budapest Puppet Theatre**; see Budapest for Children in the Facts for the Visitor chapter for details.

SPECTATOR SPORTS

Hungarians love attending sporting matches as well as watching them on TV. The most popular spectator sports are football and water polo, though horse racing and motor racing also have their fans.

Football

Hungary's descent from being on top of the heap of European football to a béka segge alatt ('under the arse of the frog' as the Hungarians describe something really far down) remains one of life's great mysteries. Hungary's defeat of the England team, both at Wembley (6-3) in 1953 and at home (7-1) the following year, is still talked about as if the winning goals were scored yesterday.

There are four premier league football teams in Budapest out of a total 12 nationwide, including: Kispest-Honvéd, which plays at **Bozsik Stadium** (Map 1; ☎ 282 9791; XIX Új temető út 1-3; bus No 36); MTK at **Hungária Stadium** (Map 3; ☎ 333 6758; VIII Hungária körút 12-14; tram No 37 or 37/a); and UTE at **UTE Stadium** (Map 2; ☎ 369 7333; IV Megyeri út 13; bus No 47 or 96). But none dominates Hungarian football like Ferencváros (FTC), the country's loudest and brashest team and its only hope. You either love the Fradi boys in green and white or you hate them. Watch them play at **FTC Stadium** (Map 7; ☎ 215 1013; IX Üllői út 129; metro M3 Népliget). The daily sports paper Nemzeti Sport (National Sport; 79Ft) has the game schedules.

Water Polo

Hungary has dominated the European (12 times) and Olympic (six times) water polo championships for decades (W www.water polo.hu, Hungarian only) so it's worthwhile catching a professional or amateur match of this exciting seven-a-side sport (if for no other reason than to watch a bunch of guys in skimpy bathing suits horse around). The Hungarian Water Polo Association (Magyar Vízilabda Szövetség, MVLSZ) is based at the **Alfréd Hajós National Sports Pool** (Hajós Alfréd Nemzeti Sportuszoda; Map 3; ☎ 349 2357; e mvlsz@euroweb.hu; XIII Margit sziget; tram No 4 or 6, bus No 26). If you want to see a match or the lads in training, call or email the MVLSZ for times and dates or check the schedules in Nemzeti Sport.

In summer the national team usually trains at the national sports pool from 9am on weekdays; just buy a normal entrance ticket into the pool (see the special section 'Taking the Waters' in the Things to See & Do chapter) to watch. In season (September to May) the best clubs – FTC, Vasas, BVSC, Honvéd and UTE – compete here and at two other pools: the **Béla Komjádi** (Map 3; ☎ 212 2750; II Árpád fejedelem útja 8; bus No 86, tram No 17) and the **BVSC** (Map 3; ☎ 251 3888; XIV Szőnyi út 2; trolleybus No 74 or 74/a).

Horse Racing

The descendants of the nomadic Magyars are keen on horseflesh and horse racing.

The **Trotting Race Track** (Ügetőpálya; Map 1; ☎ 263 7817; X Albertirsai út 2; metro M2 Pillangó utca) is the place to go for trotting. Seven or eight races are held on Saturday and Sunday from 3pm and on Wednesday from 5pm.

Motor Racing

The **Hungarian Formula-1 Grand Prix** (for information ☎ 28-444 444; w www.hungaroring.hu), reintroduced in 1986 after a hiatus of 50 years, is part of the World Championship Series that takes place at the Hungaroring at Mogyoród, 24km northeast of Budapest. Best to buy your **tickets** (☎ 28-444 407, fax 441 860; e ticket@hungaroring.hu) directly and show the confirmation email or fax to the cashier when you pick them up.

Practice is on the Friday, the qualifying warm-up on Saturday and the race begins after morning practice at 2pm on Sunday. The only seats with views of the starting grid are Super Gold ones and cost €384 for the weekend; cheaper are Gold (€251 to €312), which are near the pit lane, and Silver (€179 to €281) tickets. Standing room costs €108 for the weekend, €98 for Sunday.

Shopping

WHAT TO BUY

Books and folk-music tapes and CDs are very affordable in Budapest by international standards, and there is an excellent selection. Traditional products include folk embroidery and ceramics, wall hangings, painted wooden toys and boxes, dolls, all types of basketry, and porcelain (especially Herend and Zsolnay). Goose feather and down pillows and duvets (comforters) are of exceptionally high quality. Foodstuffs that are expensive or difficult to buy elsewhere – goose liver (both fresh and potted), caviar and some prepared meats like Pick salami – make nice gifts (as long as you're allowed to take them home), as do the many varieties of paprika. Some of Hungary's 'boutique' wines (see the boxed text 'The Wines of Hungary' in the Places to Eat chapter) make good and relatively inexpensive gifts. A bottle of six-*puttonyos* Tokaji Aszú dessert wine always goes down a treat.

WHERE TO SHOP

Shops in Budapest are well stocked and the quality of the products is generally high. Nowadays traditional markets stand side by side with mammoth shopping malls (see the boxed text 'Magyar Malls'), with traditional umbrella or button makers next to cutting-edge fashion boutiques. Some streets or areas specialise in certain goods or products. For example, antique shops line V Falk Miksa utca and V Vitkovics Mihály utca in Pest and II Frankel Leó út in Buda. V Múzeum körút in Pest has a string of antiquarian and second-hand bookshops.

Antiques & Jewellery Shops

If you don't have time to get to the Ecseri or Petőfi Csarnok markets or it's the wrong day of the week (see Flea Markets later in this section), check any of the BÁV stores (open 10am to 6pm Monday to Friday, 9am to 1pm Saturday), essentially a chain of pawn and second-hand shops with several branches around town. Try VI Andrássy út 27 for old jewellery and bric-a-brac; V

Bécsi utca 1–3 for knick-knacks, porcelain and glassware; XIII Szent István körút 3 for chinaware and textiles; and II Frankel Leó út 13 for furniture and porcelain.

The antique shops along V Falk Miksa utca (tram No 4 or 6) and V Vitkovics Mihály utca (metro M1/2/3 Deák Ferenc tér) in Pest and II Frankel Leó út (tram No 4 or 6) in Buda (open 10am to 6pm Monday to Friday, 10am to 1pm Saturday) can be pretty expensive but you might stumble on a bargain. Among the best – at least for browsing – are the cavernous **Pintér** *(Map 5; ☎ 311 3030; V Falk Miksa utca 10)*, **Dárius** *(Map 5; ☎ 311 2603; V Falk Miksa utca 24-26)* and **Belvárosi** *(Map 6; ☎ 317 6289; V Vitkovics Mihály utca 3)*. **Anna Antikvitás** *(Map 5; ☎ 302 5461; V Falk Miksa utca 18-20)* is the place to go if you're in the market for embroidered antique tablecloths, bed linen and pillow cases.

Pless & Fox *(Map 5; ☎ 312 1238, 340 4333; XIII Szent István körút 18; tram No 4 or 6; open 10am-6pm Mon-Fri, 10am-1pm Sat)* has sublime jewellery and *objets d'art* for sale, mostly in the Art Nouveau and Secessionist styles.

Art Galleries

Polgár Gallery and Auction House *(Polgár Galéria és Aukciós-ház; Map 6; ☎ 318 6954; V Váci utca 11/b; metro M1 Vörösmarty tér; open 10am-6pm Mon-Fri, 10am-1pm Sat)*, in magnificent 1000-sq-metre premises, has antique furnishings and works by reputable Hungarian painters.

Inner Town Auction House *(Belvárosi Aukciós-ház; Map 6; ☎ 266 8374; V Váci utca 36; metro M3 Ferenciek tere; open 10am-6pm Mon-Fri, 10am-4pm Sat & Sun)* usually has themed auctions (jewellery, graphics, furniture and carpets etc), at 5pm on Monday.

Arten Gallery *(Map 6; ☎ 266 3127; V Váci utca 25, enter from Pesti Barnabás utca; metro M3 Ferenciek tere; open 10am-8pm daily)* is physically close by but, with works by such modern Hungarian artists as Ápád Müller and Endre Szász, worlds away in what it sells.

Magyar Malls

In the mid-1990s Budapest began to go mall crazy, and at last count the city had upwards of a dozen, both in the centre of town and on the fringes. However, 'mall' may not be the accurate word to describe what the Hungarians call *bevásárló és szorakoztató központ* (shopping and amusement centres); here you'll find everything from designer salons, more traditional shops and dry cleaners to food courts, casinos, multiscreen cinemas and live bands. It's a place to spend the entire day, much as you would just about anywhere else in the globalised world of the third millennium.

Though it's unlikely you've come all the way to Budapest to hang out in a generic, could-be-anywhere shopping centre, it can be fun watching Magyars and malls meet for the first time. The following are the biggest or the most central or the most exclusive or the cheapest of them all.

Duna Plaza (Map 2; ☎ 465 1666, 465 1200; XIII Váci út 178; metro M3 Gyöngyösi utca). Until the advent of the West End City Centre, this was the mother of all Magyar malls, with the requisite Greek taverna, a multiplex cinema with a dozen screens, bowling lanes and an ice-skating rink.

Europark (Map 7; ☎ 347 1607, 269 6985; XIX Üllői út 201-235; metro M3 Határ út). Conveniently (?) located on the way to/from the airport, Europark is entertainment- and gimmick-free, and for serious shoppers only.

Lurdy Ház (Map 7; ☎ 268 1288; IX Könyves Kálmán körút 12-14; bus No 103, tram No 1). This place in Ferencváros is almost a carbon copy of Duna Plaza – right down to the multiscreen cinema complex. There's a big supermarket here too.

Mammut I & **Mammut II** (Map 3; ☎ 345 8020; II Lövőház utca 2-6; metro M2 Moszkva tér). The 'Mammoths', side by side in Buda, are true 'shopping and amusement centres' with as many fitness centres, billiard parlours and cafés as shops. The Buda middle class comes here in droves.

MOM Park (Map 3; ☎ 487 6100; XII Alkotás utca, cnr Csörsz utca; tram No 61). The city's newest mall has both office and retail space, including a nine-screen cinema, recreation centre and in-house brewery pub.

Pólus Centre (Map 1; ☎ 415 2114, 414 2145; XV Szentmihályi út 131). In the far reaches of northern Pest, this mall runs its own bus every half-hour from Keleti train station. There's a big Tesco supermarket here.

West End City Centre (Map 5; ☎ 238 7777, 374 6530; VI Váci út 1; metro M3 Nyugati pályaudvar). In central Pest, this Goliath has everything you could possibly want or need, with large indoor fountains, a cultural centre and the rather stunning 230-room Hilton West End hotel.

Simonyi Galéria *(Map 6; ☎ 343 5019; VII Rumbach Sebestyén utca 7; metro M2 Astoria; open 11am-6pm Mon-Thur, 11am-5pm Fri, 11am-4pm Sun)*, a lovely gallery by the Conservative Synagogue, exhibits and sells contemporary artworks in every medium imaginable, many of them with a Jewish theme.

Bookshops

General Top of the pops for English-language bookshops in Budapest is the recently expanded **Bestsellers** *(Map 6; ☎ 312 1295; V Október 6 utca 11; metro M1/2/3 Deák Ferenc tér; open 9am-6.30pm Mon-Fri, 10am-5pm Sat, 10am-4pm Sun)*, which has novels, travel guides, Hungarica, magazines and newspapers. Under the same management is the nearby **CEU Bookshop** *(Map 6; ☎ 327 3096; V Nádor utca 9; open 9am-6pm Mon-Fri, 10am-4pm Sat)* at the Central European University, which has an excellent selection of academic and business titles with a regional focus.

The huge **Libri Könyvpalota** *(Map 5; ☎ 267 4844; VII Rákóczi út 12; metro M2 Astoria; open 10am-7.30pm Mon-Fri, 10am-3pm Sat)*, spread over two floors, really is a 'book palace', with a huge selection of English-language novels, art books, guidebooks and maps, and a café on the 1st floor. Try the more central **Libri Studium** *(Map 6; ☎ 318 5881; V Váci utca 22; metro M3 Ferenciek* *tere; open 10am-7pm Mon-Fri, 10am-3pm Sat & Sun)* for books in English on Hungarian subjects.

Pendragon *(Map 3; ☎ 340 4426; XIII Pozsonyi út 21-23; tram No 4 or 6; open 10am-6pm Mon-Fri, 10am-2pm Sat)* has an excellent selection of English books and guides (including Lonely Planet titles) as does **Kódex** *(Map 5; ☎ 331 6350; V Honvéd utca 5; metro M2 Kossuth Lajos tér; open 9am-5pm Mon-Wed, 9am-6pm Thur, 9am-4pm Fri)*, where you'll find Hungarian books on the ground floor and foreign books on the 1st floor, as well as a decent selection of classical and jazz CDs. The small **Párisi Udvar** bookshop (see Maps in the Facts for the Visitor chapter) and the **Bamako** bookshop at the Vista Travel Centre (see Travel Agencies in the Facts for the Visitor chapter) stock guides as well as maps.

The **Oxford University Press Bookshop** *(Map 6; ☎ 318 8633; V Gerlóczy utca 7; metro M3 Ferenciek tere; open 9am-5pm Mon-Fri)* has Hungarian classics in English and books for teaching English.

Atlantisz Book Island *(Atlantisz Könyvsziget; Map 6; ☎ 267 6258; V Piarista köz 1; metro M3 Ferenciek tere; open 10am-6pm Mon-Fri, 10am-2pm Sat)*, in a tiny alley at the start of the more touristy end of Váci utca, has numerous academic titles in Hungarian and paperback English-language classics for a steal. **Orisis** *(Map 6; ☎ 266 4999; V Veres Pálné utca 4-6; metro M3 Ferenciek tere; open 8am-6pm Mon-Fri, 10am-4pm Sat)* carries a small but high-quality selection of contemporary English-language works as well as those by up-and-coming Asian writers.

Writers' Bookshop *(Írók Boltja; Map 5; ☎ 322 1645; VI Andrássy út 45; metro M1 Oktogon, tram No 4 or 6; open 10am-6pm Mon-Fri, 10am-1pm Sat)* is *the* place to go for Hungarian authors in English translation. It was a popular artists' café called the Japán for most of the first half of the 20th century, and hosts readings and lectures.

Antique & Second-hand As well as others on the same street, **Központi Antikvárium** *(Map 6; ☎ 317 3514; V Múzeum körút 13-15; metro M2 Astoria; open 10am-6.30pm Mon-Fri, 10am-2pm Sat)* has an excellent choice of antique and second-hand books in Hungarian, German and English. Established in 1881, it is the largest antiquarian bookshop in Budapest. Other good *antikvárium* include **Szőnyi** *(Map 5; ☎ 311 6431; V Szent István körút 3; tram No 4 or 6; open 10am-6pm Mon-Fri, 9am-1pm Sat)*, with an excellent selection of antique prints and maps as well as books, and **Nyugat** *(Map 5; ☎ 311 9023; V Bajcsy-Zsilinszky út 34; metro M3 Arany János utca; open 9am-5pm Mon-Thur, 9am-4pm Fri)*, which stocks foreign-language titles only.

The **Red Bus Second-hand Bookstore** *(Map 6; ☎ 337 7453; V Semmelweis utca 14; metro M2 Astoria; open 10am-6pm Mon-Fri, 10am-3pm Sat)*, below the popular hostel of that name (see the Places to Stay chapter), is the only shop in town selling used English-language books.

Fashion Salons & Boutiques

Tangó Classic *(Map 6; ☎ 318 4394; V Apáczai Csere János utca 3; metro M1 Vörösmarty tér; open 10am-6pm Mon-Fri, 10am-1pm Sat)* has exclusive women's suits, blazers, jackets, evening attire and accessories with a Hungarian twist.

Manier *(Map 5; ☎ 413 0080; VI Andrássy út 27; metro M1 Opera; open 10am-6pm Mon-Fri, 10am-2pm Sat)* has wispy, slinky and silvery numbers as well as solid foundation pieces. This is the shop for some affordable and downright funky pieces from Hungarian talent Anikó Németh.

Monarchia *(Map 6; ☎ 318 3146; V Szabadsajtó út 6; metro M3 Ferenciek tere; open 10am-6.30pm Mon-Fri, Sat 10am-1.30pm)* stocks funky one-off and made-to-measure items. Another great place for up-to-the-minute casual wear is **Persona** *(Map 6; ☎ 337 9428; V Fehér Hajó utca 5; open 9am-5pm Mon-Fri, 9am-1pm Sat)*, with branches in the Duna Plaza, West End City Centre and Mammut shopping malls.

Náray Tamás *(Map 6; ☎ 266 2473; V Károlyi Mihály utca 12; metro M3 Ferenciek tere; open noon-8pm Mon-Fri, 10am-2pm Sat)*, named after the Paris-trained eponymous Hungarian designer, stocks elegant ready-to-wear and accessories for women.

Permission Granted

Budapest's antique shops and auction houses are magnets for bargain hunters from Austria and other European countries, and there are numerous outlets around V Váci utca, V Vitkovics Mihály, V Ferenciek tere and V Falk Miksa utca in Pest and II Frankel Leó út in Buda. Those with a trained eye may find the treasures of tomorrow at some of the modern galleries today, but purchases still require you to reach deep into the pocket – at least for the credit card.

Any item over 50 years old requires a permit from the Ministry of Culture for export; this involves a visit to a museum expert (see the following), photos of the piece and a National Bank form with proof-of-purchase receipts. Companies that will take care of all this for you and ship the piece(s) include **First European Shipping** (☎ 06-20 925 8400, 06-20 933 5240; **W** www.firsteuropeanshipping.com) and **Move One** (☎ 213 0018; **W** www.moveone.info). Be aware that most art shippers won't take a job for under US$350 so if the piece is not really valuable, consider taking it in your suitcase. First European Shipping quotes a price of about US$600 for obtaining export customs clearance, crating and air-freighting a small chest of drawers to JFK Airport in New York.

If you're in a DIY mood, the following are the museums and other offices you must contact for valuations and permits in order for your purchase to be allowed out of the country.

Hungarian National Gallery (Map 4; ☎ 375 7533, ext 460) Wings B, C & D, Royal Palace, I Szent György tér. For pictorial works by Hungarian artists
National Széchenyi Library (Map 4; ☎ 375 7533, ext 157) Wing F, Royal Palace, I Szent György tér. For books, printed matter, written music, hand-written items from before 1957
Museum of Fine Arts office (Map 5; ☎ 302 1785) VI Szondi utca 77. For foreign paintings, sculptures and other works of art
Ethnography Museum (Map 5; ☎ 312 4878) V Kossuth Lajos tér. For folk art and handicraft items
Applied Arts Museum (Map 3; ☎ 217 5222) IX Üllői út 33-37. For antique furniture

Vass (Map 6; ☎/fax 318 2375; V Haris köz 2; metro M3 Ferenciek tere; open 10am-6pm Mon-Fri, 10am-2pm Sat) is a traditional shoemaker that both stocks ready-to-wear and cobbles to order. Some people travel to Hungary just to have their footwear made here.

Iguana (Map 5; ☎ 317 1627; VIII Krúdy Gyula utca 9; tram No 4 or 6; open 10am-7pm Mon-Fri, 10am-2pm Sat) stocks leather, suede, velvet and 'madness pieces' from the 1960s and '70s plus new items as well.

For cut-rate new and second-hand fashion, check out the string of shops along XIII Hollán Ernő utca (Map 5) just north of Szent István körút.

Flea Markets

Ecseri Piac (Map 7; ☎ 282 9563; XIX Nagykőrösi út; open 6am-about 1pm Tues-Sat), often just called the 'piac' (market), is one of the biggest and best flea markets in Central Europe, selling everything from antique jewellery and Soviet army watches to old musical instruments and Fred Astaire–style top hats. Saturday is the best day to go. To get there, take bus No 54 from Boráros tér in Pest near Petőfi Bridge or, better, the red express bus No 54 from the Határ utca stop on the M3 metro line and get off at the Fiume utca stop and walk over the pedestrian bridge.

Petőfi Csarnok Flea Market (Városligeti Bolhapiac; Map 3; ☎ 251 7266, 343 4327; XIV Zichy Mihály út; metro M1 Széchenyi fürdő; open 7am-2pm Sat & Sun) is a huge outdoor flea market – a kind of Hungarian boot or garage sale – held next to the Petőfi Csarnok (Concert Hall) in City Park. The usual diamonds-to-rust stuff is on offer – from old records and draperies to candles, honey and herbs. Sunday is the better day.

Kínai Piac (Chinese Market; Map 2; XIII Fáy utca 60; tram No 14; open 7am-6pm daily), a rather unusual place, is a series of stalls run by Chinese, Vietnamese and Thais that offer the usual array of knock-off designer clothing and cosmetics, cigarettes and duty-free liquor. There are some decent (and authentic) Asian food stalls here.

Folk Art & Souvenir Shops

On the 1st floor of the **Great Market Hall** (Nagycsarnok; Map 6; IX Fővám tér; tram No 47 or 49) there are dozens of stalls selling Hungarian folk costumes, dolls, painted eggs, embroidered tablecloths, carved hunting knives and so on. If you prefer your prices clearly labelled, head for the **Folkart Centrum** (Map 6; ☎ 318 4697; V Váci utca 58; tram No 47 or 49; open 10am-7pm daily).

Other good bets are **Judit** (Map 4; ☎ 212 7050; I Tárnok utca 1; Vár Busz, bus No 16; open 10am-6.30pm daily), in the Castle District, for blue-dyed fabrics and crafts, and the nearby **Carillon Folk shop** (Map 4; ☎ 201 6692; Fortuna köz off I Fortuna utca; open 10am-6pm Mon-Fri, 10am-1pm Sat).

Near the Astoria Hotel, **Babaklinika** (Map 6; ☎ 267 2445; V Múzeum körút 5; metro M2 Astoria; open 9.30am-5.30pm Mon-Fri, 9.30am-12.30pm Sat) specialises in handmade dolls.

A favourite place to shop, **Holló Atelier** (Map 6; ☎ 317 8103; V Vitkovics Mihály utca 12; metro M1/2/3 Deák Ferenc tér; open 10am-6pm Mon-Fri, 10am-1pm Sat) has attractive folk art with a modern look.

Játékszerek Anno (Map 5; ☎ 302 6234; VI Teréz körút 54; metro M3 Nyugati pályaudvar; open 9am-6pm Mon-Fri, 9am-1pm Sat) is a wonderful little shop near Nyugati train station selling finely made reproductions of antique wind-up toys.

Food & Alcohol Stores

Gourmets will appreciate the Hungarian and other treats – shrink-wrapped and potted foie gras and goose liver paté (2400/4500Ft for 100/200g), caviar (from about 8000Ft for 60g), a good selection of dried mushrooms, garlands of dried paprika (400Ft to 500Ft), souvenir sacks and tins of paprika powder (350Ft to 850Ft), and as many kinds of honey (from 350Ft) as you care to name – available on the ground floor of the **Great Market Hall** (Nagycsarnok, Map 6; IX Fővám tér; tram No 47 or 49) at a fraction of what you'd pay in the shops on nearby Váci utca.

The **Budapest Wine Society** (Map 3; ☎ 212 2569; I Batthyány utca 59; metro M2 Moszkva tér; open 10am-8pm Mon-Fri, 10am-6pm Sat) has a retail outlet where serious oenophiles should head. No one but no one knows Hungarian wines like these guys do. There are free tastings on Saturday afternoon.

Monarchia Borászat (Map 3; ☎ 456 9817; w www.magyarborok.hu, Hungarian only; IX Kinizsi utca 30-36; metro M3 Ferenc körút; open 10am-6pm Mon-Fri, 10am-1pm Sat), opposite the Applied Arts Museum, has an extensive selection from both established and new Hungarian vintners, but the best are those bottled under their own label.

La Boutique des Vins (Map 6; ☎ 317 5919; V József Attila utca 12; metro M1/2/3 Deák Ferenc tér; open 10am-6pm Mon-Fri, 10am-3pm Sat), owned by the former sommelier at Gundel, has an excellent selection of Hungarian wines. Ask the staff to recommend a label if you feel lost. **Prés Ház** (Map 6; ☎ 266 1100; V Váci utca 10; metro M1 Vörösmarty tér; open 10am-7pm Mon-Fri, 10am-2pm Sat), a more central (and expensive) place than La Boutique des Vins, has over 300 wines in an 18th-century courtyard cellar, knowledgeable staff and bottles open for tasting. The **House of Hungarian Wines** (Magyar Borok Háza; Map 4; ☎ 212 1030, 212 1031; I Szentháromság tér 6) has an even larger selection.

Lokomos Csemege (Map 6; ☎ 267 8544; V Váci utca 48; metro M3 Ferenciek tere; open 7am-8.30pm Mon-Fri, 7am-7pm Sat & Sun), on the corner of Nyáry Pál utca, is the place for Hungarian spirits: Zwack Unicum, pálinka (brandy) distilled from plums, pears or apricots and so on.

Lekvárium (Map 5; ☎ 321 6543; VII Dohány utca 39; metro M2 Blaha Lujza tér; open 10am-6pm Mon-Fri), which stocks homemade jam as well as bottled fruit and honey, is the place to check out if you haven't been able to pick up a jar or two of Hungary's greatest contribution to humanity – traditionally made lekvár (fruit jam), especially the apricot variety – at any of the food markets (see the Self-Catering sections in the Places to Eat chapter).

Szamos Marcipán (Map 6; ☎ 317 3643; V Párizsi utca 3; metro M3 Ferenciek tere; open

10am-7pm daily) sells marzipan in all shapes and sizes. Its ice cream is also a major magnet.

Glassware & Porcelain Shops

Ajka Crystal (Ajka Kristály; Map 5; ☎ 332 4541; VI Teréz körút 50; metro M3 Nyugati pályaudvar; open 10am-6pm Mon-Wed & Fri, 10am-7pm Thur, 10am-1pm Sat) has Hungarian-made lead crystal pieces and stemware in both modern and traditional designs.

For fine porcelain, check out the **Zsolnay** (Map 6; ☎ 318 3712; V Kigyó utca 4; metro M3 Ferenciek tere; open 10am-6pm Mon-Fri, 10am-1pm Sat) and **Herend** (Map 6; ☎ 317 2622, 318 9200; V József nádor tér 11; metro M1 Vörösmarty tér; open 10am-6pm Mon-Fri, 9am-1pm Sat) outlets. **Haas & Czjzek** (Map 5; ☎ 311 4094; VI Bajcsy-Zsilinszky út 23; metro M3 Arany János utca; open 9am-6pm Mon-Fri, 10am-3pm Sat), just up from Deák Ferenc tér, sells more affordable Hungarian-made Hollóháza and Alföldi porcelain as well as Zsolnay pieces.

Herend Village Pottery (Map 3; ☎ 356 7899; II Bem rakpart 37; metro M2 Batthyány tér; open 9am-5pm Mon-Fri, 9am-noon Sat) is an alternative to prissy, fragile Herend flatware. It stocks the same manufacturer's ceramic pottery and dishes decorated with bold fruit patterns.

Music Shops

Many record shops sell CDs and tapes of traditional folk music, including **Rózsavölgyi** (Map 6; ☎ 318 3500; V Szervita tér 5; metro M1/2/3 Deák Ferenc tér; open 9.30am-7pm Mon-Fri, 10am-5pm Sat). For locally produced classical CDs, tapes and vinyl, try the wonderful **Concerto** (Map 6; ☎ 268 9631; VII Dob utca 33; metro M2 Astoria; open noon-7pm Mon-Fri, noon-4pm Sun), which is always full of treasures, or **Ferenc Liszt Music Shop** (Liszt Ferenc Zeneműbolt; Map 5; ☎ 322 4091; VI Andrássy út 45; metro M1 Oktogon; open 10am-6pm Mon-Fri, 10am-1pm Sat), next to the Writers' Bookshop (see Bookshops earlier).

Wave Music (Map 6; ☎ 302 2927, 269 4231; VI Révay köz 2; metro M1 Bajcsy-Zsilinszky út; open 11am-7pm Mon-Fri, 11am-3pm Sat) and **INDIeGO** (Map 5; ☎ 266 6427; VIII Krúdy Gyula utca 7; tram No 4 or 6; open 10am-8pm Mon-Sat) are two good places for indie and alternative music.

Other Shops

Goose feather or down products like pillows (from 6000Ft) or duvets (comforters; from 20,000Ft) are of excellent quality in Hungary and a highly recommended purchase. **Nádortex** (Map 6; ☎ 317 0030; V József nádor tér 12; metro M1 Vörösmarty tér; open 10am-6pm Mon-Fri) has some of the best prices, with pure down 1000g duvets measuring 135cm x 200cm for around 35,000Ft. **Billerbeck** (Map 5; ☎ 322 3606; VII Dob utca 49; tram No 4 or 6; open 10am-6pm Mon-Fri, 9.30am-1pm Sat), with several branches around town, has a larger selection but somewhat higher prices.

Hephaistos Háza (Map 6; ☎ 266 1550; V Molnár utca 27; tram No 47 or 49; open 11am-6pm Mon-Fri, 10am-2pm Sat) has a zany collection of furniture, fittings and household goods in wrought iron, a medium in which the Hungarians have traditionally excelled.

Selene (Map 6; ☎ 266 0143; V Irányi utca 7; metro M3 Ferenciek tere; open 10am-6pm Mon-Fri, 9am-1pm Sat) sells everything and anything you might need to kit you and a horse out for riding.

Excursions

An awful lot in Hungary is within easy striking distance of Budapest, and many of the towns and cities in the Danube Bend (to the north of Budapest), Transdanubia (west), Northern Uplands (north and northeast) and even the Great Plain (east and southeast) could be visited on a day trip from the capital. You can get to Szentendre to the north in less than an hour by the HÉV commuter rail, for example, and Eger, a lovely Mediterranean-like town lying between the Bükk and Mátra Hills to the northeast, is just 1½ hours away by InterCity train.

This chapter assumes you'll be returning to Budapest after a day of sightseeing, though we've included a couple of accommodation options in each section in case you miss your train or bus or simply decide you like the place and want to stay on. For fuller treatment of these and other destinations, see Lonely Planet's *Hungary*.

SZENTENDRE
☎ 26 • postcode 2000 • pop 21,400

Just 19km north of Budapest, Szentendre (St Andrew; w www.szentendre.hu) is the southern gateway to the Danube Bend, the S-shaped curve in the Danube River that begins just below Esztergom and twists for 20km before reaching the capital. As an art colony turned lucrative tourist centre, Szentendre strikes many as a little too 'cutesy', and the town can be crowded and relatively expensive. Still, it's an easy getaway from Budapest, and the town's many art museums, galleries and Serbian Orthodox churches are well worth the trip. Just try to avoid it on summer weekends.

Tourinform (☎ 317 965, fax 317 966; e szentendre@tourinform.hu; Dumtsa Jenő utca 22; open 9.30am-4.30pm Mon-Fri year-round, 10am-2pm Sat & Sun mid-Mar–Oct) can help with information and advice.

Things to See
Right in the centre of **Fő tér**, the colourful heart of Szentendre surrounded by 18th- and

Highlights

- The Hungarian Open-Air Ethnographical Museum at Szentendre, Hungary's largest – and most complete – *skanzen* (open-air museum)
- The meticulously restored Royal Mansion at Gödöllő
- A summertime concert in the park grounds of Brunswick Mansion in Martonvásár
- The Museum of Naive Artists in Kecskemét
- Castle Hill in Veszprém and its wonderful architecture and views
- Just about everything in Eger: its castle, its architecture, its wine

EXCURSIONS

19th-century burghers' houses, stands the **Plague Cross** (Pestis-kereszt), an iron cross decorated with icons on a marble base, erected in 1763 as a votive. Across the square to the northeast is the Serbian Orthodox **Blagoveš tenska Church** (☎ 310 554; admission 100Ft; open 10am-5pm daily mid-Mar–Oct), built in 1752. The church, with fine baroque and rococo elements, hardly looks 'eastern' from the outside (it was designed by András Mayerhoffer), but once you are inside, the ornate iconostasis and elaborate 18th-century furnishings give it away.

If you descend Görög utca and turn south (right) onto Vastagh György utca, you'll reach the entrance to the **Margit Kovács Museum** (☎ 310 224; Vastagh György utca 1; adult/student or child 450/220Ft; open 10am-6pm daily Feb-Oct, 10am-4pm Tues-Sun Nov-Jan), Szentendre's biggest draw and one of the few museums open all year. Kovács (1902–77) was a ceramicist who combined Hungarian folk, religious and modern themes to create elongated, Gothic-like figures. Some of her works are overly sentimental, but many are very powerful, especially the later ones in which she became obsessed with mortality.

Castle Hill (Vár-domb), which can be reached via the Váralja lépcső, the narrow set of steps between Fő tér 8 and 9, was the site of a fortress in the Middle Ages, but all that's left of it is the **Parish Church of St John** (Szent János plébániatemplom; Templom tér; open 10am-4pm Tues-Sun Apr-Oct), from where you can enjoy views of the town. The red tower of **Belgrade Cathedral** (Belgrád székesegyház; Alkotmány utca; open daily), seat of the Serbian Orthodox bishop in Hungary and built in 1764, rises from within a walled courtyard to the north. One of the church outbuildings contains the **Serbian Ecclesiastical Art Collection** (Szerb egyházművészeti gyűjtemény; ☎ 312 399; Pátriárka utca 5; adult/child 200/100Ft; open 10am-4pm Tues-Sun Mar-Apr & Oct-Nov, 10am-6pm Tues-Sun May-Sept, 10am-4pm Fri-Sun Dec-Feb), a treasure trove of icons, vestments and other sacred objects in precious metals.

The **Hungarian Open-Air Ethnographical Museum** (Magyar szabadtéri néprajzi múzeum; ☎ 502 500, 312 304; Sztaravodai út 1; adult/child 600/300Ft; open 9am-5pm Tues-Sun Apr-June & Sept–early Nov, 9am-7pm Tues-Sun July & Aug), 3km northwest of the centre and accessible by bus, is Hungary's most ambitious open-air museum. While plans ultimately call for some 300 farmhouses, churches, bell towers, mills and so on to be set up in 10 regional units, so far there are six: the Upper Tisza area of Northeast Hungary, the Kisalföld and Őrség regions of Western Transdanubia, the Bakony and Balaton Uplands of Central Transdanubia and a market town from the Alföld.

Places to Stay & Eat

Pap-sziget Camping (☎ 310 697, fax 313 777; tent site/adult/child 1900/900/500Ft, single/double hostel rooms 2600/3800Ft, bungalows & motel rooms for up to 4 persons 6000Ft; pension doubles 5000Ft; open May–mid-Oct), some 2km north of Szentendre on Pap Island, has a wide range of accommodation possibilities. Prices include admission to the swimming pool next door.

For a **private room**, look for 'Zimmer frei' signs on the Dunakanyar körút ring road; prices start at around 3000Ft per person.

Bükkös (☎ 312 021, fax 310 782; e buk kosh@matavnet.hu; Bükkös part 16; singles/doubles €40/45) is a friendly 16-room place halfway between the bus and HÉV stations and Fő tér.

Pizza Andreas (☎ 310 530; Duna korzó 5, pizzas from 700Ft) is a simple pizzeria close to the Danube. **Görög Kancsó** (Greek Jug; ☎ 301 729; Görög utca 1; mains 1200-2500Ft) is somewhat ambitiously named but manages tzatziki and Greek salads. **Aranysárkány** (Golden Dragon; ☎ 301 479; Alkotmány 1/a; mains around 1800Ft) may sound Chinese but it serves superb Hungarian and Austrian dishes at above-average prices.

Getting There & Away

The easiest way to reach Szentendre from Budapest is to catch the HÉV suburban train from Batthyány tér in Buda, which takes just 40 minutes. You'll never wait longer than 20 minutes (half that in rush hour), and the last train leaves Szentendre for Budapest at 11.10pm. Remember that a yellow city bus/metro ticket is good only as far as the Békásmegyer stop on the way up; you'll have to pay extra to get to Szentendre. Buses from Budapest's Árpád híd station, which is on the M3 metro line, run to Szentendre at least once an hour throughout the day.

The HÉV train and bus stations lie side by side south of the town centre; from here walk through the subway and north along Kossuth Lajos utca and Dumtsa Jenő utca to Fő tér.

GÖDÖLLŐ

☎ 28 • postcode 2100 • pop 29,900

Just 27km to the northeast and easily accessible on the HÉV, Gödöllő (roughly pronounced '**good**-duh-ler') is an easy day trip from Budapest. The main draw here is the Royal Mansion completed in the 1760s, which is Hungary's largest baroque manor house. Even the town of Gödöllő (w www.godollo.hu) itself, full of lovely baroque buildings and monuments and home to the seminal Gödöllő Artists' Colony (1901–20), is worth the trip alone.

Just inside the entrance to the Royal Mansion is **Tourinform** (☎ 415 403, fax 415 402; e godollo@tourinform.hu; open 10am-5pm

Tues-Sun Apr-Oct, 10am-4pm Tues-Sun Nov-Mar).

Royal Mansion

The Royal Mansion (Királyi kastély; ☎ 410 124, fax 423 159; ⓦ www.kiralyikastely.hu; Szabadság tér 1; adult/child/family Apr-Oct 1000/350/1800Ft, Nov-Mar 750/350/1200Ft; open 10am-6pm Tues-Sun Apr-Oct, 10am-5pm Tues-Sun Nov-Mar), sometimes called the Grassalkovich Mansion after its commissioner, Antal Grassalkovich (1694–1771), count and confidante of Empress Maria Theresa, was designed by András Mayerhoffer and completed in 1741. After the formation of the Dual Monarchy, the mansion (or palace) was enlarged as a summer retreat for Emperor Franz Joseph and soon became the favoured residence of his consort, the much beloved Habsburg empress and Hungarian queen, Elizabeth (1837–98), affectionately known as Sissy. Between the two world wars, the regent, Admiral Miklós Horthy, also used it as a summer residence, but after the communists came to power, part of the mansion was used as a Soviet barracks, as an old people's home and then as temporary housing. The rest was left to decay.

Partial renovation of the mansion began in 1994 and today more than a dozen rooms are open to the public on the 1st floor. They have been restored (some would say too heavily) to when the imperial couple were in residence, and Franz Joseph's suites (done up in manly greys and golds) and Sissy's lavender-coloured private apartments are impressive. Check out the **Decorative Hall**, all gold tracery and chandeliers, where concerts are held year-round but especially in late June and early July during the Palace Concerts Chamber Music Festival; the **Queen's Salon**, with a Romantic-style oil painting of Sissy patriotically repairing the coronation robe with needle and thread; and the **Study Annexe**, with a restored ceiling painting and an 18th-century tapestry of the huntress Diana.

A guided tour that also includes rooms and outbuildings not yet reconstructed (the palace chapel, theatre, stables etc) costs 1200/500/2200Ft for adults/children/families.

Places to Stay & Eat

GATE College (☎ 420 200, fax 432 937; ⓔ gatekollegium@freemail.hu; Páter Károly utca 1; dorm beds 1500Ft), a short distance east of the HÉV terminus, has dormitory accommodation available from June to August.

Galéria (☎/fax 418 691; Szabadság tér 8; doubles from 9000Ft), a five-room pension 300m northeast of the Royal Manor, is as central a place as you'll find to spend the night in Gödöllő. **Silver Club** (☎ 420 345, fax 432 410; ⓔ silver-tours@axelero.hu; Isaszegi út 7; doubles 7000Ft, bungalows 8500-10,500Ft) is a 12-room guesthouse with bungalows 3km to the south of central Gödöllő.

Tourinform has sample menus from restaurants around town and distributes discount vouchers. **Palazzo** (Szabadság tér; pizzas 450-900Ft; open 11am-11pm daily) is conveniently attached to the HÉV station. **Pelikán** (☎ 412 658; Kossuth Lajos utca 31-33; starters 300-480Ft, mains 600-1480Ft; open noon-11pm Sun-Thur, noon-midnight Fri & Sat), to the northwest, serves decent Hungarian fare. **Galéria** (☎ 418 691; Szabadság tér 8; starters 410-880Ft, 695-1200Ft; open 11am-11pm daily), attached to the pension of that name, is more upmarket.

Getting There & Away

HÉV trains from Örs vezér tere at the terminus of the M2 metro link Budapest with Gödöllő (40 minutes) about once every half-hour throughout the day. Make sure you get off at the Szabadság tér stop in Gödöllő, which is the third from the last. The last train leaves for Budapest just after 9pm daily. In addition, buses leave Népstadion station in Budapest about every 30 minutes for Gödöllő (40 minutes). The last bus back is just after 7pm (8.12pm on Sunday).

MARTONVÁSÁR

☎ 22 • postcode 2462 • pop 4840

Lying almost exactly halfway between Budapest and the Central Transdanubian city of Székesfehérvár and easily accessible by train, Martonvásár is the site of the former **Brunswick Mansion** (Brunszvik-kastély; Brunszvik út 2), one of the loveliest summertime concert venues in Hungary. The mansion was built in 1775 for Count Antal Brunswick (Magyarised as Brunszvik), the patriarch of a family of liberal reformers and patrons of the arts (Teréz Brunszvik established Hungary's first nursery school in Pest in 1828).

Beethoven was a frequent visitor to the manse, and it is believed that Jozefin, Teréz's sister, was the inspiration for his *Appassionata* and *Moonlight* sonatas, which the great Ludwig composed here.

Brunswick Mansion was rebuilt in neo-Gothic style in 1875 and restored to its ivory and sky-blue glory a century later. It now houses the Agricultural Research Institute of the Academy of Sciences, but you can see at least part of the mansion by visiting the small **Beethoven Memorial Museum** (*Beethoven Emlékmúzeum;* ☎ 569 500; *adult/student or child 120/60Ft; open 10am-noon & 2pm-4pm Tues-Fri, 10am-4pm Sat & Sun May-Oct; 10am-noon & 2pm-4pm Tues-Fri, 10am-4pm Sat & Sun Nov-Apr*) to the left of the main entrance.

A walk around the **park grounds** (*adult/ student or child 250/120Ft; open 8am-6pm daily summer, 8am-4pm daily winter*) – one of Hungary's first 'English parks' to be laid out when these were all the rage here in the early 19th century – is a pleasant way to spend a warm summer's afternoon. The highlight of the so-called Martonvásár Days (Martonvásár Napok), a 10-day festival in July, are the Beethoven Evenings (Beethoven-estjei) on Saturdays, when concerts are held on the small island in the middle of the lake (reached by a wooden footbridge).

The baroque **Catholic church**, attached to the mansion but accessible from outside the grounds, has frescoes by Johannes Cymbal. There's also a small **Nursery Museum** (*Óvodamúzeum;* ☎ 569 500; *admission adult/child 120/60Ft; open 10am-4pm Tues-Sun May-Sept, 11am-3pm Tues, Fri & Sun Oct–mid-Mar*) in the park.

Places to Stay & Eat

Macska (*Cat;* ☎ 460 127; Budai út 21; singles 2500Ft, doubles 5000-6000Ft), a pension with seven rooms just north of the centre, is crawling with felines, 30 of them in fact; it's definitely not the place for hyperallergenics.

Its restaurant (*mains about 1000Ft*) serves not feline under glass but the standard Hungarian *csárda* (inn) dishes.

Postakocsi (☎ 460 013; *Fehérvári utca 1; mains 900-1700Ft; open 10am-10pm daily*), in the centre of town, is a convenient place for lunch and has courtyard seating.

Getting There & Away

Dozens of trains between Déli and Kelenföld train stations in Budapest and Székesfehérvár stop at Martonvásár (35 to 40 minutes) every day and, if you attend a concert, you can easily make your way back to the capital on the last train (11.35pm). The station is a 10-minute walk along Brunszvik út, northwest of the main entrance to the mansion.

KECSKEMÉT

☎ 76 • postcode 6000 • pop 108,500

Lying halfway between the Danube and the Tisza Rivers in the heart of the Southern Plain some 85km southeast of Budapest, Kecskemét (**w** www.kecskemet.hu) is ringed with vineyards and orchards that don't seem to stop at the limits of this 'garden city'. Colourful architecture, fine museums, apricot groves and the region's excellent *barackpálinka* (apricot brandy) beckon entice, and Kiskunság National Park, the puszta of the Southern Plain, is right at the back door.

Tourinform (☎/fax 481 065; **e** kecskemet@ tourinform.hu; Kossuth Lajos tér 1; open 8am-8pm Mon-Fri, 9am-1pm Sat & Sun July-Aug; 8am-5pm Mon-Fri, 9am-1pm Sat May, June & Sept; 8am-5pm Mon-Fri Oct-Apr) is on the northeast side of the town hall.

Things to See

On the eastern side of central Kossuth tér is the **Franciscan Church of St Nicholas** (Szent Miklós ferences templom), dating in part from the late 13th century; the **Zoltán Kodály Institute of Music Education** (Kodály Zoltán Zenepedagógiai Intézet; ☎ 481 518; Kéttemplom köz 1; adult/child 100/50Ft; open noon-1pm & 4pm-6pm Mon-Fri, 10am-6pm Sat & Sun), celebrated for its unique approach to musical education, occupies the baroque monastery behind it to the east. But the main building in the square is the sandy-pink **town**

Great Market Hall (Nagycsarnok)

West End City Centre

Traditional shop fronts in Pest

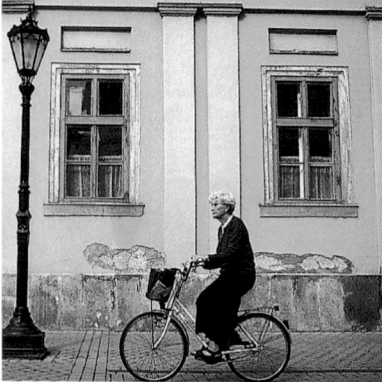

Széchenyi utca, Eger

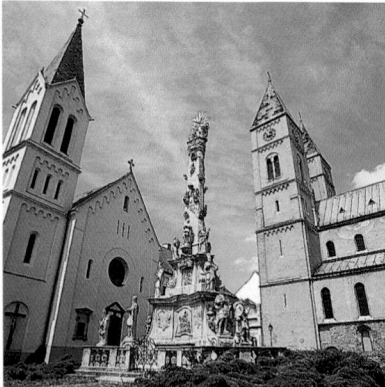

Trinity Column and Cathedral, Veszprém

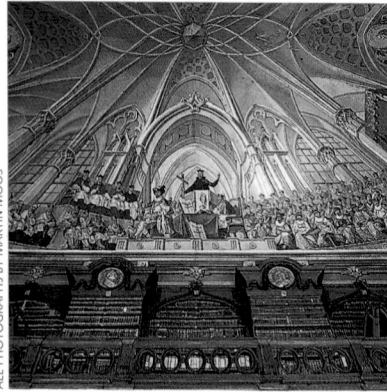

Fresco in the library of the Lyceum, Eger

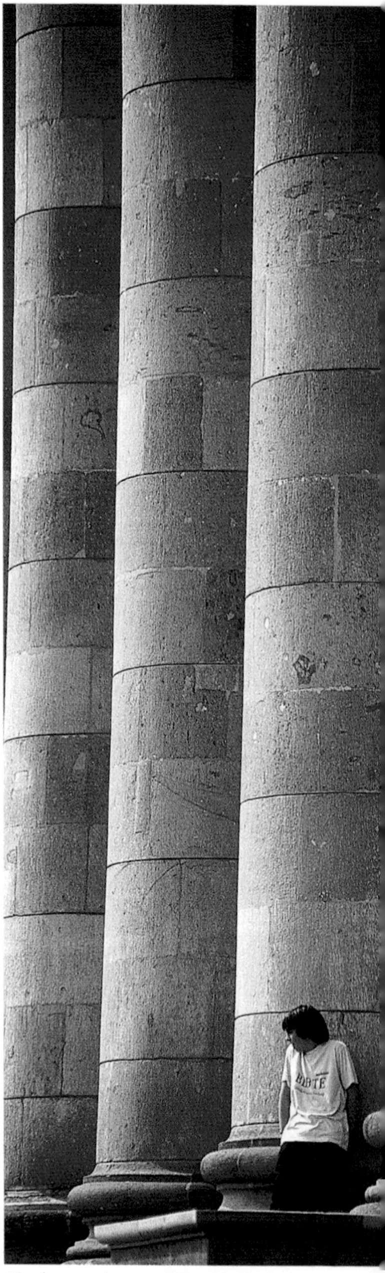

The huge columns of Eger Cathedral

ALL PHOTOGRAPHS BY MARTIN MOOS

hall (városháza), a lovely late-19th-century building designed by Ödön Lechner, who mixed Art Nouveau/Secessionist with folkloric elements to produce a uniquely Hungarian style. The town hall's carillon chimes out strains of works by Ferenc Erkel, Kodály, Mozart, Händel and Beethoven several times during the day, and groups are allowed into the spectacularly painted and decorated **Council Chamber** (☎ 483 683).

Walking northeast into Szabadság tér, you'll come to two of the Kecskemét's finest buildings. The Secessionist **Ornamental Palace** (Cifrapalota), dating from 1902 and covered in multicoloured majolica tiles, now contains the **Kecskemét Gallery** (Kecskeméti képtár; ☎ 480 776; Rákóczi út 1; adult/child 260/130Ft; open 10am-5pm Tues-Sat, 1.30pm-5pm Sun). But don't visit so much for the art; climb the steps to the aptly named **Decorative Hall** (Díszterem) to see the amazing stucco peacock, bizarre windows and more tiles. The **House of Technology** (Technika Háza; ☎ 487 611; Rákóczi út 2; admission free; open 10am-6pm Mon-Fri), a Moorish Romantic structure built in 1871, was once a synagogue but is now used for conferences and exhibitions.

Kecskemét has many museums but two stand head and shoulders above the rest. The **Hungarian Museum of Naive Artists** (Magyar Naiv Művészek Múzeuma; ☎ 324 767; Gáspár András utca 11; adult/child 150/50Ft; open 10am-5pm Tues-Sun mid-Mar–Oct) is in the Stork House (1730) just off Petőfi Sándor utca. There are lots of predictable themes here, but the warmth and craft of Rozália Albert Juhászné's work, the druglike visions of Dezső Mokry-Mészáros and the paintings of András Süli (Hungary's answer to Henri Rousseau) will hold your attention. The granddaddy of all museums in Kecskemét is the **Hungarian Folk Craft Museum** (Magyar Népi Isparművészet Múzeuma; ☎ 327 203; Serfőző utca 19a; adult/child 200/100Ft; open 10am-5pm Tues-Sat) farther to the southwest, a block in from Dózsa György út. Some 10 rooms of this old farm complex are crammed with embroidery, woodcarving, furniture, agricultural tools and textiles, so don't try to see everything.

Places to Stay & Eat

GAMF Ságvári College (☎ 510 300, fax 516 399; e koll@gamf.hu; Izsáki út 10; beds from 1250Ft) has accommodation in a four-bed room and singles and doubles are also available. Officially it's only open from mid-June to August, but you can sometimes get a bed in other months.

Fábián (☎ 477 677, fax 477 175; Kápolna utca 14; singles/doubles 5500/7500Ft), a pension with 10 modern, clean rooms with bath, is a fab place to stay, and the friendly staff speak a multitude of languages.

Három Gúnár (☎ 483 611, fax 481 253; W www.hotelharomgunar.hu; Batthyány utca 1-7; singles/doubles 10,900/12,000Ft), is a charming, friendly and small hotel formed by cobbling four old townhouses together. It has 46 smallish rooms (the best are Nos 306 to 308).

Labirintus (Kéttemplom köz 2; pizzas from 270Ft) is a cellar restaurant popular with students that has a vast array of pizza and pastas.

Görög Udvar (☎ 492 513; Széchenyi tér 9; mains 950-1500Ft) is a classy Greek restaurant worth crossing the street for and serves gyros (950Ft), souvlakia (1100Ft) and moussaka (1100Ft).

Liberté (☎ 480 350; Szabadság tér 2; mains 1000-2000Ft) is the place to go if you wanted to splurge. It's in a historical building east of the Great Church.

Getting There & Away

Kecskemét is on the central railway line linking Budapest's Nyugati train station with Szeged and there are frequent departures to and from the capital throughout the day (1¼ hours). Alternatively, there are hourly buses to/from Népliget bus station in Budapest. Kecskemét's bus and main train stations are opposite one another near József Katona Park. A 10-minute walk southwest along Nagykőrösi utca will bring you to Szabadság tér.

VESZPRÉM

☎ 88 • postcode 8200 • pop 63,900

Spreading over five hills between the northern and southern ranges of the Bakony Hills, Veszprém (W www.veszprem.hu), 110km southwest of Budapest, has one of the most dramatic locations in Central Transdanubia. The walled castle district atop a plateau, once the favourite residence of Hungary's queens, is now a living museum of baroque art and architecture, and it's a delight to stroll through the Castle Hill district's single street, admiring the embarrassment of fine churches and civic buildings. What's more, Lake Balaton, the nation's playground, is only 13km to the south and Herend, home of Hungary's finest porcelain (see boxed text 'Herend Porcelain'), is the same distance to the northwest.

Tourinform (☎/fax 404 548; e veszprem@ tourinform.hu; Vár utca 4; open 9am-6pm Mon-Fri, 11am-3pm Sat, 11am-4pm Sun June-Aug; 9am-5pm Mon-Fri Sept-May) has lots of information on the city and the surrounding town and villages, including Herend.

Things to See

As you ascend Castle Hill (Vár-hegy) and its sole street, Vár utca, you'll pass under **He-roes' Gate** (Hősök kapuja), an entrance way built in 1936 from the stones of a 15th-century castle gate. To the left is the **fire-watch tower** (tűztorony; ☎ 425 204; Vár utca 9; adult/child 100/50Ft; open 10am-6pm daily mid-Mar–Oct), an architectural hybrid of Gothic, baroque and neoclassical styles, which can be climbed.

The U-shaped **Bishop's Palace** (Püspöki palota; Vár utca 16), where the queen's residence stood in the Middle Ages, faces Szentháromság tér, named for the **Trinity Column** (1751) in the centre. The palace, designed by Jakab Fellner of Tata in the mid-18th century, is not open to the public.

Next to the Bishop's Palace is the early Gothic **Gizella Chapel** (Gizella kápolna; ☎ 426 088; Vár utca 18; adult/child 100/50Ft; open 9am-5pm daily May-Oct), named after the wife of King Stephen, who was crowned near here early in the 11th century. Inside the chapel are Byzantine-influenced 13th-century frescoes of the Apostles. The **Queen Gizella Museum** (Gizella Királyné Múzeum; ☎ 426 088; Vár utca 35; adult/child 200/100Ft; open 9am-5pm daily May-Oct) of religious art is opposite.

The **cathedral** (székesegyház; ☎ 426 088; Vár utca 18-20; admission free; open 9am-5pm daily May-Oct), dedicated to St Michael, is on the site of the first bishop's palace. Parts of it date from the beginning of the 11th century, but the cathedral has been rebuilt many times since then. The early Gothic crypt is original, though. Beside the cathedral, the octagonal foundation of the 13th-century **Chapel of St George** (Szent György kápolna; ☎ 426 088; adult/child 100/50Ft; open 10am-5pm daily May-Oct) sits under a glass dome.

From the rampart known as **World's End** at the end of Vár utca, you can gaze north to craggy Benedict Hill (Benedek hegy) and the Séd Stream and west to the concrete viaduct (now St Stephen's Valley Bridge) over the Betekints Valley. Below you, in Margit tér, are the ruins of the medieval **Dominican Convent of St Catherine** and to the west what little remains of the 11th-century **Veszprém Valley Convent**, whose erstwhile cloistered residents are said to have stitched Stephen's crimson silk coronation robe in 1031. The **statues of King Stephen and Queen Gizella** at World's End were erected in 1938 to mark the 900th anniversary of Stephen's death.

Places to Stay & Eat

Balatontourist (☎ 544 400; w www.balaton tourist.hu; Kossuth Lajos utca 25; open 8.30am-4.30pm Mon-Fri year-round; until noon Sat in summer) can help with private rooms (2500Ft per person) and flats (from 7000Ft). **Péter Pál** (☎ 567 790, fax 328 091; e info@peterpal.hu; Dózsa György utca 3; singles/doubles/triples 6000/7700/10,00Ft) is by far and away the best pension in town, with 12 very well-kept rooms, a lovely garden, an excellent restaurant and very friendly and helpful staff.

Elefánt Bisztró (Óváros tér 6; mains from 1000Ft) doesn't serve gigantic portions like the name would suggest, but the food – from steaks to salads – is altogether top-notch. There are very few places to eat on Castle Hill, but you might try **Tűztorony** (☎ 326 220; Vár utca 1; mains under 1000Ft), a Chinese restaurant between the firewatch tower and Heroes' Gate. It is a friendly place with a cheap lunch menu (480Ft).

Getting There & Away

Veszprém is on the train line linking Szombathely and Budapest's Déli train station via Székesfehérvár, and there are between eight and 10 trains a day to/from the capital (two hours). In general, bus connections are excellent to/from Veszprém, with hourly departures each day to/from Népliget bus station in Budapest, including five expresses and many more departures via Székesfehérvár.

The bus station is on Piac tér, a few minutes' walk northeast from Kossuth Lajos utca, a pedestrian street of shops and travel agencies. If you turn north at the end of Kossuth Lajos utca at Szabadság tér, and walk along Rákóczi utca you'll soon reach Óváros tér and the entrance to Castle Hill. The train station is 3km north of the bus station at the end of Jutasi út.

EGER

☎ 36 • postcode 3300 • pop 61,500

Everyone loves Eger, and it's immediately apparent why: the beautifully preserved baroque architecture gives the town a relaxed, almost Mediterranean, feel; it is the home of the celebrated Egri Bikavér (Eger Bull's Blood) wine known the world over; and it is flanked by two of the Northern Uplands' most beautiful ranges of hills. Hungarians visit Eger for those reasons and more, for it was here that István Dobó and his troops fended off the Turks for the first time during the 170 years of occupation in 1552 (see boxed text 'The Siege of Eger').

Tourinform (☎ 517 715, fax 518 815; e eger@tourinform.hu; Bajcsy-Zsilinszky utca 9; open 9am-7pm Mon-Fri, 10am-6pm Sat & Sun June-Aug, 9am-5pm Mon-Fri, 9am-1pm Sat Sept-May) can supply all the information you need and recommend agencies dealing with private accommodation.

Eger Castle

The best overview of the city can be had by climbing up the cobblestone lane from Dózsa György tér to Eger Castle (Egri Vár; ☎ 312 744; Vár 1; adult/student or child castle & grounds 500/250Ft, grounds only 200/100Ft;

Herend Porcelain

Herend porcelain is among the finest of all goods produced in Hungary and makes a wonderful gift or memento. The stuff also has a long and fascinating pedigree.

A terracotta factory was set up in Herend in 1826 and began producing porcelain 13 years later under Mór Farkasházi Fischer of Tata in Western Transdanubia. Initially it specialised in copying and replacing the nobles' broken chinaware settings imported from Asia, and you'll see some pretty kooky 19th-century interpretations of Japanese art and Chinese faces on display at the **Porcelánium** (☎ 523 100; w www.pocelanium.com; Kossuth Lajos utca 140; adult/child factory & museum 1000/400Ft, museum only 300/100Ft; open 9am-5.30pm daily Apr-Oct, 9am-4.30pm Mon-Sat (mini-factory closed on Monday) Nov-Mar), a museum that displays the most prized pieces of the rich Herend collection and a mini-factory where you can witness first-hand how ugly clumps of clay become delicate porcelain.

The factory soon began producing its own patterns; many, like the Rothschild bird and petites roses, were inspired by Meissen and Sèvres designs from Germany and France. The popular Victoria pattern of butterflies and wild flowers was designed for the eponymous English queen after she admired a display of Herend pieces at the Great Exhibition in London in 1851.

To avoid bankruptcy in the 1870s, the Herend factory began mass production; tastes ran from kitschy pastoral and hunting scenes to the animal figurines with the distinctive scale-like triangle patterns still popular today.

In 1993, 75% of the factory was purchased by its 1500 workers and became one of the first companies in Hungary privatised through an employee stock-ownership plan. The state owns the other 25%.

EXCURSIONS

open 8am-8pm Tues-Sun Apr-Aug, 8am-7pm Tues-Sun Sept, 8am-6pm Tues-Sun Oct & Mar, 8am-5pm Tues-Sun Nov-Feb), which was erected in the 13th century after the Mongol invasion. Much of the castle is of modern construction, but you can still see the foundations of 12th-century St John's Cathedral. Models and drawings in the István Dobó Museum, housed in the former Bishop's Palace (1470), show how it once looked. On the ground floor, a statue of Dobó takes pride of place in Heroes' Hall. The 19th-century building on the north-western side of the courtyard houses the Eger Art Gallery, with several works by Mihály Munkácsy.

Beneath the castle are casemates hewn from solid rock, which you may tour with a Hungarian-speaking guide included in the price (English-language guide 400Ft extra). Other exhibits, including the Waxworks (250/150Ft) and Minting Exhibit (100/50Ft) cost extra. You can still tour the castle grounds on Monday, when all the other exhibits are closed.

Eszterházy tér

Back in town, you can begin a walking tour of the city at neoclassical Eger Cathedral

The Siege of Eger

The story of the Turkish attempt to take Eger Castle is the stuff of legend. Under the command of István Dobó, a mixed bag of 2000 soldiers held out against more than 100,000 Turks for a month in 1552. As every Hungarian kid in short trousers can tell you, the women of Eger played a crucial role in the battle, pouring boiling oil and pitch on the invaders from the ramparts. A painting by Bertalan Székely called The Women of Eger in the castle's art gallery pays tribute to these brave ladies.

Also significant was Eger's wine, if we're to believe the tale. It seems that Dobó sustained his soldiers with the ruby-red vintage. When they fought on with increased vigour – and stained beards – rumours began to circulate among the Turks that the defenders were gaining strength by drinking the blood of bulls. The name Bikavér (Bull's Blood) was born.

(Egri főszékesegyház; Pyrker János tér 1; open 9am-7pm Mon-Sat, 1pm-5pm Sun), a neoclassical monolith designed in 1836 by József Hild. Despite the cathedral's size and ornate altars, the interior is surprisingly light and airy.

Directly opposite the cathedral is the sprawling Zopf-style Lyceum (Líceum; ☎ 520 400; Eszterházy tér 1; open 9.30am-3pm Tues-Sun Apr-Sept, 9.30am-1.30pm Sat & Sun Oct-Mar) dating from 1765. The 20,000-volume library (adult/student or child 300/150Ft) on the 1st floor of the south wing contains hundreds of priceless manuscripts and codices. The ceiling fresco (1778) here is a trompe l'œil masterpiece depicting the Counter-Reformation's Council of Trent (1545–63) and a lightning bolt setting heretical manuscripts ablaze.

The Astronomy Museum (adult/student or child 300/150Ft) on the 6th floor of the east wing contains 18th-century astronomical equipment and an observatory; climb three more floors up to the observation deck for a great view of the city and to try out the camera obscura, the 'eye of Eger' designed in 1776 to spy on the town and to entertain townspeople.

Other Attractions

On the southern side of central Dobó István tér stands the Minorite church (Minorita templom), built in 1771 and one of the most glorious baroque buildings in the world. The altarpiece of the Virgin Mary and St Anthony of Padua is by Johann Kracker, the Bohemian painter who also did the fire-and-brimstone ceiling fresco in the Lyceum library. Statues of István Dobó and his comrades-in-arms routing the Turks in 1552 fill the square in front of the church.

To the north of the square is the 40m-high minaret (Knézich Károly utca; admission 100Ft; open 9am-6pm daily Apr-Oct) topped with a cross. Only non-claustrophobes will brave the 97 narrow spiral steps to the top. To the south of Dobó István tér is Kossuth Lajos utca, a tree-lined street with dozens of architectural gems. The former Orthodox synagogue (Ortodox zsinagóga; Kossuth Lajos utca 17), built in 1893, is now a furniture store backing onto a shopping mall. You'll pass several baroque and eclectic buildings, including the **county hall** *(megyeháza; Kossuth Lajos utca 9)*, with a wrought-iron grid above the main door of Faith, Hope and Charity by Henrik Fazola, a Rhinelander who settled in Eger in the mid-18th century. Walk down the passageway, and you'll see more of his magnificent work – two baroque wrought-iron gates. The one on the right shows the seal of Heves County and has a comical figure on its handle. The more graceful gate on the left is decorated with grapes. The wrought-iron balcony and window grilles of the rococo **Provost's Palace** *(Kispréposti palota; Kossuth Lajos utca 4)* were also done by Fazola.

Wine Tasting

By no means should you miss visiting the wine cellars of the evocatively named **Valley of the Beautiful Women** (Szépasszony-völgy) to the southwest of the centre. From the western end of the cathedral, walk south on Trinitárius utca to Bartók Béla tér and then west along Király utca to Szépasszony-völgy utca. Veer to the left as you descend the hill past the large Talizmán restaurant and into the valley, and you'll see dozens of cellars. This is the place to sample Bull's Blood – one of very few reds produced in Eger – or any of the whites: Leányka, Olaszrizling and Hárslevelű from nearby Debrő.

The choice of wine cellars can be a bit daunting and their characters can change so walk around and have a look yourself. Nos 6, 17, 29 and 48 are always popular; for schmaltzy Gypsy music, try No 32 or 42. But if you're interested in good wine, visit cellar Nos 5, 13, 18, 23 and 31. Be careful though; those 100mL glasses (about 50Ft) go down easily. Hours are erratic, but a few cellars are sure to be open till the early evening. The taxi fare back to Eger centre is about 500Ft.

Places to Stay & Eat

Egertourist *(☎ 510 270, fax 411 225; Bajcsy-Zsilinszky utca 9; open 9am-5pm Mon-Fri year-round, 9am-1pm Sat Jun-Sept)* and **Ibusz** *(☎ 311 451, fax 312 652; Széchenyi utca 9; open 8am-4pm Mon-Fri year-round,*

9am-1pm Sat Jun-Sept) can organise private rooms for between 2000Ft and 3000Ft a night per person.

Tourist *(☎ 411 101, fax 429 014; Mekcsey István utca 2; singles/doubles/triples/quads with shared bath 3000/5000/6000/7000Ft)* is a frayed though spotlessly clean and friendly motel south of the castle with 34 rooms.

Romantik *(☎ 310 456, fax 516 362;* **e** *romantik-eger@axelero.hu; Csíky Sándor utca 26; singles €35-55, doubles €40-65, triples € 50-75, suites €55-80)* is a very friendly and cosy 16-room hotel with a pretty back garden.

Senator Ház *(☎/fax 320 466;* **e** *hotel sen@axelero.hu; Dobó István tér 11; singles €27.50-48, doubles €39-57)* is a delightful 18th-century inn with 11 rooms in Eger's main square that many – including me – consider to be the finest small hotel in provincial Hungary.

Gyros *(☎ 310 135; Széchenyi utca 10; open noon-10pm daily)* is a local café-restaurant on a pedestrian street with Greek salads (360Ft), moussaka (750Ft) and souvlakia (750Ft). **Pizza Club** *(☎ 427 606; Dr Hibay Károly utca 8; pizzas 650-1200Ft; open noon-10pm daily)*, just off Dobó István tér, can be recommended for a cheap and light meal.

Elefanto *(☎ 411 031; Katona István tér 2; mains 950-1800Ft; open noon-midnight daily)* perched high above the market, with a non-smoking interior and covered balcony for alfresco dining, is a great new place. The food is very good.

Getting There & Away

Eger is on a minor railway linking Putnok and Füzesabony; you usually have to change at the latter to/from the capital. There are, however, up to five direct trains a day to and from Budapest's Keleti station (2½ hours) that do not require a change. Bus services are good, with buses running every hour or so to/from Népstadion bus station in Budapest via the M3 motorway. The bus station is on Pyrker János tér, just a few minutes on foot from Dobó István tér. To reach the centre from the main train station on Vasút utca, walk north along Deák Ferenc utca to pedestrian Széchenyi István utca. Dobó István tér is to the east.

Language

Hungarian (Magyar) is a member of the Ugric group of the Uralic family of languages that is related very, very distantly to Finnish (with five million speakers), Estonian (one million) and about a dozen other minority languages in Russia and western Siberia (with far fewer speakers). It's not an Indo-European language, meaning that English is actually closer to French, Russian and Hindi in vocabulary and structure than it is to Hungarian. As a result you'll come across very few recognisable words – with the exception of borrowings like *disco*, *szex* or *hello*, which is the slangy way young Hungarians say 'goodbye'.

There are also a fair number of misleading homophones (words with the same sound but different meanings) in Hungarian: *test* is not a quiz but 'body'; *fog* is 'tooth'; *comb* is 'thigh'; and *part* is 'shore'. *Ifjúság*, pronounced (very roughly) 'if you shag', means 'youth'; *sajt* (pronounced 'shite'), as in every visiting Briton's favourite *sajtburger*, means 'cheese'.

For more Hungarian words and phrases than there is space for here, get a copy of Lonely Planet's *Eastern* or *Central Europe* phrasebook.

Pronunciation

Hungarian isn't difficult to pronounce – though it may look strange with all those accents. Unlike English, it's a 'one-for-one' language: the pronunciation of each vowel and consonant is almost always consistent. Stress falls on the first syllable (no exceptions), making the language sound a bit staccato at first.

Consonants

Consonants in Hungarian are pronounced more or less as in English, with the exceptions listed below. The double consonants (**ll**, **tt**, **dd**) are not pronounced as one letter as in English, but lengthened so you can almost hear them as separate sounds. Also, what are called consonant clusters (**cs**, **zs**, **gy** and **sz**) are considered separate letters in

Hungarian and appear that way in the telephone directory and alphabetical listings. For example, the word *cukor* (sugar) appears in the dictionary before *csak* (only).

c	as the 'ts' in 'hats'
cs	as the 'ch' in 'church'
gy	as the 'j' in 'jury' with the tongue pressed against the roof of the mouth
j	as the 'y' in 'yes'
ly	also as the 'y' in 'yes', but with a slight 'l' sound
ny	as the 'ni' in 'onion'
r	pronounced with the tip of the tongue; a slightly trilled 'r' as found in Spanish or Scottish
s	as the 'sh' in 'shop'
sz	as the 's' in 'salt'
ty	as the 'tu' in 'tube' in British English
w	as the 'v' in 'vat' (found in foreign words only)
zs	as the 's' in 'pleasure'

Vowels

Vowels are quite tricky in Hungarian, and the difference between an **a**, **e** or **o** with and without an accent mark is great. *Hát* means 'back' while *hat* means 'six'; *kérek* means 'I want' while *kerek* means 'round'. Try to imagine a Briton with a standard television accent or an American from Boston pronouncing the following sounds:

a	as the 'o' in hot
á	as the 'a' in 'father' or 'shah'
e	as in 'get'
é	as the 'e' in 'they' (without the 'y' sound)
i	similar to the 'i' in 'hit'
í	as the 'i' in 'police'
o	as in 'open'
ó	a longer version of **o** above
ö	as the 'o' in 'worse' (without any 'r' sound)
ő	a longer version of **ö** above
u	as in 'pull'
ú	as the 'oo' in 'food'

| ü | a tough one; similar to the 'u' in 'flute' or as in German *fünf* |
| ű | a longer, breathier version of ü above |

Polite & Informal Address

As in many other Western languages, verbs in Hungarian have polite and informal forms in the singular and plural. The polite address (marked as 'pol' in this section) is used with strangers, older people, officials and service staff. The informal address (marked as 'inf') is reserved for friends, pets, children and sometimes foreigners, but is used much more frequently and sooner than its equivalent in, say, French. Almost all young people use it among themselves – even with strangers.

In the following phrases, the polite 'you' (*Ön* and *Önök*) is given except for situations where you might wish to establish a more personal relationship.

Greetings & Civilities

Hello.	*Jó napot kívánok.* (pol)
Hi.	*Szia/Szervusz.* (inf)
Goodbye.	*Viszontlátásra.* (pol)
	Szia/Szervusz. (inf)
Good day.	*Jó napot.*
Good morning.	*Jó reggelt.*
Good evening.	*Jó estét.*

Small Talk

How are you?	*Hogy van?* (pol)
	Hogy vagy? (inf)
I'm fine, thanks.	*Köszönöm, jól.*
What's your name?	*Hogy hívják?* (pol)
	Mi a neved? (inf)
My name is ...	*A nevem ...*
I'm a tourist/	*Turista/diák vagyok.*
student.	
Are you married?	*Ön férjezett?* (to women)
	Ön nős? (to men)
Do you like Hungary?	*Tetszik önnek Magyarország?*
I like it very much.	*Nagyon tetszik.*
Where are you from?	*Honnan jön?*
I'm ...	*... vagyok.*
American	*amerikai*
British	*brit*

Signs

Bejárat	Entrance
Felvilágosítás	Information
Foglalt	Reserved/ Occupied
Hideg	Cold
Információ	Information
Kijárat	Exit
Meleg	Hot
Nyitva	Open
Szoba Kiadó	Rooms Available
Tilos	Prohibited
Tilos Belépni	No Entry
Tilos a Dohányzás	No Smoking
Vészkijárat	Emergency Exit
WC/Toalett	Toilets
Férfiak	Men
Nők	Women
Zárva	Closed

Australian	*ausztrál*
Canadian	*kanadai*
New Zealander	*új-zélandi*

How old are you?	*Hány éves vagy?* (inf)
	Hány éves? (pol)
I'm 25 years old.	*Húszonöt éves vagyok.*
Just a minute.	*Egy pillanat.*
May I?	*Lehet?* (general permission)
	Szabad? (eg, asking for a chair)
It's all right.	*Rendben van.*
No problem.	*Semmi baj.*

Essentials

Yes.	*Igen.*
No.	*Nem.*
Maybe.	*Talán.*
Please.	*Kérem.* (when asking for something)
	Tessék. (when inviting or offering something)
Thank you (very much).	*Köszönöm (szépen).*
Thanks.	*Köszi.* (inf)
You're welcome.	*Szívesen.*

Excuse me.	*Legyen szíves.* (for attention)
	Bocsánat. (apology)
I'm sorry.	*Sajnálom/Elnézést.*

Language Difficulties

Do you speak ...?	*Beszél ...?*
English	*angolul*
French	*franciául*
German	*németül*
Italian	*olaszul*

Does anyone here speak English?
  Van itt valaki, aki angolul beszél?
I understand.
  Értem.
I don't understand.
  Nem értem.
I don't speak Hungarian.
  Nem beszélek magyarul.
How do you say ... in Hungarian?
  Hogy mondják magyarul ...?
Please write it down.
  Kérem, írja le.
Would you please show me (on the map)?
  Meg tudná nekem mutatni (a térképen)?

Getting Around

What time does ... leave/arrive?	*Mikor indul/érkezik ...?*
the boat	*a hajó*
the bus	*az autóbusz*
the ferry	*a komp*
the train	*a vonat*
the tram	*a villamos*
the plane	*a repülőgép*

The train is ...	*A vonat ...*
delayed	*késik*
on time	*pontosan érkezik*
early	*korábban érkezik*
cancelled	*nem jár*

I want to go to ...	*... akarok menni.*
Esztergom	*Esztergomba*
Debrecen	*Debrecenbe*
Pécs	*Pécsre*

I want to book a seat to Prague.
  Szeretnék helyet foglalni Prágába.

How long does the trip take?
  Mennyi ideig tart az út?
Do I need to change trains?
  Át kell szállnom?
You must change trains.
  Át kell szállni.
You must change platforms.
  Másik vágányhoz kell menni.

train station	*vasútállomás/pályaudvar*
bus station	*autóbuszállomás*
platform	*vágány*
ticket	*jegy*
one-way ticket	*egy útra/csak oda*
return ticket	*oda-vissza/retúrjegy*
ticket office	*jegyiroda/pénztár*
timetable	*menetrend*
left-luggage	*csomagmegőrző*

The following may appear in bus and train timetables: *naponta* (daily), *hétköznap* (weekdays), *munkanap* (workdays), *szabadnap* (Saturday), *szabad és munkaszünetes nap* (Saturday and holidays), *munkaszünetes nap* (holidays), *iskolai nap* (school days), *szabadnap kivételével naponta* (daily except Saturday), *munkaszünetes nap kivételével naponta* (daily except holidays).

I'd like to hire a ...	*... szeretnék kölcsönözni.*
bicycle	*kerékpárt*
motorcycle	*motorkerékpárt*
horse	*lovat*

I'd like to hire a car.
  Autót szeretnék bérelni.
I'd like to hire a guide.
  Szeretnék kérni egy idegenvezetőt.
I have a visa/permit.
  Nekem van vízum/engedélyem.

Directions

How do I get to ...?	*Hogy jutok ...?*
Where is ...?	*Hol van ...?*
Is it near/far?	*Közel/messze van?*

What ... is this?	*Ez melyik ...?*
street/road	*utca/út*
street number	*házszám*

city district	*kerület*
town/city	*város*
village	*falu/község*
(Go) straight ahead.	*(Menyen) egyenesen előre.*
(Turn) left.	*(Forduljon) balra.*
(Turn) right.	*(Forduljon) jobbra.*
at the next traffic lights	*a közlekedési lámpánál*
at the next/second/ third corner	*következő/második/ harmadik saroknál*
up/down	*fent/lent*
behind/in front	*mögött/előtt*
opposite	*szemben*
here/there	*itt/ott*
everywhere	*mindenhol*
north	*észak*
south	*dél*
east	*kelet*
west	*nyugat*

Around Town

Where is ...?	*Hol van ...?*
a bank	*bank*
an exchange office	*pénzváltó*
the city centre	*a város központ/ a centrum*
the ... embassy	*a ... nagykövetség*
the hospital	*a kórház*
the market	*a piac*
the police station	*a rendőrkapitányság*
the post office	*a posta*
a public toilet	*nyilvános WC*
a restaurant	*étterem*
the tourist office	*az idegenforgalmi iroda*

bridge	*híd*
beach	*strand*
castle	*vár*
cathedral	*székesegyház*
church	*templom*
island	*sziget*
lake	*tó*
(main) square	*(fő) tér*
market	*piac*
palace	*palota*
mansion	*kastély*
ruin/ruins	*rom/romok*
synagogue	*zsinagóga*
tower	*torony*

Emergencies

Help!	*Segítség!*
It's an emergency!	*Sürgős!*
There's been an accident!	*Baleset történt!*
Call a doctor!	*Hívjon egy orvost!*
Call an ambulance!	*Hívja a mentőket!*
Call the police!	*Hívja a rendőrséget!*
I've been raped.	*Megerőszakoltak.*
I've been robbed.	*Kiraboltak.*
I'm lost.	*Eltévedtem.*
Go away!	*Menjen el!*
Where are the toilets?	*Hol van a WC?*

Accommodation

I'm looking for ...	*... keresek.*
a camping ground	*campinget/ kempinget*
a guesthouse	*fogadót*
a youth hostel	*ifjúsági szállót*
a hotel	*szállodát*
the manager	*a főnököt*
the owner	*a tulajdonost*
Do you have a ... available?	*Van szabad ...?*
bed	*ágyuk*
cheap room	*olcsó szobájuk*
single room	*egyágyas szobájuk*
double room	*kétágyas szobájuk*

What is the address?
Mi a cím?
How much is it per person/night?
Mennyibe kerül személyenként/ éjszakánként?
for one/two nights
egy/két éjszakára
Is service included?
A kiszolgálás benne van?
May I see the room?
Megnézhetem a szobát?
Where is the toilet/bathroom?
Hol van a WC/fürdőszoba?
It is very dirty/noisy/expensive.
Ez nagyon piskos/zajos/drága.
I'm/We're leaving.
El megyek/megyünk.

Do you have ...? | *Van ...?*
a clean sheet | *tiszta lepedő*
hot water | *meleg víz*
a key | *kulcs*
a shower | *zuhany*

Shopping

I'm looking for ... | *Keresem ...*
the chemist/ | *a patikát*
pharmacy |
clothing | *ruhát*
souvenirs | *emléktárgyat*

I'd like to buy this. | *Szeretném megvenni ezt.*
How much is it? | *Mennyibe kerül?*
It's too expensive. | *Ez túl drága.*
Can I look at it? | *Megnézhetem?*
I'm just looking. | *Csak nézegetek.*

Time & Dates

When? | *Mikor?*
At what time? | *Hány órakor?*
What time is it? | *Hány óra?*

It's ... o'clock. | *... óra van.*
1.15 | *negyed kettő*
1.30 | *fél kettő*
1.45 | *háromnegyed kettő*

in the morning | *reggel*
in the evening | *este*
today | *ma*
tonight | *ma este*
tomorrow | *holnap*
day after tomorrow | *holnapután*
yesterday | *tegnap*
all day | *egész nap*
every day | *minden nap*

Monday | *hétfő*
Tuesday | *kedd*
Wednesday | *szerda*
Thursday | *csütörtök*
Friday | *péntek*
Saturday | *szombat*
Sunday | *vasárnap*

January | *január*
February | *február*
March | *március*
April | *április*

May | *május*
June | *június*
July | *július*
August | *augusztus*
September | *szeptember*
October | *október*
November | *november*
December | *december*

Numbers

0 | *nulla*
1 | *egy*
2 | *kettő* (*két* before nouns)
3 | *három*
4 | *négy*
5 | *öt*
6 | *hat*
7 | *hét*
8 | *nyolc*
9 | *kilenc*
10 | *tíz*
11 | *tizenegy*
12 | *tizenkettő*
13 | *tizenhárom*
14 | *tizennégy*
15 | *tizenöt*
16 | *tizenhat*
17 | *tizenhét*
18 | *tizennyolc*
19 | *tizenkilenc*
20 | *húsz*
21 | *huszonegy*
22 | *huszonkettő*
30 | *harminc*
40 | *negyven*
50 | *ötven*
60 | *hatvan*
70 | *hetven*
80 | *nyolcvan*
90 | *kilencven*
100 | *száz*
101 | *százegy*
110 | *száztíz*
1000 | *ezer*

one million | *egy millió*

Health

I'm ... | *... vagyok.*
diabetic | *cukorbeteg*
epileptic | *epilepsziás*
asthmatic | *asztmás*

I'm allergic to ...	... allergiás vagyok.
penicillin	penicillinre
antibiotics	antibiotikumra

I've got diarrhoea.	Hasmenésem van.
I feel nauseous.	Hányingerem van.
antiseptic	fertőzésgátló
aspirin	aszpirin
condoms	óvszer/gumi
contraceptive	fogamzásgátló
insect repellent	rovarírtó
medicine	orvosság
suntan lotion	napozókrém
sunblock cream	fényvédőkrém
tampons	tampon

FOOD

restaurant	étterem/vendéglő
food stall	laci konyha or pecsenyesütő
grocery store	élelmiszer
delicatessen	csemege
market	piac
breakfast	reggeli
lunch	ebéd
dinner/supper	vacsora
the menu	az étlap
set/daily menu	napi menü

At the Restaurant

I'm hungry.	Éhes vagyok.
I'm thirsty.	Szomjas vagyok.
The menu, please.	Az étlapot, kérem.
I'd like today's menu, please.	Mai menüt, kérnék.
Is service included in the bill?	Az ár tartalmazza a kiszolgálást?
I'm a vegetarian.	Vegetáriánus vagyok.
I'd like some ...	Kérnék ...
Another ... please.	Még (egy) ..., kérek.
The bill, please.	A számlát, kérem/ Fizetek.

bread	kenyér
chicken	csirke
eggs	tojás
fish	hal
food	étel
fruit	gyümölcs
meat	hús
pepper	bors
pork	disznóhús
salt	só
soup	leves
sugar	cukor
vegetables	zöldség

hot/cold	meleg/hideg
with/without ice	jéggel/jég nélkül
with/without sugar	cukorral/cukor nélkül

DRINKS

| Cheers! | Egészségére! |

apple juice	almalé
apricot brandy	barackpálinka
bottle	üveg
cappuccino	tejes kávé
champagne/ sparkling wine	pezsgő
coffee	kávé
draught beer	csapolt sör
drinks list	itallap
glass of beer (.3L)	pohár sör
glass of wine	pohár bor
lager	világos sör
lemonade	limonádé
mineral water	ásvány víz
mug of beer (.5L)	korsó sör
orange juice	narancslé
pear brandy	körtepálinka
plum brandy	szilvapálinka
red wine	vörös bor
spritzer	fröccs
sweet wine	édes bor
white wine	fehér bor
wine	bor

Glossary

If you can't find the word you're looking for in the Glossary, try the previous Language section.

ÁEV – Állami Erdei Vasutak; State Forest Railways

ÁFA – Általános Forgalmi Adó; value-added tax (VAT)

Alföld – the Great Plain (same as *Nagyalföld* and *pustza*)

aszú – key ingredient in the preparation of Tokaj sweet wine

Ausgleich – German for 'reconciliation'; the Compromise of 1867

autóbusz – bus

áutóbuszállomás – bus station

Avars – a people of the Caucasus who invaded Europe in the 6th century

ÁVO – Államvédelmi Ostály; Rákosi's hated secret police in the early years of communism; later renamed ÁVH (Államvédelmi Hivatal)

bábolna – large breed of horse ridden by *csikósok* in the *puszta*

bal – left

bejárat – entrance

borozó – wine bar; any place serving wine

BKV – Budapesti Közlekedési Vállalat; Budapest Transport Company

bolhapiac – flea market

Bp – abbreviation for Budapest

búcsú – farewell; also, a church patronal festival

büfé – snack bar

centrum – town or city centre

Compromise of 1867 – agreement which created the dual monarchy of Austria-Hungary

Copf – a transitional architectural style between late baroque and neoclassicism (same as *Zopf*)

Csángó – group of ethnic Hungarians living in eastern Transylvania and Moldavia famed for their traditional music

csárda – a Hungarian-style inn or restaurant

csatorna – canal

csikós – cowboy from the *puszta*

csomagmegőrző – left-luggage office

cukrászda – cake shop or patisserie

D – map/compass abbreviation for *dél*

Dacia – Latin name for Romania and lands east of the Tisza River

db or **drb** – piece (measurement used in markets)

de – am; in the morning

dél – south

du – pm; in the afternoon/evening

É – map/compass abbreviation for *észak*

Eclectic – an art and architectural style popular in Hungary in the Romantic period, drawing from sources both indigenous and foreign

élelmiszer – grocery shop; convenience store

előszoba – vestibule or anteroom; one of three rooms in a traditional Hungarian cottage

em – abbreviation for *emelet*

emelet – floor or storey

erdő – forest

érkezés – arrivals

észak – north

eszpresszó – coffee shop, often also selling alcoholic drinks and snacks; strong, black coffee; same as *presszó*

étkezde – canteen with simple dishes

étterem – restaurant

falu – village

fasor – boulevard, avenue

felvilágosítás – information

fogas – pike-perch fish indigenous to Lake Balaton

főkapitányság – main police station

földszint – ground floor

folyó – river

forint – Hungary's monetary unit

főváros – main city or capital

fsz – abbreviation for *földszint*

Ft – abbreviation for forint (see also *HUF*)

gyógyfürdő – bath or spa
gyógyvíz – medicinal drinking water
gyűjtemény – collection
gyula – chief military commander of the early Magyar

hajdúk – Hungarian for *Heyducks*
hajó – boat
hajóállomás – ferry pier or landing
ház – house
hegy – hill, mountain
HÉV – Helyiérdekű Vasút; suburban commuter train in Budapest
Heyducks – drovers and outlaws from the *puszta* who fought as mercenaries against the Habsburgs
helyi autóbusz pályaudvar – local bus station
híd – bridge
HNTO – Hungarian National Tourism Office
hőforrás – thermal spring
honfoglalás – conquest of the Carpathian Basin by the Magyars in the late 9th century
HUF – international currency code for the Hungarian forint
Huns – a Mongol tribe that swept across Europe under Attila in the 5th century AD

Ibusz – Hungarian national network of travel agencies
ifjúsági szálló – youth hostel
illeték – duty or tax
indulás – departures

jobb – right

K – map/compass abbreviation for *kelet*
kamra – workshop or shed; one of three rooms in a traditional Hungarian cottage
kastély – manor house or mansion (see *vár*)
kb – abbreviation for *körülbelül*
kékfestő – cotton fabric dyed a rich indigo blue
kelet – east
kemping – camp site
képtár – picture gallery
kerület – city district
khas – towns of the Ottoman period under direct rule of the sultan
kijárat – exit
kincstár – treasury

Kiskörút – 'Little Ring Road' in Budapest
kocsma – pub or saloon
kolostor – monastery or cloister
komp – ferry
könyvesbolt – bookshop
könyvtár – library
kórház – hospital
körülbelül – approximately
körút – ring road
korzó – embankment or promenade
köz – alley, mews, lane
központ – centre
krt – abbreviation for *körút*
kúria – mansion or manor
kuruc – Hungarian mercenaries, partisans or insurrectionists who resisted the expansion of Habsburg rule in Hungary after the withdrawal of the Turks (late 17th and early 18th centuries)

lángos – deep-fried dough with toppings
lekvár – fruit jam
lépcső – stairs, steps
liget – park

Mahart – Magyar Hajózási Részvénytársaság; Hungarian passenger ferry company
Malév – Magyar Légiközlekedési Vállalat; Hungary's national airline
MÁV – Magyar Államvasutak; Hungarian State Railways
megye – county
menetrend – timetable
mihrab – prayer niche in mosque facing Mecca
MNB – Magyar Nemzeti Bank; National Bank of Hungary
Moorish Romantic – an art style popular in the decoration of 19th-century Hungarian synagogues
mozi – cinema
műemlék – memorial, monument
munkavállalási engedély – work permit

Nagyalföld – the Great Plain (same as the *Alföld* and *puszta*)
Nagykörút – 'Big Ring Road' in Budapest
Nonius – Hungarian breed of horse
Ny – map/compass abbreviation for *nyugat*
nyitva – open
nyugat – west

ó – abbreviation for *óra*
önkiszolgáló – self-service
óra – hour, o'clock
osztály – department
OTP – Országos Takarékpenztár; National Savings Bank
Ottoman Empire – the Turkish empire that took over from the Byzantine Empire when it captured Constantinople (Istanbul) in 1453, and expanded into southeastern Europe

pálinka – Hungarian fruit brandy
palota – palace
pályaudvar – train station
Pannonia – Roman name for the lands south and west of the Danube River
panzió – pension, guesthouse
part – embankment
patika – pharmacy
patyolat – laundry
pénztár – cashier
pénzváltó – exchange office
piac – market
pince – wine cellar
plébánia – rectory, parish house
polgármester – mayor
porta – type of farmhouse in Transdanubia
presszó – see *eszpresszó*
pu – abbreviation for *pályaudvar*
puli – Hungarian breed of sheepdog with shaggy coat
puszta – literally 'deserted'; other name for the Great Plain (see *Alföld* and *Nagyalföld*)
puttony – the number of 'butts' of sweet *aszú* essence added to other base wines in making Tokaj wine

racka – sheep on the Great Plain with distinctive corkscrew horns
rakpart – quay, embankment
rendőrkapitányság – police station
repülőtér – airport
Romany – the language and culture of the Roma (Gypsy) people

Secessionism – art and architectural style similar to Art Nouveau
sedile (pl sedilia) – medieval stone niche with seats
sétány – walkway, promenade

shahoof – distinctive sweep-pole well found only on the Great Plain (Hungarian: *gémeskút*)
skanzen – open-air museum displaying village architecture
söröző – beer bar or pub
stb – abbreviation of *és a többi* (and so on) equivalent to English 'etc'
strand – grassy 'beach' near a river or lake
sugárút – avenue
szálló – hotel
szálloda – same as *szálló*
székesegyház – cathedral
sziget – island
színház – theatre
szoba kiadó – room for rent
szűr – long embroidered felt cloak or cape traditionally worn by Hungarian shepherds

Tanácsköztársaság – the 1919 Communist Republic of Councils under Béla Kun
táncház – folk music and dance workshop
tanya – homestead or ranch
tartózkodási engedély – residence permit
távolsági autóbusz pályaudvar – long-distance bus station
templom – church
tér – town or market square
tere – genitive form of *tér* as in Hősök tere (Heroes' Square)
tilos – prohibited, forbidden
tista szoba – parlour; one of three rooms in a traditional Hungarian cottage
tó – lake
toalett – toilet
Trianon Treaty – 1920 treaty imposed on Hungary by the victorious Allies, which reduced the country to one-third of its former size
Triple Alliance – 1882–1914 alliance between Germany, Austria-Hungary and Italy – not to be confused with the WWI Allies (members of the *Triple Entente* and their supporters)
Triple Entente – agreement among Britain, France and Russia, intended as a counter-balance to the *Triple Alliance*, lasting until the Russian Revolution of 1917
turul – eagle-like totem of the ancient Magyars and now a national symbol

u – abbreviation for *utca*
udvar – court
ünnep – public holiday
úszoda – swimming pool
út – road
utca – street
utcája – genitive form of *utca* as in Ferencesek utcája (Street of the Franciscans)
útja – genitive form of *út* as in Mártíroká útja (Street of the Martyrs)
üzlet – shop

va – abbreviation for *vasútállomás*
vágány – train station platform
vár – castle

város – city
városház, városháza – town hall
vasútállomás – train station
vendéglő – a type of restaurant
vm – abbreviations for *vasútállomás*
Volán – Steering Wheel; Hungarian bus company
vonat – train

WC – toilet (see *toalett*)

zárva – closed
Zimmer frei – German for 'room for rent'
Zopf – German and more commonly used word for *Copf*

Alternative Place Names

(C) Croatian, (E) English, (G) German, (H) Hungarian, (R) Romanian, (S) Serbian, (Slk) Slovak, (Slo) Slovene, (U) Ukrainian

Alba Iulia (R) – Gyula Fehérvár (H), Karlsburg/Weissenburg (G)

Baia Mare (R) – Nagybánya (H)
Balaton (H) – Plattensee (G)
Belgrade (E) – Beograd (S), Nándorfehérvár (H)
Berehove (U) – Beregszász (H)
Braşov (R) – Brassó (H), Kronstadt (G)
Bratislava (Slk) – Pozsony (H), Pressburg (G)

Carei (R) – Nagykároly (H)
Cluj-Napoca (R) – Kolozsvár (H), Klausenburg (G)

Danube (E) – Duna (H), Donau (G)
Danube Bend (E) – Dunakanyar (H), Donauknie (G)
Debrecen (H) – Debrezin (G)

Eger (H) – Erlau (G)
Eisenstadt (G) – Kismárton (H)
Esztergom (H) – Gran (G)

Great Plain (E) – Nagyalföld, Alföld, Puszta (H)
Győr (H) – Raab (G)

Hungary (E) – Magyarország (H), Ungarn (G)

Kisalföld (H) – Little Plain (E)
Komárom (H) – Komárno (Slk)
Košice (Slk) – Kassa (H), Kaschau (G)
Kőszeg (H) – Güns (G)
Lendava (Slo) – Lendva (H)
Lučenec (Slk) – Losonc (H)

Mattersburg (G) – Nagymárton (H)
Mukačevo (U) – Munkács (H)
Murska Sobota (Slo) – Muraszombat (H)

Northern Uplands (E) – Északi Felföld (H)

Oradea (R) – Nagyvárad (H), Grosswardein (G)
Osijek (C) – Eszék (H)

Pécs (H) – Fünfkirchen (G)

Rožnava (Slk) – Rozsnyó (H)

Satu Mare (R) – Szatmárnémeti (H)
Senta (S) – Zenta (H)
Sibiu (R) – Nagyszében (H), Hermannstadt (G)
Sic (R) – Szék (H)
Sighişoara (R) – Szegesvár (H), Schässburg (G)
Sopron (H) – Ödenburg (G)
Štúrovo (Slk) – Párkány (H)
Subotica (S) – Szabadka (H)
Szeged (H) – Segedin (G)
Székesfehérvár (H) – Stuhlweissenburg (G)
Szombathely (H) – Steinamanger (G)

Tata (H) – Totis (G)
Timişoara (R) – Temesvár (H)
Tirgu Mureş (R) – Marosvásárhely (H)
Transdanubia (E) – Dunántúl (H)
Transylvania (R) – Erdély (H), Siebenbürgen (G)
Trnava (Slk) – Nagyszombat (H)

Užgorod (U) – Ungvár (H)

Vác (H) – Wartzen (G)
Vienna (E) – Wien (G), Bécs (H)
Villány (H) – Wieland (G)
Villánykövesd (H) – Growisch (G)

Wiener Neustadt (G) – Bécsújhely (H)

LONELY PLANET

ON THE ROAD

Travel Guides explore cities, regions and countries, and supply information on transport, restaurants and accommodation, covering all budgets. They come with reliable, easy-to-use maps, practical advice, cultural and historical facts and a rundown on attractions both on and off the beaten track. There are over 200 titles in this classic series, covering nearly every country in the world.

 Lonely Planet Upgrades extend the shelf life of existing travel guides by detailing any changes that may affect travel in a region since a book has been published. Upgrades can be downloaded for free from **www.lonelyplanet.com/upgrades**

For travellers with more time than money, **Shoestring** guides offer dependable, first-hand information with hundreds of detailed maps, plus insider tips for stretching money as far as possible. Covering entire continents in most cases, the six-volume shoestring guides are known around the world as 'backpackers bibles'.

For the discerning short-term visitor, **Condensed** guides highlight the best a destination has to offer in a full-colour, pocket-sized format designed for quick access. They include everything from top sights and walking tours to opinionated reviews of where to eat, stay, shop and have fun.

CitySync lets travellers use their Palm™ or Visor™ hand-held computers to guide them through a city with handy tips on transport, history, cultural life, major sights, and shopping and entertainment options. It can also quickly search and sort hundreds of reviews of hotels, restaurants and attractions, and pinpoint their location on scrollable street maps. CitySync can be downloaded from **www.citysync.com**

MAPS & ATLASES

Lonely Planet's **City Maps** feature downtown and metropolitan maps, as well as transit routes and walking tours. The maps come complete with an index of streets, a listing of sights and a plastic coat for extra durability.

Road Atlases are an essential navigation tool for serious travellers. Cross-referenced with the guidebooks, they also feature distance and climate charts and a complete site index.

LONELY PLANET

ESSENTIALS

Read This First books help new travellers to hit the road with confidence. These invaluable predeparture guides give step-by-step advice on preparing for a trip, budgeting, arranging a visa, planning an itinerary and staying safe while still getting off the beaten track.

Healthy Travel pocket guides offer a regional rundown on disease hot spots and practical advice on predeparture health measures, staying well on the road and what to do in emergencies. The guides come with a user-friendly design and helpful diagrams and tables.

Lonely Planet's **Phrasebooks** cover the essential words and phrases travellers need when they're strangers in a strange land. They come in a pocket-sized format with colour tabs for quick reference, extensive vocabulary lists, easy-to-follow pronunciation keys and two-way dictionaries.

Miffed by blurry photos of the Taj Mahal? Tired of the classic 'top of the head cut off' shot? **Travel Photography: A Guide to Taking Better Pictures** will help you turn ordinary holiday snaps into striking images and give you the know-how to capture every scene, from frenetic festivals to peaceful beach sunrises.

Lonely Planet's **Travel Journal** is a lightweight but sturdy travel diary for jotting down all those on-the-road observations and significant travel moments. It comes with a handy time-zone wheel, a world map and useful travel information.

Lonely Planet's eKno is an all-in-one communication service developed especially for travellers. It offers low-cost international calls and free email and voicemail so that you can keep in touch while on the road. Check it out on **www.ekno.lonelyplanet.com**

FOOD & RESTAURANT GUIDES

Lonely Planet's **Out to Eat** guides recommend the brightest and best places to eat and drink in top international cities. These gourmet companions are arranged by neighbourhood, packed with dependable maps, garnished with scene-setting photos and served with quirky features.

For people who live to eat, drink and travel, **World Food** guides explore the culinary culture of each country. Entertaining and adventurous, each guide is packed with detail on staples and specialities, regional cuisine and local markets, as well as sumptuous recipes, comprehensive culinary dictionaries and lavish photos good enough to eat.

OUTDOOR GUIDES

For those who believe the best way to see the world is on foot, Lonely Planet's **Walking Guides** detail everything from family strolls to difficult treks, with 'when to go and how to do it' advice supplemented by reliable maps and essential travel information.

Cycling Guides map a destination's best bike tours, long and short, in day-by-day detail. They contain all the information a cyclist needs, including advice on bike maintenance, places to eat and stay, innovative maps with detailed cues to the rides, and elevation charts.

The **Watching Wildlife** series is perfect for travellers who want authoritative information but don't want to tote a heavy field guide. Packed with advice on where, when and how to view a region's wildlife, each title features photos of over 300 species and contains engaging comments on the local flora and fauna.

With underwater colour photos throughout, **Pisces Books** explore the world's best diving and snorkelling areas. Each book contains listings of diving services and dive resorts, detailed information on depth, visibility and difficulty of dives, and a roundup of the marine life you're likely to see through your mask.

OFF THE ROAD

Journeys, the travel literature series written by renowned travel authors, capture the spirit of a place or illuminate a culture with a journalist's attention to detail and a novelist's flair for words. These are tales to soak up while you're actually on the road or dip into as an at-home armchair indulgence.

The range of lavishly illustrated **Pictorial** books is just the ticket for both travellers and dreamers. Off-beat tales and vivid photographs bring the adventure of travel to your doorstep long before the journey begins and long after it is over.

Lonely Planet **Videos** encourage the same independent, tough-minded approach as the guidebooks. Currently airing throughout the world, this award-winning series features innovative footage and an original soundtrack.

Yes, we know, work is tough, so do a little bit of deskside dreaming with the spiral-bound Lonely Planet **Diary** or a Lonely Planet **Wall Calendar**, filled with great photos from around the world.

TRAVELLERS NETWORK

Lonely Planet Online. Lonely Planet's award-winning Web site has insider information on hundreds of destinations, from Amsterdam to Zimbabwe, complete with interactive maps and relevant links. The site also offers the latest travel news, recent reports from travellers on the road, guidebook upgrades, a travel links site, an online book-buying option and a lively travellers bulletin board. It can be viewed at **www.lonelyplanet.com** or AOL keyword: lp.

Planet Talk is a quarterly print newsletter, full of gossip, advice, anecdotes and author articles. It provides an antidote to the being-at-home blues and lets you plan and dream for the next trip. Contact the nearest Lonely Planet office for your free copy.

Comet, the free Lonely Planet newsletter, comes via email once a month. It's loaded with travel news, advice, dispatches from authors, travel competitions and letters from readers. To subscribe, click on the Comet subscription link on the front page of the Web site.

Lonely Planet Guides by Region

Lonely Planet is known worldwide for publishing practical, reliable and no-nonsense travel information in our guides and on our Web site. The Lonely Planet list covers just about every accessible part of the world. Currently there are 16 series: Travel guides, Shoestring guides, Condensed guides, Phrasebooks, Read This First, Healthy Travel, Walking guides, Cycling guides, Watching Wildlife guides, Pisces Diving & Snorkeling guides, City Maps, Road Atlases, Out to Eat, World Food, Journeys travel literature and Pictorials.

AFRICA Africa on a shoestring • Botswana • Cairo • Cairo City Map • Cape Town • Cape Town City Map • East Africa • Egypt • Egyptian Arabic phrasebook • Ethiopia, Eritrea & Djibouti • Ethiopian Amharic phrasebook • The Gambia & Senegal • Healthy Travel Africa • Kenya • Malawi • Morocco • Moroccan Arabic phrasebook • Mozambique • Namibia • Read This First: Africa • South Africa, Lesotho & Swaziland • Southern Africa • Southern Africa Road Atlas • Swahili phrasebook • Tanzania, Zanzibar & Pemba • Trekking in East Africa • Tunisia • Watching Wildlife East Africa • Watching Wildlife Southern Africa • West Africa • World Food Morocco • Zambia • Zimbabwe, Botswana & Namibia
Travel Literature: Mali Blues: Traveling to an African Beat • The Rainbird: A Central African Journey • Songs to an African Sunset: A Zimbabwean Story

AUSTRALIA & THE PACIFIC Aboriginal Australia & the Torres Strait Islands •Auckland • Australia • Australian phrasebook • Australia Road Atlas • Cycling Australia • Cycling New Zealand • Fiji • Fijian phrasebook • Healthy Travel Australia, NZ & the Pacific • Islands of Australia's Great Barrier Reef • Melbourne • Melbourne City Map • Micronesia • New Caledonia • New South Wales • New Zealand • Northern Territory • Outback Australia • Out to Eat – Melbourne • Out to Eat – Sydney • Papua New Guinea • Pidgin phrasebook • Queensland • Rarotonga & the Cook Islands • Samoa • Solomon Islands • South Australia • South Pacific • South Pacific phrasebook • Sydney • Sydney City Map • Sydney Condensed • Tahiti & French Polynesia • Tasmania • Tonga • Tramping in New Zealand • Vanuatu • Victoria • Walking in Australia • Watching Wildlife Australia • Western Australia
Travel Literature: Islands in the Clouds: Travels in the Highlands of New Guinea • Kiwi Tracks: A New Zealand Journey • Sean & David's Long Drive

CENTRAL AMERICA & THE CARIBBEAN Bahamas, Turks & Caicos • Baja California • Belize, Guatemala & Yucatán • Bermuda • Central America on a shoestring • Costa Rica • Costa Rica Spanish phrasebook • Cuba • Cycling Cuba • Dominican Republic & Haiti • Eastern Caribbean • Guatemala • Havana • Healthy Travel Central & South America • Jamaica • Mexico • Mexico City • Panama • Puerto Rico • Read This First: Central & South America • Virgin Islands • World Food Caribbean • World Food Mexico • Yucatán
Travel Literature: Green Dreams: Travels in Central America

EUROPE Amsterdam • Amsterdam City Map • Amsterdam Condensed • Andalucía • Athens • Austria • Baltic States phrasebook • Barcelona • Barcelona City Map • Belgium & Luxembourg • Berlin • Berlin City Map • Britain • British phrasebook • Brussels, Bruges & Antwerp • Brussels City Map • Budapest • Budapest City Map • Canary Islands • Catalunya & the Costa Brava • Central Europe • Central Europe phrasebook • Copenhagen • Corfu & the Ionians • Corsica • Crete • Crete Condensed • Croatia • Cycling Britain • Cycling France • Cyprus • Czech & Slovak Republics • Czech phrasebook • Denmark • Dublin • Dublin City Map • Dublin Condensed • Eastern Europe • Eastern Europe phrasebook • Edinburgh • Edinburgh City Map • England • Estonia, Latvia & Lithuania • Europe on a shoestring • Europe phrasebook • Finland • Florence • Florence City Map • France • Frankfurt City Map • Frankfurt Condensed • French phrasebook • Georgia, Armenia & Azerbaijan • Germany • German phrasebook • Greece • Greek Islands • Greek phrasebook • Hungary • Iceland, Greenland & the Faroe Islands • Ireland • Italian phrasebook • Italy • Kraków • Lisbon • The Loire • London • London City Map • London Condensed • Madrid • Madrid City Map • Malta • Mediterranean Europe • Milan, Turin & Genoa • Moscow • Munich • Netherlands • Normandy • Norway • Out to Eat – London • Out to Eat – Paris • Paris • Paris City Map • Paris Condensed • Poland • Polish phrasebook • Portugal • Portuguese phrasebook • Prague • Prague City Map • Provence & the Côte d'Azur • Read This First: Europe • Rhodes & the Dodecanese • Romania & Moldova • Rome • Rome City Map • Rome Condensed • Russia, Ukraine & Belarus • Russian phrasebook • Scandinavian & Baltic Europe • Scandinavian phrasebook • Scotland • Sicily • Slovenia • South-West France • Spain • Spanish phrasebook • Stockholm • St Petersburg • St Petersburg City Map • Sweden • Switzerland • Tuscany • Ukrainian phrasebook • Venice • Vienna • Wales • Walking in Britain • Walking in France • Walking in Ireland • Walking in Italy • Walking in Scotland • Walking in Spain • Walking in Switzerland • Western Europe • World Food France • World Food Greece • World Food Ireland • World Food Italy • World Food Spain **Travel Literature:** After Yugoslavia • Love and War in the Apennines • The Olive Grove: Travels in Greece • On the Shores of the Mediterranean • Round Ireland in Low Gear • A Small Place in Italy

Lonely Planet Mail Order

Lonely Planet products are distributed worldwide. They are also available by mail order from Lonely Planet, so if you have difficulty finding a title please write to us. North and South American residents should write to 150 Linden St, Oakland, CA 94607, USA; European and African residents should write to 72-82 Rosebery Ave, London, EC1R 4RW, UK; and residents of other countries to Locked Bag 1, Footscray, Victoria 3011, Australia.

INDIAN SUBCONTINENT & THE INDIAN OCEAN Bangladesh • Bengali phrasebook • Bhutan • Delhi • Goa • Healthy Travel Asia & India • Hindi & Urdu phrasebook • India • India & Bangladesh City Map • Indian Himalaya • Karakoram Highway • Kathmandu City Map • Kerala • Madagascar • Maldives • Mauritius, Réunion & Seychelles • Mumbai (Bombay) • Nepal • Nepali phrasebook • North India • Pakistan • Rajasthan • Read This First: Asia & India • South India • Sri Lanka • Sri Lanka phrasebook • Tibet • Tibetan phrasebook • Trekking in the Indian Himalaya • Trekking in the Karakoram & Hindukush • Trekking in the Nepal Himalaya • World Food India **Travel Literature**: The Age of Kali: Indian Travels and Encounters • Hello Goodnight: A Life of Goa • In Rajasthan • Maverick in Madagascar • A Season in Heaven: True Tales from the Road to Kathmandu • Shopping for Buddhas • A Short Walk in the Hindu Kush • Slowly Down the Ganges

MIDDLE EAST & CENTRAL ASIA Bahrain, Kuwait & Qatar • Central Asia • Central Asia phrasebook • Dubai • Farsi (Persian) phrasebook • Hebrew phrasebook • Iran • Israel & the Palestinian Territories • Istanbul • Istanbul City Map • Istanbul to Cairo • Istanbul to Kathmandu • Jerusalem • Jerusalem City Map • Jordan • Lebanon • Middle East • Oman & the United Arab Emirates • Syria • Turkey • Turkish phrasebook • World Food Turkey • Yemen **Travel Literature**: Black on Black: Iran Revisited • Breaking Ranks: Turbulent Travels in the Promised Land • The Gates of Damascus • Kingdom of the Film Stars: Journey into Jordan

NORTH AMERICA Alaska • Boston • Boston City Map • Boston Condensed • British Columbia • California & Nevada • California Condensed • Canada • Chicago • Chicago City Map • Chicago Condensed • Florida • Georgia & the Carolinas • Great Lakes • Hawaii • Hiking in Alaska • Hiking in the USA • Honolulu & Oahu City Map • Las Vegas • Los Angeles • Los Angeles City Map • Louisiana & the Deep South • Miami • Miami City Map • Montreal • New England • New Orleans • New Orleans City Map • New York City • New York City Map • New York City Condensed • New York, New Jersey & Pennsylvania • Oahu • Out to Eat – San Francisco • Pacific Northwest • Rocky Mountains • San Diego & Tijuana • San Francisco • San Francisco City Map • Seattle • Seattle City Map • Southwest • Texas • Toronto • USA • USA phrasebook • Vancouver • Vancouver City Map • Virginia & the Capital Region • Washington, DC • Washington, DC City Map • World Food New Orleans **Travel Literature**: Caught Inside: A Surfer's Year on the California Coast • Drive Thru America

NORTH-EAST ASIA Beijing • Beijing City Map • Cantonese phrasebook • China • Hiking in Japan • Hong Kong & Macau • Hong Kong City Map • Hong Kong Condensed • Japan • Japanese phrasebook • Korea • Korean phrasebook • Kyoto • Mandarin phrasebook • Mongolia • Mongolian phrasebook • Seoul • Shanghai • South-West China • Taiwan • Tokyo • Tokyo Condensed • World Food Hong Kong • World Food Japan **Travel Literature**: In Xanadu: A Quest • Lost Japan

SOUTH AMERICA Argentina, Uruguay & Paraguay • Bolivia • Brazil • Brazilian phrasebook • Buenos Aires • Buenos Aires City Map • Chile & Easter Island • Colombia • Ecuador & the Galapagos Islands • Healthy Travel Central & South America • Latin American Spanish phrasebook • Peru • Quechua phrasebook • Read This First: Central & South America • Rio de Janeiro • Rio de Janeiro City Map • Santiago de Chile • South America on a shoestring • Trekking in the Patagonian Andes • Venezuela **Travel Literature**: Full Circle: A South American Journey

SOUTH-EAST ASIA Bali & Lombok • Bangkok • Bangkok City Map • Burmese phrasebook • Cambodia • Cycling Vietnam, Laos & Cambodia • East Timor phrasebook • Hanoi • Healthy Travel Asia & India • Hill Tribes phrasebook • Ho Chi Minh City (Saigon) • Indonesia • Indonesian phrasebook • Indonesia's Eastern Islands • Java • Lao phrasebook • Laos • Malay phrasebook • Malaysia, Singapore & Brunei • Myanmar (Burma) • Philippines • Pilipino (Tagalog) phrasebook • Read This First: Asia & India • Singapore • Singapore City Map • South-East Asia on a shoestring • South-East Asia phrasebook • Thailand • Thailand's Islands & Beaches • Thailand, Vietnam, Laos & Cambodia Road Atlas • Thai phrasebook • Vietnam • Vietnamese phrasebook • World Food Indonesia • World Food Thailand • World Food Vietnam

ALSO AVAILABLE: Antarctica • The Arctic • The Blue Man: Tales of Travel, Love and Coffee • Brief Encounters: Stories of Love, Sex & Travel • Buddhist Stupas in Asia: The Shape of Perfection • Chasing Rickshaws • The Last Grain Race • Lonely Planet ... On the Edge: Adventurous Escapades from Around the World • Lonely Planet Unpacked • Lonely Planet Unpacked Again • Not the Only Planet: Science Fiction Travel Stories • Ports of Call: A Journey by Sea • Sacred India • Travel Photography: A Guide to Taking Better Pictures • Travel with Children • Tuvalu: Portrait of an Island Nation

Index

Text

Bold indicates maps.

Boxed Text

Places to Stay

Places to Eat

MARTIN MOOS

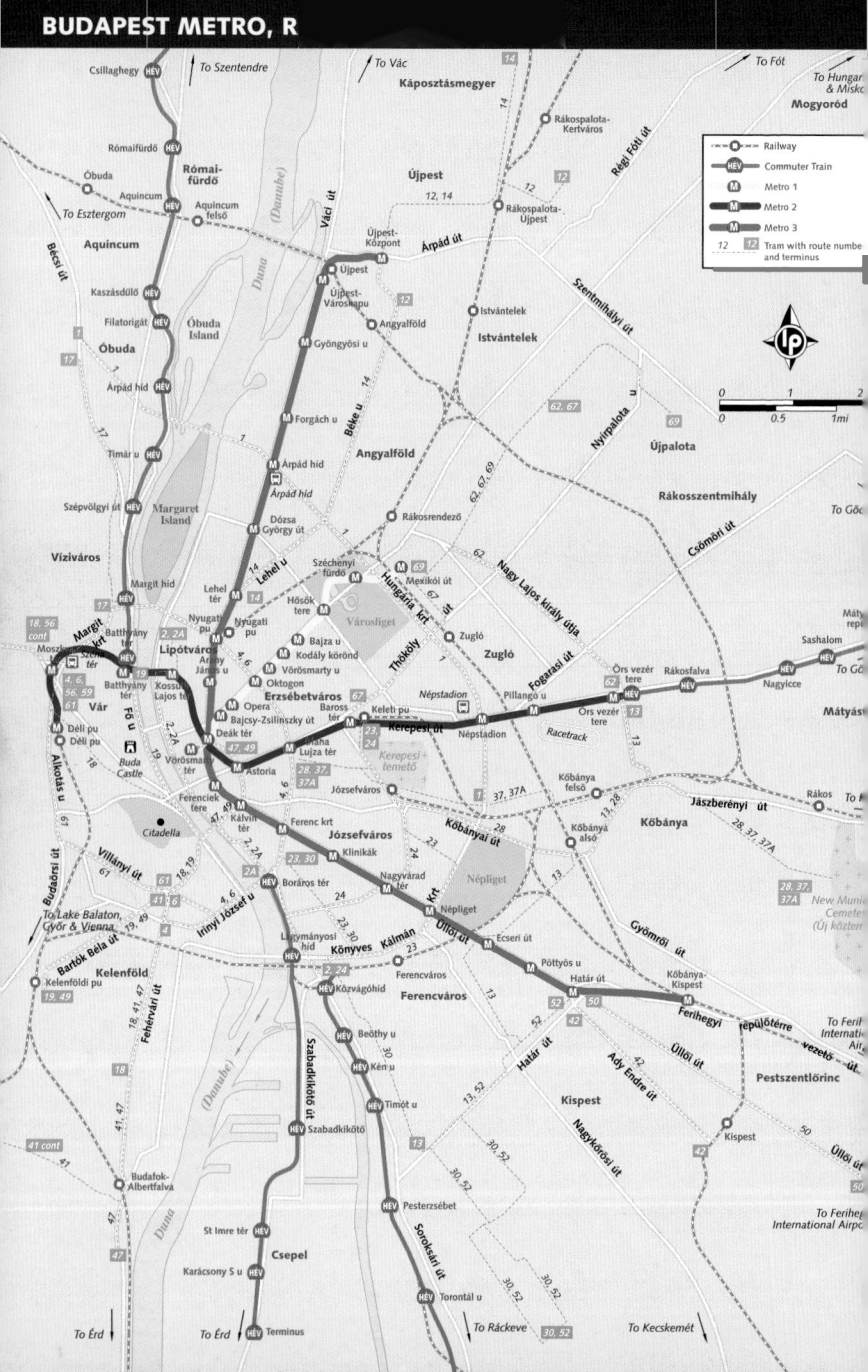

BUDAPEST METRO, R

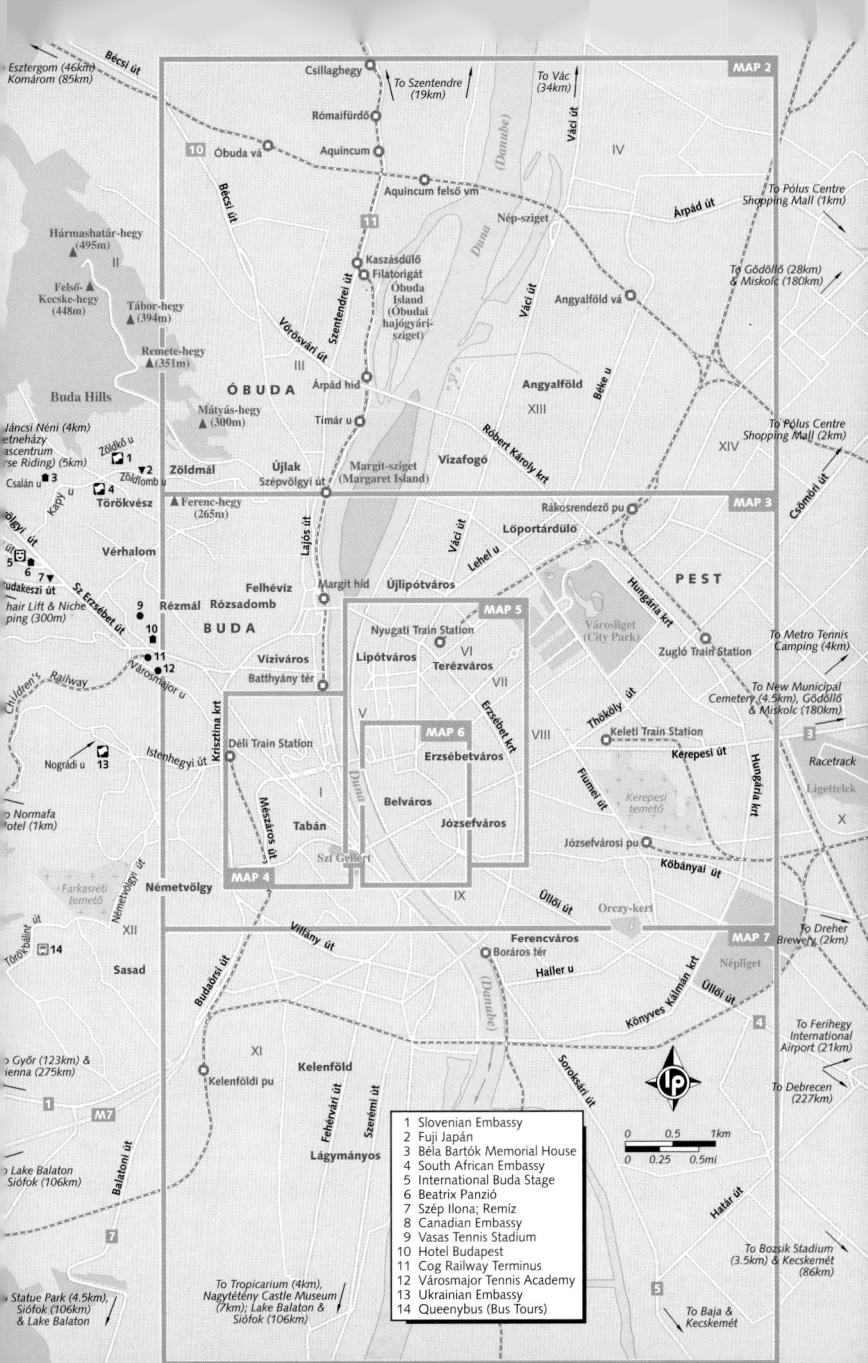

MAP 2
MAP 3
MAP 5
MAP 6
MAP 4
MAP 7

To Esztergom (46km);
Komárom (85km)

Bécsi út

Csillaghegy

To Szentendre (19km)

To Vác (34km)

Váci út

IV

Rómaifürdő

Óbuda vá

10

Aquincum

Bécsi út

Aquincum felső vm

Nép-sziget

To Pólus Centre Shopping Mall (1km)

Árpád út

Hármashatár-hegy
(495m)

II

Felső-
Kecske-hegy
(448m)

Tábor-hegy
(394m)

Remete-hegy
(351m)

Vörösvári út

Szentendrei út

11

Kaszásdűlő

Filatorigát

Óbuda
Island
(Óbudai
hajógyári-
sziget)

Duna

To Gödöllő (28km)
& Miskolc (180km)

Váci út

Angyalföld vá

Buda Hills

III

Árpád híd

Timár u

Mátyás-hegy
(300m)

Béke u

Angyalföld

XIII

Róbert Károly krt

ÓBUDA

Jánosi Néni (4km)
etneházy
ascentrum
rse Riding) (5km)

Zöldkő u

1

Csalán u

3

Kepy u

2

Zöldlomb u

Zöldmál

Törökvész

Ferenc-hegy
(265m)

Újlak

Szépvölgyi út

Lajos út

Margit-sziget
(Margaret Island)

Vizafogó

Vizafogó

Rákosrendező pu

Lóportárdülő

PEST

Csömöri út

XIV

To Pólus Centre
Shopping Mall (2km)

5

6 7

Budakeszi út

Sz Erzsébet út

Vérhalom

Felhéviz

Rózsadomb

Margit híd

Újlipótváros

Váci út

Lehel út

Hungária krt

Rézmál

9

10

BUDA

11

12

Vízíváros

Batthyány tér

Nyugati Train Station

Lipótváros

VI

Terézváros

VII

Erzsébet krt

Városliget
(City Park)

Zugló Train Station

To Metro Tennis
Camping (4km)

hair Lift & Niche
ping (300m)

Children's

Railway

Városmajor u

Istenhegyi út

Krisztina krt

Déli Train Station

V

MAP 6

Erzsébetváros

Thököly út

To New Municipal
Cemetery (4.5km), Gödöllő
& Miskolc (180km)

Keleti Train Station

Kerepesi út

3

Racetrack

Nógrádi u

13

Mészáros u

I

Tabán

Duna

Belváros

Józsefváros

Kerepesi
temető

Fiumei út

Hungária krt

Ligettelek

X

To Normafa
otel (1km)

Farkasréti
temető

XII

Némethegyi út

Némethegy

Szt Gellért

IX

Józsefvárosi pu

Kőbányai út

Üllői út

Orczy-kert

14

Törökbálint út

Sasad

Budaörsi út

Villány út

Ferencváros

Boráros tér

Haller u

Könyves Kálmán krt

Üllői út

Népliget

To Dreher
Brewery (2km)

4

To Ferihegy
International
Airport (21km)

o Győr (123km) &
Vienna (275km)

1

M7

Balaton út

XI

Kelenföld

Kelenföldi pu

Felhévári út

Soroksári út

Sorkári út

To Debrecen
(227km)

0   0.5   1km
0 0.25 0.5mi

To Lake Balaton
Siófok (106km)

7

Lágymányos

1 Slovenian Embassy
2 Fuji Japán
3 Béla Bartók Memorial House
4 South African Embassy
5 International Buda Stage
6 Beatrix Panzió
7 Szép Ilona; Remíz
8 Canadian Embassy
9 Vasas Tennis Stadium
10 Hotel Budapest
11 Cog Railway Terminus
12 Városmajor Tennis Academy
13 Ukrainian Embassy
14 Queenybus (Bus Tours)

IP

Határ út

To Bozsik Stadium
(3.5km) & Kecskemét
(86km)

Statue Park (4.5km),
Siófok (106km)
& Lake Balaton

To Tropicarium (4km),
Nagytétény Castle Museum
(7km); Lake Balaton &
Siófok (106km)

5

To Baja &
Kecskemét

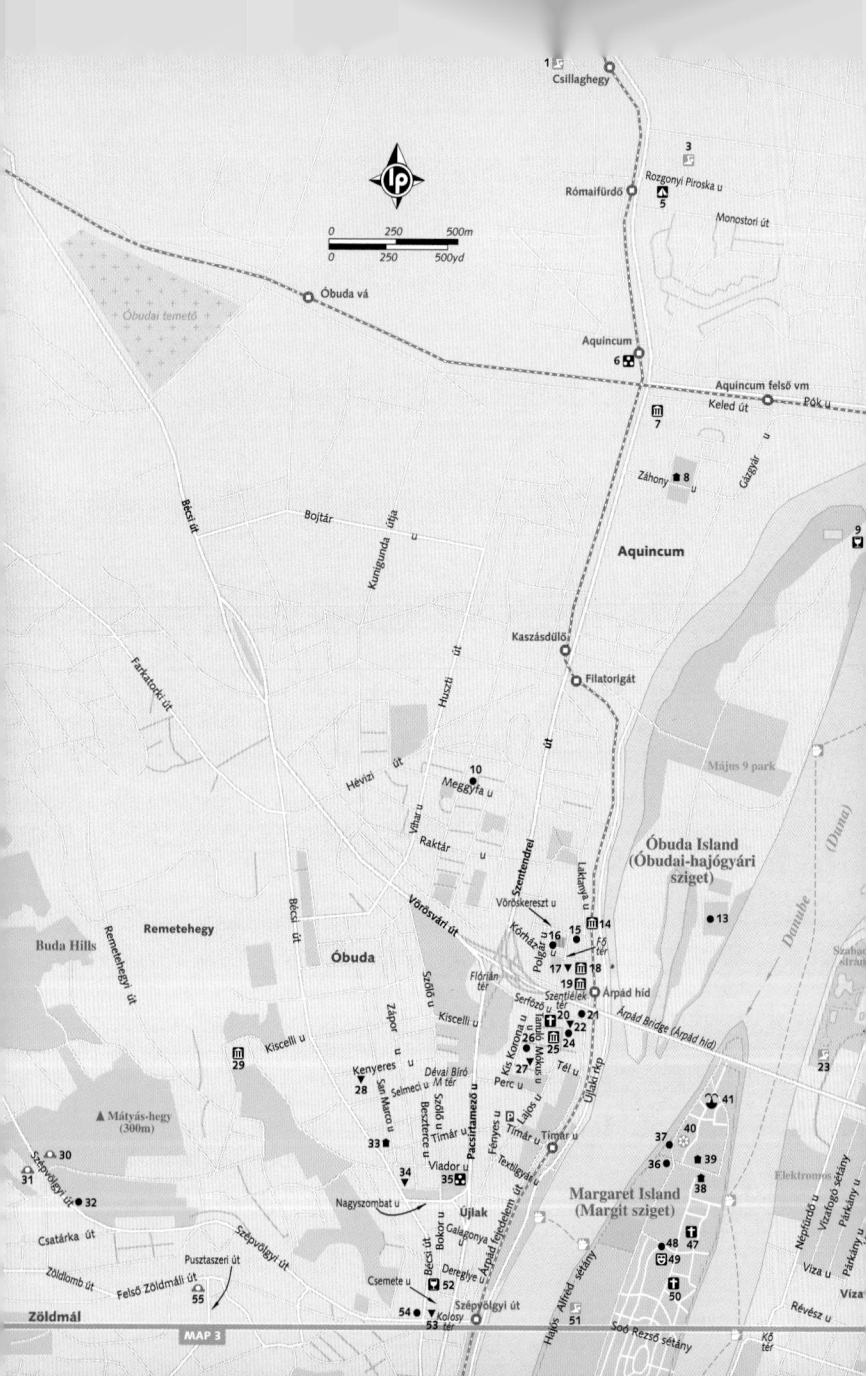

MAP 3

Csillaghegy 1

3

Rozgonyi Piroska u
Rómaifürdő
5
Monostori út

Óbuda vá

Óbudai temető

Aquincum
6

Aquincum felső vm
Keled út
Pók u
7

Záhony u 8

9

Aquincum

Bojtár útja

Kunigunda útja

Huszti út

Bécsi út

Kaszásdűlő

Filatorigát

Május 9 park

Farkastorki út

Hévizi út

10
Meggyfa u

Raktár u

Vihar u

Óbuda Island
(Óbudai-hajógyári
sziget)

Szentendrei út

Buda Hills

Remetehegy

Remetehegy út

Bécsi út

Óbuda

Vörösvári út

Vöröskereszt u
15
16
Kórház u 17
19
14
Fő tér
18

13

Danube (Duna)

Szabad
strå

Kiscelli u

Zápor u

Kiscelli u

Flórián tér

Serfőző u
Szentlélek tér
20
22
23

Árpád híd
Árpád Bridge (Árpád híd)

29

Kenyeres u
28

Dévai Bíró
M tér

Kis Korona u
26
25
27
24
Tél u

Újlaki rkp

Mátyás-hegy
(300m)

San Marco u

Beszterce u

Szőlő u

Pacsirtamező u

Perc u

Lajos u

Margaret Island
(Margit sziget)

41

37
40
36
39
38

Elektromos sétány

Népfürdő u

Vízafogó sétány

Patkány u

33

Timár u
Fényes u

Timár u

34
Viador u
35

Nagyszombat u

Textilgyár u

Szépvölgyi út
30
31
32

Csatárka út

Szépvölgyi út

Zöldlomb út

Felső Zöldmáli út

Pusztaszeri út

Kolosy
tér
52
Csemete u
54 53

Újlak

Bokor u
Galagonya u

Bécsi út

Árpád fejedelem útja

Deregnye u

Szépvölgyi út

48 47
49

50

51

Hajós Alfréd sétány

Sód Rezső sétány

Kő tér

Viza u

Révész u

Patkány u

Zöldmál

0   250   500m
0   250   500yd

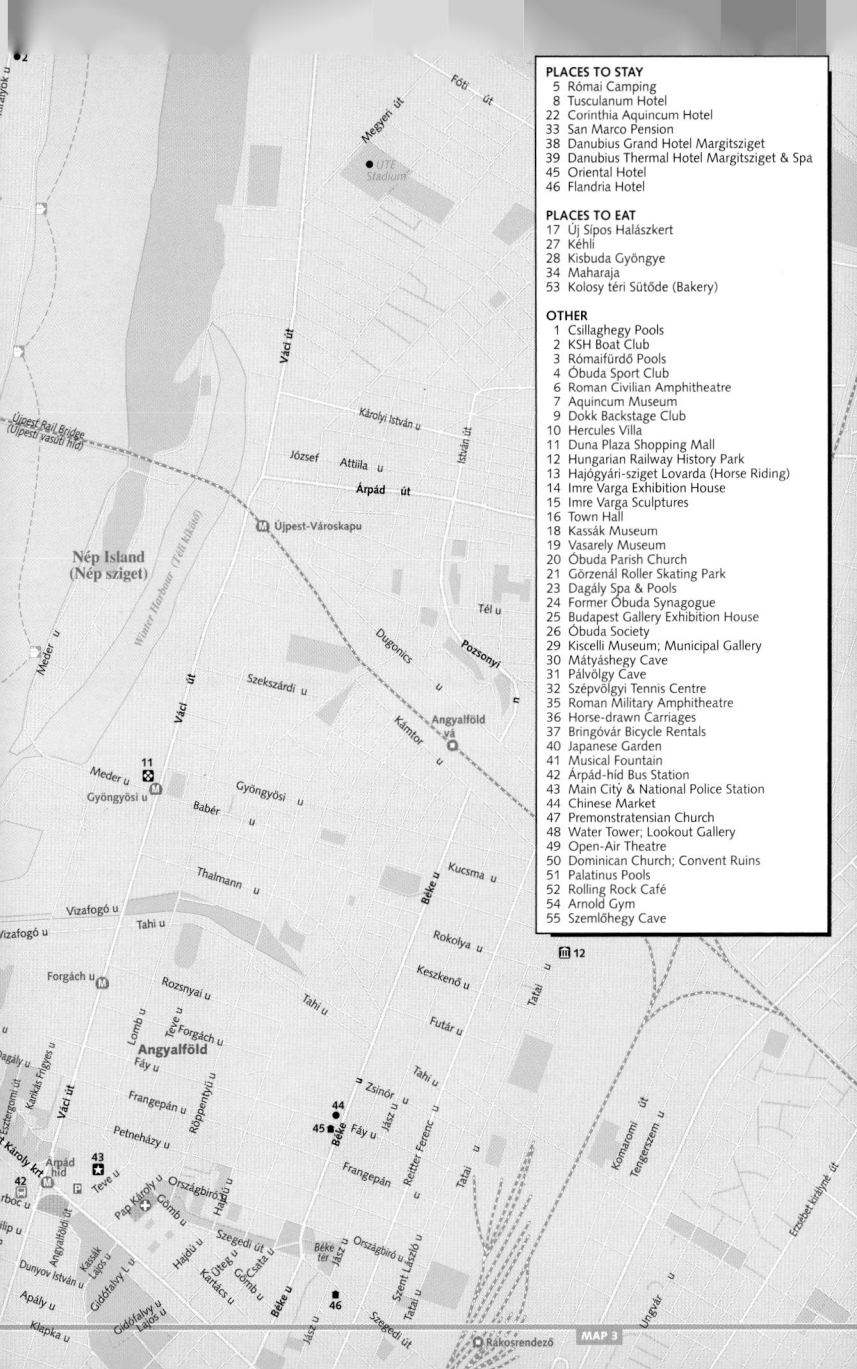

MAP 3

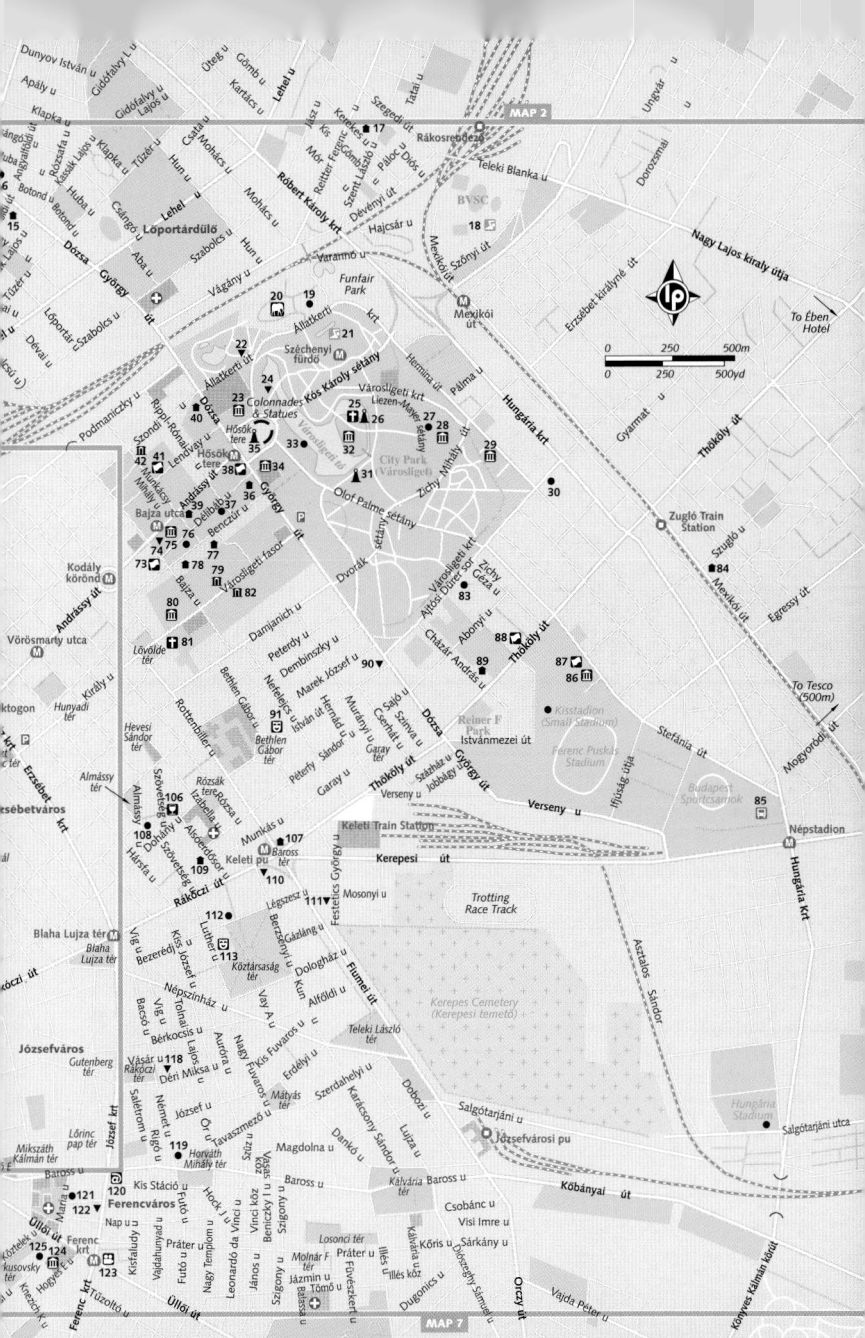

MAP 3 – BUDA & PEST

PLACES TO STAY
5 Margitsziget Hotel
8 Sirály Hostel
11 Sydney Apartment Hotel
12 Peter's Apartments
15 Diákspont Hostel
17 Góliát Hotel
36 Délibáb Hotel
39 Andrássy Hotel
40 Liget Hotel
58 Papillon Hotel
77 Benczúr Hotel; Pedagógus Hotel
78 Radio Inn
84 Station Guesthouse
89 Dominik Panzió
92 Garzonház Serviced Apartments
94 Hostel Bakfark
101 Büro Panzió
107 Hotel Baross Panzió
109 Aquarium Youth Hostel
130 K.M. Saga Guest Residence
135 Citadella Hostel & Hotel

PLACES TO EAT
1 Vadrózsa
13 Leroy's Country Pub
22 Bagolyvár & Borvendéglő 1894
24 Robinson
44 Lehel Csarnok
45 Móri Borozó
46 Pozsonyi Kisvendéglő
47 Firkász Restaurant
54 Gasztró Hús-Hentesáru (Butcher Shop); BÁV Shop
56 Café Gusto
60 Marxim
71 Kacsa
74 Premier Restaurant
90 Kilenc Sárkány Chinese Restaurant
97 Íz-É Faloda
99 Fény utca Market
100 Demmer's Teahouse
103 Nagyi Palacsintázója
110 Nonstop Shop
111 Rosenstein Restaurant
114 Il Treno
116 Mongolian Barbecue
117 Nonstop Shop
118 Rákóczi tér Market
122 Stex Alfred
126 Pink Cadillac Pizzeria; Paris, Texas
127 Coquan's Café
128 Shiraz (Takeaway)
129 Shiraz (Restaurant)

MUSEUMS
23 Museum of Fine Arts
28 Aviation Museum
29 Transport Museum
32 Hungarian Agricultural Museum; Vajdahunyad Castle
34 Palace of Art
66 Foundry Museum
75 Ferenc Hopp Museum of East Asian Art
80 György Ráth Museum
86 Geology Institute; National Geological Museum
124 Applied Arts Museum

OTHER
2 Poco Loco Pub
3 Újlak Synagogue
4 Alfréd Hajós National Sports Pool
6 Franciscan Church; Monastery Ruins
7 Margaret Island Crystal Water
9 Raoul Wallenberg Memorial
10 Hélia Thermal Hotel Spa & Pools
14 Palace of Wonders
16 Americana Rent-a-Car
18 BVSC Swimming Pool
19 Municipal Great Circus
20 City Zoo; Botanical Garden
21 Széchenyi Bath
25 Ják Chapel
26 Anonymous Statue
27 Petőfi Csarnok
30 National Institute for the Blind
31 George Washington Statue
33 Ice-Skating Rink (Winter Only)
35 Millenary Monument
37 Hungarian Language School
38 Serbia and Montenegro Embassy
41 Croatian Embassy
42 Sonnenberg Mansion
43 Lehel Church
48 Pendragon Bookshop
49 Centennial Monument
50 Sétacikli Bike Rental
51 Béla Komjádi Swimming Pool
52 Lukács Bath
53 Gül Baba's Tomb
55 Friends of Nature Bicycle Touring Association
57 Hungarian Automobile Club
59 International House Language School
61 City Squash
62 Marczibányi tér Cultural Centre
63 Millennium Exhibition Hall
64 Millennium Park
65 Gay.Pont Club
67 St Florian Chapel
68 Király Baths
69 Former Military Court of Justice; Fő utca Prison
70 Herend Village Pottery
72 Foreign Ministry
73 Austrian Embassy
76 British Council
79 Egger Villa
81 Városliget Calvinist Church
82 Vidor Villa
83 America House Library
85 Népstadion Bus Station
87 Slovakian Embassy
88 Romanian Embassy
91 Central Europe Dance Theatre
93 American Clinics
95 Széna tér Bus Station
96 Mammut II Shopping Mall; Kaméleon Club
98 Mammut I Shopping Mall; Top Squash
102 Oscar's American Bar
104 Budapest Wine Society Shop
105 Déli Gyógyszertár (Pharmacy)
106 Angel Club
108 Almássy tér Recreation Centre
112 Former Communist Party Headquarters
113 Erkel Theatre
115 Australian Embassy
119 Former Telephone Exchange Building
120 Private Link Internet Café
121 Magnum Sauna & Gym
123 Corvin Film Palace
125 Monarchia Wine Shop
131 Budapest Economics University; Közgáz Klub
132 Cliff Chapel
133 Former Swedish Embassy
134 Independence Monument
136 Budapest Congress Centre
137 MOM Park Shopping Mall

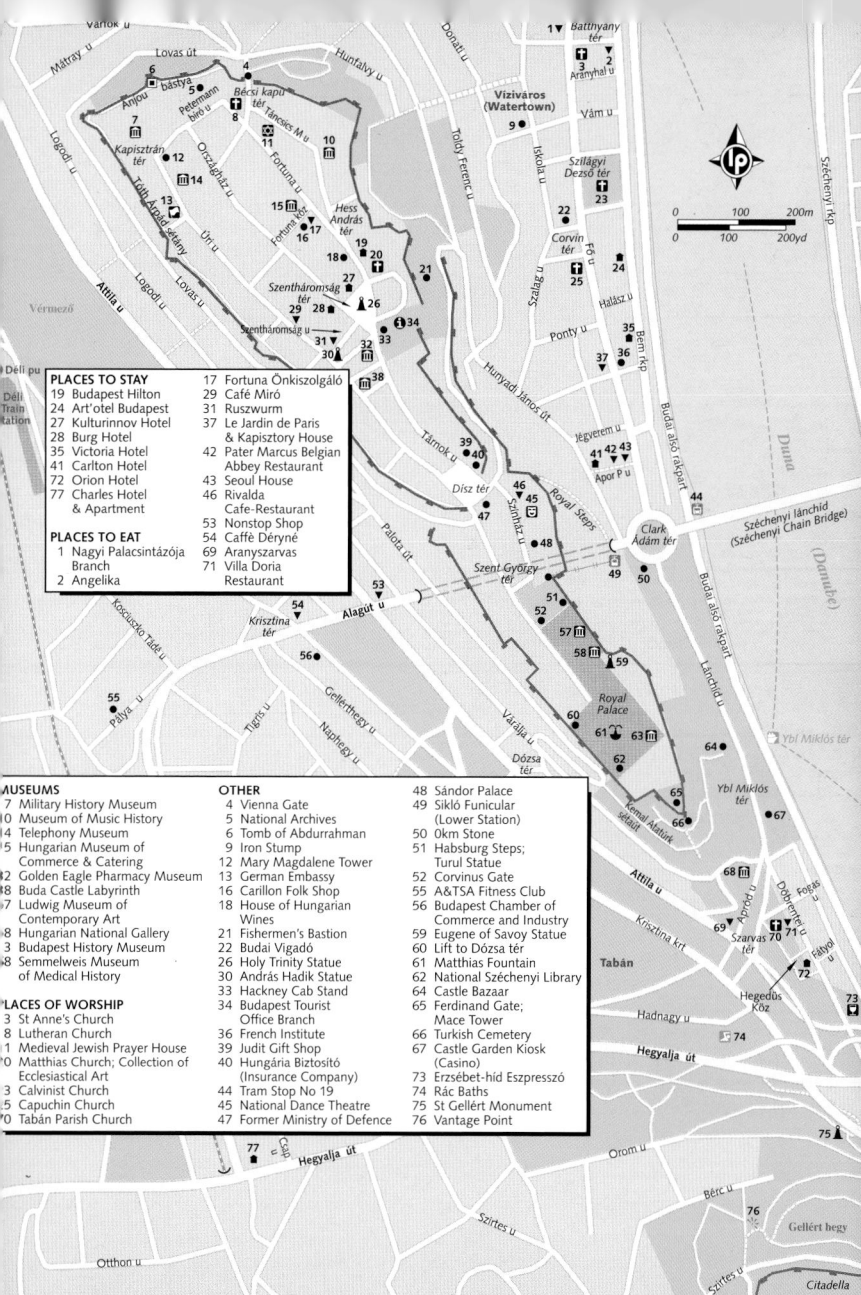

PLACES TO STAY
19 Budapest Hilton
24 Art'otel Budapest
27 Kulturinnov Hotel
28 Burg Hotel
35 Victoria Hotel
41 Carlton Hotel
72 Orion Hotel
77 Charles Hotel
   & Apartment

PLACES TO EAT
1 Nagyi Palacsintázója
   Branch
2 Angelika

17 Fortuna Önkiszolgáló
29 Café Miró
31 Ruszwurm
37 Le Jardin de Paris
   & Kapisztory House
42 Pater Marcus Belgian
   Abbey Restaurant
43 Seoul House
46 Rivalda
   Cafe-Restaurant
53 Nonstop Shop
54 Caffè Déryné
69 Aranyszarvas
71 Villa Doria
   Restaurant

MUSEUMS
7 Military History Museum
10 Museum of Music History
14 Telephony Museum
15 Hungarian Museum of
   Commerce & Catering
12 Golden Eagle Pharmacy Museum
13 Buda Castle Labyrinth
17 Ludwig Museum of
   Contemporary Art
18 Hungarian National Gallery
3 Budapest History Museum
8 Semmelweis Museum
   of Medical History

PLACES OF WORSHIP
3 St Anne's Church
8 Lutheran Church
1 Medieval Jewish Prayer House
0 Matthias Church; Collection of
   Ecclesiastical Art
3 Calvinist Church
5 Capuchin Church
0 Tabán Parish Church

OTHER
4 Vienna Gate
5 National Archives
6 Tomb of Abdurrahman
9 Iron Stump
12 Mary Magdalene Tower
13 German Embassy
16 Carillon Folk Shop
18 House of Hungarian
   Wines
21 Fishermen's Bastion
22 Budai Vigadó
26 Holy Trinity Statue
30 András Hadik Statue
33 Hackney Cab Stand
34 Budapest Tourist
   Office Branch
36 French Institute
39 Judit Gift Shop
40 Hungária Biztosító
   (Insurance Company)
44 Tram Stop No 19
45 National Dance Theatre
47 Former Ministry of Defence

48 Sándor Palace
49 Sikló Funicular
   (Lower Station)
50 0km Stone
51 Habsburg Steps;
   Turul Statue
52 Corvinus Gate
55 A&TSA Fitness Club
56 Budapest Chamber of
   Commerce and Industry
59 Eugene of Savoy Statue
60 Lift to Dózsa tér
61 Matthias Fountain
62 National Széchényi Library
63 Castle Bazaar
65 Ferdinand Gate;
   Mace Tower
66 Turkish Cemetery
67 Castle Garden Kiosk
   (Casino)
73 Erzsébet-híd Eszpresszó
74 Rác Baths
75 St Gellért Monument
76 Vantage Point

PLACES TO STAY
9 Hilton West End
12 Metro Hotel
28 City Panzió Ring
44 Radisson SAS Béke Hotel
46 Best Hostel
48 Yellow Submarine Youth Hostel
50 Hostel Bánki
74 Medosz Hotel
85 Garibaldi Guesthouse & Apartments
94 Caterina Hostel
141 Cosy Guest House
144 King's Hotel & Restaurant
151 Hostel Marco Polo
154 Emke Hotel
157 Mercure Nemzeti Hotel
170 Museum Castle Guest House

PLACES TO EAT
2 Mézes Kuckó Bakery
3 Rothschild Supermarket
6 Művész Bohém
14 Wabisabi
15 Okay Italia
23 Szeráj
24 Chicago Rib Shack
27 Három Testvér Branch
32 Kaiser's Supermarket
33 Okay Italia Branch
34 Don Pepe Pizzeria
36 Szalai Café
42 Lukács Café
49 Demmer's Teahouse
52 Semiramis
60 Marquis de Salade
63 Három Testvér Branch
64 Arigato
71 McDonald's (24 Hours)
72 Butterfly Ice Cream Shop
73 Teaház a Vörös Oroszlánhoz
76 Krizia
78 Non-stop Shop
83 Pick Ház
87 Chapter One
88 Iguana Restaurant
90 Hold utca Market
92 Soho Palacsintabár
96 Fortuca
97 Café Vian
98 Bombay Palace
101 Articsóka
110 Smatch Supermarket
111 Vörös és Fehér
113 San Marzano Pizzeria
116 Incognito Café; Pompeii Pizzeria
117 Víg Chinese Restaurant
119 La Tasca
122 Falafel Faloda
124 Művész Café
127 Happy Bank
132 Két Szerecsen Café
133 Frici Papa Kifőzdéje
136 Shalimar
138 Mini Étkezde
140 Kádár Canteen
142 Három Testvér
143 La Bodega
148 Arany Folyó Chinese Restaurant
150 Grill 99
155 Match Supermarket
164 Budapest Blue Café
168 Kalocsa

PUBS, BARS & CLUBS
7 Rigoletto Club
22 Süss Fél Nap
25 Trocadero Club
31 Bank Music Club
39 Pótkulcs
51 Becketts Irish Pub
61 New Orleans Music Club
69 Hades Jazztaurant
75 Heaven 51
77 Piaf
79 Picasso Point
93 Cactus Juice
103 Mystery Bar & Internet Café
134 Szimpla
139 Sark Café
146 Old Man's Music Pub
152 Chaos Music Pub
159 Portside Pub
161 M4 Music Club
167 Darshan Café
171 Darshan Udvar; BioPont Restaurant; INDIeGO Music Shop

TOURIST, ACCOMMODATION & BOOKING OFFICES
10 Fine Arts Museum Permit Office
37 Cooptourist
86 Express Branch
95 Budapest Tourist Office Branch
123 MÁV Central Ticket Office
173 Ticket Express

MUSEUMS
40 Zoltán Kodály Memorial Museum
57 Ethnography Museum
65 House of Terror
68 Franz Liszt Memorial Museum & Old Music Academy
121 Stamp Museum

SHOPPING
4 Clothing Shops
8 West End City Centre Shopping Mall
17 Fotex Photo Shop
18 BÁV Shop
19 Szőnyi Antikvárium
20 Dárius Antiques
21 Anna Antikvitás
26 Pless & Fox Jewellers
35 Pintér Antiques
45 Ajka Crystal
47 Játékszerek Anno
81 Kódex Bookshop
91 Cartographia Map Shop
102 Nyugat Antiquarian Bookshop
114 Ferenc Liszt Music Shop
115 Writers' Bookshop
126 Haas & Czjzek Porcelain
131 BÁV Shop; Manier
137 Billerbeck Duvet Shop
153 Lekvárium Jam Shop
162 Libri Könyvpalota Bookshop
172 Iguana Clothing Shop

OTHER
1 Debrecen Summer University; Palatinus House
5 Comedy Theatre
11 Lédere Mansion
13 I&I Records
16 Szindbád Cinema
29 Canadian Chamber of Commerce
30 Lindenbaum Apartment Houses
38 Post Office
41 Kolibri Pince Theatre
43 Teréz Patika (Pharmacy)
53 Copy General
54 CopyCat
55 Inner Town Police Station
56 Economy Ministry
58 Parliament
59 Cityrama Bus Tours
62 Művész Cinema
66 Budapest Puppet Theatre
67 Academy of Fine Arts
70 Rothschild Supermarket
80 Bedő House
82 Imre Nagy Monument
84 Hungarian Chamber of Commerce and Industry
89 Soviet Army Memorial
99 Budapest Operetta Theatre
100 Thália Theatre
104 Former Postal Savings Bank
105 US Embassy
106 MTV Headquarters
107 National Bank of Hungary
108 British Chamber of Commerce
109 House of Hungarian Photographers
112 Fashion House
118 Ferenc Liszt Music Academy
120 Art Nouveau Primary School
125 Goethe Institute
128 Irish Embassy
129 Top Clean Laundry
130 Hungarian State Opera House
135 Örökmozgó Film Museum Cinema
145 BKV Lost and Found Office
147 New York Palace
149 Narancs Internet Café
156 Csillag Gyógyszertár (Pharmacy)
158 St Rókus Chapel
160 Astoria Fitness Centre
163 Uránia National Cinema
165 Kenguru Ride Service
166 Former Hungarian Radio Headquarters
169 Ervin Szabó Library

PLACES TO STAY
6 K+K Hotel Opera
11 Connection Guest House
12 Club Hotel Ambra
26 Starlight Suiten Hotel
50 Hotel Fiesta
63 Budapest Inter-Continental Hotel
66 Kempinski Hotel Corvinus
67 Le Meridien; Program Centrum
74 Carmen Mini Hotel
98 Red Bus Hostel; Bookstore
107 Budapest Marriott Hotel
116 Astoria Hotel
122 City Panzió Pilvax
126 Millennium Court Apartment Hotel
132 Leó Panzió
157 Hostel Apáczai
158 Erzsébet Hotel
160 City Panzió Mátyás
168 Hotel Art
186 Ibis Centrum Hotel
198 K.M. Saga II Guest Residence

PLACES TO EAT
1 Nagy Fal (Chinese Fast Food)
4 Kisharang
5 Café Kör
15 Spaghetti Ice Gelateria
19 Durcin Sandwich Bar
20 Lou Lou
21 Gandhi
28 Coquan's Café
29 Xi Hu Chinese Restaurant
31 La Fontaine
36 Kővári Kosher Delicatessen
37 Al-Amir
41 Mokka
46 Durcin Sandwich Bar
47 Pesti Vendéglő
49 Mozaik Teahouse
51 Zazie
54 Carmel Pince
55 Fröhlich Cake Shop
57 Kosher Bakery
61 Sushi An
64 Gerbeaud
72 Kinor David
82 Resti Kocsma
84 Cosmo
93 Fausto's
96 Papageno Restaurant
101 Nagy Tamás Cheese Shop
119 Auguszt Café
135 Baraka Restaurant
141 Kárpátia Restaurant
143 Múzeum Café Restaurant
151 Vegetarium Restaurant
152 Centrál Kávéház
156 Károlyi Restaurant
180 Sole d'Italia
183 CD Fú Teázó
184 Képíró Restaurant
187 Non-stop Shop
189 1000 Tea
191 Trattoria Toscana
195 Taverna Dionysos
195 Pireus Taverna
196 Bangkok House Restaurant
200 Marie Kristensen Sandwich Bar
201 Teaház a Vörös Oroszlánhoz
202 Soul Café

PUBS, BARS & CLUBS
2 Garage Café
8 Morrison's Music Pub
34 Szent Jupát Söröző (Wichmann)
80 Columbus Irish Pub
92 Champs Sports Bar
94 Bar Martinez
97 Café Eklektika
133 Darling Bar
154 Action Bar
163 Darshan Cafeeling
165 Extra Caffè
167 Irish Cat Pub
170 Fat Mo's Music Club
177 Capella Café
185 Cha Cha Cha Bar
194 Limo Café
197 Jazz Garden
199 Mojito

TOURIST, ACCOMMODATION & BOOKING OFFICES
3 To-Ma Travel Agency
7 Ticket Express
14 Central Ticket Office
30 National Philharmonic Ticket Office
32 Budatours
38 Vista Visitor Center; Vista Internet Café; Pocok Media
39 Vista Travel Center
68 Tourinform Branch
77 Vigadó Ticket Office
78 Malév Ticket Office
79 Tourinform (Main Branch)
90 Ibusz Branch
109 Tribus Non-stop Hotel Service
117 Express
130 Ibusz (Main Office)
139 Starting Point Tourist Service
147 Pegazus Tours
166 Music Mix
176 Mahart PassNave Ticket Office
188 Hungarian Equestrian Tourism Association

MUSEUMS
33 Postal Museum
56 Hungarian Electrotechnology Museum
59 Underground Railway Museum
91 Jewish Museum
153 Hungarian National Museum
155 Petőfi Literary Museum

SHOPPING
16 Wave Music Shop
18 Bestsellers Bookshop
35 Kosher Wine Shop
40 Térképkirály Map Shop
42 La Boutique des Vins Wine Shop
44 Herend
45 Nádortex Duvet Shop
53 Concerto Music Shop
70 Simonyi Galéria
85 Persona Fashion Shop
99 Holló Atelier
100 Oxford University Press Bookshop
102 Belvárosi Antiques
104 Rózsavölgyi House & Music Shop
106 Prés Ház Wine Shop
108 Tangó Classic
110 Polgár Gallery; Thonet House
111 Philanthia Flower Shop
114 Fotex Photo Shop
123 Szamos Marcipán Shop
124 Libri Studium Bookshop
127 Arten Gallery
128 Vass Shoemakers
131 Párisi Udvar Bookshop
134 Babaklinika Gift Shop
136 Zsolnay Shop
137 Atlantisz Book Island
140 Monarchia
142 Központi Antikvárium
145 Náray Tamás
150 Orisis Bookshop
159 Inner Town Auction House
162 Lokomos Csemege
172 Selene Equestrian Shop
181 Folkart Centrum
190 Hephaistos Háza Furniture
203 Great Market Hall; Fakanál

OTHER
9 Drechsler House
10 Church of St Teresa
13 New Theatre
17 St Stephen's Basilica
22 Hungarian Academy of Sciences
23 Central European University Bookshop and Cafetaria
24 Duna Palota
25 Gresham Palace
27 OTP Bank
43 Ferenc Deák Statue
48 S.O.S. Dental Service
52 Orthodox Synagogue; Hanna Restaurant
58 Rumbach Sebestyén utca Synagogue
60 UK Embassy
62 Finance Ministry
65 Citibank
69 Deák tér Calvinist Church
71 Carl Lutz Monument
73 Holocaust Memorial
75 American Express; American Chamber of Commerce
76 Outdoor News Kiosk
81 Pesti Vigadó
83 Bank Palace
86 Avis
87 Municipal Council Office
88 Merlin Theatre
89 Currency Exchange Machine
95 Great Synagogue
103 Matáv Telepont Internet Kávézó
105 Török Bank House
112 Main Post Office
113 Pest County Hall
115 East-West Business Centre
118 Puskin Cinema
120 World Press House
121 Irisz Szalon
125 Netvillage Internet Café
129 József Katona Theatre; Kamra
138 Budapest Exhibition Hall
144 Italian Institute of Culture
146 University Library
148 Friends of the City Cycling Group
149 Inner Town Parish Church
161 Ami Internet Coffee; K&H Bank
164 University Church
169 Budapest Net Internet Café
171 St Michael's Church
173 Queen Elizabeth Statue
174 Pump Room
175 Rudas Baths; Cinetrip Water-Movie; Rudas Romkert Beer Garden
178 National Foreign Language Library
179 Aranytíz Youth Centre; Kalamajka Táncház
182 Serbian Orthodox Church
193 International Ferry Pier

MAP 7 – SOUTH BUD

MAP 3

Hegyalja út
Schweidel u
Ramvány u
Kelenhegyi út
Jubilee Park
Independence
Imre
Mátyás
Czucz
Közl

Nedecvár u
Frics u
Ménesi út
Somlói út
Kelenhegyi út
Reszeda u
Minerva u
Pipacs u
Vereitek u
Kelenhegyi út
Szabadság
Szt Gellért tér
Szt Gellért bér
Műegyetem rkp

Karolina út
alsó hegy u
Villányi út
Badögh út
Mányoki u
Orlay u
Budafoki u
Csiky u
7

Diószegi út
David Ferenc
Tas vezér
Fencketlen-tó
Ménesi út
Hímfy u
Mészöly u
Bartök Béla út
Bertalan
Zenta u
Kemenes u
5
6
4
Lajos
Sztoczek József u
Petőfi

24
Móricz Zsigmond körtér
23
22
21
19
18
Kruspér u
20
27
28

Bocskai út
Kosztolányi Dezső tér
25
Karinthy Frigyes út
Irinyi József u
39

Nagyszölös u
Takus M u
41
Bercsényi u
26
Október 23 u
40
Köröny József u
Baranyai u
Budafoki út

Hamzsabégi út
Sárbogárdi út
Kanizsai u

Budaörsi
Bartók
Béla
42
Frakno u
Halmi utca
Bártfai u
43
Dombóvári u
Andal

Kelenföldi pu
Etele tér
Etele út
Kelenföld
Mérnök u
Etele út
Galambóc u
Fehérvári
Bánát u
Lecke u
Hengermalom ut
Vízpart u
44

Menyecske u
Bikszádi út
Sopron u
Sztregova u
46
Naborfejérvári u
Szeréni út
Lágymányos
Barazda u

Mikes Kelemen u
Örmezei út
Csákvár u
Andor u
Tétényi út
Allende park
Csurgól
Zsombor u
Galvani u
Budafoki

To Statue Park (5km)
Péter-hegyi út
Kardhegy u
Hunyadi János
 Adács u
Mátyás út
Latinca Sándor u
Szabados Sándor u
Kondorosi út
Temesvár u
47

Kelenvölgy
Teréds I u
Körmend u
Sáfrány u
Építész u
Fehérvári út

Ady Endre út
Kunhegyes u
48
Vegyész u
Szeréni u
Hunyadi János

49
Rózsavölgy
Ady Endre út
Budafok-Albertfalva vá
Kitérő út

Duna (Danube)

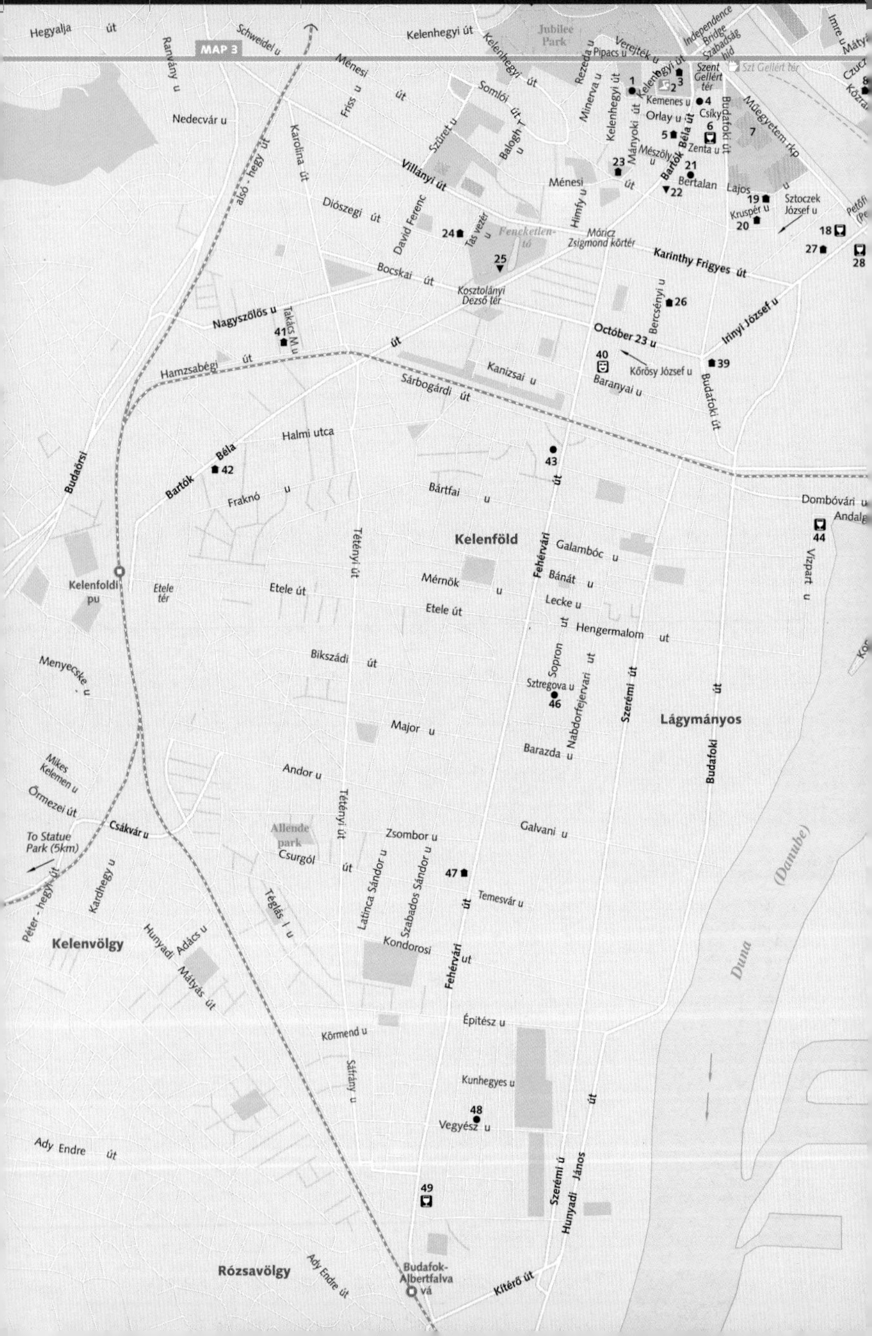

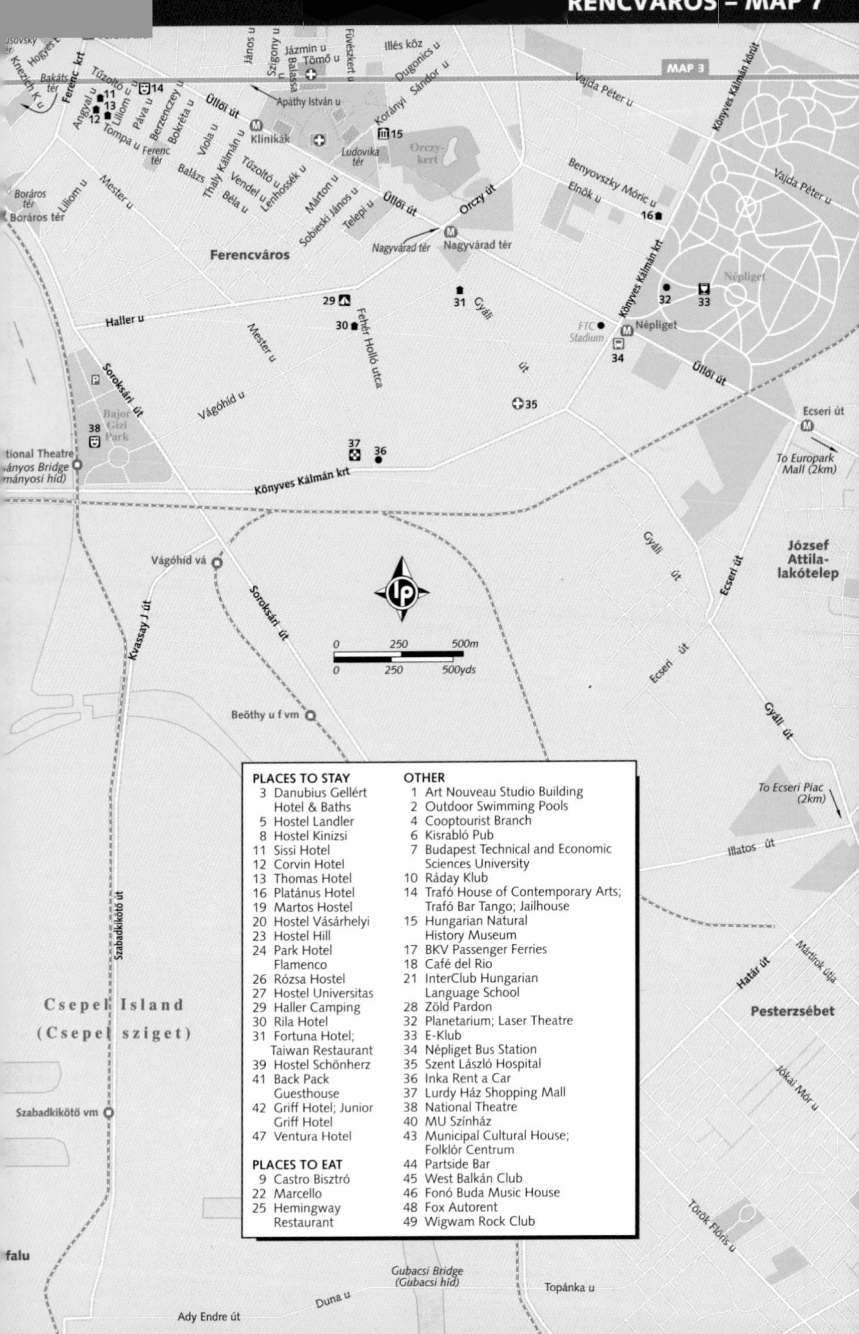

MAP 3

Illés köz

Jázmin u
Tömő u
Füvészkert u

Apáthy István u

Korányi Sándor u

Vajda Péter u

Könyves Kálmán köz

János u

Szigony u

Balázs Béla u

Üllői út

Klinikák

Ludovika tér

Orczy-kert

Benyovszky Móric u

Elnök u

Vajda Péter u

Kliníkák

15

Béla u

Telepi u

Sobieski János u

Márton u

Üllői út

Orczy út

Nagyvárad tér

Nagyvárad tér

16

Könyves Kálmán krt

Mester u

Lilom u

Tompa u

Tűzoltó u

Ferenc tér

Ferencváros

29

31 Gyáli

32

33

Néptliget

Haller u

30

Fehér Holló utca

FTC Stadium

34

Néptliget

Üllői út

Ecseri út

To Europark Mall (2km)

Mester u

Vágóhíd u

út

35

Sorok sári út

Bajor Gizi Park

National Theatre
ányos Bridge
mányosi híd)

38

37

36

Könyves Kálmán krt

József Attila-lakótelep

Gyáli

út

Vágóhíd vá

Sorok sári út

Ecseri út

Beöthy u f vm

Gyáli út

To Ecseri Piac (2km)

Kvassay J út

0   250   500m
0   250   500yds

Illatos út

Csepel Island
(Csepel sziget)

Szabadkikötő út

Határ út

Mártírok útja

Pesterzsébet

Jókai Mór u

Szabadkikötő vm

Török Flóris u

falu

Gubacsi Bridge
(Gubacsi híd)

Duna u

Topánka u

Ady Endre út

PLACES TO STAY

3 Danubius Gellért Hotel & Baths
5 Hostel Landler
8 Hostel Kinizsi
11 Sissi Hotel
12 Corvin Hotel
13 Thomas Hotel
16 Plátanus Hotel
19 Martos Hostel
20 Hostel Vásárhelyi
23 Hostel Hill
24 Park Hotel Flamenco
26 Rózsa Hostel
27 Hostel Universitas
29 Haller Camping
30 Rila Hotel
31 Fortuna Hotel; Taiwan Restaurant
39 Hostel Schönherz
41 Back Pack Guesthouse
42 Griff Hotel; Junior Griff Hotel
47 Ventura Hotel

PLACES TO EAT

9 Castro Bisztró
22 Marcello
25 Hemingway Restaurant

OTHER

1 Art Nouveau Studio Building
2 Outdoor Swimming Pools
4 Cooptourist Branch
6 Kisrabló Pub
7 Budapest Technical and Economic Sciences University
10 Ráday Klub
14 Trafó House of Contemporary Arts; Trafó Bar Tango; Jailhouse
15 Hungarian Natural History Museum
17 BKV Passenger Ferries
18 Café del Rio
21 InterClub Hungarian Language School
28 Zöld Pardon
32 Planetarium; Laser Theatre
33 E-Klub
34 Néptliget Bus Station
35 Szent László Hospital
36 Inka Rent a Car
37 Lurdy Ház Shopping Mall
38 National Theatre
40 MU Színház
43 Municipal Cultural House; Folklór Centrum
44 Partside Bar
45 West Balkán Club
46 Fonó Buda Music House
48 Fox Autorent
49 Wigwam Rock Club

MAP LEGEND

CITY ROUTES

Freeway	Freeway		Unsealed Road
Highway	Primary Road	—+—	One Way Street
Road	Secondary Road		Pedestrian Street
Street	Street		Stepped Street
Lane	Lane	)= = =	Tunnel
	On/Off Ramp		Footbridge

REGIONAL ROUTES

Tollway, Freeway	
Primary Road	
Secondary Road	
Minor Road	

BOUNDARIES

—·—·—	International
—··—··—	State
— — —	Disputed
▬▬▬	Fortified Wall

HYDROGRAPHY

	River, Creek		Dry Lake; Salt Lake
	Canal		Spring; Rapids
	Lake		Waterfalls

TRANSPORT ROUTES & STATIONS

—O—	Train	—□	Ferry
	Underground Train		Walking Trail
— M —	Metro	· · · · ·	Walking Tour
	Tramway		Path
↦↦↤↤↦	Cable Car, Chairlift	——	Pier or Jetty

AREA FEATURES

	Building		Market	↗	Beach		Forest
❋	Park, Gardens		Sports Ground	+ + +	Cemetery		Plaza

POPULATION SYMBOLS

◌ **CAPITAL**	National Capital	● **CITY**	City	● Village	Village
◉ **CAPITAL**	State Capital	● **Town**	Town		Urban Area

MAP SYMBOLS

■	Place to Stay	▼	Place to Eat	●	Point of Interest

✈	Airport	⊞	Cinema	🏛	Museum		Swimming Pool
❸	Bank	📷	Embassy, Consulate	✚	Police Station		Synagogue
⊕	Border Crossing	☎	Fountain	✉	Post Office		Theatre
	Bus Stop, Station	✛	Hospital		Pub or Bar		Tomb
⌂	Castle, Chateau	@	Internet Cafe		Ruins	❶	Tourist Information
✝	Cathedral, Church	▲	Monument	✿	Shopping Centre		Winery
⌂	Cave	☾	Mosque		Stately Home		Zoo

Note: not all symbols displayed above appear in this book

LONELY PLANET OFFICES

Australia
Locked Bag 1, Footscray, Victoria 3011
☎ 03 8379 8000 fax 03 8379 8111
email: talk2us@lonelyplanet.com.au

UK
72-82 Rosebery Ave, London, EC1R 4RW
☎ 020 7841 9000 fax 020 7841 9001
email: go@lonelyplanet.co.uk

USA
150 Linden St, Oakland, CA 94607
☎ 510 893 8555 TOLL FREE: 800 275 8555
fax 510 893 8572
email: info@lonelyplanet.com

France
1 rue du Dahomey, 75011 Paris
☎ 01 55 25 33 00 fax 01 55 25 33 01
email: bip@lonelyplanet.fr
www.lonelyplanet.fr

**World Wide Web: www.lonelyplanet.com *or* AOL keyword: lp
Lonely Planet Images: www.lonelyplanetimages.com**